COGNITIVE RESPONSES IN PERSUASION

Edited by
RICHARD E. PETTY
University of Missouri-Columbia

THOMAS M. OSTROM
TIMOTHY C. BROCK
Ohio State University

 LAWRENCE ERLBAUM ASSOCIATES, PUBLISHERS
1981   Hillsdale, New Jersey

Lawrence Erlbaum Associates, Inc., Publishers
365 Broadway
Hillsdale, New Jersey 07642

Library of Congress Cataloging in Publication Data

Main entry under title:

Cognitive responses in persuasion.

  Bibliography:
  Includes index.
  1. Persuasion (Psychology)   2. Attitude change.
3. Cognition.   I. Petty, Richard E.   II. Ostrom,
Thomas M., 1936-   III. Brock, Timothy C., 1935-
BF323.C5C63   153.8'52   80-26388
ISBN 0-89859-025-6

Printed in the United States of America

Contents

250352

v

Foreword

Back in the mid-1930s, just before I began to study psychology, Gordon Allport, one of the great psychologists of his time, called *attitudes* the central topic of social psychology. Maybe it was, but there was then pitiably little by way of theory and method to back up the claim. Social psychology itself was still more a dream and a program than an accomplishment.

During World War II, a good deal of serious practical social psychology got done, and in the immediate postwar years, social psychology like clinical psychology consolidated itself as a self-conscious subdiscipline. A major work of that period, *Communication and Persuasion* (1953) by Carl Hovland, Irving Janis, and Harold Kelley, all then at Yale, is the most direct ancestor of the present work. The strongest praise that I can give to the book before you is that it is a worthy successor to Hovland-Janis-Kelley, almost 3 decades later. Were you to read *both* books (a good idea), you would find that the psychology of attitudes, attitude change, and persuasion has made real progress over the quarter century. This book, a collaborative product of leading contributors to attitude research and theory, should itself help to move things ahead.

At about the time that my friends at Yale were opening up the systematic experimental study of persuasive communication, my colleagues Jerome Bruner, Robert White, and I at Harvard were trying to counterbalance the schematic simplifications of pro-con attitude measurement and of single-factor theories of attitude change in a "naturalistic" approach to the embeddedness of people's opinions in their ongoing adaptive enterprises of living (*Opinions and Personality,* 1956). In retrospect, the *Zeitgeist* gave much more support to Hovland-Janis-Kelley than to Smith-Bruner-White. In the years since, social psychologists have invested almost exclusively in the strategies of theory-testing in the laboratory in contrast with qualitative or "clinical" observation, and the present book both exemplifies and reaps the products of this mainstream tradition of experimental social psychology. It represents experimental social psychology at its best. It does not try to establish contact with the content-oriented strategies of survey research, which have developed in regrettable independence of the laboratory study of persuasion processes.

All the same, the distinctive focus that binds the book together, a stress on people's *cognitive responses* during exposure to persuasive communication as in some way mediating or qualifying the impact of the persuasive message, seems to me a welcome return to concerns that Bruner, White, and I had very much in mind but were in no position to deal with so systematically. Once more we are dealing with the idiosyncratic opinion processes of active persons, persons who do not merely "receive" messages but resist, select, and interpret them in their commerce with what we called their informational environment.

What is radically different in the *psychological* environment of social psychology today as compared with the 1950s is the general prevalence of cognitive psychology. In the '50s and earlier, the byways of social psychology provided a haven for deviant psychologists who would not give up the idea of people as active thinkers and knowers. Now, cognitive psychologists of information processing *are* the mainstream. In accommodating to this new theoretical environment, the recent experimental social psychology of persuasion has returned to some of the issues raised but not settled in *Opinions and Personality* and is in a position to deal with them more adequately.

Although the editors and authors share a common interest in "cognitive responses," this is not a monolithic book. It is not the documented presentation of a single theory. From my outsider's perspective, the editors have taken their unifying theme with just the right degree of semi-seriousness. It *does* bind the book together, but the book also stands as a fair and responsible summary of the state of research on persuasive communication a quarter century after Hovland, Janis, and Kelley, a representative presentation of the main competing theoretical perspectives (the editors and authors by no means all agree, and the rough edges are fortunately not all smoothed out), and a rich and sensitive treatment of the methodological issues that beset the attempt to figure out and formulate what goes on "in people's heads" when, sometimes, they are persuaded—and when, sometimes, they resist persuasion. I know of no better source from which to gain sophisticated acquaintance with the present state of attitude research and theory.

A further recurrent theme in the book delights me: renewed interest in and respect for the *content* of persuasive messages as a centrally relevant consideration in understanding the persuasion process. For long it had seemed to me that the "new rhetoric" stemming from research in the style of Hovland-Janis-Kelley was dealing with everything *except* the essentials of persuasive argument: The focus was so heavily on peripheral contextual matters. Now we may be ready to concern ourselves with the central processes of persuasion, a wonderful, perplexing blend of the rational, the nonrational, and the irrational. The authors of this book are mainly concerned with general formulations, theoretical or methodological, and that is entirely proper. If social psychologists are to involve themselves increasingly in applied settings, dealing with current history from their distinctive perspective and with their distinctive competences, respect for the actual content of communication seems to me essential.

Cognitive Responses in Persuasion is a credit to the editors and authors who have represented their field of inquiry so well and are nudging its development ahead in promising ways. It should be valuable to students and practitioners of social psychology. It captures and communicates the ferment in the field. It helps to restore the psychology of attitudes toward a central position.

M. Brewster Smith
Santa Cruz, California

Preface

The idea for this volume began in informal discussions among the three editors at Ohio State University. We felt that the 1970s had brought a fundamental change to traditional work in social psychology on the problems of attitudes and persuasion. There seemed to be a shift in the problems being studied and the conceptual bases used to understand these new issues. Existing textbooks generally mirrored only the conceptual orientations that had been developed in the 1950s and 1960s. Yet contemporary research seemed less and less related to those traditional approaches.

We concluded that it would be useful at this point in the evolution of attitude research to try to identify the underlying commonalities that were emerging. Such an effort, although bound to be imperfect in some ways, should have several desirable effects. It should provide students with a textbook that does more than convey past history. It should bring coherence to their reading of contemporary attitude research as well as present them with the more enduring features of the earlier conceptual approaches. For active researchers, this volume should increase their awareness of converging lines of research and further encourage them to break away from the traditional research pathways.

Edited volumes on attitude change have historically played an important role through the education of students and guidance of subsequent research. Previously, the Hovland volumes (e.g., Hovland & Janis, 1959; Hovland, Luchins, Mandell, Campbell, Brock, McGuire, Feierabend, & Anderson, 1957) represented well the emergence of "attitude change" as an empirical science in the 1950s, and were instrumental in leading the field into the 1960s. In the late 1960s, the various volumes on consistency motives (e.g., Abelson, Aronson, McGuire, Newcomb, Rosenberg, & Tannenbaum, 1968; Feldman, 1966) represented the dominant trend in the area, and paved the way for the recent refinements in dissonance and balance theories made in the 1970s. Other volumes in the late 1960s documented the variety of noncognitive consistency orientations (Greenwald, Brock, & Ostrom, 1968) and perceptual-judgmental approaches (Sherif & Sherif, 1967) that pertained to the functioning of attitudes.

Although there are still quite a large number of empirical approaches and theories vying for the attention of the discipline, the late 1970s have brought a remarkable coalesence around what has been called a "cognitive response" (Greenwald, 1968a) or an "information-processing" (cf. Eagly & Himmelfarb, 1978; Fishbein & Ajzen, 1975; McGuire, 1978; Wyer, 1974) approach to the study of attitudes and persuasion. In the last 10 years, the approach has been used extensively by persuasion researchers in social psychology and consumer behavior. The present volume brings this research and thinking together in one place for the first time.

The cognitive response approach emphasizes that the recipient of a communication is an active information processor who manipulates, elaborates, and integrates the information as it is received. Thus, the nature of the thoughts that pass through a person's mind as a message is anticipated, received, or reflected upon, and the manner in which these thoughts are combined and integrated with previous information are a major focus of research.

In order to present the accumulated research and thinking about the cognitive response approach, we asked active researchers from social psychology and consumer behavior to contribute original chapters on particular topics that highlighted the most recent work in the field. We asked also that the authors discuss the classic persuasion studies upon which the more recent work was based. All of the authors we initially contacted agreed to contribute, and we believe that their chapters provide a contemporary introduction to attitude change processes for advanced undergraduate and graduate students. Instructors will find that this book gives expanded coverage to important material not traditionally found in attitude change texts, including electrophysiological correlates of attitudes and cognition, effects of group discussion on persuasion, and the effectiveness of advertising communications.

We have divided the book into three sections. Each section begins with an editor's overview that sets the stage for the chapters in that section. Part I begins with the history of the cognitive response approach. Next, the nature of attitudes and cognitions is discussed, as well as the relationship of these concepts to overt behaviors. Various techniques for measuring attitudes and cognitive responses are described. The logic of the attitude change experiment is also presented in Part I along with an analysis of the methodological difficulties in investigating the cognitive mediation of persuasion. Part II presents a cognitive response analysis of the major independent variables in persuasion research. The following basic question is addressed in this section: How does the source (message, receiver, modality of presentation, etc.) affect information processing and persuasion? In addition to highlighting important theoretical findings, applications of the cognitive response approach to advertising communications is given considerable attention. In Part III, four influential cognitive theories of attitude change are presented in detail. McGuire presents his probabilogical model; Insko presents an updated analysis of cognitive consistency approaches in balance theory terms; Fishbein and Ajzen present their theory of reasoned action; and Anderson presents his information integration theory. In the last chapter in Part III, the relevance of some specific principles from experimental cognitive psychology for attitude formation and change are discussed.

Finally, we should note that this volume represents something of a hybrid between an attitude change "textbook" and a book of independent chapters on persuasion. Because there is no monolithic "cognitive response theory" at present, this volume does not purport to provide an integrated synthesis of the field. In fact, several of the chapter authors disagree with each other on some key points. To conceal this controversy would be misleading and premature. On the other hand, for didactic purposes, we have attempted to standardize terminology, cross-reference material where possible, and avoid unnecessary duplication among chapters. We are indebted to our authors for cooperating in this endeavor.

R. E. Petty

T. M. Ostrom

T. C. Brock

Contributors

Icek Ajzen, *University of Massachusetts—Amherst*
Norman H. Anderson, *University of California—San Diego*
Timothy C. Brock, *Ohio State University*
Eugene Burnstein, *University of Michigan*
John T. Cacioppo, *University of Iowa*
Robert B. Cialdini, *Arizona State University*
Debbra E. Colman, *University of Southern California*
Alice H. Eagly, *Purdue University*
Martin Fishbein, *University of Illinois at Urbana-Champaign*
Anthony G. Greenwald, *Ohio State University*
Stephen G. Harkins, *Northeastern University*
R. Glen Hass, *City University of New York (Brooklyn College)*
Chester A. Insko, *University of North Carolina—Chapel Hill*
John H. Lingle, *Rutgers University*
William J. McGuire, *Yale University*
Norman Miller, *University of Southern California*
Thomas M. Ostrom, *Ohio State University*
Richard E. Petty, *University of Missouri—Columbia*
Curt A. Sandman, *University of California—Irvine*
Alan Sawyer, *Ohio State University*
Keith Sentis, *University of Michigan*
Peter Wright, *Stanford University*

COGNITIVE RESPONSES IN PERSUASION

HISTORICAL AND METHODOLOGICAL PERSPECTIVES IN THE ANALYSIS OF COGNITIVE RESPONSES: AN INTRODUCTION

Timothy C. Brock
Ohio State University

It has been almost half a century since Gordon Allport (1935) wrote that "attitude is probably the most distinctive and indispensable concept in contemporary social psychology [p. 798]." A quick perusal of the contents of any current text in social psychology will reveal that more attention is devoted to the topic of attitudes and persuasion than to any other area. Social psychologists have emphasized the empirical investigation of attitudes because of the directing role attitudes play in determining social behaviors. Other disciplines are interested in the study of attitudes and persuasion because of its direct practical relevance for understanding and predicting such phenomena as consumer behavior, the effectiveness of advertising campaigns, the results of political elections, jury decisions, psychotherapy outcomes, and so forth.

This volume is an advanced undergraduate/introductory graduate textbook dealing with attitude change from the perspective of mediating and accompanying cognitive responses. Cognitive response analysis, the volume's unifying theme, stems from the long-standing and widespread interest in elucidating the fundamental cognitive processes that are instigated by a persuasive message. In his excellent chapter on attitudes and persuasion in *The Handbook of Social Psychology*, McGuire (1969a) proposed that two schools of research techniques and interests have

1

emerged—the "Hovlanders" (from Carl Hovland, who began the first systematic persuasion experiments during World War II and later at Yale) and the "Festingerians" (named after Leon Festinger, the originator of the influential theory of cognitive dissonance). Despite the many differences between these schools noted by McGuire, one point of substantial agreement is that attitude change can best be explained by taking into account the mental processes that ensue once a persuasive stimulus has impinged upon a thinking recipient (cf. Festinger & Maccoby, 1964; Hovland, Lumsdaine, & Sheffield, 1949). The authors who have contributed to this volume share the view that people are active processors of the information they receive.

Despite the heavy explanatory roles cognitive mediating responses have been assumed to play in producing persuasion, the traditional foci of attitude change texts have been on presenting diverse theories of attitude change or on encyclopedic renditions of empirical findings. Analyses of the cognitive processes that underlie attitude changes have been relatively ignored. In fact, it is only within the past decade that the implications of an information-processing view have been carefully applied to the study of persuasion. In that short period of time, however, techniques for the measurement of mediating cognitive responses have been developed, and the information-processing approach has shown its ability to integrate a wide body of existing data under one conceptual framework, to provide insights into the microprocesses involved in persuasion, and to generate unique and nonobvious predictions. This volume highlights the past decade of research and theory on cognitive responses in persuasion.

The goal of Part I of this book is to provide an introduction to the cognitive response approach to the study of persuasion. In Chapter 1, the editors present a brief history of the attitude concept and the cognitive response approach to persuasion. The cognitive response approach is compared to the four traditional approaches to persuasion (learning, functional, perceptual, and consistency), and the classic early research findings that documented the importance of cognitive processes for understanding attitude change are cited. In Chapter 2, Cacioppo, Harkins, and Petty give the concepts of attitude and cognitive response a precise meaning and popular techniques for the measurement of these internal constructs are presented.

Most of the knowledge that psychologists have about attitude change processes comes from experimental research. In Chapter 3, Petty and Brock introduce the experimental method and show how a hypothesis about the importance of a person's thoughts in producing persuasion can be tested and validated. In Chapter 4, Cacioppo and Sandman relate attitudes and cognitive responses to physiological responses. Physiological techniques for the measurement of attitudes and cognitive processes are discussed, and a model that relates attitudes and cognitive responses to bodily processes is presented.

Chapter 5, by Miller and Colman, presents a critical evaluation of the cognitive response approach to persuasion. Methodological and conceptual problems in analyzing the cognitive mediation of persuasion are addressed, and various remedial recommendations are made. Greenwald, in Chapter 6, evaluates the direction that research on *cognitive responses* has taken since he first introduced the term in 1968 and speculates about some future gains of continued use of the approach. Both Chapters 5 and 6 are somewhat more technical than the preceding four chapters and may be of interest primarily to graduate students and researchers in the field. Other readers may wish to omit these chapters and proceed directly to Part II, which presents a cognitive response analysis of the major research findings on persuasion.

1 Historical Foundations of the Cognitive Response Approach to Attitudes and Persuasion

Richard E. Petty
University of Missouri-Columbia

Thomas M. Ostrom
Timothy C. Brock
Ohio State University

INTRODUCTION

How do you feel about sentencing criminals to the electric chair? Is the death penalty a positive weapon against crime? A necessary evil? A disgusting anachronism? How would you describe your attitude? What would make you change your mind? This book explores the cognitive processes involved in attitude change. Let's say that you and three friends have been asked how you feel about capital punishment by a national opinion-polling organization. Each of your friends indicates on an attitude scale (the one shown in Table 1.1 is typical of those used in attitude research) that he or she feels "somewhat unfavorable." What does this tell you about their attitudes? Should you assume that each person has the same attitude? What roles do their attitudes play in their lives? How could you persuade them to change their attitudes?

Even though the attitudes of your friends came out the same on the scale, their attitudes are probably not identical. You'd find this out if you asked them to talk

TABLE 1.1
Sample Attitude Scale Response to the Issue: Capital Punishment

	X						
Strongly Unfavorable	Somewhat Unfavorable	Mildly Unfavorable	Neutral	Mildly Favorable	Somewhat Favorable	Strongly Favorable

about their attitudes toward the electric chair. During the conversation you could probably list several thoughts they would express. Table 1.2 presents some thoughts from three different persons. Person A appears to be unfavorable because she opposes the death penalty in general and can give reasoned arguments to support that position. Person C, on the other hand, feels that the electric chair is not severe enough. Person B has mixed feelings, but his emotional responses against the death penalty carry the greatest weight.

Although each person's response is identical on the attitude scale, the thoughts behind the ratings are different. Some responses are emotional; others are rational. Some attack persons who support capital punishment; others attack arguments that might be used to support the concept. Some responses seem consistent with each other; others appear contradictory. Some are elaborations of previous thoughts; others are specifications. Some relate the attitude to other attitudes; others relate it to friendships and social relationships. Some are almost identical to the attitude scale statement; others are zany, illogical, or unrelated to the attitude scale statement.

The particular focus of this text is on the thoughts behind attitudes. We emphasize thought mechanisms to explain the process of persuasion, or how

TABLE 1.2
Cognitive Responses to the Issue: Capital Punishment

PERSON A

1. Studies have shown that capital punishment is not an effective crime deterrent, since states with capital punishment have identical crime rates as those without.
2. There is always the possibility that the wrong person will be executed.
3. I just read the other day that the state of Utah mistakenly executed an innocent man in 1954.
4. It is generally the poor who end up being executed, since they don't have the resources to hire a good attorney.
5. If society condones the death penalty, it decreases the value of human life.
6. Other civilized societies, like Great Britain, have eliminated the death penalty without any harmful consequences.

PERSON B

1. The thought of killing another person makes me sick.
2. How is capital punishment different from abortion, which is disgusting?
3. The electric chair is the most economical way to deal with repeat criminals, though.
4. Only racists and Republicans favor capital punishment.

PERSON C

1. I am somewhat unfavorable toward capital punishment.
2. I've written to the governor that the electric chair is too good for most criminals.
3. The Bible says, "an eye for an eye and a tooth for a tooth."
4. We should bring back public hanging, firing squads, and the guillotine!
5. All my friends agree that anyone who commits a bloody crime deserves an equally bloody death.
6. Whoever likes capital punishment is really stupid.
7. I can't help but wonder if capital punishment is always given in capital cities.
8. I wasn't punished much as a child.

people change other people's minds. An understanding of the effectiveness of persuasive communications depends on an understanding of the cognitive responses that arise in the persuasion context. By a cognitive response to a communication, we mean to include all of the thoughts that pass through a person's mind while he or she anticipates a communication, listens to a communication, or reflects on a communication. If we presented each of your three friends with a Supreme Court opinion arguing in favor of the death penalty, we would want to know his or her thoughts during and following examination of the court opinion, each individual's cognitive reactions. Merely manipulating experimentally features of the persuasion setting (for example, the trustworthiness of the source) or measuring responses on rating scales is not an adequate research technique to assess the dynamics of how an attitude is changed. Yet this is the primary strategy researchers have used during the past 30 years to test theories of attitude change. The validity of the theory being tested, even theories about the thoughts people have in response to communications, was determined primarily by whether or not the theory could accurately predict how the attitude scales would be affected. The thoughts that accompanied the attitude were typically not measured. In this chapter we review research on cognitive responses to persuasion from World War II to the mid-1960s. The following chapters bring us to the present. But first, let us turn to a history of the concept of *attitude*. The term has not always meant what we think of today.

A BRIEF HISTORY OF
THE ATTITUDE CONCEPT[1]

The word *attitude* first came into English about 1710 from the French *attitude*, which came from the Italian *attitudine*, which in turn came from the Latin *aptus*, meaning "fitness" or "adaptedness." In the 18th century the term was used primarily to refer to the posture or bodily position of a statue or figure in a painting. The word today, of course, still refers to a general orientation toward something (like your orientation toward, or view of, the death penalty).

Although the sociologist Herbert Spencer employed the term as a mental concept (e.g., having the "right" attitude) in his *First Principles* in 1862, a more influential usage occurred in Charles Darwin's *Expressions of the Emotions in Man and Animals* in 1872. Darwin used *attitude* as a motor concept—the physical expression of an emotion (e.g., a scowling face signifying a "hostile attitude"). To Darwin, an attitude was a biological mobilization to respond. In 1888 the experimental psychologist L. Lange discovered in a reaction-time experiment that subjects who were consciously prepared to press a telegraph key to

---

[1]We are indebted to Allport's (1935) and Fleming's (1967) histories of the attitude concept in preparing this section.

a signal reacted more quickly than subjects whose primary attention was focused on the incoming signal rather than the response. He called this reaction a "task-attitude" or *aufgabe*. To Lange, the task-attitude was a musculature preparation to respond (e.g., an "alert attitude"). The English neurophysiologist, Charles Sherrington referred (1906) to attitude, not as the occasional manifestation of a strong emotion or a certain task set, but as one's normal pose or posture (e.g., an "upright attitude"). Although Darwin, Lange, and Sherrington viewed attitudes as motor states, the mental (or cognitive) view was destined to take prominence.

The first indication of this came from the German Würzburg school of psychology, whose mentors included Külpe, Wündt, Titchener, Watt, and Ach. The aim of this school was to study the phenomenon of thought—a traditional theme handed down from the ancient Greeks. The Würzburg school regarded an attitude as a task set, as did Lange; but instead of focusing on the motor aspect, they focused on the mental, or abstract, and logical aspects. As a result of the Würzburg work, most psychologists came to accept "attitude" as an indispensable concept, though not all believed attitudes to be reducible to purely mental events.

Margaret Washburn (1916), Titchener's first doctoral student, tried to combine both the mental and motor conceptions of attitude. In *Movement and Mental Imagery*, she proposed that all intellectual processes were accompanied by motor impulses, however slight (i.e., mental work was physical). Washburn's book strengthened the association of attitude with mental activities without diminishing the motor aspect. At about the same time, John B. Watson (1919), the founder of the behaviorist school of psychology, was arguing that all thinking could in principle be correlated with movements of the larynx (and emotions with tremors of the genitals). Chapter 4 in this book presents some current thinking about the relations among physiological activity, mental processes, and attitudes.

The mental view of attitudes was given a large boost in 1918 with the publishing of a landmark in social research, *The Polish Peasant in Europe and America*, a study of the problems Polish immigrants faced in coming to the United States. A key concept in this work (1927 edition) by sociologist William I. Thomas and poet-philosopher Florian Znaniecki was *attitude*, which they defined as "a process of individual consciousness which determines real or possible activity of the individual in the social world [p. 22]." For Thomas and Znaniecki, an attitude was always a feeling directed toward some object. Thus "love of children," "hatred of criminals," and "respect for science" were possible attitudes. This view of attitude was important historically not only because attitudes had acquired an "object" but also because Thomas and Znaniecki had stripped attitude of its physiological content. This non-physiological, more cognitive view of attitude became acceptable to psychologists in large part because the influential psychologists of the 1930s (e.g., Hull, Tolman, Skinner) were neo-behaviorists who postulated nothing about physiology. Also, during the mid-thirties and in the years beyond, researchers began to explore the similarities between attitude and psychophysical judgments—the earliest area of mental investigation in experimental psychology (e.g., Sherif, 1935; Sherif & Cantril 1945, 1946; Tresselt & Volkmann, 1942).

At the same time, however, by making attitudes less physiological and more cognitive, Thomas and Znaniecki removed the part that made attitudes observable. The concept of attitude would surely decline in empirical science if it were not measurable. Fortunately, theory and techniques for the measurement of attitudes were soon developed by L. L. Thurstone (1928), a University of Chicago psychologist whose primary interest had been in psychophysics, and by Rensis Likert (1932), a statistician with the U. S. Department of Agriculture. Both Thurstone and Likert introduced direct methods of measuring the pro-con or evaluative property of attitudes. These techniques were soon followed by others, including Moreno's *sociometric choices* in 1934, Guttman's *cumulative scaling method* in 1941, Coombs' *unfolding technique* in 1952, and Osgood, Suci, and Tannenbaum's *semantic differential* in 1957. The popular techniques for measuring attitudes are presented in the next chapter.

The first notable effort to achieve a significant sampling of public attitudes on a variety of topics appeared in 1929 in Robert and Helen Lynd's *Middletown,* an in-depth discussion of life in Muncie, Indiana, which became the first sociological best-seller. Public awareness of attitude surveys increased in 1936, when the now defunct *Literary Digest* attempted to predict, through a nationwide postcard poll, the winner of the presidential election (they failed miserably, however, because their sample of affluent respondents contained a much higher percentage of Republicans than appeared in the electorate). By World War II, the cognitive conception of attitude was well entrenched in American scientific and lay vocabularies.

TRADITIONAL APPROACHES TO THE STUDY OF PERSUASION

Once the concept of attitude was firmly established, attention turned to the interesting question of attitude change. Although the first known set of principles governing the art of persuasion was recorded in the fourth century B.C. by Aristotle in his *Rhetoric,* it was not until the present century that attitude change was investigated experimentally (cf. Chen, 1935; Knower, 1935, 1936; Lund, 1925). The first large-scale, systematic, experimental investigations of attitude change were conducted by Carl Hovland and his colleagues during World War II. Hovland interested a number of psychologists in attitude research during the war while experimenting on the persuasive impact of various U. S. Army morale and training films (Hovland, Lumsdaine, & Sheffield, 1949). After the war, Hovland established the Attitude Change and Communication Research Project at Yale, which helped to make the study of attitudes and persuasion one of the most important topics in psychology. Four general theoretical approaches can be identified in the work on persuasion since World War II (McGuire, 1969a, 1972; Smith, 1968). They are the learning approach, perceptual approach, functional approach, and consistency approach. After a brief discussion of each, we discuss the cognitive response approach to persuasion.

Learning Theory Approach to Persuasion

The learning theory approach assumes that learning processes are responsible for attitude change. One of the first investigators in persuasion to take the learning approach was Doob (1947), who suggested that attitudes were nonobservable responses that were learned and changed through the application of rewards and punishments, just like all other responses.

The notion that attitudes could be changed through the application of reinforcers suggested that the principles of classical and instrumental conditioning could be applied to attitude change. For example, in an experiment employing the classical conditioning approach, Zanna, Kiesler, and Pilkonis (1970) demonstrated that a word that signaled the onset of an electric shock over a series of trials was rated less favorably on an attitude scale than a word associated with the cessation of the shocks. In classical conditioning terms, the electric shock was an *unconditioned stimulus* that produced the *unconditioned response* of discomfort and pain. By pairing the originally neutral word (or *conditioned stimulus*) with the electric shock over a series of trials, eventually the negative affect, which was previously associated only with the electric shock was elicited by the word. Thus, the previously neutral attitude toward the word had become a negative one through classical conditioning (see Staats, 1967, for more information on the classical conditioning of attitudes).

In classical conditioning, the response to be learned is initially elicited by the unconditioned stimulus. In instrumental conditioning, the person initially emits a variety of different responses, one of which is rewarded. For example, Insko (1965), interviewed students over the telephone about initiating a campus festival. Half of the students were rewarded with a comment like "good" whenever they made statements favorable to the festival, and half were rewarded whenever they made unfavorable statements. When their opinions on creating the festival were measured 1 week later, the results indicated that the telephone verbal reinforcement had a significant effect on the students' attitudes. (See Lott & Lott, 1968, for more on instrumental conditioning of attitudes.)

The major concern with conditioning procedures is the question of whether subjects are aware of the stimulus–response connection that the experimenter is trying to establish (Page, 1969). If the subject is aware of the connection, then the effects may be best explained by a more cognitive theory. In Chapter 14, Insko presents a cognitive interpretation of attitudinal verbal reinforcement effects.

Some of the most influential attitude researchers employing the learning approach were those working in Hovland's Communication Research Program at Yale, from which several important volumes of research resulted. The most thorough presentation of their conceptual approach is *Communication and Persuasion* (Hovland, Janis, & Kelley, 1953). Because of their learning orientation, which emphasized stimulus–response connections, Hovland and his co-workers focused on stimulus variables in the persuasion situation that would determine the responses of attending, comprehending, and yielding to the message facts and arguments. Aspects of the source of the message, the content of the message, the mode of message presentation, and characteristics of the audience assumed particular importance. These variables are given considerable attention in Part II of this volume.

In general, learning theorists propose that it is learning to associate positive or negative attributes with the attitude object that is crucial in achieving persuasion. This approach includes learning message facts and arguments, as well as acquiring affective emotional responses through conditioning.

Perceptual Theory Approach to Persuasion

The perceptual approach emphasizes the meaning that the persuasive communication has for the subject. Thus, if we want to predict what effect a certain communication will have on attitude, we need to know how the person perceives it. For example, Asch (1948) suggests that the actual meaning of a statement is determined by who says it. Take the statement, "I hold it that a little rebellion now and then is a good thing, and as necessary in the political world as storms are in the physical." Asch (1948) argues that the meaning of this statement can be different depending on whether it is attributed to Thomas Jefferson (the actual author) or Vladimir Lenin. The statement may be more persuasive when it is attributed to Jefferson, because when he is the author, subjects interpret the statement to mean that people should be independent; they should not be afraid to stand up for what they feel is right. When Lenin is the author, however, the statement is interpreted to mean that people should engage in revolution and overthrow the government.

Sherif and Cantril (1945, 1946), in describing the effect of perception on attitude change, have noted two general classes of effects—selectivity of perception and frame of reference. Selectivity of perception concerns investigating the portion of the objective world to which the individual is actually paying attention. Frame of reference concerns contextual factors thought to influence judgments, such as the distribution of stimuli that have previously been encountered in the judgment setting. The most popular perceptual theory is undoubtedly Sherif and Hovland's (1961) social judgment theory, which is discussed briefly in Chapter 8 of this volume.

Functional Theory Approach to Persuasion

The functional approach emphasizes the relationship of the position advocated in the persuasive communication to the person's underlying motivational and personality needs. If the communication addresses a different need from the one on which the relevant attitude is based, then persuasion may not occur. For example, let us assume that an Anglo-American dislikes a Chicano because this allows him to feel superior. Functional theorists would argue that this attitude can only be changed if the person is shown the connections between his attitude and underlying ego-defensive motives. A communication designed merely to provide factual information about Chicanos would not be effective, as our hypothetical person's attitude serves an "ego-defensive" function rather than a "knowledge" function. This ego-defensive attitude protects the person from acknowledging basic truths about himself or realities in the external world (Katz, 1960). An attitude serving a "knowledge" function is based upon an individual's need for meaningful cognitive organization, consistency, and clarity. An attitude can also serve a "utilitarian" function, in which the aim is to maximize external rewards and minimize punishments; or a "value expression" function, in which the attitude is aimed at maintaining self-identity or enhancing favorable self-image. Although other functions have been suggested, functionalists are united in the belief that attitude change depends on the extent to which the persuasive communication is relevant to a personal or social need. Investigators who have worked within the functional framework include Adorno, Frenkel-Brunswik, Levinson, and Sanford (1950), Katz and Stotland (1959), Kelman (1961), Sarnoff (1960), and Smith, Bruner, and White (1956).

Consistency Theory Approach to Persuasion

Consistency theorists hold that a person may adjust a personal attitude in order to maintain internal harmony in the belief system. Attitudes change when some fact, behavior, or event produces inconsistency within the system. For example, when a smoker hears a message that says it is harmful to one's health to smoke, this idea is inconsistent with the already held belief that "I like to smoke" or with the behavior of smoking. This message may cause the smoker's attitude toward smoking to change to make it more consistent with the new information. The smoker, of course, may maintain consistency in other ways. She might reject the message as untrue, or she might adopt the new belief that "one's health isn't very important." In any case, the person is thought to be motivated to maintain consistency. The three most popular consistency theories are Heider's (1946) balance theory, Festinger's (1957) dissonance theory (both discussed in Chapter 14), and Osgood and Tannenbaum's (1955) congruity theory (discussed in Chapter 7).

THE COGNITIVE RESPONSE APPROACH
TO PERSUASION

Each of these approaches to persuasion—learning, perceptual, functional, and consistency—has its advantages and adherents. In this volume we focus on another approach that emphasizes the importance of cognitive responses in persuasion. Most current research on persuasion employs such "cold" attitude measures as the simple evaluative ticks on a scale (illustrated in Table 1.1) and thereby neglects "hot" cognitions (as illustrated in Table 1.2) (Abelson, 1963). The cognitive response approach (as originally outlined by Greenwald, 1968a) postulates that when people receive persuasive communications, they will attempt to relate the new information to their existing knowledge about the topic. In doing this, the person may consider much cognitive material that is not in the communication itself. These additional self-generated cognitions may agree with the proposals of the source, disagree, or be entirely irrelevant to the communication. To the extent that the communication evokes cognitive responses that are supportive, the subject will tend to agree with the source. To the extent that the communication evokes antagonistic cognitive responses, because the self-generated cognitions either refute the arguments of the source or support a position other than the one advocated, the subject will disagree. It is also possible that the subject's own antagonistic cognitive responses may be so much more persuasive than the message's arguments that the subject may come away with an attitude opposite to that advocated (referred to as *boomerang*).

The notion that a person's cognitive responses are an important mediator of persuasion and thus should be studied is not new. In 1949, Hovland, Lumsdaine, and Sheffield suggested that an audience may protect itself against persuasion by going over its own arguments against the position while hearing a presentation. Hovland later (1951) emphasized that the best way to study the internal process of attitude change was to have subjects "verbalize as completely as possible their thoughts as they responded to the communication [p. 430]." Other researchers continued to stress that an audience is not passive but counterargues, constructs positions opposing what it is hearing, anticipates what will come, and carries on its own concurrent discourse (Brock, 1967; Festinger & Maccoby, 1964; Freedman & Sears, 1965; Kelman, 1953).

By 1968, the call for research on the implicit cognitive responses that accompany attitude change had become a chorus. McGuire (1968b) emphasized the need to allow the subject "complete freedom" in formulating and expressing the propositions that make up his or her belief system. "A study of these subject-generated propositions might suggest the rules of inference which he is following [p. 155]." Both Greenwald (1968a) and Weiss (1968) also stressed that an understanding of the attitudinal impact of a message must take into account the self-generated arguments of subjects in hearing the message; the impact of the message may well be reduced if subjects counterattack it with their own arguments.

Although many have recognized the importance of cognitive responses in understanding attitude formation and change, theoretical and empirical work on cognitive response is only now gaining prominence. Theoretical treatments have appeared in scattered sources and have usually not dealt with recipient thoughts. A primary objective of this volume is to survey past theoretical and empirical work as well as current research that employs thought-listing measures. We aim to promote a better understanding of what is known and to highlight directions for future research.

Relation of the Cognitive Response Approach to Other Approaches

The learning, perceptual, functional, and consistency approaches have often been viewed as separate (and competing) theoretical orientations. To the extent that one was correct, the others were viewed as wrong. The cognitive response approach is not offered as a fifth competing approach but as complementary to the others. In fact, it has its roots in the other approaches. Each of the four traditional approaches can be discussed in cognitive response terms, although the focus of each is different. For example, a learning theorist would propose that a persuasive communication is effective to the extent that the recipients adopt the message's arguments as their own cognitive responses. Perceptual theorists would be interested in how a person's preexisting repertoire of cognitions influences the meaning given to a message. Functional theorists would expect people to have different cognitive responses to the same communication depending on how the communication relates to underlying needs. Consistency theorists would focus on the consistency or inconsistency between the responses elicited by the message and already existing cognitions. In large part, the cognitive response approach can be viewed as an attempt to bring the four traditional approaches together by examining the thoughts elicited when a person anticipates, receives, or reflects on a communication.

Although each of the four traditional approaches to persuasion suggests ways in which cognitive responses can mediate attitude change, researchers have paid little attention to the actual cognitive responses produced in the persuasion setting. The cognitive response approach emphasizes such questions as: What variables facilitate and inhibit the generation of cognitive responses? What variables associated with a persuasive appeal are likely to produce favorable cognitive responses? What variables are likely to produce negative responses? What kinds of cognitive responses are mediators of persuasion, and what kinds are irrelevant? To repeat: The cognitive response approach holds that an understanding of the contents of the thoughts produced in the persuasion context is essential if the process of attitude change is to be understood fully.

Early Attempts at Measuring Cognitive Responses

Before cognitive responses could be analyzed in detail, however, an effective means for measuring thoughts had to be developed. The introspectionist school (of which Würzburg school was part) was the first to report success. The school's founder, Wilhelm Wündt, established the first laboratory dedicated to experimental psychology in 1879 in Leipzig, Germany. He studied mental events by training subjects to report the elements of their conscious experience. Another important influence on the measurement of cognitive responses was Sigmund Freud's (1900/1939) method of free association used in the interpretation of dreams. In free association, a person is encouraged to say everything that enters the mind without censoring it.

Attitude researchers have employed various methods to assess cognitive responses. Hovland, Lumsdaine, and Sheffield (1949) used a technique previously employed in radio research (Hallonquist & Suchman, 1944) and currently used in audience tests of new television programs. Subjects were provided with a pair of push buttons during the showing of a movie and were instructed to press one button during portions of the film that they liked and the other during portions they did not like. Oral reports have also been tried. In one experiment, subjects gave their impressions of a persuasive communication vocally while they were reading it. The results indicated that a "low-threat" communication on smoking and cancer elicited fewer verbal criticisms and more attitude change than did a "high-threat" communication that strongly emphasized the seriousness of lung cancer (Janis & Terwilliger, 1962).

Perhaps the most elaborate study of attitudes, which also probed cognitive responses, was conducted by Smith, Bruner, and White (1956). These investigators wanted to analyze in detail the interrelationship of attitude and personality, believing that if one "looks far enough into the origins of any opinion, one will find not just an opinion, but a sample of how the holder of that opinion copes with the world [p. 40]." Their study, aimed at investigating attitudes about Russia, involved 10 men who were put through 28 procedures requiring 15 weekly 2-hour sessions. The subjects responded to open-ended interviews about the Soviet Union (in which respondents were encouraged to tell as much as they could about their feelings toward Russia), *information apperception tests* (in which subjects gave the meaning of 10 "loaded" statements, such as: "In 1939, more books were published in Russia than in any other country—including many translations of such writers as Shakespeare''), *stress interviews* (in which interviewers alternated attacking and defending the subjects' views and recorded their cognitive reactions), and other projective and free-response procedures.

But most early attempts to measure cognitive responses were not as extensive as those of Smith, Bruner, and White (1956). Generally, the research employed open-ended questions instead of, or in addition to, fixed-response attitude scales. In their influential social psychology text, Krech and Crutchfield (1948) advocated the use of open-ended questions over fixed-response items because they allow "the utmost opportunity for the individual to express his opinions in his own terms and from his own point of view [p. 282]." Thus, although some early attitude researchers did measure cognitive responses, a full understanding of the role of such responses awaited the advances in techniques of measurement and conceptualization that are discussed in the next chapter. Let us look at how cognitive response measures were used in each of the traditional approaches to persuasion we have discussed.

Learning Approach. A measure of particular importance to learning theorists is a measure of free recall. According to the learning view, the amount of persuasion should be related to the amount of material retained from the persuasive communication. Insko (1964) had subjects listen to the prosecution and defense arguments from a supposedly real bigamy trial. One communication was presented either immediately, 2 days, 1 week, or 2 weeks after the other. Measures of opinion and free recall of arguments were taken either immediately, 2 days, or 1 week after the second communication. When the measures were taken immediately after the second communication, the longer the time interval between the two communications, the greater the persuasive impact of the second communication and the more numerous the arguments that could be recalled from the second communication (a recency effect). Other results generally indicated that the pattern of recall paralleled the pattern of opinion. However, the fact that the average within-cell correlation between recall and opinion was low ($r = .10$) and nonsignificant (indicating that for any given experimental group, attitude could not be predicted by knowing how many message arguments a person recalled) led Insko to conclude that message retention did not appear to mediate the effect of time upon opinion. Insko proposed that time independently affected both opinion and retention. Similar results were obtained by Miller and Campbell (1959) and by Watts and McGuire (1964).

Studies of person perception have produced similar results. Anderson and Hubert (1963) found that an impression formed on the basis of trait adjectives provided by an experimenter did not depend on the ability to recall those adjectives. These experiments suggest that persistence of attitude change does not depend on the ability to recall specific message features. More recent data suggest that persistence may depend instead on the ability to recall the cognitive responses that were initially elicited by the persuasive communication (Greenwald, 1968a; Petty, 1977a).

Perceptual Approach.   Perceptual theorists focus on the meaning of stimuli. In one experiment, subjects were asked to read statements attributed to various authors and then to write down what they thought the authors' motives were (Horowitz & Pastore, 1955). The greater the esteem for the author, the more subjects agreed with the statement and the more their thoughts reflected an attribution of good motives to the author. In another experiment, Horowitz (1963) gave subjects one of three motives for an American prisoner of war in Korea to have accepted anti-United States propaganda. Some subjects were told that the "betrayal" had occurred under torture, others that it occurred to make life more comfortable, and others that it occurred impulsively. After being given this information, subjects were asked to respond to three open-ended questions designed to assess feelings about the soldier, his act, and its consequences. An analysis of the responses showed that different cognitive themes emerged with the different motives. Horowitz concluded that the motive provided for the treasonous act contributed to the meaning of that act, which in turn influenced subjects' subsequent evaluations of the soldier involved. In addition, Horowitz reported that subjects tried to interpret the acts to match their preexisting cognitions.

Functional Approach.   A functional theorist would contend that the only new responses a person would add to an existing cognitive structure are ones that would serve some function for the person. Jones and Aneshansel (1956) asked students who were in favor of and opposed to segregation to learn 11 brief antisegregation statements and then tested them for free recall. Generally, those opposed to segregation were able to recall the statements more accurately than those in favor. However, when the prosegregationists were told that in a subsequent second task they would be required to *counterargue* a prosegregationist position, they recalled the antisegregation statements more accurately than the antisegregationists. Presumably, the prosegregationists had a utilitarian motive to put some antisegregation material "on file," whereas the antisegregationists felt less need to do this. Jones and Kohler (1958) also demonstrated a motivational basis for incorporating responses into one's cognitive structure by showing that subjects who were asked to learn plausible statements learned proattitudinal statements better than counterattitudinal ones. But when subjects were asked to learn implausible statements, they learned counterattitudinal statements better than proattitudinal ones.

Consistency Approach.   As we have seen, consistency theorists hold that a person is motivated to maintain consistency among feelings, beliefs, and behaviors. If a person engages in counterattitudinal behavior, that individual may be motived to change his or her attitude in order to restore consistency with that behavior. Early research demonstrated that feelings of inconsistency (or dissonance) were more likely to occur when persons felt they had freely chosen to engage in a discrepant action than when they felt coerced (cf. Brehm & Cohen, 1962). For example, Brock (1962) asked non-Catholic college freshmen to write an essay on "Why I would like to become a Catholic." Some subjects were told they had no choice but to write the essay, whereas others were led to believe they had a high amount of choice. In accord with a consistency theory prediction, Brock found that the greater the perception of choice in writing the counterattitudinal essay, the greater the attitude change in favor of becoming a Catholic. Brock also asked subjects to write their responses to the phrase, "For me, becoming a Catholic would mean . . . ," both before and after the counterattitudinal essays were written. Subjects were further asked to categorize their cognitions into naturally occurring groups. To indicate the bonds or relationships among the thoughts, subjects were asked to indicate which cognitions would have to be changed, modified, or excluded if any one response was changed, modified, or excluded. These response measures were taken in an attempt to determine what changes in the structure of cognitive responses accompanied attitude change. Brock reports that attitude change (i.e., a restoration of consistency) tended to correlate with an increase in the interrelatedness (i.e., bonds) among cognitions and with a decrease in the number of groupings.

THEMES IN EARLY RESEARCH
ON COGNITIVE RESPONSES

Having looked at some techniques for measuring cognitive responses employed by early researchers using different approaches, let us turn to the development of the cognitive response approach itself. The early attitude research relevant to the cognitive response approach can be divided into three broad areas. First, and perhaps most important, is work that concerns the links between an attitude and the thoughts relevant to the attitude (affective–cognitive links). Another area of research concerns the organizational structure of cognitive responses. A final area concerns individual differences in cognitive style, which may be important because individuals with different cognitive styles may produce different kinds of cognitive responses. Each of these broad areas is discussed briefly.

Affective–Cognitive Links

The notion that a person's own cognitive responses might be important in producing persuasion received support from three kinds of early experiments. In the research on active versus passive participation (which concerned whether the recipient of a persuasive communication was a passive listener or an active participant in the persuasion setting) and inoculation theory (which concerned ways of resisting the persuasive impact of a communication), no attempts were made to measure implicit cognitive responses; however, the pattern of data in these studies clearly suggested that a person's own responses were important in mediating persuasion. In a third kind of study, persons' beliefs and/or values were measured in an attempt to predict affective and evaluative reactions. We discuss each of these areas of research in turn.

Active Versus Passive Participation.   Some researchers investigated whether it was generally more effective for a person to participate actively in the persuasion process or to be a passive recipient of information. Active participation can take several forms. In a classic study in social psychology, Lewin (1947) performed experiments to compare group discussion with individual instruction. The objective of one experiment was to increase the consumption of beef hearts, kidneys, and other unusual meats during World War II. Groups of housewives participated for 45 minutes. They either listened to a persuasive lecture or participated in a group discussion. Both groups had access to the same information. A follow-up survey showed that only 3% of the women in the lecture group served one of the meats, whereas 32% of the women in the group discussion served them. Although there are several ways to explain these results, one possibility is that women in the group discussion produced their own arguments that were more persuasive than the arguments contained in the lecture.

In a more controlled experiment, Janis and King (1954) found that subjects who were instructed to give an informal talk on one of three conterattitudinal topics changed their attitudes more in the direction they advocated than did other subjects who passively listened to the talks. The experimenter's observations and subsequent interviews with the subjects revealed that on the two topics for which the greatest attitude change was produced, subjects improvised more in their talks; whereas for the topic producing the least change, subjects stayed close to the prepared outline available for each topic. Janis and King (1954) hypothesized that improvisation might be a critical factor, "perhaps because the communicatee is stimulated to think of the kinds of arguments, illustrations, and motivating appeals that he regards as most convincing [p. 215]." However, subjects also reported being more satisfied with their talks on the two high-change topics. This satisfaction might also account for the data.

King and Janis (1956) had subjects in another experiment either read a persuasive communication into a tape recorder, read and then give their own improvised version of the communication, or simply read the communication to themselves. Subjects in the improvisation condition changed their attitudes on the topic significantly more than subjects in either the oral or silent reading conditions. Subjects in the oral reading condition felt the most satisfied with their performance, however. This result further supports the view that one's own cognitive responses on a topic are the most compelling (see Harvey & Beverly,

1961; Scott, 1957; for similar results). More recently, Greenwald and Albert (1968) showed that subjects tend to accept and to recall their own improvised arguments more than comparable arguments improvised by others, and that personally improvised arguments are viewed as more original than those of others. In other words, people seem to have a higher regard for their own self-generated thoughts than for those originating externally.

Inoculation Theory.   Some research has focused on procedures for creating resistance to persuasion. McGuire (1964) used a biological analogy to suggest two basic ways to make someone resistant to counterattitudinal propaganda. One can either bolster the health of the original attitude by providing supportive information and arguments, or one can "inoculate" the attitude by presenting the individual with weak counterarguments to his or her own view, accompanied by refutations. McGuire argues that the presentation of refuted weak counterarguments will produce resistance to subsequent stronger attacks because the inoculation poses a threat that motivates the individual to develop bolstering arguments for the somewhat weakened belief. This practice in generating supportive cognitive responses and refuting attacks enables the person to resist subsequent propaganda more effectively than can nonpracticed (or noninoculated) persons.

In the first study to test the effectiveness of inoculation on resistance to persuasion, McGuire and Papageorgis (1961) collected a set of cultural truisms: It's a good idea to brush your teeth after every meal if at all possible; the effects of penicillin have been, almost without exception, of great benefit to mankind; mental illness is not contagious. Truisms should be highly susceptible to persuasion because most people have little practice in defending these beliefs. Subjects were given two defenses with which to resist potential attacks. For one truism, they were given a *supportive defense* that consisted of paragraphs containing elaborations of separate arguments in favor of the truism. For a second truism, the same subjects received a *refutational defense* that consisted of paragraphs presenting and refuting arguments against the truism. The refutational defense was, of course, the inoculation treatment. Two days after the defenses were provided, the subjects heard three counterattitudinal messages. One attacked the truism that received the supportive defense, another attacked the truism that received the refutational defense, and another attacked a truism that had received no defense. After the counterattitudinal attacks, subjects rated their attitudes on all three truisms and on a truism for which neither a defense nor a subsequent attack was provided. The results (Fig. 1.1) showed that both defenses were helpful in resisting the effects of the counterattitudinal message, but the refutational defense (inoculation treatment) was significantly more effective. To test the notion that refutational defenses motivated subjects to bolster their attitudes, subjects were asked to list thoughts in favor of their initial positions 1 week after being exposed to the defenses. More supportive thoughts were listed by subjects

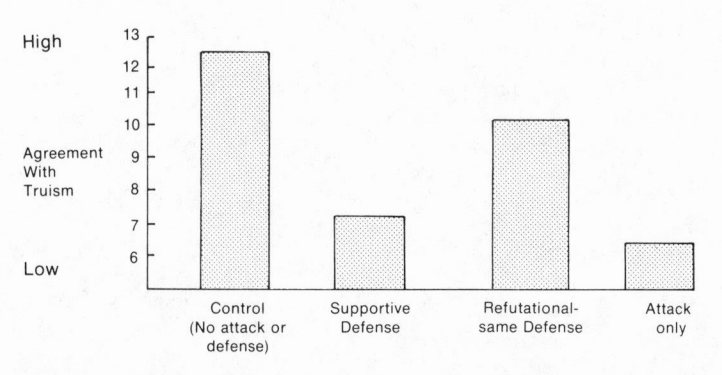

FIG. 1.1.   Resistance conferred by supportive and refutational defenses (from McGuire & Papageorgis, 1961).

who had been exposed to the refutational than to the supportive defense ($p < .10$, one-tailed).

In the study just mentioned, the arguments used in the counterattitudinal attack were those previously refuted in the refutational defense (a refutational-same defense). According to inoculation theory, however, the inoculation effect should not be confined to such cases. Papageorgis and McGuire (1961) found that inoculation defenses in which arguments other than those used in the subsequent counterattitudinal attack are refuted (a refutational-different defense) were equally effective in producing reistance, and both were superior to a supportive defense in conferring resistance.

Inoculation theory also predicts the persistence of induced resistance to persuasion over time. Supportive defenses provide arguments to support one's initial viewpoint. As these arguments are forgotten, the effectiveness of the supportive defense should diminish. Refutational-different defenses show persons how to refute arguments other than those used in later counterattitudinal propaganda. This defense works presumably because the person, in learning that his or her belief is vulnerable, is motivated to assimilate belief-bolstering material as well as to seek new information. Thus, resistance should initially increase as the person seeks new bolstering responses but should then decrease as time passes and motivation to generate supporting cognitive responses diminishes.

Refutational-same defenses enable the person to refute the very attack he or she will later receive. For this defense, persistence of resistance depends on the ability to recall the specific refuting arguments as well as the increased motivation to generate supporting cognitive responses. Combining these processes leads to the prediction that resistance should decline more in later intervals than in earlier ones. McGuire (1962) tested these predictions. The highly supportive data he obtained are graphed in Fig. 1.2. The mean belief for the supportive defenses dropped off significantly over time, as did the mean belief for the refutational-

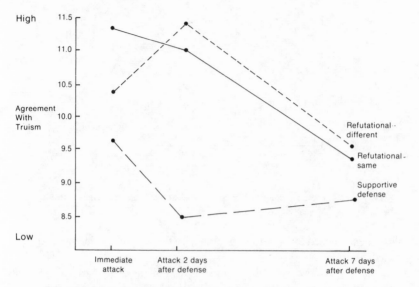

FIG. 1.2. Persistence of the resistance to persuasion conferred by three types of prior belief defenses (from McGuire, 1962).

same defenses. As predicted, the refutational-different defenses exhibited a non-monotonic trend (the rise in mean belief from immediate to 2 days is significant). Again, the refutational (inoculation) defenses produced more resistance than the supportive defenses.

McGuire also addressed the question of whether active or passive participation is more effective when one is preparing to defend one's beliefs. Under active defense conditions, persons are assigned the task of writing a defense (supportive or refutational) either from an outline or without any assistance. Under passive defense conditions, persons simply read a defense that was previously prepared by the investigator. Because individuals have so little experience in defending their beliefs on the cultural truisms, McGuire argues that they will be poorly prepared to generate cognitive defenses in the active conditions, and that passive defenses will produce more resistance to an immediate attack. However, because individuals perform so poorly in the active conditions, they become more motivated to defend their beliefs. McGuire (1964) reports that an experimental investigation revealed that although passive defenses tended to be superior when the counterattitudinal attack was immediate, active defenses (supportive, refutational-same, and refutational-different) increased in resistance conferral when the attack occurred 1 week later; whereas passive defenses (particularly supportive and refutational-same) showed a drop in resistance 1 week later. A passive refutational-different defense led to a slight increase in resistance 1 week later because presumably, like the active defenses, it posed a threat that motivated the generation of bolstering cognitive responses.

Early experiments on active versus passive participation and inoculation theory thus clearly suggested that a person's individual cognitive responses play a crucial role in mediating attitudinal changes.

Relation of Attitudes to Underlying Beliefs and Values.   Many early experiments focused on determining if any relationship existed between attitude changes and changes in underlying individual beliefs and values. Persuasive communications typically consist of arguments, examples, or illustrations designed to change a person's beliefs about an attitude object (like the death penalty). Thus, early attitude theorists postulated that attitude change was primarily due to changes in beliefs about attitude objects (Cartwright & Harary, 1956; Smith, Bruner, & White, 1956). Numerous empirical studies have related the affective disposition toward an object (attitude) to a person's beliefs about the object itself, or its value-attaining powers.

Cartwright (1949), for example, reported that during the Seventh War Loan Campaign (in World War II), which was designed to get Americans to buy U.S. savings bonds, people who could give more reasons (favorable cognitive responses) for buying bonds in an interview were more likely to have actually bought bonds. In a similar linking of beliefs with affect, Smith (1949) reported that the extent of positive or negative feeling toward the Soviet Union could be predicted from the person's pattern of values and his or her beliefs about how these values are influenced by the Soviet Union (see also Woodruff, 1942; Woodruff & DiVesta, 1948).

Kelman (1953) presented seventh graders with a counterattitudinal communication that argued against Superman comic books and in favor of Tarzan comic books. He then asked the students to write an essay in favor of the Tarzan books and promised them either a certain reward, a low probability of a reward, or no reward. The greatest attitude change toward the Tarzan books was produced in the group that had a low probability of receiving a reward. In analyzing the quality of the essays, Kelman found that students writing under the low-probability-of-reward conditions wrote the best essays (presumably because under the low-probability conditions, the quality of the essay would enhance the probability of a reward). In Kelman's terms, the students who produced the most supporting and least interfering responses in their essays evidenced the most attitude change in the direction of their essays.

In an ambitious early investigation of the relationship between attitudes and cognitive responses, Peak and Morrison (1958) had college students read and think about either pro- or antisegregation arguments after measuring their initial attitudes. A control group worked on an irrelevant task. Three weeks later, attitudes were again measured, and subjects were classified as either pro- or antisegregation depending on how they rated themselves on this second attitude measure. Subjects were also asked to list all the good and bad consequences that might result from desegregation and to underline the consequences that they personally accepted. Only the antisegregation arguments were found to produce attitude change. In addition, antisegregation subjects who had earlier been exposed to the antisegregation arguments generated more good consequences of desegregation that they personally accepted than did anti-segregation controls who had not been previously exposed to the antisegregation arguments. Furthermore, prosegregation subjects exposed to the antisegregation arguments generated fewer bad consequences of desegregation than did prosegregation controls. These data suggest that the antisegregation arguments were effective in producing attitude change because they modified subjects' personal beliefs about the consequences of desegregation.

Some researchers have prepared messages specifically designed to change underlying beliefs and values in order to show that attitude change would follow changes in relevant cognitions. Carlson (1956) found that by making moderately prejudiced college students aware of how desegregation would lead to the attainment of four important goals (e.g., greater American prestige in other countries), more favorable attitudes toward integration could be produced. In an experiment by Stotland, Katz, and Patchen (1959), college coeds read a communication designed to give insight into the psychodynamics of racial prejudice and, in addition, were subjected to various manipulations aimed at facilitating the internal restructuring of beliefs (e.g., ordering statements about prejudice into cause-and-effect sequences). There was no reduction in prejudice immediately after the inductions, but a significant reduction was shown in a measure taken 3 to 4 weeks later, suggesting that restructuring of responses takes some time to occur. The Stotland et. al. and Carlson experiments are particularly interesting, because the investigators were apparently able to produce a change in affect, not through the use of persuasive messages attacking racial prejudice directly, but by attacking the cognitive foundations of the prejudice.

Before concluding this section on affective–cognitive links, we should mention the mathematical models developed to describe the affective–cognitive linkages. The most frequently cited are those of Rosenberg (1956), Anderson (1959), and Fishbein (1963). Rosenberg (1956) proposed that an attitude toward a particular object is a function of (1) the probability that the object leads to good or bad consequences and (2) the degree of satisfaction or dissatisfaction expected from these consequences. An "index of affective loading" can be derived from the sum of the products for each goal of (1) a number corresponding to the satisfaction value of the goal (or consequence) and (2) a number corresponding to the instrumental probability that the attitude object leads to the goal. If, for example, a subject rated the goal of reducing property values as -10 and saw integration as having a 0.9 probability of reducing property values, the contribution of that goal item to the affective loading index for the concept integration would be -9.0. This would be added to the contributions for all other goal items. Rosenberg (1956) found a high positive correlation between his affective loading index and a measure of attitudes. Consistent with the cognitive response approach, Rosenberg also reported that an index based on goals generated by the individual subjects to a verbal probe showed a stronger relation to attitude than indices based on a standard set of experimenter-provided goals.

Whereas most early researchers focused on the question of whether belief and value changes would produce subsequent attitudinal changes, Rosenberg (1960b) sought to determine if attitudinal changes would produce subsequent belief changes as measured by his affective loading index. In one experiment, Rosenberg (1960b) hypnotized susceptible subjects and told them that they would feel bad whenever they thought or heard about giving aid to foreign countries. This posthypnotic suggestion was designed to change directly the subjects' attitudes about foreign aid. Measures of attitude and affective loading were administered to the experimental group and to an unhypnotized control group immediately after and 2, 4, and 7 days after the experimental subjects were given the posthypnotic suggestion. At each of the latter three testing periods, the experimental group changed more than the control group both in attitude and on the index of affective loading. Changing affect then seems to result in a persistent change in related cognitions. Incidentally, Rosenberg reports that after the removal of the posthypnotic suggestion, most subjects regained their former attitudes, although there was some tendency for a few subjects to retain the induced attitudes in a weakened form.

The mathematical models proposed by Fishbein and Anderson agree with Rosenberg in that there are two parameters necessary to map the cognitive foundation of an attitude. One parameter generally corresponds to an evaluative component (how positive or negative one feels about some goal or attribute), whereas the other parameter generally corresponds to an importance or strength component (e.g., the likelihood that an object possesses some attribute). The models of Fishbein and Anderson are presented in detail in Chapters 15 and 16 of this volume.

Organizational Structure of Cognitive Responses

Cognitive structure refers to the extent to which a person's cognitions concerning some attitude object are organized and interrelated. Various measures of cognitive structure have been proposed (cf. French, 1947; Scott, 1963; Zajonc, 1960), and some of these are discussed in the next chapter. In this section we consider briefly some of the early work focusing on how cognitions are structured.

Peak (1958) proposed a theory of motivation in which relations among cognitions play a key role in determining behavior. She discusses cognitive structure in terms of the position of the cognitions, the psychological distance among them, and those points that receive activation from some other source. In contrast to Peak's focus on individual cognitions, Rokeach (1960) has sought to characterize an entire cognitive structure or belief–disbelief system as "open" or "closed."

Persons with open systems can process information unencumbered by irrelevant factors such as "unrelated habits, beliefs, irrational ego motives, power needs . . . [p. 57]." Persons with closed systems would presumably have less accurate perceptions of incoming stimulus information. In addition to his work on open and closed cognitive systems, Rokeach (1963) has discussed how deeply rooted in the structure some beliefs are and has reported that under hypnosis, the amount of change that could be produced was inversely proportional to the "centrality" of the belief (the extent to which the belief was connected to other beliefs).

Numerous researchers have analyzed the effects of consistent (the person's beliefs follow from one another) versus inconsistent (some beliefs are contradictory) structures on attitude change. Scott (1959) asked subjects to take a position opposite to their own in a debate. After the debate, Scott found that cognitively inconsistent subjects [as measured by how well the direction and strength of their predebate attitude could be predicted from Rosenberg's (1956) affective loading index] changed their attitudes more (both toward and away from the advocated position) than cognitively consistent subjects, who tended to resist any changes. Hardyck (1963) also found that cognitively consistent subjects were more resistant to persuasion than inconsistent subjects. This was especially true when the subjects were led to believe that the separate opinions they held were relevant to the key persuasion issue.

Gollin (1954) was interested in how an individual's cognitive responses to contradictory information would be organized. Gollin showed male undergraduates a movie in which a young woman behaved in a promiscuous manner in some scenes and in other scenes behaved in a manner suggesting that she was exceedingly kind. After viewing the movie, subjects reported their impressions of the young woman on a rating scale and, in addition, were asked to write detailed impressions of her personality. Gollin was able to sort the written impressions into three organizational structures. Of the 79 subjects tested, 23% attempted to assimilate the conflicting information into an integrated characterization (*related* impressions); 29% mentioned but did not reconcile the conflicting behaviors (*aggregated* impressions); and 48% wrote *simplified* impressions in which either only positive or only negative behaviors were mentioned. Subjects who wrote simplified impressions judged the woman in the film more extremely on the rating scale measure (both favorably and unfavorably) than subjects who wrote aggregate or related impressions. Gollin's research indicates that the formation of an attitude is a function not only of the objective information provided but also of the underlying cognitive organizing process of the observer.

Finally, Abelson and Rosenberg (1958), Abelson (1959), and McGuire (1960c) have discussed how the interrelationship among cognitive responses can produce new responses. Influenced by Heider's (1946) abstract system for representing cognition–sentiment relations (discussed further in Chapter 14), Abelson and Rosenberg (1958) proposed the rules of *psycho-logic*. These rules, which differ from the rules of formal logic, are presumed to operate whenever someone is motivated to think about the cognitive elements in his or her belief system. The rules allow an individual to discover new cognitive responses by combining two old responses with a common element. For example, according to the rules of psycho-logic, the two cognitions, "Al likes Bill" and "Bill likes Chuck," imply a third cognition: "Al likes Chuck." Application of the rules of psycho-logic has been used to predict successfully the resolution of experimentally induced cognitive inconsistency (e.g., Rosenberg & Abelson, 1960). In addition to the rules of psycho-logic, Abelson (1959) proposed several other modes of resolving cognitive inconsistency. For example, a person may engage in *denial,* which involves the alteration of one or more cognitive relations. Or the individual may develop additional consistent relations with one or the other of the inconsistent cognitive units (*bolstering*). Bolstering does not really resolve the inconsistency but simply drowns it out. McGuire (1960c) has shown that merely asking people to express their opinions on logically related issues (i.e., making their cognitive responses on a given topic salient) sets off a tendency to bring these beliefs into greater logical consistency with one another. This *Socratic effect* is discussed in more detail in Chapter 13.

Cognitive Styles

A cognitive style refers to a consistent difference among individuals in the ways in which they process the information available to them. Various styles have been identified.

Cohen (1957) refers to a *need for cognition* variable (based on a measure of how much information is sought in understanding hypothetical situations). Cohen divided a sample of students into those with high and low needs for cognition and then attempted to arouse experimentally a need for cognition either before or after delivering a persuasive message. The experimental need-arousal induction was in fact a fear-arousing oral communication that cited problems with the grading system at Yale. The persuasive message, delivered either before or after the need-arousal induction, advocated "grading on a curve" and presented this method of grading as an excellent way to resolve some of the difficulties of the current system. In general, the message was designed to satisfy specifically the needs aroused by the experimental induction. The results indicated that subjects with a high need for cognitive clarity changed their attitudes toward accepting the solution of grading on a curve to the same extent whether the solution was offered before or after the need-arousal induction. For subjects with low needs for cognitive clarity, the order of presentation made a difference. More change in the direction of the communication occurred when the need-arousal induction came first. Perhaps subjects with weak cognitive needs have to be motivated to process the incoming information, whereas subjects with strong cognitive needs are generally self-motivated to process.

Kelman and Cohler (1959) have distinguished between levelers and sharpeners. *Sharpeners* are people who emphasize unique distinguishing details, whereas *levelers* characteristically ignore such details and seek to simplify their environment. These researchers found that in a persuasion situation, sharpeners showed greater acceptance of the recommendations of a communication than did levelers, and this difference was greatest for those with a high need for cognitive clarity. In explaining these results, Cohen (1964) argued that sharpeners with a high need for cognitive clarity should be especially active in processing all information in a communication, whereas levelers with a high need for cognitive clarity should be especially unobservant in order to avoid ambiguity. Thus, the differences in message processing between levelers and sharpeners should be maximal when they have strong needs for cognitive clarity.

A good deal of research has been done on a style referred to as *cognitive complexity* (Bieri, 1955; Scott, 1962) or conceptual differentiation (Gardner & Schoen, 1962). Scott (1968) refers to cognitive complexity as the "elaboration of the cognitive component of an attitude—the richness of the ideational content, or the number of ideas the person has about the object [p. 207]." Complexity has been positively correlated with cognitive flexibility (the ability to change concepts or categories) (Scott, 1962) and negatively correlated with an index of cognitive balance or consistency (Scott, 1963). Berkowitz and Lundy (1957) have reported that persons with more complexity of constructs showed more change in response to an influence attempt than did simple subjects. These authors hypothesized that complex subjects find more "meaning" in the persuasive communication. It is interesting to speculate that those who find the most "meaning" in a communication (e.g., sharpeners, high complexity) might show the least attitude change if the communication contained simplistic, flawed arguments rather than sound, reasoned ones. In any case, an examination of the cognitive responses generated by persons varying in cognitive style would be helpful in gaining a more precise understanding of how persons differing in style might differ in their manner of processing persuasive communications.

CHAPTER SUMMARY

Even though the expressed attitudes of two persons may appear to be identical, the cognitive foundations of those attitudes may be quite different. In order to understand the effectiveness of persuasive communications, it is necessary to understand the nature of the thoughts that pass through a person's mind as he or she anticipates, receives, or reflects on a communication.

The word *attitude* has always referred to a general orientation toward something, but its origins are as a physical or physiological, rather than as a cognitive, concept. The current view of attitude as a purely mental concept gained acceptance in part from the successful development of new measurement techniques.

In the 50 years in which experimental investigations of persuasion have been conducted, four approaches have emerged. The approaches differ primarily in the aspect of the persuasion situation that is targeted for emphasis. Learning approaches focus on the importance of learning message facts and arguments, or learning to associate various positive (pleasure) or negative (pain) stimuli with the attitude object. Perceptual approaches focus on how a message recipient interprets, understands, and/or distorts the information that is provided. Functional approaches focus on persuasion as a matter of changing a person's underlying motivational or personality needs rather than the amount of objective information or the person's perceptions of that information. Consistency approaches focus on how a person adjusts personal beliefs, attitudes, and behavior in order to keep a maximum degree of internal harmony within the cognitive system.

The cognitive response approach is one that is compatible with each of the traditional approaches, although its focus is somewhat different. The approach postulates that attitude change processes can best be understood by taking into account the thoughts that arise in the persuasion situation. To the extent that the persuasion situation elicits thoughts that are favorable, attitude change in the direction advocated should be facilitated; but if negative thoughts are elicited, attitude change should be inhibited. Methods of measuring a person's thoughts about an attitude issue have ranged from a simple button-pushing technique to an elaborate, multisession interview procedure. Researchers favoring each of the traditional approaches to persuasion have found it useful to employ open-ended assessments of recipients' message-relevant cognitions.

The early research relevant to the cognitive response approach was divided into three subgroupings. The first area concerned links between attitudes and underlying cognitions (beliefs and values). Within this first area, the research on active versus passive participation demonstrated that active involvement in the persuasion process (generating one's own arguments) was more effective than passive exposure to external arguments in producing persuasion. Similarly, the research on inoculation theory indicated that the generation of one's own counterarguments was an important technique for resisting persuasion. Additional early support for affective–cognitive linkages was provided by numerous experiments demonstrating that a person's affective response to an attitude issue could be predicted from that individual's beliefs on that issue. A second area of research focused on the organizational structure of cognitive responses and indicated that attitudes depended not only on the number and type of attitude-relevant thoughts a person possessed but also on how those cognitions were organized and interrelated. A third area of research stressed the need for examining consistent individual differences in the method of processing incoming information (cognitive styles) in order to understand the persuasion process fully.

2 The Nature of Attitudes and Cognitive Responses and Their Relationships to Behavior

John T. Cacioppo
University of Iowa

Stephen G. Harkins
Northeastern University

Richard E. Petty
University of Missouri-Columbia

INTRODUCTION

In the first chapter, the cognitive response approach to the study of attitude change was introduced, and the prominent role that early theorists and researchers gave to the cognitive mediation of persuasion was documented. In this chapter, we define the concepts of attitude and cognitive response more precisely and discuss the most common techniques of measurement. Finally, we discuss the relationships between attitudes, cognitive responses, and behaviors.

The originator of modern attitude measurement, Thurstone (1931), conceived of an attitude as the amount of affect or feeling for or against a stimulus. The attitude concept was subsequently broadened to include dimensions other than the affective one. In their classic investigation of opinions and personality discussed in Chapter 1, Smith, Bruner, and White (1956) conceived of an attitude as containing seven properties. For example, *salience* concerned the extent to which a particular attitude was central in the everyday concerns of a person; *object value* was the affective tone engendered by the attitude; and *orientation* concerned the action or behavioral tendencies aroused by the attitude. Scott (1968) subsequently provided an even more extensive list of 11 features of attitudes (e.g., direction, cognitive complexity, overtness, and so on).

The properties of an attitude described by Smith et al. (1956), Scott (1968), and others can be conceptualized as denoting three classes of responses: (1) *affect*—an individual's general feelings about a stimulus; (2) *cognition*—an individual's thoughts, ideas, associations, and images pertaining to a stimulus; and (3) *conation*—an individual's behavioral responses that are evoked by a stimulus. Numerous researchers have incorporated two or all three types of responses into their definitions of attitude (Allport, 1935; Harding, Kutner, Proshansky, & Chein, 1954; Katz & Stotland, 1959; Rosenberg & Hovland, 1960).

Ostrom (1969) noted that each of the three classes of responses could be used to assess how a person evaluated an object. Thus, affect would concern whether the person had positive or negative feelings toward an object; cognition would concern whether the person associated positive or negative attributes (e.g., qualities, images, and so forth) with the object; and conation would concern whether the person behaved in a positive or negative manner toward the attitude object. Ostrom (1969) concluded that although each type of response could be used to measure an evaluative reaction to an object, the responses were conceptually independent (i. e., each class of response had its own unique determinants).

Recently, there has been a trend back toward the restricted Thurstone (1931) definition. Consider the following recent definitions of attitude:

Attitudes are likes and dislikes [Bem, 1970, p. 14].

[An attitude] is a feeling that an attitude object is good or bad, fair or unfair [Collins, 1970, p. 71].

[Attitudes] are dispositions to evaluate objects favorably or unfavorably [Insko & Schopler, 1972, p. 1].

... the major characteristic that distinguishes attitude from other concepts is its evaluative or affective nature (Fishbein & Ajzen, 1975, p. 11).

Attitudes are the core of our likes and dislikes for certain people, groups, situations, objects, and intangible ideas [Zimbardo, Ebbesen, & Maslach, 1977, p. 20].

These restricted definitions identify the attitude concept most closely with affect, or a general evaluative reaction. Thus, one's global feelings about an object, which constitute the attitude ("I like candy"), can be distinguished from one's cognitions ("Candy is sweet"; "Candy prices are rising") and conations ("I eat candy often"). Although we define *attitude* as a *general and enduring favorable or unfavorable feeling about an object or issue,* this does not mean that cognitive and behavioral responses are ignored. Rather, they are accorded independent conceptual status, and this chapter is devoted to a consideration of the meaning and measurement of, and the interrelationships between, cognitions, behaviors, and attitudes.

THE MEASUREMENT OF ATTITUDES

Ever since Thurstone developed the first attitude scale, attitude measurement techniques have focused on assessing a general evaluation of, or affective response to, an attitude object. They have focused on measuring how much one likes or dislikes, or feels generally favorable or unfavorable toward, some object or issue.

Classic Techniques

Thurstone (1928) measured attitudes by presenting a set of statements to subjects and asking them to indicate the ones with which they agreed. The statements expressed evaluations ranging from very unfavorable toward the attitude object to very favorable. To construct a Thurstone scale, a large number of statements is initially given to a panel of judges who are instructed to place each statement objectively into one of 11 equally spaced categories depending on the degree of favorableness or unfavorableness expressed by each statement toward the attitude object. Each statement is assigned the median scale value chosen by the panel of judges. A person's attitude score on a Thurstone scale is determined by computing the median favorability value of all the statements the subject endorses. Table 2.1 contains an abbreviated version of a Thurstone scale measuring attitudes toward capital punishment. Of course, in actual use of the measure, the scale values would not appear with the statements.

Thurstone scaling has the advantage of assigning subjects an attitude score that is meaningful in terms of an underlying evaluative continuum. However, there are many cases in which this absolute information is not needed; cases in which one need only know who is relatively favorable or unfavorable toward a particular object or issue. Likert (1932) suggested a method that provides such "relative" scores and is less time-consuming to implement than the Thurstone scale because it does not involve determining objective scale values for each of the statements used in the measure. Further, its ability to estimate "relative" scores is just as reliable as that of the Thurstone method. With Thurstone's method, scale construction and scale administration are two distinct steps. With Likert's method, construction and administration can occur simultaneously; no preliminary judging is required. Instead, subjects rate how much they personally agree with each of a series of statements similar to those found in the Thurstone scale (rather than rating each item's objective favorableness). The subject's ratings for each of the items are then correlated with the sum of all the ratings. A person's final attitude score on the Likert scale is his or her total score for the subset of the items (e.g., 6 to 10 statements) whose ratings correlate best with the total score. Table 2.1 includes an abbreviated version of a Likert scale.

TABLE 2.1
Five Types of Scales for Measuring Attitudes
Toward Capital Punishment

Thurstone Equal Appearing Interval[a]
Check all the statements with which you agree.
(1.5) ____ We can't call ourselves civilized as long as we have capital punishment.
(10.4) ____ Any person, man or woman, young or old, who commits murder should pay with his own life.
(5.5) ____ It doesn't make any difference to me whether we have capital punishment or not.
(2.4) ____ Capital punishment cannot be regarded as a sane method of dealing with crime.
(7.2) ____ Capital punishment may be wrong, but it is the best preventative to crime.

Note. Scale values for each item are given in parentheses. A person's attitude score is the median scale value of the statements checked.
[a] Adapted from Shaw and Wright (1967).

Likert Scale
Circle the response that best represents your opinion.
SA—Strongly Agree   A—Agree   U—Undecided   D—Disagree   SD—Strongly Disagree

(4)	(3)	(2)	(1)	(0)	
SA	A	U	D	SD	Capital punishment is just and necessary.
(0)	(1)	(2)	(3)	(4)	
SA	A	U	D	SD	I do not believe in capital punishment under any circumstances.
(0)	(1)	(2)	(3)	(4)	
SA	A	U	D	SD	We cannot call ourselves civilized as long as we have capital punishment.
(4)	(3)	(2)	(1)	(0)	
SA	A	U	D	SD	Capital punishment should be used more often than it is.

Note. For each statement, an item score from 4 to 0 is assigned depending on the response circled. A person's attitude score is the sum of the item scores. Note that items unfavorable to capital punishment are reverse scored, so that disagreeing with these items is like agreeing with a favorable item.

(continued)

A third classic technique was developed by Guttman (1944). Basic to Guttman scaling is the notion of passing all lesser hurdles if one passes a higher one. Take, for example, a set of math problems, each of which is more difficult than the one that precedes it. A person with the ability to solve a difficult problem has the ability to solve all the easier problems. Similarly, think of a set of attitude statements ordered so that agreement with each succeeding one indicates an increasingly more favorable attitude. Just as a person who solves the difficult math problem would be expected to solve the less difficult ones, a person willing to agree to a very favorable attitude statement would be expected to agree also to less favorable ones. To the extent that this occurs, the items form a Guttman scale. For instance, a person agreeing with Item 2 in Table 2.1 would probably agree with Item 1 but may or may not agree with Items 3 and 4. This method works best typically with statements that vary in some quantitative way. For example,

TABLE 2.1—*Continued*

Guttman Scale

Indicate whether you agree or disagree with each statement by circling the appropriate alternative.

Agree	Disagree	Capital punishment should be used only for the most extreme crimes (e.g., multiple murders).
Agree	Disagree	Capital punishment is justified for premeditated murder.
Agree	Disagree	Capital punishment is just and necessary.
Agree	Disagree	Every criminal should be executed.

Note. A person's attitude score is the number of statements with which he or she agrees.

Semantic Differential

Capital punishment is:

Good____ : ____ : ____ : ____ : ____ : ____ : ____Bad

Fair____ : ____ : ____ : ____ : ____ : ____ : ____Unfair

Note. For each scale, a score is assigned from -3 to $+3$ depending on the category checked. (The numbers typically do not appear on the scale, but the blank closest to the negative adjective— e.g., bad—is assigned a value of -3, the next blank is assigned a -2, and so forth.) A person's attitude score is the sum of the scale scores.

Self-Rating Scale

How favorable or unfavorable do you feel toward capital punishment?

1	2	3	4	5	6	7	8	9	10	11
Very Favorable									Very Unfavorable	

Note. A person's attitude score is the number circled on the scale.

statements like "I would be willing to give at least $5 ($10, $15, $20) to the NAACP" are most likely to result in a Guttman scale. A person's final attitude score on a Guttman scale is obtained by summing the number of statements to which he or she gives a pro response. (For more details on scale construction, see Edwards, 1957b; and Lemon, 1973.)

Contemporary Techniques

The classic techniques of attitude measurement appear more often in textbooks than in actual experiments. They are respected but little-used procedures. Researchers have discovered that for most research purposes, an adequate measure of a person's general evaluative reaction can be obtained in a simpler and more straightforward manner by simply asking the person to rate on one or a small number of scales how positive or negative he or she feels about the attitude object.

One popular method resulted from Osgood, Suci, and Tannenbaum's (1957) work on the connotative or implied meaning of words. They found that words could be classified along three dimensions: (1) evaluative dimension (e.g., good–bad, fair–unfair), (2) potency dimension (e.g., strong–weak, large–small), and (3) activity dimension (e.g., fast–slow, active–passive). Osgood et al.'s evaluative dimension coincides with the characteristic of an attitude measured by the Thurstone, Likert, and Guttman techniques. The subject is asked to rate the attitude object on a set of three to six 7-point evaluative rating scales anchored by bipolar adjectives such as *good–bad, kind–cruel, fair–unfair*. These bipolar adjectives have been selected via factor analysis and have been used across cultures and attitude objects (Osgood, 1965). (Two evaluative scales are presented in Table 2.1.) The response to each scale is assigned a score from −3 to +3 depending on the category checked. The subject's ratings on the different scales are then summed, and this sum represents the subject's attitude score. This response scale is called the *semantic differential,* since Osgood's initial effort was directed at categorizing the dimensions along which words had meaning (i.e., differentiating semantic space). Attitudes on virtually any topic can be assessed easily by using the semantic differential. An advantage of this technique is that it can be used to compare a person's attitude toward a variety of objects (e.g., the individual favors capital punishment more than prison reform).

Employed even more widely to assess attitudes are the single-item self-rating scales. Although rating scales vary in appearance (they may be represented by continuous lines, by lines broken by slashes, by numbers, and/or by explanatory phrases), the end points of the scale are always labeled. Table 2.1 includes a rating scale similar to those used in nationwide surveys such as the Gallup and Harris polls. The subject's task is to select the number that describes most accurately his or her opinion. Because construction time is negligible and the information provided is adequate for most research purposes, single-item self-rating scales are often used in both public opinion polling and laboratory research.

Indirect Techniques

The attitude measures discussed up to this point are constructed for use with respondents who wish to give accurate accounts of their attitudes. To the extent that respondents are unable or unwilling to give accurate accounts, the measures are not valid indicants of attitude (cf. Cook & Sellitz, 1964). For example, a *response set* refers to a biased and consistent way of responding to an attitude scale that reflects a characteristic of the respondent other than his or her evaluative reaction to the attitude object. Two of the most researched response sets are *acquiescence*— the tendency to agree with any item regardless of its content (Couch & Keniston, 1960)—and *social desirability*—the tendency to give the most socially acceptable answer to a question (Edwards, 1957a). To circumvent the response bias problem, indirect attitude measurement techniques have been developed. These techniques are meant to tap the attitude while leaving the respondent unaware of this purpose. For example, in a *projective test* the respondent is shown a picture and is asked to tell a story about it. It is assumed that the content of the respondent's story will reflect the underlying attitude (Proshansky, 1943). Another type of indirect measure is the *information error test,* which is presented as a multiple-choice test. In this test, all the alternatives are incorrect, but the answers depart from the correct responses in ways that are consistent with either a positive or negative attitude toward the object. The answer selected is assumed to reflect the person's attitude (Hammond, 1948; Weschler, 1950). *Logical reasoning tests* have also been used as disguised measures. For example, arguments with faulty conclusions are presented, and presumably, if the respondent's attitude is consistent with the bias, he or she will judge the faulty conclusion as logically following from the premises (Waly & Cook, 1965). Finally, *physiological tests* have been employed as indirect measures of attitudes and are discussed in Chapter 4.

Indirect or disguised measures have not been used widely, partly because they are unwieldy and are often unsuitable for group administration. When reliability and validity checks have been made, the indirect measures have often been inferior to the direct attitude scales (Lemon, 1973). Although the primary advantage of indirect measures is that they control for response biases, direct attitude scales can also be constructed to minimize or control for the effects of response sets. For example, to minimize the effects of an acquiescence response set, an equal number of statements of the attitude scale may be worded and keyed in the positive and negative directions. To control for social desirability, the subjects may be required to choose between items that are equal in social deisrability but that differ in the attitude represented. Finally, the validity of the direct measures is enhanced to the extent that the subjects are convinced that their responses are anonymous and that there are no right or wrong answers, because attitude items involve matters of opinion, not fact. For additional information about the problems of assessing attitudes, see Cook and Sellitz (1964).

WHAT IS A COGNITIVE RESPONSE?

An attitude refers to a general and enduring favorable or unfavorable feeling about an object or issue, whereas a cognitive response refers to a unit of information pertaining to an object or issue that is the result of cognitive processing. Cognitive processes refer to such information-processing and -structuring activity as perceiving, abstracting, judging, elaborating, rehearsing, and recalling from memory (D. A. Norman, 1976; Posner, 1973). Cognitive responses are the results of information-processing and -structuring activity and thus consist of responses such as recognitions, associations, elaborations, ideas, and images. To the extent that motivation affects cognitive processing, it affects cognitive responses (cf. Simon, 1967); to the extent that cognitive processing is inhibited, cognitive responses are inhibited (see Chapter 3). A useful method of monitoring cognitive processing, then, is to monitor the end result of that processing—the cognitive response.

What is the nature of cognitive response in persuasion? Clearly, various persuasive stimuli evoke a variety of cognitive processes and responses. For example, some responses are the results of straightforward identifications of a simple stimulus (e.g., recognizing sounds as a message); some result from rehearsal of the attributes of the stimulus (e.g., memory of the arguments in a persuasive appeal); and some result from elaborations of the stimulus (e.g., counterarguing the communication). All these reactions are included in the study of cognitive responses in persuasion. Some kinds of cognitive responses have not been studied in a persuasion context, however. For example, although there is some evidence from the experimental study of cognition that cognitive responses need be neither conscious (Treisman, 1964) nor semantically encodable (Neisser, 1967), the roles of these cognitive responses in persuasion have not been delineated.

THE MEASUREMENT OF
COGNITIVE RESPONSES

How does one study objectively something as unobservable as a cognitive response to a stimulus? In the following sections, techniques for obtaining, categorizing, judging, weighting, and structuring cognitive responses are considered.

Obtaining Cognitive Responses

The first task in the measurement of "cognitive responses" is to obtain a physical representation of their existence. The method used to obtain cognitive responses should provide access to responses elicited naturally by the stimulus (e.g., a persuasive appeal) rather than by the measurement instrument. Procedures for obtaining cognitive responses are discussed next.

Mechanical Techniques. Techniques building upon Hovland, Lumsdaine, and Sheffield's button-pushing procedure (1949; noted in Chapter 1) have been employed (Beaber, 1975; Carter, Ruggels, Jackson, & Heffner, 1973). For instance, Carter and Simpson (1970) delivered printed messages to subjects at a computer console. Subjects were instructed to press keys at the console to stop the message momentarily to agree or disagree with a particular argument. They found that subjects stopped more to agree than to disagree with the message when the information contained in the message was proattitudinal and that the opposite was true when the information conatined in the message was counterattitudinal.

The average number of stops to agree and disagree did not differ when the information was neutral. These results suggest the signal-stopping technique may prove useful in future research on cognitive response to persuasion. (See Chapter 5 for a description of a similar recording technique employed by Beaber, 1975.)

A potential problem with procedures that require subjects to "do something" before, during, or after the presentation of a persuasive appeal in order to tap cognitive responses is that the request itself may elicit or alter the cognitive responses measured. The use of electrophysiological and pupillographic techniques to measure cognitive processing and/or responses provides a means of assessing the extent of this problem, because the purpose of these measures is not obvious to subjects. That is, subjects are not asked to respond; instead, the natural bodily responses elicited by the persuasive appeal are monitored without the subjects' awareness of the purpose or meaning of the measurements. These physiological procedures have been used to provide evidence that cognitive processing was actually enhanced when subjects reported verbally that cognitive responses were elicited (Cacioppo & Petty, in 1979a; see Chapter 4 for a discussion).

Reaction-time procedures, employed commonly in the study of verbal learning and verbal behavior by experimental psychologists, have also been employed recently in the study of cognitive responses in impression formation (Lingle & Ostrom, 1979; see Chapter 17) and may serve as yet another nonobvious measure of cognitive responses. This procedure, like the physiological procedures, however, has not yet provided information about the type of thoughts elicited. To date, the profile of cognitive responses has been ascertainable only by using the listing or reporting procedures discussed next.

Oral and Written Listing Techniques.   By far the most common means of obtaining cognitive responses has been to instruct subjects either to list (write) or to report verbally their thoughts; each of these techniques of obtaining cognitive responses has its merits (cf. Wright, 1974a). Verbal measures are advantageous because they can be obtained quickly (it is easier to speak than write), minimizing the forgetting of one's actual responses to a communication. The written listing procedure, though slower, can be administered easily in group settings and requires only pencil and paper. The administration of these and other measures of cognitive responses is usually done in such a manner that the public nature of the measure is minimized so that subjects are less guarded about what they report.

Both oral and written measures have been used in empirical studies. For instance, as noted in Chapter 1, Janis and Terwilliger (1962) instructed subjects to read a message aloud and to verbalize all their thoughts pertaining to the message into a tape recorder. But oral measures have been used infrequently. Employed more commonly have been methods of obtaining written thought listings (Brock, 1967). For example, Greenwald (1968a) asked subjects to "collect their thoughts'' on an issue about which they had just read a communication and then to list those thoughts. Subjects were willing and able to provide listings of cognitive responses in accordance with these instructions.

Type of Thought Requested.   Investigators have tried different instructions for obtaining the cognitive responses elicited by a persuasive appeal. Three different types of instructions have been used most commonly. The researchers have asked for a listing of: (1) thoughts elicited by the communication (e.g., Roberts & Maccoby, 1973); (2) general thoughts on the topic of the communication (e.g., Greenwald, 1968b); or (3) all thoughts that occurred to an individual during the communication (e.g., Petty & Cacioppo, 1977). Although it is unlikely that the subjects responded differently to the first two types of instructions, the request to list the thoughts elicited by the communication (i.e., the first procedure) assumes that subjects are able to distinguish those thoughts that are elicited by the communication from those that are not. Thus, it is necessary to assume that subjects are able to determine the cognitive effects of the stimulus (i.e., the communication). Recent research indicates that this assumption is dubious (cf. Nisbett & Wilson, 1977a). In the latter two instructional procedures, subjects are not asked to identify the cognitive effects of the stimulus. Instead, the well-founded assumption is made that subjects are aware of their thoughts rather than their thought processes (cf. Ericsson & Simon, 1980).

This does not mean that the latter two listing procedures yield identical results, however. For example, in a study that employed a counterattitudinal communication (Petty & Cacioppo, 1977), it was found that when subjects were instructed to "try to record only those ideas that you were thinking during the last few minutes [p. 648]," the demand to produce any particular type of cognitive response was minimal; the thoughts listed were predominantly unfavorable to the issue or neutral. However, when subjects were asked to list their thoughts on the particular topic of the communication, significantly more favorable and fewer neutral thoughts were reported. The "topic instructions" produced an experimental demand for subjects to report responses relevant to the topic and may have compelled them to show their "open-mindedness" and/or "intelligence" by generating thoughts on both sides of the issue. Because each of these profiles of thoughts may be of interest to an investigator, the instructions that provide the most useful results depend on the aims of the particular experiment.

Measurement Time.   Another factor that influences the profile of cognitive responses that is obtained is the amount of time given to subjects to report their responses (Miller & Baron, 1973; Osterhouse & Brock, 1970; Wright, 1974a). In general, investigators want to assess the cognitive responses elicited by a persuasive appeal in order to study their role in the mediation of persuasion. The purpose of imposing a time limit on listing thoughts is to increase the likelihood that only those responses that have been elicited by the persuasive appeal are measured.

The time provided for listing cognitive responses has ranged from 45 seconds (Miller & Baron, 1973) to 10 minutes or longer (Greenwald, 1968b); the time interval used most commonly has been 2 to 3 minutes (Wright, 1973), but the optimal time interval depends on the purpose of the particular experiment and the nature of the experimental materials (e.g., the length of the message). For instance, if only the most salient thoughts are desired, a very brief time interval would be better than one so long that a subject would have time to reflect and select among cognitive responses or to generate new responses.

Besides the consideration of the time interval allowed to list thoughts, another concern is whether the profile of cognitive responses differs as a function of when the responses are obtained. There is a paucity of evidence concerning this question, and what exists is conflicting; some research indicates the responses measured during and after a presentation are very similar (Greenwald, 1968b), and other research suggests the responses to a persuasive appeal after its presentation are more unfavorable than responses during its presentation (Roberts & Maccoby, 1973). One issue at stake is whether the responses reported during or after the persuasive appeal reflect more accurately the cognitive responses elicited normally by the persuasive appeal. Obtaining cognitive responses after the communication can be done unexpectedly to the subject and does not require interruption of or distraction from the presentation of the communication. Obtaining responses during the communication, however, requires that the subjects know during the persuasive appeal that their cognitive reactions to the communication are being monitored. Furthermore, subjects must either interrupt the presentation of the persuasive appeal, or they must distract themselves from it to report their cognitive reactions. Consequently, measurement during the persuasive appeal may alter the responses elicited naturally by the persuasive appeal more than an unexpected measure of cognitive response obtained after the communication (Wright, 1974a). Research has indicated that including a measure of cognitive response after the advocacy does not affect the attitude reported (Insko, Turnbull, & Yandell, 1974; Petty, Wells, & Brock, 1976).

Categorizing a Cognitive Response

Once cognitive responses have been obtained, it is necessary to define categories in which to place them so that they can be analyzed statistically. Researchers have in the past coded thoughts into various categories, including "counterarguments" (Brock, 1967), "defensive reactions" (Janis & Terwilliger, 1962), "source derogations" (Wright, 1974a), "favorable thoughts" (Insko et al., 1974), "disaffirmations" (Beaber, 1975), "neutral thoughts" (Petty & Cacioppo, 1977), "point comments" (Roberts & Maccoby, 1973), "supportive thoughts" (Cialdini, Levy, Herman, Kozlowski, & Petty, 1976), "recipient-generated thoughts" (Greenwald, 1968b), and "connections" to one's personal life (Krugman, 1967).

Proposed here are three dimensions that have characterized the classification of responses in past research: (1) *polarity*—the degree to which the statement is in favor of or opposed to the advocacy; (2) *origin*—the primary source of the information contained in the person's response; and (3) *target*—the focus at which the comment is directed. These three orthogonal dimensions are proposed as a method of categorizing more systematically the cognitive responses to persuasion.

Polarity Dimension.   The most reliable finding in cognitive response research has been that there is a consistent relationship between the polarity of the responses elicited by, and the yielding to, a persuasive appeal (e.g., Brock, 1967; Greenwald, 1968b; Wright, 1974a; see also Chapter 5). There are three types of polarity comments: (1) *favorable thoughts*—statements that support the advocacy; (2) *neutral thoughts*—statements that neither favor nor oppose the advocacy; and (3) *unfavorable thoughts*—statements that oppose the advocacy. Most of the research to date has concerned unfavorable thought production and persuasion, although the term *counterargument* has been used instead of *unfavorable thought*. The term *counterargument*, however, implies that the response counters an argument contained in the persuasive appeal (i.e., it has both polarity and target dimensions). Furthermore, although counterargumentation was operationally defined originally as "a declarative statement directed specifically against [the advocacy] that mentions a specific *unfavorable* or *undesirable* consequence that was not simply a restatement or paraphrase of the fact of [the advocacy]" (Brock, 1967, p. 301), it has been used recently to include a variety of statements that are unfavorable to the advocacy (Osterhouse and Brock, 1970; Petty & Cacioppo, 1977). The terms *favorable, unfavorable,* and *neutral thoughts* are preferred here because these terms describe accurately the attributes that characterize the polarity dimension and because classification in this manner maintains independent conceptual status for the three dimensions.

Origin Dimension.   Classifying cognitive responses according to their *origin* was first proposed by Greenwald (1968b). Three classifications of origin follow: (1) *message-originated thoughts*—statements that are direct restatements or paraphrases of the communication (i.e., message recall); (2) *modified message-originated thoughts*—statements that are reactions to, qualifications of, or illustrations of the material in the communication (e.g., elaborations of, or replies to, message arguments); and (3) *recipient-generated thoughts*—statements expressing ideas or reactions not traceable directly to the communication (e.g., responses pertinent to the issue but not to a specific argument in the message).

Research employing a similar origin classification system has produced results indicating that in some cases, recipient-generated thoughts were most related to persuasion (Greenwald, 1968b; Roberts & Maccoby, 1973), and in other cases message-originated thoughts were most related (Calder, Insko, & Yandell, 1974; Insko et al., 1974). Various factors such as the subjects' prior knowledge about the message topic, availability of a schema concerning the advocacy, or ability to generate responses may all affect whether recipient-generated or message-originated thoughts are most important in persuasion (cf. Tesser, 1978). For instance, recipient-generated comments might be most important when subjects find it easy and adaptive to generate responses to an advocacy and when they have some prior knowledge on the topic (e.g., eliminating editorial comments in the news media; Roberts & Maccoby, 1973). In support of this contention are the results of numerous experiments on active versus passive participation, which demonstrate that when subjects have some prior familiarity with a topic, more persuasion results when arguments are actively self-generated than when arguments are passively received (see Chapter 1).

When subjects have little prior knowledge on an issue, as when judging a defendant's guilt in a hypothetical case (Calder et al., 1974), they probably have to rely on the information contained in the message rather than on their own belief systems, because no responses to the specific case exist prior to exposure to the persuasive appeal. (During jury selection, judges attempt to select jurors who are characterized by just such a cognitive and attitudinal state.) Experimental evidence for this view is provided by McGuire's (1962) experiments on inoculation theory, which demonstrated that when subjects have little familiarity with defending their positions on an issue (as on cultural truisms), externally provided defenses (passive) are initially superior to self-generated defenses (active) (see Chapter 1). Thus, the discrepancy that exists concerning the relative importance of recipient-generated and message-originated thoughts may be due in part to differences in the knowledge subjects have about the topic of the persuasive appeal prior to the advocacy.

Target Dimension. The *target* of the cognitive responses provides information about the effect of the persuasive appeal on the recipient's focus of attention. Empirically, targets have been classified into the following categories: (1) *message-topic thoughts*—statements pertaining to the topic of the appeal or pertaining to arguments either stated or implied in the message; (2) *source thoughts*—statements pertaining to the communicator and his or her style of communication; and (3) *audience thoughts*—statements pertaining to the recipients or potential recipients of the persuasive appeal, including oneself and significant others. Roberts and Maccoby (1973) investigated various targets and found that message and source targets accounted for most of the responses listed. Lasswell's (1948) and McGuire's (1968b, 1969a) analyses of the persuasion process suggest that an examination of *channel thoughts*—statements pertaining to the media or modality through which the appeal is transmitted—might also be fruitful.

Potential Dimensions.   There are, no doubt, a variety of other dimensions that may be important, including saliency (i.e., how often the cognitive response is elicited—Smith et al., 1956) and processing mode (i.e., the emotionality of the response—Miller & Baron, 1973). For instance, concerning the latter, cognitive responses might be classified along a continuum ranging from the objective (e.g., logical ramifications) to the emotional (e.g., profane exclamations). Investigations of the processing mode may provide information about the frequency of and conditions under which reasoned, rather than emotional, belief defenses are employed and about their relative effectiveness. Information about personality characteristics (e.g., dogmatism) might also be obtained from these analyses. To date, however, only calls for classification along these dimensions exist (Miller & Baron, 1973; Smith et al., 1956; Wright, 1974a).

Judging and Weighting Cognitive Responses

Once cognitive responses have been obtained and classification dimensions have been selected, there is the need to judge the responses (i.e., assign each response to a particular category along each dimension) and to combine the responses along each dimension to obtain an index of each individual's cognitions.

With respect to the task of categorizing the responses, three methods have been employed:

1. *Judge rating*—individuals who are familiar with the scoring categories, but not with the experimental hypotheses, assign each response to a particular category (within each dimension) on the basis of their understanding of the meaning of the response (Brock, 1967; Cook, 1969; Insko et al., 1974; Roberts & Maccoby, 1973).

2. *Subject rating*—after completing the dependent variables, subjects are instructed how to categorize their responses (e.g., "Place a plus sign next to thoughts that favor the advocacy") and are asked to look back at their listed thoughts to classify them (Calder et al., 1974; Cialdini et al., 1976; Greenwald, 1968b).

3. *Judge and subject ratings*—both subjects and judges rate the responses; if there is disagreement between the independent judges' ratings, the subject's rating is employed (Cacioppo & Petty, 1979b; Petty et al., 1976).

Independent judges usually demonstrate a high degree of agreement in their classification of responses (e.g., Insko et al., 1974), but occasionally, unacceptably low concordance between raters is found (e.g., Greenwald, 1968b). Although ratings by subjects and judges are correlated highly (Petty et al., 1976), having subjects rate their own responses circumvents both the problem of low interrater reliability and the problem of judges misinterpreting the meaning of responses. Unfortunately, subjects are not always willing and/or able to comply with the request to classify their thoughts; this problem is accentuated by the selection of several dimensions along which subjects must classify their thoughts, because subjects may either become bored with the procedure (and thus be less willing to comply) or forget what they mean by a response (and thus be less able to comply). The procedure of using both judges' ratings and subjects' ratings represents a compromise method.

Some of the listed cognitive responses may appear to be more "weighted" (e.g., more favorable or unfavorable) than others. However, research indicates that weighting the responses empirically according to their "extremity," or "favorability/unfavorability," neither alters nor strengthens the relationships found by using straightforward counts of the number of various types of comments produced. This is true both when subjects' ratings (Calder et al., 1974; Cullen, 1968; Greenwald, 1968b) and when judges' ratings (Roberts & Maccoby, 1973) are employed.

However, Petty (1977a) has demonstrated that if cognitive responses to persuasive messages are weighted by the subjects' certainty that the response is true along with extremity, then enhanced correlations with attitude are obtained both on an immediate and a delayed (1 week) posttest.

The Reliability and Validity of Cognitive Response Measures

Almost every standard reference on attitude measurement (cf. Edwards, 1957b; Lemon, 1973) stresses the importance of reliable and valid assessment. These concepts are of equal importance when measuring cognitive responses. *Reliability* refers to the extent to which a measure contains random error. A person's score should change only when the "true score" has changed and not when the weather changes or the experimenter changes. A perfectly reliable measure is internally consistent (split-half reliability) and yields the same results on repeated testings (test–retest reliability). Cullen (1968) compared the reliability of some standard attitude scales with a measure of cognitive responses. Subjects completed a Likert scale and a Thurstone scale and listed their thoughts on one of two topics, with order of assessment counterbalanced across subjects. Spearman–Brown split-half reliability coefficients and test–retest correlations indicated that all measures showed acceptably high reliabilities. Averaged over both issues (birth control and segregation), the cognitive response measure had a reliability that fell between the two attitude scales (see Table 2.2).

Validity refers to the degree to which a measuring device taps the true score that it was designed to measure. We have already noted how certain "response sets" might render an attitude measure invalid. For a measure of cognitive responses, the question of validity centers on whether or not subjects can accurately report their thoughts. Some have cautioned that there are "serious methodological questions concerning the validity of subject reports as a tool of social

TABLE 2.2
Comparisons of the Reliability of Listed Thoughts with
Likert and Thurstone Attitude Scales[a]

	Split-Half Reliabilities	
	Birth Control	Segregation
Listed thoughts	.445	.906
Likert	.830	.837
Thurstone	.667	.439

	Test–Retest Reliabilities	
	Birth Control	Segregation
Listed thoughts	.664	.624
Likert	.824	.848
Thurstone	.448	.624

[a] Adapted from Cullen, 1968.

science investigation'' (Nisbett & Bellows, 1977, p. 624). Most of this alarm comes from the finding that subjects are often unable to report the effect that some stimulus had on their behavior (Nisbett & Wilson, 1977b). As noted previously, however, it is not necessary to assume that a subject is aware of the cognitive or behavioral effects of a stimulus for self-report techniques to be useful in experimentation. It has long been argued that individuals are unaware of many of their motives and behaviors; yet their motives and behaviors may be ascertainable through analyses of their self-reports (e.g., Freud, 1924). Indeed, psychologists would have little to do if individuals could report accurately what the cognitive and behavioral effects of stimuli were. The cognitive response analysis described in the preceding sections makes no assumptions about a person's accessibility to stimulus–response connections; it does provide a method of studying objectively and quantitatively the cognitive mediation of persuasion, however. For example, even if a person were totally unaware of the fact that distraction inhibited one's ability to counterargue a message, it would still be possible to measure the number of counterarguments distracted and nondistracted subjects were able to generate after hearing a communication and to show that fewer cognitive responses were generated by distracted subjects (Petty et al., 1976; see also Chapter 3).

To summarize our extended discussion on cognitive response measurement, it appears that an unexpected request to list everything about which a subject thought during the presentation of a persuasive appeal, with strict time limits imposed for listing (e.g., 3 minutes), provides a useful indication of the cognitive responses elicited naturally by the persuasive appeal. The classification of the cognitive responses may be done by judges, subjects, or both. Frequency counts of the items within each category of cognitive responses provide a satisfactory measure of the relative prominence or profile of the different cognitive response categories.

MEASURING COGNITIVE STRUCTURE

Cognitive structures provide the means by which persons organize objects and events in their environment. In order to measure cognitive structure, Zajonc (1960) had subjects describe a stimulus person "by freely listing the qualities and attributes that characterized [p. 160]" a person about whom they had read a letter. In other words, Zajonc (1960) obtained the cognitive responses (one per index card) elicited by the stimulus person. Four measures of cognitive structure were suggested: (1) *Differentiation* is a measure of the extent to which a person is capable of identifying and discriminating objects and events. The simple total of characteristics listed is the measure of differentiation. If one were interested in studying the structure of cognitive responses to a persuasive communication, the total number of topic-relevant thoughts listed could serve as the measure. (2) The cognitive responses that subjects list can come from a single category or multiple categories. The number of categories used determines *complexity*. For example, a person whose cognitive responses about capital punishment all related to one theme or category (e.g., a moral code theme: "It's immoral to kill"; "It violates God's law to take a life") would show less complexity than a person whose reactions related to several themes or categories (e.g., a moral code theme: "It's wrong to kill"; a legal theme: "The death penalty is cruel and unusual punishment and thus prohibited by the Constitution"; and an economic theme: "It costs more money to kill the killers than to have them serve life sentences"). (3) *Unity* is a measure of the interdependence of the cognitive responses. It is assessed by having the subjects indicate which cognitive responses would change if any given cognitive response were changed or untrue. The greater the number of changes resulting from a change in each of the cognitive responses, the greater the unity. (4) *Organization* is the degree to which one cognitive response or set of cognitive responses is central or dominates the relationship among the cognitive responses. For example, if changing a person's view of the morality of capital punishment led to changes in cognitive responses concerned with legal and economic aspects of capital punishment, this would indicate that the morality theme was central.

Although the structure of cognitive responses could quite easily be examined using Zajonc's measures, little work has been done on a structural analysis of cognitive responses. One exception to this is a study by Brock (1962, noted in Chapter 1). Of course, other techniques for assessing cognitive organization are adaptable to a cognitive response analysis (e.g., Scott, 1974; Wyer, 1974).

In sum, the research to date concerning the measurement of cognitive responses to persuasion has focused on a variety of empirical means of obtaining and analyzing cognitive reactions to a stimulus. Most of this work has been conducted on the level of analyzing and classifying single responses. The work on cognitive structure offers a potentially rich area of research in which structural alterations in response to a persuasive appeal might be investigated.

RELATIONSHIPS BETWEEN COGNITIVE RESPONSES, ATTITUDES, AND BEHAVIORS

Having discussed how attitudes and cognitive responses can be measured, next considered are the relationships between cognitive, attitudinal, and behavioral responses. There are two basic methods for assessing such relationships: (1) *correlational procedures*, which involve measuring the variables of interest and assessing the relationships with statistical analyses; and (2) *experimental procedures*, which involve manipulating a variable to assess its effects on a measured (dependent) variable (see Chapter 3 for a discussion of this procedure). In the next sections, the conceptual status of, and the interrelationships between, attitudes, cognitive responses, and behaviors are discussed.

Attitudes and Cognitive Responses

As noted earlier, one of the most replicated findings in the research on cognitive responses is that the favorable thoughts elicited by a communication correlate positively with attitude change, whereas the unfavorable thoughts elicited by a communication show a strong negative relationship with persuasion (see Table 5.1, Chapter 5).

Although attitudes and cognitive responses (that are scored along the polarity dimension) are related highly, they are not the same thing. As stated previously, cognitive responses are the specific products of information-processing activity that occurs at a particular moment in time, whereas an attitude represents an enduring favorable or unfavorable feeling about an object or issue. An attitude is capable of influencing (Abelson, 1963; Simon, 1967) as well as being influenced by cognitions (Petty et al., 1976; Tesser, 1978). Also, just as a cake is more than a sum of ingredients, an attitude can be more than a simple summary of cognitive responses: In the case of each, the final product (e.g., cake or attitude) may have properties not predictable on the basis of a simple listing of "ingredients" prior to mixture. For both, any alteration of the natural "cooking" process (increasing the baking temperature or limiting the time for thought) can change the nature of the end result.

What, then, is the relationship between attitude change and cognitive responses? Recall from Chapter 1 that the cognitive response approach views the recipient of a persuasive appeal as an active information processor. Cognitive responses are the results of thinking about the persuasive material presented, and the thoughts elicited by a message are believed to mediate or shape the amount of persuasion that results. In support of the view that cognitive responses mediate attitude change are the numerous studies using statistical and experimental procedures, which have revealed that (1) high correlations exist between polar cognitive responses and the amount of persuasion produced; and the more important the topic of the persuasion attempt is to the recipient, the stronger the relationship between the cognitive responses elicited and the amount of attitude change that results (Petty & Cacioppo, 1979a, 1979b); (2) manipulations that affect cognitive responses also affect persuasion (Calder et al., 1974; Petty et al., 1976; Roberts & Maccoby, 1973); and (3) implementation of statistical procedures to assess causal orderings of cognitive responses and persuasion has indicated that cognitive responses may have mediated yielding to persuasion (e.g., Greenwald, 1968b; Osterhouse & Brock, 1970) but that the reverse causal ordering was not operating (Cacioppo & Petty, 1979a, 1979b; Petty & Cacioppo, 1977).

The most parsimonious account of these findings is that cognitive responding can mediate yielding to persuasion. This does not mean that a third variable is not mediating both cognitive responses and yielding to persuasion in some contexts. It means only that the simplest account of a wide body of literature is that cognitive responding influences the final attitude. Because the chapters in Part II of this volume discuss the mediational role played by cognitive responses in attitude change produced by such variables as source credibility, message forewarnings, message repetitions, group discussion, and so forth, mediation is not discussed further here.

Cognitive Responses and Behaviors

As noted previously, cognitive responses are the product of information-processing activity. Behaviors, on the other hand, refer to any and all observable acts (i.e., response executions). Investigations of the relationship between cognitive responses and behavior have indicated that general cognitive responses aimed at changing behavior (i.e., global self-instructions) have not been correlated highly with actual behavior change (Levinger, 1970; Meichenbaum & Cameron, 1973).

Levinger (1970, 1974) has provided evidence that when cognitive responses are specific and behavioral implications are straightforward (i.e., there are few intervening events between the cognitive and behavioral responses), a relationship between the cognitive and behavioral responses is found. For instance, the simple but diffuse cognitive response, "Stop eating," is likely to fail to lead to weight loss because persons may forget or judge not applicable this intention in a given specific situation, may succumb to habit, and so on. However, specific cognitive responses, such as "I will leave the room as soon as the main course is completed," more often lead to completion of the specific behavior and thereby to the general behavioral goal (in this case, losing weight).

Fishbein and Ajzen (1975) discuss three factors that affect the association that may be found between cognitive responses (e.g., behavioral intentions) and behaviors in empirical investigations:

1. *Measurement specificity*—Do the measures of cognitive response and behavior tap equally specific events? The greater the correspondence between the specificities of the measures, the greater the expected association between cognitive and behavioral responses (e.g., Fishbein, 1966).

2. *Response stability*—Is the cognitive response that was measured the same as the one that would be obtained immediately prior to the behavior? The greater the length of time or the greater the number of events that transpire between the measurements of the cognitive and behavioral responses, the greater the likelihood is that an event can occur that would alter the cognitive response. Thus, the behavior may be consistent with the response that existed immediately prior to the behavior but not with a response measured at a much earlier time (e.g., Ajzen & Fishbein, 1974).

3. *Behavioral ability*—Is the person able to control the occurrence of the behavior? The control a person has over the execution of a behavior can range from (relatively) complete (e.g., when selecting a candidate for whom to vote) to almost none (e.g., when the behavior is required by a drug addiction or habit). The greater a person's ability to choose to execute a behavior, the greater the expected association between the cognitive and behavioral responses.

Hoyt and Janis (1975) provided evidence that cognitive responses are not only related to behavior but also influence behavior. During a telephone interview with women who were enrolled in an exercise class, subjects completed a "balance sheet" in which they considered carefully the pros and cons of a personal decision. Half the subjects thought about the consequences of attending class regularly, and half the subjects thought about reducing or abstaining from cigarette smoking (an irrelevant balance-sheet task). Even though all the women had committed themselves to attending the class, attendance (assessed over a 7-week period) was much greater for women who had engaged in cognitive responding about the consequences of attending regularly (relevant and specific cognitive responding) than for women who had responded cognitively about smoking (i.e., irrelevant cognitive processing).

This should not be taken to imply that in some situations, cognitive responses are not used to rationalize a behavior (Kiesler, 1977) or that cognitive responses invariably accompany behavior. For instance, well-practiced (automated) behaviors (e.g., walking, riding a bicycle) require very little cognitive processing and are not easily disrupted by a distractor; behaviors that are not automated completely, however, require more extensive cognitive processing and are more easily disrupted by a distractor (cf. LaBerge, 1975; Schneider & Shiffrin, 1977). Nevertheless, a significant portion of a person's behavior is not automated and is accompanied by cognitive responses.

Attitudes and Behaviors

Most attitude theorists have assumed that attitudes and overt behavior should be closely related. That is, one should be able to predict a person's behavior from his or her attitude. In fact, this hypothesized relationship is incorporated into some definitions of attitude. Thus, attitudes are sometimes defined as predispositions to respond (Osgood, Suci, & Tannenbaum, 1957) or dispositions to react (Sarnoff, 1960). Allport's (1935) classic definition suggests that attitudes exert a directive and energizing effect on behavior. However, a number of studies have questioned the notion that attitudes direct behavior. In a now classic study, LaPiere (1934) found that although in response to a mailed survey, hotel and restaurant owners indicated negative feelings about serving Chinese, they allowed a Chinese couple accompanied by a Caucasian to frequent their establishments. Similarly, Kutner, Wilkins, and Yarrow (1952) found that restaurant owners would seat a black woman who arrived late to join her companions, but when asked for reservations for a group that included a black woman, they refused.

Carr and Roberts (1965) measured Black-American college students' attitudes toward civil rights activities and their actual participation in civil rights activities. The highest correlation for males and females between attitudes and behavior was only .29. Corey (1937) obtained measures of attitudes toward cheating and actual cheating behavior and found them essentially unrelated ($r = .02$). Wicker (1969), in his extensive review, concluded that there is "little evidence to support the postulated existence of stable, underlying attitudes in the individual which influence both his verbal expression and his actions [p. 75]." Abelson (1972) likewise concluded that there is little evidence to support the assumption that attitudes have systematic effects on behaviors.

Examination of other work in this area, however, indicates that these views are too pessimistic. As Dillehay (1973) has noted, at least two of the classic studies in the area suffer from grave methodological shortcomings. In the studies of both LaPiere (1934) and Kutner et al. (1952), there is reason to believe that different sets of people responded to the written and to the face-to-face requests. The managers of the hotels and restaurants in all likelihood responded to the requests for reservations, whereas desk clerks and hostesses engaged in the face-to-face encounters. Because different people were sampled for the verbal and behavioral measures, there is no particular reason to expect attitude–behavior correspondence.

Two other methodological shortcomings of research in this area may be responsible for other failures to find attitude–behavior correspondence. First, Fishbein (1967, 1973) has pointed out that verbal attitudes are often measured with respect to a general class, whereas behaviors are measured with respect to a specific member of that class. For example, a person is asked about blacks in general and then is asked to engage in some behavior with one particular black. If both measures are specific, the discrepancy between attitude and behavior is diminished (cf. Heberlein & Black, 1976; Weigel, Vernon, & Tognacci, 1974; Wicker & Pomazal, 1971). The problem of one measure (attitude) being much more general than the other measure (behavior) was also a problem in correlating behaviors with cognitive responses, and appears again in Chapter 8 in correlating personality variables with attitudes.

Second, the measures of behavior with which attitude measures are to be correlated are typically single acts chosen "on an intuitive and arbitrary basis" (Fishbein & Ajzen, 1974, p. 65). Persons with the same attitude may behave quite differently toward the attitude object in any single setting (i.e., single-act criterion) because of peculiar attributes of the setting rather than the attitude object. However, these persons would be expected to behave similarly toward the attitude object if their behaviors were observed in a variety of settings, because the attitude object rather than peculiarities about a particular setting would be influencing this measure of behavior (i.e., multiple-act criterion).

As Fishbein and Ajzen (1974) note: "A person's attitude towards an object need not be related to any single behavior that may be performed with respect to the [attitude] object" but "it should be related to the overall pattern of his behaviors [p. 61]." Fishbein and Ajzen go on to show that for church-related behaviors (e.g., attendance, contributions), when single acts are correlated with the attitude measures, nonsignificant relationships are obtained. When indices of multiple behaviors (i.e., "Did he not only contribute money, but did he additionally attend church, or buy a raffle ticket?") were used, the correlations between attitude and behavior were much higher (cf. Weigel & Newman, 1976).

Ajzen and Fishbein (1977) have recently reviewed the attitude–behavior literature and have found that in those studies in which the attitude and behavior measures were of differing specificity and/or single behavioral criteria were used, the correlations between attitudes and behaviors were not significant. In those studies in which appropriate measures were employed, in 26 of 26 studies, significant correlations were obtained between attitudes and behaviors. The systematic work of Fishbein and Ajzen has been instrumental in clarifying the relationship between attitudes and behavior. It has led to the conclusion that when the attitude and behavior measures are equally specific and/or equally general, as when multiple behavioral criteria are used, the relationship between attitude and behavior is reasonably strong.

Beyond these methodological considerations, recent research has shown that the attitude–behavior link may be further strengthened by taking other factors into account. For example, Regan and Fazio (1977) have shown that people who form their attitudes on the basis of direct behavioral interaction with the attitude object show greater attitude–behavior consistency than individuals whose attitudes are formed by other means. Schwartz (1978) has shown that a source of attitude–behavior discrepancy is temporal instability in attitudes. That is, attitudes may change in the time between their measurement and the measurement of the behavior, leading to an apparent discrepancy. This discrepancy can be reduced by reducing the time between measurement of the attitude and of the behavior. Interestingly, it appears that the correspondence between attitudes and behaviors can also be increased by getting subjects to think about their attitudes or past behaviors before responding (e.g., Carver, 1975; Snyder & Swann, 1976). Finally, some researchers have indicated that a consideration of personality factors may also enhance understanding of the relationship between attitudes and behaviors. For example, Snyder and his colleagues (Snyder & Monson, 1975; Snyder & Tanke, 1976) have reported that low self-monitoring individuals (those who guide their behavioral choices on the basis of salient information from relevant internal states) show greater attitude–behavior consistency than high self-monitors (those who monitor their behavioral choices on the basis of situational information).

It appears that the pessimism arising from early failures to predict behavior from attitudes may have been unwarranted. When methodological and other relevant factors are taken into account, the attitude–behavior relationship appears relatively robust.

CHAPTER SUMMARY

An *attitude* is a general and enduring favorable or unfavorable feeling about an object or issue. A variety of procedures have been developed to measure an attitude, including the Thurstone, Likert, Guttman, semantic differential, self-report scales, and indirect measures. Each of these techniques is designed to assess an individual's general evaluative reaction to an attitude object (e.g., capital punishment); however, the obtrusiveness and accuracy with which the attitude is measured varies with the technique employed. For instance, although indirect measures may be the most useful in controlling for response biases, they may also be the least accurate assessors of attitude. Although the complex scaling techniques are venerated, the simple self-report scale is used most often.

Cognitive responses are units of information pertaining to an object or issue that are the results of information-processing activity. Cognitive responses have been measured using mechanical, physiological, and oral techniques, but the most popular procedure has been to ask subjects to list their thoughts after hearing a communication. Because investigators have most often been interested in measuring the most salient responses to a communication, time limits on reporting thoughts have usually been imposed.

Once obtained, cognitive responses can be classified into whatever categories are of interest. Responses have been categorized most often along the *polarity* (Is the response in favor of or opposed to the advocacy?), *origin* (Did the response originate in the message or in the recipient?), and *target* (At what is the response directed?) dimensions. Quantification of these categorized responses can range from simple frequency counts of the responses in each category to elaborate weighting and combination techniques. To date, the simpler frequency-count method has provided as satisfactory a measure of cognitive responses to persuasion as the more elaborate techniques. The thought-listing measure of cognitive responses appears to be be about as *reliable* (the extent to which a measure contains random error) and *valid* (the extent to which a measure assesses what it is supposed to assess) as traditional measures of attitude. The thought-listing procedure can also be employed to obtain a measure of *cognitive structure* (the extent to which a person's cognitions are organized and interrelated).

Attitudes and cognitive responses are highly related, and each influences the other in some instances. Concordance between cognitive responses and behaviors also exists, although the manner in which the responses are measured affects the extent to which these variables are related. For instance, the specificity of the cognitive and behavioral responses, the stability of the cognitive responses, and the ability of the individual to control the occurrence of the behaviors affect the degree to which these responses covary linearly. The relationship between attitudes and behaviors is also affected by the measurement procedures employed. When the measures of attitudes and behaviors are equally specific, the correlation between these responses is greater than when the measurements of the responses are not equally specific. Furthermore, measurement of multiple attitudinal and behavioral items (i.e., multiple-act criterion) provides more reliable indications of these responses and typically increases the extent to which knowledge of attitudes allows prediction of behavior.

Finally, the attitude–behavior relationship is stronger when the relevant attitude has been formed as a result of direct behavioral interaction with the attitude object, when the lapse between the measurements of attitude and behavior is brief, and when persons are encouraged to think about their attitudes prior to responding.

3

Thought Disruption and Persuasion: Assessing the Validity of Attitude Change Experiments

Richard E. Petty
University of Missouri-Columbia

Timothy C. Brock
Ohio State University

INTRODUCTION

Now that the necessary background material has been covered and it is clear that attitudes and cognitive responses can be measured, some fundamental questions about persuasion may be addressed: How is attitude change studied experimentally? How can the cognitive response approach help in understanding the process of persuasion? What kinds of predictions can the cognitive response approach generate? How can these hypotheses be tested? Consider the following two examples:

> A man who is a heavy smoker is driving home from work. A public service message comes on the radio and discusses the undesirable consequences of smoking. The man is attempting to listen to the message, but at the same time he is watching the other cars on the busy freeway and trying not to miss his exit.
>
> A woman who considers herself an agnostic is at an outdoor religious rally listening to a world-famous evangelist discuss the merits of Christianity and the Bible. Suddenly, it begins to drizzle slowly. Although the woman can clearly hear the message over the loudspeaker system, she is diverted from thinking about its contents to thinking about how to keep herself dry.

What these two situations have in common is that a person who is the target of a possible persuasive influence attempt is distracted by some external stimuli from paying full attention to, and thinking in any great depth about, the arguments in the persuasive communication. A researcher employing the cognitive response approach might analyze the foregoing situations in the following manner. Under normal circumstances,the heavy smoker and the agnostic would resist the persuasion attempt by silently arguing against (counterarguing) the points in the communication. Under the specific conditions cited, however, the normal counterargumentation process is being disrupted by some external distraction. This inability to counterargue is likely to lead to some attitude change in the direction of the advocated position. Our hypothesis is that counterargument disruption produces persuasion. This hypothesis follows directly from the cognitive response approach outlined in the preceding chapters. Negative thoughts help in resisting persuasion (recall McGuire's work on *inoculation theory* discussed in Chapter 1). By disrupting the negative thoughts, resistance should be weakened, and attitude change should result.

A primary purpose of this chapter is to document the contention that the thoughts elicited by a communication are important in mediating attitude changes. Other goals, however, are to discuss how experimental research in persuasion is conducted and to describe how hypotheses are put to an empirical test. We meet these goals by reviewing some evidence for the notion that thoughts mediate persuasion in a manner that illuminates the qualities that make a piece of research a convincing test of a hypothesis. Although we focus our discussion on the effects of thought disruption on persuasion, since this issue is crucial to the cognitive response approach, our remarks on the evaluation of experiments are applicable generally to research in the field of persuasion and in the social and behavioral sciences. We begin the discussion with a distinction between the conceptual and operational levels of research.

CONCEPTUAL AND OPERATIONAL
LEVELS OF RESEARCH

A simple research effort can be diagramed as in Table 3.1. The relationship above the dividing line represents the conceptual level. It is what the theory or hypothesis states is happening. Below the line is the *operationalization* of the theoretical constructs (how the theoretical variables were translated into variables that could be manipulated and measured). This level represents what is observed to happen. For example, our hypothesis is that "inhibition of counterargumenta-

TABLE 3.1
Theoretical Network Representing a Simple Research Effort

CONCEPTUAL LEVEL	Theoretical Causal Variable (TCV) ⟶	Theoretical Dependent Variable (TDV)
OPERATIONAL LEVEL	Operational Causal Variable (OCV) ⟶	Operational Dependent Variable (ODV)

tion'' (the theoretical causal variable) leads to ''persuasion'' in the direction of the advocacy (the theoretical dependent variable). One crucial difference in testing this hypothesis in an experiment rather than in a correlational study is that in an experimental study, the theoretical causal variable is manipulated, whereas in a correlational study it is simply measured. In both cases, the theoretical dependent variable is measured.

Two types of experimental designs have been used generally in the laboratory to assess attitude change: the *pretest–posttest* control group design and the *posttest–only* control group design (Campbell & Stanley, 1966). The former design may be summarized as follows:

$$\text{Experimental Group} \quad R\ O_1\ X\ O_2$$
$$\text{Control Group} \quad\quad R\ O_3\quad O_4$$

Subjects are assigned randomly (R) to one of two groups, the experimental or the control group (i.e., any given subject has an equal change of being assigned to either group). The pretest attitudes of the experimental group (O_1) and the control group (O_3) are measured using any of the attitude measurement techniques mentioned in the last chapter. Some *treatment* or *manipulation* (X) is presented to the experimental group and is followed by a posttest measurement of the attitudes of the experimental (O_2) and control groups (O_4). Because the subjects are assigned randomly to experimental and control groups, they should have similar attitudes on the average at pretest $(O_1$ and $O_3)$. Attitude change is defined as a change from the pretest (O_1) to the posttest measurement (O_2) that occurs in the experimental group as a result of the manipulation (X). Of course, something in addition to the treatment (X) could occur between O_1 and O_2 to change their attitudes. This explanation is untenable if the control group shows no change from O_3 to O_4, because extraneous events should affect the control group as they do the experimental group. If some extraneous event occurs in addition to the manipulation (X), then the change in control group attitudes from O_3 to O_4 allows an estimation of the amount of change due to the extraneous event and that due to the treatment.

The posttest-only control group design takes the following form:

$$\text{Experimental Group} \quad R\ X\ O_1$$
$$\text{Control Group} \quad\quad R\quad O_2$$

Subjects are assigned randomly (R) to an experimental and a control group. The experimental group receives the treatment (X) followed by a posttest attitude measurement for the experimental (O_1) and control groups (O_2). Attitude change is defined as a difference in measured attitude between the posttest attitude scores of the experimental (O_1) and control groups (O_2). Because the groups are constituted randomly and are treated identically except for the manipulation (X), there should be nothing contributing to the differences between the attitude measures

(O_1 and O_2) except the effects of the manipulation. Of course, these basic designs may be extended to include more than one experimental and control group.

Festinger and Maccoby (1964) reported the first experimental test of the hypothesis that a disruption of counterarguing would lead to attitude change in the direction of the advocacy. In one of their experiments, 179 fraternity men and 114 independents at the University of Southern California were assigned randomly to one of three rooms. A different condition was run in each of the rooms. In all the rooms, the fraternity men and independents were told that they were going to view Part 4 of a movie about university life dealing with college fraternities. The beginning of the movie showed various scenes of campus buildings and students walking on college campuses. In the "ordinary film" condition, the initial scenes dissolved to a scene of a young college professor who argued for the abolition of college fraternities, stating that they encourage cheating and dishonesty, social snobbishness and racial discrimination, and are antithetical to the purposes of a university. In the "distracting film" condition, the initial scenes dissolved into an amusing film entitled *Day of the Painter*. The original sound track of the amusing film (which contained sound effects and music) was replaced with the sound track of the antifraternity film. Thus, subjects in both conditions heard the same persuasive sound track but saw different films. After watching the appropriate film, subjects in both conditions responded to four self-rating scales designed to assess their attitudes toward fraternities. In the third room, a "control" condition was run in which the students responded to the attitude scales before seeing a film. In this experiment, employing a posttest-only design, Festinger and Maccoby attempted to manipulate directly their subjects' ability to counterargue by distracting them with an amusing film. If the distracted subjects were prevented from counterarguing, and if an inhibition of counterarguing produces persuasion (i.e., the hypothesis is correct), then the postfilm attitudes of "distracted" students should be more antifraternity than those in the "ordinary film" and "control" conditions. Table 3.2 presents a theoretical network representing the Festinger and Maccoby experiment. The diagram indicates how the theoretical constructs have been operationalized. The term *treatment* refers to what the experimenter does to treat an experimental group differently from a control group. In the ideal case, the two groups should

TABLE 3.2
Theoretical Network Representing the Festinger and Maccoby
(1964) Experiment

CONCEPTUAL LEVEL	Disruption of counterarguing (TCV) ⟶	Persuasion (TDV)
OPERATIONAL LEVEL	Watch an amusing film during presentation of a message (OCV) ⟶	Sum of four attitude scales on fraternities (ODV)

differ only in that the experimental group receives the operational causal variable whereas the control group does not.

In the Festinger and Maccoby experiment, the data for the independents showed no appreciable differences in attitude among conditions, although the data for the fraternity men did. The average attitude score for fraternity men in the distracting film condition was 23.5; for fraternity men in the ordinary film condition, 24.6; and for fraternity men in the control condition, 24.8. Because low numbers were indicative of an antifraternity response on the scales, the data for fraternity men appear to support Festinger and Maccoby's hypothesis that disruption of counterarguing leads to persuasion. However, as will become clear shortly, this interpretation of the findings is only one of many competing alternative explanations as to what happened. The goal of research is to rule out as many plausible alternative explanations for an observed effect as possible (Campbell, 1969; Platt, 1964; Stinchcombe, 1968). If all plausible alternative explanations can be ruled out, then the investigator's hypothesis remains as the only viable interpretation of the observed effect. In the remainder of this chapter, we discuss the classes of alternative explanations that can threaten the validity of an experiment.

THREATS TO THE VALIDITY
OF AN EXPERIMENT

In evaluating an experiment like the one conducted by Festinger and Maccoby, four kinds of questions can be posed:

1. Was there a reliable difference between conditions?
2. Was the treatment necessary to produce the observed effect?
3. Does the effect generalize to other subjects, times, and settings?
4. Do the treatment and dependent measures reflect the theoretical constructs of interest?

These questions correspond respectively to Cook and Campbell's (1976) four kinds of experimental validity: conclusion, internal, external, and construct. The questions specify the classes of alternative hypotheses that threaten the validity of an experiment.

Statistical Conclusion Validity

Statistical conclusion validity concerns the question of whether any true differences among the various conditions in the experiment were obtained. Recall that in the Festinger and Maccoby study, fraternity men in the distracted group had a mean attitude score of 23.5, the ordinary film group a mean of 24.6, and the control group a mean attitude of 24.8. There are always two possible explanations for observed differences among randomly assigned groups that have been treated differently: (1) The observed effect may represent a real difference among the groups, or (2) the observed effect may be due to chance. Even though random assignment took place, it is likely that the groups will differ to some extent on the dependent measure even if no treatment had been given. Statistical analyses allow the investigator to specify how often any particular observed difference will occur simply by chance when the subjects have been assigned to conditions randomly.

The convention in the social sciences is that no difference is accepted as true if a statistical analysis indicates it could have been produced by chance alone more than 5 time in 100. Adopting this convention means that there is a .05 probability or less ($p < .05$) that an investigator will conclude that a difference is real when it is in fact due to chance. This kind of error is referred to as a *Type I* or *Alpha* error. On the other hand, if an experimenter uses too few subjects or has unreliable measures, another kind of error can be made—concluding that the observed difference is due to chance when it is in fact real. This is referred to as a *Type II* or *Beta* error (see Cohen, 1977, for calculation procedures).

A statistical analysis of the Festinger and Maccoby data indicated that the probability that the attitudes of the fraternity men in the distracting film group and the ordinary film group differed because of chance alone was .06. This does not quite reach the conventional level of statistical significance, and thus chance (Type I error) must be considered a plausible hypothesis to account for the difference between these two groups. The attitude of the fraternity men in the distracting film group did differ significantly from the attitude of the control group, however ($p < .05$), but the attitude of the ordinary film group did not.[1]

Internal Validity

Let us assume for the moment that the difference between the distracting film and the ordinary film conditions did reach conventional levels of statistical significance [as was the case when Festinger and Maccoby (1964) repeated or *replicated* the experiment by showing the same distracting and ordinary films to fraternity men at San José State College]. This would tell us that something other than chance produced the difference in attitude between the two groups. It would

---

[1]Festinger and Maccoby inappropriately performed statistical analyses that assumed that each subject was an independent unit. This assumption is problematic, because all the distracting film subjects were run in one room, all the ordinary film subjects in a different room, and control subjects in a third room. This problem has plagued a number of other distraction experiments (e.g., Haaland & Venkatesan, 1968; Silverman & Regula, 1968). If it is necessary to run subjects in groups, they should not be allowed to have visual or auditory contact with each other (e.g., Petty, Wells, & Brock, 1976). For purposes of exposition, however, we discuss these experiments as if the appropriate analyses had been performed.

not tell us that the treatment (watching an amusing film) was responsible. *Internal validity* poses the question of whether or not the specific treatment employed in the experiment was necessary to produce the observed effect.

If some extraneous causal variable produced the observed effect and the treatment was not necessary, the experiment is not internally valid. Campbell and Stanley (1966) have proposed eight specific threats to the internal validity of an experiment. These threats all propose that some extraneous causal variable (like a historical event, a maturation process, or nonequivalence of the subjects in the various conditions) is responsible for the observed effect rather than the treatment. All the threats to internal validity can be ruled out by employing appropriate control groups and by randomly assigning subjects to conditions. Because a control group is treated identically to the experimental group except for the treatment, if the two groups are found to differ, this difference must either be attributed to the treatment or to the fact that the two groups have different kinds of subjects. By randomly assigning subjects to conditions, we can eliminate the latter possibility and conclude that the treatment was necessary to produce the observed effect.

External Validity

Even though we are able to conclude that the treatment was necessary to produce the observed effect, we cannot be certain that the treatment was sufficient. The treatment may only produce the observed difference when certain kinds of subjects are tested, or only at certain times of the year, or only in the laboratory and not in the field. The question of how generalizable the research findings are is one of *external validity*. If the Festinger and Maccoby experiments were the only ones examining the effect of external distraction on persuasion, we could not be sure of how robust the effect is. For example, in their series of experiments, Festinger and Maccoby found that the effect tended to work on fraternity men at the University of Southern California and San José State, but it did not work on independents at the University of Southern California or on fraternity men at the University of Minnesota. How generalizable is the distraction effect found by Festinger and Maccoby?

Generalizing Across Subject Populations

Table 3.3 lists 22 published experiments examining the effect of external distraction on persuasion. The effect has been shown with high school students and college students in at least 15 universities. Yet if the counterargument disruption hypothesis is correct, the effect should not generalize to *all* subject populations. Festinger and Maccoby argued that if distraction enhances persuasion by disrupting counterarguing, the effect should be obtained only for subjects who are motivated to counterargue. If subjects are not counterarguing during the presentation of the message, then it is impossible for the distraction to interfere

TABLE 3.3

The Effects of External Distraction on Persuasion[a]

Source	Subjects	Message	Distraction	Decreased Counter-argumentation Under Distraction?	Increased Persuasion Under Distraction?
1. Festinger & Maccoby (1964)	Univ. of Minnesota, Univ. of So. California, and San Jose State male undergraduates	Against college fraternities	An amusing film	(Not assessed)	Yes—for San Jose State fraternity men
2. Janis, Kaye, & Kirschner (1965)	Yale undergraduates	Four unpopular positions (e.g., reducing armed forces by 85%)	Eating Pepsi and peanuts	(Not assessed)	Yes
3. Rosenblatt (1966)	University of Missouri—Columbia undergraduates	Opposed to yearly TB chest X-rays	Slides of dental hygiene or general psychology slides	(Not assessed)	Yes
4. Silverman & Regula (1968)	S.U.N.Y. (Buffalo) undergraduates	Tuition increase	Tapes with static	(Not assessed)	Yes—when distraction was thought to be intentional
5. Kiesler & Mathog (1968)	Michigan State University coeds	Several counter-attitudinal topics (e.g., requiring uniforms, bed checks)	Copying lists of two-digit numbers	(Not assessed)	Yes—for highly credible speaker
6. Vohs & Garrett (1968)	University of Montana undergraduates	Presented the Ku Klux Klan favorably	Operations on geometric figures or simple arithmetic	(Not assessed)	No
7. Haaland & Venkatesan (1968)	University of New Hampshire undergraduates	Lowering voting age to 18, and opposed to lowering it	Humorous film, or filled out questionnaire	(Not assessed)	No

8. Shamo & Meador (1969)	Memphis State University undergraduates	In favor of racial segregation	Slides of scenery, sporting events, etc.	(Not assessed)	Yes
9. Osterhouse & Brock (1970)	Ohio State University undergraduates	Tuition increase	Monitoring a panel of flashing lights	Yes	Yes
10. Rule & Rehill (1970)	University of Alberta undergraduates who showed extreme disagreement to topic on pretest	Increased use of television in high schools	Tape of 22 different sounds (whistle, car, laughter, etc.)	(Not assessed)	Yes—for high self-esteem groups
11. Zimbardo & Ebbesen (1970)	Stanford undergraduates selected to be moderately extreme on the topic	Required military service, and shorter summer vacations	Delayed auditory feedback	(Not assessed)	Yes
12. Zimbardo, Snyder, Thomas, Gold, & Gurwitz (1970)	New York University and Stanford University undergraduates	Giving state aid to sectarian schools, and shorter summer vacations	Number summation task	(Not assessed)	Yes—when instructed that attention to message was primary task
13. Keating & Latané (1972)	Ohio State University undergraduates	Against all-volunteer army or for censorship of pornography	Intermittent or continuous distortion of television reception	(Not assessed)	Yes—under intermittent distortion conditions
14. Regan & Cheng (1973)	Cornell University coeds	Simple or complex message advocating less tooth brushing and seat-belt use	Alternating classical and popular music	(Not assessed)	Yes—for simple messages
15. Bither & Wright (1973)	Male college students	Pro-Ford, anti-Chevrolet automobile commercial	Irrelevant visual to accompany the audio	(Not assessed)	Yes—for moderate and high self-confident subjects
16. Keating & Brock (1974)	Ohio State University undergraduates	Tuition increase	Manually or vocally monitoring a panel of flashing lights	Yes	Yes

(continued)

TABLE 3.3—*Continued*

Source	Subjects	Message	Distraction	Decreased Counter-argumentation Under Distraction?	Increase Persuasion Under Distraction?
17. Insko, Turnbull, & Yandell (1974)	University of North Carolina male undergraduates	Shorter summer vacations	Number summation task	Yes—when focus was on message, not task	Yes—when focus was on message, not task
18. Haslett (1976)	Birmingham University, England, male undergraduates	Advocated compulsory male sterilization	Writing or verbalizing the values of flashing numbers	Yes	Yes
19. Petty, Wells, & Brock (1976)	Ohio State University undergraduates	Easy or difficult-to-counterargue message on increasing and reducing tuition	Monitoring a screen of flashing X's	Yes—for easy-to-counterargue messages	Yes—for easy-to-counterargue messages
20. Watts & Holt (1979)	High school students	Contemporary issues (e.g., nuclear proliferation)	Message printed in white type on black background	(Not assessed)	Yes—on an immediate but not a delayed measure
21. Romer (1979)	University of Sheffield, England, and University of Illinois-Chicago Circle undergraduates	Favoring student loans over grants; a tuition increase	Beep sounds on the taped message	Yes—for moderate, but not high distraction	Yes—for moderate, but not high distraction
22. Lammers & Becker (1980)	University of Missouri—Columbia undergraduates	In favor of or against increasing tuition	Rating the pleasantness of various slides	Yes—for the counterattitudinal message	Yes—rated counterattitudinal message as closer to own position

a Adapted from Petty (1975).

with these negative cognitive responses and lead to enhanced persuasion. Independents would not be strongly motivated to defend the fraternity system; nor would fraternity men at an institution where the fraternity system was weak (as it was at the University of Minnesota at the time the study was conducted). Festinger and Maccoby argue that this lack of motivation would account for their failure to find the effect in these groups.

Thus, the treatment (distraction by an amusing film) per se was not sufficient to produce the observed effect. The effect also appeared to depend on testing subjects who were motivated to counterargue. This fact limits the generalizability of the distraction effect but at the same time provides support for the counterargument disruption explanation of the effect.

Other investigations have suggested that the distraction effect may be limited to subjects who have high self-confidence (e.g., Bither & Wright, 1973) or high self-esteem (e.g., Rule & Rehill, 1970). Since Wright (1971) has demonstrated that high self-confident subjects are more active in generating counterarguments than those with less self-confidence, it is likely that this limiting condition is just another demonstration of the fact that the distraction effect will occur only if subjects are attempting to counterargue the persuasive appeal.

Generalizing Across Experimental Settings and Materials

Distraction has been shown to facilitate persuasion in a large number of experiments, although field studies have been rare. The experiments were conducted in different physical locations, at different times, and by different experimenters, indicating that the effect is quite robust. However, a careful examination of Table 3.3 indicates that there are at least three factors that may limit the generalizability of the distraction effect. First, although distraction has enhanced persuasion on a wide variety of message topics, a common feature of the messages employed is that they are counterattitudinal and generally on highly involving topics. Research that has manipulated the counterarguability of the messages (Lammers & Becker, 1980; Petty, Wells, & Brock, 1976) indicates that distraction enhances persuasion only for messages that elicit counterargumentation. Second, distraction appears to enhance persuasion only when the subjects' primary attention is on the message and not on the extraneous distraction (e. g., Insko, Turnbull, & Yandell, 1974; Zimbardo, Snyder, Thomas, Gold, & Gurwitz, 1970). It is likely that subjects are most apt to attempt to generate counterarguments when their attention is on the message rather than on the distraction. Finally, there is research indicating that distraction will enhance persuasion when the source of the message is highly credible but not when the source is of low credibility (Kiesler & Mathog, 1968). Hass (1972) has demonstrated that when the message topic is highly involving, subjects are more apt to counterargue a source of high rather than low credibility (see Chapter 7). Thus, a common feature of all these limiting conditions is that they specify conditions under which counterarguing is most likely to occur. Like the limiting subject-characteristics already mentioned, these characteristics of the experimental materials limit the generalizability of the distraction effect but at the same time provide particular support for the counterargument disruption hypothesis. In sum, the external validity of an effect can be assessed by testing the treatment on a wide variety of subjects, in a wide variety of settings, employing a wide variety of experimental materials.

Construct Validity

Once we have determined that we have observed a reliable difference between our experimental groups (conclusion validity), that our treatment was necessary to produce this difference (internal validity), and the limiting conditions under which the treatment will produce the effect (external validity), we can ask the most important theoretical question: Does our treatment (operational causal variable) truly represent the theoretical causal variable? This is a question of *construct validity*.[2] In the case of the Festinger and Maccoby experiment, the question is whether the experimental treatment represented disruption of counterarguing or whether it represented something else. For example, the amusing film may not have disrupted counterarguing; it may simply have put the subjects in a good mood, and this good mood may have made the fraternity men more likely to agree with the speaker's position. It is important to note that this explanation says that the treatment is necessary to produce the effect, but the treatment doesn't represent the theoretical causal variable. Because treatments are complex and unlikely to evoke only one process, it is always possible that some extraneous causal variable covaries with, or is *confounded* with, the treatment. The problem of determining exactly what a treatment represents (the core concern of construct validity) typically generates the most controversy in the interpretation of an experiment. In this section, we discuss four methods of checking on the construct validity of a treatment:

1. eliminating biasing effects
2. multiple operations of the treatment
3. manipulation checks
4. eliminating alternative theories

Eliminating Biasing Effects

Because, as we just noted, treatments are complex, it may sometimes be unclear what particular aspect of the treatment was responsible for producing the observed effect. We discuss three major varieties of bias that might be responsi-

---

[2]Construct validity also poses the question of whether or not the operational dependent variable represents the theoretical dependent variable. Since the last chapter discussed threats to the validity of attitude and cognitive response measures (e.g., social desirability and acquiescence response sets), we do not discuss the matter further here.

ble for producing the observed effect rather than the treatment: demand charac-teristics, evaluation apprehension, and experimenter bias.

Demand Characteristics.   Orne (1962) has argued that many subjects in an experiment try to find out what the experiment is about. The notion is that the subject wants to modify his or her behavior so that it will conform to what the experimenter expects (i.e., the subject will behave so as to confirm the experi-menter's hypothesis). Whenever the experimental treatment gives the subject a hint about the "correct" response, *demand characteristics* are confounded with the experimental manipulation.

The notion that subjects will go out of their way to please the experimenter by providing the data they think is desired stems from research indicating that subjects are extermely cooperative in research settings. For example, Orne (1962) told subjects that the "experiment" required them to complete a page of simple arithmetic problems, then to tear the answer sheet in 32 pieces and throw them away. This nonsensical activity was repeated until the subject expressed a desire to stop. All subjects worked for several hours, none showing any inclina-tion to discontinue the activity. In another study (Orne & Evans, 1965), subjects complied with an "experimenter's" instructions to reach bare-handed into a jar labeled (falsely) "nitric acid." The fact that subjects are willing to perform monotonous or dangerous tasks when asked to do so by an experimenter does not necessarily mean that they are trying to figure out what the experimental hypothesis is so that they can support it, however. Subjects may simply assume that there is a point to the apparently pointless tasks and that apparently danger-ous tasks are really safe (which is true).

Weber and Cook (1972) reviewed seven experiments in which some subjects were given the hypothesis of interest whereas others were not. These experiments indicated that subjects behaved in accord with the hypothesis only when the behavior required was socially desirable. If confirming the hypothesis required responses that would not put the subjects in a favorable light, the subjects' behavior did not confirm the hypothesis. Thus, subjects appeared to be more concerned with presenting a favorable impression of themselves than they were with supporting the investigator's theory.

Evaluation Apprehension.   As already noted, subjects' intentions may not be to confirm an investigator's hypothesis but instead may be to present themselves as competent, psychologically healthy persons. Rosenberg (1969) has argued that in many experiments, subjects are apprehensive or anxious about being evaluated by experimenters who are presumably experts in human behavior. This *evaluation apprehension* leads subjects to distort their behavior in a socially desirable fashion. If an experimental treatment makes subjects especially anxious or aware that they are being observed and evaluated, evaluation apprehension is confounded with the experimental manipulation.

Silverman (1977) has proposed that evaluation apprehension may account for the effects of distraction on persuasion. The notion is that distracted subjects surmise that the experimenter is trying to impair their ability to concentrate. In order to prove that their power of concentration is not affected and therefore to appear to be quite skillful at the task, subjects report agreement with the message. Presumably, agreement with the communication allows subjects to demonstrate to the experimenter that they attended well enough to the message to be persuaded. In an experiment designed to test this explanation (Silverman & Regula, 1968), some subjects were told that the distraction (static on a tape recording that advocated an increase in tuition) was intentional (i.e., it was part of the experiment), whereas others were told that it was unintentional (i.e., it was inadvertently acquired in transcribing the talk from a radio broadcast). If the distraction effect is due to evaluation apprehension, only subjects in the intentional conditions should show the effect. In the unintentional conditions, the distraction should not cue evaluation apprehension, because in this condition, subjects do not think that the distraction has anything to do with the experiment. As expected, when the distraction was intentional, a higher degree of distraction produced more attitude change. In contradiction to the evaluation apprehension explanation, however, the same effect tended to occur when the distraction was unintentional. Furthermore, the evaluation apprehension explanation does not justify why the effect of distraction interacts with such variables as credibility of the speaker and self-esteem of the subject. Thus, this biasing factor does not seem to be a parsimonious (i.e., economical) explanation for the effect of distraction on persuasion.

In most persuasion research, both evaluation apprehension and demand characteristics are minimized by employing the following techniques: (1) giving the subjects a false hypothesis, (2) removing the dependent measure from the experimental setting, (3) keeping the subjects unaware of being in an experiment, (4) using a bias-reducing design like the posttest-only rather than the pretest–posttest, (5) testing nonobvious hypotheses, (6) using treatments that are absorbing enough to make subjects oblivious to role behavior—called *experimental realism* by Aronson and Carlsmith (1968), and (7) reducing the status difference between experimenter and subject.

Experimenter Bias.   The first two kinds of bias discussed were the result of the subject either trying to please the experimenter by confirming the hypothesis, or trying to impress the experimenter by behaving in a socially desirable manner. The third form of bias involves the experimenter's behavior. Rosenthal (1966) has argued that an experimenter's expectation as to how the data will come out can bias the data that is obtained. The notion is that the experimenter's desires are transmitted to the subjects by means of unintentional cues (such as changes in the experimenter's posture or facial expressions) and that these expectancies influence the subjects' responses. Although some experiments have demonstrated that experimenters' expectancies can influence subjects' responses (e.g., McFall & Schenkein, 1970; Zobel & Lehman, 1969), as Barber (1976) notes, there are more than 40 studies that looked for, but failed to find, an experimenter expectancy effect. Furthermore, of those that have claimed to demonstrate the effect, some have defects in data analysis (e.g., Rosenthal, Persinger, Mulry, Vikan-Kline, & Grothe, 1964), and others are open to the criticism that the experimenters who served as subjects either failed to follow the experimental protocols, misrecorded the data, or actually made up the data (e.g., Rosenthal & Fode, 1963).

Experimenter bias is probably not as prevalent as was once feared. In any case, if the experimenters are kept blind to the experimental condition they are running, and if experimental procedures are clearly specified and/or automated, this bias should not be a problem. Further details on techniques for eliminating the three kinds of bias, as well as discussions of the ethics of various experimental procedures, can be found in Carlsmith, Ellsworth, and Aronson (1976), Crano and Brewer (1973), and Rosenthal and Rosnow (1969).

Miltuple Operations of the Treatment

In the section on external validity, we said that it is a good idea to repeat the experiment on different groups of subjects, at different times, in different settings to see if the same results are observed. It is also a good idea to try several different treatments, all of which are thought to represent the same theoretical causal variable. This is referred to as *multiple operationism*. Complex treatments are characterized by "multiple meaning" (Aronson & Carlsmith, 1968), and single examples or operationalizations of a theoretical concept are unlikely to be pure. That is, as noted earlier, the impact of a treatment can be due to any of several factors, many of which—like demand characteristics or evaluation apprehension—are extraneous to the theoretical variables of interest. A series of experiments should be conducted in which the theoretical variable is operationalized by a number of techniques that differ as much as possible from each other but have the theoretical variable in common. If these procedures produce identical results, attributing the effect to the common conceptual variable is reasonable.

As Table 3.3 indicates, researchers have attempted to disrupt counterarguing with distractions that were visual (Shamo & Meador, 1969), auditory (Rule & Rehill, 1970), and gustatory (Janis, Kaye, & Kirschner, 1965). The distractions have required a manual response (Haslett, 1976), a vocal response (Keating & Brock, 1974), or no response (Regan & Cheng, 1973); they have been pleasant (Festinger & Maccoby, 1964), unpleasant (Rosenblatt, 1966), and neutral (Watts & Holt, 1979). In all these cases, distraction was found to enhance attitude change in the direction of the advocacy. In addition, many different experimenters and *cover stories* (a rationale given to subjects to explain their participation in the experiment that masks the investigator's true purpose) have been employed, making it highly unlikely that the same extraneous variable was present in every replication.

Our primary goal in assessing the validity of distraction as an operationalization of counterargument disruption is determining whether or not distraction is capable of inhibiting thoughts. In addition to employing different types of distractions while subjects hear a persuasive communication, another way one can assess whether distraction is an adequate operationalization of the theoretical causal variable is to test whether distraction inhibits thinking in other contexts. If distraction is a valid *thought disrupter*, it should inhibit different thoughts in different contexts.

Inhibition of Self-Generated Attitude Change. In a series of experiments, Tesser and his colleagues used distraction as a means of preventing subjects from thinking about an attitude object or issue when no persuasive communication was delivered (cf. Tesser, 1978). In one study (Sadler & Tesser, 1973) subjects were exposed to either a likable or a dislikable partner. Unknown to the subject, the "partner" was simulated with one of two tape recordings. The likable partner complimented the subject and described himself in positive terms without appearing to brag. The dislikable partner criticized the subject and was arrogant and insulting. After exposure to one of the partners, half the subjects were instructed to think about their partners, and the remaining subjects were given an irrelevant distraction task designed to keep them from thinking about their partners. Finally, subjects rated their partners on a series of attitude scales and listed their thoughts about him. Nondistracted subjects evaluated the likable stimulus person more favorably and generated more positive thoughts about him than distracted subjects. Also, nondistracted subjects evaluated the dislikable stimulus person more unfavorably and generated more negative thoughts about him than distracted subjects. Distraction was apparently successful in inhibiting the cognitive responses that created the observed attitude polarization.

Inhibition of Sexual Thoughts. As a second example of how distraction appears to be a general "thought disrupter," we turn to a study in which an attempt was made to interfere with the sexual thoughts of male undergraduates. It has long been known that whereas the basis of sexual arousal for lower animals is mainly physiological, for humans, there is a large cognitive component (Beach, 1969). For example, pornographic materials are thought to be arousing because they stimulate sexual thoughts, ideas, and fantasies within the individual (Byrne, 1976). Geer and Fuhr (1976) reasoned that if this is true, it should be possible to interfere with an affective response like sexual arousal by interfering with a person's cognitive responses to erotic materials. Male undergraduates wearing headphones listened to an erotic tape recording that was played in one ear. The tape was of a woman explicitly describing a sexual experience. All the men were attached to a penile plethysmograph that monitored any changes in penis volume (length and/or circumference), providing a sensitive measure of male sexual arousal (cf. Fruend, Sedlacek, & Knob, 1965). In the other ear, subjects heard a random number spoken every 3 seconds. In the nondistracted condition, the participants were told that they were free to listen to the erotic tape and could ignore the numbers. Three distraction conditions were also run. In one, subjects were asked to write down the numbers as they were spoken; in another, they had to add each successive pair of numbers; and in the third, they had to consider each pair of numbers and classify it as above or below 50, and as odd or even. The more complex the distraction task, the less aroused the males were by the erotic recording (as measured by the penile plethysmograph). The results of this experiment provide a clear demonstration of the importance of thought processes in sexual arousal. For our purposes, however, the experiment provides compelling evidence for the notion that distraction is a general "thought disrupter." If the predominant thoughts at a given moment in time are sexual in orientation, these will be disrupted, and an inhibition of sexual arousal will result.

Manipulation Checks

In the preceding section we were concerned with validating the treatment by employing multiple operations in multiple contexts. To the extent that all the different kinds of distraction in the different contexts produce the effects that would be expected if thinking were being disrupted, confidence is conferred in distraction as a manipulation of thought disruption. Of course, we are primarily interested in determining if distraction inhibits *counterarguing* in response to persuasive messages.

Perhaps the most obvious way to assess the validity of a manipulation is to measure its psychological impact directly. For example, let's assume that in an experiment, subjects hear either a highly credible source (operationalized as a "Nobel prize-winning physicist") or a source of low credibility (operationalized as a "high school senior") advocate that all nuclear weapons be abolished. Let us further assume that more attitude change is produced by the highly credible source. We can feel confident in attributing the attitude change to the fact that the source has high credibility only if we can be sure that our subjects perceive the sources as differentially credible. A question or procedure designed to check on the psychological effectiveness of an experimental manipulation is referred to as a *manipulation check*. Subjects can be asked to rate the expertise or believability of the source on a rating scale. If the highly credible source is rated as more believable than the source low in credibility, we have some evidence that the manipulation has the intended effect on the subjects.

In the case of the Festinger and Maccoby experiment, which hypothesized that distraction would inhibit counterargumentation and result in increased agreement with the advocacy, no manipulation check was taken (i.e., there was no measure of counterargumentation). Osterhouse and Brock (1970) reported the first distraction experiment in which a measure of counterargumentation was used.

The undergraduate students who served in this experiment were told that they were to simulate a pilot who must listen to audio communications while monitoring an instrument panel. The "instrument panel" consisted of a black wooden box containing four white light bulbs. While the subjects listened to a speech advocating that the tuition be doubled at their university, they were instructed to call out the number of lights that flashed at the rate of either 10, 20, or 30 times a minute. Figure 3.1 presents the results of the experiment. As expected, subjects showed increasing message acceptance with increasing distraction. In addition to expressing their attitudes, subjects were given 3 minutes to list their thoughts about the topic. When judges coded these thoughts for counterarguments, it was demonstrated that subjects showed decreasing counterargumentation with increasing distraction. Later research (e.g., Haslett, 1976; Insko et al., 1974; Keating & Brock, 1974) has also demonstrated that distraction inhibits the number of counterarguments reported during a thought-listing interval.

In addition to measuring the number of counterarguments that a subject could report during a thought-listing interval, Osterhouse and Brock took a measure of the number of message arguments that a subject could recall. This was done because Festinger and Maccoby recognized that distraction would enhance persuasion only if it were strong enough to make it quite difficult to counterargue but not so strong as to interfere with hearing the speech. Thus, the distraction should be strong enough to interfere with processing and evaluating the message arguments but not so strong as to interfere with their reception. As would be expected on the basis of a learning theory of persuasion, when distraction is so strong as to interfere severely with message reception (e.g., Haaland & Venkatesan, 1968; Romer, 1979; Vohs & Garrett, 1968) distraction does not enhance persuasion but inhibits it.

In the Osterhouse and Brock study, distraction did not affect the number of message arguments subjects could recall, though it did affect the number of

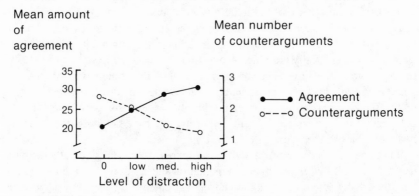

FIG. 3.1.   Mean amount of agreement and mean number of counter arguments in relation to level of distraction. Data from Osterhouse and Brock (1970).

multiple-choice questions they could answer correctly about the message. More recent experimentation has also demonstrated that distraction can enhance persuasion even when message reception is somewhat inhibited (e.g., Insko et al., 1974; Petty et al., 1976; Watts & Holt, 1979). Insko et al. (1974) suggest that there is a relatively flat slope relating recall and attitude change and that, therefore, it takes a relatively large drop in message recall before there is any associated drop in attitude change.

Eliminating Alternative Theories

The evidence in favor of the counterargument disruption explanation of the distraction effect may at this point appear overwhelming. The only threat to this hypothesis that is likely to remain is an alternative theory of the effect that can account for all the findings we have presented thus far.[3] After carefully reviewing all the distraction experiments conducted through 1972, Baron, Baron, and Miller (1973) concluded that such an alternative theory existed. This alternative theory stems from Festinger's (1957) theory of cognitive dissonance and is now discussed further.

A Dissonance Interpretation of Distraction.   Dissonance theory is a consistency theory (see Chapter 1) that concerns the relations among the elements of a person's cognitive system. Cognitive dissonance is an unpleasant motivational state brought about when a person feels responsible for bringing cognitions into an inconsistent relationship (Wicklund & Brehm, 1976). Because dissonance is aversive, persons are motivated to engage in some cognitive work designed to eliminate the inconsistency (e.g., attitude change, denial, bolstering).

Baron et al. (1973) argued that subjects who are distracted while they are listening to or reading a persuasive communication are required to exert more effort to attend to and comprehend the message than are nondistracted subjects. However, the belief that one has voluntarily exerted a great deal of effort to hear a communication should be inconsistent or dissonant with the knowledge that the communication presented a disagreeable position. Effort that is expended on an unpleasant activity (hearing a counterattitudinal speech) theoretically results in dissonance. One method of reducing the dissonance is to decide that the communication is not so disagreeable after all (i.e., to change one's attitude in the direction of the advocacy).

A number of experiments have supported the notion that subjects will change their attitudes in order to justify the effort spent on an unpleasant task. For example, Zimbardo (1965) had subjects give a counterattitudinal speech while hearing their own voices played back on a .25-second delay (high effort re-

---

[3]For example, an explanation that argued that positive affect is responsible for the distraction effect is untenable because it fails to account for the fact that both negative (Rosenblatt, 1966) and neutral (Watts & Holt, 1979) distractions have been shown to enhance persuasion.

quired), or under delayed auditory feedback of .01 seconds (low effort). The difference between pretest and posttest attitude scores indicated that significantly more attitude change in the direction of the advocacy occurred in the high-effort than in the low-effort condition. Wicklund, Cooper, and Linder (1967) demonstrated that the mere anticipation of performing an effortful task could result in attitude change. In two experiments, subjects who anticipated a relatively effortful experience (e.g., 7 minutes of running in place) before being exposed to a persuasive communication showed significant attitude change in the direction of the expected communication. Subjects who anticipated a relatively noneffortful experience (e.g., 7 minutes of sitting quietly) did not differ from the control group.

Baron et al. (1973) contended that all the distraction manipulations to date have been confounded with effort, and that effort justification is thus a viable alternative theory to account for the facilitating effect of distraction on persuasion.[4] The dissonance hypothesis is especially plausible, because it can also account for the interactions of distraction with self-esteem and with credibility of the speaker that were mentioned earlier.[5] As the confounding of distraction and effort may be unavoidable, the best way out of this methodological difficulty is to devise an experiment for which the alternative theories (counterargument disruption and effort justification) make competing predictions. An experiment that allows us to decide between two alternative theories, both of which are quite plausible, is called a *crucial experiment* (Stinchcombe, 1968).

A Thought Disruption Interpretation of Distraction.   Petty, Wells, and Brock (1976) devised two experiments for which the counterargument disruption and effort justification explanations made competing predictions. Petty et al. reasoned that the counterargument disruption hypothesis would predict an enhancing effect for distraction only for a message that is susceptible to counterar-

---

[4]Although Baron et al. (1973) speak of the effort hypothesis in dissonance terms, it is not really necessary to do so. Other orientations would also expect more attitude change with increased effort. *Self-perception theory* (Bem, 1968), for example, states that when someone can discover no salient external justification for his or her overt behavior (expending high effort), that individual comes to infer attitudes from personal behavior (e.g., "If I work this hard for so little reason, I must believe in what I am doing"). Similarly, Brock's (1968) *commodity theory* specifically states that "a message will increase in effectiveness the greater the magnitude of the recipient's effort to obtain the information or to understand it [p. 249]."

[5]Dissonance theorists account for the fact that distraction works best for subjects of high self-esteem by noting that dissonance effects are more likely when subjects have high self-esteem, because dissonance is generally created by any cognition that is inconsistent with a positive view of self (Aronson, 1968). To explain why distraction works best with speakers of high credibility, dissonance theorists argue that hearing a moron disagree with you should not produce dissonance, whereas hearing an expert disagree with you should (Baron et al., 1973). Thus, the same factors that have been shown to be associated with increased counterarguing have been shown to be associated with increased dissonance.

guing and would not predict an effect for a difficult-to-counterargue message because, presumably, here there are no counterarguments to disrupt.

Two specific messages were constructed for each of the two experiments. One message in each experiment used arguments that were logically sound and easily defendable. Pilot testing revealed that when subjects were allowed to think about the arguments, the message elicited predominantly positive thoughts on a post-message thought listing. The other message advocated the same position but used arguments that were open to refutation and skepticism, and it elicited primarily negative thoughts in pilot testing.

Explanations of the distraction effect based on effort would predict that with increasing levels of distraction (and thus effort), there would be increased acceptance of *both* messages. A cognitive response analysis yields different predictions for the two messages, however. As noted in Chapter 2, cognitive responses are the result of processing or thinking about the arguments in a communication. Distraction, as a "thought disrupter," should inhibit evaluation of the message arguments. This inhibition of processing will result in the production of fewer favorable thoughts about a high-quality communication (because subjects will not realize how "good" the arguments are) and will result in fewer negative thoughts about a low-quality communication (subjects will not realize how "poor" the arguments are). Thus, for an easy-to-counterargue message, distraction should inhibit negative cognitive responses and result in increased persuasion; but for a difficult-to-counterargue message, distraction should inhibit positive cognitive responses and result in reduced persuasion.

In one experiment, subjects listened to one of the two different messages (easy or difficult to counterargue) under either low or medium distraction. The distraction task required subjects to monitor a screen on which an X flashed in one of the four corners at either 4 (low distraction) or 12 (medium distraction) times per minute. The X's flashed in the different corners at random, and the subjects were required to record the corner in which the X appeared.

Table 3.4 presents the mean number of favorable and unfavorable thoughts subjects listed when given 2½ minutes to list their thoughts on the topic after listening to the message under either low- or medium-distraction conditions. Overall, 60% of the thoughts listed in response to the easy-to-counterargue message were unfavorable, whereas the corresponding figure for the difficult-to-counterargue message was 8%. Favorable thoughts predominated in response to the difficult-to-counterargue message: 62% of the total thoughts listed were coded as favorable. Only 27% of the thoughts listed in response to the easy-to-counterargue message were coded as favorable. More importantly, distraction inhibited the predominant cognitive response. Thus, for the easy-to-counterargue message, distraction inhibited the production of unfavorable cognitive responses; for the difficult-to-counterargue message, distraction inhibited the production of favorable cognitive responses.

TABLE 3.4
Mean Number of Favorable and Unfavorable Thoughts Generated in
Relation to Message Counterarguability and Level of Distraction[a]

| | Easy to Counterargue | | Difficult to Counterargue | |
| | Low Distraction | Medium Distraction | Low Distraction | Medium Distraction |
Measure				
Unfavorable thoughts	3.92 a	2.61 b	.38 c	.48 c
Favorable thoughts	1.15 a	1.77 a	3.69 b	2.31 c

Note. Cells in any row having a common subscript are not significantly different at the .05 level by the Duncan multiple-range test.
[a] Data from Petty, Wells, and Brock (1976), Exp. 2.

An examination of subjects' postmessage attitudes (top panel, Fig. 3.2) revealed that overall, subjects agreed more with the difficult- than with the easy-to-counterargue message. However, a Message × Distraction interaction indicated that for the easy message, distraction tended to enhance persuasion, but for the difficult message, distraction tended to reduce persuasion. It is important to note that these effects were obtained both when the messages advocated proattitudinal and counterattitudinal positions (see Fig. 3.2).[6]

The data from the two experiments reported by Petty et al. (1976) strongly support the general thought disruption hypothesis over the effort justification notion. The effect of distraction on acceptance was not dependent on the amount of effort exerted or on whether the speaker advocated pro- (reducing tuition) or counterattitudinal (increasing tuition) positions, but it did depend on the quality of the arguments in the message and on the nature of the thoughts elicited by those arguments. When distraction inhibited the production of unfavorable thoughts, increased agreement with the message resulted; but when distraction inhibited the production of favorable thoughts, decreased agreement with the message resulted. Only the general thought disruption hypothesis is able to account for the observed effects of distraction on persuasion, and until another alternative theory is proposed that can account equally well for all the data, thought disruption remains the most viable account for the effect of distraction on persuasion.

---

[6]Lammers and Becker (1980) have reported a conceptual replication of these experiments. In their experiment, subjects heard either a counterattitudinal message in favor of doubling tuition (which elicited predominantly unfavorable cognitive responses) or a proattitudinal message opposed to doubling tuition (which elicited predominantly favorable cognitive responses). After hearing the message under one of three levels of distraction, subjects rated the perceived extremity of the message's position. Under increased distraction, subjects tended to see the proattitudinal message as being further from, and the counterattitudinal message as being closer to, their own positions.

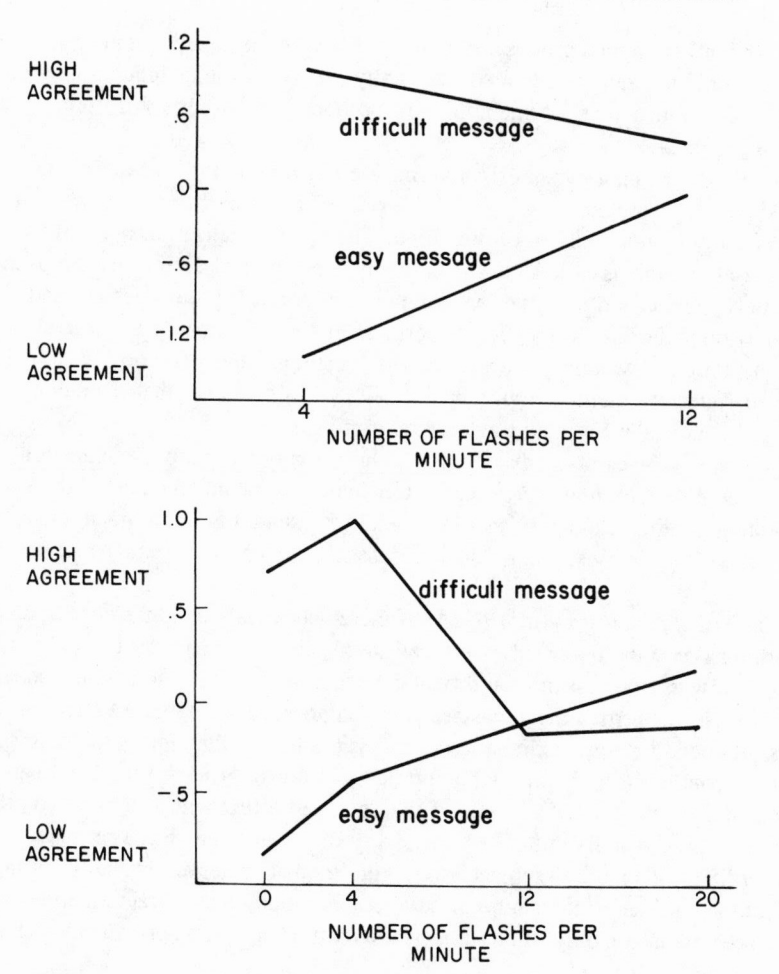

FIG. 3.2.   Top Panel: Mean attitude scores in relation to message and level of distraction for messages advocating proattitudinal position. Bottom panel: Mean attitude scores in relation to message and level of distraction for messages advocating counterattitudinal positions. Data from Petty, Wells, and Brock (1976).

CHAPTER SUMMARY

A cognitive response view of persuasion holds that the thoughts elicited by a persuasive communication (favorable or unfavorable) are important mediators of attitude changes. This view is best tested in an *experiment* in which the hypothesized causal or independent variable (a person's thoughts) is manipulated and changes in the measured or dependent variable (attitude) are monitored. If two randomly assigned groups are found to differ on the dependent measure after the manipulation and were treated identically except for the manipulation, then it can be concluded that the manipulation produced the observed difference between groups.

After generating a hypothesis, the first step in conducting an experiment is to translate the theoretical or *conceptual variables* into *operational variables* that can actually be manipulated or measured. The operationalization of the theoretical causal variable is called a *treatment*. The experimental designs used typically to study persuasion are the pretest–posttest control group design and the posttest-only design. In the first experimental investigation of the relation between thought disruption and persuasion, Festinger and Maccoby (1964) distracted fraternity men with an amusing film and concluded that distraction increased persuasion by inhibiting counterarguing.

Any single research study is susceptible to many alternative explanations of the observed effect, however, because translation of the theoretical variables into operational variables is not exact. The goal of research is to eliminate plausible alternative hypotheses. Four general classes of alternative explanations were noted.

Statistical conclusion validity asks if there was a realiable difference between conditions or if the observed effect was simply due to chance. Statistical procedures allow us to assess the viability of chance as a plausible alternative. *Internal validity* asks if the treatment was necessary to produce the observed effect or if it was produced by some extraneous causal variable. By randomly assigning subjects to conditions and employing appropriate control groups, this threat can be eliminated. *External validity* asks if the observed effect will generalize to other subjects, times, and settings. By repeating or *replicating* the experiment with many different kinds of subjects and experimental materials in many settings, limitations on the effect can be discovered. For example, distraction appears to enhance persuasion only when subjects are motivated to counterargue the persuasive appeal.

Construct validity asks if the treatment truly represents the theoretical causal variable (i.e., does distraction inhibit thought production?) and thus is crucial in theory testing. Four ways of increasing confidence in the treatment as a reflection of the theoretical causal variable were discussed. First, biasing effects like *demand characteristics* (cues in the treatment that elicit what subjects believe to be the correct response), *evaluation apprehension* (cues in the treatment that elicit socially desirable behavior), and *experimenter bias* (cues in the experimenter's behavior that elicit conformity to the hypothesis) must be eliminated. Second, *multiple operations* of the treatment (operationalizing the treatment in several ways that differ as much as possible from each other but have in common the theoretical variable) should be employed to eliminate the effects of extraneous variables that are *confounded* or covary with the treatment. The treatment might also be tested in other contexts. For example, distraction was shown to inhibit thoughts that were not in response to a persuasive message. Third, *manipulation checks* (measurement of the effectiveness of the treatment on the psychological mediator) should be taken. Thus, distraction was shown to inhibit the listing of counterarguments. Finally, alternative theories of the effect should be eliminated in *crucial experiments* (experiments for which different plausible theories make competing predictions). Thus, distraction was shown to produce effects consistent with thought disruption and not with effort justification.

In the years since the original Festinger and Maccoby experiment, more than 20 distraction–persuasion experiments have been conducted. A careful analysis of these experiments reveals that thought disruption is the most viable mediator of the distraction–persuasion relationship. Thus, the distraction experiments provide unique support for a cognitive response view of persuasion. The research demonstrates that persons often are motivated to process actively the information contained in persuasive communications, and when this processing is inhibited, the attitudinal results are modified.

4

Psychophysiological Functioning, Cognitive Responding, and Attitudes

John T. Cacioppo
University of Iowa

Curt A. Sandman
University of California-Irvine

INTRODUCTION

How are psychological phenomena such as attitudes and cognitive responses related to physiological processes? The question is thousands of years old and has frustrated generations of philosophers and scientists (cf. Uttal, 1975). Indeed, Schopenhauer (1788–1860) was moved by the magnitude and complexity of this question to call it *the world knot*. This puzzle continues to mystify philosophers and scientists. Recently, scientists, particularly psychologists, have broken this overall question down into smaller subquestions. Some of these subquestions have been deemed inappropriate for scientific study, whereas empirical evidence has been collected that bears on some of the remaining subquestions. In this chapter, we consider the present state of evidence and theory pertaining to physiological processes as they relate to attitudes and cognitive response.

In the first part of this chapter, we discuss and evaluate some popular physiological techniques for measuring attitudes. These techniques can be added to the rating scale methods discussed in Chapter 2. In the second part, we show how cognitive responses may be reflected physiologically. In addition, a psychophysiological model of cognitive responses and attitudes is presented that illustrates that internal physiological factors may affect information processing and cognitive responding much like the external factor of distraction discussed in Chapter 3.

MEASURING ATTITUDES PHYSIOLOGICALLY

The earliest definitions of attitudes were stated in terms of bodily processes. Contemporary definitions of attitudes, however, no longer contain physiological references (see Chapters 1 and 2). Bodily processes are now of interest to investigators of attitude change because of the belief that these processes may reflect the attitude (McGuire, 1966a). Westie and DeFleur (1959) designated two assumptions that were necessary when using self-report measures of attitudes: (1) People can accurately (i.e., are able to) determine their attitude toward an attitude object; and (2) people are willing to disclose this information truthfully to another person (e.g., an experimenter). How much simpler the study of attitudes would be if investigators had a window to a person's thoughts and feelings. Although there are no transparent (physiological) windows of this kind, an understanding of the relationships between cognitive and physiological processes may offer unique data from which investigators can obtain a more complete picture of attitudinal and cognitive responses. Physiological processes most often have been tapped by monitoring bioelectrical activity by placing small discs (electrodes) on various parts of the body and head. This technique, termed *electrophysiological measurement,* provides information about the activity of the nervous system.

Two approaches to the bodily (physiological) assessment of attitudes are discussed in this section. In one approach, an attempt is made to tap the naturally occurring physiological indicators of affective states. The second approach involves an attempt to tap an evaluative reaction by monitoring a classically conditioned physiological response.

Emotional Response Approach

Early researchers hypothesized that the affective (emotional) aspect of the attitudinal reaction to an object was reflected in subsequent physiological activity. This bodily response presumably indicated both the direction and the intensity of the affect associated with the attitude object (cf. Summers, 1970). Hence, attitudinal direction was assessed by monitoring the direction (or pattern) of the physiological response(s), and the strength of the attitude was assessed by measuring the intensity of the response(s). This approach shares a perspective similar to that found in the classical theoretical work of James (1890) and Lange (1888): They argued that each emotional reaction is the result of a unique physiological syndrome or pattern of responses, with the intensity of the emotional state proportional to the intensity of the physiological reaction. (The theory of emotions proposed by James and Lange differs from the emotional response approach in a simple way. The classical Jamesian approach states that the emotional reaction to an attitude object is preceded and determined by the physiological responses; the emotional response approach seeks to monitor physiological responses that could be a *consequence* of the evaluation of, or emotional reaction to, an attitude object.)

Cannon (1927) criticized the Jamesian concept that each emotional reaction was distinguishable physiologically. The critique was based primarily on anatomical grounds; he proposed instead that *all* emotional reactions were accompanied by the same pattern of general peripheral nervous system activation. He argued that emotional states were the result of a subcortical signal to the cortex that identified the emotion and simultaneously activated all the peripheral bodily responses for "fight or flight." Consequently, an emotional response model based partially on Cannon's (1927) theory of emotions might use the activation of any single physiological response to an attitude object as indicative of the strength of the attitudinal response. The direction of the attitude could not be assessed, however, and the attitudinal response would have to be extreme enough to be accompanied by an emotional reaction when elicited for assessment of attitudinal strength.

The models have in common the assumption that an attitude object elicits an affective (evaluative) reaction that, if strong enough, is accompanied by physiological activity. Most investigations employing the emotional response approach have monitored either electrodermal (skin) activity or pupillary responses. A summary of this research follows.

Electrodermal Activity and Attitudes: Novel Findings. Neurophysiologically, electrodermal activity is mediated by the sympathetic nervous system and is controlled by several *different* cortical and subcortical areas in the brain (Wang & Lu, 1930). In the past, electrodermal activity was thought to indicate the level of "arousal" of an organism. However, electrodermal responding may result from changes in one of various specific neural systems, often without corresponding changes in other responses. Consequently, "the common utilization of electrodermal activity as a relatively monolithic arousal indicator [sic] is a gross and erroneous over-simplification" (Edelberg, 1972, p. 394; see Martin & Venables, 1966; Prokasy & Raskin, 1973, for technical reviews).

Nevertheless, electrodermal activity has been one of the most frequently used physiological measures of arousal in the attitudinal response. Authors have argued that the size and/or frequency of the elctrodermal response is related directly to the strength of the affective reaction to an attitude object (cf. Mueller, 1970). The most commonly employed electrodermal measure has been the *galvanic skin response* (GSR), which refers to the varying electrical resistance of the skin to a small electrical current passing between two electrodes. Because GSR is thought to reflect the strength but not the direction of an attitude, it is a *unidirectional* measure.

One of the first studies to be conducted in this area was by Smith (1922). He monitored GSR while presenting words to persons and found that GSR deflections accompanied words with emotional meaning more often than words with neutral meaning. Almost three decades hence, McCurdy (1950) reviewed the literature concerning mental states and electrodermal activity. He found substantial correlations reported (median value was $+.75$) to exist between the size of an electrodermal response and the vividness of various subjective and emotional experiences. For instance, Dysinger (1931; reported by McCurdy, 1950) presented to subjects a list of words, each of which was rated immediately after its presentation on a 5-point scale ranging from "very pleasant" to "very unpleasant." The electrodermal response was highly correlated ($r = .85$) with the extremity of the rating but was not correlated with whether the stimuli were rated on the pleasant or unpleasant portion of the scale. In other words, the strength of the subjective reaction was reflected in the electrodermal response, whereas the affective direction was not.

Some researchers failed to find any relationship between attitudes and GSR. To account for these failures, Rankin and Campbell (1955) noted that the use of verbal representations rather than actual presentations of attitude objects may have elicited too weak an affective reaction from persons to be detected. To test their notion, Rankin and Campbell (1955) recruited subjects with either extremely favorable or unfavorable attitudes toward blacks for participation in an experiment in which a black graduate student and a white graduate student served as the experimenters (and as the attitude objects). Electrodermal responses were recorded when the black versus the white experimenter entered the room to adjust an electrode on the subject's arm. The results indicated that *all* subjects displayed greater electrodermal activity when the black rather than the white experimenter was in the room. But is this due to unreported prejudices on the part of the "unbiased" subjects or to the insensitivity of the electrodermal response to prejudice? Subsequent experimentation indicated that persons with unfavorable attitudes toward blacks displayed larger electrodermal responses to black experimenters (Porier & Lott, 1967) and photographs of blacks (Vidulich & Krevanick, 1966; Westie & DeFleur, 1959) than persons with favorable attitudes toward blacks.

This result was interpreted as meaning that a relationship between attitudes and electrodermal activity would exist only if the presentation of the attitude object elicited a strong emotional reaction. If the presentation of an attitude object elicited electrodermal responses, one might conclude that the attitude was either very favorable or very unfavorable. For instance, Cooper and Singer (1956) asked 126 subjects to rate and rank 20 ethnic and national groups. Twenty of these 126 subjects revealed extreme attitudes toward their most liked and disliked groups and served subsequently as subjects in a laboratory experiment. Each subject was tested individually, and electrodermal activity was monitored while the experimenter (1) derogated the most liked group, (2) complimented the most disliked group, (3) derogated a group toward which subjects felt neutral, and (4) complimented a group toward which subjects felt neutral. The largest electrodermal responses followed derogatory statements about the most liked group and complimentary statements about the most disliked group (see Fig. 4.1). Cooper and Singer (1956) concluded that the electrodermal activity was indicative of the emotional energy expended and that there was greater emotional energy expended in response to attitude objects with maximum strength (e.g., prejudices) than to attitude objects with minimum strength (e.g., neutral attitudes).

Cooper and Siegel (1956) and Cooper and Pollock (1959) conducted partial replications of this experiment using similar procedures to assess the relationship between electrodermal activity and negative or neutral attitudes. It was again found that increased electrodermal activity was associated with complimentary statements about the most disliked group. (There were no conditions in which the most liked group was derogated in these experiments.) Cooper (1959) stated, "Physiological tests support the thesis that prejudicial attitudes are attended by relatively strong emotion [p. 314]."

Although these studies demonstrated electrodermal activation in response to the presentation of certain attitude objects, it may not be the case that the electrodermal activity reflects emotion per se. Indeed, Lacey (1959) has argued that increased electrodermal activity does not necessarily indicate evaluative reactions, even though, as he stated, "the differential magnitude of galvanometer deflections to words is one of the most reliable phenomena in psychology today [p. 163]." For instance, the presentation of strange, novel, or unexpected stimuli

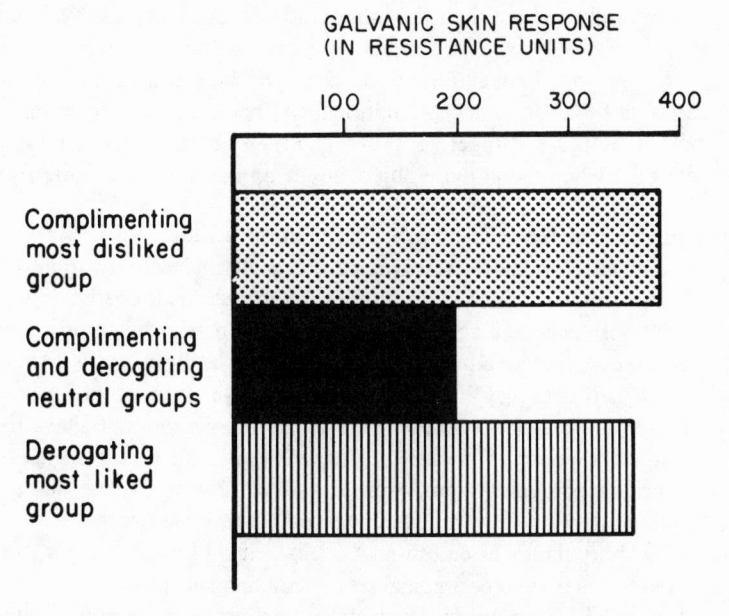

FIG. 4.1.   Mean galvanic skin response to verbal stimuli (calculated from data presented in Cooper, 1959).

has been shown to elicit an increase in electrodermal activity (Sokolov, 1963) and to be a component of the orienting or "what is it?" response (Pavlov, 1927). It is possible that the subjects in research such as that just described found an experimenter complimenting their most disliked group to be more novel or surprising than an experimenter complimenting a group toward which they felt neutral. And conversely, when subjects heard the experimenter derogate their most liked group, they possibly were more surprised by the novelty of this behavior than when he derogated a group toward which they felt neutral. Consequently, the increased electrodermal activity found in these experiments (see Fig. 4.1) could be indicative of the unexpected nature of the stimuli rather than of the "emotional energy" expended in the *attitudinal reaction* to the stimuli. Whereas in either case, the physiological measure might be used to assess an attitude, the novelty interpretation offered here ties the validity of this assessment to the peculiar attributes of these experimental settings.

Cooper and Singer (1956) and Cooper (1959) provide some evidence that supports the notion that the electrodermal responses were caused by the novelty of the stimuli. Cooper (1959) reported that there was some general agreement in the subject population concerning who were the most liked and disliked groups. If the subjects were aware that their preferences were similar to, or at least not opposite from, those of other persons with whom they interacted, they may have expected the experimenter also to have similar preferences concerning the groups. Second, and more compelling, Cooper and Singer (1956) reported that questioning subjects about their prejudices did not cause increased electrodermal activity. "It was only when a subject's positive prejudice object was cast in a derogatory light or his negative prejudice object was cast in a complimentary light that significant amounts of emotionality [increased electrodermal activity] appeared" (Cooper & Singer, 1956, p. 245). That is, electrodermal activity increased only when the attitude object appeared in a novel or unexpected context.

The novel or unexpected context in which the attitude object was presented may account also for the differences in electrodermal activity found between persons with pro- and antiblack attitudes when race-related stimuli were presented. For instance, a black experimenter may have been more novel to a prejudiced person than to a person not prejudiced; similarly, 10 to 20 years ago, photographs of blacks may have been more novel or unexpected for prejudiced than for unprejudiced persons. Thus, electrodermal activity may have indicated the attentional response of orienting rather than an evaluative response.

In further support of this proposition, it is interesting to note that Flanagan (1967) found attention to be a better intervening-variable interpretation of electrodermal activity than was emotion. A major reason for Flanagan's conclusion (in addition to his own experimental evidence) was Darrow's (1936) report that in some cases of strong emotion, electrodermal activity *decreased* rather than *increased*.

In summary, although several investigations have found that strong positive and negative attitudes are accompanied by increased electrodermal activity, it is possible that the electrodermal activity resulted from the novelty of the stimuli rather than as a simple evaluative reaction. To distinguish between these interpretations, experimentation must be conducted in which novelty is neither confounded with the initial attitude position nor with the presentation of neutral and extreme attitude objects. In any event, it seems, at best, that an attitude is reflected in increased physiological activity only if the attitude is strong enough to elicit an emotional reaction when the attitude object is presented.

The Pupillary Response and Attitudes: Interesting Phenomena.   The pupil of the eye is capable of a *bidirectional* response: It dilates when lighting is dim, and it constricts when lighting is bright. The size of the pupil is under the control of two smooth muscles in the iris. The muscle responsible for pupillary constriction is mediated by the parasympathetic nervous system (which primarily functions to maintain systems), whereas the muscle that controls pupillary dilation is under the control of the sympathetic nervous system (which primarily functions to activate systems). The pupil can range in size from 1.5 to 9.0 millimeters and can react to stimulation in as little as .2 seconds (Lowenstein & Loewenfeld, 1962). Loewenfeld (1958) provides a comprehensive review of the neurophysiological aspects of the pupillary response. Lowenstein (1920) reported that the pupils of a catatonic schizophrenic dilated to suggestion-induced states such as "pleasure," "displeasure," and to warnings of impending stress. He concluded that the pupillary response was related to internal events as well as to external environmental changes such as alterations in lighting. Hess (1965) then related the pupillary response to attitudes: (1) Pupillary constriction was said to accompany a negative attitudinal reaction to a repeatedly presented stimulus object, consequently reducing the contact with the unpleasant stimulus; (2) pupillary dilation was said to accompany a positive attitudinal reaction when a stimulus object was repeatedly presented.

The notion of pupillary constriction in response to negatively evaluated or aversive stimuli was contrary to the prevailing evidence that all emotional reactions, whether positive or negative, were associated with pupillary dilation (Loewenfeld, 1966). Hess and Polt (1960) and Hess, Seltzer, and Shlien (1965) provided evidence that pupillary dilation accompanied the viewing of pleasant and interesting stimuli, but it was not until an experiment conducted by Hess (1965) that pupillary *constriction* was thought to indicate a *negative* attitude. People viewed pictures that varied in their interest value and pleasantness. When the pictures were viewed initially, pupillary dilation was largest for the interesting pictures regardless of their affective characteristics. But with repeated presentations of the pictures, unpleasant pictures resulted in pupillary constriction. (Repeated presentations rule out a novelty interpretation, because the orienting response habituates during repeated exposure to stimuli.) These results led Hess

(1965) to hypothesize that positive affect would be associated with dilation and that negative affect would be associated with constriction of the pupils. Another less stringent statement of the hypothesis is that pupil size and attitude are positively correlated.

These hypotheses have received considerable attention since 1965 (reviews of this literature are provided by Goldwater, 1972; Hess, 1972; Janisee, 1974; Mueller, 1970; Woodmansee, 1970). Woodmansee (1965) selected persons who were either very favorable or very unfavorable toward blacks. Photographs of blacks, whites, blacks and whites together, neutral content (the numbers 1 through 4 in the corners and 5 in the center of a gray-white background), and unpleasant content (a filthy toilet and surroundings) were presented repeatedly to all subjects. The results revealed that both groups of subjects reacted similarly to the repeated presentation of all photographs, whereas it had been expected that the prejudiced subjects would react differently to the pictures of blacks and whites than would the nonprejudiced subjects. Moreover, no significant pupillary constriction was found in response to the unpleasant photograph.

Much of the subsequent experimentation failed also to support the hypothesized relationship between pupillary responses and attitudes. Woodmansee (1970) varied the number of presentations of the stimulus, the aversiveness of the stimulus, and the time at which persons rated their attitudes toward each stimulus. In two experiments, he found no evidence for a bidirectional pupillary response (i.e., dilation and constriction) to the stimuli; nor did he find that positively evaluated stimuli caused larger pupillary dilation than negatively evaluated stimuli. Pupil size has also failed to differentiate words varying on rated dimensions of good–bad and neutral–very important (Peavler & McLaughlin, 1967); and a person's verbal attitude rating of a picture and the pupillary response to the picture were found to be unrelated (Collins, Ellsworth, & Helmreich, 1967).

However, occasional support for the hypothesis of Hess is reported. Barlow (1969) found that politically liberal subjects showed dilation to pictures of Lyndon Johnson and Martin Luther King, Jr., but constriction to a picture of George Wallace, whereas conservatives showed the opposite pattern of pupillary responding. Hicks and LePage (1976) reported that subjects displayed pupillary constriction when viewing slides of disliked ethnic groups and pupillary dilation when viewing slides of liked ethnic groups, even during their initial presentation. Nevertheless, the bulk of the empirical evidence suggests that attitudes cannot be determined solely by the analysis of pupil size.

Woodmansee (1966, 1970) argued that methodological problems in pupillographic research employing visual stimuli threaten the validity of pupil size as a measure of psychological reactions. Most of the methodological issues discussed by Woodmansee concern the attributes of the testing situation and materials that cause large variations in pupil size even though they have no psychological significance. For instance, pupil size tends to decrease in size during an experiment. Thus, it is important either to randomize or counterbalance the order of the stimulus presentations. Woodmansee (1970) and Goldwater (1972) have suggested that some of these problems could be circumvented by using nonvisual stimuli in research on pupil size and psychological states (e.g., Kirby, 1968). Although the research in which nonvisual stimuli were used is more sparse, "of particular interest is Hess' own report that constriction responses were found only with visual stimuli; unpleasant-tasting liquids and disliked musical selections consistently evoked dilation" (Goldwater, 1972, p. 343).

In summary, the pupil response has been hypothesized to reflect the attitudinal reaction to stimuli. Most empirical evidence, however, suggests that the response is correlated with the interest, attention, or processing capacity elicited by a stimulus rather than with an evaluative reaction (cf. Kahneman, 1973; Libby, Lacey, & Lacey, 1973). Future research could circumvent many of the methodological problems by providing fixation points, constant illumination, and controls for prestimulus pupil size while presenting to subjects nonvisual (e.g., audio) stimuli that vary along the psychological dimensions of interest to the investigator (e.g., affect). Repeated presentations of the stimuli may also provide a means of circumventing the confounding effects of the orienting response to novel stimuli.

Summary of Research Using the Emotional Response Approaches.   Experimentation utilizing the unidirectional emotional response approach, for the most part, has concerned the relationship between electrodermal activity and attitudes. This is unfortunate, because the electrodermal response is sensitive to many irrelevant stimuli and makes properly controlled experiments difficult to conduct.

Experimentation employing the bidirectional emotional response approach has typically measured the pupillary response to visual presentations of attitude objects. The pupillary response does not appear to reflect the evaluative reaction to a stimulus consistently, although the evidence is not yet definitive on this issue. It is doubtful, however, that a *single* measure exists that differentiates affective states (see reviews by Fehr & Stern, 1970; Lang, Rice & Sternbach, 1972; Strongman, 1973).

Early research on emotions also failed to reveal consistent response *syndromes* indicating positive and negative emotional reactions. However, several recent experiments using multiple measures of physiological activity (e.g., electrodermal activity, electromyography, heart rate, respiratory activity, blood pressure) have provided some evidence for distinguishable response patterns among affective states (e.g., Averill, 1969; Ax, 1953; Sandman, 1971, 1975; Schwartz, Fair, Salt, Mandel, & Klerman, 1976a, 1976b).

For instance, Schwartz et al. (1976b) have presented evidence that the emotional states of happiness, sadness, and anger are associated with specific patterns of electromyographic (EMG) activity in the muscles of the face; these responses are not easily distinguishable by either the subject or the experimenter. They also found that patients suffering from depression displayed EMG patterns normally characteristic of sadness and anger but displayed attenuated EMG patterns characteristic of happiness. When the depressed patients were asked to think of a typical day, the EMG patterns displayed were characteristic of sadness (Schwartz et al., 1976a). These investigations, each of which relied upon the study of response patterns rather than single responses, provide an example of a research methodology that may be applicable to the study of the subtle affective states characteristic of most attitudes.[1]

Classical Conditioning Approach

The emotional response approach utilized the measurement of naturally occurring physiological responses thought to be indicative of affective states. An alternative approach involves assessing an induced (classically conditioned) physiological response to measure attitudinal reactions. Razran (1939) demonstrated that once a conditioned stimulus (CS) is classically conditioned to a response (CR), the verbal equivalent of the actual CS also elicits the CR. That is, words that have the same meaning as the CS are conditioned semantically to the CR because they elicit the CR only after conditioning. Words that have a meaning similar to the CS elicit a weaker form of the CR after conditioning, a phenomenon termed *semantic generalization.*

Investigators studying attitudes have suggested using an evaluative word such as *good* as the CS while using a physiological response as the CR. After conditioning, attitude objects could be presented to subjects. As displayed in Fig. 4.2, the magnitude of the physiological response that served as the CR could then denote the strength of the attitude toward the object (e.g., Cook & Sellitz, 1964). This approach, termed here the *classical conditioning model,* could be extended by conditioning a physiological response (e.g., vasomotor activity) to evaluative words opposite in meaning to each other (e.g., *good* vs. *bad*). The physiological response activated by the presentation of the attitude object (e.g., vasomotor dilation vs. constriction) should indicate whether the attitude is favorable or unfavorable, and the intensity of the CR should indicate the relative strength of the attitude.

---

[1]Although Cannon (1927) hypothesized that physiological functioning increased in a highly intercorrelated manner, and that any physiological measure would suffice as a measure of this "arousal," the experimental literature has failed to support this hypothesis completely (e.g., Blaylock, 1972; Darrow, 1929; Davis, 1957; Lacey, 1967; Malmo, 1972; Schwartz, 1975). Instead, there appear to be various central nervous system control centers that operate upon specific subsets of peripheral physiological responses (Cacioppo & Petty, 1979a). In other words, subarousal processes and response patterns exist (Schwartz, 1975). Hence, a multiple-measure approach appears preferable to determine the relationships between psychological functioning and physiological phenomena (cf. Cacioppo, Petty, & Snyder, 1979).

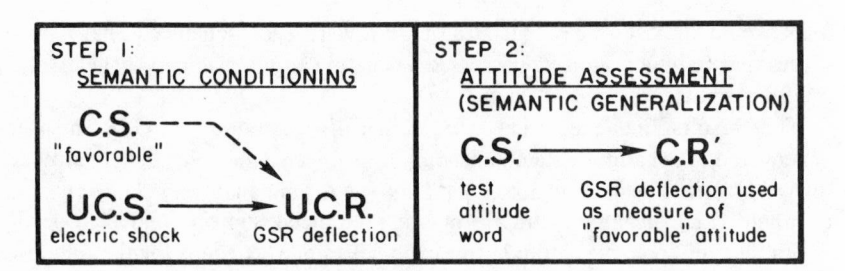

FIG. 4.2.   The classical conditioning approach.

In a review of the Russian literature on semantic conditioning, Razran (1961) reported a relevant experiment by Volkova (1953). In Volkova's study, a young boy was conditioned to salivate to the spoken word *good* but not to the word *bad*. After conditioning, the boy exhibited large salivary responses to sentences in which the word *good* was embedded and to sentences that had favorable meanings (e.g., "The Soviet army was victorious"). The same boy showed only small salivary responses to sentences with the word *bad* and to sentences that had unfavorable meanings (e.g., "The Fascists destroyed many cities"). Thus, the conditioned physiological response (salivation) appeared to reflect the boy's attitudinal reaction to the statements.

Acker and Edwards (1964) successfully conditioned 24 of 29 volunteer hospital patients to show constriction of the blood vessels in the left index finger; half the patients were conditioned to display vasoconstriction to the word *good* and half to the word *bad*. Seventy-five words rated previously by the patients on a good–bad bipolar scale were then presented to each person while vasomotor activity was monitored. Results were consistent with the classical conditioning model: Words that had been rated as bad on the pretest were accompanied by constriction of the vessels if the CS had been the word *bad*, whereas words that had been rated as good on the pretest were accompanied by constriction of the vessels only if the CS had been the word *good*.

Tognacci and Cook (1975) investigated the usefulness of the classical conditioning approach as a bidirectional indicator of attitudes by selecting persons who held either strongly favorable or unfavorable attitudes toward blacks. Galvanic skin response (GSR) served as the conditioned response (CR); negatively evaluated statements served as the conditioned stimulus (CS+); and positively evaluated statements served as the unreinforced (CS−) conditioned stimulus (i.e., the CS was not followed by the UCS). Thus, sentences evaluated negatively were conditioned to elicit GSR deflections, and sentences evaluated positively were conditioned not to elicit GSR deflections. Sentences were then presented to subjects: Some of the sentences were favorable toward blacks, some were unfavorable, and some were unrelated to racial issues. During the presentation of these "test" sentences, GSR was monitored. The expectation was that the

GSR would indicate the subjects' attitude toward each sentence. That is, sentences toward which subjects possessed a negative attitude were expected to elicit a GSR response.

The results indicated that the classically conditioned GSR measure generalized to the attitude statements only for subjects who held positive attitudes toward blacks. The authors noted that the large discrepancy between the personally held (i.e., negative) attitude of the prejudiced subjects and the socially desirable (i.e., positive) attitude toward blacks could account for the failure of the conditioned GSR to reflect their attitudes; that is, the conditioned physiological response served as an index of attitude only where the personally held attitude was also acceptable socially. This explanation assumes that a person's cognitive set or expectations can influence the classically conditioned GSR—an assumption that has been supported in recent investigations (Biferno & Dawson, 1977; Dawson & Reardon, 1969; Grings, 1973; Hill, 1967). Thus the results of the Tognacci and Cook (1975) experiment indicate that the classical conditioning approach (at least using GSR) may be applicable only if the persons are willing to report their true attitudes. This, of course, removes one of the major advantages of physiological assessment. Research using vasomotor activity or other less easily controlled physiological responses may prove more promising for this approach.

Summary of Research Using the Classical Conditioning Approach.   The classical conditioning approach to assessment of attitudes may provide a bidirectional measure that circumvents problems of response bias in self-report measures (which are totally under the voluntary control of subjects). The approach involves monitoring an induced physiological response rather than a naturally occurring physiological response to an attitude object. Accordingly, the conditioning of the response is a necessary antecedent to attitude measurement. The recent evidence that a classically conditioned autonomic response (particularly GSR) can be inhibited cognitively (cf. Grings, 1973; Lazarus, 1967) provides forewarning that the classical conditioning approach is not a cure-all for problems in attitude measurement, because subjects may be able to control both the verbal response and the physiological response.

ASSESSING AND AFFECTING
COGNITIVE RESPONSES PHYSIOLOGICALLY

As documented in the preceding section, attempts to obtain direct relationships between attitudes and physiological processes have met with only moderate success. In this section, a psychophysiological cognitive response model is presented that postulates a relationship between physiology and attitudes because of the organism's biological propensity for processing information (Cacioppo, 1977, 1979; Cacioppo & Petty, 1979a; Cacioppo, Sandman, & Walker, 1978).

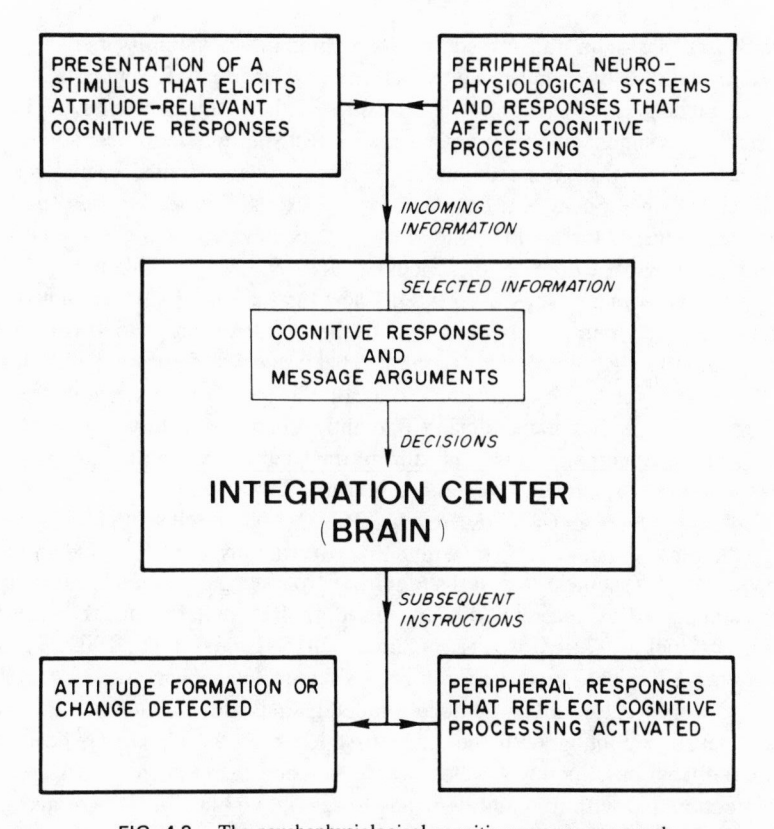

FIG. 4.3.   The psychophysiological cognitive response approach.

Peripheral neurophysiological circuits and responses can reflect and/or influence cognitive processing, either because of the effects of the afferent activity from the peripheral response on brain functioning or because of the neural commands from a subcortical system influencing both information processing and peripheral response. Hence, when cognitive responses are elicited by the presentation of an attitude object or opinion issue, the pattern of peripheral activity that is related to cognitive processing provides an indication of and perhaps an input to the cognitive responses that occur. Peripheral neurophysiological systems and responses that do not reflect cognitive processing may be irrelevant to this approach (see Fig. 4.3). Two physiological responses that have been found to be related to cognitive processing are discussed here; they are cardiac and speech-muscle activity.

Heart Rate Reflects Cognitive Processing

Bonvallet, Dell, and Hiebel (1954) and Bonvallet and Allen (1963) researched the effects of transient pressure changes associated with heart rate on cortical excitability. They found that pressure-sensitive receptors (baroreceptors) in the cardiovascular system transmitted the information of arterial pressure changes to the brain and thereby changed the excitability of the cortex (cf. Schwartz, Davidson, & Pugash, 1976). As shown in Fig. 4.3, these transient changes in the internal environment of the organism may affect the integration capabilities of the brain. Specifically, the dynamic feedback system Bonvallet and his associates described operates to increase cortical excitability temporarily (perhaps decreasing sensory thresholds) when heart rate is elevated.[2] On the basis of this neurophysiological evidence, the Laceys (Lacey & Lacey, 1974; Lacey, 1967; Lacey, Kagan, Lacey, & Moss, 1963; Lacey & Lacey, 1970) speculated that accelerated heart rate was associated with the cognitive elaboration (facilitated processing) of material whereas decelerated heart rate was associated with (facilitated) sensory intake. Experimental tests of this position have indicated that sensory intake is facilitated during operantly conditioned lowered heart rate (McCanne & Sandman, 1974) and during transient decreases in heart rate and pulse pressure (Sandman, McCanne, Kaiser, & Diamond, 1977), although conflicting evidence exists (Edwards & Alsip, 1969; Surwillo, 1971).

Several investigators using different kinds of stimulus materials have provided support for the hypothesis that tasks requiring processing of complex information are accompanied by accelerated heart rate (e.g., Baker, Sandman, & Pepinsky, 1975; Blaylock, 1972; Kaiser & Sandman, 1975; Lacey et al., 1963; Tursky, Schwartz, & Crider, 1970). For instance, when persons engage in tasks such as spelling words backwards, mental arithmetic, and constructing multiple sentences (each beginning with the same first letter of the alphabet), heart rate increased from baseline levels. However, when persons performed tasks requiring attention and with minimal demands for cognitive elaboration, storage, and retrieval (e.g., watching light flashes), heart rate decreased from baseline levels (Lacey et al., 1963). Furthermore, when persons listened to a series of digits to be used later, heart rate decelerated; when the digits were then reordered, heart rate accelerated; and the more complex the digit-transformation task, the higher the heart rate during the transforming process (Tursky et al., 1970).

We too have found evidence that increased cognitive work is associated with increased heart rate. When persons were unscrambling the letters of infrequently used words, they displayed higher heart-rate levels than when they were unscrambling the letters of frequently used words (Kaiser & Sandman, 1975). But are these increases in heart rate due to the cognitive requirements or to the stressfulness of the tasks? To address this question, we had persons view slides of autopsy, solve anagrams and arithmetic problems, and memorize digit strings (Cacioppo & Sandman, 1978). Half the problems for each of the three cognitive

---

[2]Hilton (1965) has demonstrated that the dynamic autoregulation system via the baroreceptor reflex is inactive in the case of extreme responses, such as during a strong defense reaction. Consequently, this mechanism and its psychological concomitants would be inoperative during these periods (see Lacey, 1967).

tasks required a simple solution, and half required a complex solution. If the increased heart rate was caused by the stressfulness of processing the complex problems rather than by the increased processing requirements necessary to solve them, then an accelerated heart rate should also be found when comparing the heart rate during viewing autopsy slides that were highly stressful with the heart rate during viewing slides that were slightly stressful. (Stressfulness was measured by ratings of unpleasantness, and the slides used were rated as being just as unpleasant or stressful as the cognitive problems.) As expected, we found that subjects' heart rate was higher when performing the complex (and highly stressful) cognitive tasks than when performing the simple (and slightly stressful) cognitive tasks. And, importantly, subjects' heart rate was *not* affected by the stressfulness of the slides of autopsy (during which cognitive requirements were equally low). These results suggest that the accelerated heart rate we observed was attributable to the increased cognitive processing involved in the complex cognitive tasks rather than to a stress reaction elicited by the more complex problems (see also Jones & Johnson, 1978; Leber & Johnson, 1976).

Speech-EMG Activity Reflects Cognitive Processing

The activity of the muscles used during speech represents yet another peripheral measure of cognitive processing. Sokolov (1969) reviewed a series of experiments in which the electromyographic (EMG) activity of the speech musculature was monitored during a variety of processing tasks. He found that increases in speech-EMG activity resulted when complex linguistic reasoning was required (e.g., recalling sentences) but that processing the same input repeatedly was accompanied by a return of speech-EMG activity to the baseline level. In other words, the response became automatic, requiring little thought for its elicitation; as this occurred, speech-EMG activity again became quiescent.

Sokolov (1967) hypothesized that the speech areas of the cortex are exicted by incoming (afferent) information that involves linguistic processing. These speech centers then transmit (efferent) impulses down pathways to the speech musculature and cause "covert, soundless articulation ('inner speech') [p. 6]." The muscle activity involved in inner speech then excites afferent nerves that affect cortical areas involved in linguistic processing (but see also Smith, Brown, Toman, & Goodman, 1947).

Hansen & Lehmann (1895; reported in Edfeldt, 1960) noticed that persons participating in a "mind-reading" experiment produced whispering sounds, though neither the person nor the experimenter could detect lip movements. These results, which suggested that cognitive and subvocal activity occurred together, led to more objective experimentation. McGuigan (1970, 1978) and Garrity (1977) provide comprehensive reviews of the literature investigating the involvement of speech-muscle activity during the silent performance of language tasks.

The importance of this approach is demonstrated in three experiments conducted by McGuigan and Bailey (1969). Persons performed five tasks with relaxation periods preceding each task. The tasks were silent reading, memorizing prose, listening to prose, listening to music, and listening to "nothing." The first three tasks involved linguistic processing, whereas the last two tasks did not. Speech-EMG activity increasing during the silent reading and memorization tasks and was greater during these tasks than during the performance of the nonlanguage tasks. Breathing rate and preferred-forearm-muscle activity were also greater during the performance of language tasks than nonlanguage tasks. The muscle activity in a preferred (writing) forearm during linguistic processing is due to the involvement of those muscle groups in writing (McGuigan, 1967; McGuigan & Rodier, 1968). This interpretation follows from Jacobsen's finding that persons imagining that they are exerting physical effort display an increase in muscle activity in the body part that would be involved in the physical effort (cf. Jacobsen, 1973) if it were real.

Testing the Psychophysiological Cognitive Response Model

The psychophysiological cognitive response model can be stated and tested in terms of the following propositions: (1) Peripheral responses that reflect cognitive processing (e.g., speech-EMG) should become more active during a period in which *cognitive responding* is present than during a baseline (cognitively quiet) period; (2) the increased activity in these peripheral measures should be independent of peripheral measures not related to cognitive processing (e.g., back-muscle activity); (3) the increased activity of these peripheral measures should be due to the processing task, and similar changes should not be noted during simple intake or attentional tasks not involving language stimuli; (4) the manipulation of the activity of one of these peripheral physiological measures or patterns (*ceteris paribus*) should affect cognitive responding and persuasion. Heart rate and speech-muscle activity appear to be appropriate peripheral measures of (linguistic) cognitive processing, both on neurophysiological and empirical grounds.

Physiological Assessment of Cognitive Responses.   Cacioppo & Petty (1979a) conducted a test of the first two propositions of this model. Subjects were informed that the experiment would have two parts: In the first part, they would be told the topic and position of several communications that they would be hearing; and in the second part, the communications would be presented. The purpose of the first part of the experiment, subjects were told, was to allow them time to adapt to the experimental setting and to collect their thoughts on the issues they were to hear about later.

Six forewarnings were presented to each subject. Each forewarning was attributed to a highly credible source and concerned an involving and highly counterattitudinal topic. For instance, subjects were told that the university board of regents was considering a proposal to increase student tuition by $90 per quarter. Heart rate, speech-muscle (lip, chin, and throat) activity, back-muscle (trapezius) activity, breathing rate, and the pulse amplitude of the blood flowing to the brain were monitored during the minute preceding each forewarning (during which time subjects were asked to sit quietly) and during the minute following each forewarning (during which time they were asked to "collect their thoughts"). Following the latter period, subjects were asked to list everything about which they had thought during the preceding ("collect thoughts") interval and to include only the thoughts they had had during that interval.

It was expected that subjects would generate cognitive responses concerning the forewarned opinion issues (cf. Petty & Cacioppo, 1977; see also Chapter 10). Further, it was expected that these cognitive responses would be reflected in increased activity of the heart and speech musculature but would not lead to increased activity of the nonoral muscle group in the back. The results, presented in Fig. 4.4, supported these predictions. The thought listings revealed that pre-

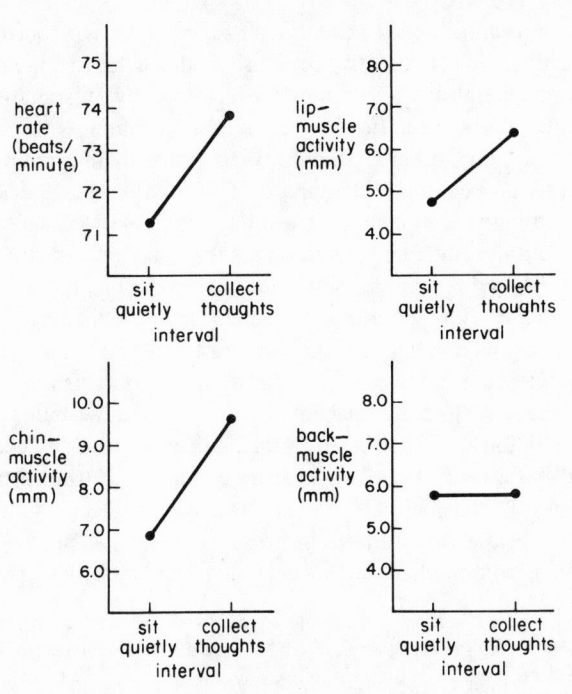

FIG. 4.4.   Cognitive responding was associated with increased heart rate (top left panel) and covert oral activity (top right and lower left panels) but not with general muscle activity (lower right panel). (Adapted from Cacioppo & Petty, 1979a.)

dominantly counterarguments were generated during the "collect thoughts" period. Heart rate, lip- and chin-muscle activity, and breathing rate increased during the "collect thoughts" interval from baseline ("sit quietly") levels, whereas back-muscle activity did not change. Furthermore, the change in heart rate was consistent with the position of the Laceys regarding cognitive elaboration and heart-rate acceleration, although the increased breathing rate may have contributed to the accelerated heart rate.

Festinger and Maccoby (1964), Brock (1967), and Keating and Brock (1974) have emphasized both the importance of counterargumentation in resistance to persuasion and the subvocal nature of counterargumentation. Analyses in the preceding experiment (Cacioppo & Petty, 1979a) indicated that counterargumentation indeed appeared to be more important than favorable or neutral thoughts in mediating the subsequent agreement with an opinion position. However, neither any single physiological response nor any combination of physiological responses obtained could differentiate among counterarguments, favorable thoughts, and neutral thoughts. Thus, these results support a more general hypothesis: Subvocalization is a correlate of cognitive responding whether it be counterarguing, favorable thinking, or neutral thinking.

Physiological Manipulation of Cognitive Responses.   The fourth proposition of the psychophysiological cognitive response model states that the manipulation of one of the peripheral measures should affect cognitive responding and, subsequently, attitudes. The specific changes in heart rate and its theoretically predictable effects on the brain's propensity to process information provide a rationale for this proposition. Cacioppo et al. (1978) conducted a test of this proposition by training 20 males over a 5-day period to increase and decrease their heart rate, reinforcing them to sustain it at the attained levels. Subjects were taught to accomplish this feat without major changes in breathing rate or muscle activity by using a systematic form of biofeedback (discriminative operant conditioning).[3] In other words, the changes in heart rate were not simply due to changes in the muscular or respiratory activity of the organism.

On the 5th day, counterattitudinal communications that were designed to elicit counterargumentation were presented to the subjects during an accelerated, decelerated, and basal (noncontrolled) heart rate trial (each trial lasting approximately 1 minute). It was expected that heart rate would affect cognitive responding and thereby affect the attitude that resulted from the presentation of the counterattitudinal communication.[4] Accelerated heart rate was expected to be

---

[3]Discriminative operant conditioning refers to a type of training in which one stimulus (e.g., a blue light) signifies that reinforcement (e.g., money) is to be given only for a desired response (e.g., accelerated heart rate), and a second stimulus (e.g., a yellow light) signifies that reinforcement is to be given only for a different desired response (e.g., decelerated heart rate).

[4]Whether the peripheral change in heart rate affected a controlling subcortical mechanism or the conditioning was accomplished as a result of changes in the subcortical mechanism, the expectation remains that the conditioned heart rate, when uncoupled from somatic and respiratory controlling mechanisms, should affect cognitive responding and persuasion.

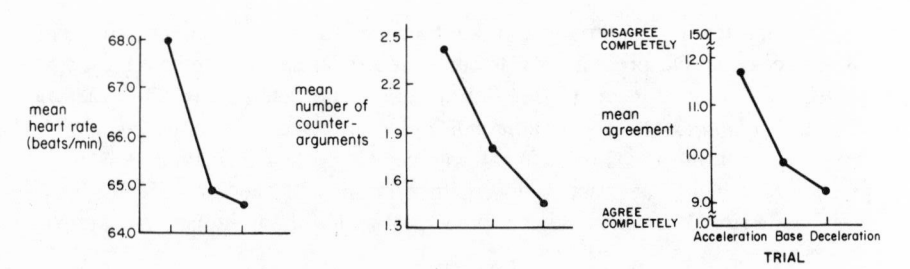

FIG. 4.5. Manipulated heart rate (left panel) significantly affected counterarguing (middle panel) and agreement (right panel) (adapted from Cacioppo, Sandman,
& Walker, 1978).

associated with increased counterargumentation and resistance to persuasion,
whereas decelerated heart rate was expected to have the opposite effects.[5] It is
important to note that transiently and specifically increased heart rate is not
associated with resistance to persuasion per se but rather with facilitated information processing. Because the presentation of the messages led pilot subjects to
generate predominantly counterarguments, increased heart rate was expected to
facilitate counterargumentation and, hence, resistance to persuasion.

The results are presented in Fig. 4.5. Conditioning of accelerated heart rate
was associated with the generation of more counterarguments and greater resistance to persuasion than decelerated heart rate. The implications of these findings
are that (1) the cognitive responding during the presentation of a persuasive
appeal (affected by the conditioning trial) affects the resistance to persuasion,
and (2) consciousness (e.g., attitudes) is associated in a predictable manner to
alterations of the internal environment (i.e., physiological states). The subjects
not only were affected differentially by the counterattitudinal communications as
a function of their (manipulated) heart rate, but they also were unaware of the
hypothesis that heart rate would influence cognitive responding and resistance to
persuasion.[6] Nor did subjects report awareness that the heart-rate manipulations
affected their reactions to the attitudinal stimuli. Thus, subjects' attitudes and
cognitive responses were altered even though subjects were unaware of any
changes in their thinking or feeling.

---

[5]The order of conditioning trials and messages was randomized to control for differences in
cognitive responding and persuasion due to the order of presentation or the message presented. After
the presentation of the three messages, subjects were asked to list what they had thought during each
of the message presentations. The thoughts listed by the subjects were counted as a counterargument
if they stated logical or emotional points against the proposal of the message or derogated the source
of the message.

[6]Postexperimental protocols revealed that subjects could not state the hypothesis that heart rate
would influence cognitive responding or that heart rate would influence attitude ratings. These
findings are consistent with the demands made by the experimenter when he asked subjects to answer
as honestly as possible by reporting their true feelings about the opinion issues when asked. Furthermore, Detweiler and Zanna (1976) found that false feedback about a subject's heart rate led to
increased attitude change whether the feedback indicated that heart rate was increasing or decreasing.
These bits of evidence together argue against a demand characteristics interpretation of the results.

A second test of the proposition that transient and specific changes in heart rate affect cognitive processing was conducted, because the methodology employed by Cacioppo et al. (1978) did not allow the determination of whether heart-rate *changes* or heart-rate *conditioning* affected counterargumentation (i.e., information processing). What was needed to test this hypothesis were persons with heart rates that could be altered transiently and specifically (i.e., without altering other physiological processes) and without the persons' knowl-

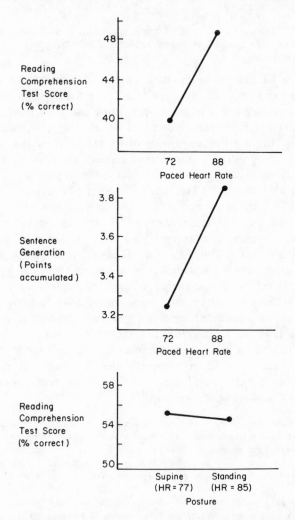

FIG. 4.6.   Pacemaker-induced heart-rate changes significantly affected reading comprehension (top panel) and marginally affected sentence generation (middle panel). Posture-induced heart-rate changes did not affect cognitive performance (bottom panel—see Cacioppo, 1979).

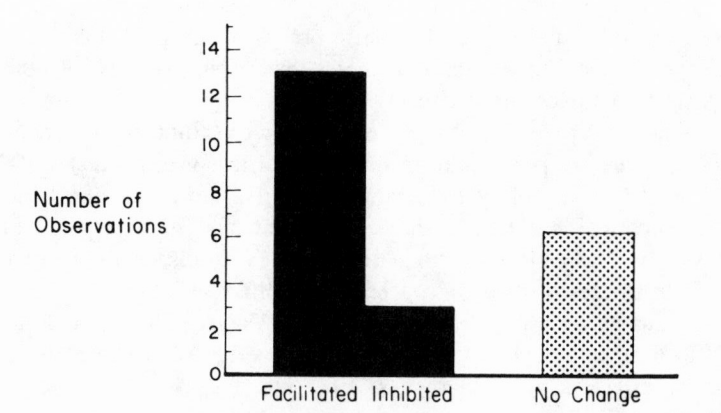

FIG. 4.7. Pacemaker-induced heart-rate changes significantly affected the number of counterarguments generated. (Adapted from Cacioppo, 1979.)

edge that their heart rates were being altered. Such an experiment was conducted using cardiac-pacemaker patients who were visiting their cardiologist for their regular (9-month) checkups (Cacioppo, 1979). All persons who participated in the experiment were articulate and in good health, consented to participate, and appeared motivated to perform well. Their basal heart rates were 72 beats per minute (bpm). But when a magnet was placed over a reed within the pacemaker, their heart rates increased immediately to 88 bpm (although subjects were not aware of whether or when their heart rates were changed). Subjects performed reading comprehension and sentence generation tasks while their heart rates were either increased (by placing an uncapped magnet over the reed) or ostensibly increased (by placing a capped magnet over the reed). As expected, the results indicated that subjects indeed processed the information better when their heart rates were accelerated than during basal heart-rate levels (see Fig. 4.6). In a second experiment, pacemaker patients read counterattitudinal communications while their heart rates were either accelerated or not. As is illustrated in Fig. 4.7, we found that an accelerated heart rate led to greater counterargumentation. And, as in the conditioning study, counterargumentation was associated with resistance to persuasion.

The foregoing model can also account for several existing experiments on persuasion and heart rate. For instance, Katz, Cadoret, and Abbey (1965) found that heart rate was faster when acceptable or unacceptable statements were presented to a subject for the first time than when neutral statements were presented. Katz et al. (1965) gave the example "There definitely is no God" as being typical of unacceptable statements, and "Most modern religions are monotheistic" as being typical of neutral statements. If it is assumed that the acceptable and unacceptable statements stimulated more cognitive activity than neutral statements (e.g., because of their more involving nature), then the increased heart rate could have resulted from greater cognitive processing during the presentation of the acceptable and unacceptable statements than during the presentation of the neutral (less controversial) statements.

Of course, experiments of the relationship between attitudes and cardiac activity exist that are not pertinent to this model. For instance, Burdick (1972) employed heart-rate variability and change scores (regardless of direction) rather than measures of the duration, direction, extent, and specificity of heart-rate responses. In another investigation, Buckhout (1966) discussed the association between heart rates that were characteristic of different individuals (rather than heart-rate changes within a person) and attitude change. These studies are mentioned to designate areas in which the cognitive response approach does not apply. Nevertheless, they do suggest other possible associations between attitudes and physiology.

Other interesting relationships exist between a person's cognitive set (e.g., attitudes, beliefs, expectations) and physiological reactions to stressful stimuli. For instance, Ikemi and Nakagawa (1962) demonstrated that when subjects were led to believe that they were being touched by the leaves of a tree to which they were allergic when in fact they were being touched by harmless leaves, all subjects displayed allergic reactions. When the subjects were led to believe they were being touched by harmless leaves when in fact they were being touched by the allergy-producing leaves, 11 of the 13 subjects did *not* show allergic reactions. Similar effects have been found by Graham (1962; Graham, Kabler, & Graham, 1962) and Lazarus (1966; Lazarus, Opton, Nomikos, & Rankin, 1965).

Physiological measures have also been used in attempts to measure arousal or motivational states relevant to attitude change, such as cognitive dissonance. For instance, finger-pulse amplitude was smaller (an indication of stress) after persons made a difficult (high-dissonance-arousing) rather than an easy (low-dissonance-arousing) choice between preferences (Gerard, 1967). Consequently, there is some evidence suggesting that a high state of cognitive dissonance is stressful. It is unclear, however, whether or not the state of cognitive dissonance leads to a general and diffuse state of physiological arousal (cf. Kiesler & Pallak, 1976).

Summary of Research Using the Cognitive Response Approach. A psychophysiological cognitive response model has been described, and experimentation testing various propositions of the model has been reviewed. This model is based on the assumption that psychological and physiological phenomena are two aspects of the same fundamental biological process. Hence, it accounts for a relationship between attitudes and physiology in terms of the organism's biological aptitude for processing information. It appears from the evidence to date that when an attitude object or opinion issue elicits cognitive responding, the state of certain physiological patterns (e.g., accelerated heart rate and quiescent nontask EMG activity) may have predictable effects on psychological states (e.g., cognition, attitudes). Further research is necessary to assess the replicability and to delineate the boundaries of this approach.

CHAPTER SUMMARY

Although the earliest definitions of attitudes were stated in terms of bodily processes, current definitions stress the general evaluative reaction individuals have to objects or issues. Physiological responses are of interest because of the belief that they may reflect the affect associated with an attitude. In the *emotional response approach* to the physiological assessment of attitudes, naturally occurring physiological responses that are thought to indicate affective states are monitored to provide information about the intensity and/or direction of the attitudes. Research using electrodermal (skin) measures (primarily GSR) has indicated that increased electrodermal activity may be more indicative of the unexpected nature of the stimuli (novelty) than of an affective reaction to those stimuli. Research employing the pupillary response suggests that this measure may be more indicative of the interest, attention, or processing capacity elicited by a stimulus than of the affective reaction. Recent evidence indicates that although no single physiological measure may tap an attitudinal reaction, different affective states may be reflected in subtle, yet distinguishable, facial electromyographic response patterns. In the *classical conditioning approach,* an induced (classically conditioned) physiological response is used to measure the intensity and direction of the attitudinal response. The fact that a classically conditioned autonomic response can be inhibited cognitively presents an assessment problem that future research must address.

A psychophysiological cognitive response model was described that posited a relationship between attitudes and bodily processes because of the organism's biological propensity for processing information. Just as increased heart rate and activity of the speech musculature have been found to accompany performance on tasks requiring processing of complex information, these same physiological responses have been shown to accompany cognitive responses elicited in anticipation and during the presentation of highly involving counterattitudinal communications. In addition, physiological manipulations were found to affect cognitive responses and persuasion. Specifically, operantly conditioned and pacemaker-induced accelerated heart rate led to the generation of more counterarguments and greater resistance to persuasion compared to basal or decelerated heart rate.

5 Methodological Issues in Analyzing the Cognitive Mediation of Persuasion

Norman Miller
Debbra E. Colman
University of Southern California

The preceding chapters have presented the foundations of the cognitive response approach to the study of persuasion. The measurement of attitudes, cognitive responses, and the role that thoughts might play in the mediation of attitude change have been discussed. In the last two chapters, the questions of how external and internal factors could affect the processing of persuasive communications were addressed. In this chapter we alert the readers to some problems that arise when we attempt to understand the mediating events in the persuasion process. We begin by critically evaluating the concepts of *attitude* and *cognitive response* and end by discussing the advantages, disadvantages, and potential pitfalls of some common strategies for assessing the causal role of cognitive responses in the mediation of persuasion.

THE ATTITUDE CONCEPT

Perhaps the most important feature of an attitude is *temporal stability*. An attitude is extended in time and space. When formed, it persists, applying to other specific objects in the same concept class but also to the same object next week or next month. Subsequently acquired information and new experience as well as future action must be integrated with it. Virtually no experimental research on attitudes formally or explicitly includes this temporal feature in its measurement procedures. Yet without it, attitude does not differ from a single evaluative judgment about any specific object at a single point in time. It is this temporal stability that gives attitude a basic similarity to personality; both are conceived as relatively stable attributes of the person. In this sense, attitude is also vulnerable to the recent criticisms of personality (Ebel, 1972; Mischel, 1968, 1973).

Part of the attack on the concept of personality emphasizes the potency of situational cues. Recent research has indicated that environmental factors may be producing effects that were previously attributed to personality dispositions (e.g., Condry & Dyer, 1976; Jellison, Jackson-White, Bruder, & Martyna, 1975). The concept of attitude is vulnerable to the same argument. Recent attacks on the attitude concept have centered on the notion that expressed attitudes are merely responses to situational cues (Jellison & Arkin, 1977; Tedeschi, Schlenker, & Bonoma, 1971). According to this view, the verbal and behavioral expressions formerly thought by other researchers to reflect an enduring social attitude not only lack any temporal consistency or generality but simply amount to opportunistic displays to garner others' approval. Attitudes are merely an exemplification of impression management or self-presentational concerns.

There are strong and weak versions of this viewpoint. The weak version has merits. It asserts that in many social psychological laboratory experiments on attitudes, the data can be interpreted in terms of subjects' concerns about optimizing the impression of themselves that they may be giving to other subjects or to the experimenter; impression management may carry some of the explanatory burden better than some theory or hypothesis about attitude formation and change. With this view, we have no argument. Why should surprise or consternation arise over the possibility that concerns about impression management and manipulation account for some variance among responses in laboratory experiments or other situations? One can interpret the literature on anticipatory belief change (discussed in detail in Chapter 10) as supporting this view (Cooper & Jones, 1970; McGuire & Millman, 1965; McGuire & Papageorgis, 1962). Strategic modifications of expressed opinion and subsequent nullifications of the shift by removing the initial reason for it have recently been demonstrated (e.g., Cialdini, Levy, Herman, Kozlowski, & Petty, 1976).

It should be emphasized that the notion that expressed attitude reflects tactical considerations does not argue for abandoning the concept of attitude. It simply posits tactical modifications of "own position" as a source of apparent changes in experiments on attitudes. Indeed, the fact that the *direction* of tactical modification of own attitude depends on the degree to which one is involved in the attitudinal issue (Cialdini et al., 1976) indirectly supports the "existence" or conceptual status of attitude as well as that of tactical modification. The direction of tactical self-presentations depends on something else—one's involvement in the attitude. In the same vein, there should be no surprise if other situational factors such as social norms (Amir, 1969; Foley, 1976; Pettigrew, 1959; Riley & Pettigrew, 1976) affect expressed attitudes.

The strong version of attack on the attitude concept (Arkin, 1976) generates more concern. It argues that we can dispense with attitude—that we do not need a concept referring to temporally stable evaluative dispositions toward a class of attitudinal objects, because there are no such dispositions. *All* variance in attitude found in so-called attitude change experiments can be attributed to the fulfillment of impression management goals or other situational variables. If true, neither this nor the other chapters in this book bear reading, much less writing. Obviously we are inclined to reject this second view. As Kelman (1974) shows, survey studies provide strong evidence of stable relations between attitudes and behavior. Furthermore, not only is there evidence of stability in political attitudes over very substantial periods of time (Newcomb, Koenig, Flacks, & Warwick, 1967), but they are even transmitted across generations (Hyman, 1959). More recently, Schaie and Parham (1976) provided additional compelling support. They examined the stability of 13 personality factors and 6 attitudinal factors over a 7-year span. Their sample contained eight age-group cohorts, with the youngest ranging from 22 to 28 and the oldest from 71 to 77. Using analyses that enabled them to separate sociocultural change, maturational effects, and cohort or generation differences, they found substantial support for a stability model. Not only was stability the rule for all but 1 of the 13 personality factors but also for 5 of the 6 attitudinal factors!

COGNITIVE MEDIATING RESPONSES

Having briefly discussed the conceptualization and measurement of attitude and its relation to persuasion, what is the bearing of cognitive mediating responses upon them? The general goals of cognitive response analysis are simple: to determine the intervening causal events in the persuasion process and/or to improve our ability to predict attitudes. Although the implications of these two goals may not be identical, rather than dwelling on the distinctions, let us first consider the kinds of cognitive responses that might intervene in the persuasion process.

Even the most simple and uncontested models of persuasion, such as McGuire's (1969a) depiction of the causal process, seem to posit several intermediary stages between stimulus input and attitudinal response. McGuire's model, resting on the earlier work of Hovland and his colleagues (Hovland, Janis, & Kelley, 1953), has been characterized as behavioral primarily because of its historical roots and the style of research that it prompted. As an experimental psychologist, Hovland spent much of his early career determining how people learn and remember verbal materials. When he turned to the study of persuasion, he quite naturally focused on variables that affect one's attention to the persuasive message and the learning of its content. In other words, his approach

Attention → Comprehension → Yielding → Retention → Action

FIG. 5.1.   Sequential steps in the persuasion process (McGuire, 1969a).

emphasized information processing. Additionally, he experimentally focused on external variables, such as a speaker's credibility or the characteristics of the persuasive message. To manipulate credibility, the message might be attributed to a believable and trustworthy source for some subjects, whereas for others, the alleged source would lack these attributes. In the first instance, subjects would presumably attend more carefully and learn the content of the message more thoroughly. Though persuasion would be the major dependent variable, measures of other variables such as perceptions of the speaker's intelligence or fairness were also often obtained. These latter measures, though typically viewed as manipulation checks, can also be viewed as cognitive mediating variables. So, too, can measures of information learned by exposure to the communication. In this sense, then, the theory or model is a cognitive one; the intervening cognitive events—judgments about the speaker's character or information and new beliefs acquired by listening to the communication—presumably play a causal role in the persuasion process. (See Chapter 7 for a full discussion of source effects in persuasion.)

Given Hovland's leadership and his focus on information, it is not surprising that conceptualizations of resistance to persuasion rested heavily upon the availability of information—information that counters that contained in the persuasive message. The extent to which the listener mustered counterarguments to refute a speaker's points came to be seen as a critical ingredient for resisting influence. For example, the research on the relative effectiveness of a one-sided versus a two-sided persuasive message seemed to place explanatory burden on covert counterarguing. The fact that a two-sided communication—one that mentioned some of the arguments opposed to the position the speaker was advocating—was more persuasive than a one-sided speech could be attributed to the possibility that it aroused less motivation to counterargue. As noted in Chapter 1, McGuire's own research on "inoculation against persuasion" also invoked covert counterarguing as an explanatory mechanism.

Other models of persuasion, though not explicitly depicted by their proponents as cognitive models, can nevertheless be viewed as much. In Sherif's (Sherif & Hovland, 1961; Sherif, Kelly, Rodgers, Sarup, & Titler, 1973; Sherif, Sherif, & Nebergall, 1965) social judgment theory (discussed further in Chapter 8), a person's ego involvement in the attitudinal topic and its effect on that individual's judgments about the acceptability or extremity of the advocated position were the critical intervening cognitions. High involvement in the issue causes a person to judge as extreme and unacceptable a speech that might appear reasonable and credible to one less involved. As a consequence of this judgment, one that exaggerates the extremity of the advocated position, the speech loses its persuasiveness. The less involved person, whose judgment about the speech's extremity is not distorted, more readily accepts influence. Thus, the judgment of where the advocated position of the speech lies on the attitudinal continuum is the critical cognitive response that mediates persuasion in this "perceptual theory" of attitude change.

Dissonance theory (Festinger, 1957), along with other cognitive consistency and balance theories (discussed further in Chapter 14), directs its attention to cognitive events that transpire following presentation of a persuasive message. Indeed, dissonance theory is exclusively concerned with the relations among cognitions. It concerns itself with the cognitive events that transpire when incompatible cognitions arise, such as those that might occur when one behaves in a way that contradicts one's beliefs.

The preceding examples show that irrespective of a theorist's own characterization of a model, all can be viewed as containing cognitive mediating mechanisms. All directly or indirectly point to cognitive processes that occur between the antecedent external events designed to affect attitude and some subsequent dependent measure of it. Whether a theorist uses an external behavioristic language or an internal perceptual, cognitive language is quite irrelevant to this point (Campbell, 1963). Likewise, the theories may differ in terms of the type of process they emphasize; they may attend to different intervening variables (Kiesler, Collins, & Miller, 1969); nevertheless, on a general conceptual level, some of the scientific questions they all raise are basically very simple. Do the postulated intervening cognitive events in fact causally mediate the relation between the independent manipulation and the dependent measure of attitude? Is there a causal sequencing among the various types of cognitions that intervene between the antecedent stimulus and the subsequent attitudinal responses?

MEASURING COGNITIVE
MEDIATING RESPONSES

Before pursuing answers to these questions, it is important to emphasize that the types of cognitions or intervening variables that are thought to causally mediate the effects of antecedent external stimulus events upon the formation or alteration of an attitude possess a basic similarity to attitude itself. Like attitude, regardless of whether they are conceptualized with an external or internal language, they are only observable as episodes of external behavior—written or spoken answers to questions posed by the experimenter or some other person. With this perspective, the issues and problems surrounding the measurement of various cognitive mediators of attitude do not differ from those that concern the measurement of attitude. The cognition is inferred from a response elicited from the subject— some external verbal-behavioral measure. Thus, we label them mediating *responses*. In terms of their role in persuasion, however, they have stimulus properties as well, in that they affect attitude. In principle, then, problems and concerns about the reliability and validity of attitude measures do not differ from those that will arise when measuring any other cognitive component of the persuasion process.

Even though two theoretical constructs may indeed have an important functional relationship (validity), unreliable measures may still preclude its discovery. This commonly acknowledged truism naturally applies to the constructs involved in cognitive response analysis as well as to any others. One cannot make statements about the ways in which cognitions are related either to each other or to attitudes until one first develops reliable and valid measures. There is little need to replow this ground here.

In Chapter 2, Cullen's (1968) finding that a measure of cognitive responses was as reliable as some standard attitude scales was reported. This information is of limited value, however. To be useful in determining the causal sequence of the persuasion process, thought listing must tap something distinct from the target attitude or action sequence that the persuasive attempt addresses. This requires demonstration of both internal consistency—evidence that the items or thoughts all reflect some one thing (factorial purity)—and discriminant validity—evidence that the items or thoughts reflect something distinct from other measures or item sets. These conceptual issues of convergent and discriminant validity, raised by Campbell and Fiske's (1959) multitrait-multimethod matrix, argue that "listed thoughts" must have an "entityness" distinct from attitude to be useful in the causal analysis of persuasion. Furthermore, as is well known, a multifactored array of test items augments stability measures of reliability, such as split-half and especially test-retest.

More recently, factor analytic techniques have been developed that seem to deal more effectively with the problem of separating method variance from trait or construct variance (Alwin & Tessler, 1974; Kenny, 1976; Rock, Linn, & Joreskog, 1976). Method variance can cause the individual items of a measure to appear to tap a single theoretical construct by virtue of the fact that they all share a common method of assessment. To know that we have indeed assessed the trait or construct of interest requires that a consistency among a person's responses emerges despite the fact that the trait has been measured by means of a variety of techniques, such as self-reports, observers' ratings, peer ratings, and so forth. As seen from this perspective, and indeed as conceptualized by Cullen herself, listed thoughts simply provide another measure of attitude and not of some separate cognitive response that mediates it. Fishbein and Ajzen's (1975) analysis of attitude measures clearly shows that Cullen's index derived from listed thoughts contains the same basic elements contained by virtually every "standard" measure of attitude—belief and evaluation. The thoughts evoked by the thought-listing instructions constitute beliefs. The ratings performed on these beliefs—the degree to which the elicited beliefs are favorable or unfavorable toward the position advocated by the communication—correspond to evaluation. In terms of the implicit programmatic goal of cognitive analysis—a causal analysis of mediators in the persuasion process—the value of a thought-listing procedure more likely lies in its potential for providing indices of cognitive structure. As such, it can in principle portray changes in the differentiation of beliefs, changes in ambivalence and consistency, and changes in total affective arousal (see Fishbein & Ajzen, 1975, p. 100). Such measures may be important for separating the effects of normative influence or self-presentational tactics on changes in expressed attitude from those changes induced by assimilation of new information.

STRATEGIES FOR ASSESSING
THE CAUSAL ROLE OF
COGNITIVE MEDIATING RESPONSES

As emphasized, the theoretical task facing those concerned with persuasion is to analyze and order the variables that affect it. Though theorists differ in their judgments about the intervening variables to which they ascribe importance, as well as the causal arrangements among them, they invariably postulate or attempt to demonstrate empirically the causal role of various intervening cognitions or cognitive processes. We now consider the kinds of procedures that they have used.

Indirect Inference

Psychology, with all its technological accoutrements, lacks a periscope into the mind. A minute-by-minute, direct internal monitoring remains a practical impossibility. Consequently, one approach to investigating causal sequencing is basically indirect. The researcher manipulates a variable that he or she hypothesizes will affect the critical cognitive mediating events in a particular way and then observes the effect on attitude. If the attitudinal effect conforms to the postulated relation between attitude and the particular cognitive mediating mechanism, the researcher assumes that the causal role of the cognitive mediator has been confirmed. Of course, several theories may predict the same effect but explain it quite differently. The point is that a researcher cannot be sure that the manipulation postulated to elicit cognitive mediating mechanism A did not invoke instead an alternate mechanism B, which nevertheless yielded the predicted result. As noted in Chapter 3, the goal of experimentation is to eliminate all plausible rival explanations for an effect. Since Chapter 3 discussed strategies for doing this, we do not deal with it further here.

Self-Report

Many dependent measures in social psychology are self-reports of one kind or another; this includes most measures of attitude. Although even the so-called direct measures of attitude, such as those developed by Guttman, Thurstone, and

Likert, are indirect in the sense that attitude is inferred and abstracted from answers to specific questions, nevertheless they are self-reports—albeit ones that primarily reflect the immediate state of affairs. Other self-reports, such as thought listing, are often hoped to be more retrospective, attempting to tap from subjects information about what was going on in their heads 15 minutes ago, while they were listening to a persuasive communication. Still others, "How often did your parents argue?" ask for information much more remote in time.

Yet even a self-report on one's current state will not always be accurate. Freudian analysts, by detailing the circumstances under which unconscious motivation will operate to produce self-deception, have not only made the tool of self-report suspect but, turning the coin over, have also provided guidelines for when it is more likely to be trustworthy. The beginnings of modern experimental psychology (Boring, 1929) have also contributed to the tainted character of self-reports. The failure of the early introspectionists to analyze sensation successfully left self-reports with an enduring stigma. As Bergman (1952) astutely notes, however, it may make considerably more sense to assign the cause of the introspectionists' failure to the task they set for themselves rather than to the method they employed. This brings us to an important point. Psychologists have tended to use self-reports in those situations where they tend to work.

The crucial question for the cognitive response approach is whether or not the typical techniques used for assessing cognitive responses in fact reflect the actual cognitions of the subject during exposure to a communication. For example, does the production of rational counterarguments when requested reflect the amount of covert counterarguing engaged in during exposure to the communication? Miller and Baron (1973) suggest that the act of scrutinizing an individual's attitude (implicit in an experimental situation where a measure of agreement and a listing of communication-relevant thoughts are temporally contingent) may lead that person to perceive the thought-listing procedure as an opportunity to justify his or her stated position. A person who has just been persuaded by a communication will not proceed to demonstrate that there are many good reasons why he or she should have disagreed and resisted influence (by listing many counterarguments and few support arguments) or that the persuasion was accomplished by an untrustworthy or unknowledgeable speaker (by listing source-derogation comments). It is just as likely that these cognitions are a response to whatever attitude change has or has not already occurred rather than its cause. If so, such measures must be considered invalid.

Two means of getting at the issue of spontaneity of cognitive responses to a persuasive communication have been proposed. First, as noted in Chapter 2, a very short time to list thoughts immediately after a communication should enhance the likelihood that those thoughts listed reflect cognitions the subject actually had during exposure to the message (Miller & Baron, 1973). Second, an ongoing direct measure of cognitive responses can be attempted. In a study purportedly designed to ascertain "what radio audiences are really thinking,"

Beaber (1975) arranged for subjects to record their thoughts as they occurred over the course of a taped communication by instructing them to use a foot pedal to interrupt it and verbalize their spontaneous thoughts onto another recorder. In this way, he obtained a temporal record of thoughts that presumably occurred while subjects listened to the communication.[1] Reports of difficulty in reporting different types of cognitions indicated an overall success rate of 65%, with speaker-oriented thoughts creating least difficulty, irrelevant thoughts providing most, and content-oriented thoughts intermediate. However, none of these pairwise comparisons differed significantly.

Although Beaber's results are marred by the failure of his manipulation of credibility to produce differential attitude change, his method may prove valuable in future research. Furthermore, a number of his empirical results were interesting. "Counterarguments" accounted for 40% of all remarks made during the communication, suggesting that in fact spontaneous counterarguing does occur *during* message reception. Yet closer examination revealed that although amount of counterarguing was related to final attitude, this relation is misleading in that it was *not* related to attitude change. The partial correlation between counterarguing and final attitude, removing the effect of subjects' initial attitude, was nonsignificant. In simpler terms, this means that countetarguing did not determine final attitudes; instead, initial attitudes determined both the amount of counterarguing and final opinion.

A much different result was found for "disaffirmations." By disaffirmations, Beaber means short exclamations or statements that evaluatively deny the speaker's point or position without further argument or explanation. These statements (e.g., "Bullshit") amount to simple rejections of message content. Like counterarguments, disaffirmations were significantly related to final attitude ($r = -.26, p < .05$). Yet they were independent of initial attitude ($r = .00$) and, of course, still related to final attitude with initial attitude partialed out. In these data, "simple disaffirmations" play an important role in successful resistance to persuasion, whereas the role of counterarguing is called into question. Closer examination of the temporal placement of categories of response, possible because of the method, show an even stronger relationship between the frequency of disaffirmations within the 1st minute and the postmeasure of agreement ($r = -.48, p < .006$). And when the effect of frequency of early disaffirmations was removed from the overall relationship between disaffirmations and attitude

---

[1]Since the novelty of the procedure might interfere with subjects' ability or motivation to report their thoughts accurately, steps were taken to reduce this possibility: The instructions emphasized recording *any* spontaneous thought; they provided extensive examples of what other people said— examples that included every category of thought, including exclamations, irrelevancies, agreements, counterarguments, incoherencies, non sequiturs, and so forth in an effort to provide social support for any type of spontaneous utterance; the instructions emphasized "a relaxed approach"; the procedures carefully provided anonymity to each subject; finally, all subjects first went through the procedure with a practice communication to assure that they were familiarized and comfortable with it.

change, the partial correlation between disaffirmations and attitude change was nonsignificant ($r = .16$, $p < .14$).

Beaber's results bear comparison with those of Roberts and Maccoby (1973). They inserted eleven 20-second pauses into their 8½-minute communication so that subjects could "collect their thoughts." Among those committed to an attitudinal position via an administration of a premeasure, they report some reduction in the resistance to persuasion conferred by the pauses when the effect of counterarguments is covaried out. Of the 10% of variance among final opinion scores estimated to be attributable to the opportunity to think (provided by the pauses), almost half is attributable to the effect of the most potent counterarguing measure. Though the results of the two studies are not directly comparable, Maccoby and Roberts interpret their data as arguing that counterarguing be accorded an important mediating role, whereas Beaber argues the opposite.

The controversy regarding the mediational role of counterarguing in the persuasion process does not find a resolution in these pages. Whatever the final verdict, we argue that the elicitation of self-reports at various points during the experimental procedure, in thoughtful coordination with the conceptual problem explored by the experimental manipulations, serves as a useful tool for understanding mediational processes. We return later to an instructive example of this point by presenting an experiment that uses self-report data in combination with experimental manipulation to clarify the mediating mechanisms evoked by fear-arousing communications.

Bivariate Correlations

Multiple regression, path analysis, and maximum-likelihood confirmatory factor analysis are statistical techniques for developing causal models. As such, they provide other approaches for evaluating causal mediators of persuasion. However, before discussing their advantages and problems, we step back a pace in history.

Until very recently, most experimental social psychologists concerned with persuasion have shown little inclination to construct causal models of the interrelations among cognitive mediators. This probably stems largely from lack of training in the techniques that underlie their use. More common has been the occasional tendency to report simple correlations. Correlation coefficients provide less information than regression coefficients. For instance, they do not directly convey what magnitude of change can be expected in a dependent measure when the independent variable changes by a given amount. Some researchers have thought that correlations are useful in suggesting the importance of a given variable. An independent variable that explains much of the variance in a dependent measure is presumably more important than one that explains little. The squared correlation, indicating the proportion of variance in one variable that is explained by another, is thus seen as speaking on this issue.

However, very misleading conclusions can be drawn from an analysis employing bivariate correlations if certain problems are ignored. For example, response biases such as acquiescence and social desirability (introduced in Chapter 2) can lead to artifactually inflated correlations. Differences in the reliability of measures as well as the range or variance of the scores can also strongly affect correlation magnitudes. These problems are discussed further in Chapter 16.

We now turn to the attitude literature and examine how researchers might use correlations to infer causal roles for cognitive mediating responses. One necessary, though by no means sufficient, requirement for establishing the causal relations between variables posited as cognitive mediating mechanisms is to demonstrate that they do correlate with attitude change in accordance with the causal directions hypothesized by the investigator. If counterarguments intervene to aid in successfully resisting persuasion, we should find negative correlations between their frequency and attitude change. If an independent variable affects attitude change but does not produce differences on some measure of cognitive response, its mediational role is called into question.

A review of much of the attitude change literature through the past decade shows two things. First, correlations between dependent measures are seldom reported. Second, when reported, the obtained within-cell correlations do not show consistent support for the various cognitive mechanisms hypothesized. Table 5.1 attempts to summarize some of the correlations reported in attitude change studies published in the major social psychological journals over the last 10 years. What does it tell us? Despite some consistent correlational relationships, it is difficult to come to any sound conclusions on the basis of the tabled information. To illustrate, examine the variable *retention*. The range of reported correlations between retention and attitude change varies from $-.16$ to $.28$. Clearly, unequivocal support for the crucial role of retention in the attitude change process fails to emerge.

In considering reported correlations, however, the distinction between within- and between-cell correlations must be kept in mind. If the independent variable had a strong impact, we should expect the between-cell correlations to be high. The independent variable clusters subjects' responses on some dependent measure *within* conditions and polarizes them *between* conditions. Figure 5.2 illustrates this point with fictitious data for an experiment manipulating a speaker's credibility and measuring retention and opinion. On the left is the scatter plot of 40 control subjects who, without having heard the message, receive the opinion measure and the information test based on the content of the message. On the right are 40 subjects, half of whom heard each speaker. The control condition depicts virtually no relation between information and opinion. Likewise, *within* each experimental condition, there is no relation. If the two experimental groups are pooled, however, the between-cell effect, which has spread the groups apart on both measures, gives the impression of a strong relation between information and persuasion. In this case, high credibility may have augmented attention,

TABLE 5.1
A Partial Summary of Within-Cell Correlations
Reported in the Attitude Change Literature

Correlations Between:	Author(s)	Average Within-Cell Correlations
Source evaluation and attitude change	Bochner and Insko (1966)	.10
	Miller and Baron (1968)	.38 (range = .28 to .56)
	Eagly (1969)	.12
Source derogation and attitude change	Miller and Levy (1967)	−.42
	Hass and Linder (1972)	−.19 (range = .08 to −.54)
	Regan and Cheng (1973)	
Counterarguments and attitude change	Brock (1967)	−.23 (range = −.13 to −.43)
	Osterhouse and Brock (1970)	−.40 (range = −.11 to −.57)
	Keating and Brock (1974)	−.63 (range = −.19 to −.70)
	Beaber (1975)	−.32
	Petty and Cacioppo (1977)	−.63 (Exp. 1), −.46 (Exp. 2)
	Cacioppo and Petty (1979)	−.56
	Petty and Cacioppo (1979)	−.22 (low involvement)
		−.73 (high involvement)
Favorable thoughts and attitude change	Petty and Cacioppo (1977)	.40 (Exp. 1), .43 (Exp. 2)
	Cacioppo and Petty (1979)	.45
	Petty and Cacioppo (1979)	.35 (low involvement)
		.64 (high involvement)
Confidence in initial attitude and attitude change	Ritchie and Phares (1969)	.19 (range = −.11 to .44)
	Hass and Linder (1972)	−.70 (range = −.45 to −.82)
Retention and attitude change	Millman (1968)	.002
	Wilson and Miller (1968)	.28
	Rule and Rehill (1970)	−.16
	Keating and Brock (1974)	.19
	Insko, Turnbull, and Yandell (1974)	−.02
	Insko, Lind, and LaTour (1976)	.001 (Exp. 1), .122 (Exp. 2)
	Cacioppo and Petty (1979)	−.01
	Petty and Cacioppo (1979)	.01 (low involvement)
		.19 (high involvement)
Counterarguments and recall	Keating and Brock (1974)	.10
	Cacioppo and Petty (1979)	.17
	Petty and Cacioppo (1979)	.09 (low involvement)
		.02 (high involvement)
Favorable thoughts and recall	Cacioppo and Petty (1979)	−.07
	Petty and Cacioppo (1979)	.06 (low involvement)
		.10 (high involvement)

(continued)

TABLE 5.1 (*Continued*)

Correlations Between:	Author(s)	Average Within-Cell Correlations
Counterarguments and favorable thoughts	Petty and Cacioppo (1977)	−.11 (Exp. 1), −.37 (Exp. 2)
	Cacioppo and Petty (1979)	−.45
	Petts and Cacioppo (1979)	−.26 (low involvement)
		−.51 (high involvement)
"Assimilation-contrast" and		
1. attitude change	Eagly (1969)	.07
2. perceived approval	Eagly (1969)	.32
3. source evaluation	Eagly (1969)	.28

thereby increasing the learning of information and at the same time independently increasing agreement. However, the lack of a within-cell relation between opinion and information would argue against any important mediating role for information. Insko, Turnbull, and Yandell (1974) recognize this problem. They note that whereas the between-cell correlations for these two measures are often significant, reflecting the large variance created between conditions (Insko, 1964; Insko et al., 1974; Miller & Campbell, 1959), the within-cell correlations are near zero. Observing the flatness of the slope relating recall to attitude change they argue that a large change in recall is necessary in order to create noticeable differential effects in attitude change.

This digression should caution the reader that despite the inconsistency among correlations in Table 5.1, cognitive responses may nevertheless play a mediating role. Problems in measurement like those pointed out can obscure relationships that do in fact exist. Taking all this into account, what can be derived from the table is the suggestion that investigators in the future systematically examine and report all the within-cell correlations between measures of their hypothesized cognitive intervening variables and attitude change. Even better, though not answering by itself the question of cause, would be standardized regression coefficients.

Why do we suggest that researchers turn to regression coefficients? Because the slope in a regression analysis is not affected by the variance or range, it seems to be more meaningful than a correlation. Nevertheless, the comparison of the steepness of the slope for various predictors can still be misleading about their relative importance, because the size of the scale units of the respective predictors does matter. For this reason, standardizing regression coefficients is thought to allow meaningful comparisons of the relations between variables despite differences in the measurement scales among variables. Again, however, this will only be true when the sampled values adequately reflect the true variance in the population.

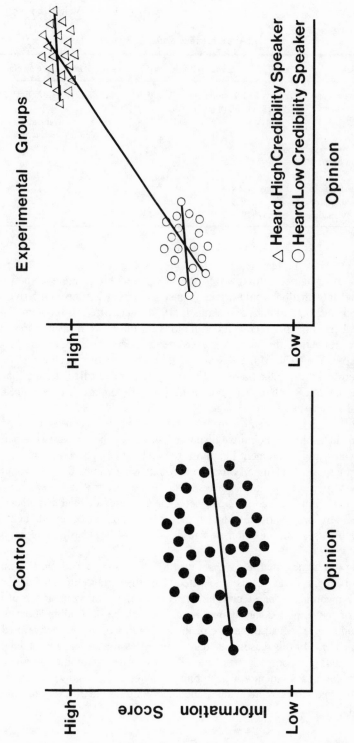

FIG. 5.2. The relation between information and opinion for a fictitious experiment manipulating credibility. (Regression slopes are eyeball approximations.)

118

Multiple Regression and Causal Modeling

The application of multiple regression and other causal modeling procedures to the task of unraveling the causal relations among cognitive mediators is fraught with problems. Despite these problems, there is something to be gained from their use, particularly in complex natural settings (McGuire, 1973). It becomes possible to consider, within a single environmental or message context, interrelations among numerous theoretically linked variables. Other advantages in their application to data collected in natural settings center around consideration of external validity (Campbell & Stanley, 1966). Many laboratory studies use topics in their designs about which people are unlikely to have attitudes of any generality or intensity. Laboratory impression-formation studies that deal with issues of information integration often fall into this category. In the laboratory setting that uses college subjects, strong implicit pressures to behave rationally may operate, whereas real-life situations lack such impetus. Judges exhibit striking discrepancies in their bail-setting behavior when they make their judgments under "experimentlike" conditions in the privacy of their chambers, as contrasted with their actual behavior on the bench. In the courtroom they ignored much of the available information that they did use in the more experimental setting. Indeed, whereas all the available information was used in the laboratorylike setting, in actual practice they virtually ignored three-fourths of the information, attending only to the district attorney's recommendation (Ebbesen & Konecni, 1975; see Chapter 16 for a further discussion of this study).

In nonlaboratory settings, strong emotion may arise in conjunction with the attitudinal issue, particularly in face-to-face discussions among peers. However, perhaps with the exception of research on effects of fear appeals, few laboratory studies of persuasion are performed in the context of emotional arousal. Fishbein and Ajzen, in recognizing this point (1975), nevertheless seem to feel that a human being may appropriately be viewed as a "rational processor of the information available to him [p. 214]."

Though they may be correct, it is clear that subjects who feel involved with an attitudinal issue behave quite differently from those who do not. Occasionally, they *appear* to respond even more strongly to demands for rational information processing than those who lack involvement—as when they make fewer intransitive judgments when they scale attitudinal statements (Koslin & Paragament, 1969). Yet this may simply reflect less carelessness among those who care. In most instances, however, they seem less "rational" than the uninvolved subject. When asked to sort statements into piles that "belong together" and "are graded in terms of their favorability toward the issue [p. 126]," they use fewer categories (show less cognitive complexity) and their modal judgment is located further from their own stand (Sherif et al., 1965). In other words, they tend to see things in simple dichotomies and, in general, as more objectionable, despite the fact that they typically possess more information (Reich & Sherif, 1963).

Such considerations emphasize the need to examine the extent to which cognitive processes elicited most strikingly in the laboratory also bear the explanatory burden in more natural conditions. Regression and correlational models are typically the tools for analyzing naturalistic data. Unfortunately, however, their usefulness can easily be overestimated. In the classic least squares regression model, the effects of all independent variables are estimated simultaneously; the effect of any one independent variable is estimated while simultaneously taking account of the effects of all other independent variables. This seems to imply an unbiased outcome with the possibility of clear-cut interpretations of results. Unfortunately, however, the estimation of parameters is affected by the multicolinearity of measures included in the model—the extent to which so-called independent variables are not independent of one another but instead are correlated.

Stepwise regression adds the effect of individual variables to the model one at a time, thereby attempting to determine whether or not a given variable significantly adds to the explanatory value of the model. If not, then presumably it plays no causal role. Unfortunately, answers to such questions depend heavily on the sequence in which measures are entered. This, too, stems from the effects of independent variables that are correlated. Typically, the obtained regression coefficients will be larger than the "true" coefficients, but moreover, the sign can even be wrong (Hoerl & Kennard, 1970).

The solutions to problems of multicolinearity are not clear and do not come easily. Whereas some researchers suggest the application of ridge regression (Lawless & Wang, 1976; Marquardt & Snee, 1975; Newman, 1977), a procedure first introduced by Hoerl (1962), others advocate factor analysis as a guide for how to cluster variables (Horst, 1965). Its routine application, however, can be very misleading. Opportunities for self-deception grow when theoretically distinct concepts share common method variance in varying amounts. Two measures of a common latent variable may exhibit a relatively minor relation when assessed with maximally different methods, each of which has substantial unique variance. Likewise, measures of two distinct latent variables may covary sufficiently to lead the unwary researcher to conclude that they reflect a single underlying latent variable—as when they are assessed at a single point in time, by a common method, in a common setting that differs sharply from the arenas in which the behaviors associated with each of the two theoretical variables typically occur. If one concluded, on the basis of a factor analysis containing the sets of items comprising these two measures, that they do reflect a single common underlying latent variable, one would be partially correct—but misleadingly so. The underlying commonality would be method specific and scientifically useless in any test of a hypothesis or theory.

Variations of this problem are found in the now expansive literature on discrepancies between attitudes and behavior (Fishbein & Ajzen, 1975; Liska, 1975; Wicker, 1969). Encouragingly, the focus of discussion seems to have shifted from bemoaning the weak relations often found to analyzing the circumstances under which strong and weak relations can be expected. Recall from

Chapter 2 Fishbein and Ajzen's (1975) argument about the effects of degree of specificity in measures of attitude and behavioral intentions. When a substantial amount of unique method variance is associated with a measure, it will not correlate very highly with anything. For example, consider the complications that may arise when one undertakes a naturalistic correlational study of the impact of a communitywide "information campaign" on attitudes and voting behavior. The researcher not only wishes to study attitudes and voting behavior but also hopes to assess the role of cognitive mediators. The investigator would probably want to include measures of: respondent's initial attitude, amount of exposure to campaign materials, perception of the source of messages, perceived normative support for own position, perceived importance or involvement in the issue, immediate social support for own position, typical level of emotional arousal or activation when the topic is introduced, past accumulated information in support of own position, judgments regarding the extremity of the source's advocated position, new information assimilated from exposure to the persuasive communication, perceived intent of source to persuade (reactance), behavioral intentions, and so forth.

Conceptually, these measures would be viewed as independent variables; final attitude and voting behavior would be dependent measures.[2] The determination of the "proper" causal sequencing will depend on one's initial theory and at the same time constitute the problem to be solved. One thing, however, is clear. Many of these measures would show high intercorrelations; from the standpoint of our earlier discussion, they are multicolinear.

How would such an array of measures be obtained? If they were self-reports—answers by the respondent to different sets of questions administered in a single interview from a single interviewer—common method factors would intrude into all answers, thereby artificially inflating their interrelation. Furthermore, answers to questions tapping the respondent's cognitions with respect to any one theoretical mediator would be highly likely to affect the individual's response to other variables due to pressures for consistency. The potency of this latter source of covariation among responses would depend on their relative temporal adjacency to one another in the interview schedule. Unfortunately, the solution for effective removal of such artificial sources of interdependency among conceptually distinct variables remains elusive.

Combining Experimental and Causal Modeling Procedures

Having pointed to an array of relevant problems in the application of multiple regression and causal modeling procedures such as path analysis to the problems of determining the details of the causal process underlying persuasion, we next

---

[2]In a theoretical sense, many or all of the mediators listed are conceptualized both as dependent and independent variables; they are responses, but they also influence other cognitive responses represented in the entire set.

present an experiment in which subjects were exposed to a fear-arousing communication that combines experimental manipulations with causal modeling procedures.

Rogers and Mewborn (1976) noted that communications typically used in "fear-appeals" studies present subjects with multifaceted stimuli. They isolated three components: (1) magnitude of noxiousness of the depicted act, (2) conditional probability that the noxious event will occur provided no adaptive activity is performed, and (3) effectiveness of a coping response that might avert the noxious event. These in turn initiate a corresponding cognitive mediating process, respectively: (1) perceived severity of the depicted event, (2) expectancy of exposure to the event, and (3) belief in the efficacy of the recommended coping response. They assumed that the three types of cognitions exert independent effects on attitude change.

In their experiment, in which all three components were manipulated, dependent measures tapping each of the three postulated cognitive mediators were included as manipulation checks: Three items assessed the "perceived severity of the depicted event" (e.g., "Lung cancer is an extremely frightening and dangerous type of disease"); three items measured "expectancy of exposure" (e.g., "I think it is likely that I will get lung cancer sometime in the years ahead"); and two measured the "perceived efficacy of the coping response" (e.g., "For a smoker, giving up cigarette smoking is extremely effective in reducing the chances of developing lung cancer"). In addition, four items assessed intentions to comply with the recommended practices (e.g., "At the present time, I intend to stop smoking completely"). Further, a measure of fear arousal consisting of six mood indicators (*fright, tension, nervousness, anxiety, discomfort,* and *nausea*) was completed immediately after viewing a film that served as the antismoking persuasive communication.

Their results demonstrated that "regardless of what the threatened event was, how noxious it was, or how likely it was to occur, the stronger the belief that a coping response could avert a danger, the more strongly people intended to adopt the communicator's recommendation [p. 59]." Of greatest interest here, however, is a multiple regression and path analysis of the dependent measures. Because the theoretical model assumes that the cognitive mediational processes are independent, a multiple regression equation was computed, entering the manipulation check items as predictors of the criterion variable—behavioral intentions. The standardized coefficients are seen as reflecting estimates of the contribution of each predictor variable in "causing" the criterion variable and providing some information about which variables are more crucial in predicting reactions to the fear-arousing communications. The coefficients obtained were: fear arousal—.13, severity—.19 ($p < .05$), expectancy of exposure—.03, belief in efficacy—.32 ($p < .01$). It is obvious that "belief in efficacy of coping responses" contributed substantially more variance than did any of the other predictors, which corroborates an analysis of variance that showed the strongest (and only consistent) main effect for "belief in efficacy." In addition, a path analysis was performed in order to determine whether these mediators affected intentions by operating *indirectly*—that is, by affecting intentions *through* its effects on one or more of the other mediating variables. The paths that were significant beyond the .05 level are presented in Fig. 5.3.

The path analysis provides valuable additional information. We can see now, for example, that although "fear arousal" was not significantly related to "intentions" in the multiple regression equation, it was importantly related to them indirectly through its significant relation to appraised severity. This makes theoretical sense for two reasons. First, research shows that experimentally aroused fear quickly dissipates. Given this fact, in combination with their spacing of measures, no effect from the fear-arousing stimulus should have been present at the time they measured behavioral intentions. Secondly, the assumptions of their theory—protection motivation theory—require the presence of sustained cognitive representations to mediate persuasion. The outcomes of the path analysis are particularly interesting in light of the absence of any analyses of variance main effects for noxiousness upon either expressed severity or intentions. Also noteworthy is the direct effect of "efficiency of coping responses" upon intentions, which meshes with the analysis of variance main effect for efficacy. If an action is seen as likely to work, people are more likely to take it. Additionally, however, the path analysis confirms the theoretically postulated independence of perceived efficacy from the other cognitive mediators— perceived severity of consequences and likelihood that they will occur. This outcome supports Leventhal's (1970) separation of fear arousal from danger-control processes and emphasizes the importance of the latter. The study thus presents empirical support for viewing appraised severity and belief in the efficacy of coping responses as specific cognitive mediating components of Leventhal's earlier parallel response model (see Chapter 8 for further discussion).

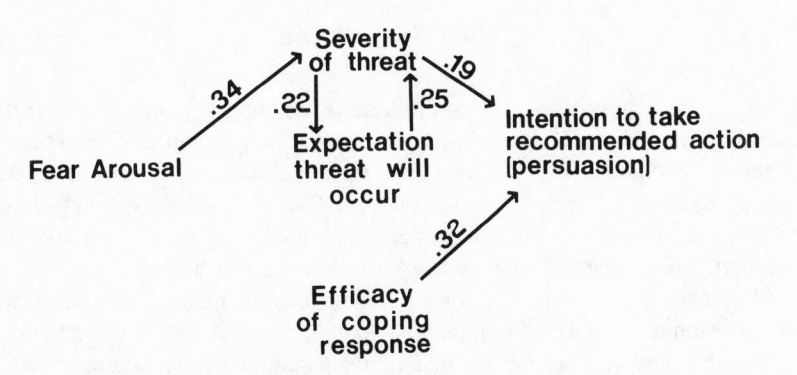

FIG. 5.3.   Significant "causal" links between cognitive mediating responses and persuasion (from Rogers & Mewborn, 1976).

Without discussing the bearing upon Rogers and Mewborn's research of some of the concerns raised earlier, particularly those concerned with "estimates of importance," it can be seen that the study provides an encouraging example of the way that experimental and correlational methodologies can profitably be combined with theory to make progress in isolating causal relations among cognitive mediators.

CONCLUSION

Our purpose in this chapter has been to alert the reader to a variety of methodological concerns and problems that arise when we attempt to understand the mediating events in the persuasion process. Unfortunately, the solutions to problems are often not readily apparent. Were they so, the problems undoubtedly would not be problems. But awareness is a start. Hopefully, our discussion will sensitize readers to issues that warrant attention.

New technologies and procedures rarely retain their initial luster when later examined from historical perspective. Moreover, the newest techniques for developing causal models with correlational data (Joreskog, 1974; Joreskog & van Thillo, 1973) can never substitute for the true experiment. At the same time, experimental social psychologists cannot be complacent about the ease with which one can mislead oneself about the relation between experimental operations and the conceptual variables to which they are presumably linked. The answer obtained from any single method, procedure, or paradigm is unlikely to be the final solution. Rather, when converging answers emerge from the application of different methodologies in both laboratory and field settings, our confidence in the validity of their role as intervening mechanisms will increase.

CHAPTER SUMMARY

The most important attribute of an attitude is temporal stability, although few researchers include this feature in their measurement procedures. Recent investigators have claimed that attitudes lack temporal consistency and are merely manifestations of self-presentational concerns. Evidence was presented to defend the position that attitudes, when properly measured can be enduring and are a useful way of conceptualizing some aspects of human behavior.

Almost all theories of persuasion posit some intervening cognitive mechanism between stimulus input and attitudinal response. In order to test these theories, reliable and valid measures of the intervening cognitive activity are necessary. It was suggested that the popular "listed thoughts" measure may simply provide another index of attitude rather than the cognitive responses that mediate it.

Various strategies for assessing the causal role of cognitive mediating responses were considered. The *indirect inference* strategy calls for manipulating a variable that is thought to affect the intervening cognitive responses in a particular way. If the persuasion effect observed conforms to the hypothesized relation between attitudes and the particular cognitive mediating mechanism, then support for the causal role of the cognitive mediator is implied. *Self-reports* of internal cognitions are a more direct assessment strategy. However, self-reported cognitions may be mere rationalizations of attitude rather than mediators. Measures of cognitive responses taken during the presentation of a message may be more valid than measures taken after a communication.

Various statistical procedures that can handle multiple variables were described, as well as the potential problems that are inherent in their use. The need to examine the extent to which cognitive processes elicited in the laboratory also bear the explanatory burden in more natural conditions was stressed. Finally, an experiment that meaningfully employed both experimental and multivariate correlational procedures was described.

6 Cognitive Response Analysis: An Appraisal

Anthony G. Greenwald
Ohio State University

A major achievement of the past decade has been the accumulation of enough data (well represented in the chapters of this volume) to make clear the value of regarding the communication audience member as an active information processor rather than a passive recipient. The major achievement of the next decade should be the unfolding of the implications of this view for the analysis of persisting and delayed impacts of persuasive communications.

RETROSPECT AND CRITIQUE

The label *cognitive response analysis* was first attached to the view that the communication recipient is an active information processor—an alterer or modifier of the information content of the communication—in the context of an attempt to salvage an associative learning interpretation of persuasion (Greenwald, 1968a). In that presentation, and also in the historical introduction to this volume (Chapter 1), it is emphasized that this basic theme of cognitive response analysis was stated well before the label was attached. Accordingly, the history of cognitive response analysis substantially predates 1968. The novel element introduced in 1968 was the recognition that the audience-as-active-information-processor view could be used to account for some findings that did not previously fit well with learning theory explanations—findings that showed that differences between individuals or between experimental treatments in the persuasive impact of a given communication were unrelated to differences in the degree of learning of the information content of the communication (Anderson & Hubert, 1963; Greenwald, 1968a; Hovland, Janis, & Kelley, 1953; Insko, 1964; Miller &

Campbell, 1959; Watts & McGuire, 1964). The problem and its suggested solution were stated as follows (Greenwald, 1968a):

> It is widely accepted that cognitions bearing on the object of an attitude form a major component of the structure of the attitude toward that object.... Since the individual is not born with ... cognitions, but acquires them, there seems to be no reasonable alternative to the assumption that cognitions bearing on attitude objects are learned....
>
> Rehearsal and learning of cognitive responses to persuasion may provide a basis for explaining persisting effects of communications in terms of cognitive learning [pp. 148, 149].

Confirmation of the importance of viewing the recipient as an active information-tion processor has been obtained by the convergence of several types of evidence that are represented in various chapters of this volume. The method of *listed thoughts* has been used as an aid to observing the content of cognitive responses during persuasion. (The virtues and problems of this method are discussed in Chapters 2 and 5.) Results obtained with the listed thoughts method show that (1) the audience member's thoughts are often very rich in content that neither originates in nor agrees with the content of a just-received communication, and (2) the evaluative content of listed thoughts serves well to predict immediate and delayed posttest opinion responses. *Role-playing* methods have been used to demonstrate that people attach special importance to their own thoughts relative to those of a comparably expert other (Greenwald & Albert, 1968). Last, in experiments using *distraction* procedures, persuasive effects are consistent with the notion that the distraction interferes with the recipient's active cognitive contribution to the persuasion process (see Chapter 3).

In the prevailing conception that has just been described, cognitive responses constitute a silent, internal communication on the part of an audience member. This internal message is assumed to mediate the effect of the (external) communication on subsequent opinion. The status of the cognitive response process is therefore that of a mediating, or intervening, variable. An alternative conception is to regard cognitive responses as products of the same set of factors (communication, setting, and audience predispositions) that are usually assumed to affect postcommunication opinion. In this alternative view, cognitive responses have the conceptual status of a dependent variable rather than that of an intervening variable. Considered from this latter perspective, the repeatedly obtained evidence that cognitive response evaluative content predicts posttest opinion well can be interpreted as indicating that evaluative cognitive responses and opinion responses are conceptually equivalent. Two forms of evidence are consistent with (but don't demand) this interpretation. One is the readily obtained finding (cf. Calder, Insko, & Yandell, 1974; Greenwald, 1968a; Osterhouse & Brock, 1970) that evaluative measures of cognitive response content (that is,

scores based on numbers of agreement and/or counterargument responses) correlate strongly with measures of postcommunication (and precommunication) opinion. Second is Cullen's (1968) finding that the listed thought procedure produces
evaluative measures that correlate strongly with, and have properties similar to,
measures derived from standard attitude-scaling procedures such as Thurstone or
Likert scales.

In support of the mediating-process interpretation are some correlational results suggesting that cognitive response content is a more immediate consequence of a persuasion attempt than is measured postcommunication opinion
(e.g., Insko, Turnbull, & Yandell, 1974; Osterhouse & Brock, 1970). However,
the analyses used in these studies could support the mediating-process conclusion
spuriously *if* measures of the evaluative component of cognitive responding are
generally more reliable than are ones of postcommunication opinion. Correlational tests of the cognitive-response-as-mediator conception will become more
convincing when persuasion researchers (the author included) attend more to the
reliabilities of their measures.

PROSPECT

The conception of the communication recipient as something more than just
another medium in which the communicated information may reside brings with
it the possibility of applying the rich variety of theory and methods developed in
the study of simpler information-processing domains. Glimpses of the potential
of such applications may be seen in some of the later chapters in this volume—
particularly the ones by McGuire (Chapter 13) and by Lingle and Ostrom (Chapter 17)—in which organization of information in memory is central to the theoretical analysis. The comments that follow are intended to suggest some of the gains
that may come from application of a few particular concepts—processing set,
organization of information in memory, and retrieval cues—that can be borrowed
from theoretical analyses of the relatively simple information-processing task of
list learning.

Analysis of Enduring Effects of Communications

Most existing theory of persuasion is silent on the subject of effects of communications on opinion measures administered at a delay after exposure to the communication. As Cook and Flay (1978) have pointed out, there exist three
theoretical approaches to the analysis of these residual effects. The most prevalent and least interesting is the Ebbinghaus-curve forgetting interpretation; this
was used explicitly by Miller and Campbell (1959) and implicitly by many others
who have, in effect, assumed that the passage of time should yield a monotonic
reduction of a communication's persuasive impact. Theoretically more interest-

TABLE 6.1
Alternative Modes of Audience Processing of Communications

Informal Designation of Processing Set	Component Cognitive Processes	Illustration in Natural Settings	Laboratory Tasks That Might Produce Similar Processing
Inattention	Preattentive processing	Thumbing through print ads, conversing during TV ads, daydreaming during a lecture	Performing a distracting task that prevents focal attention to a communication
Irrelevant interest (incidental learning)	Attention but no appraisal or retention	Proofreading, taking notes for a friend at a lecture	Counting occurrences of "the" in a message, judging the personality of a speaker
Future usefulness (intentional learning)	Retention but no appraisal	Studying a text, attending a lecture, reading a consumer guide in expectation of making a purchase	Instructing subjects to expect a delayed test for retention of message content
Immediate evaluation	Appraisal but no retention	Listening to a debate, reading newspaper ads to select a film to see	Advising subjects of the persuasive intent of the speaker
Immediate evaluation and future usefulness (scholarly analysis)	Appraisal and retention	Preparing to give a lecture, to engage in a debate, or to write an editorial	Advising subjects to expect both an immediate opinion posttest and a delayed retention test

ing, but less widely used, are Kelman's (1958) analysis of three processes of influence (compliance, identification, and internalization) which is presented in Chapter 7, and McGuire's probabilogical analysis, which receives an updated presentation in Chapter 13.

Information-Processing Sets of Communication Audiences. Theoretical inactivity notwithstanding, it has been clear for some time that research on duration of communication effects may provide the basis for an eventual integration of diverse findings from experimental and survey studies of attitude change (Hovland, 1959). The problem with which Hovland was concerned in 1959 would be described in contemporary terms as that of the ecological validity of laboratory persuasion research. The analysis introduced in Table 6.1 presents a new approach to ecological validity of persuasion experiments, one that is suggested by the general orientation of cognitive response analysis. Instead of examining dimensions of *procedural* similarities and differences between laboratory methods and natural persuasion settings, this analysis examines similarities and differences in the *modes of information processing* that may be elicited by various laboratory and natural settings. In Table 6.1, communication situations are characterized in terms of audience information-processing sets that vary in the presence or absence of *appraisal* and *retention* components. This analysis indicates that communication situations can vary greatly in terms of the way the recipient is prepared to process the communicated information. These variations in processing sets can have impact both (1) on opinion responses observed immediately or after some delay, and (2) in determining whether it is the communication content or evaluative (i.e., appraisal) reactions to the communication (or both) that are retained from the persuasion episode.

Organization of Opinion-Relevant Information in Memory. In future studies of persuasion, principles of memory organization and retrieval may be applied to determine whether the information content of a communication is organized for storage in somewhat different fashion than is the content of evaluative reactions to the communication. Such research may show that the cues that are most effective in eliciting retrieval of information content of the communication may not be the same ones that are most effective in eliciting retrieval of evaluative reactions to the communication. This could provide a ready interpretation in terms of well-understood processes of memory organization and retrieval for the frequent findings of lack of correlation between opinion (i.e., evaluation) effects of a communication and audience success in recalling the information content of the communication (cf. Anderson & Hubert, 1963).

Organization of Information in Relation to the Self. A number of recent findings have pointed to the important organizing role of *self* in memory and cognition (e.g., Markus, 1977; Rogers, Kuiper, & Kirker, 1977; cf. Greenwald,

1980). Some of this research indicates that information that is organized in terms of its relevancy to self is especially easily retrieved (cf. Greenwald & Albert, 1968). It is plausible to suppose that an audience member's evaluative reactions to a communication are inherently more self-relevant than is the communication content itself. Thus, although both communication content and evaluative reactions might be equally well remembered (in the sense of being equally well retrieved, given optimal retrieval cues), nonetheless the evaluative reactions might have much the greater likelihood of spontaneous retrieval, because of self-relevancy. This reasoning suggests that experimental manipulations that affect the organization in relation to self of either communication content or evaluative reactions would, in turn, affect the likelihood that these components of the communication situation would remain influential at the time of a delayed measure of opinion.

Measurement of Cognitive Responses

Researchers interested in the cognitive processing of persuasive communications have obvious use for a measurement procedure that provides access to the content of cognitive responses while not altering the content of those responses in the process of observing them. The work on physiological measurement (see Chapter 4) indicates that known physiological indexes, such as pupil dilation, GSR, and heart rate, are insensitive to the evaluative content of cognitive responding, although they may be sensitive to the amount of effort being spent in information processing. A careful attempt by Love (1972) to discover facial or gestural indicators of the evaluative content of cognitive responding succeeded in demonstrating only that those nonverbal channels could not be used successfully for that purpose. Love's negative findings were particularly disappointing because he employed the same measures that had previously been shown by others (see Mehrabian, 1969) to provide useful indicators of facial and gestural affect in interpersonal interactions. Evidently, the nonverbal channels that convey affect in interpersonal exchanges do not express affect similarly in situations of listening to and watching a person deliver a persuasive communication.

The likelihood of developing unobtrusive measures that directly tap the content of cognitive responding continues to seem remote. In contrast, the prospects for various indirect, or inferential, measures are very promising. In the past decade, investigations of simple information-processing tasks (reviewed, e.g., in D. A. Norman, 1976) have led to the development of methods for diagnosing the organization of stored memories by inference from (1) response latencies, (2) the ordering of information produced in recall, and (3) the effectiveness of various retrieval cues in eliciting recall. Research applications of such methods to more complex information-processing tasks, including person perception (see Chapter 17) and persuasion, are now being developed in a number of laboratories.

CONCLUSION

The first decade of research on cognitive response analysis has encouraged continued development of its general theoretical orientation—that of regarding the communication recipient as an active processor of information. It is this general orientation, rather than any specific set of theoretical postulates, that is best identified as cognitive response analysis. The confinement of much of the past decade's research to a focus on immediate reactions to persuasion attempts has left untapped the full potential of the audience-as-active-information-processor view. The next decade should see an expansion of the purview of cognitive response analysis to include the interpretation of enduring effects of persuasive communications.

ACKNOWLEDGMENTS

Preparation of this chapter was facilitated by National Science Foundation Grants SOC 74 13436 and BNS 76 11175, both titled "Research in Persuasive Communication."

THE ROLE OF COGNITIVE RESPONSES IN ATTITUDE CHANGE PROCESSES

Richard E. Petty
University of Missouri-Columbia

In Part I, the cognitive response approach was outlined, techniques for the measurement of attitudes and cognitive responses were described, and the logic of experimentation was discussed. In Part II, the cognitive response approach is used to explain the effects of traditional independent variables on attitude change processes. Each of the chapters in Part II reviews an important area of research in persuasion and notes how a cognitive response analysis has been, or can be, useful in understanding why each independent variable has the effect it does.

The process of persuasion has typically been analyzed in terms of *who says what to whom, how, and with what effect* (Lasswell, 1948). "With what effect," of course, refers to whether or not any attitude change has been produced. The other four items serve to identify the four major independent variables in persuasion research. These variables are *source* (who), *message* (what), *recipient* (to whom), and *modality* (how).

Because the cognitive response approach to persuasion focuses attention on the thoughts that pass through a person's mind as a communication is anticipated, received, or reflected upon, a cognitive response analyst would seek to determine how different variables affected the manner in which a communication was processed. Figure II.1 diagrams one possible cognitive response model of attitude

135

changes that result from exposure to persuasive communications (Petty, 1977a). The model proposes that enduring changes in attitudes are the result of *cognitively responding* to the message content, whereas temporary shifts in opinion are the result of *persuasion cues*. Cognitive responding refers to overt, verbalizable thinking related to the message content, whereas a persuasion cue refers to a factor or motive inherent in the persuasion setting that may be sufficient to produce an initial attitude change without the need for thinking about the message content.

Because enduring attitude changes result from thinking about the information presented in a message, whereas temporary shifts may result without processing, it becomes crucial to delineate those factors that will lead to message processing. As Miller, Maruyama, Beaber, and Valone (1976) have noted: "It may be irrational to scrutinize the plethora of counterattitudinal messages received daily. To the extent that one possesses only a limited amount of information processing time and capacity, such scrutiny would disengage the thought processes from the exigencies of daily life [p. 623]."

According to the model, two factors will determine whether or not a person will think about the content of a message—motivation and ability. A person will not be motivated to process every message that is presented. Numerous variables may affect a person's motivation to process a stimulus. For example, messages that have high personal relevance, or that arouse dissonance, or that the recipient is solely responsible for evaluating may be particularly likely to be processed (cf. Petty & Cacioppo, 1979b; Petty, Harkins, & Williams, 1980). Recipient variables such as a person's "need for cognition" (see Chapter 1) may also affect motivation.

If a message is to be processed, however, the communication recipient must also have the ability to process the message. The complexity of a message, the number of times it is repeated, whether or not there are any extraneous distractions present—all these things may affect one's ability to process (cf. Cacioppo & Petty, 1979b; Petty, Wells, & Brock, 1976). Recipient variables such as a person's prior knowledge about, or familiarity with, an issue may also influence the ability to process a message in a meaningful fashion. If the message is incomprehensible, or the person has no schema or framework for relating the message to his or her existing beliefs and values, then no processing can occur, even if sufficient motivation is present. Only if a person has both the motivation and the ability to process a persuasive communication can *enduring* attitude change result according to the model.

When both motivation and ability are present, then the next important question concerns the nature of the information processing that occurs. What kinds of thoughts are elicited by the message? Are they generally favorable toward the position advocated or unfavorable? Variables such as the quality of the arguments presented and the person's initial attitude on the topic may affect whether predominantly favorable or unfavorable cognitions are elicited. In some instances, even though a person is motivated and able to process the message, only neutral or topic-irrelevant thoughts will be elicited. When this occurs, enduring attitude change is unlikely.

If a person generates thoughts that have favorable or unfavorable implications for the advocated position, it is likely that enduring attitude change will result if the elicited thoughts produce a lasting change in the underlying cognitive foundation of the attitude. In other words, if several new, favorable implications of the advocated position are uncovered by thinking about the message, but none of them enters long-term memory, enduring attitude change is unlikely. The number of favorable and unfavorable cognitive responses generated and the amount of rehersal of the thoughts that occurs may both ultimately affect whether or not any *new* cognitions will be stored in memory. When the new cognitions stored are more positive than those available prior to message exposure, an enduring positive attitude change (persuasion) is likely; and when the new cognitions stored are more negative than those available prior to message exposure, an enduring negative attitude change (boomerang) is likely.

Clearly, the cognitive response model in Fig. II.1 indicates that it is quite difficult to produce an enduring attitude change. The recipient of a persuasive message must have both the motivation and the ability to process the information contained in the communication; cognitions that have favorable or unfavorable implications for the advocated position must be elicited; and finally, these cognitive responses must supplement or supplant the cognitions existing previously in memory.

Of course, measurable attitude change sometimes occurs in response to a message even though *none* of the foregoing conditions are met. Returning to Fig. II.1, it can be seen that if a person lacks either the motivation or the ability to process a message, a temporary shift in attitudes may result if a persuasion cue is present. For example, if a young man were motivated to please his date, he might shift certain uninvolving attitudes to agree with hers regardless of the arguments she puts forth, or even if no arguments were presented. Attitude shifts that are the result of persuasion cue processes will endure only as long as the operative cue(s) remain(s) salient (i.e., only as long as the young man wants to impress his date).

Many of the attitude changes observed in the psychological laboratory are probably the result of persuasion cue processes (as are many of the attitude shifts observed in the "real world") (Cialdini, Levy, Herman, Kozlowski, & Petty, 1976). For example, one reliable lab finding is that subjects will readily shift their opinions on very esoteric and complex issues in order to agree with the position advocated by a highly prestigious and expert source. Yet these changes generally do not persist when measured only 1 week later (cf. Cook & Flay, 1978). According to the cognitive response model, enduring change should not be expected in this case, because the initial attitude change was not likely to be based on an extensive processing of the information provided by the source. When the source is no longer salient, the attitude shift disappears.

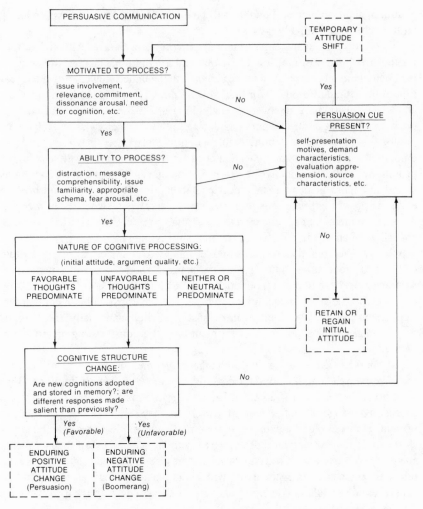

FIG. II.1. A cognitive response model of enduring and temporary attitude shifts that result from exposure to persuasive communications. Adapted from Petty (1977a).

In sum, the cognitive response approach to attitude change processes outlined in Fig. II.1 holds true the following:

1. If the communication recipient has the motivation and ability to process the message, and the message processing leads to changes in cognitive structure, then any attitude change produced is likely to be enduring.
2. If motivation or ability are absent, or if no cognitive structure change results from processing the message, then an attitude change may still occur if a persuasion cue is present.

3. Attitude shifts that result from persuasion cue processes are likely to be rather temporary unless the cue remains salient, or unless the person subsequently becomes motivated or acquires the ability to process the message.
4. If neither motivation, nor ability, nor persuasion cues are present, no attitude change will occur as a result of exposure to the communication.

The chapters in Part II of this volume discuss how the four traditional independent variables in persuasion research—source, recipient, message, and modality—can affect the manner in which a communication is processed. Figure II.1 may provide a useful organizing device for thinking about the chapters in this section.

In Chapter 7, Hass discusses the effects of source characteristics on the cognitive processing of persuasive communications; that is, do highly credible sources motivate more processing or less? The cognitive processes mediating the effects of expert, attractive, and powerful sources are described. Chapter 8 by Eagly is on recipient characteristics as determinants of responses to persuasive messages. Three different strategies for assessing the relationship between personal characteristics and cognitive responses are outlined and critiqued. In addition to the emphasis on source and recipient factors in Chapters 7 and 8, message variables are discussed when appropriate. Thus, for example, Hass explains that the optimal level of message discrepancy depends on the level of source credibility, and Eagly notes that the relative effectiveness of one- and two-sided messages depends on the educational level of the recipient. Message variables are also covered in relevant sections of the remaining chapters.

Chapter 9 by Burnstein and Sentis examines attitude changes that result from group interaction. Theories based on normative processes (approval seeking) and cognitive/informational processes are compared and evaluated. In Chapter 10, Cialdini and Petty explore the cognitive and attitudinal effects of simply expecting to receive or present a persuasive message. Again, the roles of normative and informational factors are discussed, and the antecedents of both enduring and temporary anticipatory attitude shifts are described.

The last two chapters in Part II apply the cognitive response approach to two variables that are of particular interest to advertising and marketing researchers. In Chapter 11, Sawyer examines the effects of message repetition on cognitive responding and persuasion; and in Chapter 12, Wright investigates the effects of the modality of a message (e.g., print, radio, TV) on cognitive responses and persuasion.

7 Effects of Source Characteristics on Cognitive Responses and Persuasion

R. Glen Hass
Brooklyn College, City University of New York

INTRODUCTION

A high proportion of the knowledge and attitudes that each of us possesses about our world was obtained from other people, and some persons who provide us with information have an easier time persuading us than others. The recognition that the persuasive impact of a communication can differ depending on the characteristics of its source stimulated some of the first carefully controlled experiments on the attitude change process (e.g., Hovland, Janis, & Kelley, 1953; Hovland, Lumsdaine, & Sheffield, 1949). The goal of those early experiments and much of the research on the persuasiveness of message sources during the next three decades was to identify specific characteristics of persuasive sources rather than to develop theoretical explanations for the phenomena.

Of course, it is important to know the characteristics that make a source more influential and the limits of those effects from situation to situation. This knowledge is important for many practical purposes. For example, who would you rather have act as your defense attorney before a jury in a small town—a well-known, prestigious New York lawyer or a country lawyer from the same small town? Who would be the better choice as the communicator in a television commercial for a new family car—a well-known actor or actress, an engineer, or the members of a "typical family"? Or in a commercial encouraging people to use car pools—the actor or actress, a respected political figure, an environmental scientist, or an "average" commuter?

However, the knowledge of the persuasive effects of source characteristics and their limitations is also important for subsequent theory building. This chapter reviews some of the major findings of research designed to investigate the effects of the characteristics of the source of a message on persuasion, and it shows how a cognitive response analysis may provide a starting point for explaining some of those effects.

WHAT IS A MESSAGE SOURCE?

It may be obvious to the point of seeming trival that the source of a message is simply the answer to the question, "Who says so?" But the meaning of the term *source* has been interpreted broadly by experimenters (McGuire, 1969a). A message source may be a person, a group, or even a label that has a favorable or unfavorable connotation for the message recipient. Messages used in research have been attributed to known individuals about whom subjects are expected to have well-developed attitudes (such as Walter Cronkite or Thomas Jefferson) and to unknown individuals whose credibility has been manipulated by giving information about them (such as information about their experience on the topic, or information that might arouse suspicion about the source's motives or biases in advocating a particular position). Messages have been attributed to groups (such as the American Medical Association, a random sample of the U.S. population, or a group of students at a local high school). And messages have been given labels designed to suggest other characteristics or beliefs of an otherwise unidentified source (such as the "conservative" position or the "environmentalist" position).

According to current beliefs, there are three sets of characteristics that affect the persuasive impact of a message when they are attributed to its source: the source's *credibility, attractiveness,* and *power.* Each of these qualities may enhance the amount of attitude change produced by a source, but they operate through different psychological processes of persuasion, and each has different behavioral implications. These three categories of source characteristics, as well as the antecedent circumstances that produce each of them, and their behavioral and attitudinal consequences were first conceptualized by Kelman (1961). Their importance also was demonstrated by William McGuire (1969a), who used them effectively to organize the enormous and diffuse literature on source characteristics.

Although the three categories are conceptually distinct, they are combined in most natural situations. A personal experience may illustrate the difficulty in separating the three categories of source characteristics outside the laboratory. My 4-year-old son and I often go for a walk in a large park near our home. Several times during our walks, we have talked about the importance of putting any trash we had in the litter baskets that are available or putting it in our pockets until we found a litter basket, rather than dropping it on the ground.

On one particular day, my son came over to me as we were walking, pointed in the direction of a man who was some distance away from us, and reported that the man had done a "bad thing" because he had dropped a paper cup on the ground. I quickly agreed that the man should have put the cup in one of the nearby litter baskets, and we walked on. I was pleased that the attitude he had expressed agreed with the position I had recommended in previous "communications." As we continued to walk, I reflected on my "persuasive success" as a message source and realized that the influence I had had could have resulted from any one or a combination of all three characteristics—my credibility, attractiveness, or parental power.

Credibility of the Source

The credibility of the source refers both to the source's expertise on the topic and trustworthiness as a communicator—in other words, the extent to which the source is perceived to know the "correct" position on the issue and the extent to which she or he is motivated to communicate that position. A credible source is one who is perceived to possess information that is "correct" and who is perceived to be willing to communicate that information without bias. Because the ability to obtain desired outcomes often depends on possessing accurate information, persons are likely to be quite open to messages that update or improve their view of reality.

Credibility produces attitude change through a psychological process that Kelman (1961) called *internalization*. Internalization occurs when an attitude is learned and adopted as the receiver's own by being integrated into that individual's belief and value system. Internalization is the process most people usually have in mind when they talk about attitude change in the sense of changing a person's beliefs or convictions. Once an attitude or attitude change has been internalized, the person will tend to maintain that new attitude even if the source of the message is forgotten and even if the source switches to a new position. As we shall see, these last two effects distinguish persuasion produced in response to a source's credibility from attitude change that results from a source's attractiveness or power.

As I walked with my son, I hoped that the antilittering attitude he had expressed was one that he had internalized. I also recognized that my credibility as a source for him was of an unusual sort and one that might become increasingly limited in the coming years. Beginning at birth, children are dependent on others, particularly their parents, for information about their environment. Of course, they learn a great deal by manipulating and exploring their surroundings, but much information is mediated by the communications and teachings of others (Jones & Gerard, 1967). Mediation of information by others is especially important in areas that would be difficult or impossible for children to experience alone, such as historical events or the existence of places they have never been. For the first few years of life, a child's parents have a virtual monopoly on the information provided. Gradually children come to realize that people other than their parents can offer explanations about their environment. They come to learn also that discrepancies may occur in explanations, that explanations can be biased, and that some sources may be more accurate and reliable than others. They become interested in the source's knowledge, skill, or experience in the topic, and they become wary of any vested interest that might influence a source's motivation to present information that is distorted or incomplete. And so, perhaps, develops a person's attentiveness to a communicator's expertise and trustworthiness, two of the components of source credibility.

Attractiveness of the Source

Attractiveness is the second category of source characteristics that affects persuasion. Individuals respond to the credibility of a source in order to increase the verity of their beliefs. They respond to a source's attractiveness in order to enhance their self-concepts. To the extent that a source is someone (or a group) we like or admire, we might choose to take on similar interests, preferences, behaviors, or attitudes. By adopting the characteristics of people we view favorably, or by perceiving ourselves as associated with them, we may affect positively our self-image and self-esteem. Kelman (1961) called this process *identification* with the source, and he described it in terms of a desire to establish gratifying role relationships with the source. The role relationship can be in the traditional sense of identification, in which an individual adopts the same attitude as the source; or it may take the form of a complementary role relationship, in which an individual adopts characteristics that are different but form a compatible counterpart to those of the source. Adopting the same attitude as the source is probably the most common effect of source attractiveness, but holding an attitude that supplements the source's may make the relationship more satisfying when complementary roles are involved, such as teacher–student, author–editor, pitcher–catcher, husband–wife, or father–son.

Although attitudes acquired or changed through identification with an attractive source are accepted by the recipient, as are internalized attitudes, they are not incorporated into the individual's system of beliefs and values; nor are they maintained independent of the message source. Unlike attitude change produced by a credible source, persuasion by an attractive source is not dependent on the validity of the recommended position and the existence of evidence to support it. For example, R. Norman (1976) found that a source described as an expert was more persuasive when he gave six arguments supporting the opinion that people sleep more than necessary than when he simply stated his belief without the supporting arguments. When an attractive source advocated the same opinion, he was equally persuasive whether or not he offered reasons for the belief. The attitude of an attractive source is accepted because of who advocates it, rather than because of the perceived truth value of the reasons that support it. Therefore, the maintenance of the new belief depends on the source's continued advocacy of the position, as well as the continuation and salience of the psychological link between the source and the recipient. A change in the attitude of an attractive source is sufficient to produce corresponding attitude change in the recipient. Similarly, if the source loses his or her attractiveness to the recipient, the changed attitudes may revert to their earlier positions.

In practice, it is not always so easy as it might sound here to make the distinction between acceptance of a position because of who advocated it (identification) and acceptance of a position for the reasons that support it (internalization). For example, consider a situation in which a source who is a highly knowledgeable expert on a topic has carefully analyzed evidence that we may not feel qualified to evaluate; that source then recommends a particular position. We might adopt the source's position without requiring any reasons other than that the source believed it. We might even change our position again to correspond with a later change in the source's position. This process seems to satisfy the criteria of attitude change produced by identification rather than internalization. But the source's position may have been accepted because we believe the source has given us valid information that conforms to reality, rather than to establish a gratifying role relationship. We might even dislike the source but accept his or her summary of complex material. In short, ''because an acknowledged expert believes it'' can be a persuasive argument regardless of what we think about the attractiveness of the source.

A further complication in the relationship between source attractiveness and attitude change via processes of internalization and identification has been found in an experiment by Chaiken (1979). Not only are attractive sources able to stimulate message recipients to adopt a communicator's position through a process of identification, attractive communicators also may possess characteristics or skills that dispose them to be particularly persuasive sources of information and internalized attitude change. Rather than using the usual procedure of manipulating the subjects' *perception* of the attractiveness of the source while holding constant the actual message and its delivery, Chaiken (1979) compared attractive and unattractive communicators in genuine interpersonal situations. She found that the more attractive communicators possessed greater communication skills, higher educational accomplishments, and more self-assurance than the less attractive sources. Since these characteristics are often related to persuasiveness, the results obtained by Chaiken (1979) suggest that attractive people frequently possess behavioral styles that may facilitate internalized attitude change in addition to attitude change they may produce by processes of identification.

As I walked with my son, I smiled at the implications of analyzing his expression of an antilittering attitude in terms of the attractiveness of the source. One of the gratifying and sometimes embarrassing things about parenting is to see your attitudes and behaviors appear in your offspring—imitated just because they are yours. Although the effects of the attractiveness of a source may be seen quite readily in the behavior of children vis-à-vis their parents, they continue to occur as we get older, though perhaps not so slavishly.

Reference groups, either membership or normative (Kelley, 1952), are also sources that commonly influence us through our perception of their attractiveness and our desire to maintain them as part of our identities. For example, a person who considers himself or herself a liberal might be influenced to accept a recommendation labeled ''the liberal position.'' But we also use the attractiveness of a source as a guide to what not to believe (Osgood & Tannenbaum, 1955). For example, people who consider themselves conservatives might be influenced to reject the recommendation labeled ''the liberal position.'' We may strive to dissociate ourselves from individuals or groups we consider offensive. This phenomenon has been demonstrated by Cooper and Jones (1969), who found that subjects were prompted to change their opinions to show their distinctiveness from an obnoxious person who was otherwise similar to themselves. When the obnoxious other person was obviously dissimilar to the subjects to begin with, the desire to dissociate themselves by expressing a divergent opinion was reduced.

Aside from the work on reference groups, most of the consistency theories of attitude change also predict that the more someone likes the source of a persuasive message, the more that individual will adopt the source's position. For example, Heider's balance theory (1958) predicts that if person p likes person o (the source, in this case), and p believes that o likes object x (the source's position on the topic), then p will come to like x also (adopt the source's position; see Chapter 14 for further elaboration of balance theory).

The theory that has applied the consistency notion to the typical persuasion situation with the greatest detail is Osgood and Tannenbaum's congruity theory (1955). According to congruity theory, when a source advocates a position, there is a tendency for the recipient's evaluations of both the source and the position to shift toward a point of equilibrium or congruity, and those shifts are inversely related to the extremity of the initial evaluation.

Congruity Theory.   Congruity theory (Osgood & Tannenbaum, 1955) specifically applies the notion of cognitive balance or consistency to the problem of acceptance of a persuasive communication. The theory makes predictions about both the direction and the amount of attitude change that will occur.

According to the congruity principle, whenever a source and an attitude (toward an object, event, person, or matter) are linked, pressures toward attitudinal congruence arise. If a source expresses a *favorable* attitude on a topic (the President endorses national health insurance), congruence occurs when the recipient holds the same attitude toward both the source and the topic. If a source makes an *unfavorable* assertion toward the topic of the communication (the President vetoes national health insurance), congruence occurs when the recipient holds attitudes toward the source and the topic that are equally intense but opposite in direction. (The theory does not allow for different degrees of favorable or unfavorable assertions.) Furthermore, the theory predicts that if attitude change is necessary to restore congruity, then both one's attitude toward the source *and* one's attitude on the topic will change, with the one that is more extreme changing less. More precisely, the degree of change of one's attitude toward the source or the topic will be inversely proportional to the initial polarity of those attitudes (distance from the neutral point).

For example, consider a person whose evaluation of the President is +2 (on a scale ranging from −3 to +3) and whose evaluation of national health insurance is −1. After exposure to an assertion, the point of conflict resolution for the object can be obtained from the following formula:

$$R_0 = \frac{|A_0|}{|A_0| + |A_s|} A_0 + (d) \frac{|A_s|}{|A_0| + |A_s|} A_s$$

where A_0 is the attitude toward the object (−1), A_s is the attitude toward the source (+2), and d is the direction of the assertion (+1 if favorable and −1 if unfavorable). The point of resolution for the source is identical to the point of resolution for the object if the assertion is favorable and opposite in sign if the assertion is unfavorable.

These two examples are represented in Fig. 7.1. It is worth noticing that the example of the President speaking against national health insurance is also an

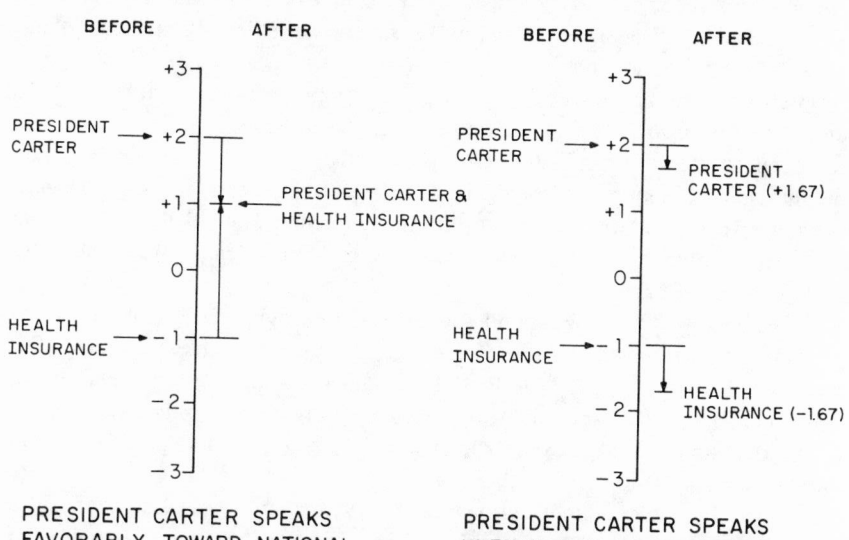

PRESIDENT CARTER SPEAKS FAVORABLY TOWARD NATIONAL HEALTH INSURANCE

PRESIDENT CARTER SPEAKS UNFAVORABLY TOWARD NATIONAL HEALTH INSURANCE

FIG. 7.1.   Examples of congruity theory predictions. The President (initially rated +2) speaks favorably or unfavorably toward national health insurance (initially rated −1).

example of a situation that is balanced but not congruous. This result is possible because congruity theory allows for degrees of favorability and unfavorability of an attitude, whereas balance theory does not.

It is important to observe that congruity theory makes the reasonable-sounding prediction that linking a source with an attitudinal position may change a message recipient's evaluation of the source, as well as his or her attitude on the issue. Most conceptualizations and research on the effects of source characteristics on persuasion implicitly assume that the evaluation of the source remains constant. Or at best, they ignore the possibility that the receiver's view of the source could change in addition to, or instead of, changes in attitude. In fairness, it is probably true that in most cases, the recipient's attitude on the topic is more likely to change than his or her evaluation of the source. For example, Osgood and Tannenbaum found that although evaluations of the source do change, they do not change as much as the theory originally predicted. They took this result into account by adjusting congruity theory predictions by a numerical value they called an *assertion constant*. Nevertheless, possible changes in evaluation of the source of a message should not be overlooked when considering the effects of a persuasive communication.

A noteworthy exception among the consistency theory predictions of increased acceptance of a source's position accompanying greater liking for the source is Festinger's (1957, 1964) theory of cognitive dissonance. The theory predicts that under certain circumstances, a source will produce more attitude change as the recipient's dislike for the source increases (Brehm & Cohen, 1962). The prediction applies to situations in which individuals voluntarily choose to expose themselves to a persuasive communication, and it is based on the process through which they justify that choice to themselves. If the source is someone the message recipient does not like or believes to be disreputable, then the individual cannot justify the decision to listen to the message on the basis of the worthiness of the source. As a result, the recipient is more likely to justify the decision by believing that the message itself was worth listening to and therefore will be more influenced by it.

Jones and Brehm (1967) found support for this cognitive dissonance theory prediction by demonstrating that in a no-choice situation, a likable source who advocated a position contrary to that of the subjects was more influential than a dislikable source. But when the subjects were subtly induced to choose to listen to the counterattitudinal message, the dislikable source was more persuasive than the likable source.

Support for the cognitive dissonance theory prediction was also found in a memorable experiment conducted by Zimbardo, Weisenberg, Firestone, and Levy (1965). The authors found that subjects who agreed to eat fried grasshoppers upon the request of an unfriendly experimenter came to believe that the grasshoppers tasted better than did subjects who ate grasshoppers for a pleasant experimenter. Similarly, subjects who refused to eat grasshoppers for the likable experimenter decided that eating the insects was more repulsive than those subjects who refused the request of the dislikable experimenter. According to dissonance theory, those subjects who complied with the nice experimenter and those who refused the unpleasant experimenter could justify their behavior to themselves on the basis of their liking for the friendly experimenter or their dislike of the unfriendly experimenter. But those subjects who agreed to eat a grasshopper despite the experimenter's obnoxiousness and those who refused the friendly experimenter's request had to justify their behavior in another way. Deciding that fried grasshoppers do not taste so bad (when they were eaten at the request of the obnoxious experimenter) or coming to believe that eating grasshoppers is even more disgusting (when refusing the request of the pleasant experimenter) are ways they could justify their behavior to themselves. If we voluntarily choose to comply with the recommendation of a less credible source, we may become more favorable to the communicator's position than if the same message were presented by a more highly credible source.

Power of the Source

The third characteristic through which a source may influence a message recipient is the source's *power* over the recipient. The source, by being able to control the delivery of rewards and punishments to the recipient, may be able to induce *compliance* with the position advocated by the source (Kelman, 1961). Attitude change expressed from compliance pressures represents a public adoption of the source's position without private acceptance of it. The opinions are not adopted because the individual believes in their content but simply to acquire external incentives. In order to gain membership in a group, secure a promotion, or obtain the approval of a professor, for example, an individual might be careful to express only certain "correct" opinions advocated by the higher power source.

Because compliance produces only an overt expression of attitude change without private acceptance, maintaining the new attitude depends on several severely limiting requirements. The new attitude will continue to be expressed only so long as (1) the recipient perceives the source as having the power to deliver the positive or negative sanctions; (2) the recipient perceives the source as caring whether or not the recipient complies; and (3) the recipient perceives himself or herself as being under the surveillance of the source (Kelman, 1961; McGuire, 1969a).

As I walked with my son thinking about attitude change through the process of compliance, I realized that his expression of an antilittering attitude might have been just for my benefit. He knew that I thought people in the park should throw their trash in the litter baskets and that I wanted him to agree. So he may have anticipated my favorable response toward him when he noticed the man littering and spontaneously criticized the man's action. His criticism could have come from a general desire for approval, or it could have been stimulated by his desire for a *Star Wars* T-shirt for which he was campaigning.

But alas, I cannot know precisely which of the source characteristics provoked my son to voice his opposition to littering. I have heard that he has made similar statements at other times when I was not there to monitor what he was saying, and he had no reason to think what he said would be reported back to me (even after he got his *Star Wars* T-shirt). So I probably can rule out compliance as the sole cause of his behavior. But that does not mean that his desire to gain his father's approval played no part in the attitude he exhibited. In fact, his attitude probably was not a pure example of the result of any of these source characteristics: credibility, attractiveness, or power. More likely it came from a mixture of all three, as do the majority of changes in attitude that occur outside the laboratory.

Just as the three categories of source characteristics may be mixed in non-laboratory settings, their attitudinal effects probably do not remain distinct either. Attitudes produced or changed because of the source's attractiveness (identification) or power (compliance) may come to be privately accepted (internalized) by a message recipient after a lapse of time.

An attitude accepted only because it was advocated by an attractive source would be difficult to maintain in isolation from all other beliefs and values. Thus, the individual may adjust previously existing attitudes and perhaps invent reasons and rationalizations for the new attitude (McGuire, 1969a); Rosenberg, 1960a, 1960b).

Similarly, attitudes expressed because of compliance pressures may become internalized. Expressing an attitude with which one does not agree and expressing it only when one's behavior is being monitored by the high power source creates problems for one's own feeling of attitudinal consistency. In fact, one of the important implications of cognitive dissonance theory (Festinger, 1957, 1964) is that one way to change people's attitudes is to change their behavior first—that an attitude initially expressed as overt compliance will become internalized. According to the theory, inconsistency among one's cognitions is aversive. When such cognitive dissonance occurs, one will alter one's cognitions to restore a consistent relationship. How one has behaved in the past (or, more precisely, a cognition about past behavior) is very difficult to change; thus, a person is more likely to change her or his attitude to be consistent with the behavior. As a result, the expression of a behavior due to compliance pressures can lead to the subsequent adoption of an internalized attitude that is consistent with the person's actions.

There is, however, an interesting relationship between the expression of an attitude because of pressures to comply and the subsequent internalization of that position. Not surprisingly, the more powerful the external pressures for compliance, the greater will be the expression of agreement with the source. But increasing the external pressure for compliance makes it less likely that the expressed attitude will be internalized. The greater the external justification for expressing an attitude, the lower is the need for establishing internal justification by actually coming to agree with it ("I said it because I was forced to"). Conversely, the lower the external justification, the greater is the need to establish internal justification ("I wasn't forced to say it, therefore I must agree with it"). This relationship has been experimentally confirmed many times in situations in which the individual does comply. Researchers have found greater attitude change, the weaker the positive incentives for compliance (cf. Festinger & Carlsmith, 1959; Linder, Cooper, & Jones, 1967) or the milder the threats for not complying (cf. Aronson & Carlsmith, 1963). If the person refuses to comply, on the other hand, the attitude change processes reverse direction. The individual must justify a refusal to comply in the face of positive incentives or threats to induce compliance. Attitude change in a direction opposite to that advocated is the predicted result (Festinger & Freedman, 1964).

The three categories of characteristics that can affect persuasion when attributed to the source of a communication, the psychological mechanisms through which they operate, and their attitudinal products at first may have seemed readily distinguishable. However, we have seen that both conceptually and in practice, they are complex and interwoven, as the analysis of my son's expression of an antilittering attitude has illustrated. The three characteristics may be mixed in one source. The resulting attitudes of the message recipient may overtly appear to have changed, though covertly they have not. And attitudes that began as products of identification or compliance may become internalized. We turn now to another important example of conceptual and practical overlapping of the three categories of source characteristics: the similarity of the source and the recipient.

SIMILARITY BETWEEN THE SOURCE
AND THE RECIPIENT

Another characteristic that has been found to affect persuasion is the perceived *similarity* between the source and the recipient. There is considerable evidence that individuals are more likely to be influenced by a persuasive message to the extent that they perceive it as coming from a source similar to themselves (McGuire, 1969a). However, rather than being a separate category of source characteristic, similarity bridges the gap between source credibility and source attractiveness. That is to say, the perceived similarity of the source and the recipient can increase the persuasiveness of a message by making the source seem more attractive to the recipient and/or by conferring a type of credibility on the source.

Similarity and Attractiveness of the Source

A great deal of research has shown consistently that liking for another person increases along with the number of attitudes, perferences, and other characteristics individuals share (Byrne, 1961, 1969). When the characteristics that the recipient and the source have in common are irrelevant or only slightly relevant to the topic of the message, similarity probably increases a global or general feeling of attractiveness of the source and facilitates persuasion via the process of identification (Berscheid, 1966). For example, Burnstein, Stotland, and Zander (1961) found that an adult communicator who was a deep-sea diver was more successful at influencing the sea-diving preferences of a group of children when he was described as having a similar background (growing up in the same town, swimming and fishing in the same places, and in general having a childhood very similar to their own), than when he was described as having a very different background (being raised in a large city elsewhere in the country and having amusements and pursuits quite foreign to those with which the children were familiar). However, similarity between the source and the recipient can affect the persuasiveness of a message independent of any changes in the attractiveness of the source perceived by the recipient.

Similarity and Source Credibility

Similarities between the source and the recipient can increase attractiveness whether or not the similarities are relevant to the topic of the message. However, when the qualities shared by the source and the recipient are relevant to the source's influence attempt, similarity can increase the persuasiveness of a message even when attractiveness is controlled. For example, Berscheid (1966) found that when feelings of attractiveness for the source were held constant, subjects were influenced more on an education issue than on an international affairs issue when they believed they shared the source's values on education. Conversely, subjects who were led to believe that they and the same source had similar values on international affairs were more influenced on the international affairs issue than on the education issue. With attractiveness controlled, the source was more persuasive when his similarities to the recipient were relevant to the influence attempt.

Source-recipient similarities that are relevant to the topic of a persuasive message can sometimes make a source more credible than one who has much more experience on the topic. For example, Brock (1965) conducted an experiment in the paint department of a retail store and found that a salesman whose paint use was similar to that of a customer was more effective than a dissimilar salesman (whose paint use was 20 times that of the customer) in getting buyers to change their minds about the brand of paint they wanted to purchase.

Just as two sources may differ in credibility on a topic because they vary in the amount of experience they have, sources may also vary in credibility with regard to their effect on the belief and value components of an attitude. Characteristics that increase a source's credibility for changing beliefs are very different from those that affect a source's credibility for changing values. As used here, the term *belief* refers to a person's knowledge and factual cognitions. *Values* are evaluative and attach an emotion of liking or disliking to a cognition. Attitude changes often accompany changes in beliefs and values that are relevant to the attitudinal object.

When a source is interested in changing a belief, the recipient's interest is in being confident that the advocated attitude is a verifiably correct assertion. As a result, a credible source will be one who has had experience on the topic—an expert. In contrast, when the issue is one of value, the recipient must determine the subjective goodness or badness of the entity or state of affairs. Consequently, a credible source will be someone with whom the recipient shares mutual interests, goals, needs, and perspectives—a co-oriented peer (Jones & Gerard, 1967). An expert affects our attitudes by influencing our beliefs with facts. An expert functions as a source of information regarding how things are, not in defining whether they are enjoyable. Co-oriented peers affect our attitudes by influencing our values. Information from a co-oriented peer is given less weight in interpreting reality than information from an expert. However, someone who is similar to the recipient on relevant dimensions ("one of us") will have more influence on the recipient's likes and dislikes than an expert. A brewmaster may know lots of reasons why one brand of beer is better than another, but your friends will probably have a bigger influence on which brand you prefer, or on whether you like beer at all.

The importance of different aspects of source credibility in influencing beliefs and values has been shown in an experiment by Goethals and Nelson (1973). Subjects' confidence in their judgment of the relative academic success of two students (belief) was increased more by agreement from another person they thought was dissimilar to themselves than by agreement from someone who was similar. Agreement by a dissimilar other increases one's confidence on a belief issue by demonstrating that the belief is supported by others with different perspectives. If a belief is held by a broad and heterogeneous consensus, it must be correct. In contrast, when the subjects were asked which of the two students they liked more (value), their confidence in their judgment was increased more by agreement from someone they believed was similar to themselves than by agreement from a dissimilar other. Agreement by a similar other increases one's confidence in a value by providing relevant social support for the evaluation. Our likes and dislikes are most influenced by the preferences of someone else who has similar tastes. Parallel results were obtained in an experiment conducted by Mills and Kimble (1973), who found that when subjects were led to believe that rankings of poetry were an objective matter of artistic knowledge (belief), their rankings were more influenced by a dissimilar other than by a similar other. When they were led to believe that poetry ranking was a subjective matter of personal taste (value), subjects' rankings were more influenced by a person described as similar to themselves than by a dissimilar other. Likewise, Goethals (1972) found that agreement from someone who is dissimilar increases one's confidence in a belief, whereas Brock (1965) and Berscheid (1966), in studies cited earlier, and Darley and Aronson (1966) demonstrated the greater impact of a similar other on the recipient's values.

To summarize, perceived similarity between the source and recipient can increase the persuasive force of a message. When the similarities are irrelevant to the influence attempt, greater persuasion results from increased attractiveness of the message source. When the similarities are relevant to the message topic, persuasion is increased via the credibility co-oriented peers have for influencing one's values.

SOURCE EXPERTISE AND TRUSTWORTHINESS

Although co-orientation is a very important aspect of source credibility, most of the research on credibility has focused on the expertise and trustworthiness of the communicator. This unplanned choice probably evolved because it is easier in a brief laboratory encounter to produce measurable changes in the factual beliefs of message recipients than changes in their values. The choice also may have grown out of the use of informational communications in attitude change research. And the most credible source for influencing one's attitudes via their belief or informational component is a trusted expert.

A persuasive appeal designed to alter an individual's beliefs is an attempt to induce the recipient to adjust her or his view of external reality. A source who is credible for that purpose will be an expert in that area of reality who knows the "correct" view and can be trusted to communicate it. Few areas of research in social psychology have produced results as consistent as the findings that sources high in expertise and/or trustworthiness are more persuasive than those low in these qualities (Insko, 1967; McGuire 1969a), though we will see that the addition of such related concepts as persuasive intent complicates the picture somewhat.

The expertise and trustworthiness of a message source were among the topics studied by Hovland and his associates in their seminal research on attitude change. For example, Hovland and Weiss (1951) demonstrated that a communication represented as coming from a high-credibility source is more persuasive than the same communication when attributed to a low-credibility source. Four different topics were used: the advisability of selling antihistamines without a prescription, whether or not the steel industry was to blame for the then-extant steel shortage, the effect of television on the future of movie theaters, and the practicality of building an atomic-powered submarine. The communications were described as coming from a high- or a low-credibility source for different groups of subjects. For instance, the high-credibility source for the antihistamine issue was the *New England Journal of Biology and Medicine,* and the low-credibility source was a mass-circulation, monthly pictorial magazine. As expected, significantly more of the subjects were influenced by the high-credibility than by the low-credibility sources.

Because the persuasive superiority of high-credibility over low-credibility sources has been such a pervasive finding, most research on source credibility has attempted to locate the limits of the phenomenon and to identify variables that interact with it. For example, recent research has suggested that the persuasion-enhancing effect of source credibility may work best with counterattitudinal communications. Sternthal, Dholakia, and Leavitt (1978) reported that a low-credibility source induced greater persuasion than one of high credibility when the issue was one toward which subjects had a positive initial disposition. Presumably, the less credible source engendered the motivation to generate supporting arguments to bolster the advocacy; whereas a highly credible source produced the feeling that the position was already adequately represented, and further bolstering was not needed (Sternthal, Phillips, & Dholakia, 1978).

Sleeper Effect

Another limitation on the usual source credibility effect was investigated by Hovland and Weiss (1951). A secondary objective of their study was to investigate the extent to which opinions derived from high- and low-credibility sources were maintained over a period of time. In an earlier experiment, Hovland, Lumsdaine, and Sheffield (1949) had found some evidence that a communication from a low-credibility source had greater persuasive impact after a lapse of time than it did immediately following exposure. The message influenced the recipients only after they had "slept on it." Hovland, Lumsdaine, and Sheffield termed the result the *sleeper effect* (see Fig. 7.2). In order to test further this phenomenon, Hovland and Weiss (1951) measured their subjects' attitudes again 4 weeks later and found that the difference between the high-credibility and low-credibility conditions had disappeared. The number of subjects influenced by the high-credibility source had decreased, and the number influenced by the low-credibility source had increased somewhat. The difference in change of direction for the two groups was significant.

In subsequent years the sleeper effect became one of the most frequently cited phenomena of the effects of the source on attitude change, and many experiments were conducted to study it. However, Gillig and Greenwald (1974) pointed out that a significant sleeper effect, as originally defined (an increase over time in the persuasive impact of a message from a low-credibility source), has *never* been reported since the original Hovland, Lumsdaine, and Sheffield (1949) research. Instead, what typically has been found is a statistically significant interaction between source credibility and the passage of time since the message was pre-

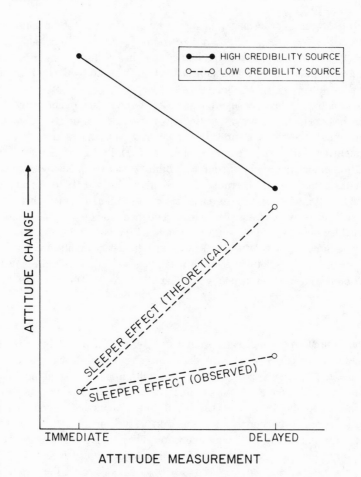

FIG. 7.2.   Attitude change as a function of source credibility and time of posttest—the sleeper effect (theoretical and observed).

sented (see Fig. 7.2). The interaction has been obtained by contrasting a nonsignificant (or absent) delayed impact in the low-credibility condition with a substantial decrease in persuasion over time in the high-credibility condition (e.g, Gillig & Greenwald, 1974; Hovland & Weiss, 1951; Kelman & Hovland, 1953; Watts & McGuire, 1964).

Recently, however, Gruder, Cook, Hennigan, Flay, Alessis, and Halamaj (1978) have provoked renewed interest in the sleeper effect. By specifying precisely the circumstances necessary in order to produce a sleeper effect, Gruder et al. have successfully produced the elusive absolute increases in persuasion following a delay period. Unfortunately for our present discussion, low communicator credibility was not the variable used to produce the delayed persuasion. Instead, Gruder et al. included a statement following the message that claimed that the conclusion of the message was false. After a delay of 5 or 6 weeks, the initial persuasion-inhibiting effects of the statement had worn off, and the impact of the message had increased. Although these results are suggestive, whether or not gains in persuasion over time can be obtained merely because the communicator has low credibility remains an open question.

Although the original conceptualization of the sleeper effect seems uncertain, the disappearance after a few weeks of differences in persuasion produced by high-credibility and low-credibility sources remains an interesting and reliable phenomenon. Initially, Hovland and his colleagues believed that the convergence over time of attitudes of subjects in high- and low-credibility-source conditions occurred because subjects forgot the identity of the source more rapidly than they forgot the persuasive content of a message, leaving the content of the message to have whatever persuasive effect it could on its own. However, subsequent experiments (Kelman & Hovland, 1953; Watts & McGuire, 1964) have shown that the convergence of opinion over time is not due to any simple tendency to forget the source of a message. Instead, subjects remain aware of both the source and the content but gradually fail to associate the two spontaneously. Furthermore, Gillig and Greenwald (1974) found evidence that the dissipation of attitude change in the high-credibility conditions took place because subjects in those conditions were unprepared or unwilling to counterargue with the communication. When subjects were provided with a counterargument defense prior to receiving the message, both the significant decrease in agreement over time in the high-credibility conditions and the interaction between source credibility and time of posttest disappeared.

We might speculate that as an individual begins to dissociate a high-credibility source from a message, he or she may spontaneously review the content of the message more critically than before the dissociation took place. It may well be this examination and counterarguing with the information presented in the message, along with some forgetting of the content, that produces the decrease in persuasion over time when the source is highly credible. (There is more on the relationship between source characteristics and counterarguing later in this chapter.)

Source–Recipient Discrepancy

Another variable that has been found to interact with source credibility is the discrepancy between the recipient's initial attitude and the position recommended by the source. Studies that have explored the relationship between source credibility and source-recipient discrepancy have typically found the following: (1) A high-credibility source is more persuasive than a low-credibility source. (2) The more attitude change advocated by the source, the more attitude change evoked, up to a point. Beyond that point, additional discrepancy between the source and the recipient not only does not continue to increase persuasion; it may actually decrease the amount of attitude change produced. (3) This point of asymptote or drop-off occurs at a more extreme source–recipient discrepancy for a high-credibility source than for a low-credibility source (e.g., Aronson, Turner, & Carlsmith, 1963; Bergin, 1962; Bochner & Insko, 1966). For example, Aronson, Turner, and Carlsmith (1963) asked female subjects to rank nine stanzas from obscure modern poems, all of which contained alliteration, and then to read an essay entitled, "The Use of Alliteration in Poetry." For one-third of the subjects, the communication discussed the stanzas ranked eighth by the subjects as average (small discrepancy); for one-third, the eighth-ranked stanza was presented as superior to all but two of the nine examples (moderate discrepancy); and for the final third, the eighth-ranked stanza was claimed the best example of alliteration in the sample (extreme discrepancy). Half of each of these three groups of subjects were told that the communication was written by T. S. Eliot (highly credible source), and the other half were told that the communication was written by Miss Agnes Stearns, a college student who was studying to become a high school English teacher (mildly credible source). After reading the essay, subjects were told that their initial ranking of the stanzas was merely to acquaint them with the poetry and the ranking procedure, and they were asked to rank the poems a second time.

The results indicated that the highly credible source was more persuasive than the mildly credible source at every level of discrepancy (see Fig. 7.3). Furthermore, for the highly credible source, the greater the discrepancy, the greater the amount of attitude change, although the increase in persuasion at the extreme discrepancy was very small, and it appeared as if the amount of change had reached an asymptote. In sharp contrast, when the communication was attributed to the mildly credible source, widening discrepancy increased persuasion only to a point. As the discrepancy became more extreme, the degree of opinion change decreased to the point that at the extreme discrepancy, there was no more persuasion than there had been in the slight-discrepancy conditions.

Source Trustworthiness

A trustworthy source should be more influential than a source that we suspect might not be motivated to present valid information fairly. The idea seems obvious, but the evidence is somewhat contradictory.

If a source advocates a position knowing it will be popular with his or her audience, a neutral recipient might tend to doubt the source's sincerity or suspect the position was taken just to please the audience. If, on the other hand, the neutral recipient feels that the communicator knows the communication will be unpopular with the audience, the recipient would be less likely to question the source's motives and might be more influenced. Mills and Jellison (1967) found support for this hypothesis. College students read a speech favoring tripling truck-licensing fees. Some subjects were told the speech had been delivered to

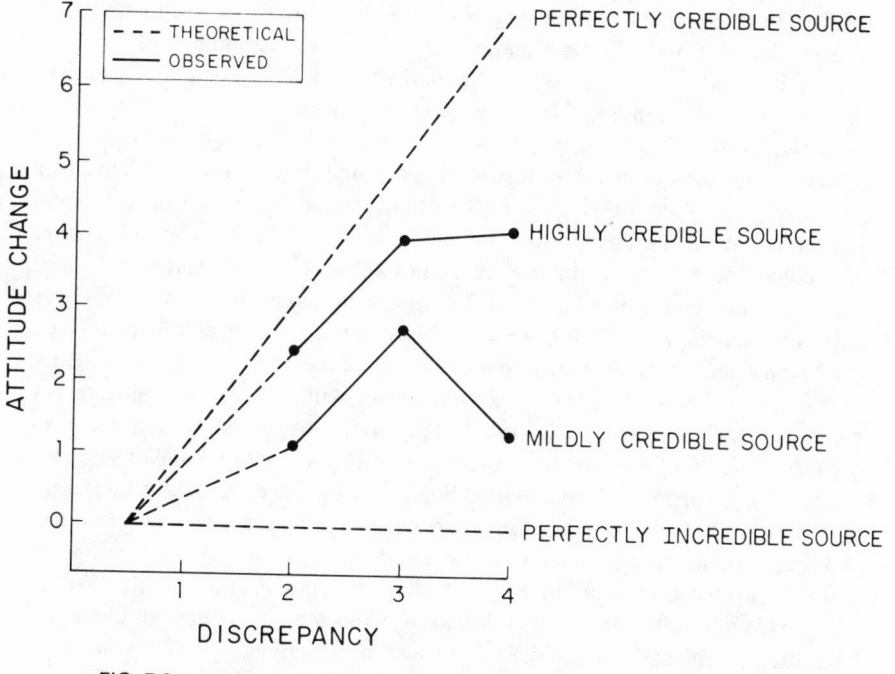

FIG. 7.3 Attitude change as a function of source credibility and extent of message discrepancy—theoretical and observed curves (from Aronson, Turner, & Carlsmith, 1963).

railway men (desirable condition). Others were told that it had been delivered to truck drivers (undesirable condition). As hypothesized, subjects agreed with the position advocated in the message more in the undesirable condition than in the desirable condition.

Walster and Festinger (1962) found that subjects were more influenced by a message when they thought the speakers were unaware that they were being overheard and therefore could not have intended to persuade the recipient. However, in this study and in a follow-up experiment by Brock and Becker (1965), overheard communications have produced increased persuasion only when the topic was involving and the advocated position was desirable for the recipients.

Unfortunately, the results of research on source trustworthiness are not straightforwardly consistent. Several of the studies on source credibility conducted by Hovland and his colleagues found that a source who stood to profit from persuading the subject was judged as less fair and tended to produce less opinion change. However, opinion change differences occurred only when the disinterested source was also an expert (Hovland & Weiss, 1951; Kelman & Hovland, 1953). Hovland and Mandell (1952) held expertise more nearly constant by comparing persuasion induced by a source described either as an academic economist or the head of an import firm on a message urging lower tariffs. The communication was judged more fair but produced no more opinion change when attributed to the economist than to the businessman. Advocating a self-serving position failed to reduce the source's persuasiveness in these studies, contrary to expectation and the results of other research.

Eagly, Wood, and Chaiken (1978) have proposed an attribution analysis of communicator effects that may lead to a better understanding of the impact of trustworthiness of the source. In some situations, an individual may have a strong expectation about the position a communicator will advocate. The expectation may come about because the communicator is perceived as having a strong, sincere preference for one side of an issue (termed *knowledge bias* by Eagly et al.). For example, one might infer that a black communicator will favor relaxed admission standards for minority applicants to graduate and professional schools. In the case of knowledge bias, a communicator will be viewed as sincere but biased nonetheless. An expectation about the communicator's position may also occur because of a belief that the communicator is unwilling to convey accurate information (termed *reporting bias*). For example, an extremely polite communicator, or a one who is addressing an audience whose members are extreme in their opinion, may shade his or her communication to avoid offending or antagonizing those present. In a test of their conceptualization, Eagly, Wood, and Chaiken (1978) demonstrated that if expectations based on the communicator's personal characteristics or based on situational pressures are confirmed, the persuasiveness of the message will suffer. On the other hand, if the communicator advocates a position contrary to the one expected (such as Ralph Nader speaking favorably of the automotive safety practices of General Motors), the message recipient will perceive the content of the message to reflect external reality accurately, and persuasion will be enhanced.

The concept of reporting bias corresponds closely to the concept of trustworthiness, because both view the communicator as failing to convey his or her true beliefs. Knowledge bias is a concept that falls between expertise and trustworthiness. Communicators are viewed as presenting faithfully their true beliefs; but (unlike expert communicators) because their convictions are so strong, they are seen as unversed or unsympathetic to the other side of the issue and biased as a result. The inconsistency in results of research on the trustworthiness concept probably has occurred because the concept is more complicated than originally viewed, as Eagly et al. have shown.

In the same complicated vein, although most experiments have demonstrated that when subjects are forewarned of the persuasive intent of the speaker, persuasion is inhibited (e.g., Hass & Grady, 1975; Kiesler & Kiesler, 1964; see also Chapter 10), some experiments have found that awareness of a desire to influence can facilitate attitude change in certain circumstances. For example, Mills and Aronson (1965) found that a physically attractive female source was more persuasive to male subjects when she expressed a desire to influence them, even though the subjects thought the source would never know how they responded. It appears that when a source is particularly likable, a stated desire to influence can clarify what the recipient must do to ingratiate (Jones, 1964) or identify with the source. Similarly, when a source appears genuinely concerned about the recipient's welfare (Mills, 1966) or is arguing against his or her own self-interest (Walster, Aronson, & Abrahams, 1966), an earnest desire to influence may increase persuasion.

From our present vantage point, it appears that the concept of the trustworthiness of the source and related concepts such as disinterestedness, objectivity, sincerity, persuasive intent, and bias are not related in a simple way to the persuasive impact of a message. It is probably true that a source's persuasiveness will suffer if the source is perceived to have something to gain by persuading the recipient, especially if the source's gain comes at the recipient's expense. Likewise, a source who is perceived to be councealing relevant information (not telling the whole story) or as having undisclosed motives will be less persuasive than one who is perceived as forthright in his or her presentation. On the other hand, there are situations in which these relationships do not hold and others in which they actually reverse.

At present, the literature on source credibility can be summarized by saying that there is considerable evidence that the perceived competence of the source adds to the impact of the communication on the informational portion of recipients' attitudes, evidence that the co-orientation of the source facilitates changes in recipients' likes and dislikes, and the qualified suggestion that confidence in the source's trustworthiness enhances persuasion.

COGNITIVE RESPONSE ANALYSIS OF SOURCE CREDIBILITY EFFECTS

Research interest in source variables stems from the common observation that some people are more persuasive than others, and most of the experiments discussed so far have been attempts to identify characteristics of successful communicators. By calling them *source characteristics* we are focusing our attention on the source and implying that it is changes in the source that alter the persuasive effectiveness of a message. However, such an orientation overlooks an important insight that may be gained from these studies. Research on source characteristics has (appropriately) presented subjects with the very same message, communicated exactly the same way, in the same context. As a result, the research has shown conclusively that the persuasiveness of the message is affected by what the message recipient *believes* about the source—regardless of the actual characteristics of the communicator.[1] In other words, the same message presented by the same source in the same way may be more or less persuasive because of differences in attributions about the source. So, although research on source effects has focused almost exclusively on the communicator (his or her trustworthiness, expertise, similarity, power, or attractiveness, to recall a few)

---

[1]A noteworthy exception is the experiment by Chaiken (1979) mentioned earlier in this chapter.

and we speak of *source* effects, we are more properly dealing with changes in the *recipient* that depend on beliefs about the source. By altering an individual's belief about the communicator, the same message will be processed differently when it is received by the recipient, thereby affecting its persuasive impact. We now shift our orientation back to the recipient and differences in how a message is cognitively processed depending on beliefs about the source.

Hovland and his colleagues initially believed that differences in persuasion produced by such source characteristics as credibility were mediated by differences in learning the content of the communication: A high-credibility source was more persuasive because the recipient was more motivated to learn the arguments presented. However, there is very little evidence that differences in source persuasiveness are accompanied by differences in comprehension (Hovland, Janis, & Kelly, 1953; McGuire, 1969a). People seem quite willing to learn the content of a message and then decide they disagree with it. Therefore, the characteristics of the source seem to affect attitude change not through differences in learning the arguments in the communication but by making the arguments seem stronger or weaker depending on who is believed to have presented them.

The remainder of this chapter considers cognitive processes through which incoming information and arguments are evaluated—processes that may help explain why the amount a recipient yields to a persuasive message is affected by who the source is purported to be. Since our cognitive response analysis focuses on the processing of factual information in a persuasive attempt, it necessarily also focuses on attempts to persuade via the beliefs or cognitive structure associated with an attitude as opposed to the values underlying an attitude. Consequently, source characteristics such as expertise and trustworthiness are central to our cognitive response analysis.

A Two-Function Model of Counterarguing Behavior

Most research on cognitive processes that mediate attitude change has focused on the ability of the message recipient to generate counterarguments to the position and arguments advocated by the source. It is assumed that the more able the recipient is to counterargue covertly with the points raised in the message, the less he or she will be persuaded.[2] The research implicitly has considered coun-

---

[2]An attitude is sometimes viewed as the syllogistic conclusion that follows from a belief premise and a value premise (Bem, 1970; Jones & Gerard, 1967; Rosenberg, 1960b). For example, the belief "smoking causes lung cancer" and the value "lung cancer is bad" produce the attitude "smoking is bad." In this conceptualization, the resistance of an attitude to change is an increasing function of the number of attitudinal syllogisms that lead to the same attitude (have the same conclusion). For example, the syllogism "smoking lessens one's sensitivity to the taste of food, reduced sensitivity to taste is bad, therefore smoking is bad" and the syllogism "smoking annoys strangers nearby, annoying strangers is bad, therefore smoking is bad" increase the strength of one's antismoking attitude. In other words, the greater the number of distinct cognitions supporting an attitude, the more resistant it will be to a persuasive attempt.

terarguments as primarily a device for resisting persuasive attempts, something an individual calls into play when he or she is already inclined to reject the advocated position. This view seems too limited. Persons utilize the information they possess for more than merely resisting persuasion. Counterarguing represents a process of summoning forth information possessed and probably *is* used for the purpose of justifying rejection of arguments supporting a counterattitudinal position. However, in many instances a recipient may gather familiar information during a persuasive attempt, even when not specifically aroused beforehand to reject the source's arguments, in order to determine if the new information "fits" with what he or she already knows about the world. New information is compared with old in order to determine the worth or subjective correctness of the new. Although the counterarguments may indeed result in reduced persuasion, they may have been aroused to defend one's own position, or simply to compare the content of the incoming message to that which is already known.

These two tendencies correspond to the paradox in requirements for human behavior that Jones and Gerard (1967) have called the *basic antinomy*. It is useful to be open to new information that correctly improves our view of physical and social reality. On the other hand, rejection of new information has survival value as well. Treating every situation as new and unique and constantly revising our beliefs inhibits ready action. Persistent attitudes facilitate behavior and promote the stability necessary for optimal social interaction. According to Jones and Gerard, these two tendencies are related to one's committing actions. When a person is minimally committed to a position, openness, flexibility, and redefinition dominate. When the individual has taken strong committing actions, closedness, stability, and self-protection prevail.

Hass (1972) has suggested that the arousal of counterarguments by a recipient while processing a persuasive message may be related to the basic antinomy. When uncommitted, or on the open side of the basic antinomy, one may be less interested in defending a position than in *examining* the persuasive content to determine the best position to take. One may inspect the content for logical flaws and contradictions that require no knowledge of the topic itself. Or, to the extent that arguments on the issue are known, one also may counter in a relatively objective manner with arguments that support an opposing view. When uncommitted, such cognitive activity is designed primarily for the purpose of establishing verity.

On the other hand, when committed to a position through previous decisions and actions, a person is much less tolerant of opposing views. A defensive posture is assumed, and one *resists* any attempted persuasion away from one's committed stand. In a more argumentative tone, probing for logical flaws will occur, but in addition one actively strives to call forth arguments supporting one's own position and refuting that of the source. In other words, the purpose of mustering counterarguments may be to resist persuasion or to examine the message content, or, more often, it may be some combination of the two.

Counterarguing and Source Credibility

Conceptualizing counterarguing as resulting from functional processes of examination and resistance leads to some interesting predictions of the relationship between source credibility and arousal of counterarguments during the reception of a persuasive message.

When an individual is uncommitted and open to persuasion, incoming information will be scrutinized in order to determine its validity. Any cue that leads the recipient to suspect the accuracy of the information will stimulate a more stringent examination of it. Since a low-credibility source has a higher probability of being wrong, a position advocated by such a source will be examined more closely in terms of other information the recipient possesses. People are less likely to anticipate erroneous statements from a highly credible communicator. Therefore, they are more likely to be unprepared or disinclined to examine information from a highly credible source by mustering counterarguments. So, when an individual is uncommitted on the message topic and open to new information, an inverse relationship between source credibility and counterarguing should be expected. The greater the expertise and trustworthiness of the communicator, the less stringently the message content will be examined—an experto crede effect (Hass, 1972).

In contrast, when the recipient is committed and disinclined to yield her or his conviction, the process of resistance may lead to a very different relationship between characteristics of the source and arousal of counterarguments. Tendencies to produce counterarguments for the purpose of resisting should occur when negative outcomes accrue for changing opinion. When one is deeply committed to a view, changing it might provoke negative outcomes for oneself in the form of lessening of esteem from others, admission of previous error, reduction of credibility as a source of information, or blame for misleading others. Furthermore, a change of opinion when one has been strongly committed reinstates uneconomic conflict in choosing a course of action.

For resistance to persuasion to be successful, it must be in proportion to the force of the persuasive attack. As a result, if it is assumed that a more competent source is perceived as able to present a stronger attack, to the extent that one is behaviorally committed, more counterarguing will occur in the presence of a highly credible source than a less credible source. This is just the reverse of the predicted relationship when the recipient is uncommitted: more counterarguing to a low-credibility source when commitment is low but more counterarguing to a high-credibility source when commitment is high (Hass, 1972).[3]

---

[3]However, this is *not* to predict that when a recipient is highly committed, a low-credibility source will be more persuasive than a high-credibility source. It is generally true that the more the recipient is aware of arguments that rebut a source's statements, or buttress her or his own opinion, the less persuasive impact a message will have. Still, no simple translation of attitude change and counterargument proposals is currently possible. For example, regardless of numerical differences in coun-

Furthermore, counterarguing should be more intensive when the recipient is strongly committed than when one is uncommitted or neutral on the topic. When uncommitted, one produces counterarguments only when the veracity of the message is in doubt. When committed, one counterargues to resist persuasion whether or not the specific arguments supporting the position recommended are perceived as valid.

Existing research evidence has provided support for these predictions. In a situation in which it is doubtful that subjects felt highly committed to their viewpoint, Baron and Miller (1969) found that subjects generated fewer counterarguments in anticipation of a message from a high-credibility source than when anticipating the same message from a low-credibility source.

In a pair of experiments, Cook (1969) also used a topic on which subjects have been found to be open to persuasion and measured counterarguments during presentation of a written message by asking subjects to write them down in space provided next to the message. The message, on the topic of the recommended frequency with which people should brush their teeth, was attributed either to a renowned dental researcher and professor from the Stanford Medical School or to a high school student with poor grades and few intellectual interests.[3] The high-credibility source proved to be the more persuasive, and strong support for an

---

terargument production, the source's arguments may be given more weight when they are believed to come from a high-credibility source than from a low-credibility source. Such a result would enhance the difference in persuasiveness due to differences in counterarguing to high- and low-credibility sources when recipient commitment is low but would reduce the difference in persuasiveness when commitment is high. An effect of this type might be part of the explanation for the observation that differences in the persuasiveness of high- and low-credibility sources, shown so reliably in the laboratory, are often not found in nonlaboratory research (Hovland, 1959). Unfamiliar issues—topics on which recipient attitudes are neutral and their commitment is low—are typically used in laboratory experiments. In contrast, nonlaboratory research frequently investigates topics on which recipients are strongly committed and have firm convictions.

In addition, when commitment is low, cognitive examination of new information is probably a dominant psychological concern. When commitment is high, cognitive resistance through counterarguing is only one of many powerful psychological forces that may affect persuasion, making the translation from counterarguing to persuasion even more difficult. Examples of other forces that might operate when recipient commitment is high include ego involvement (Ostrom & Brock, 1968) and motivational forces such as cognitive dissonance (Gerard, 1968) and psychological reactance (Brehm, 1966).

Despite these complications, counterargument production in response to a persuasive message is significant in its own right. It is part of the psychological mechanism of processing incoming information and is intimately, but not simply, related to attitudes and persuasion (Weiss, 1968).

[3]The topic of brushing our teeth is an example of what McGuire (1964) has called *cultural truisms*—beliefs pervasively held by persons in our society without their questioning the possibility that a contrary position might exist. Recall from Chapter 1 that such beliefs are quite vulnerable to persuasion because people have few readily available counterarguments to support them. So, although most people are committed to brushing their teeth, for example, that commitment apparently confers resistance only to the extent that the individual recognizes that the issue is controversial at the time of the committing behavior.

inverse relationship between source credibility and counterarguing was indicated by a significantly higher number of counterarguments written when the message was attributed to the less competent source. Comparison of these results with a control condition in which no information on the source was given indicated that high source credibility caused decreased recipient counterarguing, whereas low credibility did not increase it. The finding offers further confirmation that when open to persuasion, we tend to "trust the experience of experts" (experto crede).

A series of seven experiments by Gillig and Greenwald (1974) also provides impressive support for the *experto crede* phenomenon. As in the previously cited experiments, subjects produced more counterarguments in response to a low-credibility source than to a high-credibility source. In addition, however, Gillig and Greenwald found that providing subjects with counterarguments beforehand increased their use of counterarguments only when the source was low in credibility. Providing subjects with arguments that opposed the source's position did not increase counterarguing when the source was highly credible. The authors concluded that "the effectiveness of a communication from a high credibility source may in part be due to suppression of counter-arguments of which the audience is aware [p. 137]."

Some evidence for the predicted relationship between source credibility and counterargument production when the recipient is strongly committed to his or her point of view comes from an experiment reported by Brock (1967). The topic of the message used in the experiment was a proposed tuition increase at the subjects' university—a position strongly opposed by the students. Any opinion change in the direction of accepting higher tuition would involve powerful negative outcomes for the students in the form of monetary expenditure and social sanction. Brock found that the message recipients generated more counterarguments to the source they perceived to be more qualified ("Faculty Council of the Academic Affairs Committee") than to the source they perceived as less qualified ("a graduate seminar in journalism"). The difference was significant only when the message advocated a large tuition increase, but that is precisely where the effects of committed opposition and resistance should be strongest. Unfortunately for our current purpose (Brock's interests were different from those being discussed here), the more credible source was presented as having greater persuasive intent than the less credible source, making an unambiguous interpretation of the effects of source credibility difficult.

Of course, the most convincing evidence for the reversal of the relationship between source credibility and counterargument production depending on the level of recipient commitment would come from directly manipulating both credibility and commitment, as was done in an experiment conducted by Hass (1972). Within the bogus context of preparing materials for use in future research, each subject tape-recorded a statement congruent with his or her own opinion on the issue of the relative time professors should spend on teaching and research. Subjects either recorded their names on the tape and signed releases allowing use of their identities with the statement of opinion (high commitment), or they made the same recordings anonymously and were assured their identities would not be divulged (low commitment). Following commitment, subjects were led to anticipate hearing a message advocating a position opposed to their own on the topic of professors' apportionment of time. The impending message was attributed either to a qualified source who had studied the issue for several years or to a group of high school students with no special knowledge of the issue. While awaiting exposure to the message, subjects wrote their "thoughts and ideas" on the topic.

The results supported the proposed model of counterarguing (see Fig. 7.4). When commitment was low, more counterarguments were generated in anticipation of the less qualified source, confirming the examination or experto crede

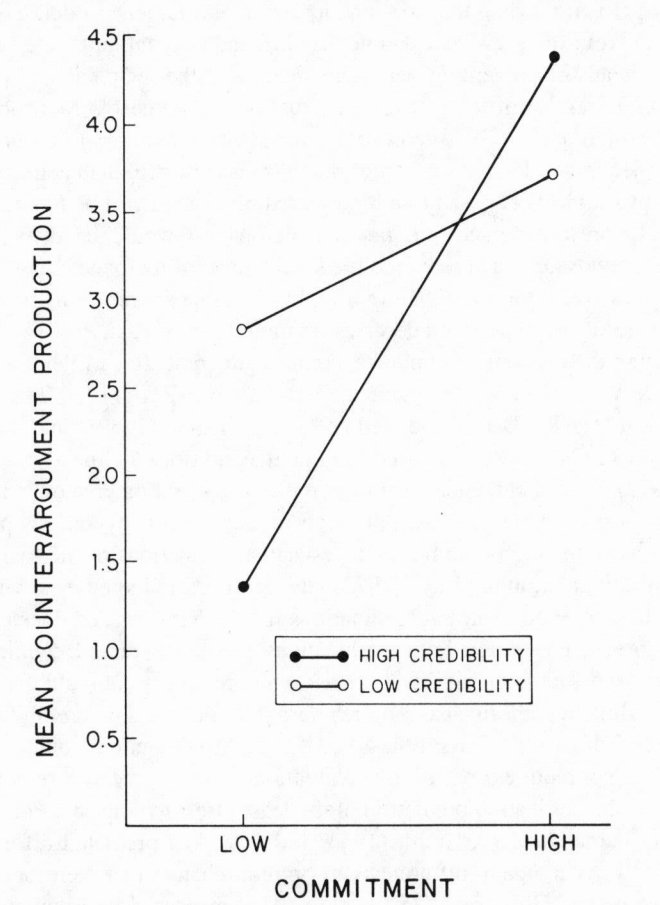

FIG 7.4 Counterargument production as a function of source credibility and recipient commitment (Hass, 1972).

prediction. High commitment increased counterarguing for both the expert and inexpert sources, as predicted. Although production of counterarguments to the expert source was not significantly greater than to the unqualified source when the recipients were highly committed to their position, a significant interaction between source credibility and recipient commitment supported the hypothesized two-function model of counterarguing activity. Furthermore, combining the results of the several experiments reviewed offers encouraging support for resistance and examination as precipitating factors in counterargument production.

Least-Effort Hypothesis

Another hypothesis generated by a different set of assumptions makes quite different predictions than the two-function counterargument model. The predictions stem from the view that counterarguing and derogation of the source are alternate means of preventing persuasion, and that the recipient will engage in whichever is less effortful in a given situation (Festinger & Maccoby, 1964; Kiesler & Mathog, 1968). Accordingly, for subjects exposed to an unqualified source, rejection or derogation of the source is less effortful than counterarguing. Conversely, subjects exposed to a highly credible source will be forced to counterargue to prevent persuasion, because derogation would be difficult. Consequently, exposure to a barely credible source, according to the hypothesis, will result in less counterarguing than to a highly credible source. This prediction is the opposite of the experto crede or examination hypothesis.

Although the least-effort hypothesis retains adherents (cf. Miller, Maruyama, Beaber, & Valone, 1976), the evidence for it seems weak at best. The results of the experiments by Baron and Miller (1969), Cook (1969), and Gillig and Greenwald (1974) and the low-commitment conditions of the experiment by Hass (1972) contradict the least-effort hypothesis by finding greater counterarguing to the less credible sources. Although the least-effort hypothesis prediction coincides with the high-commitment, resistance predictions of the two-function model of counterarguing (Hass, 1972), the least-effort hypothesis will require greater elaboration to identify the situations in which it does and does not apply. Furthermore, even though both explanations predict increased counterarguing with increased source credibility (at least when recipient commitment is high), the least-effort hypothesis also requires derogation of the low-credibility source (Aronson, Turner, & Carlsmith, 1963). The two-function counterargument model does not require a negative reevaluation of the source. There is also little support for the derogation prediction of the least-effort hypothesis. For example, Aronson, Turner, and Carlsmith (1963) failed to find predicted differences in derogation to accompany differences in opinion change that were obtained. In their experiment, Gillig and Greenwald (1974) measured both counterarguing and discounting responses. Discounting responses were defined as "rejection of an argument on the basis of context rather than content, such as when the argument is attributed to a distrusted-source [p. 133]." In direct opposition to the least-effort hypothesis, Gillig and Greenwald found that *both* counterarguing *and* discounting increased when the source was low in credibility.

Before- and After-Message Description of the Source

When recipient commitment is not high, presenting the communicator as highly credible reduces counterarguing and increases persuasion (experto crede), whereas attributing low credibility to the source increases counterarguing and reduces attitude change. If one assumes that the ability of counterarguments to reduce persuasion is greatest when they are aroused prior to or in conjunction with presentation of the message (i.e., retroactive effects of counterarguing are weak), then several interesting predictions follow with regard to the time of notification of source characteristics. Taking no knowledge of communicator characteristics as a baseline, a highly credible source inhibits counterarguing when recipient commitment is low; therefore, greater persuasion should follow description of the source *before* the message rather than after. On the other hand, an unqualified source stimulates counterarguing and should be more persuasive when that source's lack of qualifications is not revealed until *after* the communication rather than before.

Several experiments have demonstrated these phenomena. Greenberg and Tannenbaum (1961) found that early identification of a positive source produced greater acceptance of the advocated position than late mention or no mention at all. Mills and Harvey (1972) also found that agreement with an expert source was higher when the information about the source preceded the message than when the information followed the message. But they found, in addition, that persuasion by an attractive source was not affected by the "before" or "after" placement of the description of the source. Since attitude change through identification with an attractive source is irrelevant to the information content of the message, it mattered little whether the source was described before or after the communication.

By contrast, an unqualified source stimulates counterarguing (assuming low commitment) and should be more persuasive when his or her lack of qualifications is not revealed until *after* the communication rather than before it. Support for this hypothesis was found in two experiments by Greenberg and Miller (1966). In a third experiment they tested both high- and low-credibility sources identified either before or after the communication. A significant interaction between source credibility and time of identification on final opinions offered further support for the hypotheses.

Effects of Counterpersuasion

If the increased persuasion produced by a highly competent source results from a decrease in examination of the evidence prior to accepting it, an interesting prediction may follow. An attitude that is held without having been critically examined may be quite vulnerable to counterpersuasion, as McGuire (1964) found in the case of what he called *cultural truisms*. Perhaps a similar effect might be found depending on the source of the communication that originally established the attitude. That is, even though a high-credibility source may elicit almost complete acceptance of the position advocated when one is open to persuasion, an individual may then be quite vulnerable to a counterpersuasive attempt. Being unchallenged before acceptance, the new attitude may be as difficult to defend as were the truisms (see McGuire, 1964).

The effect of a second counterpersuasive appeal following an initial message attributed to communicators varying in credibility was explored in an experiment conducted by Hilibrand and reported by Bauer (1965). The first message was attributed to communicators who varied in competence on the topic and trustworthiness. As expected, the high-competence–high-trust source produced the greatest acceptance of the position advocated in the first message. But when the countercommunication was presented 2½ weeks later, these subjects proved so vulnerable to counterpersuasion that they came to have the least favorable attitude on the topic. Not only was their initial advantage lost, but as a group they were surpassed by subjects in all other experimental conditions in capacity to resist counterpersuasion. Presumably, the lack of expertise or objectivity on the part of the other sources of the first communication stimulated the subjects to examine critically the content of the initial message and to appreciate more fully its strengths and weaknesses. That examination then served to inoculate them against later counterpersuasions.

Interaction of Source Characteristics and Message Structure

A cognitive, information-processing approach has also been successful in accounting for some effects of message structure on persuasion (Hass, in press). Combining the results of research on source characteristics and research on message structure leads to some interesting predictions concerning the relative persuasive effectiveness of different message structures for different sources.

Research on message structure has shown that a message is likely to be more persuasive if it can be structured to disarm a recipient's counterarguments early in the message and to avoid suggesting new counterarguments to the recipient until late in the message or not at all. For example, Hass and Linder (1972) found that when a source implicitly refuted counterarguments at the beginning of a message (acknowledged the existence of counterarguments but claimed without elaboration that they were outweighed by arguments on the other side), more persuasion occurred for subjects who were aware of counterarguments than when the implicit refutation came at the end of the message. Overcoming their cognitive defenses early in the message produced more persuasion than leaving those defenses intact until the end of the message. The source used in this experiment was probably regarded by the subjects as highly qualified on the topic.

If, as we have seen, people who are open to persuasion accept what an expert says with less critical examination than a message from a low-credibility source, then an implicit refutation might be a more successful persuasive device, the greater the credibility of the source. Whereas an implicit refutation by an expert might be given persuasive weight by a message recipient, an implicit refutation from a low-credibility source is more likely to be doubted or challenged, making it less effective at overcoming counterargument defenses. In fact, the low-credibility source might even reduce his or her persuasiveness by unconvincingly discrediting the counterarguments. The implicit refutation from a low-credibility source might reduce the persuasiveness of the message by reminding the recipient of forgotten counterarguments (without overcoming them) or by making known counterarguments seem stronger because the source has failed to overcome them.

These hypotheses have been tested in a recent experiment by Hass and Reichig (1977). Subjects viewed a videotape of a televised editorial reply arguing that forest fires in wilderness areas may have beneficial effects on woodlands and should be allowed to burn themselves out when they do not threaten human life or property. The message was attributed to either a professor of forestry (high credibility on the topic) or a concerned citizen who was a pharmacist (low credibility on the topic). For half of the subjects, the message began with an acknowledgment and implicit refutation of common arguments against forest fires. For the other half of the subjects, the implicit refutation was omitted. As hypothesized, the high-credibility source was more persuasive than the low-credibility source overall. In addition, the high-credibility source was *more* presuasive when he implicitly refuted counterarguments at the beginning of the message than when the implicit refutation was omitted. The low-credibility source, however, was *less* persuasive when the implicit refutation was included than when it was omitted. The observed relationship between source credibility and message structure followed the counterargument prediction.

CHAPTER SUMMARY

Some people are more persuasive than others when they deliver a communication. The qualities of the source that seem to have an important effect on attitude change include the communicator's credibility, attractiveness, and power. Highly *credible sources* are though to change attitudes through a process of *internalization*, in which a person integrates the new attitude into his or her preexisting belief and value system. *Attractive sources* change attitudes through *identification*, in which a new attitude is adopted in order to establish a gratifying role relationship with the source. Most consistency theories hold that the greater the liking for a source, the more attitude change will result. Dissonance theory, however, predicts that if a person has the perception of freely choosing to hear a discrepant communication, attitude change will increase with the recipient's dislike for the source. Congruity theory makes the specific prediction that when a source is linked to some attitude object, both the evaluation of the object and of the source will change. *Powerful sources* change attitudes through *compliance*, in which a recipient publicly adopts a source's position (because of the rewards or punishments available) without privately accepting it. The perceived similarity of the source and the recipient also affects persuasion, either by increasing the source's attractiveness or by increasing the source's credibility with regard to changing the values associated with an attitude.

Source credibility also combines with other variables to affect the persuasive impact of a message. For example, source credibility interacts with both time of attitude measurement and with the discrepancy of the communication. The first interaction indicates that although highly credible sources produce more immediate attitude change than sources of low credibility, this difference disappears after a few weeks as the change produced by the high-credibility source decays. The second interaction results from the fact that the more attitude change a source advocates, the more change is produced up to a point; after this point, change does not continue to increase and may decrease. The point of asymptote occurs at higher levels of discrepancy for higher levels of source credibility.

A cognitive response analysis of source credibility effects examines how the knowledge of a source affects the manner in which the incoming information in the communication is processed by a message recipient. A two-function cognitive response model was proposed. When an individual is uncommitted to an attitudinal position and is open to persuasion, information from a low-credibility source is cognitively examined more stringently (counterargued) than when the same message is presented by a high-credibility source. In contrast, when the recipient is committed and disinclined to yield, more counterarguing will occur in the presence of a highly credible source than a less credible source. Empirical research was found to support the model.

Over the years most attitude change research has investigated variables that are believed to *increase* persuasion. The approach has been one of "why *do* people change their attitudes?" In the case of source characteristics, following McGuire's (1969a) suggestion to turn the question around and investigate factors that inhibit acceptance of a persuasive message has led to new insights. In the long run, it may even prove more fruitful.

ACKNOWLEDGMENTS

Helpful comments on an earlier version of this chapter were made by Michael Wolff and Barbara Brooks.

8 Recipient Characteristics as Determinants of Responses to Persuasion

Alice H. Eagly
*University of Massachusetts-Amherst**

INTRODUCTION

The idea that people differ in their cognitive responses to persuasive communications has such a ring of obvious truth to it that it scarcely needs documentation. A simple proof could be obtained in many ways. One could ask a number of people for their reactions to a particular persuasive communication. Despite an identical stimulus situation established by receiving the same message from the same communicator under the same conditions, each person's response would probably be unique and would differ in at least some respect from those of all the others. For example, people no doubt would agree with the communication to differing extents, and they would react differently to the communicator. Individuals might also differ in their responses to arguments the message contains, with some analyzing and reacting to each argument and others reacting mainly to the communicator or to the communication's overall point rather than to the argumentation. Thus, both agreement with the communication and cognitive responses such as counterarguing and evaluation of the communicator might differ among individuals.

It is hardly surprising that reactions to communications are often highly variable, because individuals differ in the prior experiences they have had in relationship to topics, communicators, and social contexts in which influence is exerted. Differing experiences lay the groundwork for differing responses in the present.

Researchers who study persuasion often attempt to take into account differences in recipients' past experience by examining predispositions that they bring with them to the communication situation. Such researchers may regard

*Now at Purdue University.

message recipients as endowed with enduring characteristics (e.g., psychological traits such as intelligence, cognitive styles, and personality traits, as well as chronic social characteristics such as sex and social class). Researchers may also postulate more transient characteristics (e.g., moods, temporary states of anxiety or arousal) that predispose recipients to react in particular ways. From such a perspective, it is assumed that responses to communications can be predicted more exactly when relevant predispositions are taken into account than they can when responses are predicted exclusively from characteristics of the situation.

What characteristics of individuals should be taken into account in predicting persuasibility? That researchers face an abundance of possibilities is illustrated by the fact that a number of years ago, Donald Campbell (1963) was able to list 76 general terms that psychologists and other researchers had used to describe classes of personal dispositions, or—to use Campbell's term—types of *acquired behavioral dispositions* (e.g., frame of reference, habit, need disposition, motive, personality trait, schema, tendency). Further, persuasion researchers may decide to formulate *new* recipient characteristics to serve special purposes. Decisions concerning which characteristics to utilize in research are critical, and so are decisions concerning research designs to test hypotheses about influenceability. This chapter suggests that decisions on these matters should be informed by knowledge of a variety of theoretical and methodological issues.

To limit somewhat the domain of the chapter, its focus is on enduring rather than transient characteristics and on *persuasibility* rather than the broader concept of *influenceability*. Persuasibility signifies individual differences in the tendency to change attitudes and beliefs as a result of exposure to persuasive communications, and influenceability signifies individual differences in the tendency to change attitudes, beliefs, or behaviors in response to any of a variety of types of influence inductions that might occur, for example, in verbal conditioning, conformity, social learning, role playing, persuasion, or other contexts (cf. McGuire, 1968b). As this chapter documents, achieving the ability to make reasonably exact predictions of responses to persuasive communications from knowledge of recipient characteristics has remained an elusive goal. However, before discussing some of the reasons that personality–persuasibility relationships have often proven weak, this chapter provides examples of research illustrating three general strategies for understanding the effects of recipient predispositions. The first, or *personality strategy*, invokes a personality theory to suggest both a personality trait that may affect attitude change and a mechanism via which the trait affects persuasion. The second, or *attitude change strategy*, relies upon an attitude theory to suggest both a structural, or process, variable along which individuals differ and a mechanism by which the variable accounts for their differing reactions to inductions of influence. The third, or *personality–attitude change strategy*, attempts a combination of the prior two approaches by using personality theory as a source of suggestions concerning relevant traits but invoking attitude theory to specify the mechanisms by which such traits affect attitude change. As we shall see, the personality strategy often fails to elaborate the role of cognitive responses, whereas the latter two approaches—because they both invoke attitude theory—usually give at least some attention to the issue of how cognitive responses mediate attitude change.

THE PERSONALITY STRATEGY

The personality approach to understanding individual differences in persuasibility is associated with a number of theories of personality that feature one or more personality characteristics as their central predictive device and then employ these characteristics as recipient predispositions to account for variability in responses to persuasion. Frequently, a personality theory suggests that persons high (or low) on a featured personality trait are likely to be especially susceptible to social influence or may even specify the conditions under which a trait is likely to produce stronger or weaker effects on social influence. To be included as an exemplar of the personality strategy, such derivations are made in the context of the personality theory itself and do not involve theories of attitude change.

To illustrate the personality approach, social influence research pertaining to any of a variety of personal dispositions might be described—for example, authoritarianism (e.g., Johnson & Izzett, 1969; Johnson, Torcivia, & Poprick, 1968), intelligence (e.g., Hovland, Janis, & Kelly, 1953; Janis & Hovland, 1959), or anxiety (e.g., Janis, 1954; Millman, 1968). However, this chapter reviews research relating to two variables: *internal-external control* and *self-esteem*. These variables are especially informative because they have generated a larger body of empirical work concerning their relationships to persuasion than have most other recipient characteristics, and this empirical work illustrates particularly well many of the issues that are typically associated with persuasion research inspired by personality theory.

Internal-External Control

The idea that people differ in the extent to which they believe they control their environment has appeared in the psychological literature in several guises, but its most systematic development is in terms of a personality dimension called *internal-external control* or *locus of control*. This personality variable was formulated by Julian Rotter (1954, 1966) and was linked to his social learning theory of personality.

Rotter, reasoning in expectancy-value terms, hypothesized that the likelihood that a person will engage in a behavior is a function of (1) the person's expectancy that the behavior will secure the rewards available in the situation, and (2) the value of these rewards for him or her. The internal-external control dimension represents the first or expectancy link in Rotter's theory—the relationship between a behavior and its outcomes. Expectancies are treated as a personality trait by specifying them in a generalized way rather than for a particular situation. Thus, internal–external control represents the extent to which, across a variety of situations, an individual believes that he or she possesses personal control over rewards. Internal individuals believe that events occur as a consequence of their own actions and are under their own control, and external individuals believe that events are unrelated to their behavior and are therefore beyond their personal control.

The best known scale for measuring locus of control is the Internal–External Control Scale (Rotter, 1966). Each of 23 items presents the respondent with a forced choice between an internal and an external interpretation of an event. For example, one item presents the following alternatives: (1) Many times I feel that I have little influence over the things that happen to me; and (2) It is impossible for me to believe that chance or luck plays an important role in my life. The first alternative is considered external and the second internal. A variety of other measuring instruments are also in use (e.g., Collins, 1974; Nowicki & Strickland, 1973).

What implications does this personality trait have for predicting responses to persuasive communications? The straightforward derivation made by locus-of-control researchers (e.g., Lefcourt, 1972; Phares, 1973) builds on the idea that persuasion and other forms of social influence are generally exerted from outside the individual by an external influencing agent. Therefore, internals are likely to be more resistant to influence than externals, because they view themselves in active control of their own fates. This logic, then, predicts a positive relationship between externality and amount of change induced by influence attempts. Without more elaborate theorizing, there is little allowance for possible interactions with features of the situation except for the idea that the locus-of-control effect should reverse direction (i.e., internal persons would be relatively more influenced) if people perceive influence as emanating from themselves rather than from an external source. Indeed, such a reversal has been reported when subjects generated their own communications taking counterattitudinal positions (Sherman, 1973). It should be noted that no specification is provided of cognitive mediation of opinion change except for the idea that the correspondence between the locus of the influence induction (i.e., external or internal to the recipient of influence) and the recipient's beliefs about control determine acceptance of the message.

Given these ideas, persuasion studies would be expected to show that externally controlled individuals change more toward messages than do internally controlled individuals. Despite some support for this proposition, studies have proven far from consistent (cf. Chaiken, 1975). Some studies have demonstrated that externals were more persuaded than internals (e.g., Biondo & MacDonald, 1971; Hjelle & Clouser, 1970; Snyder & Larson, 1972), but another has reported the reverse relationship (e.g., James, Woodruff, & Werner, 1965).[1] Still other studies failed to obtain overall differences in persuasibility between externals and internals (e.g., Dembroski, 1969; Hamid & Flay, 1974; Sherman, 1973). Two such studies, however, found locus-of-control effects contingent on communicator credibility: (1) Ritchie and Phares (1969) reported that externally controlled subjects were more influenced by a high- than a low-prestige communicator but that prestige had no impact on internals; (2) McGinnies and Ward (1974) reported a significant interaction between source credibility and locus of control only in one country (Australia) in their five-country cross-national study, but with internals—not externals—more persuaded by a high- than by a low-credibility communicator.

In general, then, the hypothesis of greater persuasibility among external persons has received some support but among a minority of studies. The prediction that communicator characteristics should interact with internal–external control also failed to receive consistent support. Finally, it might be noted that findings concerning the effect of internal–external control on conformity, another type of social influence behavior, are also somewhat inconsistent (cf. Crowne & Liverant, 1963; Ryckman, Rodda, & Sherman, 1972).

Self-Esteem

Self-esteem, a personality trait important in several theories of personality and of social behavior, is generally considered to be one aspect of an individual's concept of self. This aspect is the individual's evaluation of him- or herself. People have high self-esteem to the extent that they evaluate themselves positively and low self-esteem to the extent that they evaluate themselves negatively.

Among theories of self-esteem and the self-concept, an early tradition (e.g., Cooley, 1902; Mead, 1934) emphasized that the self-concept evolves from observing the ways that others behave toward us. From this perspective, the self develops by a reflected appraisal process whereby we learn what other people believe about us and take over their views. Festinger (1954) and other social scientists emphasized another social aspect of the self by arguing that the standards by which we view ourselves are relative in the sense that people evaluate themselves in comparison to other people. Other theorists, such as Carl Rogers (1951, 1959), have claimed that a favorable self-concept is a necessary condition for positive mental health and have assumed that a motive to seek positive self-evaluations from others is central to human behavior. Many other psycholo-

---

[1]However, James, Woodruff, and Werner (1965) predicted that internal individuals would change their smoking behavior more than external individuals, presumably because changes in habitual behavior may require the active control of one's own life rather than mere compliance with an external influencing agent.

gists agree that people are usually motivated to view themselves positively (e.g., Cohen, 1959; Epstein, 1973; Festinger, 1954; Pepitone, 1964).

Given that these and many other theorists have featured self-esteem as a central concept, it is not surprising that numerous measuring instruments have been designed to assess the trait (cf. Crandall, 1973). Most such instruments inquire about respondents' evaluative beliefs concerning themselves. For example, a measure commonly used in persuasion studies is Janis and Field's (1959) Feelings of Inadequacy Scale, which contains 23 items such as the following: "How often do you feel inferior to most of the people you know? How often do you have the feeling that there is *nothing* you can do well [p. 300]?"

The most commonly encountered derivation concerning the relationship between self-esteem and influenceability (e.g., Hovland et al., 1953) is that high-self-esteem persons are more resistant to social influence than their low-self-esteem counterparts. The usual reasons cited for this difference are that high-self-esteem individuals know others think well of them, and they view themselves favorably when relative comparisons are made. Their resulting confidence encourages them to trust their own judgment and to rely less on others' views. In contrast, low-self-esteem people are less confident, and as suggested by Hovland et al. (1953), they may be especially sensitive to immediate threats of social disapproval. Such a derivation provides little, if any, specification of the cognitive mediation of opinion change but, instead, assumes that message recipients' beliefs about themselves establish a generalized readiness to be receptive or resistant to influence inductions.

Empirical relationships between self-esteem and susceptibility to influence show considerable variability. High-self-esteem persons have proven to be less influenced than low-self-esteem persons in many persuasion studies (Cohen, 1959; Janis, 1954, 1955; Janis & Field, 1959; Janis & Rife, 1959; Linton & Graham, 1959) as well as in conformity studies (Crutchfield, 1955; Lesser & Abelson, 1959). However, nonmonotonic relationships in the form of an inverted U are also quite common. Such relationships were found in one or more experimental conditions of several persuasion studies (Cox & Bauer, 1964; Nisbett & Gordon, 1967; Silverman, Ford, & Morganti, 1966) and conformity studies (Eagly, 1969; Gergen & Bauer, 1967). Positive relationships (e.g., Ziller, 1973) are less common. Even a nonmonotonic U-shaped relationship was reported in one conformity study (Silverman, 1964) utilizing an unusual subject population (male Veterans Administration domiciliary residents).

The effect of self-esteem on persuasibility has been reported to be dependent on the favorability of the position advocated. Several studies (Eagly, 1967; Eagly & Whitehead, 1972; Leventhal & Perloe, 1962; Stroebe, Eagly, & Stroebe, 1977) reported that high- compared to low-self-esteem individuals are more likely to be receptive to information with favorable implications for themselves and that low- (vs. high-) self-esteem individuals are more likely to be receptive to information with unfavorable implications. Although such findings may be troublesome in relation to many theorists' suggestions that people generally strive for a positive self-concept, they are in line with Cohen's (1959) psychoanalytic theorizing. Cohen argued that high-self-esteem persons use avoidance defense mechanisms, such as reaction formation, which are thought to block the expression of unacceptable impulses and thereby preserve an insulated but positive self-concept; whereas low-self-esteem persons use expressive defenses, such as projection, which are thought to permit unacceptable impulses to be acted out and may thereby make persons vulnerable to the influence of situations and events.

Comments on Personality Strategy

There are two respects in which the research on locus of control and on self-esteem illustrates important characteristics of persuasibility research utilizing classic personality variables as predictors. The first respect pertains to the manner in which persuasibility hypotheses are derived: The derivations stem from personality theory and have little to do with other forms of theory that have developed concerning how attitudes and beliefs change. For locus of control, for example, the internal–external idea is metaphorically extended to the domain of social influence in such a way that most forms of influence are regarded as "external" in origin. For self-esteem, ideas about perceived competence and resulting self-confidence are translated into hypotheses about susceptibility to influence. Because knowledge that has evolved among attitude theorists concerning the cognitive antecedents of opinion change is not considered, the personality strategy is likely to be a limited approach to the extent that accurate prediction of opinion change requires detailed understanding of cognitive mediation.

A second respect in which these two research areas typify persuasibility research based on personality theories is in the inconsistencies shown in empirical findings. Substantiating this point further is the fact that other reviews of influenceability research utilizing classic personality and ability variables have reported similar patterns of inconsistency. For example, McGuire's (1968b) review of studies on the impact of anxiety and of intelligence on influenceability yielded a comparable mix of findings. Steiner's (1966) survey of the effect of personality variables on conformity behavior also noted the high frequency of inconsistent findings. Even if it is acknowledged that it is difficult to set standards concerning the level of consistency necessary to consider findings established, it seems fair to conclude that personality variables have seldom shown unitary relationships to social-influence dependent variables and that few findings can be considered well established. In fact, given "first-order" hypotheses that concern the effects of classic personality variables on persuasion but ignore situational variability, the success rate usually appears to be relatively low. Given the presumed tendency of journals to publish studies that obtain significant findings (Greenwald, 1975), the published literature may overestimate the true success rate.

Another front for research of this genre is the formulation of "second-order" hypotheses predicting interactions between personality variables and situational characteristics. The formulation of these more detailed hypotheses generally marks more elaborate theorizing, as illustrated for locus of control by Ritchie and Phares' (1969) ideas concerning communicator characteristics. Although this interactionist approach seems to provide no guarantee of more consistent findings, it is worthy of further consideration and is discussed later.

THE ATTITUDE CHANGE STRATEGY

The second, or *attitude change strategy,* involves developing attitude change theories' implications for individual differences. Several attitude theories feature one or more key structural or process variables that are held to mediate responses to persuasive communications. It is sometimes possible to view people as varying in terms of such a structure or process and therefore having differing reactions to inductions of influence. Classic personality variables, formulated in terms of personality theory, are *not* considered by this approach. Rather, recipient characteristics are formulated directly in the terms given by an attitude theory. Pure types of this strategy are few, but perhaps the best example is associated with Sherif's (M. Sherif & Hovland, 1961; C. W. Sherif, M. Sherif, & Nebergall, 1965) social judgment theory.

Social Judgment Theory

Sherif's social judgment theory assumes that the structure of attitudes is an important determinant of change toward persuasive communications. Structure is specified in terms of a latitude of acceptance (the range of positions that an individual accepts) and a latitude of rejection (the range of positions rejected) and, in later formulations (e.g., Sherif et al., 1965), a latitude of noncommitment (the range of positions to which an individual is indifferent). According to the theory, if a message is judged to be within the latitude of acceptance, attitude change toward the message occurs; whereas if a message is judged to be within the latitude of rejection, little or no change takes place, or attitude change away from the advocated position may occur. Research has shown that attitude change is maximal for messages judged to be within the latitude of acceptance (Atkins, Deaux, & Bieri, 1967) or located at the beginning of the latitude of rejection (Peterson & Koulack, 1969).

If the theory is scanned for implications concerning recipient predispositions, the most striking derivation is that persons who differ in the widths of latitudes of acceptance and rejection on a particular issue should differ in attitude change. Thus, persons with a relatively wide latitude of acceptance and a narrow latitude of rejection are more likely to change toward a message than persons with a narrow latitude of acceptance and a wide latitude of rejection.

Experimental evidence related to this derivation was provided by Miller and Devine (reported in Kiesler, Collins, & Miller, 1969), who found that the subjects with typically broad latitudes of rejection (averaged across 30 attitudes) resisted persuasion more strongly than did subjects with typically narrow latitudes of rejection. In addition, Zimbardo (1960) reported that subjects who changed their opinions toward a friend's position had initially accepted a wider range of statements on the issue and had rejected a narrower range than had subjects who did not change toward the friend's position. Although this finding supports social judgment predictions, the messages presented to wide-latitude-of-acceptance subjects may have been more discrepant from subjects' initial positions than the messages presented to narrow-latitude-of-acceptance subjects, because the messages were "tailored" to fall within each subject's latitude of acceptance in one condition and latitude of rejection in another condition.

To provide a more detailed test of social judgment theory's implications for individual differences in attitude change, Eagly and Telaak (1972) took into account both latitude width and message discrepancy (the distance between a subject's initial position and the position advocated in the message). Messages were located so that the mildly discrepant messages fell in the latitude of acceptance for all subjects, and the strongly discrepant messages fell in the latitude of rejection for almost all subjects. Only the moderately discrepant messages had a variable location in relationship to the latitudes (in the latitude of rejection for narrow-latitude subjects and in the latitude of acceptance for increasing proportions of medium- and wide-latitude subjects). Thus, social judgment theory predicts that individuals will differ in attitude change as a product of latitude width primarily for the moderately discrepant messages, because they were located in differing latitudes depending on latitude width. Little difference in attitude change should occur with the mildly or strongly discrepant messages, because they fell almost exclusively in latitudes of acceptance or rejection, respectively, for all subjects regardless of latitude width.

Eagly and Telaak (1972) found that for all three levels of discrepancy, subjects with wide latitudes of acceptance showed greater attitude change than did subjects with either narrow or medium latitudes of acceptance, but the effect of latitude width was not contingent on the discrepancy of the message. Thus, latitude-of-acceptance width determined persuasibility, but the pattern of findings was not consistent in a detailed way with social judgment theory predictions concerning the interaction of latitude width and discrepancy size. This and other findings of the study led Eagly and Telaak to conclude that latitude-of-acceptance width is an issue-specific index of influenceability, not for the reasons specified in social judgment theory, but perhaps because it taps subjects' certainty and confidence concerning their initial attitude positions. Thus, wide latitudes may be associated with low certainty and confidence, and narrow latitudes may be associated with high certainty and confidence.

Comments on Attitude Change Strategy

Individual-differences research following from a particular attitude change theory is likely to be no more successful than the theory on which it is based, because its hypotheses are derived directly from the theory. Even though research on social judgment theory has yielded only mixed support, further tests are needed. Social judgment predictions have been challenged on other grounds, however (cf. Himmelfarb & Eagly, 1974), and it may be that weak empirical support in the individual-differences area reflects limitations of the theory.

The advantage of the attitude theory approach to understanding persuasibility is that it often provides a relatively detailed model of the psychological processes by which attitudes and beliefs are changed. Although a particular theory may specify these processes in a narrow way, it is likely that at least in the long run, predictions will be improved by a detailed specification of underlying cognitive and motivational processes. In contrast, the personality theory approach generally proceeds on the basis of molar ideas concerning how social influence takes place and ignores the underlying microprocess of cognitive and other responses to persuasion.

A disadvantage of the attitude change approach, however, is that it leaves unanswered many questions about how classic personality variables such as self-esteem affect persuasion. Much of the interest in persuasibility research has traditionally been focused on such variables, not on new variables that might be derived from attitude theories. Research fitting the attitude change strategy can be expanded to incorporate personality traits, however. To do so, it is necessary to specify in detail how such traits relate to the intervening states specified by the attitude theory. Approaches attempting this transition are discussed in the next section.

THE PERSONALITY–ATTITUDE CHANGE STRATEGY

A third, hybrid strategy has been the source of the more recent theoretical advances in persuasibility research. The approach proceeds by grafting a personality variable formulated in terms of personality theory onto a theory of attitude change. In the personality approach, ideas about how the trait affects social influence are given in the personality theory itself, but this third, hybrid approach uses personality theory as a source of ideas about traits and not as a source of ideas about how attitude change takes place. The trait's implications for social influence are worked out through an attitude theory's specification of how attitudes and beliefs are changed, and the trait is assumed to affect persuasion through its impact on the mediating processes specified by the theory. Approaches in this tradition hold promise of dealing with a wide array of personality variables and linking them with theoretical propositions developed by attitude change theorists. The most thoroughly developed example of a research framework proceeding along these lines is the information-processing model of influenceability developed by McGuire (1968b, 1969a).

Information-Processing Model of Influenceability

McGuire's approach builds on Hovland, Janis, and Kelley's (1953) suggestion that persuasion can be studied in terms of a set of sequential processes. Hovland et al. argued that independent variables influencing attitude change may act not only on tendencies to accept messages but also on prior processes such as attention to the message and comprehension of its content. To examine these prior message-reception processes empirically, they often included in their experiments measures assessing recipients' learning of the content of messages (e.g., Hovland & Weiss, 1951).

The role of attention and comprehension has been more extensively developed by McGuire in his "information-processing" theory, formulated in the 1960s. Recall from Chapter 5 that McGuire suggested that persuasive impact is a product of five sequential steps: (1) attention, (2) comprehension, (3) yielding, (4) retention, and (5) action. However, only the first three steps need be considered in relationship to the typical persuasion study, which assesses change immediately after the message. Also, the first two steps are generally combined into a single step of reception because of the empirical difficulty of separating attention and comprehension within a persuasion study. In most applications, then, the approach specifies two intervening processes—reception and yielding—that mediate the effect of independent variables on message persuasiveness.

McGuire pointed out that personality–persuasibility hypotheses usually fail to take into account cognitive mediating processes prior to yielding, and thus fail to consider that personality variables might relate to the capacity to receive information as well as to the likelihood that recipients yield to what they receive. This point might be noted in relationship to the locus-of-control and self-esteem research reviewed earlier in this chapter. The logic of hypotheses concerning these two variables derived from general ideas about accepting influence and not from any consideration of information processing.

McGuire also argued that most individual-difference variables, such as self-esteem and intelligence, relate positively to reception (i.e., persons higher in self-esteem and intelligence are better able to receive information) and negatively to yielding (i.e., persons low in self-esteem and intelligence are less likely to counterargue and thus are more likely to yield to the communicator's view).

Because reception of message content generally enhances acceptance of persuasive messages (Eagly, 1974), these opposing reception and yielding effects would, he noted, often result in an overall nonmonotonic relationship, with individuals with moderate positions on personality variables most likely to be influenced.

The information-processing model has additional power to account for persuasibility because of the assumption that the relative importance of the reception and yielding mediators of personality variables changes with the nature of the situation. Thus, self-esteem, for example, might in general have its impact on persuasibility through both reception and yielding and therefore would most often be nonmonotonically related to persuasibility in the form of an inverted U. Yet in some situations (e.g., complex, well-argued message), the impact of self-esteem would be primarily a function of its effect on reception, and in other situations (e.g., simple, less well-argued message), its impact on yielding would be of most importance (cf. Nisbett & Gordon, 1967). Given that high-self-esteem individuals comprehend better but yield less readily than their low-self-esteem counterparts, a positive linear relationship between self-esteem and persuasibility might be obtained with complex, well-argued messages, but a negative linear relationship with simpler, less well argued messages. McGuire (1968b) proposed that such personality–situation interactions account for the inconsistencies observed in the self-esteem–persuasibility relationship.

Empirically, the theory has fared only moderately well in the several tests that have been conducted (Eagly & Warren, 1976; Johnson & Izzett, 1969; Johnson & Stanicek, 1969; Johnson, Torcivia, & Poprick, 1968; Lehman, 1970; Millman, 1968; Nisbett & Gordon, 1967; Zellner, 1970). These studies concerned anxiety, authoritarianism, intelligence, and self-esteem, and their findings are difficult to survey briefly. The studies involved a variety of situational manipulations, and several included experimental manipulations of traits as well as assessment of their chronic levels.[2] In each study, some predictions were confirmed and others not, and most positive findings were relatively weak in magnitude.

A key issue in these experiments is obtaining confirmation of the mediating role of comprehension. However, little direct evidence of the success of comprehension (or reception) mediation of personality–persuasibility relationships was in fact obtained. Only four studies assessed comprehension (Eagly & Warren, 1976; Johnson et al., 1968; Millman, 1968; Zellner, 1970). Only the

---

[2]Experimental manipulations of traits attempt to establish situations that elicit psychological states that are chronic in persons having a high (vs. low) level of particular traits. For example, to manipulate self-esteem, a researcher might provide subjects in a high-self-esteem experimental group with favorable feedback on their personalities by telling them that they are mature, creative, and highly intelligent. Subjects in the low-self-esteem group might be told that they are immature, lack creativity, and are unintelligent. (Thorough debriefing is, of course, a necessity after such a procedure.)

Johnson et al. and the Eagly and Warren studies found positive relationships between chronic levels of personality traits and comprehension, and only the latter finding is free from the criticism that the relationship may have been a product of premessage informational differences between persons high and low on the trait. Despite this and other reservations about empirical support the model has generated, it has enormous heuristic value in suggesting how frameworks might be generated that link classic personality variables to attitude theory in a relatively systematic fashion.

Parallel Response Model of Reactions to Fear-Arousing Communications

Another approach that links individual-difference variables to attitude change theory is Leventhal's (1970) parallel response model of reactions to fear-arousing communications. Ever since interest in fear appeals was sparked by the now-classic Janis and Feshbach (1953) experiment on responses to a fear-arousing dental hygiene communication, social psychologists have conducted numerous experiments addressed to understanding how fear-producing argumentation can function to enhance the effectiveness of persuasive messages. As Higbee's (1969) useful review of this research indicates, most experimentation in this area has followed the theoretical lead of Janis and Feshbach by assuming that fear motivates attitude change. This approach, based on learning theory assumptions, is commonly known as the *fear-as-a-drive* or *fear-drive* model. It pertains to situations in which a communication's description of threatening events arouses recipients' fears, but the fear-producing stimuli are followed by reassuring recommendations instructing recipients on how to cope with the dangers that were described. Mental rehearsal of the reassuring recommendations is assumed to reduce the fear and thereby reinforce belief in the recommendations. The fear-drive model predicts that ordinarily higher rather than lower degrees of fear are more effective in inducing persuasion because of the greater magnitude of reinforcement from reducing the higher level of fear. However, the approach recognizes that in some situations, the recommendations a message contains may not be sufficiently reassuring to have much impact on the fear that has been aroused. Then recipients may reduce fear by denying or ignoring the danger—a response that would be accompanied by resistance to, rather than acceptance of, the communicator's recommendations.

Although this fear-drive approach to persuasion has guided the design of numerous experiments (cf. Janis, 1967), many of the more detailed predictions following from the model have not been confirmed (cf. Leventhal, 1970). In an effort to achieve better prediction, Leventhal proposed an alternate *parallel response model* of response to fear communications. It suggests that fear communications produce two parallel and relatively independent reactions: *fear control* and *danger control*. Thus, the message recipient is motivated to control and reduce his or her fear reaction as well as to cope with the danger described in the message. Accepting the message's recommendations is ordinarily considered part of the danger-coping response. The emotional reaction (fear) is not a causal antecedent of coping with the danger, as suggested by the fear-drive model. Rather, the two responses are regarded as parallel and contemporaneous. Under some circumstances, however, there may be some relationship between fear control and danger control. According to Leventhal, especially with serious threats that elicit strong emotional responses and strong coping reactions, one response may interfere with the other. For example, a very strong, immediate emotional reaction to a message may delay or interfere with coping reactions, and strong coping behavior may delay or interfere with emotional response.

One important area where the parallel response model is in competition with the fear-drive model is individual differences in response. Leventhal argued that individuals differ in their ability to cope with stress and that people who have difficulty coping with a particular problem are likely to experience a strong emotional reaction; and especially immediately after a relevant communication, they would be likely to engage in fear-control responses to such an extent that danger-control responses (and, hence, acceptance of the communication) would be inhibited.

Personality traits that might affect coping behavior include *self-esteem* (with low-self-esteem persons generally more vulnerable and less able to cope with dangers) and a specific personality variable—*copers* versus *avoiders,* which assesses individuals' ability to relate to (vs. to deny) their own emotional reactions. In a study classifying subjects as copers or avoiders (Goldstein, 1959), avoiders but not copers were less accepting of recommendations when given in a high-fear compared to a low-fear message. Similarly, several studies have shown that high- but not low-self-esteem recipients are more likely to accept recommendations of high-fear compared to low-fear messages (e.g., Dabbs & Leventhal, 1966; Leventhal & Trembly, 1968). Other experiments have involved classifications of recipients according to their vulnerability to diseases such as lung cancer (Leventhal & Watts, 1966) as well as vulnerability to automobile accidents (Berkowitz & Cottingham, 1960). These studies showed that vulnerable people (e.g., smokers for antismoking communications; regular drivers for seat-belt-use communications) were relatively less likely to be influenced by higher fear communications than were less vulnerable persons (e.g., nonsmokers, nondrivers). These findings are, then, consistent with the parallel response approach.

Although this approach is not as formal as the McGuire information-processing model, and hypotheses seem more difficult to derive unambiguously from the framework's theoretical propositions, the approach holds promise for understanding how emotional reactions link to acceptance of persuasive communications and how individual differences in such reactions affect persuasion. So far, however, empirical support for the approach largely relies on the classification of past research in terms of the model and not on a priori tests of its adequacy.

Comments on Personality–Attitude Change Strategy

The information-processing and the parallel response frameworks illustrate psychologists' growing sophistication concerning how personality variables may be linked with attitude change theories. Other attitude theories could possibly be developed along these lines. For example, dissonance theory has received some attention in terms of linkages to classic personality variables (cf. reviews by Glass, 1968; Wicklund & Brehm, 1976). Katz's (e.g., 1960) functional theory ideas have received some exploration in an individual-differences framework, particularly in regard to the ego-defensive function that Katz presumed attitudes may serve (e.g., Katz, McClintock, & Sarnoff, 1957). In addition, Kelman's (e.g., 1961) processes of opinion change described in the last chapter (internalization, identification, and compliance) could provide a useful approach to studying persuasibility if individuals were regarded as engaging in the processes to varying extents. Then personality variables could be used to assess proclivities to favor one process or the other, and a number of predictions would follow. Despite some forays in this area (e.g., Kelman & Cohler, 1959), Kelman's model has not been extended very far in this direction.

The approaches reviewed in this section suggest that it is not sufficient to assume that traits affect susceptibility to social influence without considering the nature of individuals' responses to social influence. Attitude change is ordinarily not usefully conceptualized as a unitary response but is best approached more precisely through an understanding of its cognitive and motivational antecedents and consequences. If causally prior responses such as information reception are considered, or parallel and contemporaneous responses such as counterarguing or emotional reactions are postulated, the relationship of individual-difference variables to each of these components should be taken systematically into account. Predictions should thereby be more exact than they would be if only relationships to opinion change are considered. Thus, the hybrid approach to personality–persuasibility predictions holds considerable promise and seems an advance over theorizing encapsulated within personality theory traditions.

Despite the attractiveness of this general approach, there are several barriers to easy empirical successes. Success is, of course, limited by the validity of the attitude theory and personality variable being investigated. Additional difficulties may stem from many personality traits' weak impact on the intervening processes postulated by a theory. For example, some of the empirical weakness of the McGuire model might possibly be explained in terms of (1) the relatively flat slope of the function relating number of arguments comprehended to persuasion (Calder, Insko, & Yandell, 1974; Insko, Lind, & LaTour, 1976), which means that it takes a large difference in comprehension before any corresponding change in attitude is observed; and (2) the weak impact of many personality variables on the comprehension process. It follows that only personality variables having a major impact on comprehension can be expected to behave in a manner approximated by McGuire's hypotheses. In view of these considerations, intelligence (Eagly & Warren, 1976) may be the best candidate to provide support for the approach because of its strong relationship to comprehension of verbal messages.

DEALING WITH THE EMPIRICAL INCONSISTENCIES OF EXISTING PERSUASIBILITY RESEARCH

This chapter has described several types of persuasibility research and noted that all tend to be characterized by a mixed pattern of empirical successes and failures. Further, most positive findings, although significant, are of quite low magnitude in terms of variance accounted for. Although both the attitude change strategy and the personality–attitude change strategy are promising because they often take account of current knowledge concerning the nature of the psychological processes relevant to persuasion, so far even the most sophisticated of these approaches do not yield impressively strong or consistent empirical findings.

A difficulty in accounting for a large amount of variability in dependent measures is an attribute that persuasibility research shares with other personality research. The usefulness of personality traits in predicting behavior has been the focus of considerable debate in recent years. This controversy gained momentum with Walter Mischel's (1968) claim that traits have little predictive value. If it is valid to assume that behavior is organized in terms of traits, Mischel argued, then different manifestations of the same trait should cohere. For example, if honesty is a trait, then persons who are honest in one situation should be honest in another situation. Yet, as Mischel (1968) documented in relation to several traits, correlations between relevant behaviors across situations are usually quite low. In addition, personality traits inferred from questionnaire measures generally fail to predict specific behaviors with much accuracy. Mischel noted that correlations of greater than .30 between traits and presumably relevant behaviors are seldom attained.

Since much persuasibility research consists of studies in which specific social-influence dependent variables are predicted from general personality traits, Mischel's critique has considerable relevance. Yet it will be argued that the absence of strong predictability of specific behaviors by general personality dispositions should not be surprising, in view of the methodology ordinarily used in persuasibility research; nor are there insurmountable barriers to improved predictability. Three methods of improving predictability are considered: (1)

defining personality independent variables and persuasibility dependent variables at equivalent levels of generality; (2) using a large and representative sample of studies as a basis for conclusions about the effects of general traits on specific behaviors; (3) adopting an interactionist position that takes simultaneous account of personality and situational variables.

Level of Generality of Personality and of Persuasibility

In Chapter 2, it was noted that one problem that led to weak correlations between attitude measures and behavioral measures was that one measure often was more general than another. This same problem arises in assessing the influence of personality variables on persuasion. Many personality characteristics, such as self-esteem, are defined extremely generally and are presumed to affect most aspects of individuals' behavior. Yet some general traits have alternate operational definitions, differing in specificity. For example, to assess locus of control, Rotter's (1966) general scale can be used, or an instrument can be chosen that breaks up the general dimension into two or more specific dimensions (e.g., Collins, 1974). Still other variables may be defined quite narrowly so that they pertain to a circumscribed domain of objects. Examples of dispositions that relate specifically to particular issues and message content are the issue-specific latitude-width variables used in the Eagly and Telaak (1972) study and the disease vulnerability variables used in some fear-appeal studies.

Persuasibility can also be defined more generally or more specifically. When agreement with a message is assessed by a single response to a message at a single point of time, persuasibility is specifically defined, whereas averaging agreement responses over a larger sample of relevant items, situations, and occasions establishes a more general definition.

What is the relevance of generality–specificity in traits and in behaviors predicted from traits? The following propositions are suggested: Generally defined personality characteristics often predict general dependent variables with considerable success; more specifically defined traits often predict specific dependent variables with considerable success. In other words, defining independent and dependent variables at comparable levels of generality is likely to yield stronger relationships, and the mismatching of levels of generality tends to generate weak relationships.

In support of these propositions, it should be noted that a sample of relevant behaviors (taken over time or over situations) provides a much more reliable estimate of a behavioral tendency than does a single behavior. Among personality theorists, Epstein (1977, 1979) has recognized that much of the difficulty in obtaining strong relationships of behaviors to each other and of general traits to behavioral dependent variables stems from inadequate sampling of behavior. And, as noted earlier, attitude research has demonstrated that general attitudes usually predict single behaviors only weakly but are much more successful in predicting larger sets of related behaviors (Fishbein & Ajzen, 1974; Weigel & Newman, 1977).

This perspective shows how unfortunate it is that researchers have seldom followed the lead of the pioneering persuasibility research of the Yale communication and persuasion school (Hovland & Janis, 1959) by sampling the domain of agreement responses over sets of questionnaire items and stimulus materials. Given the fact that later researchers tended to use single messages and often single-response dependent variables along with general personality variables such as self-esteem, it is not surprising that personality–persuasibility relationships are often weak and frequently not replicable.

An alternate approach to increasing the magnitude of personality-persuasibility relations is to increase the specificity of the personality variables that are the object of research and maintain a relatively specific definition of the persuasibility dependent variable. There are several ways in which personality variables can be made more narrowly relevant to the dependent variables used in persuasibility research. For example, traits may be defined in such a way that they are relevant only to social situations, only to social influence situations, or perhaps only to message content of a particular type. If investigators demur because their attraction to personality variables stems from the advantages of working with broad, enduring dispositions with a wide range of potential situational relevance, they then should seriously consider choosing similarly broad behavioral criteria.

Drawing Conclusions from Large and Representative Samples of Studies

The typical persuasibility study examines the relationship between one or more relatively general dispositions of the message recipient and one or more responses to a single set of stimulus materials, with responses observed on a single occasion (or, in pre–post designs, on two occasions). In view of the considerations already discussed, it is unlikely that findings from such studies will often prove replicable; nor will they have much generality when considered over broader ranges of stimulus materials and situations. The advice that general dispositions be investigated with larger research designs that sample situations or occasions requires considerable effort from researchers; and for already complex research questions involving several independent variables, studies of this type may be so unwieldy as to be virtually impossible. An alternate solution is to achieve generalizability by examining findings over large and representative samples of related experiments to determine whether some findings emerge as more stable and replicable than others.

There are often barriers to gaining access to an adequate sample of studies; for example, only a few studies may have been carried out, or there may be a systematic bias restricting the nature of the studies that appear in the literature. Yet there are at least a few recipient characteristics for which this goal can be approximated. One such characteristic is the sex of the recipient of influence: A large number of past social influence studies have employed subjects of both sexes and have reported the presence or absence of sex differences. Because until recently, sex-difference findings were generally peripheral to researchers' major hypotheses and reported only as secondary findings, the usual biases restricting the nature of the findings appearing in the published literature should be less severe. Whether or not social influence studies were published was determined, for the most part, by their main findings—not by those having to do with sex differences.

What pattern of findings is revealed by a survey of the large body of studies reporting presence or absence of sex differences? Textbooks in social psychology and related fields generally claim—often on the basis of citations of only one or a very few studies—that women are more easily influenced than men and explain the presumed sex difference in terms of a propensity to yield inherent in the female gender role. Yet a thorough literature survey (Eagly, 1978) revealed that this widely cited generalization needs revision. In fact, for persuasion research and for conformity research not involving group pressure, there is scant empirical support for a sex difference. However, for group pressure conformity studies (e.g., the Asch situation), there is stronger support, with 34 percent of the studies reporting women significantly more conforming than men.

The unusually large sample of studies reporting the effect of recipients' sex also made it possible to examine the stability of at least some interactions between subject sex and contextual features of the social influence situation. One of these interactions, involving the content area of the influence attempt, appeared to be quite stable: Each sex is more influenceable in areas in which the other sex is perceived as more expert (e.g., Sistrunk & McDavid, 1971). Another contextual feature, the extent to which the influencing agent has surveillance over the recipient, may also be important and may account for the limitation of influenceability sex differences primarily to group pressure conformity situations in which influencing agents, who are the other group members, have surveillance over recipients.

The work on influenceability sex differences illustrates how misleading it can be to interpret the effects of recipient characteristics on the basis of single studies or even a small number of studies. Yet reasonable inferences can be drawn if a large number of studies are available to provide a base for generalizations, especially if independent tests of hypotheses are combined by a reviewer through meta-analysis techniques that involve combining probabilities (Rosenthal, 1978) and averaging effect sizes (Cohen, 1977). Thus, the difficulties created by the use of single-response dependent measures and very narrow sampling of settings and stimulus materials can be compensated by the reviewer's opportunity to survey findings across a large number of relatively unselected studies.

Taking Situational Variation into Account

Yet another approach to accounting for substantial variability in persuasibility involves taking situational determinants of behavior into account along with personality variables. This interactionist strategy is especially important if researchers continue to design studies that attempt to predict relatively specific dependent variables from general personality characteristics. Because predictability on the basis of recipient characteristics is then likely to remain low, one appropriate strategy for accounting for more variability is to consider simultaneously characteristics of the social situation.

In this chapter there has so far been little consideration of how situational variables relate to persuasion. Yet, as any review of the attitude change literature (e.g., Eagly & Himmelfarb, 1978; McGuire, 1969a) suggests, many situational variables—features of the message, communicator, and the social context in which communication takes place—have been shown to affect attitude change. For example, recall the well-known findings presented in the last chapter that demonstrate that credible communicators are more persuasive than less credible communicators (e.g., Hovland & Weiss, 1951).

Despite such moderately generalizable conclusions concerning a few situational variables, however, studies on other situational independent variables are frequently inconsistent across studies, much as findings often are concerning the effects of personality variables. Researchers have attempted to explicate inconsistencies by specifying that differing intervening processes can be elicited by manipulations of the same situational variable. Research on distraction has been particularly successful in this regard, with the variable shown to have multiple impact on intervening cognitive processes. Thus, as discussed in Chapter 3, distraction can interfere with both the reception mechanism (commonly assessed by argument recall) and the yielding mechanism (commonly assessed by counterarguing). Chaiken and Eagly's (1976) recent work on communication modality (i.e., written vs. audiotaped vs. videotaped messages) made a similar point by showing that modality affects both message comprehension and yielding to the message.

Because both personality and situational characteristics often affect attitude change, taking variables of both types into consideration should usually account for more variability in agreement behavior than consideration of only one type of variable. Personality psychologists (e.g., Endler & Magnusson, 1976) have often favored such an interactionist position, and it should be given careful consideration in persuasibility research because it offers a third route to dealing with the fact that personality traits' impact on persuasion often differs widely across situations. The two routes discussed—cumulating responses over settings and occasions, and basing generalizations on sets of related findings—handle the problem of such situational interactions by averaging across situations, with the effect that unrelated sources of situational variability tend to cancel each other's impact. In their simplest applications, these two approaches in fact ignore differing sources of situational variability by the technique of averaging responses over situations. In contrast, the interactionist solution requires that the joint impact of personality and situational variables be understood, so that it can be taken systematically into account. The interactionist approach constitutes the most demanding solution to improving predictability, because effective theory concerning the joint impact of personality and situational characteristics is not easily achieved, given the current state of knowledge concerning attitude change.

Researchers adopting an interactionist position generally treat either personality predictions or situational predictions as their primary interest, and then regard variables of the secondary class as altering the processes by which variables of the primary class affect persuasibility. One of the clearest examples of starting with personality variables and considering situational variables as establishing contingency conditions for personality predictions is provided by McGuire's (1968b) information-processing approach to influenceability. As already noted, this model focuses on the effects of personality characteristics on reception and yielding processes and assumes that the relative importance of these intervening processes depends on the level of relevant situational variables.

If a researcher's primary focus is on the effect of situational variables on attitude change, then levels along a personality variable may be regarded as providing contingency conditions affecting the impact of situational variables. Some of the classic persuasion research conducted by Hovland and his associates provides illustrations of this approach. For example, a few of these studies probed whether messages that explicitly draw the conclusion from their premises are more effective than those that leave the conclusions implicit. Hovland and Mandell (1952) and the majority of subsequent studies demonstrated the superiority of explicit-conclusion messages. Yet if this finding is explained by the fact that many recipients are not intelligent enough to draw the conclusion for themselves, the superiority of explicit-conclusion messages should be more pronounced for recipients of lower rather than higher intelligence. Some support for this interaction was obtained by Cooper and Dinerman (1951), although not by Hovland and Mandell (1952), perhaps because of insufficient variability in intelligence among their college student subjects. Similarly, Hovland and his associates (Hovland, Lumsdaine, & Sheffield, 1949) compared one-sided messages—which ignore opposition arguments—to two-sided messages—which acknowledge and refute opposition arguments. Although neither one- nor two-sided messages had a clear persuasive advantage in Hovland's or most subsequent research, an interesting interaction with recipients' educational level was obtained such that two-sided messages were more effective with better educated recipients and one-sided messages with less educated recipients (Hovland, Lumsdaine, & Sheffield, 1949).

Thus, past research suggests the importance of considering that dispositional and situational variables interact in their impact on persuasion. Yet the success of research on personality–situation interactions depends on adequate theory about how variables of these two classes link to intervening psychological processes. In view of the incompleteness of current knowledge, it must be recognized that many situational variables' impact on personality–persuasibility relationships is unknown or not correctly understood. Because researchers are therefore unable to take more than partial account of personality–situation interactions, findings generated in an interactionist framework will probably not cumulate in any more simple or straightforward fashion than other persuasion findings. To deal successfully with unknown and poorly understood situational determinants of personality–persuasibility relationships, interactionist researchers would benefit from the recommendations noted earlier involving averaging responses across situations and occasions. Then the generalizability of those interactions that are understood could be demonstrated across appropriately selected settings and occasions, as indeed was illustrated earlier in relation to some of the interactions involving sex of the message recipient.

CHAPTER SUMMARY

This chapter reviewed studies illustrating three differing styles of research concerning the relationship between personal characteristics of message recipients and responses to persuasive messages. The *personality strategy* invokes a personality theory to suggest a relevant personality trait and a mechanism by which the trait affects attitude change. Research relating locus of control (internal vs. external) and self-esteem to persuasibility has yielded inconsistent results. The personality strategy may be of limited utility because it fails to consider the cognitive antecedents of persuasion. The *attitude change strategy* accounts for reactions to persuasive communications by relying upon an attitude theory to suggest a variable along which individuals differ. For example, social judgment theory assumes that the structure of attitudes is an important determinant of change toward persuasive messages. Individual differences in attitude structure are viewed in social judgment terms as differences in the widths of latitudes of acceptance and rejection, and the perceived location of a message in relation to these latitudes determines whether or not attitude change occurs. The *personality–attitude change strategy* uses personality theory to define a relevant recipient characteristic but relies on attitude theory to specify the mechanism by which the characteristic affects reactions to persuasive communications. For example, McGuire, in his information-processing model, argued that self-esteem is related positively to reception and negatively to yielding. In persuasion settings in which reception is more important (e.g., complex, well-argued message), high-self-esteem persons are expected to show most persuasibility; whereas in situations in which yielding is more important (e.g., simple, less well argued message), low-self-esteem persons should be more persuasible. Settings in which both reception are yielding are important should produce an inverted-U relationship between self-esteem and persuasion. Although research traditions illustrating all three strategies have been characterized by a mixed history of empirical successes and failures, the two approaches invoking attitude theory are more promising in that they give more thorough consideration to the underlying cognitive and other responses that may mediate reactions to persuasive communications.

The study of individual differences in persuasion and other social influence behaviors is not as popular an area of research as it was in the 1950s and 1960s. This chapter suggested that methodological difficulties may account for this decline of interest. In particular, most influenceability studies have attempted to relate a general personality disposition to one or more very specifically defined social influence behaviors, even though such findings have a high probability of being relatively weak and difficult to replicate. This chapter suggested some of the reasons for this weak predictability and the instability of many findings and recommended several routes to greater success. These recommendations involved (1) defining personality independent variables and persuasibility dependent variables at equivalent levels of generality; (2) using large and representative samples of studies to examine the effects of general traits on specific behaviors; and (3) taking simultaneous account of recipient characteristics and situational variables. The utility of the third approach can be seen in some early research that demonstrated that the superiority of explicit-conclusion messages was more pronounced for recipients of lower rather than higher intelligence, and that two-sided messages were more effective with better educated recipients and one-sided messages with less educated recipients. It is hoped that the recommendations given in this chapter will help renew interest in persuasibility research, so that individual-differences implications of recent theories of attitude change will be effectively explored.

9 Attitude Polarization in Groups

Eugene Burnstein
Keith Sentis
University of Michigan

INTRODUCTION

Why would Senator Goldwater have beseeched us: "Extremism in defense of liberty is no vice!"'? One conjecture is that this *cri de coeur* arose from the belated recognition of a common belief that people whose attitudes tend toward the farthest limit are unsound. After all, the balanced mind is supposed to carefully appraise ideas before uttering them. Appreciating this, the ambitious politician of overweening principle and uninhibited tongue must combat the inference in the mind of the electorate that extremism is a disqualification for high office. Whether or not people do in fact equate moderation with sound thinking, there is rather good empirical evidence that in groups, they often exert a moderating influence on extreme members. Group members taking fringe positions are usually persuaded (or at least act as though they are persuaded) to the majority position.

A notorious example of this phenomenon is the process by which President Kennedy and his closest advisers decided to attack Cuba at the Bay of Pigs: The invasion force of 1,400 daring exiles was completely wiped out in three days. Here we have a group of very intelligent and sophisticated individuals making an ignominious or, at best, a very unwise decision. President Kennedy put the question aptly, "How could we have been so stupid?" The process leading up to the decision to invade has been labeled *groupthink* by Janis (1972). The term is appropriately Orwellian, referring as it does to a set of techniques that still individual disagreement and amplify consensus. For example, at the beginning of their deliberations, the advisory group adopted the rather simple procedural rule that decisions were to be unanimous. In retrospect this turned out to be an insidious source of groupthink. First, it inhibited the incisive questioning required for an objective analysis of the situation. The pressure on members to achieve unanimity made a critical attitude untenable, as no one wished to appear carping or disloyal. Moreover, it allowed those who controlled the agenda to present with impunity a description of the situation biased toward one particular course of action:

> At each meeting, instead of opening up the agenda to permit a full airing of the opposing considerations, he [Kennedy] allowed the CIA representatives to dominate the entire discussion. The President permitted them to refute immediately each tentative doubt that one of the others might express, instead of asking whether anyone else had the same doubt or wanted to pursue the implications of the new worrisome issue that had been raised [Janis, 1972, p. 43].

Finally, the unanimity rule produced self-censorship. Those who deplored the invasion suppressed their attitude. As an example Janis noted the following remark by Arthur Schlesinger:

> In the months after the Bay of Pigs, I bitterly reproached myself for having kept so silent during those crucial discussions in the cabinet room. . . . I can only explain my failure to do more than raise a few timid questions by reporting that one's impulse to blow the whistle on this nonsense was simply undone by the circumstances of the discussion [Schlesinger, 1965, p. 255]

Indeed the research literature (as well as political life) was so replete with such instances that most of us who studied social processes tacitly assumed that groups necessarily have the power to move extreme members toward the majority and inevitably use it. As a result we were taken aback (and intrigued) some years ago by a series of findings demonstrating that extreme members are often able to move the majority toward their position. In short, polarization is just as natural a consequence of social discourse as moderation or compromise.

In this context, *polarization* refers to instances in which posterior attitudes (those held after group discussion) are more extreme than prior attitudes (those held before group discussion). Two classes of theories have recently been proposed to explain this phenomenon, one focusing on normative processes, the other on informational processes. The purpose of our chapter is to describe and assess these theories. It would be remiss, however, not to recall that some of the earliest experiments in social psychology were, in fact if not in name, concerned with polarization. Soon after the first world war, Bechterew and deLange (1924)[1] carried out studies in group decision making that produced some striking results that foreshadow current analyses based on informational processes. For example, in deciding what should be done about a boy who is caught stealing, 78% of the

---

[1]The authors thank Michael Berbaum for his skillful translation of this article.

members after discussion had the idea: "If he's hungry, he shouldn't be punished." Prior to discussion, only 13% had thought of this on their own. Before discussion, only 5% could imagine that "beating is barbarous"; after discussion, however, over 90% had such an idea. Bechterew and deLange suggested that when discussion leads to the dissemination of uncommon but persuasive ideas, a marked shift in attitude (e.g., toward leniency) is likely to follow. Somewhat later, other researchers observed polarization following discussions involving matters of social value, fact, logic, and aesthetics (e.g., Shaw, 1932; Thorndike, 1938a, 1938b; Timmons, 1939). Indeed, Thorndike (1938b) was one of the first to make explicit *the* issue that is the current focus of debate in research on polarization—namely, whether this effect is due "to the intellectual give and take of discussion [informational influence] . . . (or) . . . to knowing the opinion of the other members of the group and shifting to conform to it [normative influence] [p. 343]."

Informational influence reflects the impact of cogent ideas. Although such ideas at first may be available to only a few members, in the course of discussion they become widely known. As a result, the benighted change their mind. This is the most common explanation for shifts toward accuracy (or inaccuracy) in group problem solving. To illustrate, Miller and Brownell (1975) had second graders discuss some standard problems used by Piaget and his co-workers in their research on intellectual development. It was found that postdiscussion individual solutions were more likely to be correct than the solutions advocated by the average child prior to discussion, and this shift toward accuracy came about because the ideas expressed by the correct children happened to be more persuasive than those put forth by the incorrect children (also see Davis, 1973; Laughlin & Bitz, 1975; Laughlin, Kerr, Davis, Halff, Marciniak, 1975). In contrast, normative processes describe the impact of rewards and punishments, actual or anticipated. When a person values membership in a group and finds that his or her position on an important issue differs from that of other members, that individual is likely to experience a variety of distressful emotions (e.g., fear of disapproval, shame, loss in self-esteem). Such a person will then abandon the prior position and shift toward the consensus in order to reduce such threats (Deutsch & Gerard, 1955; Festinger, 1954; Sanders & Baron, 1977).

THEORIES BASED ON NORMATIVE INFLUENCE

The current interest in polarization began with Stoner's (1961) discovery of the "risky shift." He presented to subjects 12 hypothetical problems called *choice-dilemmas*. Each of these items tells of a sorely perplexed hero who must choose between two courses of action, only one of whose outcomes is certain. The dilemma rests on the fact that the certain outcome is less attractive than what would be achieved *if* the uncertain course succeeds.

Sample Choice-Dilemma Problems

The following are two examples of choice-dilemma items. The first, from Kogan and Wallach (1964, p. 258) typically polarizes toward risk, the second, from Stoner (1968, p. 446), toward caution.

1. Mr. B. is currently a college senior who is very eager to pursue graduate study in chemistry leading to the Doctor of Philosophy degree. He has been accepted by both University X and University Y. University X has a world-wide reputation for excellence in chemistry. While a degree from University X would signify outstanding training in this field, the standards are so very rigorous that only a fraction of the degree candidates actually receive the degree. University Y, on the other hand, has much less of a reputation in chemistry, but almost everyone admitted is awarded the Doctor of Philosophy degree, though the degree has much less prestige than the corresponding degree from University X.

Imagine that you are advising Mr. B. Check the lowest probability that you would consider acceptable to make it worthwhile for Mr. B to enroll in University X rather than University Y.

2. Mr. E is about to board a plane at the airport at the beginning of his overseas vacation. Although he has been looking forward to this trip for some time, he is troubled because he awoke in the morning with a severe abdominal pain. Because he has never flown before, he thinks that the pain may simply be an upset stomach brought on by anticipation of the flight. Although he is not far from a hospital where he knows he will obtain quick attention, he realizes that a visit to the hospital will cause him to miss his flight which in turn will seriously disrupt his vacation plans. The pain has gotten more severe in the last few minutes.

Imagine that you are advising Mr. E. Check the *lowest* probability that you would consider acceptable for Mr. E to board the plane.

Below each dilemma was a response scale of the following kind:

1. Mr. F should enroll an University X if the chances are at least
   _____ 1 in 10 that Mr. F would receive a degree from University X
   _____ 2 in 10 that Mr. F would receive a degree from University X
   .
   .
   .
   _____ 9 in 10 that Mr. F would receive a degree from University X
   _____ Place a check here if you think Mr. F should not enroll in University X, no matter what the probabilities.
2. Mr. E should board the plane if chances are least
   _____ 1 in 10 that his abdominal pain will not become more severe during the trip

_____ 2 in 10 that his abdominal pain will not become more severe during the trip

.

.

.

_____ 9 in 10 that his abdominal pain will not become more severe during the trip

_____ Place a check here if you think Mr. E should *not* board the plane, no matter what the probabilities.

Although the choice-dilemmas are widely used, polarization has been observed with a large variety of items. Many of them involve issues that have nothing to do with risk (see the review by Myers & Lamm, 1976). In fact, identical results are obtained with the choice-dilemmas when a Likert-type attitude scale is substituted for the probability values, say, ranging from "I very strongly prefer alternative J" to "I very strongly prefer alternative K" (Gouge & Fraser, 1972; Stroebe & Fraser, 1971).

Stoner's (1961) subjects first decided individually how sure success must be in order to commend the uncertain course of action to the hero. They were then divided into groups that discussed the same problems and came to agreement about the correct solution to each dilemma. Group decisions were found to be more risky than those made by the individuals alone; that is, the minimum probability of success acceptable to the group was *less* than that acceptable to the average member prior to discussion. Furthermore, members revised their own preferences in similar fashion. Indeed, shifts in individual attitudes following discussion are equally robust whether or not there is an explicit group decision.

One of the first significant explanations of the "risky shift" held that in a group situation, the sense of personal responsibility for the results of a decision is reduced to the extent that the decision is shared (Wallach, Kogan, & Bem, 1962). A collective choice enables members to anticipate that in the case of failure, they will be less blameworthy than when they choose alone and must assume sole responsibility for the consequences. A variety of procedures were used to test this hypothesis. Some experimenters directly varied the extent to which responsibility was shared (e.g., whether the decision was made for the group by a single member whom the experimenter designated, or by the membership as a whole). They found little or no support for the diffusion of responsibility hypothesis; that is, polarization occurred whether or not responsibility was shared (e.g., Marquis, 1962). There were additional findings that produced further difficulties. For instance, full risky shifts are obtained when subjects only listen to a taped group discussion (e.g., Kogan & Wallach, 1967; Lamm, 1967). It is hard to see how a subject can share the responsibility with a group that he or she will not meet or that no longer exists. Finally, soon after the diffusion of responsibility hypothesis was proposed, further analyses of the choice-dilemmas revealed that a few of these items reliably polarized toward caution (cf. Brown, 1965). Many researchers since have been able to construct new dilemmas that also give reliable cautious shifts. There seems no way for a process of responsibility diffusion to explain the polarization of attitudes in a cautious direction. In light of such evidence, the diffusion of responsibility hypothesis has been abandoned as an explanation of polarization.

Although the diffusion of responsibility explanation attributed the shifts to normative processes—the group reduces one's uneasiness about being blamed for a mishap—it does require discussion or at least some form of interaction for "sharing" to occur. There is a more popular set of explanations for polarization that do *not* require group members to interact. They merely assume that each person learns the initial attitude of others and is able to *compare* his or her own attitude to theirs. Of course, this information about others is usually communicated during discussion. But from the point of view of these theories, it could just as well have been announced by the experimenter, written on the blackboard, or the like. The earliest comparison formulation was made by Brown (1965). His principal assumption was that relatively extreme attitudes are socially desirable and that people who present themselves in this fashion thus gain in social approval as well as in self-esteem. The attractiveness of extreme attitudes is said to stem from particular values in Western culture. According to Brown, when confronted with certain kinds of problems, we value riskiness and want to appear appropriately risky. Given other kinds of problems, caution is valued, and we desire the appearance of caution. But in any particular setting, what is appropriately risky (or cautious) may be unclear. Nevertheless, the person initially assumes an attitude that he or she believes is sufficiently daring (or prudent). In a group, however, the individual is likely to be confronted by others who are even more extreme. A comparison between the personal choice and those of the other members quickly informs the individual that he or she has been too moderate. Distressed by that moderation, fearful of disapproval, the person changes his or her initial attitude and accepts a more extreme course of action.

Other versions of social comparison theory have been proposed since Brown (1965) to explain polarization. The Jellison and Riskind formulation makes the classical social comparison assumption (Festinger, 1954) that individuals wish to perceive themselves as slightly more able than their peers. If we believe, as Jellison and Riskind do, that the person's attitude toward risk implies his or her level of ability, then it follows that "When a person learns . . . the level of risk he has initially chosen is at or below the group average, he has learned that he is defining himself as only as able, or less able, than the other group members" (Jellison & Riskind, 1970, p. 377). In order to appear slightly more able than others, people change their initial preferences for something more risky—ergo, the "risky shift." As in the case of responsibility diffusion, it is difficult for the Jellison–Riskind formulation to handle polarization toward caution or polarization of risk-free attitudes. In the past few years several researchers have put special stress on Brown's point about self-presentation, arguing that the person will move toward the socially rewarding position—that is, the one that will elicit the most approval from other group members (Jellison & Arkin, 1977; Sanders & Baron, 1977). Finally there are a small number of investigators who believe that the attitude a person expresses is a compromise. Some say it is between the ideal preference, the choice he or she would really like to make, and what the individual thinks is the group standard (Levinger & Schneider, 1969). Others assert that the compromise is between an individual's ideal preference and the value he or she attaches to being a person of moderation and reasonableness, one not given to extremes (Pruitt, 1971). The former has been called the *pluralistic-ignorance hypothesis* and the latter, the *release hypothesis*. According to pluralistic ignorance, prior attitudes fall between the individual's ideal and the assumed group standard. Knowledge of others' attitudes presumably leads to a reevaluation of the group standard and, thus, to a shift in the person's preference. The release hypothesis also implies that polarization follows from learning that there are group members who are more extreme than oneself. Knowing that such people exist is supposed to liberate individuals from the constraints of moderation, allowing them to act the way they would really like, to express a more extreme attitude.

THEORIES BASED ON
INFORMATIONAL INFLUENCE

Another set of explanations for polarization assign primary importance to informational influence. This paper focuses on one version, called *persuasive-arguments theory*. Similar versions of informational influence have been proposed by Bishop and Myers (1974) as well as by Anderson and Graesser (1976; see also Chapter 16). The basic idea of persuasive-arguments theory is that when the person evaluates (or reevaluates) alternative J relative to alternative K, he or she generates arguments, ideas, images, or thoughts (i.e., cognitive responses) describing the attributes of J and K. This is based on the assumption that there exists a culturally given pool of arguments speaking to each alternative. In order to judge the relative merits of these alternatives, the person samples (retrieves arguments) from this pool. Arguments may vary in availability (the probability of their coming to mind), direction (pro-J or pro-K), and persuasiveness. When the preponderance of arguments in the pool favors a particular alternative, the average prior attitude reflects the direction and magnitude of this preponderance. Further thought or discussion leads to polarization toward the alternative that initially elicits more and/or better arguments. The extent of polarization will depend on whether the initial argument samples (1) overlap or (2) exhaust the larger pool. This implies that polarization will approach a maximum when a person begins to *rethink* the issue and there still remain many arguments that have not yet come to mind, or when several individuals *discuss* the issue with each other and the arguments that have come to mind are only partially shared.

A persuasive-arguments analysis of discussion effects may be illustrated with a simple example. Consider a choice in which the culturally given pool contains six pro-J arguments—*a, b, c, d, e,* and *f,*—and three pro-K arguments—*l, m,* and *n.* One of several distinct outcomes would be expected *depending on the distribution of arguments among members.* Suppose all three of our discussants had thought of the same arguments. In this case their prior attitude toward J would be identical, and discussion would produce no change. On the other hand, if *a, b,* and *m* had come to mind in one discussant; *c, d,* and *m* in the second; and *e, f,* and *m* in the third (i.e., if each has different pro-J arguments but the same pro-K arguments), then although they again hold identical prior attitudes, the discussion would produce marked polarization toward J. Finally, polarization toward K would be predicted if one member had generated *a, b,* and *l;* another *a, b,* and *m;* and the third *a, b,* and *n* (i.e., if each had initially thought of the same pro-J but different pro-K arguments). Normally, individual argument samples are representative of the larger pool (Vinokur & Burnstein, 1974). There-fore, average prediscussion preferences can be estimated from the balance of pro-J and pro-K arguments in the pool. Postdiscussion preferences can be pre-dicted just as readily if, in addition, we know the degree of partial sharing—that is, the extent of overlap among individual argument samples.

By assuming that polarization is the result of partial sharing, we imply that it is highly dependent on group size. That is to say, the extent to which persuasive arguments must be shared in order to produce a full shift in attitude decreases rapidly as group size increases. The reason, of course, is that a large group is more likely to contain a member who possesses a rare but persuasive argument than is a small group. A formal model has been constructed to reflect this line of reasoning. It specifies in mathematical terms the set of relations that were already discussed in a somewhat informal fashion—namely, how availability, persua-siveness, and group size interact to determine attitude polarization. A description of the model and supporting data can be found in Vinokur and Burnstein (1974) and in Vinokur, Trope, and Burnstein (1975). For additional evidence on the relationship between the distribution of persuasive arguments among group members and polarization, see Ebbesen and Bowers (1974), Kaplan (1976, 1977), Kaplan and Miller (1976), Morgan and Aram (1975), and Silverthorne (1971).

INFORMATIONAL VERSUS NORMATIVE INFLUENCE

Some have proposed that persuasive argumentation plays a subsidiary or, at best, a complementary role to social comparison and especially to self-presentation. From this point of view, argumentation merely facilitates the shift that was produced by comparison processes in the first case (e.g., Sanders & Baron,

1977). There are two reasons for rejecting this proposal. The first is a matter of parsimony. Persuasive-arguments theory says that attitude polarization is fundamentally an informational phenomenon. Normative influences are relatively remote, meaning that they operate on polarization, if at all, through cognition. For example, if a person were distressed because others held more extreme attitudes and he or she were about to shift toward their position, this state of affairs would be reflected in ideation, in the content of the argument sample, and could be taken into account at that point. In fact, we have observed, somewhat to our suprise, that when the real attitudes of others are sharply opposed to the ideas they express, only the latter predicts the direction of polarization (Burnstein & Vinokur, 1973, Experiment II). Hence, for the purpose of explaining polarization, comparison theory may be excess baggage.

The proposal that argumentation merely complements (facilitates) comparison effects is also difficult to justify in the light of past research. There is little evidence for normative process having any *direct* effect on polarization. The evidence for informational influence, however, is reasonably strong. The remainder of this chapter is concerned with that issue.

Polarization and the Social Desirability of Extreme Attitudes

In an unpublished study, we presented several choice-dilemmas to subjects and asked them to predict the distribution of choices of "100 people like you" over the response scale. On the average they believed that 30% would hold more extreme attitudes than their own. The assumption that an individual will be surprised and piqued to discover that one or two members of a five-person group prefer a more drastic course than he or she does, thus, seems unconvincing. Indeed, there is absolutely no evidence of an increase in distress when such a discovery is made. Nor is there any sign of relief when the individual shifts toward a more extreme position. Because these propositions about changes in emotional state are easily tested, the absence of published research on this point is worrisome, especially given that when individuals shift toward more extreme positions, they do not think that their posterior attitudes are any more socially desirable than their relatively moderate prior attitudes (Kahan, 1975). Moreover, diligent attempts to relate polarization and the belief that one is more extreme than one's peers have been singularly unsuccessful (e.g., Lamm, Trommsdorff, & Rost-Schaude, 1972). Thus, polarization is no greater for those who hold such a belief than for those who do not. Our own interest in the issue led us to ask subjects on a postexperimental questionnaire to describe their states of mind upon learning that their attitudes differed from those of other members (Burnstein & Vinokur, 1975). Reports of pique or embarrassment were rare and unrelated to polarization. However, polarization was correlated with the extent to which the person tried to explain the difference and with the amount of thought given to reasons why others made the choices they did (as well as with the number of such reasons subjects actually generated). Although the mental processes these people described are not those one would anticipate on the basis of a social comparison analysis, they are just what would be expected on the basis of persuasive-arguments theory.

A second line of evidence comes from several experiments that use a subjective expected utility (SEU) model as a framework for analyzing the effects of persuasive argumentation on preferences involving uncertainty (e.g., on the choice-dilemmas). By itself, the SEU model is simply a set of rules for making wise (rational) decisions—it tells how to integrate what we know or believe about the alternatives in question so as best to choose between them. In respect to the choice-dilemmas, the SEU formulation stipulates that the person will favor the risky alternative (R) over the cautious alternative (C) to the extent that the likely results of choosing R (i.e., the subjective expected utility of R, or SEU_r) is more appealing than that of choosing C (i.e., the subjective expected utility of C, or SEU_c). Whether SEU_r is large or small depends on (1) the perceived likelihood of R being successful, relative to the likelihood of failure, weighted by (2) the perceived value or utility of success (U_s), relative to the utility of failure (U_f). By definition, the outcome of C is certain, or unity; therefore, SEU_c is always equal to the perceived values of C (U_c). The implication is that the person's attitude will polarize toward R as SEU_r increases in comparison to SEU_c. The latter happens if one (or all) of the following events occur: an increase in the perceived probability of success, a decrease in the perceived probability of failure, an increase in U_s or in U_f, or, finally, a decrease in U_c. How the SEU model actually works can be seen when it is stated a little more rigorously. Thus, let p, q, designate, respectively, the *subjective* probabilities that the risky alternative will be successful or unsuccessful. Assume (1) $U_s > U_c > U_f$, (2) $p + q = 1$ (i.e., $q = 1 - p$) for every subject. Then, the subjective expected utility of the risky alternative: $SEU_r = pU_s + (1 - p) U_f$; and the subjective expected utility of the certain alternative: $SEU_c = 1 \cdot U_c$. A basic assumption of the model is that people will maximize the subjective expected utility; that is, the choice of the risky alternative follows only when its SEU is equal to or greater than the SEU of the certain (cautious) alternative, when $SEU_r \geq SEU_c$. Or, equivalently, the risky alternative should be chosen if and only if $pU_s + (1 - p) U_f \geq 1 \cdot U_c$; or, solving for p, when

$$p \geqq \frac{U_c - U_f}{U_s - U_f} \tag{1}$$

In other words, according to the SEU model, the *lowest* probability of success that a subject will accept (i.e., the individual's risk-level preference) in order to attempt the risky alternative is

$$\hat{p} = \frac{U_c - U_f}{U_s - U_f} \tag{2}$$

Note that $\hat{p}$ is the ratio of the utilities of the outcomes and serves as a predictor of the subject's actual risk-level preference, p.

Two important consequences of the SEU model are indicated by Equation 1. First keep in mind that the p that maximizes SEU is not determined by the absolute utility of any single outcome alone but by the relative differences between all the utilities—that is, by the ratio of the utilities ($\hat{p}$). Thus, if the ratio of the utilities is known, then we should be able to predict an individual's attitude toward R or C (i.e., his or her risk-level preference). Moreover, if the change in this ratio is known, then we should be able to predict the magnitude of polarization toward R or C. Finally, the SEU model is especially useful in a persuasive-arguments analysis, because it tells us that if the person changes his or her attitude toward R or C—say, after discussing it with others—and if this change is due to receiving new ideas regarding R and C, then these ideas must have a particular content that caused the individual to revise his or her opinion about U_s, U_f, or U_c. In fact, it has been shown that attitudes will polarize toward R when a person learns in discussion that failure at R is really not so bad (thereby increasing U_f and making it less negative), that success on R is wonderful (thereby increasing U_s), or that the certain outcome is distinctly mediocre (thereby decreasing U_c and minimizing the $U_c - U_f$ difference). Similarly, polarization toward caution has been found when arguments are made for a decrease in U_f or U_s or for an increase in U_c (Vinokur, Trope, & Burnstein, 1975),. This is precisely what Equation 2 would predict.

Furthermore, in one study using the SEU model, a content analysis was performed on the ideas that come to mind while people formulate their attitudes on the choice-dilemmas as well as the ideas they express during discussion (Vinokur, Trope, & Burnstein, 1975). As suggested earlier, it was possible to identify several classes of arguments having to do with (1) the perceived utility of success and failure associated with the uncertain alternative, and (2) the perceived utility of the certain alternative, both of which were called *outcome utilities*. In addition, because social comparison theory assumes that an extreme choice is in itself attractive, there should be utilities associated with, or inherent to, taking the "risky" or "cautious" action that are independent of the outcomes actually specified in choice-dilemma items. Arguments of this type, called *action utilities*, were also identified. (For example, consider the choice between going to a highly prestigious university where a good proportion flunk out or to a mediocre one where no one does. In the face of this dilemma, two common arguments regarding outcome utilities are "you can always transfer to the easy school" and "you ought to be sure of getting your degree"; the former, of course, supporting the choice of the uncertain alternative, the latter supporting the certain alternative. Examples of arguments concerned with action utilities are "life is no fun unless you take a chance" of "being cautious is a sign of wisdom.") Well over two-thirds of these arguments were concerned with outcome utilities (70% of those generated privately, 72% of those emitted in discussion) and less than a tenth with action utilities (9% in private and 6% in discussion). Outcome utilities were significantly and substantially correlated with polarization ($r = .63$), but the correlation between action utilities and polarization was weak and insignificant ($r = .16$). Finally, when outcome utilities (the persuasive-arguments variable) and action utilities (the social comparison variable) were combined to predict polarization, the correlation ($r = .62$) was no higher than when only outcome utilities were used. If what people think about, as well as what they say, reflects the relative significance of argumentation and social comparison, then these results demonstrate that the former process by itself has considerable impact on polarization, whereas the latter has very little.

The Necessity of Argumentation

From the very beginning, the dispute about the relative importance of informational and normative processes was reduced to the following simple question: Does polarization depend on argumentation or on knowing the attitudes of others? Sometimes the positions taken were even more starkly simple. Witness Brown's (1965) description of analyses based on normative processes that assert the "content of the discussion, the arguments pro and con are of no importance. It is the information about people's answers [their risk preferences] that makes individuals move toward greater risk after group discussion [p. 702]." The research also partook of this simplicity. To separate out the effects of knowing others' attitudes from the effects of argumentation, group members were required either (1) to discuss an issue without revealing their own attitudes, or (2) to reveal their attitudes and achieve consensus without discussing the issue—say, by repeated shows of hands. The former procedure did produce substantial polarization (Clark, Crockett, & Archer, 1971; St. Jean, 1970). However, reasonably accurate inferences probably could be made about where other members actually stood from what they said in disucssion, even without them making explicit statements to that effect. The latter procedure, as can be imagined, was rather awkward. Some researchers observed weak shifts (Clark & Willems, 1969; Stokes, 1971; Teger & Pruitt, 1967); others found no polarization at all (Bell & Jamieson, 1970; Clark et al., 1971; St. Jean & Percival, 1974; Wallach & Kogan, 1965).

Somewhat later, different procedures were devised to avoid such difficulties. In one study (Burnstein & Vinokur, 1973, Experiment I) subjects knew that when discussing some issues, they must argue for their actual positions, and when discussing others, they must argue for the opposite. They were aware that this was the case for the other members as well. However, in any given discussion they did not know who was or who was not arguing for their actual positions. Thus subjects' true attitudes could not be inferred from what they said. A second study (Burnstein & Vinokur, 1973, Experiment II) permitted individuals to determine readily and precisely another member's real position. The latter was always the exact mirror image of the position the member explicitly advocated during group discussion, and the mirror image conversion rule was well known. Theories based on social comparison processes predict that polarization will *not* occur as long as members remain ignorant of each other's true attitudes; it will be observed, however, when they possess such knowledge, independent of discussion. Persuasive-arguments theory leads one to have different expectations. It assumes that people will choose positions for which they have the greatest number of persuasive arguments. In our first experiment (Burnstein & Vinokur, 1973, Experiment I), subjects occasionally needed to argue for positions they previously had rejected. This required them to advocate the (relatively) unadvocable—that is, to support courses of action for which they had few persuasive arguments. Cogent discourse would be unlikely in these circumstances. As a result, polarization should not be observed. Polarization, however, should occur if all members argue for their true attitudes, whether or not they are aware of this fact. On the whole, the findings were quite consistent with persuasive-arguments theory. When members did not know whether others were advocating their real positions or the opposite, and the former was the case, polarization was obtained. However, when members could easily ascertain each other's true attitudes but were required to argue for their mirror images, polarization was not obtained.

The design as well as the reasoning employed in the two experiments just described are rather complex. Fortunately there is an elementary but important difference between social comparison theory and persuasive-arguments theory that can be tested in straightforward fashion. Consider an experimental design in which (1) the number of others' attitudes available for comparison is varied independently of (2) the number of arguments others present in support of these attitudes. Social comparison theory would predict the magnitude of polarization to be a function of the former and not the latter, whereas persuasive-arguments theory would predict the opposite. When such an experiment was performed (Burnstein, Vinokur, & Trope, 1973), none of the effects based on the number of others' attitudes approached significance. The only reliable main effect was based on the number of arguments that were made available to the person.

Finally, although comparison theories in general assume that argumentation is unimportant for polarization (i.e., knowledge of others' positions is sufficient), those that specifically rely on self-presentation processes (Jellison & Arkin, 1977; Sanders & Baron, 1977) assume, in addition, that others in the situation must be able to deliver rewards such as social approval. In respect to this latter assumption, recall that there are several studies that attempt to demonstrate the significance of argumentation by having subjects peruse a list of cogent ideas (e.g., Burnstein, Vinokur, & Trope, 1973; Vinokur & Burnstein, 1974) or listen to a tape of a group discussion (e.g., Kogan & Wallach, 1967; Lamm, 1967). In no case did subjects know the people who generated the ideas or participated in the discussion; nor was there any prospect of meeting them. Obviously the possibility of obtaining, say, social approval from these others was nil. Nevertheless, typical polarization effects were observed.

The Depolarization of Attitudes

It should not be forgotten that following discussion, attitudes depolarize (converge) as well as polarize. In fact, among the dozen standard choice-dilemmas, there are a few so-called neutral items that do not polarize but exhibit *only* depolarization. This happens because neutral items have argument pools containing a similar number of ideas favoring the certain and uncertain course of action; as a result, each member tends to have available about as many (partially shared) prorisk as procaution arguments (Vinokur & Burnstein, 1974; Vinokur, Trope, & Burnstein, 1975). On occasion, the identical state of affairs may occur with items that are known to polarize. Consider an item that typically shifts toward K. According to persuasive-arguments theory, this means that the average individual will have access to more pro-K than pro-J arguments. Due to this, of course, that individual's prior attitude will be pro-K. Suppose there is an unusual group in which half the members are pro-J (and thus for the moment have more pro-J than pro-K arguments) and half are pro-K (and thus for the moment have more pro-K than pro-J arguments). Even though discussion typically leads to polarization toward K, the partial sharing model must predict that depolarization will occur in this group: Pro-J members will become more pro-K; pro-K members, more pro-J; and there will be little or no polarization. Furthermore, if the proportion of pro-J and pro-K arguments in the larger pool is known, even roughly, then an estimate can be made of which subgroup will depolarize the most following discussion. For example, on dilemmas that usually polarize toward risk, the number of prorisk arguments in the pool is larger than the number of procaution arguments. Thus, in discussion, prorisk members are likely to generate a greater number of additional arguments supporting their position (and to have more impact on procaution members) than the reverse. As a result, procaution individuals should shift (toward risk) more than prorisk individuals (toward caution). A similar line of reasoning would predict that prorisk members will exhibit a greater shift (toward caution) than procaution members (toward risk) on dilemmas that typically polarize in a cautious direction. Finally, on neutral dilemmas, the proportion of prorisk and procaution arguments in the larger pool is similar. According to persuasive-arguments theory, therefore, prorisk and procaution subgroups should depolarize to the same extent.

From the point of view of social comparison theories, the fact that attitudes generally polarize toward K signifies that this alternative is more socially desirable and thus potentially more rewarding than J. Given our hypothetical half-pro-J and half-pro-K group, these theories suggest two possible outcomes, both of which differ from that proposed by persuasive-arguments theory. First, upon observing that others prefer K, pro-J members may realize their faux pas and change in the socially desirable direction—polarization toward K will occur. A second possibility is that pro-J members will find pro-K members too dissimilar for purposes of comparison or approval, and vice versa. By categorizing the other attitude subgroup as noncomparable, pro-J members in effect define J (not K) as the socially desirable alternative, whereas pro-K members define K (not J) as the socially desirable alternative. This implies that comparisons would be made within, not between, the two attitude subgroups. As a result, pro-J members will become increasingly pro-J, and pro-K members increasingly pro-K. The first derivation from social comparison theory suggests, therefore, that polarization will be unidirectional; the second, that polarization will be bidirectional. Neither, however, leads one to expect depolarization.

An experiment was recently performed involving groups similar in composition to the hypothetical one just described (Vinokur & Burnstein, 1978b). Subjects were selected according to their prior attitudes on the choice-dilemmas so as to constitute two attitudinally distinct subgroups within the larger discussion group. One subgroup was composed of three individuals strongly in favor of the uncertain course of action (they preferred a probability level of 3/10 or 2/10 on the 10-point scale ranging from 1/10 to 10/10); the other subgroup was composed of three individuals strongly in favor of the certain course (they preferred a probability level of 7/10 or 8/10 on this scale). In one condition, no mention was made to subjects of the sharp difference in prior attitude. In a second condtion, the difference in attitude was stressed (e.g., subjects were informed that two subgroups existed with markedly discrepant attitudes; one subgroup was seated at the opposite end of the table from the other; and a card in front of each subject identified that individual as belonging to the prorisk or procaution camp). Our expectation was that if comparison processes operated at all, it would be apparent in the latter condition. Nevertheless, no differences were found between stressing and not stressing the existence of distinct attitudinal subgroups. In both conditions, we observed a marked depolarization of attitudes. Following discussion, pro-J members become more pro-K, and pro-K members became more pro-J. In addition, on risky items, the procaution subgroups depolarized more (toward risk) than the prorisk subgroup (toward caution), and vice versa on cautious items. Finally, on neutral items, both subgroups depolarized to a similar extent. In no case did polarization, bidirectional or unidirectional, occur. Thus, the data provided strong support for persuasive-arguments theory over a social comparison interpretation.

Polarization in the Absence of Discussion

Let us briefly return to the experiment in which the number of arguments was varied independently of the number of others' attitudes (Burnstein, Vinokur, & Trope, 1974). In one particular condition of the experiment, when argumentation was minimal but the positions of several individuals were known, some polarization could be noticed. This shift in attitude, however, was much too modest to be reflected in the statistical treatment of the data. Nevertheless, we (Burnstein, Vinokur, & Trope, 1973) were puzzled and spent a little time musing over the persistence of such weak social comparison effects:

> It may well be the case that when a person reconsiders an initial choice, his first preference is to do this in the light of information contained in the arguments—if for no other reason than these statements provide better or more information for evaluating alternatives than the mere choices of others. However, when only the latter are available they will be put to use. . . . Knowledge that others' choices are discrepant from his own may induce the person to reconstruct a line of reasoning which he thinks could have produced such choices. This is to say, knowing others have chosen differently stimulates the person to generate arguments which could explain (and thus would support) their choices. (Hence) . . . informing the person that others took a position more extreme than his own does not serve so much to threaten his self-esteem or to legitimize some suppressed yearning but rather induces him to find a reasonable explanation for the difference [p. 244].

An experiment was then performed to check our musings (Burnstein & Vinokur, 1975). It consisted of three conditions. In the first, after indicating their own attitude toward J, individuals learned of the attitudes of others and immediately afterward generated arguments in respect to J. In the second, individuals also learned of the attitudes of others regarding J, but immediately afterward they had to generate arguments in respect to a completely unrelated issue. Individuals in the third condition did not find out about others' attitudes; they merely indicated their own attitude toward J and then generated arguments relevant to J. Our analysis suggests that in the absence of discussion, knowing the positions of others will lead to polarization only when this knowledge induces the person to think of arguments that might explain their positions. The implication is that polarization will occur solely in the first condition. In the other conditions, a person is either distracted from generating relevant arguments by having to deal with a different issue, or that individual simply does not know the positions of others.

In fact, polarization occurred only in the first condition, where individuals *knew* and *thought about* the attitudes of others. Furthermore, the more arguments that came to mind explaining why others might have taken the positions they did, the more likely the individual was to revise his or her own attitude accordingly. Recall from Chapter 3 that these findings are similar to those recently obtained by Tesser and his colleagues (cf. Tesser, 1978), who observed that if a moderately pro-J individual simply thinks about the issue, this alone is sufficient to polarize his or her attitude toward J. However, in no instance did these effects depend on knowledge about the attitudes of others. They appeared, in short, without there being any possibility of social comparison.

GENERALIZING PERSUASIVE-ARGUMENTS THEORY

Recently we have begun to examine the theoretical basis for an argument being persuasive and have ventured that this property might be based on an argument's *validity* and *originality*. It has been assumed that in formulating his or her position, a person generates arguments. The latter are assertions or inferences that follow from a line of reasoning. The validity of an inference (argument), thus, would depend on its soundness. Does it follow, is it justified, given the line of reasoning? The line of reasoning itself involves a string of inferences that has as its premise the information available to the person when he or she begins to think about the issue. Ordinarily, this preliminary information is contained in the way the issue is stated, in the facts given therein or immediately suggested, in what the person knows about the positions of others, and so on. The originality of an argument is defined by the number of steps in a line of reasoning. This is a rather important property because we assume that at each step, from premise to assertion, additional ideas are recruited and made accessible to the person. Therefore, when one either *generates* or *comprehends* a valid argument, the greater its originality, the more additional arguments are brought to mind. So far it has been possible to demonstrate crudely that if an argument is valid, its perceived as well as its actual persuasiveness increases with its originality (Vinokur & Burnstein, 1978b). In this study arguments were rated by judges for their validity [defined as "the extent to which the argument is true and accepted as such by most people" (p. 338)] and originality [defined as "the extent to which the argument relies on information which is already contained in the item describing the choice dilemmas situation or is new and novel" (p. 339)].

In our first experiment, the prerated arguments were presented to a large number of subjects who judged their persuasiveness. In a second experiment, subjects expressed their attitudes after receiving either (1) several valid and *original* prorisk arguments and several valid but *unoriginal* procaution arguments, or (2) several valid but *unoriginal* prorisk arguments and several valid and *original* procaution arguments. The results were straightforward. First, valid and original arguments were perceived as more persuasive than either valid and unoriginal arguments or invalid and original arguments. Second, after reading the samples of arguments, the subject's attitude polarized toward the position advocated by the original arguments rather than toward that advocated by the unoriginal arguments.

Informational processes of the type we have been discussing sometimes may seem irrelevant in the light of common sense. After all, are there not well-known experimental situations in which shifts in attitude do occur but where there seems to be virtually no information available with which to think about (or discuss) one's attitude (e.g., Sherif's autokinetic paradigm), or where the information that is available appears to argue for an attitude quite different from the one actually observed (e.g., Asch's line judgment paradigm)? Before accepting that in such cases, persuasive argumentation must be beside the point, keep in mind that there may be a mental representation of a line of reasoning, even though one has difficulty describing the information it contains in words or images (see Natsoulas, 1970; Pylyshyn, 1973). Perhaps persuasive-arguments theory should not be dismissed just because introspection suggests that informational processes are feeble. Our speculations in this respect are confined to the Asch conformity situation, where naive subjects judge which of two lines matches a third line in length after hearing some experimental accomplices, posing as real subjects, give incorrect answers. Whether or not the line judgment task is in fact "unthinkable" and "undiscussable," we will assume for the moment that argumentation does occur but is difficult to tap directly. Let us now show that this assumption has testable implications.

A number of situational factors guide (bias) the person in generating arguments. For instance, knowing that a disagreement with the majority will be made public may change the pool of relevant arguments and lead the individual to consider ideas that would never have entered his or her mind were the disagreement to remain private. Indeed, in terms of a persuasive-arguments analysis, some widely used experimental procedures for changing attitudes may actually do so because they introduce new information that redefines the universe of relevant arguments for the subject. As a consequence, ideas that were inaccessible, or that had no bearing on the issue, become accessible or pertinent. Redefining the pool, in the sense of enlarging it, may be critical for polarization when otherwise, there would be few arguments on hand with which to formulate an attitude (e.g., when the person is uninformed about the issue or when it is inherently "unarguable"). Suppose a person is asked to state his or her opinion about something quite unfamiliar—say, kumquats. Then, before discussing that opinion with others, the individual learns that this fruit has been condemned by a highly credible source—say, a group of gourmet oncologists. Although the person's familiarity with kumquats has not increased, in all likelihood, this additional information would greatly enlarge the universe of kumquat-relevant arguments, so that the number and kind of ideas contained in subsequent samples (e.g., those expressed in discussion) will be markedly different from those contained in the initial sample.

The biases that concern us here stem from the fact that individuals know the attitudes of their peers. Let us briefly consider the effects of such knowledge in relation to some well-known results from Asch (1951, 1956) having to do with the size of a majority (for an analysis of other results from Asch, see Burnstein & Vinokur, 1977). A still puzzling finding is that agreement with a unanimous majority increased with the size of the majority but only up to the size of 3 (Asch, 1956). Hence, a unanimous majority need not be large to exert all of its potential influence. Keep in mind, however, that individual attitudes are revealed in series. Since the critical subject was always next to last, that individual received more information about the preferences of others and had a greater amount of time to generate arguments as majority size increased. The knowledge that another prefers, say, alternative J rather than K focuses the person's attention on the former. The larger the majority, the more this alternative will monopolize the subject's attention and lead him or her to generate a disproportionately large number of arguments explaining why J might be preferred. Therefore, the tendency to agree with a majority would continue to increase over a large range of sizes. Asch, as we know, did not obtain such an effect. Persuasive-arguments theory suggests why: While others reveal their preference for J, the person, at some point in this string of revelations, will have exhausted the pool of pro-J arguments. From that instant, knowing that still another member favors J can have no impact because the person simply will be unable to think of additional reasons for being pro-J. Whether this point occurs early or late in the series obviously depends on the number of pro-J arguments in the pool. In the Asch conformity studies, the alternative preferred by the majority is unlikely to elicit many favorable arguments. Hence, according to persuasive-arguments theory, under these conditions the tendency to conform will not increase with the majority size beyond some relatively small value.

CHAPTER SUMMARY

Contrary to what many believe—that groups overvalue compromise and stifle radical ideas—participation in even simple social activities such as group discussion often allows a person to take a more extreme (rather than a more moderate) position on an issue than would otherwise be the case. This phenomenon, called *polarization,* has been the focus of much of the recent research on group processes and attitude change. The present chapter reviews this work and tries to arrive at some conclusions as to why polarization occurs. In so doing, two sets of theories are compared. According to one set, polarization is due mainly to affective (*normative*) processes. There is, these theories assert, a common need to increase social approval and to enhance self-esteem. Polarization is a straightforward consequence of this assumption, given also that extreme attitudes are socially desirable. That is, a member will experience a rise in social approval and self-esteem by shifting from a moderate to an extreme position. The second set of theories holds that polarization is primarily the result of cognitive (*informational*) processes. This effect will be observed when a person is deciding between different courses of action and gains access to ideas (heretofore inaccessible) that are persuasive in respect to one of the alternatives. Attitudes are especially likely to polarize in a group, according to these theories, because very often there are persuasive ideas that come to mind in only a few members. When these rare but cogent bits of wisdom are shared with others—say, in discussion—a marked shift in attitude must take place. The basic issue that concerns us, thus, is the conditions under which polarization does and does not occur. For example, will it appear if one position is no more socially desirable than another or if discussion is prevented? Our analysis of the research on questions of this type suggests that theories based on cognitive processes offer the more adequate explanation of attitude polarization.

Normative influence, as described by theories of social comparison, seems to be neither a necessary nor a sufficient condition for attitude polarization. At present, this phenomenon seems explicable in terms of cognitive processes, as described by persuasive-arguments theory. From a broader theoretical perspective, however, the relationship between persuasive-arguments theory and social comparison theory might be conceptualized as one in which the former deals with the more immediate determinants of polarization and the latter, with relatively remote determinants. In short, comparison processes may influence, say, the argument sample a person generates and, thus, indirectly affect polarization. Finally, it was suggested that persuasive-arguments theory might be extended beyond the typical polarization situation to those involving ostensibly "undiscussable" issues, where argumentation seems virtually unimaginable. Traditional analyses of social influence would have us believe that in these circumstances, changes in attitude must be due to normative processes. If this extension is warranted, it suggests rather that social influence, in general, is essentially informational.

10 Anticipatory Opinion Effects

Robert B. Cialdini
Arizona State University

Richard E. Petty
University of Missouri-Columbia

Most of the research described in previous chapters of this book involved an examination of what happens to one's opinions after a persuasive message on some topic has been encountered. Sometimes the messages come from external sources, and sometimes (as in the active participation experiments described in Chapter 1) the person constructs his or her own communication. But in each case, the focus is on what happens after the communication has been received. The work to be covered in the present chapter, however, involves a different question: *What are the effects of simply expecting to have to deal with a persuasive communication?* For example, if the President of the United States wanted to convince the public that taxes should be raised, would he be more effective if the public were forewarned of his position, or if his message took them by surprise?

There is considerable evidence that the mere anticipation of presenting or receiving a communication can produce reliable opinion effects, and under some conditions these effects can be comparable in size to those resulting from the actual receipt of a persuasive attack. Compared with the long history of research on the effects of a message upon attitude, the literature describing the influence of an expectation upon attitude is relatively recent, beginning systematically in the early 1960s. Nonetheless, a substantial number of studies have since investigated anticipatory effects, so that we now know quite a bit about them. It seems a proper initial step, then, to begin with a description of what it is that we now know about the phenomenon of anticipatory effects in persuasion.

EXPECTATIONS THAT PRODUCE
ANTICIPATORY OPINION EFFECTS

We are using the term *anticipatory opinion effect* to refer to any opinion effect that occurs as a result of simply expecting to have to deal with a persuasive communication. As we will see shortly, sometimes these anticipatory effects take the form of increased persuasion and sometimes of decreased persuasion; sometimes the effects are measured before any communication is presented and sometimes after. Before discussing the determinants and direction of these anticipatory effects, we discuss three different types of expectations with the ability to influence opinion: expecting to present a persuasive message, expecting to receive a persuasive message, and expecting to exchange views on a topic.

Expecting to Present
a Persuasive Message

Just as the act of publicly presenting a communication on a topic has been found to influence one's position on the topic (e.g., Cialdini, 1971; Janis & King, 1954; see Chapter 1), so has the anticipation of performing such an act (e.g., Brock & Blackwood, 1962; Greenwald, 1968; Jellison & Mills, 1969). In the instances of studies wherein subjects expected to state publicly a position on an issue, the reliable finding has been attitude movement in the direction of the to-be-advocated position. So when subjects have committed themselves to deliver communications that are contrary to their initial opinions, the commitment has resulted in movement toward the to-be-advocated position (e.g., Brock & Blackwood, 1962); and when subjects have intended to advocate publicly their own attitude positions, the intention has caused them to become even more extreme on the side of their initial positions (e.g., Jellison & Mills, 1969).

A possible explanation for anticipatory opinion shifts of this sort is that the commitment to public advocacy of a topic position might cause subjects to rehearse, generate, and critically evaluate the arguments they will have to use in the public presentation. This consideration of arguments in favor of the to-be-advocated position can lead to opinion shifts. If a person generates and rehearses arguments favorable to his or her initial position, the individual may become even more extreme in that view; but if arguments opposed to the person's initial position are generated and rehearsed, movement away from the initial position would be expected. Further, because one will want to make a good showing (as a communicator) in the eyes of the audience, one may be inclined to view those arguments in favor of the to-be-advocated position as more valid than before.

Data that are consistent with such an interpretation can be found in two studies. In the first (Greenwald, 1968b), subjects were assigned to write an essay favoring either specialized or general education. It was found that subjects merely expecting to write in support of specialized education became more favorable in opinion to specialized education, whereas those expecting to write in support of general education became more favorable to general education. It is also interesting to note that not only did subjects shift their opinions toward the side of the issue they expected to advocate, but they also rated statements favorable to their assigned side as more valid than did a control group. Because subjects wanted to make a good showing in their essays, they may have been inclined to view arguments that favored the to-be-advocated position as more valid than before.

The second study (Cialdini, 1971) showed that intending to advocate a position publicly did not result in opinion change when subjects did not have to construct, rehearse, or critically evaluate topic-related arguments in order to advocate a position. In the Cialdini (1971) experiment, subjects did not have to write an essay, make a speech, or engage in a discussion in order to advocate the assigned position. Instead, they only expected to have to provide a one-word description of opinion (responding "good" to various belief statements). This type of advocacy did not require the processing of topic-related arguments in preparation for a presentation of opinion, and no anticipatory opinion effect was found.

Taken together, the findings of Greenwald (1968) and Cialdini (1971) suggest that the anticipation of advocating an issue position produces opinion change by causing subjects to consider arguments related to the issue and to bias their perceptions of the validity of these arguments. This distortion of the validity of topic-relevant arguments may result from a subject's desire to be seen by the audience (usually the experimenter) as someone able to present a cogent, valid communication on an issue. However, when the vehicle for advocacy does not require a consideration or presentation of arguments, the biasing process does not occur, and no anticipatory change results.

Expecting to Receive a Persuasive Message

By far, most of the data on anticipatory effects in persuasion have come from studies in which subjects expected to receive a persuasive communication. The process whereby subjects are informed of an upcoming communication is called *forewarning*. Papageorgis (1968) has distinguished two types of forewarning employed by researchers in this area. In the first sort, subjects are told that they will be presented with a message that is designed to influence their position on some topic. We can call this procedure "forewarning of persuasive intent." It is clear to such subjects that someone, either the communicator or the experimenter, is interested in whether they will be persuaded. These forewarnings have led typically to resistance to persuasion (e.g., Hass & Grady, 1975).

In the second kind of forewarning, subjects are informed that they will be receiving a communication, the topic and/or position of which is described. We can call this procedure "forewarning of message content." Here, the subjects are not told that the purpose of the communication is to persuade them. Forewarnings of this type have sometimes led to resistance to persuasion and sometimes to susceptibility. We discuss the conditions under which each type of effect occurs shortly.

Expecting to Exchange Views on a Topic

The third type of expectation that has been found to lead to position shifts is the expectation of engaging another person in some kind of exchange of views on an issue. These anticipated exchanges are usually cast in the form of discussion or debate. Expectations of this variety have been shown to be quite powerful in influencing opinions. For example, in one experiment, subjects were asked to judge the cause of a behavior for which they had served as either a participant or an observer. When the judgments were to be made privately, participants and observers differed widely in their causal perceptions. But when a discussion of the behavior was anticipated, the actor–observer differences were eliminated (Wells, Petty, Harkins, Kagehiro, & Harvey, 1977). In another study, subjects expected to discuss a jury verdict in an affirmative action case with a partner. When subjects' attitudes toward affirmative action were made salient prior to the expected discussion, subjects moderated their positions in anticipation of that discussion. This occurred both when disagreement from the partner was expected and when no information about the partner was known (Snyder & Swann, 1976).

In the relevant conditions of a study by Deaux (1968), coeds who expected to have to defend their own opinions after watching a movie that advocated a military draft of females changed more as a consequence of that expectation than those who only anticipated having to watch the movie. Sears (1967) showed that the size of shifts resulting from the expectation of discussion was increased if the discussion involved face-to-face communication. Subjects who expected to discuss their opinions on the future of the U.S. economy with an opponent were more persuaded by a prediscussion message on the issue than were subjects who expected to communicate with, but not physically face, an opponent. It was also found that expecting to face a highly critical discussion partner led to more change than expecting to face a less critical opponent. In all, it appears that expecting to engage in an exchange of views is a strong and reliable motivator of opinion change.

DETERMINING THE DIRECTION
OF ANTICIPATORY SHIFTS

One aspect of anticipatory opinion effects that was puzzling during the initial years of research on the phenomenon was the seemingly unpredictable direction that the effects would take. As we noted earlier, some studies indicated that forewarning of the onset of a persuasive communication produced *less* change in the direction of the message than no such warning, but others indicated that forewarning produced *more* change in the direction of the expected communication.

Timing of Measurement

The confusion was compounded because some researchers measured the effect of the forewarning on attitude change before any communication was presented, whereas others measured attitudes after the communication. In the typical post-communication assessment, the subjects were led to expect exposure to a counterattitudinal message on a specific topic; the message was then delivered; and finally, the amount of opinion movement resulting from the message was measured. Both significantly increased (e.g., Sears, 1967) and significantly decreased (e.g., Freedman & Sears, 1965) susceptibilities to the communication have been obtained from this set of procedures.

In the typical precommunication assessment experiment, subjects were informed that a persuasive communication would be provided; but before the communication was delivered, subjects' positions on the issue were measured. In this way, the immediate effect of simply expecting to receive a persuasive attack could be determined. Again, experiments employing this sequence of procedures have demonstrated more opinion movement in the direction of the anticipated communication in some instances (e.g., Cooper & Jones, 1970) but less change in the direction of the communication in other instances (e.g., Petty & Cialdini, 1976). So, although procedural differences in the way anticipatory effects have been measured have complicated the picture, both positive and negative influences of forewarning on opinion movement have been obtained. Thus, the direction of such movement cannot be explained through an examination of whether anticipatory effects have been assessed in terms of pre- or postcommunication attitude change.

Issue Importance

If the timing of the attitude measurement does not influence the direction of the attitude change, what does? One factor that now appears to play a decisive role can be seen in the data of the Allyn and Festinger (1961) experiment, a study that is regarded as the first investigation of the forewarning phenomenon. The study is usually described as showing that high school students who were warned about an antiteenage driving speech were less persuaded by it than those who were not forewarned. It is the case, however, that with all subjects included in the analysis, there was no significant difference between the groups. It was only when Allyn and Festinger examined separately those subjects for whom having a driver's license was important that the persuasion-inhibiting effect of forewarning became significant.

Personal Involvement

The relationship is not quite so simple as the previous paragraph would suggest, however. For instance, several studies have found forewarning to increase persuasion on such important topics as the future of the American economy (Sears, 1967) and the likelihood of a third World War (Papageorgis, 1967). It seems that it is one special type of issue importance that influences the direction of preliminary opinion shifts—direct, *personal* importance. It is when subjects are *personally involved* with the topic that forewarning reduces opinion movement in the direction of a counterattitudinal persuasive message. When the topic is not of strong personal relevance, forewarning increases such movement. From this perspective, it is not surprising that on such generally important but personally noninvolving issues as the probability of finding a cure for cancer (McGuire & Millman, 1965), the expansion of federal government into state activities (Cooper & Jones, 1970), or man's destruction of the ecological system (Gaes & Tedeschi, 1978), forewarning has led to greater anticipatory change in the direction advocated; whereas on a generally unimportant but personally relevant issue such as raising by 15 cents the fare for New York subways (the subjects were New York City college students), forewarning has led to less persuasion (Hass & Grady, 1975).

Research that has specifically manipulated the personal relevance of the topic has shown the extent to which the subject's involvement with the issue is necessary for forewarning to produce less persuasion. Apsler and Sears (1968) warned their college student subjects of the advent of a communication advocating that a large number of undergraduate courses be taught by teaching assistants rather than professors. Half the subjects were informed that the communication proposed that the new policy should take effect in the next year, thereby affecting the subjects personally; these were the high-involvement subjects. The other half of the subjects were told that the communication argued that the policy should take effect in 12 years; these were the low-involvement subjects. It was found that the forewarning manipulation had opposite effects on the two groups. The low-involvement subjects changed a good deal *more* in the direction of the message as a result of being forewarned, whereas the high-involvement subjects changed slightly *less* than the comparable unwarned groups.

Public Commitment

Freedman, Sears, and O'Connor (1964) as well as Jones and Kiesler (Kiesler, 1971) varied the topic involvement of their subjects in a different manner. By arranging for subjects to be publicly committed to their initial issue positions, the personal relevance of the issue was increased. The pattern of results in both studies indicated that forewarning led to greater persuasion with low personal involvement but to less persuasion with high personal involvement. In sum, it now appears that a prime determinant of the direction of anticipatory opinion shifts is the extent to which the topic is personally important (i.e., involving) for the subject. Opinions tend to shift more in the direction of an anticipated message when the topic is not personally involving but to shift less in that direction when the topic is personally involving.

MEDIATION OF ANTICIPATORY SHIFTS

In the first part of this chapter, we described several known features of anticipatory opinion effects. In the next part, we discuss the ways in which researchers in the area, on the basis of these and other such features, have speculated about the basic nature of the shifts and the mechanisms that bring them about. These speculations have differed for anticipatory effects leading to decreased persuasion and for anticipatory effects leading to increased persuasion. Consequently, we consider each category of effect separately.

Factors Leading to Decreased Persuasion

Forewarning of Message Content

McGuire and Papageorgis (1962) hypothesized that the persuasion-inhibiting effect of expecting to receive a persuasive attack could be explained in terms of a counterargumentation process. The warning that a counterattitudinal communication is about to be delivered might stimulate one to begin rehearsing and generating thoughts that would counter the arguments of the inpending message and support one's own position on the topic. Once fortified in this fashion, one would be better able to resist the attack; thus, persuasion would be reduced. This counterargumentation hypothesis has received confirmation in a number of ways.

Time to Generate Defenses. One source of support comes from the apparent fact that forewarning of the content of an upcoming message has produced less change in the direction of the message only when some delay (of at least 2 minutes) has separated the warning and the onset of the message. Consistent with the counterargumentation hypothesis, then, only when subjects have been given sufficient time to build a cognitive defense has forewarning of the content of a persuasion attempt blunted the impact of the attack. Most studies of this sort have simply imposed a delay between the warning and the message (e.g., Allyn & Festinger, 1961; Apsler & Sears, 1968).

Some experimenters, however, have manipulated the amount of time allotted to subjects after the warning but before the message. Presumably, the longer the delay, the more will subjects be able to engage in counterresponding to the anticipated communication, and the more resistance to persuasion will result. Freedman and Sears (1965) tested this prediction with a modification of the Allyn and Festinger (1961) procedure. High school students were told to expect to hear a talk that strongly opposed teenage driving. Then, 0, 2, or 10 minutes later, they heard the speech. Exactly according to prediction, subjects who experienced no delay were least resistant to the influence of the speech, whereas those who experienced the 10-minute delay were most resistant. Subsequent experiments (e.g., Hass & Grady, 1975; Petty & Cacioppo, 1977) have replicated this effect.

Anticipatory Counterargumentation.   Additional support for the anticipatory counterargumentation hypothesis can be seen in studies that have measured cognitive responses while subjects were expecting to encounter an attack on their issue positions. In a study by Brock (1967), undergraduates expected to read a communication advocating an increase in tuition at their university. Subjects were forewarned that the communication would advocate either a $10, $125, or $275 increase in fees and were given 10 minutes to write down all their thoughts about the issue before receiving the message. The results indicated that subjects listed counterarguments to the tuition increase in anticipation of the message, and the number of counterarguments recorded increased with communication discrepancy. Correlations between the measures of counterarguing and subsequent message acceptance suggested that anticipatory counterargumentation increased resistance to the communication.

Similar evidence for anticipatory counterargumentation was obtained by Petty and Cacioppo (1977) even when subjects were not specifically instructed to record thoughts on the topic. Instead, in some conditions, subjects were asked to list only those thoughts that actually occurred to them after the warning but preceding the message. In two experiments, subjects who were forewarned of counterattitudinal communications on highly involving topics were changed less by the communication than nonforewarned subjects. The forewarning also caused greater counterargumentation to occur before the communication was received. To further test the counterargument explanation, these authors included a group of subjects who were asked to list their thoughts about the message topic, although they did not expect to receive any communication on that topic. This group showed resistance to persuasion equivalent to that of a forewarned group, indicating that anticipatory thinking about an involving counterattitudinal advocacy is sufficient to produce resistance.

The preceding experiments suggest that expecting to be exposed to a counterattitudinal message on a personally involving topic produces a tendency to generate arguments favorable to one's side of the topic and unfavorable to the other side. This anticipatory thinking solidifies one's initial position prior to the message and reduces subsequent susceptibility to persuasion.

Forewarning of Persuasive Intent

It is informative to note that the anticipatory counterargumentation hypothesis seems only able to explain anticipatory opinion resistance effects when subjects have been forewarned about the *content* of an upcoming message. In studies that have demonstrated reduced persuasion as a result of warning subjects of the communicator's persuasive intent, a different mechanism appears to apply. Recall that the distinction between forewarning of message content and forewarning of persuasive intent is the one articulated by Papageorgis (1968) and described at the outset of this chapter. Unlike studies employing forewarning of message content, studies examining the effects of forewarning of persuasive intent have not required that a delay period exist between the warning and the message.

For example, Hass and Grady (1975) showed equally strong reductions in susceptibility to a communication when there was no delay and when there was a 10-minute delay between the information that the communication was designed to change attitudes and the onset of the communication. Thus, because there was no time in the no-delay condition for subjects to prepare arguments to counter the persuasive message in advance of the communication (and without a warning of message content, subjects are not even aware of what the communication is about), some mechanism other than anticipatory counterargumentation likely accounts for the increased resistance. One possibility is that a communicator who appears to be specifically interested in persuading the subjects is seen as a less trustworthy source of the truth about the topic. That is, the information presented in the message may be suspect because its primary intent is to persuade rather than to represent reality accurately. The subjects' tendency, then, might be to discount and derogate the arguments of the communication as they are heard.

This explanation suggests that forewarnings of persuasive intent may produce resistance to persuasion by motivating subjects to engage in increased counterargumentation and derogation *during* the receipt of the message. Several studies support this interpretation. Kiesler and Kiesler (1964) showed that subjects who were informed at the beginning of a communication that it had a persuasive purpose were more resistant than those who were so informed at the end of the communication (when it was too late to increase counterarguing). Watts and Holt (1979) demonstrated that a forewarning of persuasive intent did not confer resistance if the subjects were distracted during the presentation of the message, although it had the usual effect when no distraction was present. The distraction presumably inhibited the subjects' ability to counterargue during the message, thereby eliminating the effect of the forewarning. Petty and Cacioppo (1979) hypothesized that a forewarning of persuasive intent instills *reactance* in subjects and motivates them to counterargue in order to assert their freedom to hold a contrary attitude. Because greater reactance should be aroused, the greater the personal relevance of the attitude under attack (Brehm, 1966), a forewarning of persuasive intent should produce greater inhibition of persuasion for a counterattitudinal message on a topic of high rather than low personal relevance. This result was obtained. In addition, this study found that high-involvement subjects generated more counterarguments to the message when warned of the communicator's persuasive intent than when unwarned.

Factors Leading to Increased Persuasion

As noted earlier in this chapter, a number of studies have shown that anticipation of exposure to a persuasive message (either self- or externally originated) results in greater opinion movement in the direction of the expected message. It is perhaps important to note that what all these studies have in common is that subjects believed from the outset that their opinions would be monitored. Thus, a critical factor determining whether these anticipatory movements will occur may be whether subjects can infer that their attitudinal reactions to the impending message will be observed.

Direct evidence for this statement can be seen in an experiment by Cooper and Jones (1970, Study 2). They informed one group of subjects that they were about to receive a counterattitudinal message on a specific topic and that the experimenters were interested in measuring opinion change that resulted from hearing the message. A second group of subjects were also led to expect the counterattitudinal message but were told that the experimenters were interested in examining how people can recall and recognize various aspects of a communication. Only the subjects who expected to receive the communication in the context of an experiment on persuasion showed any anticipatory opinion change as compared to a control group. Thus, it was only when the experimenter was monitoring the subjects' opinions that forewarning of the content of a message had an influence on those opinions.

A subsequent study by Cialdini, Levy, Herman, and Evenbeck (1973) indicated that the experimenter is not the only person whose ability to observe a subject's position after receipt of a message can bring about anticipatory opinion change. In this study, the *communicator's* capability of observing subjects' opinion responses produced an effect on opinion when subjects expected to receive the communication, and this was so even though the experimenter was purportedly not interested in opinion change.

Cooper and Jones (1970, Study 1) also demonstrated that mere knowledge that a persuasive communication existed did not cause opinion change to occur. It was only when such knowledge was combined with subjects' expectations that they would actually be exposed to the communication, and that their opinions would be observed afterward, that subjects shifted their positions on the issue. We now turn to some of the explanations that have been proposed to account for anticipatory opinion changes in the direction of the expected communication.

Self-Esteem

McGuire and Millman (1965) suggested a self-esteem mechanism as the process that accounted for anticipatory shifts. The expectation of exposure to a counterattitudinal message includes the possibility that one will be persuaded by the message, an event that could be damaging to self-esteem. In order to minimize any influence directly attributable to the message, a useful tactic would be to change in the communicator's direction prior to the message, thereby reducing the apparent impact of the message and salvaging self-esteem. Although certain results can be seen as supportive of the self-esteem hypothesis (e.g., Dinner, Lewkowicz, & Cooper, 1972), not all the relevant data have been supportive (e.g., Cooper & Jones, 1970; Deaux, 1972).

Cognitive Consistency

Papageorgis (1967) has proposed a cognitive consistency mechanism to account for the effect. He suggested that the knowledge that an opposing communication is forthcoming informs the subject that someone holds an antagonistic position. This information presumably causes an unbalanced cognitive state and a tendency to restore balance by changing opinion immediately. It now appears, contrary to Papageorgis' formulation, that the mere knowledge that an opposing argument exists does not produce the anticipatory shift; it is also necessary to expect to be exposed to a communication (e.g., Cooper & Jones, 1970; Hass & Mann, 1976). Consequently, the interpretation of Papageorgis (1967) does not seem to be a likely explanation.

Conformity

Another possibility is that the anticipatory shift is due to conformity pressures. Pressures to conform are more apt to be present if a person is actually to be confronted with a counterattitudinal communication rather than merely learning of its existence. Although there are many different conceptualizations and definitions of conformity, most definitions include a component of movement or change in beliefs or behavior due to the influence of another person or group that results in increased similarity between the individual and the other person or group. In general terms, conformity is thought to occur because of the implicit assumption that behaving like others will elicit approval, whereas dissimilar behavior will bring negative consequences (cf. Allen, 1965; Kiesler & Kiesler, 1969). More specifically, conformity in judgments and opinions may occur as a tactic of ingratiation, an attempt to increase one's own attractiveness in the eyes of another (Jones, 1964); or conformity may be an attempt to increase one's certainty about one's own physical or social reality (Festinger, 1954).

Numerous researchers have documented the conditions under which persons will shift their opinions and judgments after learning of the beliefs held by other people (e.g., Hovland & Pritzker, 1957; White, 1975). More germane to the current chapter, however, is that research has demonstrated that persons will shift their judgments to conform to those of other persons in *anticipation* of hearing those opinions (cf. Fisher, Rubinstein, & Freeman, 1956). This conformity process may explain why expecting to hear a persuasive message can cause anticipatory opinion change in the direction of the communication. The target person may simply change in order to conform with the communicator's expected position.

Moderation

A fourth possibility is that anticipatory shifts are a result of movement toward a more neutral position rather than a conformity shift toward the communicator's expected opinion. Cialdini et al. (1973) noted that all the prior research demonstrating anticipatory opinion shifts in the direction of a communicator had employed communicators whose opinions were on the side of the topic opposite to the subject's own; that is, the expected messages were always counterattitudinal. It seemed conceivable, then, that the repeatedly observed shifts obtained when a persuasive message was expected did not represent movement toward the communicator's opinion after all but, rather, movement toward a more moderate, middle position on the opinion scale. Because the communicator's position and the middle portion of the scale were always in the same direction relative to the subject's initial position, it was never possible to determine whether the anticipatory change constituted an attempt to conform to the communicator's opinion or an attempt to shift toward the middle of the scale. The latter possibility was termed a *moderation shift*.

Reasons for Moderation.   For a number of reasons, someone expecting a persuasive message may wish to move toward a more neutral point on the topic prior to message receipt. A middle position is quite a flexible one. For example, if one is expecting a discussion on the topic with the communicator, holding a central position enables one to reduce the possibility of an embarrassing defeat in the discussion; such a position allows the greatest number of arguments and counterarguments to be put forth. The middle is advantageous—no matter what the opponent's position—for someone wishing to be viewed as an able discussant, because defensive arguments can be selected from both sides of the issue without the appearance of inconsistency. Further, a moderate stance is usually associated with broad-mindedness—an ideal trait to project in an exchange if one is interested in conveying a favorable impression. Finally, if one wishes to assess the validity of anticipated information in an unbiased fashion, a neutral stance affords just such an opportunity.

Conformity versus Moderation.   Cialdini et al. (1973) tested the extent to which a tendency for movement toward the opponent's opinion and movement toward a moderate opinion accounted for anticipatory shifts in their subjects who expected to discuss an issue with a peer. As in the other experiments obtaining anticipatory shifts away from subjects' initial opinions, the topics employed were not of high personal relevance. The conformity and moderation explanations were tested against one another in two ways, both involving the stated opinion of the expected discussion partner.

In the first test, one group of subjects were told that they would discuss a certain issue with a fellow subject. Although the issue was described, the subjects were not told what the other's position would be on the issue. If conformity were the only process operating, then these subjects should not have moved their positions toward the other side of the issue, because they did not know where their discussion partner would stand. The moderation hypothesis, on the other hand, would predict movement toward the center of the scale, because moderation is viewed as advantageous no matter what the other's opinion. In support of the moderation hypothesis, substantial shifts toward the middle of the opinion scale were found in these subjects prior to discussion. A study by Hass (1975) has replicated this finding in a standard forewarning setting where subjects only expected to hear a taped message. Subjects who were informed of the nature of the topic ("The Future U.S. Economic Situation"), but who were not told the communicator's position, showed significant change toward the center of the scale before message receipt.

The second test pitted the two explanations against one another by including a group of subjects who were told that they would discuss the topic with a peer who was on the same side of the issue as they were but who was more extreme. Here, a conformity interpretation of anticipatory shifts would predict that these subjects would move in the direction of the discussant's position and, thus, would polarize their own views. The moderation interpretation, however, would continue to expect movement toward the middle of the opinion scale. Cialdini et al. (1973) found such subjects to shift toward the middle of the scale in anticipation of discussion. Although this result is consistent with the moderation hypothesis, the size of the moderation shift in these subjects was smaller than usual. The reduced magnitude of change caused the authors to suggest that both moderation and conformity pressures were operative.

When the expected opponent holds a view that is similar but more extreme than the subject's, conformity and moderation pressures will work against each other and may result in smaller change; when the opponent holds a position on the other side of the issue, however, the pressures to move toward the middle and to move toward the opponent will not cancel themselves out, and a larger shift will result. Confirmation of the tendency for a similar but more extreme communicator to bring about lessened anticipatory change than a dissimilar communicator can be seen in a pair of experiments by Hass (1975), who again merely forewarned subjects of an impending communication. Hass (1975) argued that if the subjects were comparing their own attitude positions with the extreme stance to be taken by the communicator, they may have felt relatively moderate to begin with and thus felt no need to move further toward the middle of the scale.

THE STRATEGIC NATURE
OF ANTICIPATORY SHIFTS

Although theorizing about the character of anticipatory opinion effects has been limited, for the most part, either to effects leading to decreased persuasion or effects leading to enhanced persuasion, one group of workers in the area has generated a general formulation of anticipatory shifts. Cialdini et al. (1973) suggested a conceptualization of anticipatory shifts as different from attitude change. There were two main findings of that study. First, subjects expecting to discuss an uninvolving issue with a peer became more moderate on the issue than did subjects who did not expect to discuss it; further, the moderation tendency occurred even when the other's position on the issue was unknown, and even (but to a lesser degree) when the other's position was on the same side as the subjects' but was more extreme. Second, when subjects were then told that they would not have to engage in a discussion of the issue after all, the changes they had exhibited while expecting discussion disappeared; they reverted back to their initial positions without any apparent residual effects.

The first set of findings from Cialdini et al. (1973) suggested that opinion shifts were tactical in character. The moderation shifts seemed to be attempts to seize the middle of the opinion scale and thereby afford subjects a safe, defensible position in the expected discussion. The second finding—that the preliminary opinion movement disappeared when the anticipation of discussion was cancelled—implied something else about these shifts. Not only did they seem tactical in nature, but they appeared to be elastic as well. When the situational pressures that had brought about a position shift were released, a subject's issue position snaped back to its original form much in the manner of an elastic band. Together, these qualities of anticipatory shifts suggested that they were different from attitude change as it is traditionally characterized. Attitudes are usually seen to be relatively durable, consistent tendencies to respond evaluatively to some object over various situations and points in time. However, the new issue positions assumed by subjects in anticipation of discussion showed none of the stability normally associated with an attitude. Rather, they seemed temporary, plastic, and contingent on the immediate reward context.

From these results, Cialdini et al. (1973) proposed a conceptualization of anticipatory shifts as strategic maneuvers designed to maximize the rewards of the impending situation. According to the strategic view, when a moderation shift will serve to maximize the upcoming situational rewards, a person will assume a more neutral stance; but when a polarization shift will serve to maximize such rewards, a person will become more extreme in opinion. In addition to occurring primarily in the interest of situational utility, the shifts are conceived as having, by themselves, little or no effect upon true attitude. Like an elastic band, one's position on an issue may be stretched and distorted under situational pressures (e.g., the desire to look good in an imminent discussion of the issue), only to revert to its initial form as soon as the pressures are removed. Consistent with the view that anticipatory shifts are strategic in nature, Turner (1977) found that anticipatory moderation was greater for subjects who were high in social anxiety (indicating a general discomfort in the presence of others) than for those who were not socially anxious. Finally, it might be noted that anticipatory shifts do not necessarily represent a conscious strategy of distortion. Subjects may be completely unaware that they are shifting; or, as Hass, Mann, and Stevens (1977) explain, subjects may merely be emphasizing a different aspect of their attitudes within their latitudes of acceptance.

An Experimental Test of the Strategic View

Cialdini, Levy, Herman, Kozlowski, and Petty (1976) conducted two experiments employing several different opinion topics that were designed to test the strategic conception of anticipatory opinion change. They reasoned that if anticipatory shifts were to be viewed best as tactics designed to maximize situational rewards, then by manipulating the rewards that would result from the anticipatory opinion change in a situation, it should be possible to influence the kinds of anticipatory shifts that occurred. In each experiment, the situational rewards were manipulated by varying the extent of personal involvement with the issue. It was felt that when the issue to be discussed was not an important one for a subject, the prime concern would not be a strong presentation of his or her own opinion on the topic but would be a strong presentation of a defensible and admirable position in the discussion. In such a situation, where maintenance of a positive image is the major situational goal, a moderate issue position would be most conducive to the achievement of that goal. Consequently, moderation shifts should occur in anticipation of discussion. When subjects anticipate the discussion of an issue of high personal importance, however, the concern with projecting an image should be dwarfed by pressures associated with the topic itself. That is, one would not wish to take a weak public stand on an issue with which one was highly involved. In fact, the prospect of having to argue publicly one's position on a personally important topic might cause one to become even more extreme on the topic. Thus, it was thought that the direction of anticipatory shifts that occur in expectation of discussion would depend on the personal relevance of the issue for the subjects.

Another way to test the conception of anticipatory shifts as operating only to enhance the accomplishment of situational goals would be to arrange a situation in which such ends could not be immediately attained through a change in issue position. That is, if a person were anticipating immediate discussion, tactical position shifts would be expected to take place at once, so as to maximize the receipt of positive outcomes in the upcoming discussion. However, if one were anticipating a long wait before the onset of discussion, such shifts would be less likely to occur, because holding a position that is different from one's true attitude for an extended time would involve substantial cognitive effort and would serve no immediate situational purpose. Here, a discussant might be expected to refrain from anticipatory position change until a time shortly before the start of discussion. According to the foregoing analysis, then, the expectation of discussion should produce moderation only when the onset of discussion is imminent and the topic is not personally important.

Experimental Results

In their two experiments, Cialdini et al. (1976) had half their subjects expect to discuss a personally important issue and half, an unimportant one; additionally, half the subjects anticipated immediate discussion, whereas the other half

thought the discussion would occur 1 week later. As predicted, opinion moderation was found only when subjects expected immediate discussion of a noninvolving issue. This result lends support to the contention that the anticipatory
moderation shifts of earlier studies were strategic in nature, occurring only in the
interest of situational utility. That is, when the situational contingencies did not
favor moderation or did not require immediate moderation, no such shifts took
place. Subjects in each of the other experimental conditions tended to polarize
their positions in expectation of discussion (i.e., they moved away from the
middle of the scale, taking more extreme views on their own sides of the issue).

Opinion Snapback.   A final result was that—as in the Cialdini et al. (1973)
study—when the expectation of discussion was canceled, there was a tendency
for all subjects to snap back to their initial positions on the issue. This snapback
effect again suggests that anticipatory opinion changes are tactical and elastic in
character. With the cancellation of discussion, the situational pressures producing the preliminary shifts were removed, and subjects reverted to their original
positions. However, the subjects in one experimental condition (i.e., those expecting to discuss a personally important issue immediately) were decidedly less
susceptible to a snapback effect than those in the other conditions. The data from
these experiments can be seen in Table 10.1.

Cognitive Responses Produce Resistance to Snapback.   The finding that subjects expecting immediate discussion of a personally relevant issue were resistant
to a snapback effect suggested that the manner in which the anticipatory shifts
occurred in these subjects made the initial change relatively nonelastic. Perhaps

TABLE 10.1
Polarization and Moderation Shifts

| | Personal Relevance of Issue | | | |
| | High | | Low | |
	Immediate Discussion	Delayed Discussion	Immediate Discussion	Delayed Discussion
	Experiment 1			
Discussion anticipated	1.79	1.68	−1.67	1.72
Discussion canceled	1.33	0.22	0.58	0.52
	Experiment 2			
Discussion anticipated	1.76	1.63	−2.67	0.86
Discussion canceled	1.48	0.00	−0.55	−0.58
Supportive thoughts	3.78	2.77	2.87	2.27

Note. Positive means for the discussion-anticipated and discussion-canceled measures indicate
polarization shifts; negative means indicate moderation shifts. Data adapted from Cialdini, Levy,
Herman, Kozlowski, and Petty (1976).

only these subjects were motivated to undertake cognitive activity in support of their new positions. That is, subjects in each of the other conditions were expecting a discussion on a topic of little importance to them, or a discussion that would not take place for a week, or both; thus, they may not have been willing to do the cognitive work necessary to solidify their positions. A cognitive response analysis of persuasion suggests that persisting persuasion effects are a function of one's cognitive responses to an issue or message. Genuine shifts in an attitude position are said to occur to the extent that one engages in cognitive activity supportive of that position Greenwald (1968b). For example, Petty (1977a) has demonstrated that subjects who memorized their own cognitive responses to a message showed greater persistence of persuasion than subjects who memorized the message arguments or neutral statements. It may have been, then, that for subjects who expected immediate discussion of a personally relevant topic, their tendency to generate and rehearse thoughts that supported their side of the issue caused their anticipatory polarization shifts to become nonelastic, real changes in attitude. The situational contingencies in the other three conditions, however, may not have motivated subjects to do the cognitive work necessary to make their position shifts durable; thus, when the discussion was canceled and the discussion-related influences were removed, the shifts disappeared as well.

In order to test this possibility, the second experiment of Cialdini et al. (1976) included a measure of the kind of cognitive activity the subjects were engaging in while they were still expecting the discussion. Subjects were asked to record any thoughts they were having concerning the discussion issue. It was found that the subjects expecting an immediate discussion on an involving topic exhibited a greater degree of cognitive activity in support of their own sides of the issue. That is, they recorded significantly more *supportive thoughts* concerning their positions than did the subjects in the other cells. The measure of supportive thoughts consisted of the number of thoughts recorded that either favored the subject's own position or that attacked the opposing position (see Table 10.1).

In a subsequent experiment, Petty and Cialdini (1976, cited in Petty, 1977) obtained more direct support for the view that the persistence of attitude polarization depends on the generation and/or rehearsal of supportive thoughts. In this experiment, all subjects were led to expect an immediate discussion on a highly involving topic with an opponent. Half the subjects were distracted from thinking about the topic in the prediscussion interval, and half were not. Although all subjects showed anticipatory attitude polarization, only the nondistracted group persisted in the polarized view when the discussion expectation was canceled.

Concluding Remarks

It may well be that the concept of elastic shifts is relevant to much more of the literature on persuasion than that concerning anticipatory shifts. That is, much of the experimental laboratory literature on attitude change may tell us nothing about the manner in which true attitudes are modified but, rather, may inform us only as to when and how people shift their positions on various issues so as to maximize situational outcomes. Thus, it is conceivable that the majority of variables and procedures said to produce attitude change may have little influence on lasting attitude; instead, they may only affect transient, tactical position shifts. Perhaps these variables and procedures bring about new stances that approach the status of attitudes only to the extent that they provide the motivation and opportunity for cognitive activity supportive of the new positions.

Such a possibility is consistent with the conclusions of reviews of the literature on the persistence of experimentally induced attitude change (Cook & Flay, 1978; Petty, 1977a). We do not wish to imply, however, that such a conceptualization of traditional attitude change research renders it unimportant. On the contrary, it is our feeling that a great majority of everyday interaction on one issue or another involves the strategic shifting about of one's position rather than genuine changes in attitude. Hence, the great part of the research on "attitude change" is just as relevant as ever. However, it is our belief that the research may well embody a mislabeling of the phenomenon under investigation, and that a clearer understanding of the phenomenon's identity will result in a clearer understanding of the processes involved in its occurrence.

CHAPTER SUMMARY

In the beginning of this chapter, we defined an *anticipatory opinion effect* as any opinion effect that occurs as a result of simply expecting to have to deal with a persuasive communication, whether that communication is to be self-originated or externally originated. Three kinds of expectations have been shown to produce such effects—expecting (1) to present a persuasive message, (2) to receive a persuasive message, and (3) to exchange views on a topic.

When a person expects to present a persuasive message but does not expect to hear information on the topic from any other source, anticipatory movement in the direction of the to-be-advocated position occurs. This shift is thought to be due to the anticipatory rehearsal and positive evaluation of cognitive responses that favor the to-be-advocated view.

If the person does expect to hear further information on a topic, however—as when he or she is forewarned of the content of an impending message—or if an exchange of views is anticipated, the direction of the anticipatory effect appears to depend on the personal importance of the attitude topic. The effects of forewarning on opinion shifts have been measured both before and after the communication has been presented.

Results from studies employing the postcommunication assessment procedure indicate that when a person expects to receive a counterattitudinal communication on a topic of high personal relevance, resistance to the persuasive message will occur if the person has time to generate counterarguments before being exposed to the communication. Susceptibility to the communication is more likely if there is no time to generate defenses before receiving the message, or if the topic is one of low personal relevance. If a person is forewarned that the communicator has a persuasive intent, resistance to persuasion also occurs and may be due to increased counterargumentation during receipt of the message.

If attitudes are measured before the expected communication is delivered, the direction of the anticipatory opinion change is again determined by issue involvement. On topics of low involvement, anticipatory moderation occurs, but on topics of high involvement, anticipatory polarization is more likely. These anticipatory opinion shifts were viewed as strategic responses designed to facilitate personal rewards.

Anticipatory opinion changes have only been shown to appear when the subject can infer beforehand that his or her opinion response will be evaluated by someone. This finding fits the strategic response model in that the personal goals postulated to bring about the shifts—the protection of public image and the avoidance of a weak public stand on a personally relevant issue—involve the presence of observers of one's reactions. When such evaluating observers are not present, the reasons for anticipatory change are removed, and the shifts do not occur.

Another major finding of the research on anticipatory opinion movement concerns its elastic quality. When the expectation that leads to anticipatory moderation shifts is removed, the shifts disappear as well. This suggests that the shifts are active responses to the demands of the impending situation. When the new opinions that were strategically stretched to fit the anticipated reward contingencies are no longer useful, subjects snap back to their initial positions. One exception to the temporary quality of anticipatory change has been shown when the demands of the impending situation require both preliminary change and cognitive activity in support of that change. When supportive cognitive responses accompany the anticipatory shifts, the shifts are solidified by the supportive activity and acquire the more durable quality of true attitude change. Finally, it was suggested that the concept of an elastic shift might be relevent to much more of the literature on persuasion than just that concerning anticipatory shifts.

11 Repetition, Cognitive Responses, and Persuasion

Alan Sawyer
Ohio State University

INTRODUCTION

Recently, *Newsweek* magazine published the following story.

> Last July, an Exeter, N.H., man named John Adams announced his candidacy for the Republican nomination in the state's First Congressional District. Adams, 61, an unemployed taxi driver who claims he was once a Massachusetts state senator, ran a do-nothing campaign. He made no speeches, issued no press releases, spent no money. "I did absolutely no campaigning," he said. "With a name like mine I didn't figure I had to."
>
> Apparently not. Last week, Adams won the primary, defeating his closest competitor, local newspaper columnist Edward Hewson, 30, by 4,000 votes. "We never saw Mr. Adams or read anything coming from him," said Hewson's campaign manager. "We have no way to evaluate why people voted for him."
>
> New Hampshire GOP chairman Gerald Carmen seemed less baffled. "When people went to the polls, they saw four names they didn't recognize," he explained. "*I guess they picked the one that sounded familiar*" [*Newsweek*, September 27, 1976; p. 36; italics added].

A few years ago, the Associated Press carried the following report from Corvallis, Oregon:

> A mysterious student has been attending a class at Oregon University for the past two months enveloped in a big black bag. Only his bare feet show. Each Monday, Wednesday, and Friday at 11:00 A.M. the Black Bag sits on a small table near the back of the classroom. The class is Speech 113—basic persuasion... Charles Goetzinger, professor of the class, knows the identity of the person inside. None of

the 20 students in the class do. Goetzinger said *the students' attitude changed from hostility toward the Black Bag to curiosity and finally to friendship.*

Both these incidents could be explained by *mere exposure theory.* This theory hypothesizes that familiar objects and people are more liked than less familiar ones, and that by merely being repetitively exposed, something initially unfamiliar will be looked upon more favorably.

Although most formal conceptualization and experimental research have been done in only the last few years, people have apparently long assumed that familiarization by repeated exposures will enhance liking. Parents repeatedly urge their children to "try a little of that spinach; you will learn to really like it." Sociologists and lawmakers have argued that racial prejudice can be reduced by integration and increased familiarity among different races and ethnic groups. Record companies were so convinced of the value of repeated exposure that they bribed radio stations and disc jockeys to play their records.

Communicators have also used repetition to gain acceptance of an idea. Repetition was an instrumental part of propaganda campaigns in Nazi Germany and in "brainwashing" attempts in North Korean prison camps. Schools use repetition for persuasion purposes, as well as for a teaching tool. Perhaps the most prominent use of repetition is by the advertising industry. Many advertisers believe that repetition of a campaign theme has almost limitless benefits and that a most common mistake is to change a good campaign idea too soon (e.g., Reeves, 1961). Certainly, exposure frequency is a much discussed element in most advertising campaigns (Krugman, 1968; Ray and Sawyer, 1971a).

However, it seems that the effects of repetition are far from uniformly and infinitely positive. Children often react negatively to parents' repeated arguments. Many highly exposed records never become hits, and most hit records eventually become tiresome and vanish from popularity lists. Although the familiarity of some political incumbents makes their reelection almost certain, other politicians become boring and irritating to their electorates. Television viewers list repetition as the single most irritating aspect of TV commercials.

Advertisers recognize that repetition effects are not uniform and that certain aspects of the product, the medium, and the ad copy and format may influence the effects of repeated exposures. Many advertisers worry that highly familiar ads may lose their effectiveness and "wear out" (Greenberg & Suttoni, 1973). Although much is known about repetition and learning, relatively little is known about how repeated advertising affects attitudes or purchase behavior.

COGNITIVE RESPONSES TO
MULTIPLE EXPOSURES

The focus of exposure research has recently been on *why* exposure enhances liking, *when* it does, and the conditions and processes underlying multiple exposure effects. Various types of cognitive responses have been hypothesized in different theories of the effects of multiple exposures. These cognitive activities include responses associated with learning and recognition, exploratory responses, meaningfulness and positiveness of associations to repeated stimuli, and counter or support arguments.

By studying the responses intervening between multiple exposures and attitudes, researchers may be able to understand and predict the myriad of attitudinal and behavioral effects that may occur with various stimulus environments, different target audiences, and other situational factors. This chapter discusses research about the relationship of exposure and attitude. As background, this chapter reviews repetition research that does not involve cognitive responses. However, the main focus is on cognitive responses either as hypothetical intervening variables or as measured dependent variables. (For more complete reviews about attitudinal responses to repeated exposure, see Harrison, 1977; Sawyer, 1974, 1977; and Stang, 1973.)

Most of the theoretical research about repetition and attitudes has involved noncommunication stimuli such as nonsense syllables and symbols. After this important work is reviewed, research about repeated advertisements and other messages is examined. Finally, research areas that might most profitably benefit from a cognitive response orientation are proposed.

MERE EXPOSURE OF NONCOMMUNICATION STIMULI

Zajonc's (1968) monograph, which reviewed past correlational and experimental research about the effects of exposure frequency on such affect dimensions as goodness and liking, was a major stimulant to repetition research. Zajonc concluded from his evidence that mere exposure of an object was sufficient to produce increased affect toward that object. His experimental evidence involved the presentation of initially unfamiliar stimuli such as foreign words, nonsense syllables, or men's photographs. For example, in one often-replicated experiment, Zajonc (1968) told subjects that they were participating in a study of foreign languages. Subjects then sat in a room watching slides of Chinese characters exposed for durations of 2 seconds each. The series of slides contained two characters that were exposed once, two others that were exposed twice, two 5 times, two 10 times, and two 25 times. The different slides were interspersed in a random fashion. After the slides were shown, the experimenter asked subjects to guess their meaning. Admitting that an exact guess would be impossible, he asked them to rate on a good–bad semantic differential scale the extent to which the characters represented something positive or negative. The resulting relationship between the number of exposures and affect was a positive one in which the increase due to repetition was greatest at low frequency levels and less, but still positive, at high frequency levels (see curve A in Fig. 11.1).

Zajonc's *exposure effects* have been replicated under many conditions (e.g., Harrison, 1968, 1969; Harrison & Zajonc, 1970; Harrison, Tutone, & McFadgen,

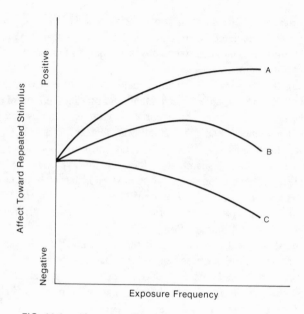

FIG. 11.1.   Alternative effects of repeated exposures on affect.

1971; Heingartner & Hall, 1974; Janisse, 1970; Matlin, 1970, 1974; Saegert & Jellison, 1970; Schick, McGlynn, & Woolam, 1972), including exposure durations as low as 1/25 of a second (Harrison & Hines, 1970) and exposure frequencies as high as 81 (Zajonc, Swap, Harrison, & Roberts, 1971) or even 243 (Zajonc, Crandall, Kail, & Swap, 1974). Simultaneous multiple exposures enhance affect just as multiple exposures presented sequentially do (Matlin, 1974).

Field experiments with nonsense words in newspapers (Zajonc & Rajecki, 1969), mailbox inserts of cards containing nonsense words (Rajecki & Wolfson, 1973), or nonsense words written on successive days on a classroom blackboard (Crandall, 1972), have indicated that exposure effects are not limited to the laboratory. For example, Zajonc and Rajecki (1969) placed nonsense words (e.g., *kadirga, saricik*) in a campus newspaper. Words were randomly assigned to exposure frequencies from 1 to 25 over a 25-day period. Single words were printed in column-inch boxes. Both mail and personal postinterviews revealed a positive exposure effect very similar to results of laboratory experiments. Finally, exposure effects in lab and field experimental results have been replicated in actual advertising campaigns (Grush, McKeough, and Ahlering, 1978).

Not all studies have found an exposure effect however. Other studies have found a *moderation effect* (curve B in Fig. 11.1) in which there is an inverted U-curve relationship between exposure and affect (e.g., Crandall, Montgomery, & Reese, 1973; Miller, 1976; Suedfeld, Rank, & Borrie, 1975). For example, Zajonc, Shaver, Tavris, and VanKreveld (1972) found that liking of abstract paintings increased from 0 to 1 to 2 exposures but then steadily decreased as the number of exposures further increased to 5, 10, and 25. Also, a few studies have found a *novelty effect* (curve C in Fig. 11.1) in which less exposed stimuli are more desired than more highly exposed ones (e.g., Cantor, 1968).

Stang's (1974b) review of past research indicates that exposure effects are very likely when (1) the stimuli are relatively complex (e.g., Reich & Moody, 1970; Saegert & Jellison, 1970; Smith & Dorfman, 1975); (2) the stimuli are not presented in homogeneous sequences (one after another until all exposures of a particular stimulus are completed; e.g., Berlyne, 1970; Harrison & Crandall, 1972); and (3) there is a delay of at least a few minutes between exposure and rating (e.g., Crandall, Harrison, & Zajonc, 1975). Exposure effects are also more likely for stimuli that are initially unfamiliar and/or neutrally evaluated (Harrison, 1977).

THEORIES OF MERE EXPOSURE

The great bulk of research supports Zajonc's contention that mere exposure is sufficient to increase liking. Several theories have been proposed that help to explain the instances in which either exposure, moderation, or novelty effects may occur. Two of these explanations are not well supported by the bulk of pertinent evidence and are only briefly summarized. However, three other theories that dwell primarily on cognitive responses intervening between exposure and affect and that are quite consistent with empirical evidence are discussed more fully.

The first explanation of past empirical results, the demand artifacts explanation, is atheoretical and focuses on the experimental procedure common to mere exposure research. The four theoretical interpretations have been labeled: (1) classical conditioning, (2) response competition, (3) optimal arousal, and (4) the two-factor theory.

Demand Artifacts

Several researchers have argued that Zajonc's positive mere exposure results may be due to subjects' adopting a behavior pattern in response to what they believe is expected or desired by the experimenter (Orne, 1969; Sawyer, 1975a). For example, in an experiment where subjects are asked to perform the very difficult task of rating whether an unfamiliar foreign word means something good or bad, they might try to guess the experimenter's purpose (more exposure is equated with either more good or more bad) in order to have some rationale for the task and then act accordingly. In several role-playing experiments, the typical Zajonc experimental paradigm, including details of the number of times an individual stimulus *would* have been exposed, was described. Then subjects' ratings of the stimuli (which were actually shown only once) were measured, along with their estimates of the experimenter's hypothesis (Sawyer, 1975b; Stang, 1974a). Consistent with a demand artifacts explanation, subjects were more apt to guess that the hypothesis equated increased exposure with increased goodness than with badness; subjects' ratings tended to be consistent with their intuitive estimates of the experimenter's hypothesis; and the overall results were very similar to those of Zajonc and his colleagues. Another experiment (Suedfeld, Epstein, Buchanan, & Landon, 1971) showed that slight differences in the experimental instructions could affect the results of a typical Zajonc experiment. In contrast to a positive set ("indicate the extent of *goodness* of the meaning of each character"), which led to an exposure effect, a negative set ("indicate the extent of *badness* of the meaning") resulted in a moderation effect.

However, demand artifacts explanations have been countered by recent evidence. Hamid (1973) was unable to replicate the results of Suedfeld et al. Moreland and Zajonc (1976) concluded that the role-playing procedures of Sawyer and Stang oversimplified the specificity and amount of exposure information to the subjects and were probably demand prone themselves. Real participants may not be able to accurately judge the frequency of a repeated stimulus (e.g., Matlin & Stang, 1975b). Also, the role-playing results may have merely meant that subjects were good predictors of their own behavior. Finally, Moreland and Zajonc (1976) and Grush (1976) found significant exposure effects in between-subjects designs in which a subject was exposed to only one level of repetition and in which it was nearly impossible to guess the experiment's intent. At this point, it seems much more profitable for researchers to focus on theoretical explanations of the effects of repeated exposures.

Classical Conditioning

Although Zajonc (1968) concluded that mere exposure was a sufficient condition to enhance affect, exposure rarely occurs in a totally neutral environment. Initial affective evaluations either of the context in which stimuli are exposed or of associations with the stimuli may increasingly become attached to the repeated stimuli as exposure increases. Burgess and Sales (1971) hypothesized that the positive nature of participating in an experiment conditioned the evaluations of the experimental stimuli, with more positiveness conditioned to those more highly exposed. Burgess and Sales found that subjects who reported that they had enjoyed their participation in a frequency experiment showed a positive effect of exposure, whereas subjects relatively negative about their participation showed no effect. A second experiment varied the initial positiveness (highly positive, moderately positive, moderately negative, highly negative) of words paired with a nonsense syllable. When each nonsense syllable–word pair was repeated up to 16 times, highly positive words in the repeated pair produced a strong exposure effect; highly negative words produced a novelty effect; and the intermediately positive and negative words produced moderation effects. Brickman, Redfield, Harrison, and Crandall (1972) found that liking of initially liked paintings increased with repetition, whereas a decrease was found for initially disliked paintings. A similar result with men's photographs linked to positive and negative occupations was found by Perlman and Oskamp (1971).

More recent evidence, however, does not support a classical conditioning explanation of exposure effects. Experiments by Stang (1974b) and Saegert, Swap, and Zajonc (1973) found positive frequency effects regardless of subjects' initial ratings of experimental participation. Zajonc et al., (1972) found that repeated stimuli that differed in their initial liking produced parallel positive frequency–affect results for all types of stimuli. Moreover, several experiments manipulating the pleasantness of the environment of the experiment on a between-subjects basis, such as forcing noxious smells and tastes on subjects during exposure, have failed to affect the positive slope of the frequency–affect curve (Johnson, 1973; Rosenblood & Ostrom, 1971; Saegert, Swap, & Zajonc, 1973).

Zajonc, Markus, and Wilson (1974a) tried to explain the varying results of repetition of stimuli with different initial affect or that are exposed in different contexts. They showed from 1 to 25 men's photographs that varied both in their initial affect (positive or negative) and in whether or not the photos were continually associated with positive or negative occupations (scientist or criminal) during exposure. Ratings of the stimuli became more positive with repetition except for a null relationship in the condition in which the repeated stimuli were associated with negative affect at every exposure. As expected, the repeated negative association served to offset the positive effects of exposure to produce a flat relationship between frequency and affect. Initial stimulus affect had no effect on the rate of increase in affect with repetition but did increase the absolute level. In other words, it seems that initial affect and exposure effects are additive, that initial affect influences only the intercept of the exposure function and not the positive slope, and repeated associations influence the slope.

Although appealing in its simplicity, the classical conditioning hypothesis does not even attempt to offer an explanation of moderation effects of repetition. A significant portion of empirical research has not supported the predictions of either positive or negative monotonic effects. Other theories involving cognitive responses to repeated stimuli seem to be more promising explanations of the repetition responses process.

Response Competition

Response competition was first offered by Harrison (1969) as an attempt to explain the cognitive processes underlying Zajonc's exposure effect and also to relate that effect to research about curiosity and exploratory behavior (Berlyne, 1960, 1966). This latter research has found that both people and animals are more apt to explore or attend to novel or relatively low-exposed stimuli than to familiar or high-frequency stimuli. Harrison reasoned that initial exposure to a novel stimulus poses a problem to an individual. With little or no past experience, one does not know how to respond to a new stimulus. Due to response generalization from other, somewhat similar stimuli encountered in the past, several tentative responses may be elicited—some of which are incompatible or even antagonistic. This coexistence of conflicting response tendencies, labeled *response competition,* is tension producing and provides negative affect and a motivation to reduce that negative tension by eliminating competing responses. Subsequent exposure, either by the person's passive presence or by active exploratory behavior, provides the opportunity to eliminate some responses and to become more sure and specific in one's response. This reduction in response competition reduces the negatively connotated tension, increases affect, and reduces motivation for exploratory behavior.

Harrison's predictions of the inverse relationships between response competition and liking and between liking and exploratory behavior have been confirmed in correlational studies (Harrison, 1968; Matlin, 1970). Also, as predicted, increased exposure that results in increased liking also leads to decreased response competition as measured either by response latencies (Harrison, 1968; Harrison & Hines, 1970; Harrison & Zajonc, 1970) or response communality or recall errors (Matlin, 1970), and to decreased exploratory behavior (Harrison & Hines, 1970; Saegert & Jellison, 1970). Other research has tried to manipulate response competition by varying the number or strength of responses associated with a stimulus and found an inverse relationship between manipulated response competition and affect (Matlin, 1970). Harrison, Tutone, and McFadgen (1971) and Zajonc, Markus, and Wilson (1974a) manipulated whether a word or picture paired with a repeated word was consistently the same or not. When the paired associate was inconsistent and changing, the overall positive frequency effect was considerably dampened. With decreases in the opportunity to reduce response competition with increased exposure, increases in affect were not nearly as great as when reductions in response competition were more easy.

Response competition is capable of explaining research results that show that exposure effects are more likely with complex than with simple stimuli, with heterogeneous rather than homogeneous exposure sequences, and with delays in measurement. An integral assumption is that reductions in response competition are not limitless or, at least, that there is a point where coinciding increases in affect taper off. Complex stimuli offer more elements to remind one initially of other past stimuli. The increased initial response competition will require more exposure than simple stimuli to reduce response competition and increase liking. Homogeneous exposure sequences avoid any confusion with other stimuli and accelerate the reduction of response competition. Finally, due to forgetting, delays in measurement are more likely at least partially to increase response competition that had previously been decreased by exposures to low-frequency stimuli than to more heavily exposed stimuli.

Response competition theory seems to be a reasonably good explanation of the bulk of past research. However, some theoretical tests have not been supportive (e.g., Brickman et al., 1972; Grush, 1976; Stang, 1975a). A major problem is that response competition as originally conceptualized does not even predict, much less explain, moderation or novelty effects. Although Saegert and Jellison (1970) revised the theory to assert that there is probably an optimal amount of reduction in initially high response competition, the theory has little predictive utility about how much exposure is needed to reach such an optimum. Also, as Stang (1975a) pointed out, response competition as operationalized may instead be measuring learning or meaningfulness.

Optimal Arousal

Two distinct schools of thought employ optimal arousal as an explanation of exposure effects. The expectancy arousal approach of J. Crandall (1970) is closely akin to the response competition explanation. Crandall hypothesizes that elements of a novel stimulus give rise to expectancies or hypotheses that may be confirmed or not with further exposure. Increased familiarity allows the subject to represent in memory and anticipate the detailed nature of the stimulus. For example, the first syllable of a word may hint at the nature of the remainder. Since a moderate amount of expectancy arousal is preferred (cf. Maddi, 1968), stimuli exposed in very low or very high frequencies will be less liked than moderately familiar ones. Unfortunately, no assessment of expectancy arousal independent of liking has been reported, and it is often difficult to distinguish predictions from expectancy arousal theory (e.g., Crandall, Montgomery, & Reese, 1973) from response competition predictions (Harrison, 1977). Crandall clearly needs some cognitive response measure to assess the validity of his hypothesis about expectancy arousal intervening between exposure and liking.

The second school of optimal arousal theory is almost psychobiological in nature. Berlyne (1960, 1966, 1971) argues that any stimulus has a certain amount of *arousal potential*. This arousal potential is the sum of the stimulus's psychophysical properties (such as brightness and intensity), ecological properties (association with other stimuli), and collative properties (such as novelty and complexity). Stimuli with moderate arousal potential are most favorable. With other stimulus properties controlled, increased exposure should decrease arousal potential. However, higher frequency levels are needed to reduce initially high arousal-potential stimuli (such as complex ones or stimuli interspersed with many other stimuli) than initially low arousal-potential stimuli. Since more exposures are necessary to lower initially high arousal potential to the optimal moderate levels, repetition of stimuli initially high in arousal potential will increase liking. Initially low arousal-potential stimuli require very few exposures to reach the optimal level; repetition will lead to a moderation or novelty effect.

Increases in exposure, depending on the initial level of arousal potential and the number of exposures, can lead to either an exposure, moderation, or novelty effect. Thus, Berlyne's arousal potential theory can post hoc explain past results quite well. However, little empirical investigation of his theory has been attempted other than confirmations that high-frequency complex objects are preferred to low-frequency complex objects. Most of Berlyne's research has focused on complexity and exploratory behavior and not on exposure and liking.

Optimal arousal theories provide potential explanations of past exposure results. However, the concept of optimal exposure levels offers very little predictive power. Such theories should perhaps not be labeled theories, because of the fact that they are nearly impossible to invalidate empirically. Arousal measures independent of repetition need to be found.

Two-Factor Theories

A major problem of response competition theory is that it cannot explain moderation or novelty effects without resorting to the ambiguous optimal reduction explanation of arousal theorists. However, a potential improvement has been suggested by Berlyne (1970) with his two-factor theory.

Figure 11.2 graphs how two opposing determinants of arousal potential might influence the effects of repetition. The first factor, *positive habituation,* is very

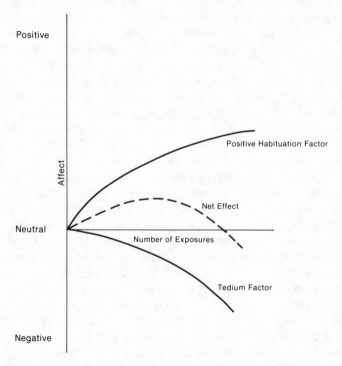

FIG. 11.2.   Berlyne's (1970) two-factor theory of liking for a repeated stimulus.

similar to reduction of response competition; exposure reduces the arousal from uncertainty and conflict and increases pleasure. The second factor, *tedium*, also increases with exposure and results in less pleasantness. Positive habituation is expected to predominate during initial repetition of a complex stimulus, because the added exposures reduce the initially high arousal potential nearer to optimally preferred levels. Repeated exposure of simple stimuli with initially low arousal potential reduces their arousal potential to levels even further from the point of maximum liking. Tedium will eventually occur at high exposure levels of complex stimuli and at relatively low frequencies of simple stimuli. Monotonous repetition as in homogeneous exposure sequences would strengthen the tedium factor relative to sequences in which several stimuli are presented in interspersed fashion. Delays in measurement after multiple exposures will decrease satiation much more rapidly than any habituation.

Stang (1973, 1974b, 1975a, 1975b) took the concept of Berlyne's two-factor theory and substituted learning for positive habituation. Stang hypothesized that exposure provides an opportunity for learning that in turn increases affect; the learning is reinforcing by itself. With increased exposure, recognition and partial learning of the stimulus leave fewer and fewer new elements to be learned. With decreased incremental learning, satiation or tedium begins to influence affect toward the stimulus negatively. Some support for the learning–affect relationship proposed by Stang has been found by Matlin (1971) and Stang (1975b) with correlational data and in frequency experiments in which the serial position of repeated stimuli influenced liking in a fashion similar to learning (Matlin, 1974; Stang, 1975b).

Certainly, the two-factor theories enjoy a lot of face validity. The importance of a tedium or satiation factor seems intuitively obvious. Much more research manipulating the two factors and comparing response competition and learning explanations is needed. The various theoretical explanations involving cognitive mediators of the frequency–affect relationship should offer important cues to the study of the effects of repeated exposures of meaningful messages.

One aspect of mere exposure research that needs some amplification concerns the question of what dimensions of stimulus affect are being measured. Typical research employs one bipolar semantic differential scale—most typically, *good–bad* or *like–dislike*. It is unfortunate that more open ended measures have not also been included. Zajonc, Crandall, Kail, and Swap (1974) used several scales including the two already mentioned plus *interesting–boring* and *harmful–beneficial*. Exposure frequencies of from 1 to 243 resulted in the traditional exposure effect on *good–bad*, a moderation effect peaking at 27 exposures for both *like–dislike* and *beneficial–harmful*, and a novelty effect on *interesting–boring*. Similar exposure effect differences in *good–bad* and *like–dislike* scales have been noted before (Saegert & Jellison, 1970), although Zajonc, Markus, and Wilson (1974a) found no differences. Zajonc and his colleagues suggested that "*good*" scales may measure permanent acceptance and afinity, whereas "*like*" scales may measure more temporary affect or curiosity.

As noted earlier, exploratory behavior and liking seem to be inversely related (e.g., Harrison, 1968, 1969). This may be due to the fact that a person may actively attend to a stimulus because it is threatening or uncertain as well as because it is pleasant (Berlyne, 1960, 1971). It has been suggested that a major difference between approach behavior signifying curiosity and that generated by affection is that the former will cease over time, whereas the latter will not (Zajonc, Crandall, Kail, & Swap, 1974; Zajonc, Markus, & Wilson, 1974b). Thus, lack of decreases or increases in approach behavior with the passage of time should indicate "true" liking. Brickman and D'Amato (1975) offer support for this conceptualization. Subjects were allowed to play a jukebox and later rated their selections. At first, subjects were likely to sample many different selections. However, later in the experiment, a set of popular selections was played quite constantly. The delayed choices were highly correlated with liking of the music, but initial exploratory behavior was not. More attempts to validate measures of both cognitive and affective effects of stimulus exposure are sorely needed.

MESSAGE REPETITION AND ATTITUDE CHANGE

The messages used in advertising and general communication research are obviously much different from the stimuli used in the mere exposure research. Communication stimuli are more complex and probably much more familiar and meaningful. Also, initial positive or negative connotations may be reinforced at each exposure and overwhelm any potential effects of exposure itself.

It should be noted that Zajonc (1968) confined his claims about the effects of mere exposure to initially unfamiliar stimuli. He readily admitted that exposure is confounded with a variety of other variables that are clearly more important and more direct determinants of evaluation. Yet Zajonc (1970) still felt compelled to speculate that much of the positive effects of persuasive messages may be due as much to the mere exposure of the communication topic as to the persuasive content. Most persuasive messages, of course, do repeatedly mention the concept or name being argued.

However, Swap (1973) found no evidence that mere exposure of the topic of a message is important. He varied the nature of a persuasive message (positive arguments, negative arguments, neutral) and the number of times the object of the persuasive message (a new automobile model, a U.S. president, and teaching machines) was mentioned within the message (1, 5, 25 times). He found no effect of repetition; 70 percent of variation of liking of the objects was accounted for by the message content alone. A second experiment replicated these results. Persuasive content and not concept-name exposure influenced attitudes about those concept-names.

Most communication and advertising research is not directly comparable to the Zajonc research, because it measures persuasion or liking of the objects or ideas presented in the message instead of liking for the message itself. However, although a controversial subject, many advertisers believe that positive achievement on the latter dimension is an important asset to attaining message acceptance (see Silk & Vavra, 1974). Of course, a key question in advertising involves whether the increased liking for a brand name due to repeated exposures transfers to the advertised product itself. Available evidence suggests that such generalization does occur in some instances. For example, Becknell, Wilson, and Baird (1963) found that repeated exposures in 1, 4, 7, and 10 frequencies of nonsense-syllable brands resulted in a positive monotone effect on both choice and ranking. Miller, Mazis, and Wright (1971) found that positive effects of 0, 2, 10, and 20 exposures of different nonsense-syllable brand names transferred to liking for different brand characteristics when the characteristics were linked to the repeated brand names. However, the positive effect of repetition on liking was eliminated when, in addition to viewing the repeated brand names, subjects tasted the food products to which the brand names were linked.

Another difference between persuasive messages and non-verbal stimuli is that, in terms of response competition and arousal, less exposures may be necessary to determine their meaning and appropriate responses. Krugman (1972) theorized that only three advertising exposures are sufficient to stimulate a buying decision. The very first exposure is dominated by "what *is* it?" cognitive responses—attempts to understand the nature of the stimulus. Krugman believed that most of the needed reduction in response competition can be accomplished in the first exposure so that, with recognition, the second elicits more evaluative and personal "what *of* it?" responses which determine the ultimate persuasive potential of the commercial. The third exposure acts primarily as a reminder—if there was an earlier meaningful response. In addition, the third exposure is the beginning of withdrawal of attention. Due to selective attention and forgetting with time, exposure frequencies greater than three are hypothesized by Krugman to be repeats of the second and third exposure effects. Several studies report that two or three advertising exposures attain the peak in effectiveness including lab studies of eye movement exploration of print advertisements (Krugman, 1968) and of viewing choice (Grass and Wallace, 1969) and advertising surveys which correlate television viewing histories, ad campaign media placement, and brand purchases as recorded in diaries (MacDonald, 1970; Maloney, 1966). However, no direct test of Krugman's hypothesis has been reported.

REPETITION AND COGNITIVE RESPONSE

Unfortunately, only a few studies have gone beyond speculation and measured open-ended cognitive responses to repeated stimuli and their referents. The first such study was by Matlin (1970), who manipulated the exposure frequency of foreign characters and words previously used by Zajonc. After subjects were exposed to different stimuli either 1, 2, 5, 10, or 25 times, subjects were asked for their free associations to each of the exposed stimuli. Ten minutes later, after an intervening unrelated task, subjects were shown each stimulus once more and were asked to recall their first free associate. Three measures—latency of first free association, errors in recall of free association, and latency of recall (thought to be inversely related to response competition)—were all increased by exposure frequency.

Stang (1975) pointed out that results such as Matlin's could occur if increased frequency resulted in a greater number of free associations. An increased number of associations could coincide with longer latencies to free associate as well as with recall errors and latencies. Grush's (1976) experiment offered support for Stang's hypothesis. Grush varied the exposure level from 2 to 4 to 8 to 16 of two types of stimuli: (1) initially positive words (e.g., *acrobat, gardenia*) and (2) initially negative words (e.g., *depravity, corrosive*). After exposure, subjects rated the test words on four semantic differentials of affect, generated associations to the words, and evaluated the goodness–badness of the associations on a 7-point scale. As Stang hypothesized and contrary to response competition theory, increased exposure coincided with more associations and not less. Concerning the ratings of the words, there was a significant interaction between exposure and word type. Ratings of negative words became significantly more negative with exposure, and positive words became (insignificantly) more positive. When the summed evaluations of each association to the test words were calculated as formulated by Fishbein (1967; see Chapter 15), these summed evaluations related to exposure frequency and word type in a manner virtually identical to the affect ratings.

Four studies have examined directly the effects of repeated messages on cognitive responses. Rothschild and Ray (1974) tested a hypothesis about involvement with an advertising topic and repetition. Slides of print political advertisements were exposed either 0, 1, 2, 4, or 6 times for three political elections in descending order of voter involvement—a presidential election, a U.S. congressional election, and a state Assembly election. Dependent measures included free recall, voting intention, and message connections. The latter variable was the "connections" cognitive response measure suggested by Krugman (1966, 1967) as a measure of involvement. Connections measure whether a viewer has connected the message copy to his or her own personal life. As hypothesized, ads for the more highly involving presidential election led to more connections of the ads' content to viewers' personal lives than did advertising for the other two elections. Overall, personal connections were unaffected by advertising repetition, however.

Cacioppo and Petty (1979) tested the effects of repetition of audio messages that advocated a position that was either consistent with or contrary to the subject's initial attitude. Both messages presented to student subjects contained the same set of eight persuasive arguments to increase university expenditures; the pro or counter position was varied by whether the message argued that the increased expenditures should be financed by a state tourist tax (pro) or by an increase in tuition (counter). The messages were exposed either one, three, or five times on a between-subjects basis. In one experiment, the prime dependent variable was agreement with the message. The result was a moderation effect of exposure frequency on agreement. An increase in agreement was produced by one and three exposures, but there was a decrease when exposures increased to five. There was a main effect of message type (more agreement with pro messages), but message type did not influence the shape of the exposure–agreement curve. A second identical experiment measured subjects' thoughts concerning the advocacy in addition to agreement. As in the first experiment, agreement increased and then decreased as exposure increased. The nature of the cognitive responses varied like agreement. Favorable thoughts showed an insignificant increase-then-decrease trend, whereas counterarguing responses exhibited a significant decrease-then-increase trend. Neutral thoughts increased with exposure. Cacioppo and Petty suggested that a message containing valid arguments initially elicits both favorable and unfavorable cognitions. With repetition, favorable thoughts increase, and negative thoughts decrease as the good arguments are evaluated and processed. With further repetition, however, evaluation of the arguments is completed, and boredom and/or tedium sets in. At this point, subjects begin to attack cognitively the now-obnoxious stimulus. This accounts for the initial increase and subsequent decrease in agreement with the communications as repetition increased.

McCullough and Ostrom (1974) also reported a direct test of the effects of repetition on cognitive responses. Subjects saw five different print ads either from a product campaign (Yardley after-shave) or a charity contribution-solicitation campaign (U.S.O.). Each ad within each campaign used the same four arguments but with different emphasis and distinct copy phrasing and picture format. The dependent variable was the number of positive and negative thoughts listed. Unlike the Rothschild and Ray (1974) or Cacioppo and Petty (1979) studies, subjects' thoughts were measured directly after each exposure to the advertisements. As can be seen in Table 11.1, repetition significantly decreased the negativeness of the net response. Although the U.S.O. campaign resulted in significantly more overall positiveness, no significant differences in the effects of the two campaigns with added exposures were found. Although subjects tended to respond relatively negatively toward the ads, this negativeness decreased with exposure. Table 11.1 indicates, however, that the decreased negativeness resulted not just because of a reduction in the number of negative responses but also because, at the same time, the average number of positive responses increased. Thus, as in the Cacioppo and Petty study, initial repetition decreased negative thoughts and increased positive ones. McCullough and Ostrom did not find a tedium effect, however, probably because unlike the Cacioppo and Petty study, McCullough and Ostrom showed slightly different ads at each exposure. In addition, there was no evidence for a decrease in attention as

TABLE 11.1
Cognitive Response as a Function of Repeated Advertising Exposures[a]

	Number of Exposures				
	1	2	3	4	5
Net cognitive response[c]					
Yardley ads[b]	−3.12	−2.44	−1.24	−.84	−1.88
U.S.O. ads[b]	−.64	.24	.28	.92	1.40
All ads[c]	−1.88	−1.10	−.48	.04	−.24
Number of positive responses	2.76	3.24	3.22	3.58	3.70
Number of negative responses	4.64	4.34	3.70	3.54	3.44
Total number of responses	7.40	7.58	6.92	7.12	7.64
Positive percentage of total	37.3	42.7	46.5	40.3	48.4

[a] From McCullough and Ostrom (1974).
[b] $n = 10$ per cell; for all other measures, $n = 20$
[c] Number of positive responses minus number of negative responses.

exposure increased, because the total number of cognitions generated tended to increase with repetition.

A somewhat similar test of viewers' reactions to television commercials was reported by Calder and Sternthal (in press). Their research was designed to test whether commercial wearout—the eventual decrease in effectiveness at high frequency levels—was the outcome of either decreasing attention or an active processing of reactions to the repeated commercial. Calder and Sternthal experimentally varied the number of commercials viewed for two products (3, 9, or 18), the variety of repeated test commercials (the same commercial or three different commercials for the same product), and the variety of other commercials also seen. These commercials were embedded in six 1-hour television shows viewed over a 3-week period. Dependent measures included semantic differential ratings of the stimulus commercials, the advertised products, and the attributes of the advertised products. In addition, cognitive responses were measured by asking subjects to list all product-relevant feelings and thoughts that came to mind in a 3-minute period. After the listing was finished, subjects rated the favorability of these thoughts and their certainty in the truth of the thoughts.

The various semantic differential ratings were first factor analyzed to reduce the number of dependent variables and to facilitate interpretation of their meaning. An interesting factor was product evaluation because this was the attitude the commercials were designed to influence. For both products, evaluation exhibited a moderation effect of commercial frequency with a slight increase in product evaluation from 3 to 9 commercials followed by a relatively large decrease from 9 to 18, replicating the pattern found by Cacioppo and Petty. For the number of negative thoughts listed about the products, a significant three-way interaction was found between frequency, variety of the test commercial, and variety of the background materials. This interaction represented the fact that whereas negative thoughts increased with frequency in nearly every variety condition, a decrease followed by an increase was found in the condition of only one repeated commercial and high-variety background commercials.

Like the Cacioppo and Petty (1979) and McCullough and Ostrom (1974) results, the results of Calder and Sternthal argue against a passive inattention reaction to multiple exposures of television commercials. However, unlike the other studies, no strong corresponding patterns between cognitive responses and the product ratings (which were not influenced by frequency) were found. Perhaps, as Calder and Sternthal argued similarly to Ray (1977), cognitive responses may not be belief specific or very salient in the low-involving mass-communication situation.

COGNITIVE RESPONSE EXPLANATIONS OF ATTITUDINAL EFFECTS OF REPETITION

As Harrison (1977) pointed out, positive effects of frequency of noncommunication stimuli can be obtained even where cognitive responses are very unlikely. First, exposure effects have been found for organisms such as newly born birds and grasshoppers that may not have the cognitive capacity for elaborate responses (Harrison & Fisicaro, 1974; Rajecki, 1973; Zajonc, Markus, & Wilson, 1974b; Zajonc, Reimer, & Hausser, 1973). Second, although stimulus recognition would seem to be a prerequisite for elaborate cognitive processes to occur, the exposure effect may occur without recognition (Birnbaum & Mellers, 1979a, 1979b; Moreland & Zajonc, 1977; 1979; Wilson, 1979).

Despite the fact that all exposure effects do not depend on intervening cognitive processing, cognitive responses do appear to offer the best available explanation of the attitudinal effects of repetition of persuasive messages—especially those that are at least somewhat involving. Fishbein and Ajzen (1975) described an attitude formation theory to describe the mere exposure process. It appears that repeated exposures of initially unfamiliar and neutrally evaluated stimuli evoke a number of cognitive responses to each exposure. The number and strength of these responses to the repeated stimulus combine with the connotative meaning of the generated associations to determine the attitudinal effects of mere exposure. Repetition of highly familiar stimuli are less likely to generate any new responses or beliefs and thus will not affect attitudes. Although the number of generated associations may increase with exposure (Matlin, 1970) or remain quite constant (Cacioppo & Petty, 1979; Calder & Sternthal, in press; McCullough & Ostrom, 1974), there is no empirical evidence that the number of responses will decrease. Stimuli initially evaluated as negative may become more negative with exposure if that exposure increases the number of negative associations (e.g., Brickman et al., 1972; Grush, 1976; Perlman & Oskamp, 1971).

However, the attitude formation theory does not theorize *why* repetition often leads to a positive exposure effect or to an inverted U-curve moderation effect with initially neutral stimuli. Currently, there are only speculative untested theoretical explanations. One explanation is the Pollyanna hypothesis, which asserts that there is a universal tendency to think and talk about positive aspects of life (Boucher & Osgood, 1969). Matlin and Stang (1975a) have shown that early free associations tend to be more evaluatively positive than later associations. With a limit to the number of possible positive associations, later associations would necessarily become more negative. As the number of available positive associations increased, one would expect a delayed attainment of the point where exposure leads to fewer positive associations and more negative ones.

Another explanation of the common inverted U-curve moderation effect would assert that either a tedium or reactance response to higher exposure levels would generalize to negative responses to the stimulus and contained message arguments (e.g., Cacioppo & Petty, 1979). Stang (1974b) argued that positive affect will accompany increases in learning of new responses (presumably either positive or negative). Only when associative learning nears completion will continued exposure result in satiation and a decrease in positive affect.

The conciseness and flexibility of the attitude formation theory is appealing. It also integrates well with Fishbein and Ajzen's (1975) more general theory of attitudes and persuasion (see Chapter 15). However, neither the Pollyanna hypothesis nor a tedium/reactance explanation can explain why the majority of responses to the first exposures of the advertisements studied by McCullough and Ostrom (1974) were negative. Positive attitude change due to repetition was due to a greater number of positive responses to later exposures, whereas the total number of responses remained quite stable. Perhaps advertisements and other persuasive messages in contexts of obvious manipulative intent always encounter a majority of negative defensive responses at first. Once expressed, these defensive responses may dissipate and allow other associations to the message. The quality and believability of the message claims may dictate whether these responses at subsequent exposures are positive or negative.

FUTURE RESEARCH

Future research about the effects of repetition on cognitive responses should focus on two areas. The first area concerns replications of the main effects of repetition; the second involves the cognitive effects of interactions between repeated message exposures and the type of message appeal. Much more research employing cognitive response measures is needed. What cognitive responses are elicited by repetition of the same message or advertisement? Over what range of exposures does the positive relationship found by McCullough and Ostrom hold?

What are the effects of temporarily spaced exposures? What happens to cognitive responses to repeated exposures over time, and how are persisting responses related to opinion and behavior measures? Can communication cognitive response measures be devised to operationalize such hypothetical intervening variables as arousal, tedium, and reactance? More knowledge about the relationship of communication liking to communication persuasiveness and how each dimension is influenced by multiple exposures is needed.

Research is also needed to assess where the attitudinal effects of repetition interact with different messages and other communication factors. Differences in the effects of exposure are likely to involve the following communication factors and message appeals: message involvement, familiarity, variation, complexity, two-sided appeals, fear appeals, and time of measurement.

Message Involvement

Noting the many similarities between the learning of nonsense syllables and television commercials (e.g., Krugman, 1962; Ray, 1969), Krugman (1965) argued that both types of stimuli have in common two factors: More than one exposure is often encountered, and the stimuli are quite uninvolving to the viewers. Due to the low level of involvement of many products and their advertisements, Krugman believed that many researchers may overestimate the degree of active, conscious cognitive reactions. Instead, with uninvolving messages, gradual changes in perception of the advertised brands that may fall short of persuasion or attitude change may occur. One way this change may occur is by subtle shifts in the relative importance of various brand attributes emphasized in the advertising.

Krugman believed that these slight changes will be noticeable only in an appropriate behavior opportunity such as an in-store purchase situation (1965).

> The significance of conditions of low or high involvement is not that one is better than the other, but that the processes of communication impact are different. That is, there is a difference in the change processes that are at work. Thus, with low involvement one might look for gradual shifts in perceptual structure, aided by repetition, activated by behavioral-choice situations, and *followed* at some time by attitude change. With high involvement one would look for the classic, more dramatic, and more familiar conflict of ideas at the level of conscious opinion and attitude that precedes changes in overt behavior [p. 353].

Krugman's hypothesized differences in the order of communication effects for low- and high-involvement situations have gained some support from Ray and his colleagues (Rothschild & Ray, 1974). For example, Ray and Sawyer (1971b) varied whether repeated brand advertisements were for low-priced convenience products (hand soap, canned soup, mouthwash) or for higher-priced products (lingerie, portable television sets, washing machines). As Krugman would have predicted, the more involving latter group showed a more classic learning–affect–behavior order of repetition effect, whereas the less involving convenience product group did not. Also, when subjects were grouped into "involved" and "uninvolved" categories according to their differentiation of the brands on the brand evaluation measure, brand evaluation increased with repetition for the involved group but not for the latter (Sawyer, 1971).

Familiarity

Familiar messages or advertisements for familiar products might differ from less familiar stimuli in attitudinal effectiveness of repetition. Zajonc predicts that familiar objects should be more liked initially but should increase less with repetition than unfamiliar ones, because the latter offer more opportunity for response competition reduction.

This hypothesis has received some support for both nonmessage stimuli (Amster & Glassman, 1966; Sawyer, 1976) and persuasive messages (Winter, 1973). However, contrary to Zajonc's prediction, Politz (1960) found that two exposures of ads for established brands produced four times the increased willingness to buy that two exposures of less well known brands did. Ray and Sawyer (1971b) similarly found that purchase intention was initially greater for well-known than less familiar brands, and that six exposures significantly increased purchase intention for the former, whereas no repetition effect on the latter was found. Simultaneous measurement of cognitive responses would have been quite informative. With persuasive communications, repeated familiar stimuli may lead to more positive cognitive responses than unfamiliar messages. Perhaps familiar messages are perceived as more credible and provoke less source derogation and counterarguments.

One economist who has studied advertising effectiveness has hypothesized a type of familiarity–cognitive response explanation of the effects of repetitive advertising. Nelson (1974) asserts that consumers attribute product quality to the perceived amount of advertising. In his conceptualization, consumers explicitly or implicitly believe that the brand that advertises the most must be the best; the more advertising for a brand, the more likely it is that the consumer perceives it to be heavily advertised and, hence, a high-quality product. Due to the relatively high costs in relation to the likely value of gathering information for low-cost products, these perceptions are often sufficient determinants of purchase choice.

A field experiment by Kapferer (1975) lends credibility to Nelson's theory that cognitive reactions to the number of exposures of a repeated communication may be important mediations of behavior. Kapferer's study involved the mailing of either one or three letters to college students urging them to go to the Student Health Service for a free blood pressure checkup. Repetition increased students' perception of relevance of high blood pressure and students' attributions of efficiency to the High Blood Pressure Detection Program. Also, the extent to which blood pressure checkups were actually taken significantly increased from 4.9% in the one-letter condition to 15.2% for those who received three letters. However, no effect of repetition was found on free recall, recognition, evaluation of the act of getting a blood pressure test, behavioral intention, or other attributions. Kapferer reported that many of the open-ended cognitive responses mentioned the fact that merely receiving more than one letter served to emphasize the importance of the test and the concern of the health center. From other questions, it seemed apparent that most students did not carefully read the letters; thus, the specific content did not seem to be a determining factor. However, in a manner somewhat analogous to that proposed by Nelson, the perception of receiving more than one letter may have by itself served to positively influence subjects' perceptions and behavior.

Fishbein and Ajzen (1975) argue that the only way repetition of a message can produce positive attitude change is by a process in which an unfamiliar stimulus becomes associated with positive attributes due to learning opportunities provided by repeated exposures. However, as noted earlier, Krugman's theory suggests that, with such passively attended and uninvolving messages as an ad for a brand of hand soap or a vote solicitation from a local political official, a very salient attribute may be the mere fact that brand or person is recognizable.

Repetition with Variation

McCullough and Ostrom attributed their strong exposure effect to the fact that the repeated ads were not identical but varied in format. It is well established that repetition of similar but nonidentical ads is more effective than repetition of identical ads in terms of both recall (Adams, 1916; Poffenberger, 1925) and persuasion (Heeler, 1972). In terms of Stang's two-factor theory, repeated exposures of varied messages would maximize the probability that new associations would occur and would certainly help stave off boredom. Such variation might also result in sustained optimal levels of arousal potential.

Message Complexity

Stimulus complexity is an important factor in the Zajonc mere exposure research. It seems plausible that, like Zajonc's noncommunication stimuli, repetition will more positively influence the persuasiveness of complex messages than of simple messages. Complex messages might include ones that do not have an explicit and direct conclusion but, instead, depend on the audience's indirect conclusions about the advocated position. One type of advertising is known as "soft-sell" advertising because of its subtle, indirect copy, which relies as much on a pleasing mood in the message as on any verbal persuasiveness. Krugman (1962) hypothesized that repetition of soft-sell ads would increase persuasion more than repetition of irritating, direct, hard-sell advertising. Consistent with Stang's two-factor model of frequency–affect, Krugman cited the fact that there was relatively little left to be learned from repeated exposures of simple, hard-sell copy, whereas repeated exposures of soft-sell advertising offered the opportunity for more varied interpretation and personal reaction to the ad's contents.

Two studies offered some support for this hypothesis. Ray and Sawyer (1971b) found that six exposures of "grabber" ads judged as intrusive and apt to communicate all their selling message in a single exposure produced no effect in purchase intention, whereas purchase intention was increased by repeated soft-sell, "nongrabber" ads. Silk and Vavra (1974) found a similar trend for two exposures of hard-sell and soft-sell radio commercials. The magnitude of increase in recall from one to two exposures was greater for the soft-sell commercial; and although the difference in brand evaluation was not significant, the second exposure of the soft-sell commercial resulted in an increase in attitude, whereas a slight decrease was found for the hard-sell ad. Perhaps a clearer relationship would have emerged if a higher number of ad exposures had been tested. With only one exposure, an unstructured soft-sell ad produced more total and more positive thoughts per subject than a highly structured hard-sell ad (Krugman, 1968). Cognitive response measures in the foregoing repetition studies could have helped to explain why the soft-sell and hard-sell ads fared differently with repeated exposures.

Two–Sided and Refutational Appeals

A two-sided appeal that presents opposing arguments as well as the advocated position is likely to be more effective with repetition than a one-sided appeal. Recall from Chapter 8 that a particular two-sided appeal—the refutational appeal that explicitly counterargues the presented opposing side—is more effective for more highly educated and initially opposed audiences (e.g., Faison, 1961; Hovland, Lumsdaine, & Sheffield, 1949; Lumsdaine & Janis, 1953). This effect has been explained by various cognitive response interpretations such as less perceived bias of the refutational appeals (Chu, 1967; Insko, 1962), more source derogation of later attacking messages (Tannenbaum, 1967), reduced psychological reactance or resistance due to the presentation of both sides (Jones & Brehm, 1970), and more curiosity and motivation to practice belief-bolstering defenses (McGuire, 1964). Greenwald (1968b) measured the effects of a one-sided and two-sided message on cognitive responses and attitudes in a group of college students. He found more positive recipient-modified thoughts and greater attitude change for the two-sided appeal.

McGuire's (1964) inoculation theory research (described in Chapter 1)—which showed that the greater the number of refuted arguments a person was exposed to, the greater the resistance to subsequent attacks—suggests that repetition of refutational messages would be highly effective. Sawyer (1973) tested the prediction that repetition would increase the persuasiveness of refutational advertisements more than for one-sided, supportive advertisements. He hypothesized that the repetition of the more complex, two-sided appeal, because of increased understanding, less perceived bias, greater reduction in credibility of the competition, and less psychological reactance, would lead to greater persuasion than repetition of the simpler supportive appeal. Overall, no differences in purchase intention over six exposures to the two ad appeals were found. However, it was further hypothesized that, due to less counterarguing, the repeated refutational appeal would be most effective for people who did not use the advertised brand but did use a competing product. For the same reason, repetition of the supportive appeal was hypothesized to be more effective for people who used the advertised brand. The results were as predicted. The effects of repeated exposures of the refutational and supportive ads varied for different subjects, who, because of their brand usage, were likely to differ in initial attitude and cognitive responses to the messages. Similar research that also included cognitive response measures could assess the replicability of Sawyer's results and also examine whether the intervening responses between message exposure and purchase intention were as speculated.

Delayed Effects

Two-factor theories explain the fact that positive repetition results are more likely to result when measures are delayed than when they are immediate by asserting that the negative effects of tedium will dissipate much more quickly over time than the positive effects of arousal, reduced response competition, or learning.

Crandall, Harrison, and Zajonc (1975) found that the immediate negative effects on stimulus liking of from 1 to 27 exposures became more positive when measured after a 1-week delay and even more positive after 1 month. They hypothesized that the positive effects of mere exposure persist longer than the boredom created by high exposure levels. Silk and Vavra (1974) theorized that any negative persuasive effects due to disliking of an advertisement itself might be temporary and that more message acceptance might occur with the passage of time. As noted earlier, Krugman (1965) believed that positive attitudinal effects of uninvolving messages might happen only after a delay when an appropriate behavior opportunity occurred.

Other research that has examined the persuasive effects of repeated message exposures has found that the prime effect of repetition is not so much to increase immediate acceptance over that of a single message exposure but to increase the permanence of any achieved increase. This finding has been noted with two exposures and 11 days (Cook & Insko, 1968), three exposures and a 1-week delay between exposure and measurement (Wilson & Miller, 1968), and five exposures and a 4-week interval (Johnson & Watkins, 1971), but not with five exposures and a 10-week interval (Johnson & Watkins, 1970). The commonly held explanation is that the greater delayed retention of learned message content enabled the subjects to retain their changed beliefs. However, when learning is manipulated by repeated message exposures, the relationship with persuasion measures is not strong (Greenwald, 1968b; Sawyer, 1971).

There seems to be a much stronger relationship between retention of cognitive responses to a message and immediate and delayed persuasion than between learning of the content of a message and persuasion (Greenwald, 1968b; Leavitt, Waddell, & Wells, 1970; Petty, 1977b; Wright, 1974a). Perhaps there is selective retention of positive cognitive responses. Another possibility is that the negative effects of satiation repress the potentially greater immediate message acceptance but not in the delayed measurement conditions.

CHAPTER SUMMARY

The goal of this chapter was to show how the effects of repetition might be explained by various cognitive responses. Research employing noncommunication stimuli (nonsense words and designs) has typically found that liking increases with repetition of the stimuli (an *exposure effect*). However, *moderation effects* (an increase, then decrease, in liking) and *novelty effects* (a decrease in liking with repetition) have also been reported. Empirical research has argued against *demand artifacts* (repetition effects are due to subjects guessing the experimenter's hypothesis) and *classical conditioning* (repetition effects are due to positive or negative features of the environment being repeatedly paired with the stimuli) interpretations of the effects of repetition. The *response competition* explanation (repetition produces liking by allowing conflicting response tendencies to be reduced) is unable to account for moderation and novelty effects. *Optimal arousal* theory (repetition works by controlling the level of arousal elicited by a stimulus) was criticized on the grounds that it could not make a priori predictions and was difficult to distinguish from response competition notions.

The *two-factor* theories hold the most promise for explaining repetition effects. These theories involve either arousal reduction or association generation in addition to a tedium or reactance factor, and they predict a moderation effect. Research that measured cognitive responses to persuasive communications led to a two-factor theory that incorporated a tedium factor along with the notion that the positiveness of the associations to repeated stimuli will determine whether there are initial positive effects of exposure. Much more research that measures the effects of multiple message exposures on cognitive responses is needed to determine the factors that lead to positive and negative responses.

Finally, the following was suggested:

1. Repetition produces attitude change before behavior change on high-involvement topics, but the reverse may occur on low-involvement topics.

2. Exposure effects are greater when the stimuli are varied on each presentation rather than identical.
3. Repetition of soft-sell ads would increase persuasion more than repetition of hard-sell ads.
4. Repetition increases the persuasiveness of refutational ads more than of one-sided ads.
5. Repetition increases the permanence of induced attitude changes.

It is the author's hope that this chapter has convinced the reader of the potential utility of cognitive responses as both predicting and explaining attitudinal effects of repetition. Typically, persuasion attempts are encountered not once but several times, and further study of repetition and cognitive response is likely to reveal needed insights into the total communication process.

12 Cognitive Responses to Mass Media Advocacy

Peter Wright
Stanford University

INTRODUCTION

The previous chapters in this text have described in considerable detail the cognitive response approach to persuasion, and how this approach is useful in understanding the accumulated experiments on attitude change. In this chapter, we use the cognitive response approach to understand an applied problem—the persuasiveness of mass media advocacy attempts. McGuire (1979a) attributed the scarcity of theoretically interesting media effects research in the attitude change literature to the way the attitude change theories popular in social psychology had evolved. The cognitive response approach differs from traditional approaches in ways that make it potentially conducive to investigating media effects. The emphasis on active processing activities draws attention to the audience member's limited processing abilities and, consequently, to reception environment factors that inhibit the person's ability to generate thoughts. Cognitive response researchers have gravitated toward examining factors that can strain audience response opportunity more so than researchers stimulated by other theoretical models. Media differences may affect audience response activities largely by creating reception environments that differ significantly in the strain they place on audience response opportunities. Evidence on such effects is reviewed in this chapter. The cognitive response model also provides a natural theoretical bridge between persuasion theory and choice theory. Formal models of the choice process typically depict someone actively processing information during pre-choice deliberations (e.g., Coombs, Dawes, & Tversky, 1970; Newell & Simon, 1972), not simply referring back to already formed global attitudes to make a choice. Theoretically, relating the thinking activities an ad evokes from an audience member to that person's subsequent deliberations as a decision maker should be productive.

Consider the following scenario from the vantage point of someone planning an advocacy campaign on television. A young woman is watching television and is exposed to four "key" ads in the midst of several hours of TV programming. In the following weeks, she makes decisions about the type of options that were discussed in those ads.

As the scenario opens, she has been intermittently watching and/or listening to TV for an hour. In that period, 46 minutes of programming, 24 ads totaling 12 minutes, and six station announcements were transmitted. A program is ending. Several characters exchange dialogue. The color video shows actors continually using facial and body language to express emotions. Our heroine is fairly attentive, since she seeks entertainment and humor at the moment. The program ends. In the next 3 minutes, there are two announcements of upcoming events and four audiovisual 30-second ads on topics of varying interest. A new program begins. After 2 minutes, the program tailgates directly into our first "key" ad. There is no forewarning on its topic. For 30 seconds, Ad A's 50-word text describes attributes of Contac, an over-the-counter drug for hay fever. Four video scenes are also shown. In two scenes, actors talk. In two others, an announcer talks while the actors act. Our heroine is not acutely motivated to respond to Ad A because the hay fever problem is not salient. By casual inspection, she notes to herself the brand and features discussed. Ad A tailgates directly into our second key ad. Its topic is a food innovation—a low-cost, high-protein product made from soybeans to simulate meat in taste and appearance. The product is unfamiliar. Once she realizes what the topic is, the woman tries to attend to both the audio text and the video scenes. She is interested in nutrition, her family's reactions to foods, and managing a tight budget. Ad B's 85-word audio text discusses four aspects of the product in 20 seconds while concurrent motion picture scenes show the food being grown, prepared, served, and eaten. Immediately afterward, a 60-second ad for a candidate for the U.S. Senate begins (key Ad C). The woman has to curtail thinking about the food ad to detect what the new ad discusses. She then becomes attentive to the new ad, since the election is imminent and the candidate is a woman she knows little about. Ad C transmits 160 words of audio text in 60 seconds, discussing several issues and attributes of the candidate. Concurrently, eight video scenes of things like wild animals, oil spills, and street crimes are shown. A print message is superimposed over the motion pictures for the final 15 seconds of the audio text. The program begins immediately. In the next break, 30-second ads for a toothpaste and the U.S. Army lead into key Ad D. Its 40-word audio text discusses a Honda motor scooter while 30 seconds of magnificent color photography depicts Big Sur, raccoons, and young people. The woman is moderately intrigued by the topic.

Immediately, another ad on an unannounced topic begins. Then, more programming and announcements. Over the 30 minutes that we observed her, our heroine tried to attend partially to every ad. She also conversed intermittently with her husband. He walked in front of her to let the cat out. She idly thought about shouts from a neighbor's yard and about her upcoming night class.

Four days later, when a head cold prompts her to stop at a pharmacy, she engages in a brief episode of in-store deliberation before choosing one of the cold remedies on the store shelves. She also stops at the meat counter in a supermarket, where the soybean product is displayed. She has made two dozen food category and brand choices in the last 20 minutes and expects to make two dozen more before leaving the store to hurry home, stash the food, and drive to a night class. She is surrounded by distracting noise. She deliberates only briefly before choosing her meats. For the 2 days before the primary election, scheduled 2 weeks after Ad C was received, the woman on several occasions mulls over her thoughts about what candidate to choose. Deliberations intensify as the commitment point nears, and she spends a minute in final deliberation in the silence of the voting booth. Over the 2 months following Ad D's transmission, she thinks about motor scooters off and on. A second personal transportation vehicle seems desirable in her family. She solicits data from some dealers and advice about some brands from friends, organizes her ideas on how to choose one brand, takes some test rides, saves some money, and buys a scooter for her birthday.

Now consider the ad reception environment in which our heroine had to operate. What about it makes it unique as an arena in which an advocate may try to bias her future choices? Her conscious ad-stimulated thoughts are of central concern. The volume and the nature of the thoughts she can produce depends, in general, on (1) her inherent cognitive ability; (2) her store of topic-relevant beliefs in memory, from which to fashion thoughts; (3) her acute motivation to produce thoughts, since thinking takes effort; and (4) her opportunity to think, because thinking takes time, because she has limits on her capacity to process different streams of information concurrently, and because she must allocate attention among competing cognitive tasks (Roberts & Maccoby, 1973; Wright, 1975). Her inherent cognitive ability is not different when she receives a TV ad than when she receives a message via radio, magazine, or through an interpersonal conversation. Her topical knowledgeability also does not vary depending on which medium the message uses. The topics addressed in the ads in our scenario represented a cross section of those that mass media advocates address. Some are familiar and others new. Some are simple and others multifaceted. Some raise the specter of imminent penalty costs if one's own judgments on problem solutions are incorrect; others involve distant or trivial penalty costs. All these variables may affect how acutely motivated an audience member is to think in response to an ad; yet it is not clear how someone's processing motivation is affected by the ad's medium per se. Different media allow an advocate to try different types of non-topic-related attention-getting tactics, but the media choice per se cannot convert a mundane topic to an involving one or vice versa.

The outstanding feature of the TV reception situation was perhaps the potential strain it imposed on the woman's opportunity to respond extensively to an ad that piqued her interest. Television ads are curt as an economic necessity. Each one presents competing stimuli that vie for someone's attention. Each ad is embedded in a continuing audiovisual transmission, so that messages on unrelated but potentially interesting topics bracket an ad. There is often no forewarning of the topics of upcoming announcements, hence no time for anticipatory preparation of critical responses. Producing many or elaborate thoughts in response to every marginally interesting ad may not be an easy task. The text of any ad is but one fleeting stimulus in a cluttered, changing stream of stimuli. In contrast, the reception environments created by other media—like newspapers, magazines, or radio—typically allow more opportunity to think extensively about whatever ads arouse interest. Note that this need not imply that a TV viewer necessarily *feels* considerable mental strain. Being adaptive, the viewer can simplify processing and response tasks by not attending to, decoding, or critically thinking about some or most of the stimuli that confront him or her. If such simplifying occurs, the person's expected (or average) production of thoughts to a set of TV ads should be lower than his or her expected production of thoughts to ads that use the same texts but are transmitted in a different medium.

Several questions of central interest to a cognitive response theorist concerned with media effects in general and with mass media applications in particular can now be identified:

1. What are the effects of the ad reception environment on immediate cognitive responses? How do media differences and the level of concurrent and surrounding distractions affect the volume and nature of the thoughts audiences emit?

2. In absolute terms, how much thinking do radio and TV audiences accomplish? Are there environments where the expected output of ad-stimulated thoughts is virtually nil? Can the cognitive response approach be retained if the proportion of audience members who manage to emit a thought or two is quite low?

3. Assuming that audience members are adaptive, what types of strategies do they develop for processing evidence in strainful reception environments? Which types of thoughts are successfully generated when generating any thoughts is difficult? Do people attend more to certain types of thoughts when their opportunity to integrate thoughts is curtailed? And finally, is there theoretical justification for believing that the thoughts elicited in strainful reception environments can seriously bias someone's future choices?

The remainder of this chapter considers these questions.

THE EFFECTS OF THE
AD RECEPTION ENVIRONMENT ON
IMMEDIATE COGNITIVE RESPONSES

Of interest are studies that varied the medium by which an ad was transmitted or that varied a factor theoretically related to differences in the reception environments different media create. It is first useful to analyze what factors differentiate ad reception environments in terms of an audience member's response opportunity.

Consider first a single isolated ad to which someone is exposed. The transmission mode of the ad's text is the one variable typically singled out as a media factor. The print text versus audio text distinction is of central interest. The most striking difference between these modes relevant to our purposes is that mass media broadcast ads use *preprogrammed* texts. The message is spoken in a continuous linear way, with no opportunity for an audience member to cause it to slow down or stop momentarily or to refer back to an earlier part. Any segment of the text—for example, a specific assertion—may be viewed as embedded in the longer ongoing text. A person's attempt to decode it and generate thoughts in response to it is potentially inhibited by (1) his or her processing of the preceding part of the text, to which the person still may be trying to respond; (2) the processing task relevant to this ongoing assertion itself; or (3) his or her processing tasks relevant to the next assertion, which begins immediately after the current one ends. A mass media print ad typically creates an environment where the audience member can examine the text at whatever pace he or she chooses and refer back to earlier parts of it easily. Technically, any printed assertion is also embedded, but the audience member so controls the reception environment that the embedding exerts much less constraint on response opportunity.

Note that we discuss here the differences between generic types of mass media reception environments common *today*. We do not try to reduce the print versus audio distinction to a "pure" variable. The distinction already discussed does not necessarily apply to all print and audio texts. For example, a television ad may show a print message, but the advocate would control the text exposure pace, not the audience member. Or the exposure pace of an audio text could be controlled by an audience member if that individual is playing back a videotape taken from an earlier television transmission. Note also that the pace of an audio text or its scheduling of new assertions is a variable and hence is controllable. By varying these factors (e.g., Miller, Maruyama, Beaber, & Valone, 1976; Roberts & Maccoby, 1973), one might approximate in some respects a print text's reception environment with an audio text.

Another relevant feature of the ad is its nontext transmissions. These function as potential distractors an audience member may try to process concurrently with the text. Print media allow pictures plus text; radio allows audio noises plus text; and television allows motion pictures, background noise, and/or superimposed print plus text. It is not incumbent on an advocate to use the multimode technical capability of a medium. One can imagine magazine ads, radio ads, or TV ads that present only the text. But if nontext stimuli are to be part of an ad, then the number and complexity of the potential distractors in a television transmission exceeds the maximum for radio, which probably exceeds the maximum for magazines. In both broadcast media, the distractors are controlled by the advocate, so a person cannot pace the immediate mental workload by referring back and forth from text to nontext distractor as efficiently as with a print ad.

A more dynamic view of the reception environment requires that we include the transmission segment in which a given ad is embedded. The earlier discussion of the complexity in responding to a single mid-ad assertion applies to the problem of responding to an embedded message as a whole. Responses to the current ad may be inhibited by processing activities evoked by the preceding transmission segment or by the ensuing transmission segment. The reader of a print ad controls the exposure pace of preceding and ensuing media stimuli. The listener to a radio or TV ad does not. The transmissions that invariably bracket a radio or TV ad, over which an advocate has little control, also vary in the complexity of their multimode sound and light shows. The bracketing segments found on TV typically (but not necessarily) offer a higher average workload potential in terms of multiple distractors than those on radio.

Text Mode Effects

Several studies have applied a thought-sampling methodology to try teasing out the effects on audience responses of reception environment variations like those described. Perhaps the most direct text mode manipulation was by Wright (1974b, 1975). Adult women were presented either an audio or print version of the text of an ad for a soybean-based food innovation. The ad followed a lead-in message on an unrelated topic. Subjects' thoughts in reaction to the ad were unexpectedly sampled during the 3 minutes immediately after its transmission. The other factor manipulated in the 2 × 2 design was the women's acute motivation to process the ad. All the women were asked to treat the entire transmission segment as they naturally would in responding to mass media transmissions in their home. Half were also told that the upcoming ad would discuss a topic about which they must soon make a personal decision. This heightened the amount of attention given to the ad versus the other message, as shown by reliable differences on a postmessage question. The transmission medium caused significant main effects on the women's total thought outputs and outputs of support arguments or source derogations (see Table 12.1). They averaged about 25% more total thoughts and twice as many support arguments or source derogations when the text was print as when it was audio. Counterargument generation was not affected by the text medium per se, but the medium × involvement interaction

TABLE 12.1
Mean Thought Outputs

	Audio Version		Print Version	
	High Involvement	Low Involvement	High Involvement	Low Involvement
Total thoughts	3.1	3.0	4.1	3.4
Counterarguments	1.2	1.2	1.6	.8
Support arguments	.6	.5	1.2	1.4
Source derogations	.1	.3	.3	.5

[a] Wright (1974c).

was significant. Print ad subjects generated more counters than audio ad subjects when both groups were acutely motivated to try to process the ad, and fewer when both were not acutely interested. Wright argued that the audio ad's pace discouraged extensive counterarguing, since that was presumably a difficult activity, given the unfamiliarity of the product being touted. But it is harder for someone to totally ignore an obtrusive audio ad than a print ad. So an audio ad may elicit counters even from some not-too-interested receivers who could more easily ignore a print version. The data were consistent with the notion that the range of outputs of more tedious thoughts elicited by an audio ad will be smaller than by a print ad, *ceteris paribus.*

The women's scores on multi-item measures of "general social confidence" (Janis & Field, 1959; Nisbett & Gordon, 1967) and "information-processing confidence" were correlated with their thought outputs. The former measure asks one to assess one's own abilities to handle message reception when a situation carries a sense of social confrontation. Both cognitive skills and social skills would be relevant in that case. The latter measure asks one to indicate the speed and efficiency of one's own information-processing capability. Wright reasoned that processing and responding to a print message is so easy that audience-member differences in general social confidence or information-processing confidence would not cause different levels of thought production. Indeed, the correlations between the scores and the outputs of thoughts were trivial when a print ad was the stimulus. However, an audio message may be more difficult to process and may create more of a sense of responding to another person, as in a social confrontation. So differences between people in response skills or techniques should cause differences in reactions to the audio message. When an audience member is not very interested in the ad, inherent processing ability (as reflected by information-processing confidence scores) should play a major role in determining the volume of thoughts one can emit. But when a person is quite interested in the ad, the sense of social confrontation is more pronounced. In that case, the mixture of skills relevant to handling social interactions (as reflected by the general social confidence scores) should be the major determinant. The data were consistent with this reasoning. Among the less involved women, the correlation between information-processing confidence scores and counterarguing was .45, but the correlation involving general social confidence was not significant. Among the acutely involved women, the correlation between general social confidence and counterargument volume was .51, but the correlation involving information-processing confidence scores was not significant.

In summary, the pattern of results indicates that differences among audience members in acute motivation to process the ad can strongly bias thought generation when the reception situation is relatively strain free, but when the reception situation is fairly strainful, as with a broadcast transmission, acute motivation differences may be less important in determining thought levels than inherent response ability differences.

Krugman (1967) also examined how media variations may bias audience thought outputs, although the limited statistical analysis reported means the data are at best suggestive. Adult women were presented with short ads for several brand-name products (e.g., a margarine, an airline). A TV version and a magazine version of the same basic ad for a given brand were contrasted. These were both embedded in other unrelated material that the subject inspected. A thought sampling about the key ad was taken soon after its inspection. The data reported were the generation of thoughts coded as "connections" (thoughts linking the message content to one's personal experiences). The women averaged 2.5 times more connections to a print ad than to a TV ad for the same brand. Since they averaged 20 seconds reading the print ad versus 60 seconds listening to and watching the TV ad, they generated eight times more thoughts per second of exposure to the print ad. Krugman argued that his data implied TV is inherently a "low-involvement" medium. However, if the differences observed were reliable, they would be consistent with the hypothesis that an embedded, multimode TV ad can create a much more strainful response environment than an embedded print ad; hence, TV is a "low-opportunity" medium.

Chaiken and Eagly (1976) contrasted the responses of students to a print-text, audio-text, or audio-text-plus-visual-distractors version of a message arguing one side in a legal case. Each subject first read a print background discussion on the case before receiving the isolated advocacy message. No reliable differences were found in counterargument outputs. Several aspects of the experiment may have contributed to this result. The subject's reading time was limited to the time it took to speak the audio version of the message, thus eliminating the key "self-paced versus preprogrammed pace" factor which normally differentiates between print and audio messages. The unfamiliar topic may also have contributed to the uniformly low levels of counterarguing observed.

Concurrent Distractors

The print ad versus audio ad manipulations in Wright (1974b, 1975) and Chaiken and Eagly (1976) varied just the text's mode; the print ad versus audiovisual ad manipulations in Krugman (1967) and Chaiken and Eagly (1976) varied both text mode and the distractors concurrent to the text. As argued, one way in which TV, radio, and magazines may differ is in the intensity of the concurrent distractors an audience member must cope with in order to respond to the text. The presence of such distractors does not guarantee that the individual will feel more overloaded. However, if actue interest level and personal cognitive ability are held constant, one would expect that ads featuring concurrent distractors place more strain on opportunity to respond to the text than those without distractors. And the pace of the distractor or the number of modes in which concurrent distractors are transmitted should affect how difficult responding to the text is. Various distractors have been manipulated in studies testing whether or when a distracted audience member becomes more favorable to the advocate's position than an undistracted one. This research is reviewed in depth in Chapter 3 of this book. For our purposes, it is useful merely to note that counterargument outputs and support argument outputs have been attenuated by concurrent visual and audio distractors in a number of studies (e.g., Insko, Turnbull, & Yandell, 1974; Osterhouse & Brock, 1970; Petty, Wells & Brock, 1976).

Preceding and Ensuing Distractors

Some data from Krugman's (1967) study, described earlier, indicate that ad-stimulated responses can be depressed when attention-getting material surrounds a broadcast ad. The margarine and airlines ads were embedded in program segments that dealt with different topics. In one treatment, the bracketing material consisted of discussions on sociopolitical topics, like "the future of the Arkansas River Basin." In the other, the bracketing material consisted of celebrity interviews and performances. When the ads were embedded in the celebrity material, they evoked an average of 30% to 40% *fewer* connections from the homemaker audience. Krugman interpreted this to mean that the lead-in sociopolitical material had first induced the audience members into a "heavy thinking" mood, and that this carried over to produce more active thinking about the ads for the products. However, assuming the differences between the treatments were reliable, an alternate interpretation would be that the celebrity material stirred greater interest in this type audience, thereby causing more distraction. The lower thought production to the ads sandwiched between the celebrity interviews could have been caused by subjects continuing to respond to the lead-in celebrity interview even though the ad had begun, or curtailing response to the key ad as soon as the next celebrity interview began. The relative interest levels evoked by the celebrity and sociopolitical materials were not documented, so the data are best viewed as suggestive.

Roberts and Maccoby (1973) used a relevant manipulation. Some subjects were given 20-second pauses in which to think every 40 seconds during an 8-minute audio transmission. Others were not. Comparing the responses of those given the pauses with those not given them is analogous to comparing responses to a series of 40-second ads not bracketed by pre-ad and post-ad messages with responses to the same ads tailgated into each other. Subjects given the mid-transmission pauses expressed twice as many counters during the transmission as those not given the pauses, and significantly more counters to specific message assertions and "self-generated" counters in an undistracted thought sampling taken after the transmission ended. So those data also suggest that responses to an audio ad are suppressed when audio material brackets that ad, and responses to a given audio assertion are suppressed when other text material brackets it.

Other insight on the effects of embedding an audio ad comes from the volume of thoughts generated by subjects in pilot studies who have been given different amounts of undistracted post-ad time to report thoughts evoked by an audio message. First, note that even when time limits on post-ad thought samplings have been imposed, they have been fairly lenient. Giving someone 2.5 to 4 minutes of *undistracted response time* (e.g., Osterhouse & Brock, 1970; Petty et al., 1976; Wright, 1974b, 1975) may seem strict in comparison to giving them 10 minutes (Calder, Insko, & Yandells, 1974) or unlimited time (Insko et al., 1974; Roberts & Maccoby, 1973). But it is a fairly long respite when viewed in the context of continuous radio or television broadcasts. Osterhouse and Brock (1970) noted that a 1-minute time limit on the undistracted post-ad thought sampling in a pilot study so reduced counterargument outputs that there were too little data to warrant analysis! A similar effect due to a short time limit was found in other pilot studies (Mazis, 1976; Wright, 1974a). The data from the pilot studies were not analyzed in detail, so these reports remain only suggestive. They do suggest that an audience member needs nontrivial time to produce thoughts, and that thought output is directly related to how long the individual can block out ensuing transmissions to think about an ad's assertions during the immediate post-ad period.

In prior studies, immediate post-ad thought samples have invariably been extracted during periods free from concurrent distractors. In distraction-effect studies, the distraction lasted only while the message text was being inspected. In future research, an interesting way to take thought samples that reflect the embedded-ad effect would be to keep an audio or audiovisual transmission going during the immediate post-ad thought sampling.

A person may also anticipate potentially interesting upcoming messages in a broadcast transmission and curtail ongoing cognitive reactions so that he or she can identify and be responsive to whatever occurs next. This issue has not yet been directly studied, but Cullen's (1968) data are suggestive. Four experiments were run in which the subject population, message, and pre-ad instructions were apparently similar. Subjects in the first two experiments averaged about 30% more thoughts on the post-ad thought sampling than those in the last two. The causal factor may be that subjects in the last two experiments were asked to answer added questions after their thought reporting. If this added response task was foreseeable (e.g., if subjects noted extra pages in the questionnaire), the lower thought outputs might have been due to the subjects' anticipation of future cognitive work. Interestingly, control group subjects who gave thoughts on the ad's topic without reading the ad and answered the same extra questions also displayed lower thought outputs in the latter two experiments. Though hardly conclusive, these data suggest that the way a person budgets his or her message response effort is sensitive to the ad's embedding context.

RECEPTION ENVIRONMENTS THAT SEVERELY LIMIT RESPONSE OPPORTUNITY

In several studies, researchers have established reception environments more like those typically faced by a mass media audience than is the case in most lab experiments. Ray, Ward, and Lesser (1973) showed adolescents and adults a TV program in which 30-second ads were embedded, some of which were anti-drug-abuse ads. Taped conversations were played in the background at different loudness levels to simulate the noisy home environment with which a TV viewer must sometimes contend. Rothschild (1975) showed subjects numerous slides of print ads for branded products and political candidates, for 10 seconds apiece, to simulate the situation where someone casually flips through a magazine and inspects the ads only briefly. The number of repetitions of a stimulus ad was the manipulated variable. Webb (1980) encouraged small groups of female acquaintances to talk, read magazines, or fix coffee during exposure to a TV program containing embedded ads. The manipulated variables were the number of ads clustered with the key ad in a program break and the number of repetitions of the key ad. To try capturing the natural involvement levels displayed by mass media audiences, the ads in these studies represented a cross-section of the topics and creative formats typical in magazine or TV advertising, the key ads were disguised, and the thought sampling was postponed until the program's end, at which time subjects reported thoughts evoked by the ads they recalled seeing. The average number of recalled thoughts per subject for the recalled ads was low, ranging from about .1 (Rothschild, 1975) to about .7 (Ray et al., 1973), and the manipulations of distraction, repetition, or program-break "clutter" did not affect the thought outputs. This could imply that those factors only marginally affected the already difficult response task.

However, Calder and Sternthal (1980) found that repetition did affect thought output in a TV viewing situation. In that case, subjects reported their *current* thoughts about the advertised product following exposure to programs in which the ads were embedded, not thoughts they recalled being evoked during the exposure per se. Differences between the latter study and the former ones in stimuli (ads; repetition schedules) or thought sampling procedures could underlie the different results.

Sometimes in these low-opportunity reception situations, exposure effects have been observed on some measure of overt behavior when no effects on thought-verbalizations were observed. For example, Wright (1979) had adults view a TV program under the guise of eliciting their ideas about what made the show successful, to direct attention to the program per se. Embedded in the program were ads for some branded antacids, onto which were edited brief audiovisual segments urging viewers to read the package warnings before buying. These varied in the concreteness of the verbal action recommendation and whether or not the in-store package inspection activity was visually modeled, factors expected to influence the viewer's mental action planning activities. Subjects subsequently shopped for an antacid in a retail pharmacy, where their package inspection behavior was unobtrusively observed. Exposure to the warning segment using the concrete language and the visual action enactment caused increased package inspection by subjects who shopped soon after seeing the program. However, a group of pilot study subjects who reported thoughts evoked by the final minutes of the TV transmission, which included two of the antacid ads, expressed no thoughts at all related to the ads, the products, or the warnings. Similarly, Rothschild (1975) found that repetition of political candidates' ads heightened subjects' reported intent to vote in the election without any corresponding effect in a retrospective sampling of message-evoked thoughts.

These results illustrate a dilemma in using thought verbalization measures in research where audience responses under naturalistic, low-opportunity reception conditions are at issue. Asking for retrospective reports of one's earlier message-evoked thoughts is an effort to expose message processing activity without obtrusively interrupting the transmission when the ad appears. However, the validity of such reports remains questionable. It could be that some important mental activities mediating behavioral effects like those in Wright (1979) or Rothschild (1975) are not at all amenable to reporting. For example, people may simply not be conscious of their mental action planning activities, even as these are occuring. Or it may be that people cannot or will not retrieve memories of such thoughts to report on a retrospective thought sampling. How thought verbalizing measures should be adapted to the mass broadcast media setting remains to be seen. Calder and Sternthal (1980) used the post-program thought sampling as a surrogate product-attitude measure, like Cullen (1968), rather than to expose message processing activity; perhaps this limited use of such measures is realistic in the TV viewing setting.

Summary

The available evidence already reviewed is consistent with the idea that different media can create reception environments that differ markedly in how much opportunity for active thinking is provided. The combination of the separate factors cited should be most oppressive. This would be a reception environment where the text is audio, the transmission is multimode, the message is embedded in a continuous transmission populated by other multimode messages, and the audience member is aware that upcoming messages may be worth considering and hence may require exertion for some processing work. In theory, television as we know it today fits this description.

The reader may wonder whether advertising agencies who test mass media ads have produced a fund of empirical evidence about media effects on cognitive responses. The answer, unfortunately, is no. Agency strategiests continue to bemoan their lack of data about media differences on audience responses. Advertising researchers have collected "thought verbatims" from audience members as part of ad campaign pretesting for decades. However, the thought samples have been given subordinate status in a bevy of other measures and are usually taken a long time after the ad's exposure. For example, Bogart, Tolley, & Orenstein (1970) and Leavitt, Waddell, & Wells (1970) reported on agency research in which retrospective thought samples were taken during "day-after" interviews. As argued, this measurement schedule tends to negate a thought sampling's potential sensitivity to the original reception environment effects.

HOW MUCH THINKING DO TV AND RADIO AUDIENCES ACCOMPLISH?

In a previous section, we tried to synthesize single experiments for insight on how the reception environment affects cognitive response outputs. One dissatisfaction with that approach is that the range of reception conditions sampled in any given study was limited. A second is that the parameters held constant in one study usually differed greatly from those held constant in another and often were not established with a generic real-world reception environment in mind. The study-by-study analysis suggested that mass media broadcasts, on TV in particular, are received in a situation that combines many potential response inhibitors. If audience thinking dwindles severely in such settings, an advocate and theorist must ponder how audiences cope with such strains and what type thoughts are likely. Before pursuing this, a relevant question is: In absolute terms, how much thinking do audiences accomplish in such settings?

One might hypothesize that strainful reception conditions, at least at the levels captured in TV reception settings, can be readily overcome by an acutely involved audience member. Or one might hypothesize the opposite—that response

TABLE 12.2
Average Thought Outputs in Cognitive Response Experiments on Persuasion

Thought Sampling Procedure	Isolated or Embedded Print Ad	Message Reception/Response Environment		
		Isolated Audio Ad, No Distractors	Isolated Audio Ad, Distractors	Embedded Audiovisual Ad
Immediate post-ad undistracted thought sample; no explicit time limit[a]	Janis & Terwilliger →15[b] Cullen, Exp. 1 & Exp. 2 →9.2 Cullen, Exp. 3 & Exp. 4 →6.6 Calder et al. →7.8 McCullough & Ostrom →7.3 Cook, 10 paragraphs →6.0 8 paragraphs →4.0 2 paragraphs →1.8 1 paragraph →.8	Roberts & Maccoby →7.0 Insko et al. →4.9	Insko et al. →5.3	
Immediate post-ad undistracted thought sample; explicit time limit (2.5–4 minutes)	Wright →3.8	Petty et al. →5.2 Keating & Brock →4.4[c] Osterhouse & Brock →2.6[c] Wright →3.0 Mazis →2.2	Petty et al., Exp. 1 & Exp. 2 →4.7 Keating & Brock →2.7[c] Osterhouse & Brock →1.8[c]	
Delayed post-ad thought sample	Krugman, Exp. 1 →1.5 Krugman, Exp. 3 →.3			Krugman, Exp. 1 & Exp. 2 →.6 Ray et al., Exp. 1 & Exp. 2 →.7[d] Webb →.4[d] Leavitt et al. →.4[d] Bogart et al. →.2[d] Rothschild →.1[d]

[a] Exception: Calder et al. used a long 10-minute limit.
[b] Number of paragraphs evoking at least one thought.
[c] Only counterarguments
[d] Mean thoughts per *recalled* ad.

opportunity so dominates response motivation that even interested audiences cannot manage many thoughts in such situations. For insight on this, the absolute levels of cognitive response outputs observed in experiments can be examined. To pursue this, the author first identified four types of media situations represented in prior cognitive response experiments: (1) a print text, (2) an isolated audio text, (3) an isolated audio text plus concurrent visual distractors, and (4) an embedded audio text plus concurrent visual distractors. Then the absolute thought outputs observed in the experimental treatments falling in each category were inspected. But the varied thought-sampling procedures used in different studies made this one-dimensional categorization inconclusive. Treatments were then also categorized according to whether the thought sampling had been (1) immediate, but with no time limit; (2) immediate, but with a time limit (4 minutes or less); or (3) delayed, with other transmissions and questions filling the interim. Distributing the more than two dozen treatments in the resulting 4×3 matrix (see Table 12.2) made it obvious that attributing the levels of absolute outputs observed to the media environment factor per se would be impossible. There were no treatments in one-third of the cells and only one in three others. Hence, we observe a steep drop in thought outputs as the media situation moved from print to embedded audiovisual ads; but almost all treatments that used a print ad also used immediate, unlimited-time thought reporting, whereas all that used an embedded audiovisual ad took the thought sampling after several other messages and on a lengthy questionnaire.

Perhaps the most useful insight gained was that our sampling of persuasion settings has been so biased in cognitive response research (and, generally, in laboratory experiments on persuasion). For example, the cases where observed thought outputs were fairly high, in addition to using less strainful media, also used bright young college students as subjects, texts much longer than those feasible in mass media ads, topics intentionally picked to be involving, and messages usually structured to be counterattitudinal. Acute involvement levels of the audiences were empirically monitored only rarely, leaving us to guess about that important situational parameter. But in many of the lab experiments that produced high thought outputs, the researchers commented that they had sought high-involvement topics and in some cases had uniformly induced high attention by telling subjects to expect a post-message test of their thoughts (Roberts & Maccoby, 1973), a post-message ad-comprehension test (Insko et al., 1974; Osterhouse & Brock, 1970), or a post-message group discussion of their ideas (Calder et al., 1974). So, in cases where audience thought outputs were observed to be higher, many parameters of the situation were set so as to encourage audience thinking. In contrast, the immediate thought outputs of a heterogeneous audience reacting to embedded audiovisual ads when not hypermotivated have not been measured.

Even so, it is instructive to highlight the thought outputs in some individual studies. Earlier we noted the very low outputs alluded to by Osterhouse and

Brock (1970) when a 1-minute undistracted sampling was taken. In one treatment of that study, students were given an isolated 6-minute audio message presenting 7 arguments, each about 50 words long, on why their tuition should be raised. They averaged 2.6 counterarguments when given an undistracted 3-minute post-ad period for reporting. Extrapolating from Petty et al.'s (1976) data obtained from similar subjects and similar topic, one might estimate that Osterhouse and Brock's subjects averaged about 5 to 6 total thoughts apiece. One can speculatively adjust the observed outputs downward to account for changes in that situation that would make it comparable to a radio audience's situation. What if the topic had not been picked to be especially involving; no comprehension test was promised; the audience was not of higher-than-average intellect; the ad's length was cut by 80% to 90%, to approximate a 30-second or 60-second commercial; and an audio transmission had played during the post-ad thought sampling? It does not seem unreasonable to speculate that the mean would drop to under 1 thought per subject. Roberts and Maccoby (1973) carved an 8.5-minute audio ad into 13 segments lasting about 40 seconds each. In effect, one can view this as 13 ads of length comparable to a normal radio ad. These subjects were forewarned that their thoughts were of interest, and the mid-ad samplings drove home this point. When they were given 20-second undistracted breaks for thought expression after each segment, they averaged about 10 thoughts, or less than 1 per break. When these breaks were eliminated, so each segment tailgated into the next, less than 6 thoughts on average were induced by the entire transmission. Wright's (1974b) homemaker audience averaged 3 thoughts to an audio ad that was 90 seconds long and preceded by only one other message, when they were given an undistracted post-ad 3 minutes for reporting.

These figures suggest that mass audiences may well have difficulty producing much thinking about the brief embedded audio or audiovisual ads they confront in an otherwise potentially distractive environment. They also call in question the argument that heightened processing motivation compensates much for low response opportunity in such settings.

AUDIENCE RESPONSE TENDENCIES IN
STRAINFUL RECEPTION ENVIRONMENTS

How might audiences adapt to the strains encountered in processing mass media message streams? Two hypotheses are offered here, and evidence supporting them is reviewed. The first is that people let negative reactions color their global response to the advocated option more so than in less strainful environments. The second is that people attend to and react to the way advocates "frame" the judgment problem, implicitly or explicitly, in touting their respective options, and that thoughts on this help shape how the audience members later attack the problem of judging preference within that domain of options.

Negative Thoughts

A series of studies suggests that in situations where opportunity to respond to assertions about an option's attributes is limited, more attention is given to negative responses than would otherwise be the case. The first study employed thought verbalization data (Wright, 1973). Recall that the design crossed a Print text—Audio text manipulation with a high Involvement—Lower Involvement manipulation. The correlations of different types of thoughts with post-exposure attitudes, measured by attitude scales, were computed, and between-cell differences in these correlations were analyzed. The correlation between counterarguing and attitude toward the advocated product was significantly stronger among subjects receiving the audio ad than among those receiving the print version. Only when highly involved subjects received the print version was there evidence that both supportarguing and counterarguing explained post-exposure attitude differences across subjects.

In two subsequent studies, subjects were shown a series of profiled automobiles (Wright, 1974c) or of birth-control devices (Wright & Weitz, 1977) and asked to react to each. The amount of time allowed was varied. This task is similar in many ways to that faced in responding to media ads. Both the profile and the ad are, in essence, just explicit assertions about product attributes; most media ads do little more than cite the attributes of the touted product (Wright & Barbour, 1975). Tactics for coping with limited response opportunity should be similar, whether the message uses a skeletal or an embellished format.

In Wright (1974c), young men reacted to each profiled car (not identified by brand name) in either 10 seconds or taking as much time as they wished. The relationship between variations in the cars' attributes and variations in a subject's global ratings of the cars was analyzed. A statistical model that overweighted the impact of negative features gave the best fit for a majority of the men who operated under time pressure. This was not the case among those given more time to respond. In a second experiment, men who had to respond while background noise was fairly loud showed more of a tendency to overweight negative evidence than those who did not have to cope with distractors. Wright and Weitz (1977) replicated this time-pressure effect in a study where young women reacted to profiled birth-control devices in 10 seconds or 40 seconds per profile. Statistical estimates of each subject's reactions showed that reactions to moderately undesirable features were more extreme when processing time was short.

While the tendency to overweight negative thoughts in strainful processing situations seems widespread (see also, Wright, 1979b), we should not conclude that mass media advocates should therefore avoid evoking negative reactions at all costs. First, it must be understood that the overweighting of negative reactions occurs only when a subject attempts resolving thoughts into an overall attitude or impression. Second, the underlying explanation for this overweighting is that it affords a conservative simplifying tactic, which should be appealing mainly when one is concerned about being "talked into" an overly favorable attitude at a time when one's facilities for critical message processing are overtaxed. Hence, the overweighting may only occur when an audience member is sufficiently concerned over the message content to bother generating reactions and integrating those into an overall impression, and to worry about making errors in this. Less concerned audience members are more likely to simplify by just not generating reactions or working out any attitude revision based on reactions generated. Consistent with this, Wright and Weitz (1977) found that women who reviewed profiled birth-control devices while considering the purchase decision a distant event did not let reactions to undesirable features color their overall ratings as strongly as did those who felt purchase was imminent. And, in both Wright (1973) and Petty and Cacioppa (1979b), counterarguing (and message-evoked thoughts in general) explained much more variance in post-exposure attitude expressions among subjects interested in message processing than among those less involved.

Broadcast media advocates apparently must arouse enough interest to stimulate active response, and handle the audience's tendency to overweight negative thoughts by reducing the processing strain (e.g., shortening the message text; pausing between assertions; reducing video distractions) or using uniformly persuasive texts. There is even some evidence that stimulating some immediate counterarguing beats not attracting any attention. Wright (1974a) compared immediate post-message thought samples to those taken 48 hours after exposure. The subjects who had most emphasized counterarguing while processing the audio message showed a significant decrease in counterarguing and an increase in "curiosity" thoughts in their later thinking. Many thoughts originally expressed as counters were expressed as questions later on. This finding is intriguing, and the issue of how immediate message responses relate to later topic-related thinking deserves more study.

Problem-framing Responses

Persuasion experiments usually focus on response to a single advocate's message, treating post-exposure beliefs, attitude, or behavior toward the particular option advocated as the only criteria for guaging exposure effects. A different view is to consider the *message stream*, comprised of messages from different advocates touting competing options, as the stimulus, and to examine how exposure to a mass media message stream affects the basic approach receivers take to judging preference between the competing options. In particular, exposure to message streams in which the advocates focus their discussion on the same factors or display the same comparison procedure in arguing the superiority of their respective options may induce receivers to focus on those same factors or try the same comparison method when they begin their own preference deliberations.

Wright and Rip (1979) exposed high school sophomores to a stream of college promotional brochures, then had the students rank profiled colleges according to personal preference. In one study, the brochures displayed either high or low consensus in the attributes highlighted. In a second, they displayed either high or low consensus in both the attributes highlighted and the comparison method each advocate adopted. Thought verbalizations during the preference ranking and statistical descriptions of the weights given to different factors in the ranking revealed that subjects had modeled how they framed the decision problem in part on what was observed in the message stream. However, thought verbalizations during the last part of the message stream did not reveal the message response activities that mediated those effects.

In those studies, print messages were used, but it seems likely that similar effects will occur due to exposure to product-class TV or radio advertising. Indeed, strainful reception environments which curtail elaborate responses to an ad's specific assertions may at least allow someone to note how the advocate framed the problem, e.g., "he's discussing Factor A"; "he's screening out candidates using Factor B." In any case, casting the communication process in terms of message stream effects on problem-framing porcesses, and using thought sampling during the preference judgment episode as one criterion measures, may open new vistas on how mass media advocacy affects audience decision processes. Whether the message response activities that mediate effects on problem-framing practices, which may include normative attributions or self-instructions on future mental activities, will be revealed in thought verbalizations during message processing remains to be seen.

CHAPTER SUMMARY

Cognitive response theorizing focuses attention on the audience member's need for a reception environment hospitable to thought production. An analysis of the factors that contribute to inhibiting ad-stimulated thinking suggested that mass media broadcasts may not give someone very much response opportunity. Audio ads were found to elicit fewer total thoughts than identical print ads. It was suggested that audience members' acute interest in the ad may increase thought production only when the reception situation is relatively strain free (e.g., print mode), but when the reception situation is more strainful (e.g., audio mode), motivational differences may be less important than inherent cognitive ability in determining thought levels. Experiments that have manipulated media-related factors (concurrent and surrounding distractors, anticipation of future cognitive work) and sampled audience thoughts have produced evidence that the factors operating in a normal TV-viewing environment can suppress cognitive responses. These studies also indicated that a thought-sampling methodology can tease out reception environment effects as long as the thought samples are taken during or immediately after the stimulus ad and some attention is given to time controls during the sampling. The thought outputs observed in these experiments can be interpreted as indicating that thought outputs may often approach zero when broadcast ads are transmitted, even when the ad's topic is intriguing.

Presumably, audiences adopt strategies to cope with strainful reception environments. One possibility that has empirical support from a series of studies is that people tend to focus more on their negative responses under strainful processing conditions. The long-term effects of this are not yet clear. Another possibility is that problem-framing thoughts are more likely to survive in strainful reception environments than are thoughts relevant to assertions about an object's properties. Theoretically, these thoughts can act as significant influences on the outcome of future choice episodes.

THEORETICAL PERSPECTIVES IN THE ANALYSIS OF COGNITIVE RESPONSES

Thomas M. Ostrom
Ohio State University

Attitudes are embedded within and conveyed through a wonderful diversity of thoughts. It might be well for the reader at this point to return to the illustration of that diversity provided in Table 1.2 at the beginning of Chapter 1. The table illustrates the wide differences that can exist between the cognitive responses of three different persons, each of whose attitudes would be called identical when measured by a simple rating scale. When people are invited to express their attitudes in informal conversation, they rarely are satisfied with a simple statement of pro-ness or con-ness. In fact, people sometimes resist being labeled as *pro* or *con*. For some, such labels are misleading, and for other people, the labels are viewed as simply missing the point. Since most attitude objects are multifaceted, and because people have a sizable store of information about and experiences with the object, it is likely that they will be focusing on those features of the attitude object rather than on some overall pro–con categorization of the self.

There can be little question that such cognitive responses are actively evoked when a person is in a persuasion setting (or any other context in which the attitude object is salient). Attitude-relevant thoughts arise whether a person is passively listening to a persuasion message or actively engaged in a discussion about the attitude object with one or more other persons. Indeed, the need to discuss and share attitudinal views is viewed by some (e.g., Festinger, 1954) as being fundamental to the psychological makeup of persons. Despite this obvious prominence of diverse cognitive responses, past theorizing in the area of attitudes has not advanced very greatly in understanding such attitude-relevant responses.

FOUR DISTINGUISHING CHARACTERISTICS OF THE COGNITIVE RESPONSE APPROACH

Most theoretical efforts over the past 25 years have been directed toward understanding how people acquire and change their evaluative disposition toward the attitude object. That is, how do people become in some overall sense favorable or unfavorable toward the attitude object? The cognitive response approach argues that such global dispositions cannot be understood in isolation from the surrounding thought processes; theories of attitude must ultimately intermesh with more general theories of thought.

In Parts I and II of this book, the reader has encountered a wide variety of applications of the cognitive response approach. These should be viewed, however, as only a beginning. The cognitive response approach will continue to uncover new phenomena and to provide new theoretical insights.

Enough research has accumulated by this point that it is useful to examine the ways in which the cognitive response approach differs from previous theoretical approaches. This exercise may help guide the future development of attitude theory as well as aid the reader in evaluating the theoretical contributions in Part III of the text. At least four distinguishing characteristics of the cognitive response approach can be identified.

Theories of Inference versus Production

Most past attitude research has studied what can be called "inference" tasks. These are tasks in which the experimenter provides a dimension of judgment and asks the subject to place the attitude object (or beliefs about the object) on the scale. Such inferential judgments are made on scales selected because of their theoretical interest to the investigators. Most typically, these are either judgments of belief (e.g., How much do you agree with an attitude item?) or judgments of evaluation (e.g., describing oneself as being for or against the attitude object).

The main difficulty with such inferential tasks is that they impose a structure (or constraints) on the cognitive response that is almost certainly different from the responses as they naturally emerge in most persuasion settings. Inference tasks correspond to the subset of naturally occurring situations in which a person is not only given a dimension of response (e.g., "Are you pro or con on the issue?") but is also forced to reply in the questioner's terminology (e.g., one may not be allowed to respond "I'm a little bit of both") and is forbidden from either clarifying, elaborating, or qualifying his or her reply. It would seem that there are very few naturally occurring situations (especially in interpersonal persuasion) with these characteristics.

The cognitive response approach focuses attention on "production" tasks, settings in which people have the opportunity to express (or produce for experimental examination) any or all salient thoughts. An adequate theory of cognitive response, then, is one that should be able to cope with cognitive responses as they are naturally produced. The remaining three distinctions in this section are ones that become germane as one explores the importance of understanding processes involved in thought production.

Univariate versus Multivariate Theory

With few exceptions (e.g., Smith, Bruner, & White, 1956), past attitude theories have attempted to explain only one feature of attitudes at a time and were usually restricted to the belief and/or evaluative dimensions. Such univariate theories aspire solely to explaining people's responses on a single dimension. Although the assessment of a person's location on such a dimension could be either through inference or production tasks, it has typically been through the use of inference tasks. Regardless of which assessment approach is employed, univariate theories are highly limited in their ability to inform us about the processes involved in cognitive response activity.

It has been widely held in the past that attitudes are multidimensional. That is, an attitude object is perceived as resting in a multidimensional space in which each dimension refers to a different attribute or belief about the attitude object. Although factor analytic, multidimensional scaling, and multivariate analysis of variance procedures are available for studying such problems of attitude multidimensionality, there do not presently exist adequate theories for understanding such processes.

Attitude theory must go beyond simply locating attitudinal responses in multiattribute space. For example, there is reason to be interested in such variables as the order in which different cognitive responses are evoked, the other responses with which they are categorized, the extent to which they serve to organize other thoughts, and the degree to which they are related to the "self." A variety of other such important variables have been described by Smith, Bruner, and White (1956) and by Scott (1968).

Quantitative versus Qualitative Theory

Theories designed to explain unidimensional properties of attitudes are normally quantitative in focus. That is, they attempt to establish the quantitative location of a person on the attitude dimension. The only issue of concern is the theory's ability to predict which variables influence how pro or con the attitude is.

The cognitive response approach encourages the development of theories that can account for qualitative differences among thoughts. The qualitative aspects of thought refer both to the existence of different categories of thoughts (and the relevance of each to attitudes and behaviors) and to the structural relations among thoughts. For example, Greenwald (1968a) found that it was important to distinguish among recipient-generated thoughts, recipient-modified thoughts, and externally (e.g., message-) originated thoughts. Whereas the former two qualitative categories were related to attitude change, the latter was only slightly related. The content of thought may be equally important as the source of the thoughts. For example, thoughts categorized as reflecting affective, cognitive, or conative responses to the attitude object (Ostrom, 1969) may relate differentially to overt reactions of an emotional, judgmental, or behavioral nature.

Once the existence of different qualitative categories is established, it becomes important to know how those categories are organized. Some may be organized in a subordinate–superordinate structure; others might be organized in a dimensional structure (as with the multidimensional attributes discussed in the previous section); and others might be organized configurally. Once the organization is identified, it becomes important to find out how people sample thoughts from this organization. Do people exhaust all thoughts from one category before moving on to another, or do they cycle through all categories before returning to the first? Finally, is the manner in which thoughts are categorized, structured, and sampled affected in any systematic way by the situational expectations of the recipient?

Information-Based versus Memory-Based Theory

A large number of attitudinal responses are made without any new information about the attitude object being received. Yet the vast bulk of research on attitudes has employed a paradigm in which attitudinal responses are sampled immediately following the receipt of new information about the attitude object. This paradigmatic feature has encouraged theorists to focus on information-based attitudinal processes, ones that deal primarily with the acceptance or rejection of new information.

The cognitive response approach invites us to go beyond the processes involved in yielding to or rejecting new information and to examine how that information is stored in memory and retrieved for use at a later point in time. Memory-based theory should inform us what kinds of thoughts people are able to draw upon when circumstances unexpectedly require them to make some decision about or response toward the attitude object. The memory-based approach also leads us to ask different questions about how people react to new information. Rather than looking solely at acceptance or rejection, we must ask which items are selected for storage in memory and seek to identify which preexisting thoughts the new items become associated with.

THE CURRENT STATE OF
COGNITIVE RESPONSE THEORY

Attitude theory appears to be in a state of transition. The period from 1930 to 1950 was spent exploring the ways in which attitudes were influenced by more basic learning, perceptual, judgmental, and motivational processes (see Ostrom, 1968). The next score of years was spent in developing theories within each of these basic areas that usually were designed to explain a small subset of attitudinal processes (see Abelson, Aronson, McGuire, Newcomb, Rosenberg, & Tannenbaum, 1968; Greenwald, Brock, & Ostrom, 1968). These "minitheories" were often identified as strongly with the name of their originator as they were with the underlying psychological processes. Indeed, the fortunes of many of these theories were more contingent on the energy, eloquence, and charisma of their progenitors than on the merit of their theoretical constructs.

The cognitive response approach represents a maturing of the discipline. It strives to uncover new complexities in the attitude process rather than live with the simplicities that necessarily accompanied the more narrowly focused univariate models developed over the last 20 years.

A good example of the kinds of advances that can be expected from the cognitive response approach is provided by work on the relationship between attitude and physiological responses. Most social psychologists doing research on this problem devoted their energies to searching for physiological correlates of attitude direction and extremity (see the discussion of the "emotional response" approach in Chapter 4). The cognitive response approach leads to a redefining of the problem, an entirely new set of relationships to be studied, and—for the first time in this area—to a conceptual framework to guide future research.

Recent work by Konečni (1975, 1978) addresses the problem of how thoughts and physiological arousal interrelate to affect behavioral responses toward the attitude object. Konečni's primary concern was with the problem of aggression and interpersonal conflict. His findings showed that cognitive activity can elevate physiological arousal, and that the level of arousal is a key determinant of the extent and intensity of negative actions directed toward a disliked target person. The cognitive responses important to Konečni's analysis include memory for aversive events, resentful and hostile thoughts, and emotional labels. It appears reasonable that the relation between attitude and behavior cannot be understood by ignoring ongoing cognitive and physiological activity.

In Part III of this book, we present five different theoretical perspectives on the problem of cognitive responses. It should be clear from the foregoing discussion that there exists no "definitive" theory of cognitive responses. Indeed, the cognitive response approach is more a conceptual orientation (or perhaps a statement of faith) toward the role of thought in attitude change and persuasion. It should not be assumed that it represents a domain that can be explained by a single, all-encompassing theory. At this point, it is reasonable to expect that a multiplicity of theories will be needed to deal with the wide variety of phenomena that permeate cognitive responses. This point is well expressed in Chapter 6 of this text by Greenwald (see Table 6.1 in that chapter).

As is true with understanding any topic, it is impossible to talk about either methodology (see Part I) or empirical findings (see Part II) without simultaneously considering theoretical issues. Consequently, the reader will have already encountered a number of theoretical concerns by this point in the text. The chapters that appear in this section (Part III) present a fairly thorough sampling of the theoretical insights that have emerged over the past 20 years that are of use in understanding cognitive responses.

Common to all these theorists is the belief that thought is important in attitude change. Indeed, all the theorists agree that attitudes are so intertwined with human thought that it is impossible to have a theory of one without simultaneously having a theory about the other. The two kinds of theories may, in fact, be ultimately indistinguishable.

A second viewpoint shared by all authors is that people are active processors of information. They do not view the human mind as a passive repository into which information is funneled. Rather, people are viewed as acting upon the information so as to selectively store it, transform it, associate it with previously acquired information, and to retrieve it from memory when needed upon future occasions. Although all authors accepted this premise, most of the resulting research (see Chapters 13 through 16) involved the use of univariate inference tasks. Despite the restrictiveness of that methodology, it is impressive to note the theoretical advances made by these investigators in understanding the more multivariate, qualitative, and memory-based aspects of cognitive responses. There is, however, a long way yet to go.

All five theoretical chapters have a third feature in common. They have identified two psychological features of cognitive responses that are of central theoretical interest. All agree that it is theoretically mandatory to posit the existence of a unit of thought. That unit is usually referred to as a cognitive element; these elements refer to any discriminable aspect of the person's world (whether physical or nonphysical) and need not be restricted to thoughts that can be expressed semantically. A second feature common to their theoretical vocabulary is the notion of a cognitive relationship. Cognitive elements do not stand in isolation but are related one to another. Of special interest to this volume, of course, are the relationships between cognitive elements and the attitude object. A wide variety of relationships are possible, and the theorists differ in the types of cognitive relations examined.

Although the five chapters share these similarities, they also offer important differences. The chapters differentially emphasize three different problem areas relevant to understanding cognitive responses. The problem of how cognitive relationships work together as a system is taken up in Chapter 13 and 14. The next two chapters (Chapters 15 and 16) address the problem of how the relevant beliefs are aggregated so as to produce an attitudinal judgment. The final chapter (Chapter 17) examines the interplay between attitudes and memory, offering a more specific analysis of memory-based attitudinal judgments.

Chapter 13 by McGuire separates out the contribution of logical processes and nonlogical processes on attitudinal thoughts. He is able to do this by restricting his theoretical focus to beliefs systems that have the potential of being totally organized through logical processes. His research employs belief systems composed of three syllogistically related beliefs. Syllogistic systems are those in which, if you accept the premises (i.e., "It never rains when the sky is blue"; and "The sky is blue today"), you are logically bound to accept the conclusion ("It will not rain today"). When dealing with attitudinal relationships, it is more meaningful to assign probability values to them rather than simple true or false judgments. The chapter explores the extent to which the laws of probability describe the interrelationship within such syllogistic systems, and the extent to which nonlogical factors must be invoked to understand the system. His work is explicitly multivariate in that he examines processes that operate within and between "truth" dimensions and "evaluative" dimensions of thought.

Chapter 14 by Insko examines the phenomenology of the cognitions surrounding an attitude object. He provides an updating and elaboration of the concepts of cognitive balance, concepts that were originally introduced by Heider (1946, 1958). These concepts underlie nearly all the various cognitive consistency formulations that were developed over the last 25 years. He explores patterns of balance and imbalance that can emerge within dyads and within triads of cognitive elements. In considering qualitative differences among cognitive responses, he distinguishes between four kinds of cognitive relations (affective, instrumental, logical, and proximity).

Chapter 15 by Fishbein and Ajzen is concerned with the prediction of behavior as well as attitude. They argue that the cognitive responses relevant to behavioral acts are qualitatively different from those relevant to overall attitude. To predict behavior, one must assess people's attitude toward the specific act as well as the normative beliefs they hold about that act. To predict attitudinal judgment, it is necessary to know the thoughts about the attitude object itself. The extent to which any given thought contributes to the overall attitude is a function of the evaluative implication of that thought and the degree of certainty or belief the subject has that that thought is true of the attitude object. Overall attitude is predicted on the basis of the summation of these weighted relevant thoughts. It can be seen, then, that their model places heavy emphasis on qualitative differences among cognitive responses.

Chapter 16 by Anderson offers a thorough analysis of the ways in which information (and thoughts) are integrated to produce an overall attitudinal judgment. His integration theory provides a vocabulary and a mode of analysis that allows the investigator to uncover whether or not thoughts are multiplied, added, or divided when combining to produce an overall attitudinal judgment. The dimensions of thought identified in this chapter are scale value (the location of each thought on the dimension of judgment) and weight (importance of each thought to the judgment). Results thus far indicate that the most prevalent form of information integration in the attitudinal domain is averaging.

Chapter 17 by Lingle and Ostrom examines the role of memory in attitudinal judgments. They provide an overview of principles of memory and cognition that are relevant to attitudes and show how those principles help understand memory-based attitudinal judgments. They show that the nature of the attitude judgment itself can influence the kinds of information about the attitude object that people can recall. Attitudinal judgments can also influence the associated thoughts people have about the attitude object. Their research also establishes that one particular kind of thought (memory for previous judgments one has made about the attitude object) can play an important part in memory-based attitudinal judgments.

CONCLUDING COMMENTS

The success of a new theory (or, in this case, a theoretical orientation) is measured by its ability to *challenge* previously accepted explanations, *resolve* preexisting controversy, *integrate* diverse empirical topics, *identify* new independent and dependent variables, and *predict* new relationships. This text illustrates the potential of the cognitive response approach to accomplish all five of these objectives. This is the first textbook on attitudes that provides an adequate beginning toward conceptually understanding such important problems as counterargumentation in persuasion (Chapter 3), the relationship between attitudinal thoughts and physiological reactions (Chapter 4), interpersonal influence in group discussions (Chapter 9), and the role of memory in attitude judgments (Chapter 17). The focus on production tasks (rather than inference tasks) should lead researchers to explore an even wider variety of topic areas in the future.

As a theory comes to satisfy the foregoing five objectives, it acquires the potential for practical application. One of the deficiencies of previous attitude theories has been their relatively limited ability to serve the interests of society.

It is in the direction of application to societal problems that we find the most exciting potential for the cognitive response approach. Given that attitudes are manifested more often in production contexts than in inference contexts, it is necessary for attitude theory to inform us about the nature and consequences of cognitive response production. Chapter 12 provides an illustration of how cognitive response analysis can be applied to persuasion through the mass media. We would hope that with the cognitive response orientation, attitude theory will become broadly germane to problems of education, value acquisition, decision making, problem solving, and human communication in general.

The Probabilogical Model of Cognitive Structure and Attitude Change

William J. McGuire
Yale University

The use of attitude change to study cognitive structure was suggested to me during my first year in graduate school. An interest in understanding the structure of thought—how our ideas are organized and what determines how one idea follows from another—had drawn me into graduate study in psychology. A course in physiological psychology dealt with the technique of teasing out the histological structure of the nervous system by putting in lesions or electrical impulses at various places in the spinal cord or brain and tracing the ramifications through the central nervous system. The analogy occurred to me that perhaps I could put in changes at focused points in the belief system and get to understand the organization of mind by tracing the ideological and behavioral ramifications of these experimentally induced, focused alterations.

Encouraged by the availability of this methodological strategy for testing our notions, we developed a theory of thought processes (McGuire, 1960a, 1960b, 1960c) that postulated probabilistic logical thinking and wishful thinking along with other mental processes described in the next section of this chapter. Derivations from the theory were tested by inducing a change on a specified belief by means of a focused persuasive communication, and then assessing the extent to which the immediate and delayed changes on related beliefs (not mentioned in the communication) showed the kinds of change predicted by our postulates of cognitive structure and functioning. The first section of this chapter describes the theory itself and the second, the empirical work designed to test and develop it.

THEORY OF THE COGNITIVE SYSTEM

Our theory of mental processes contains postulates regarding the cognitive system's components, structure, and functioning, as discussed successively in the three subsections that follow.

291

Content of Mind

The Objects of Thought.   This component of mind includes anything that we can make a judgment about. The object of thought may be simple, such as a person, place, thing, action, feeling; or it may be a complex set of the like, such as the human race, or aggressive acts; or it may be a syntactical combination of more simple elements. "An astronaut" and "Mars" would both be objects of judgment, as would "an astronaut's visiting Mars," because any of the three is a concept about which one can make a judgment (that is, can reliably discriminate from at least one other object of thought on at least one dimension of judgment).

Dimensions of Judgment.   The second aspect of mental content includes the dimensions of judgment that can be drawn through the mental space where the objects of thought are located. Any aspect with respect to which objects of thought can be perceived as differing constitutes such a dimension. Most interesting among the dimensions of judgment are the universal characteristics—that is, dimensions of mental space on which all objects of thought have some potential projection. Goodness and truth are classical examples of such transcendental characteristics. The truth dimension includes veridicality judgments about objects of thought, judgments of their likelihood, existence, occurrence, and so forth. Thus, an astronaut, Mars, the astronaut's visiting Mars, or any other object of thought can be judged as having some projection on this truth dimension. Goodness, the second universal characteristic, can be generalized as the evaluation dimension and includes judgments of desirability, liking, attractiveness, and so on. Again, all objects of thought can have a projection on this evaluation dimension. Besides goodness and truth, other universal characteristics are meaningfulness (familiarity, association value, and the like) and importance (involvement, relevance, and so on).

Many other more limited dimensions of judgment become important in subareas of mental space in that they define important characteristics for a subset of objects of thought. For example, in the domain of physical objects, dimensions of size and weight are relevant dimensions. As regards people, dimensions like intelligence and loyalty become relevant. In more mixed domains of objects of thought, hard to define denotatively, still other qualities such as dangerousness or beauty become important dimensions of judgment.

Propositions.   According to our model, the content of mind can be reduced to propositions in the form of statements that assign objects of thought to positions on dimensions of judgment. For example, a proposition such as "It is highly likely that astronauts will soon visit Mars" assigns the object of thought, "astronaut's soon visiting Mars," to a position on the expectancy (truth) dimension; another proposition—"I hope that astronauts will soon visit Mars"— assigns it to a position on the evaluation dimension of judgment. The model deals with the part of thought which can be reduced to such propositions (whether or not the thinker spontaneously tends to so reduce them). There might be aspects of thought that cannot be so verbalized, but the theory does not now deal with them.

Beliefs.   Beliefs (or attitudes) are responses that assign objects of thought to dimensions of judgment in such propositions. An individual's beliefs regarding an astronaut's visiting Mars are thus the responses by which he or she accepts or constructs propositions assigning that event to locations on such dimensions of judgment as truth or evaluation. This model and the empirical work that has grown out of it deal with thought processes that occur within belief systems made up of such propositions.

Structure of Mind

The content of mind having been mapped in terms of beliefs on propositions that assign objects of thought to dimensions of judgment, it follows that the structure of mind involves the organization among these propositions. I assume that there is a force toward structure in the mind such that the person tends to maintain connectedness (i.e., to perceive relationships among the propositions) and coherence (i.e., to prefer some patterns to others among beliefs on related propositions). Since the propositions are defined as assignments of objects of thought to positions on dimensions of judgment, I shall be concerned with mental organization within and between dimensions of judgment. The within-dimension type of structure involves mentally imposed organization among a set of propositions, all of which assign their objects of thought to the same dimension of judgment (e.g., between beliefs such as "An astronaut's visiting Mars is a good thing" and "Peace is a good thing"). The between-dimension type of structure involves the mentally required organization among propositions that assigns the same object of thought to positions on different dimensions of judgment (e.g., between beliefs such as "An astronaut's visiting Mars is a good thing" and "An astronaut's visiting Mars is likely").

Mental Functioning

The postulates regarding mental functioning are natural outgrowths of these assumptions about mental structure. We consider first postulates describing the logical aspects of mental functioning and then postulates about the nonlogical aspects of thinking.

The Probabilogical Model.   Within the theory, the best-developed postulates regarding mental functioning are those involving the projection of the objects of thought on the truth dimension. Within this domain, we make the rather sweeping assumption that the laws of thought follow the axioms of logic and probability theory, so that when a set of propositions are in a specifiable relationship as regards objective logic, we postulate that the same relationships will be reflected in the person's thought system. This point can be illustrated with syllogistically related propositions such as the following: (a) Swimming at the city beaches is a recreational activity that is becoming a serious threat to the health of the participants. (b) The city health authorities will prohibit any recreation that poses a serious threat to the health of the participants. (c) The city health authorities will prohibit swimming at the city beaches. If a person rejects either of the premises, there are no logical restraints on what the respondent's belief on the conclusion may be; but if the respondent accepts both premises, then logically (and by the postulates of our model, psychologically) the respondent must also accept the conclusion.

One immediately feels uncomfortable with this simplistic formal logic, with its stated two-value "zero *versus* one" truth matrix wherein the person either rejects or accepts each proposition absolutely. One suspects that a human lives in a more probabilistic psychological atmosphere such that one might just barely accept each of the two premises (in the sense of assigning each a probability just greater than .50 on the truth dimension, so that their joint probability could fall well below .50), and so the conclusion could be rejected without being illogical. Our probabilogical postulate of human thought differs radically from earlier logical models in recognizing this probabilistic (rather than dichotomous) nature of human thinking. Using as an example the foregoing propositions (a), (b), and (c), our probabilogical model postulates that the following relationship would obtain:

$$p(c) = [p(c/(a \& b)) \cdot p(a \& b)] + [p(c/\sim(a \& b)) \cdot p(\sim(a \& b))] \quad (1)$$

In Equation 1, the slash mark can be read as "follows on the basis of" or "given that," and & can be read as "also." Hence the term $p(c/a \& b)$ can be read as the subjective probability that c is the case, given that a and b are true. Or substituting for a, b, and c the three illustrative propositions already given, $p(c/a \& b)$ stands for the subjective probability that swimming's becoming a health hazard and the city's proclivity to proscribe unhealthy recreation imply the prohibition of swimming. The symbol $\sim$ stands for "not," so that the term $p(\sim(a \& b))$ can be read as the subjective probability that it is not the case that both a and b are true.

If the person's belief is changed on one of the premises—for example, on premise a—the probabilogically required resultant change on the conclusion, c, can be predicted. For example, if a persuasive communication aimed at major premise a produces a belief change equal to $\Delta p(a)$ by arguing effectively that the city's beaches are becoming dangerously polluted, then the probabilistic model predicts a remote impact on the unstated conclusion, $\Delta p(c)$, as follows:

$$\Delta p(c) = \Delta p(a) \cdot p(b) \cdot [p(c/(a \& b)) - p(c/\sim(a \& b))] \quad (2)$$

The empirical work on the theory uses variants of these static and dynamic equations as the definition of probabilogical thinking.[1]

The foregoing discussion, as well as much of the empirical work on the probabilogical model, has focused on syllogistically related beliefs—that is, on two premises and the conclusion that follows from them. However, the probabilogical model is not confined to syllogistically related beliefs but can be generalized to sets of beliefs in any well-formed relationship (McGuire, 1960c).

Nonlogical Functioning Postulates. The functioning postulates of the probabilogical model just presented describe the person's thought processes insofar as they are perfectly logical. To accommodate the common observation that people's thinking often falls short of perfect logic, it is postulated (McGuire, 1960c, 1968a) that additional functioning rules obtain within the thought domain. First, the model assumes that the person has a need for hedonic consistency as well as logical consistency such that an object of thought's perceived positions on the truth and evaluative dimensions tend to be positively correlated and assimilated toward one another. In terms of the syllogistic example just given, this hedonic consistency postulate implies that the person's perception of the likelihood of the conclusion, $p(c)$, is influenced by the person's perception of the conclusion's desirability. Equation 1 of the probabilogical model has already postulated that $p(c)$ is influenced by the perceived likelihood of the antecedents [by $p(a \ \& \ b)$ and $p(c/(a \ \& \ b))$, etc.]. Where hedonic consistency needs and logical consistency needs pull the perceived likelihood of the conclusion, $p(c)$, in different directions, it is postulated that the person thinks like an honest broker, so that $p(c)$ is a compromise between the logically consistent value it should have in view of the perceived likelihood of the premises from which it follows, and the hedonically consistent value it should have in view of its projection on the evaluation dimension. It is conjectured further that one tends toward a "minimax" or "least-squares" compromise, such that one's set of beliefs are adjusted to spread out the inconsistencies over the whole belief system and prevent any single belief from getting greatly out of line with the others.

Additional postulates regarding the functioning of mind posit "inertial" tendencies—both spatial and temporal. The spatial inertia postulate assumes that attitudes are chained together in a loose-link sort of way, such that pulling one end of the inference chain does exert a pull on the successively following links but only after an initial slack is taken up. Thus, if we induce a change in the first

---

[1]In our original publications on the probabilogical model (McGuire, 1960c), we formulated these equations in a more convoluted manner, the $p(k)$ term particularly causing some subsequent confusion for interpreters who did not note the subtleties of the definitions and assumptions. We prefer Wyer's (Wyer, 1974a, Wyer & Goldberg, 1970) revisions and the equations used here are a restatement of Wyer's equations in terms more directly applicable to the empirical work described here. In McGuire (1960c), the original version of Equation 1 was given as $p(c) = p(a \ \& \ b) \ p(c/a \ \& \ b) + p(k)$. Hence, the new version of Equation 1 given in this chapter follows Wyer and Goldberg (1970) in spelling out $p(k)$ as $p(\sim(a \ \& \ b)) \ p(c/\sim(a \ \& \ b))$.

link of a causal chain of propositions, there should result a remote impact on each successive link; but according to the spatial inertia postulate, the amount of this remote impact falls progressively more short of the logically required amount as we go to more distally related propositions. It should be noted that there is a diminution of impact on successive links, even if we consider strictly logical operations. That is, if premise x leads to conclusion c only via two intermediate premises, y and z, then any change induced on $p(x)$ should logically produce only a small change on $p(c)$ as defined by the logical equation: $\Delta p(c) = \Delta p(x) \cdot p(y) \cdot p(z)$. Because multiplication of probabilities is involved, the logically required $\Delta p(c)$ will fall progressively more short of the induced $\Delta p(x)$ as the length of the inference chain increases. The spatial inertia postulate adds that the actual remote impact on $p(c)$ will fall progressively more short even of this diminishing logically required impact as we go to successively more distal consequences, because part of the induced change in the prior premise will be absorbed in taking up the mental slack at each step in the implication chain.

The temporal inertia postulate states that the impact of an induced change on a premise filters down to the implied conclusions only gradually with the passage of time. Hence, the model predicts delayed action effects for the remote cognitive ramifications of induced attitude change, the delay increasing as we go to successively more distally related propositions.

A further functioning postulate has to do with salience. Objective logic assumes that the mind works like a computer in that recall is complete and all propositions are equally salient. In mental functioning, there obviously are limitations of recall, and momentary salience varies. Beliefs on a given issue may be somewhat affected by nonsalient related beliefs, but we predict here that the magnitude of their impact can be increased by enhancing their momentary salience. This postulate suggests the efficacy of a Socratic method of inducing opinion change merely by asking questions which enhance the salience of material already within the believer's cognitive system, without presenting new outside information. It also suggests techniques for inducing resistance to persuasion by directing the believer's attention to supportive beliefs already within the cognitive system. Additional alogical thinking postulates in the model are described elsewhere (McGuire, 1960c). Empirical data on the implications of the various assumptions and postulates described here are reported in the second half of this chapter.

DEVELOPMENT OF THE THEORY:
EMPIRICAL RESULTS

The varied research that has been carried out to test or develop this theory of cognitive structure and attitude change is described as regards results bearing on four successively more complex types of predictions. First, the findings regarding the initial structure of the thought system are discussed. Then we describe the results having to do with the ''Socratic effect''—that is, changing attitudes simply by eliciting contemporaneously the person's beliefs on related issues, whose enhanced salience creates pressure to adjust the related beliefs into a more coherent pattern even though no new information is communicated to the believer from any outside source. Third, research on enhancing the believer's resistance to persuasive communications by increasing the cognitive embeddedness of the belief is described. Finally, we discuss persuasive communications' remote ramifications on beliefs that are not mentioned in the communication but are related to its explicit target belief.

Relationships Among Initial Attitudes

Any belief in a person's cognitive system (for example, one's expectation that the atmosphere is getting polluted, or one's evaluation that atmospheric pollution is undesirable) is postulated to be determined by a variety of forces, two of which have been especially singled out for research attention—logical consistency and hedonic consistency. Any expectation belief, $p(c)$, shows the influence of logical consistency to the extent to which the subjective probability of an object-of-thought's occurrence is in accord with the subjective probabilities of the premises as defined by Equation 1 of the probabilogical model. The influence of hedonic consistency on that expectation belief, $p(c)$, is indicated by the correlation between $p(c)$ and belief in the desirability of c.

Initial Logical Consistency Among Beliefs.   In general, correlations of about $+0.70$ have been found between the obtained subjective probability of the consequent, $p(c)$, and the probability that would be predicted by the original model (McGuire, 1960c). With the improved formulas introduced by Wyer and Goldberg (1970), the correlation between observed and predicted $p(c)$ values has been even higher. The accord between the predicted and obtained $p(c)$ values remains high even when the sets of propositions are in relationships more complex than the syllogistic triads used in the earlier studies. For example, Henninger and Wyer (1976) found that people's estimates of the consistency of variously related sets of beliefs correlated to $+0.94$ with predictions based on the probabilogical model.

Several plausibly interacting variables have not appreciably affected the extent of this initial logical consistency. For example, several studies (Dillehay, Insko, & Smith, 1966; Holt & Watts, 1969) have found that people of varied intelligence levels show equal consistency (though, admittedly, as all these subjects were college students, the full range of intelligence found in the general population was not sampled). Also, it might be thought that manipulating the salience of the interrelations among the antecedents and consequents by grouping the triads of related propositions together (rather than scattering them in a long, randomly ordered questionnaire) would enhance the initial logical consistency.

However, Holt and Watts (1969) find almost as much logical consistency in a randomly ordered questionnaire as in a syllogistically grouped questionnaire. Most of the results reported in this chapter were found with questionnaires in which the related propositions were widely separated and in random order and where no mention of their interrelatedness or of consistency was included in the experimental procedure. Rosen and Wyer (1972) did find an increase in consistency when it was explicitly mentioned to the subjects that some of the items in the scattered questionnaire were interrelated; on the other hand, their subjects were about as consistent when no mention was made of the desirability of being consistent as when they were cautioned that well-adjusted and intelligent people tend to be more consistent in their beliefs. Effects have also been found for types of logical relations; for example, logical consistency is greater with the intersection and implication relationship than for the union relationship (Wyer, 1974b). This topic is especially deserving of further research.

Initial Hedonic Consistency.   What we here call "hedonic consistency" (that is, a positive correlation between the perceived truth and the perceived desirability of a proposition) probably reflects a causal flow in both directions—including a "wishful thinking" tendency (such that we bring our expectations in line with our desires) and a "rationalization" tendency (such that our desires are brought in line with our expectations).

Although research inspired by the present theory has concentrated less on hedonic consistency than on logical consistency, a substantial and statistically significant hedonic consistency has been demonstrated, though its magnitude is less than that obtained for logical consistency. For example, McGuire (1960c) found a hedonic consistency $r = +0.40$ and a logical consistency $r = +0.74$; and when both hedonic and logical consistency are taken into account in predicting the expectation regarding the conclusion, we get an $r = +0.96$ with grouped data.

Several studies have investigated the extent to which the magnitude of hedonic consistency is affected by interacting variables. Both Dillehay, Insko, and Smith (1966) and Watts and Holt (1970) found somewhat greater hedonic consistency in respondents of lower intelligence (though the differences are of weak statistical significance, perhaps because the variations in intelligence were only those found within the fairly homogeneous population of college students). Parenthetically, it should be mentioned that this all-too-typical use of college student respondents may contribute to the findings of more pronounced logical consistency than hedonic consistency. It should be noted, though, that this stronger strain of logical consistency is found not only among students at elite universities but also among those in high schools and community colleges (McGuire, 1960a, 1960b). The stronger logical than hedonic consistency might also reflect the focusing in these studies on the more "rational" expectation dimension of judgment. However, the probabilogical model can be applied as well to the evaluation dimension (see Wyer, 1975, pp. 234–235), and the logical consistency tendency seems as powerful (Wyer, 1974b) in accounting for initial structure among evaluative beliefs as among expectations.

The Socratic Method of Persuading

One of the most appealing lines of work emerging from the present theory is the research on producing the specifiable changes within a set of related beliefs simply by asking the person to express his or her beliefs on related propositions. This procedure can be called the Socratic method of persuasion, the eponymous term referring to Socrates' *tour de force* in attempting to demonstrate that knowledge of the Pythagorean theorem was innate. Socrates changed the beliefs of Meno's slave regarding the interrelations among triangles' dimensions simply by asking the slave questions that led him to perceive that his initial beliefs did not agree with his own accepted axioms and therefore had to be changed.

The present theory assumes that a person's momentary belief on any issue reflects many different forces in addition to the need to maintain logical consistency between it and related beliefs. Also, at any given moment many related beliefs will not be salient and thus will be exerting little influence on the given belief. The Socratic method involves asking questions about logically related issues, enhancing the salience of one's beliefs on these related issues, and increasing the strain toward logical consistency between the given belief, c, and the related elicited ones, a and b. Hence, belief on the given issue will, as a result of the questioning, move toward the $p(c)$ value specified in Equation 1.

In the research to test the model, various alternative operational definitions have been given for the Socratic effect, and its empirical track record is good with each of them. In the original study (McGuire, 1960a), the Socratic effect was tested in terms of a prediction that if people are simply asked their opinions on the likelihood of related issues on two occasions a week apart, the internal consistency among them will be greater on the second elicitation. The sensitization to any initial logical inconsistencies caused by wishful thinking is predicted to result in adjusting the set of likelihood beliefs toward greater mutual consistency by the time of the second elicitation. The prediction was confirmed in that study and in a replication by Watts and Holt (1970), though not by Dillehay, Insko, and Smith (1966). The strength of the Socratic effect is shown by its occurring in those studies even when the logically related beliefs are scattered through the questionnaire and no mention is made of their interrelatedness or of the importance of being consistent.

The Socratic effect has proved robust when a more direct test is done of the prediction that the correlation between the obtained and the logically predicted expectations on the conclusion will be greater in the second administration of the questionnaire than in the first. A dozen studies by Wyer and his students (Henninger & Wyer, 1976; Rosen & Wyer, 1972; Wyer, 1974b) have found uniformly significant evidence of the Socratic effect in these terms, though it did not appear in Holt and Watts (1969). The Socratic effect has been found whether the second elicitation follows immediately, 10 minutes, 2 days, or 7 days after the first elicitation of the interrelated opinions. This robustness allows the use of the Socratic effect to test the relative power of different cognitive consistency theories (McGuire, 1966b). Such tests (Wyer, 1974b) show that the Osgood–Tannenbaum's (1955) congruity theory, Heider's (1958) balance theory, and Abelson and Rosenberg's (1958) psycho-logic theory are not as powerful as the probabilogical model presented here in accounting for the findings.

Focus of the Socratic Effect.   The present theory has not been explicit about the focus of the Socratic effect. The related set of beliefs typically involves expectations about premises, conclusions, and the extent to which the premises imply that conclusion. The Socratic method of persuasion deals with the bottom-line effect such that on the second elicitation, this interrelated set of beliefs is expected to be more internally consistent as defined by the probabilogical model than it was on the first elicitation. The further question arises as to which beliefs are particularly likely to be the adjusted ones in accomplishing this net shift toward greater internal coherence.

The order in which the beliefs had been elicited on the first occasion could be one determinant of the focusing. The Socratic effect should be focused on the beliefs that had been elicited in the earlier part of the first session [because McGuire (1960a) predicted that the later-elicited ones would have already been somewhat adjusted even in the first elicitation]. Tentative support for this prediction has been obtained (Henninger & Wyer, 1976; Holt, 1970; McGuire, 1960a), but the results were either weak or difficult to generalize. That the evidence for a Socratic effect within a single session is less convincing than that for a Socratic effect across sessions may be due to methodological factors, or it may reflect substantive features of thought processes such as the temporal inertia postulate (discussed later, in connection with remote cognitive ramifications) that information needs some time to percolate through the cognitive system.

McGuire (1960a) also tested the possibility that there would be more Socratic effect to the extent that the belief was initially more distorted from logical consistency by wishful-thinking tendencies. However, he found no significant difference between the change toward consistency for the beliefs on the highest and lowest quartiles of the evaluation distribution as compared with the half of the propositions that were intermediate in initial desirability. He did find that significantly more of the Socratic adjustment occurred on the major premises and the conclusion than on the minor premises; the former differ from the minor premises in that only the former contain the ''predicate term'' of the syllogism— the term that tends to be most emotionally laden in syllogisms of the type used here. The overall Socratic effect having continued to prove robust, further research on these microprocesses by which it is achieved should be quite useful in testing additional postulates about cognitive functioning.

Variables Accentuating the Socratic Effect. The underlying theory from which the Socratic effect prediction is derived implies that several variables will affect the size of the Socratic effect. For example, it would follow that the greater the initial inconsistency among the beliefs, the greater the Socratic effect on the second session—a prediction confirmed by Henninger and Wyer (1976). A further prediction is that the Socratic effect will be greater when there is less initial salience of the interrelationships on the first session (because with the interrelationships more salient on the first session, there should have been less initial inconsistency to show up as a Socratic effect on the second session). The auxiliary hypothesis here has not received corroboration in that several studies have failed to demonstrate that the initial inconsistency varies with the initial salience of belief interrelationships. Perhaps for this reason, attempts to vary the amount of the Socratic effect by varying the initial salience of the interrelations among the propositions have yielded mostly negative results.

Predicting how the intelligence of the respondents should affect the magnitude of the Socratic effect is hazardous; alternative mediators would plausibly yield opposite predictions. It might be predicted that the more intelligent respondents would show less Socratic effect, because they should have greater consistency among their beliefs from the start and thus less inconsistency to correct after the initial elicitation. But on the other hand, the more intelligent can be expected to be more perceptive and more bothered by such initial inconsistencies as do occur; hence, they should tend more to correct any initial inconsistency on the second elicitation and thus show more Socratic effect. Testing this complex theoretical analysis requires a design where the relationship of intelligence would be measured with respect to initial inconsistency and to the Socratic effect, as well as to the Socratic effect while adjusting for magnitude of the initial inconsistency. So far, three studies have been done that have failed to show an interaction between intelligence and magnitude of Socratic effect, though without carrying out the full analysis suggested here. In summary, experiments have demonstrated that the Socratic effect is robust, showing up at significant levels over a wide range of conditions, though expected interactions have proven elusive.

Cognitive Linkage and Susceptibility to Persuasion

The previous two sections reviewed the empirical work on the probabilogical model that dealt with implications regarding material already within the person's cognitive system. The final two sections describe the probabilogical model's implications regarding the effect of new information that is presented to the believer from outside sources. The present section deals with how a message's impact on its explicit target belief is affected by that belief's embeddedness in a broader cognitive structure, concentrating on studies explicitly devised to test this probabilogical model and ignoring research stemming from other theoretical models by us and our students on related topics, such as producing resistance to persuasion (McGuire, 1964), or personality correlates of susceptibility to persuasion (McGuire, 1968b), or the effects of forewarning of persuasive intent and the anticipatory change phenomenon (McGuire, 1969b; McGuire & Millman, 1965). Some of these topics are discussed in other chapters of this text.

The postulate that logical consistency needs can anchor initial belief levels yields the prediction that eliciting related beliefs will sensitize the believer to any lack of logical consistency due to hedonic "distortion." Hence, when a subsequent persuasive communication argues for a change of belief on a given proposition, the prior elicitation of related beliefs will be found to have enhanced or weakened resistance to its arguments, depending on whether the change they urge is in a direction that would raise or lower consistency as defined by the probabilogical model. For example, the prior elicitation will tend to enhance the persuasion impact of a communication arguing for the likelihood of a relatively undesirable proposition and resistance to one arguing for a relatively desirable proposition (because hedonic needs would have kept expectations initially too low on undesirable and too high on desirable premises). McGuire (1960b) found support for this prediction.

It is also predicted that increasing the salience of the target issue's cognitive embeddedness should decrease the persuasive impact of communications on that issue. This prediction follows from the model's postulate that one tends to keep a given belief in logical alignment with salient related beliefs; hence, raising the salience of additional related beliefs should augment the resistance to change of the given target belief. Holt and Watts (1969) find that increasing the initial salience of the related beliefs by having a "before" questionnaire on which the interrelated propositions are grouped syllogistically results in a subsequent persuasive communication's having less attitude change impact on the target issue than when the three syllogistically related propositions are scattered throughout the "before" questionnaire. It has also been found (Watts & Holt, 1970) that the impact on this explicit premise is less when there is a before-communication measure eliciting the interrelated beliefs than when an after-only design is used. Other active and passive techniques that remind the person of related beliefs have also been found to enhance resistance to persuasion on the given belief (Holt, 1970; Nelson, 1968).

A more tenuously derived prediction is that the persuasive impact on the explicit premise will be greater if the believer, when exposed to the communication, is "cognitively tuned" (Zajonc, 1960) as a sender rather than a receiver of further messages on the topic. Believers who are prepared to be senders (that is, are instructed that they will be asked subsequently to relay the message) would tend to screen out complications of cognitive embeddedness that might interfere with effective relaying of the initial message; when they are tuned to serve as receivers of continuing messages on the topic, however, the cognitive structure of related beliefs is kept salient to facilitate encoding the high level of expected information. This cognitive-tuning prediction, that those cognitively tuned as senders tend to be less resistant to persuasion, has received strong support (Holt & Watts, 1969; Watts & Holt, 1970).

Remote Ramifications of Persuasive Communications on Unmentioned Related Beliefs

The richest set of implications of the probabilogical model has to do with the remote cognitive ramifications of persuasive communications, involving predictions that persuasive communications affect not only their explicit target belief but also the unmentioned beliefs that are related to them. By tracing the cognitive ramifications of the communication-induced attitude change on the explicit target as it spreads through the unmentioned part of the belief system, we have an opportunity to test and develop hypotheses about complex thought processes.

Evidence for Persuasive Impact on Unmentioned Consequences.   The theory predicts that a persuasive communication that affects attitudes on the proposition with which it explicitly deals will have corresponding effects on attitudes regarding logically related propositions, including those not explicitly mentioned in the message. For example, if a communication argues that the city beaches are getting polluted (thus increasing belief $p(a)$ in the example given earlier), it will tend to increase the unmentioned but implied $p(c)$ belief also—that swimming will be prohibited at these beaches. More than a dozen studies have confirmed this prediction that persuasive communications have a significant impact on unmentioned consequents that follow from their explicit target. The remote impact has been found whether it is measured immediately after the receipt of the message or at intervals ranging from 10 minutes to 1 week later; also, the remote ramifications occur over a wide range of recipients' intelligence and initial commitment. These confirmations of the assumption that there is a strong tendency to maintain structure among one's beliefs are a needed corrective to surveys of political attitudes that seem to suggest that people's belief systems are neither connected nor coherent to any appreciable extent.

Variables Accentuating the Remote Ramifications.   Other variables in the experimental situation can increase the extent of these logical ramifications. For example, McGuire (1960b) demonstrated that the remote ramifications on the unmentioned conclusion were greater when the communication argued in directions such that remote changes reduce rather than increase probabilogical inconsistency within the belief set. Watts and Holt (1970) and Holt and Watts (1969) show that the remote ramifications are greater when the person is expecting to send on the message rather than receive more information on the topic. Holt (1970) found that there was less cognitive ramification when the subjects' commitment to their initial belief on the remote issue was increased by directing their attention toward it prior to the receipt of the persuasive communication.

The Spatial Inertia Postulate.   One of the extralogical postulates of the theory is that a loose-link metaphor applies to the inference chain such that when one link in the belief chain is moved (for example, via a persuasive communication that changes the specific target belief), a certain amount of slack has to be taken up before a pull is exerted on the next belief in the chain. This picture of a loose-linked belief chain implies that the remote ramifications will fall short of the logically required amount as defined by Equation 2. The empirical evidence for such a spatial inertia is mixed. It was found in both McGuire's (1960a, 1960b) studies, in two of the three studies by Watts and Holt (1970; Holt & Watts, 1969), in one of the three McFarland and Thistlethwaite (1970) studies, and in one of the two by Dillehay, Insko, and Smith (1966). It should be noted that where the spatial inertia postulate was not confirmed, it was not because of a lack of cognitive ramification but, on the contrary, because the remote ramification on the unmentioned conclusion was so strong that it needed the full amount required by the probabilogical models, obviating any need to add this spatial inertia postulate to the probabilogical aspect of the theory.

The Temporal Inertia Postulate.   Another postulate in our theory is that, as Hugo said of God, the person sees the truth but sees it slowly, slowly. We predicted that when a persuasive communication produces a change on its explicit target belief, this change percolates through the system only gradually, thus producing delayed action changes of belief on related but unmentioned consequences. This delayed-action prediction has received only moderate empirical support. The support in studies using a 1-week delay interval are weak: In only one of the two tests by McGuire (1960a, 1960b) and one of the two by Dillehay, Insko, and Smith (1966) did the trend toward increased consistency on the conclusion approach statistical significance. However, when a shorter delay interval of 10 minutes was used by Watts and Holt (1970), they found strong evidence of delayed-action effects on the implied conclusion, with the change being significantly greater 10 minutes after the communication than immediately after. Further exploration of this time parameter is needed.

Remote Ramifications on Parallel Premises.   The assumption behind postulating remote ramifications of persuasive communications is that people try to keep their beliefs connected and coherent in the way described by the probabilogical model. Hence, when a persuasive communication raises (or lowers) the belief on the premise with which it explicitly deals, internal coherence with related but unmentioned beliefs can be maintained by adjusting the belief on the logical consequent. Alternatively, this probabilogical consistency could be maintained by adjusting the beliefs on the parallel, unmentioned auxiliary premise from which the conclusion follows. For example, in the illustrative case presented earlier, if the persuasive communication were aimed at premise *a* and did increase the belief that the beaches were becoming seriously polluted, then belief system consistency could be maintained by lowering the belief in parallel premise *b* by lessening the belief that the city health authorities would ban any dangerous recreational activity (instead of raising the belief in the undesirable conclusion *c*—that swimming would soon be prohibited—the consistency-preserving remote adjustment that we have been considering until now).

In marked contrast to the strong evidence for remote ramifications on the implied consequent, five studies have looked for remote ramifications in the form of compensatory adjustments on the implied parallel premise, and none has found any appreciable amount of it. The lack of any appreciable compensatory adjustment on the unmentioned parallel premise, in contrast to the sizable remote ramification on the unmentioned consequent, suggests that the person who receives a persuasive communication tends to think of its implications for unmentioned consequents but ignore the other (parallel) premises that are needed to infer that consequent.

Ramifications Across Dimensions of Judgment. In addition to the within-dimension consistency we have discussed so far, our theory predicts that consistency is maintained also across dimensions of judgment (for example, in the form of hedonic consistency tendencies to align our truth and evaluation beliefs regarding any object of thought). Despite our emphasis from the start (McGuire, 1960c) on both forms of consistency, most of the empirical work so far has concentrated on the within-dimensional consistency, particularly within the truth dimension. This subsequent emphasis may reflect our having discussed the truth dimension in terms of elegant probabilistic scaling, whereas the desirability dimension was initially discussed in terms of cruder ordinal scaling. However, as Wyer (1974a) has pointed out, one can measure evaluation beliefs as well as truth beliefs on a probabilistic scale. Implications of the model such as the Socratic effect seem to hold up as well for evaluations as for expectancies (Wyer, 1974b).

Almost as pronounced a neglect as that of within-dimensional consistency as regards evaluations has been the neglect of between-dimensional (from evaluation to expectancy and vice versa) hedonic consistency. McGuire (1960a) showed that a communication on expectations regarding objects of thought did have significant effects on evaluations of those objects of thought and even effects of borderline significance on the evaluations of logically related but unmentioned objects of thought. Also, Holt (1970) found that sensitizing the believer to the desirable or undesirable consequences of a premise tended to affect the initial expectation regarding the premise's object of thought, though he did not find that a message which changed expectation beliefs on the premise changed the evaluation belief on that premise. Further empirical work on the theory should give more attention to the hedonic postulates of the model, perhaps using the probabilogical model to formulate the predictions about evaluation beliefs with the same precision as has already been done for the expectation beliefs.

CONCLUSIONS

New Directions in the Work. There have been several changes in method and theoretical preoccupation of our own recent work. As regards method, we have been taking a lower profile toward describing the individual's initial belief system. Rather than, as described earlier, presenting the person with experimenter-selected sets of beliefs, we start with a potential target belief and have people generate their own perceptions of antecedents and consequents of these target beliefs. In this way, the whole net of related beliefs surrounding the initial target belief is defined inductively. Then, in the attitude change experiment itself, using a fresh wave of participants, attitude changes are induced on the original target beliefs, and the subsequent ramifications (immediate and delayed) are traced through the empirically defined surrounding belief network.

As regards theoretical changes, our current work is testing hypotheses about microprocesses of thought and cognitive structure. For example, we are testing hypotheses about asymmetry in the upward and downward remote impacts on antecedents versus consequents of induced changes on the target issue, and about asymmetrical impacts across dimensions of judgment. We expect that further changes in the probabilogical model will be suggested by current advances in modal and multivalued logics. Formal systems to deal with inferences from propositions whose truth values are "fuzzy" rather than sharply dichotomous are now developing convergently in a variety of fields—for example, the computer science work on fuzzy sets by Goguin, the decision-theory development of the preferred risk notion by R. Giles, and the analogous use of the statistical concept of error by D. Scott.

Implications for Attitude Change.   Among the theory's general implications regarding attitude change is that persuasive communications affect not just target beliefs explicitly mentioned but also unmentioned beliefs that are related to that explicit target. The work clarifies that some remote impacts are more likely than others (for example, more change on consequents than on parallel premises). It also indicates that other variables (such as the recipient's expectations and the direction of arguments) interact with logical structuring in determining the extent of these remote impacts.

More radical still, the work clarifies that attitude change can be brought about not just by presenting new information from external sources but also by eliciting information already inside the person's cognitive system—for example, by the Socratic method of asking the person questions that affect the salience of various subsets of related beliefs. The findings regarding the focus of these effects and other variables' interactions with them suggest new procedures for changing attitudes on single issues or on whole systems of beliefs. Various anchoring procedures have been described that can be used to make a belief more resistant to persuasive impact by adding or making more salient its cognitive links to other beliefs.

Implications Regarding the Nature of Thought Processes.   The robust support obtained on the Socratic effect and remote ramifications predictions suggests that there is more connectedness and coherence within the cognitive system than

some students of attitudes have thought likely. The high power of the probabilogical model in accounting for attitudinal effects suggests that the person tends to
maintain within the cognitive system a coherence similar to that described by the
axioms of logic and probability theory.

The evidence for the extralogical postulates of our theory of thought presents a
more mixed picture. The power of the probabilogical model in predicting the
outcomes and its robustness across a variety of different individual and situational variables suggest that some of the extralogical postulates of the theory may
not be needed. However, considerable variance remains to be accounted for,
especially on the level of individual belief systems, and a number of the extralogical postulates such as hedonic consistency and spatial inertia have received
considerable support. Rewarding new insights into the nature of thought would
be obtained through further work on the microprocesses underlying the predictions confirmed in this work as well as on the slight but systematic deviations
from these predictions.

ACKNOWLEDGMENTS

The preparation of this chapter and the work herein have been greatly facilitated by Grant
No. BNS 73-05401 from the Program for Social Psychology of the National Science
Foundation and Grant No. 1-RO1 MH32588 from the Committee in Social Science
Research of the National Institute of Mental Health.

14
Balance Theory and Phenomenology

Chester A. Insko
University of North Carolina-Chapel Hill

Balance theory takes as its explicit task the description of a person's phenomenology. That is, it analyzes the way in which people personally experience their world. Although embedded in the philosophical orientation of phenomenology (MacLeod, 1964), it owes its original formulation to Heider (1946, 1958). Balance theory has, from its very beginning, addressed the problem of understanding "cognitive responses."

This chapter is devoted to showing how balance theory provides a basis for understanding cognitive responses in persuasion and attitude change. The first half attempts to integrate the suggestions of Heider and others into a coherent statement of balance theory. The second half applies these concepts to selected topics in attitude change.

BALANCE THEORY

Elements, Relations, and Symbols

As Heider develops balance theory, the main concern is with *three types of elements:* the person in whose experience or phenomenology balance processes are operating, some other perceived person, and a perceived event, idea, or thing. Heider symbolizes the three elements with lowercase letters: p for the person, o for the other person, and x for the perceived event, idea, or thing.

Between any pair of the elements, *one* or *both* of *two types of relations* may exist. Heider refers to these as *sentiment relations* and *unit relations*. A sentiment is an affective or feeling relation that implies "liking" or "disliking," "approving" or "disapproving," "feeling favorable toward," or "unfavorable toward," and so forth. Sentiment relations are grossly divided into two types, positive or negative, depending on whether the affect or feeling is favorable or unfavorable. Thus "liking" and "approving" are positive sentiment relations, and "disliking" and "disapproving" are negative sentiment relations. Various theorists in the balance or consistency tradition (Feather, 1967, 1971; Osgood & Tannenbaum, 1955; Wellens & Thistlethwaite, 1971a, 1971b; Wiest, 1965) have attempted to quantify the sentiment dimension further, an effort that eventually seems necessary for a complete development of the theory.

According to Heider (1958) unit relations refer to the extent to which elements "are perceived as belonging together [p. 176]." Examples of unit relations are "similar" or "dissimilar," "close" or "far," "belongs" or "does not belong," "owns" or "does not own." Like sentiment relations, unit relations can roughly be divided into two types, positive and negative. Examples of positive unit relations are "similar," "close," and "belongs." Examples of negative unit relations are "dissimilar," "far," and "does not belong."

Cartwright and Harary (1956) have correctly pointed to an ambiguity in Heider's concept of unit relations. Their essential point is that the negation of a positive unit relation should not be construed as producing a negative unit relation. Thus if "*p* is married to *o*" is a positive unit relation, "*p* is not married to *o*" should not be considered a negative unit relation. On the other hand, "*p* is divorced from *o*" is a negative unit relation. This implies, contrary to Heider, that "does not belong" is not a negative relation.

Some tentative suggestions regarding the understanding of unit and also sentiment relations have been made by Insko and Schopler (1967). Table 14.1 is a tabular presentation of possible "cognitive relations." The column of the table labeled "affective" corresponds to Heider's concept of sentiment relation. The last three columns of the table—labeled "instrumental," "logical," and "spatial or temporal proximity"—relate to various types of unit relations.

Insko and Schopler define cognitive relations as "*any perceived relationship,* [p. 362]" and then tentatively discuss how various cognitive relations (like "ownership" and relations not stated in the present tense or relations involving moral obligation) can be conceptualized in terms of various combinations of the affective, instrumental, logical, and proximity columns in Table 14.1.

Each of the various types of cognitive relations are subdivided according to whether they are positive, null, or negative. Positive and negative relations differ in their perceptual tendency to work toward unity or disunity. In contrast to null relations, both positive and negative relations are active in the sense of movement toward or away from unity. Insko and Schopler note further that the null relations are negations of either the positive or negative relations. They involve neither a tendency toward perceptual unity nor a tendency toward perceptual disunity. The delineation of this dimension thus rests on a psychological assumption that people have tendencies that lie along an associate–dissociate continuum.

TABLE 14.1
Cognitive Relations[a]

Sign	Affective	Instrumental	Logical	Spatial or Temporal Proximity
Positive	likes	facilitates	follows from	stands by
	loves	brings about	is equivalent to	is next to
	admires	helps	is the same as	comes after
	is interested in	causes	is equal to	is close to
Null	is indifferent to	has no effect on	is not the same as	is far away
	does not interest	does not hinder	is not logically related to	does not come after
Negative	hates	hinders	is inconsistent with	moves away from*
	dislikes	acts against	contradicts	avoids
	harms	harms	is dissimilar from	

[a] Adapted from Insko and Schopler (1967).
*In Insko and Schopler's table, this "cell" was left blank because they were unable to think of an active force away from spatial or temporal proximity. "Moves away from" and "avoids," however, are, in retrospect, obvious possibilities.

Heider symbolizes a positive sentiment relation as L, a positive unit relation as U, a negative sentiment relation as nL, and a negative unit relation as nU. These positive and negative relations may exist between any two of the three elements, p, o, and x. Thus for p and o we may have pLo, pUo, $pnLo$, or $pnUo$; for p and x we have pLx, pUx, $pnLx$, or $pnUx$; and for o and x we have oLx, oUx, $onLx$, or $onUx$. It is important to realize, however, that these are relations as they exist in p's phenomenology. Thus if p perceives or thinks that o dislikes x, there is a negative sentiment relation between o and x. This is true regardless of how o actually feels toward x. Balance theory is a theory about p's phenomenology.

To the extent that attitudes are thought of as favorable or unfavorable affective responses, they would correspond to the sentiment relation in balance theory. The p–o relation refers to an attitude toward a person, and the p–x relation refers to an attitude toward an object. It is thus apparent that attitudes exist in the context of a large number of other cognitive relations.

What Is Balance?

Heider defines (1958) balance as "a harmonious state in which the entities comprising the situation and the feelings about them fit together without stress [p. 180]." The tendency toward balance is illustrated by the inclination to perceive or believe good things about our friends and bad things about our enemies. Imbalance, on the other hand, results from the perception of virtue in our enemies and vice in our friends. Balance theory does not maintain that such perceptions do not occur. Rather, it asserts that there is a *tendency* not to have such perceptions or beliefs. The ultimate in a balanced state would be a situation in which all the good people were congregated together in one place that was segregated by an eternally fixed gulf from another place in which all the bad people were congregated together. This is the traditional Judeo-Christian conception of heaven and hell.

Balance-Imbalance in the Dyad

Considering the three elements, p, o, and x, there are three possible dyads, $p-o$, $p-x$, and $o-x$. In the case of the $p-x$ dyad, balance occurs when the sentiment and unit relations are of the same sign. To quote Heider (*1946*) directly: "The cases $(pLx) + (pUx)$ and $(pnLx) + (pnUx)$ are balanced. Examples: p likes the things he made; p wants to own the things he likes; p values what he is accustomed to [p. 108]."

Determination of balance in the $p-o$ dyad is slightly more complicated than for the $p-x$ dyad. In the first place, Heider notes that the $p-o$ dyad, like the $p-x$ dyad, is balanced when both the sentiment and unit relations are of the same sign. "Analogously, the two balanced states for p and o will be $(pLo) + (pUo)$ and $(pnLo) + (pnUo)$. Examples: p likes his children, people similar to him; p is uneasy if he has to live with people he does not like; p tends to imitate admired persons; p likes to think that loved persons are similar to him" (1946, p. 108). Beyond this, however, Heider also states that balance in the $p-o$ dyad requires reciprocation of the sentiment relation. "It is in line with the general hypothesis to assume that a balanced state exists if pLo and oLp (or $pnLo$ and $onLp$) are true at the same time" (1946, p. 108).

Much of this is, of course, consistent with commonsense expectations. There are some instances, however, in which the balance theory implications do not obviously agree with common sense. Two of these instances are illustrated by the proverbs "opposites attract" and "familiarity breeds contempt." Let's consider these in order.

Balance theory, of course, implies that p should be attracted to a similar o. On the other hand, if "opposites attract," we are confronted with an apparent exception to the balance implication. It should be noted, however, that although males and females may be attracted to each other, certainly not all opposites do attract. Heider argues that when opposites do attract, it is in the special case of complementarity or oppositeness that leads to the realization of mutual goals. When two people by virtue of their differences mesh in such a way as to allow for the realization of mutual goals, there is a sense in which there is a positive unit relation between them.

The second proverb, "familiarity breeds contempt," stands in apparent opposition to the balance theory implication that p should be attracted to an o with whom there is interaction. Heider argues that interaction will lead to the formation of a positive sentiment relation only if there is not too great a dissimilarity in attitudes. "With similar attitudes proximity will increase the degree of positive sentiment; with slight dissimilarity of attitudes a mutual assimilation might be produced, and with it an increase in friendliness; with strong dissimilarities the hostility will be increased" (1958, p. 190).

In addition to the foregoing two potential problems for balance theory, both of which are discussed by Heider, there is a third potential problem that is not discussed by Heider. This has to do with the reciprocation of sentiment or, more specifically, of negative sentiment. As already indicated, Heider maintains that there is a balance tendency toward reciprocation of sentiment in the p-o dyad. In terms of Heider's scheme of positive and negative sentiment relations, there are four subsets of recriprocation: (1) p perceives that o likes p evokes p likes o, (2) p likes o evokes the perception that o likes p, (3) p perceives that o dislikes p evokes p dislikes o, and (4) p dislikes o evokes the perception that o dislikes p. The first two of these, both involving positive sentiment, are plausible. This is also true of the third, in which the initial negative sentiment is in the o to p direction. The fourth situation, in which the initial negative sentiment is in the p to o direction, however, appears to be more complicated. Does the fact that p dislikes o evoke a reciprocal tendency for p to assume that he or she is disliked by o? The situation appears to be phenomenologically complex. Part of the complexity revolves around the extent to which p holds himself or herself in high regard. Heider has developed balance theory so as to apply to a p who has high self-regard. As Heider puts (1946) it, it is assumed that "pLp [p. 111]." Given that pLp, will $pnLo$ evoke $onLp$? In this case, reciprocation of negative sentiment would produce perceived disagreement between p and o regarding the worth of p. Thus, to the extent that p is unwilling to experience disagreement regarding his or her self-worth, there should be a reluctance to assume reciprocation of the negative sentiment relation. Can such reluctance to experience disagreement be explained by balance theory? This is an interesting question that will be discussed below—after consideration of the p-o-x triad.

The remaining dyadic possibility, beyond p-x and p-o, is o-x. Although Heider does not directly discuss this dyad, one might suppose that the o-x dyad will be balanced when the unit relation and sentiment relation are of the same sign. Thus if p overhears o expressing positive sentiment for a recently purchased bicycle, the o-x dyad will be balanced (for p). This is true even if p has no strong relationship (sentiment or unit) with o.

Balance-Imbalance in the P-O-X Triad

In the case of the p-o-x triad, Heider discusses the simultaneous occurrence of the p-o, p-x, and o-x relations. Heider maintains that the triad is balanced when *all three of the relations are positive* or when *two of the relations are negative and one is positive.* This is true regardless of whether the relations are sentiment relations or unit relations. If positive sentiment and unit relations are symbolized with a + and negative sentiment and unit relations are symbolized with a −, the balanced triads can be represented as + + +, + − −, − + −, − − +. The first sign represents the p–o relation, the second the p–x relation, and the third the o–x relation. Note that in the case of two negative signs and one positive, the locus of the one positive sign is, from Heider's perspective, unimportant.

An example of the + + + triad, which involves two sentiment relations and one unit relation, is "p likes o, likes the book x, and perceives that o wrote x." An example of the − − + triad, also involving two sentiment relations and one unit relation, is "p dislikes o, dislikes the book x, and perceives that o wrote x."

As just mentioned, Heider considers the case of three positive signs balanced. Consider, however, the case of the "love triangle" or situation in which p and his male friend q both fall in love with the same girl o. Is such a triangle or triad balanced? Common sense indicates that the situation is notoriously unstable. Heider's discussion (1946) of this matter is succinct and to the point: "p does not want his girl friend o to fall in love with his boy friend q because oLq in this case implies $onLp$, which conflicts with pLo [p. 110]." It is the competitive aspect of the situation that makes the triad imbalanced. If the girl friend o falls in love with the boy friend q, there is danger that o will cease to like p, and thus p would be involved in an imbalanced dyad. The dyad would be imbalanced both because of the lack of reciprocation of the positive sentiment relation and because o's avoidance of p would create a negative unit relation. The competitive aspect of the situation thus creates the potential for p being involved in an imbalanced dyad. Heider's discussion of this matter is one of the few instances in which he recognizes the importance of dyadic relationships in the general context of triadic ones.

In terms of the possible combinations of signs in the p–o–x triad, two possibilities remain: *two positive signs and one negative sign* and *three negative signs*. The first of these possibilities (two positive signs and one negative) is imbalanced. For example: "p dislikes o, likes the book x, and perceives that o wrote x." According to Heider (*1946*) the final possibility (three negative signs) is "somewhat ambiguous [p. 110]." Heider does not indicate whether a triad of three negative signs ("p dislikes o and x and perceives that o dislikes x") is balanced or imbalanced. Heider, however, does indicate (*1958*) that "common negative attitudes toward x may readily bring about a feeling of similarity between p and o. The resulting unit (p similar to o) is in itself a positive relation, and as we have seen tends to induce a second positive relation (pLo) [p. 203]." In view of the fact that a system of three negative signs is unstable and does tend to break down into a balanced system of two negative signs and one positive sign, it has become common to assume that a triad of three negative signs is imbalanced.

Although triadic balance has been described for a system in which p is related to one person (o) and one object (x), it is equally applicable to systems that involve two persons (i.e., p–o–q) or two objects (i.e., p–x–z).

To summarize, there are four balanced triads ($+++$, $+--$, $-+-$, $--+$) and four imbalanced triads $++-$, $+-+$, $-++$, $---$). In the six cases in which there are unlike signs, Heider assumes that the permutation of the signs is unimportant. Heider also assumes that it is the sign of the relation and not the type of relation (sentiment or unit) that is important (at least in the context of triadic relations). There is some evidence (Fillenbaum, 1968), however, suggesting that within triadic situations, the preference for balance is greater when the relations are all sentiment or all unit rather than a mixture of sentiment and unit.

Cartwright and Harary (1956) have developed a simple multiplicative rule for the determination of balance or imbalance. According to this multiplicative rule, a balanced system is one in which the product of the signs is positive, and an imbalanced system is one in which the product of the signs is negative. The rule will also work for dyads. Recall that dyads are balanced if the unit and sentiment relation are of the same sign or if there is same-sign reciprocation of sentiment.

Reciprocated Sentiment—Again

In the above discussion of reciprocated sentiment in the dyad, it was pointed out that, while a tendency toward reciprocated p–o liking is very likely, a tendency toward reciprocated p–o disliking appears more problematic—particularly when the initial dislike is in the p to o direction, rather than the o to p direction. Reciprocal disliking is more problematic than reciprocal liking, possibly because reciprocal disliking produces disagreement regarding p's assumed self-worth. It was thus proposed that to the extent that p is unwilling to experience disagreement regarding his or her self-worth, there should be a reluctance to assume reciprocation of the negative sentiment relation. This proposal was followed by a question concerning whether or not such reluctance to experience disagreement could be explained by balance theory.

The answer to the above question is yes—if it can be assumed that such disagreement regarding self-worth is negatively evaluated by p. Under these circumstances it is imbalanced for the self ($+$) to be ($+$) negatively evaluated ($-$). In this instance the verb "to be" implies equality or similar grouping, and is thus a positive unit relation. The situation can be conceptualized as a triad: p likes the self, p dislikes being negatively evaluated, and the self is negatively evaluated.

The implication of the above argument is that, although reciprocated negative sentiment balances the p–o, o–p dyad, it may also imbalance a triad involving the self. When there is p to o dislike, there should thus be at least some reluctance to assume o to p dislike. On the other hand, when the initial dislike is in the *o* to *p* direction the self-related triad is already imbalanced, so there is no reason not to reciprocate the negative sentiment and balance the dyad.

Resolution of Imbalance

According to Heider, imbalance results in stress or tension, which produces a tendency for *p* to restore or create balance. Heider (1958) describes a simple study that illustrates the results of imbalance. Subjects were presented with an imbalanced social situation in which there is a positive sentiment relation, a negative sentiment relation, and a positive unit relation.

> Bob thinks Jim is very stupid and a first class bore. One day Bob reads some poetry he likes so well that he takes the trouble to track down the author in order to shake his hand. He finds that Jim wrote the poems [p. 176].

Subjects were asked to write descriptions of Bob's reactions. Coding the written descriptions of the 101 subjects resulted in five different types of response. First, 46% described Bob as feeling less negative about Jim. For example, "He grudgingly changes his mind about Jim [p. 176]." Second, 29% described Bob as feeling less positive about the poetry. For example, "He decides the poems are lousy [p. 176]." Third, 5% described Bob as doubting Jim's authorship of the poetry. For example, "Bob would probably question Jim's authorship of the poems [pp. 176-177]." Fourth, 2% described Bob as differentiating Jim. For example, "He then thinks Jim is smart in some lines but dumb in others [p. 177]." Fifth, 18% described Bob as not resolving the imbalance. Some of these subjects, however, were aware of the conflict. For example: "Bob is confused and does not know what to do. He finally briefly mentions liking of the poems to Jim without much warmth [p. 177]."

The first three of these reactions are straightforward examples of imbalance resolution. The fourth and fifth, however, need further comment. Considering these in reverse order, the fact that 18% of the subjects did not perceive Bob as resolving the imbalance illustrates a very important matter. Balance theory does not say that imbalance will necessarily be resolved. Rather, it states that there is a *tendency* to resolve imbalance. Many circumstances will undoubtedly affect the magnitude of this tendency—including perhaps individual differences in the tolerance for ambiguity.

The fourth, and in this study least frequent, reaction was differentiation. Differentiation involves the splitting apart of an element—either a person element or a nonperson element (*x*). In the foregoing case, the element was, of course, a person (Jim). In some instances differentiation appears to involve an act of creative thinking. Thus, for example, *p* may resolve the imbalance resulting from disagreement with his friend regarding the value of foreign aid by differentiating foreign aid into military aid—which he and his friend both dislike—and economic aid—which he and his friend both like.

In order for differentiation to be a completely successful mode of imbalance resolution, the unity of the element must be convincingly weakened. Thus, for the foregoing examples, there must be a clear difference between economic and foreign aid, and between the areas in which Jim is smart and dumb. An interesting question concerns the extent to which this is possible when the differentiated element is a person rather than a nonperson. One of the things that appears to make the cases involving so-called split personalities, like Jekyll and Hyde, seem so interesting is the paradoxical perception of simultaneous unity and disunity. This is a matter that is poorly understood. Stroebe, Thompson, Insko, and Reisman (1970) report a study in which subjects did differentiate a hypothetical person (Dr. M.) about whom they were given fragmentary bits of information. Thus information indicating that Dr. M. was an expert or inexpert scientist affected evaluation of a theory with which Dr. M. was associated but not of Dr. M.'s wife. On the other hand, crosscutting information indicating that Dr. M. was a nice or awful person affected evaluation of Dr. M.'s wife but not of the theory. Such results indicate that the subjects did differentiate Dr. M. the scientist from Dr. M. the person. There is reason to doubt, however, that subjects would have so clearly differentiated Dr. M. if he were an individual with whom they had contact and interaction—thereby increasing the perception of unity.

In total, Heider suggests four different modes of imbalance resolution in the p-o-x triad (a change in any one of the three relations, plus differentiation). Additional possibilities have been suggested by others. For example, Newcomb (1959) has suggested a decrease in the perceived importance of x as a mode of "strain reduction." Abelson and Rosenberg (1958) have made the reasonable suggestion that the individual may attempt to reduce "inconsistency" (their term for *imbalance*) by ceasing to think about the involved elements. Ceasing-to-think-about is suggestive of, but not the same thing as, forgetting, which has also been suggested as a possibility (e.g., Steiner, 1960). Finally, Abelson (1959) has suggested two additional possibilities—bolstering and transcendence. Bolstering involves adding further cognitive elements and relations so as to "drown out" the inconsistency or imbalance. For example, the smoker who believes that smoking causes lung cancer may attempt to handle the imbalance by telling himself or herself that smoking is enjoyable, no more dangerous than driving, an aid in the control of weight, and so forth. Transcendence involves relating the inconsistent elements to a larger superordinate element. For example, the inconsistency between science and religion may be transcended by assuming that both science and religion are necessary to achieve a deeper understanding of the universe or a fuller appreciation of life.

Such multiple consequences of imbalance, of course, make testing of the theory difficult. An obvious question for balance theory thus concerns which of these various modes of imbalance resolution will be used in any given situation. Heider himself does not address the issue, but others have made interesting suggestions. Of the various suggestions, perhaps the best known is one made by

Osgood and Tannenbaum (1955). Addressing themselves solely to the possibility of alteration of a cognitive relation, they assume that change is inversely proportional to the degree of polarization (see the discussion of the congruity principle in Chapter 7). For example, the more extreme the liking or disliking of *o,* the less likelihood there is that imbalance will be resolved through an alteration in that relation. Osgood and Tannenbaum report data that are consistent with this very plausible suggestion.

A second suggestion has been made by Abelson and Rosenberg (1958). Their concern is not with the strength, or polarization, of any one relation but with the possibility that the alteration of one or more relations so as to produce balance in one set of elements may result in imbalance with another set of elements. For example, someone who adopts the attitude of a peer may simultaneously produce balance in that relationship but imbalance in the relationship with family. Abelson and Rosenberg's suggestion is that on the assumption that all relations are equally resistant to change, the balance-achieving operation involving the fewest number of changes will be the one that occurs. This principle of least effort is certainly a reasonable suggestion.

In the general context of specifying what happens in a network of related elements, a further suggestion comes from McGuire's (1960c) cognitive inertia assumption (see Chapter 13). McGuire assumes that immediate changes in more remote relations or linkages will be less marked than in the ones that are closest to the inconsistency. However, over time the more remote relations will change further in the direction of increased consistency.

A further suggestion comes from dissonance theory, particularly as stated by Brehm and Cohen (1962). Brehm and Cohen argue for the importance of commitment to actual responses. In the present context it could be argued that a public expression of sentiment relation, for example, would make that particular relation more resistant to subsequent change.

A final suggestion, made by Abelson (1959), is that the utilization of the various modes of imbalance reduction will depend on the relative ease with which balance may be restored through the use of any one mode. Thus differentiation and transcendence will be modes of last resort after a change in a cognitive relation (which Abelson refers to as ''denial'') and bolstering have been tried unsuccessfully. The individual's initial reaction should be to change or deny the relation that originally produced the imbalance. In terms of the foregoing example, this would mean that Bob would deny or disbelieve the information indicating that Jim had written the poems. If this cannot be successfully done, the individual should then attempt bolstering. For example, Bob could consider all the additional reasons why Jim is an awful person. If this fails, further denial or change in a cognitive relation should occur. For example, Bob could change his attitude toward Jim or change his attitude toward the poems. If all this fails, the individual should then attempt differentiation and then transcendence. Transcendence might, for example, involve the development of a philosophy indicating that it is the nature of this imperfect world for good literature to be produced by bastards. What Abelson thus suggests is a hierarchy among the modes of imbalance resolution: denial, bolstering, denial (a second time), differentiation, and finally transcendence.

The Assumption of High Self-Regard

One of the more interesting, and at the same time least developed, aspects of balance theory has to do with the assumption that p holds himself or herself in high regard. Here is Heider's statement (1946) on the matter:

> High self regard of p can be expressed by pLp, low self regard by $pnLp$ (although the two p's in this expression are not strictly equivalent). All of the examples so far considered presupposed pLp. However, one also has to take into account the possibility of $pnLp$. As to be expected, it plays a role contrary to that of pLp. Examples: if p has low self regard he might reject a positive x as too good for him; if p has guilt feelings he will think he ought to be punished; if his friend admires his product he will think it only politeness [p. 111].

This statement appears to have two implications—one explicit and one implicit. The explicit implication is that the balance rules apply most obviously and accurately to people with high self-regard. The implicit implication is that the balance rules work in an opposite manner for people with genuinely low self-regard. The fact, however, that Heider devotes so little attention to this matter suggests that he believes that such people are not too common.

Actually, as Wiest (1965) has pointed out, balance theory itself implies that the frequency of genuinely negative self-regard, or self-esteem, should be low. If the second p in the pLp dyad is regarded as a self-concept with which the first p has a positive unit relation, the dyad will be balanced only if, in fact, pLp (or pLs, using Wiest's symbol of s for the self-concept).

It is clear from Heider's statement that he expects the balance rules to work more accurately for those p's with high self-regard. It is not clear, however, what should be expected for those p's with genuinely negative self-regard. This matter can be elucidated through the use of some graph theory representations (Cartwright & Harary, 1956). This also provides an opportunity to illustrate how balance theory is able to represent some of the intricate complexities that arise when considering a person's phenomenology.

In Table 14.2 there are three elements p, o, and s (p's self-concept). A solid line between any two of these elements symbolizes a positive relation, a dashed line a negative relation, a curved line a unit relation, and a straight line a sentiment relation. The arrows on the lines indicate the direction of the relation. Thus the arrow on the dashed line between p and s indicates that p dislikes s (and not that s dislikes p—whatever that would mean). Table 14.2 has been

TABLE 14.2
Balance Predictions for *o*'s Sentiment Toward
s (*p*'s Self-Concept), Assuming a *p* with
Negative Self-Regard

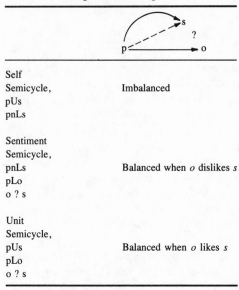

Self Semicycle, pUs pnLs	Imbalanced
Sentiment Semicycle, pnLs pLo o ? s	Balanced when *o* dislikes *s*
Unit Semicycle, pUs pLo o ? s	Balanced when *o* likes *s*

Note. A solid line represents a positive relation, a dashed line a negative relation, a curved line a unit relation, and a straight line a sentiment relation.

constructed so as to represent the situation in which *pnLs,* or *p* has negative self-regard. Consistent with Wiest's suggestion, there is a curved solid line, representing a positive unit relation, between *p* and *s*. The *pnLs* + *pUs* dyad is, of course, imbalanced. From a graph theory perspective, however, this is not a dyad but a semicycle. A semicycle is simply a closed loop—ignoring the direction of the arrows.

Table 14.2 represents the situation in which a person with negative self-regard likes some other person *o*. The theoretical question concerns the balance tendency for the *o* to *s* relation. Filling in this relation will create two additional semicycles. In Table 14.2 these are labeled "sentiment semicycle" and "unit semicycle." The sentiment semicycle is *pnLs* + *pLo* + *o?s*. Following the multiplicative rule, this semicycle is balanced when *onLs*. Consideration of the unit semicycle, however, indicates that the situation is more complicated. The unit semicycle is *pUs* + *pLo* + *o?s*. This semicycle will be balanced when *oLs*. Thus it's a toss-up as to whether a *p* with negative self-regard would want his or her friend to reciprocate the positive sentiment relation.

The representation in Table 14.2 is obviously an oversimplification. First, there is no consideration of the fact that *o* is an acquaintance with whom there is contact and interaction. Contact and interaction should result in a positive unit relation between p and o and thus produce additional semicycles. Examination of all the involved semicycles, however, indicates that making the o to s relation either positive or negative would still balance and imbalance an equal number of semicycles. Thus this added complexity does not require any revision of the foregoing conclusion regarding the ambiguity of the situation.

Second, Table 14.2 further oversimplifies the situation by not representing any of the elements or relations that account for p's maintenance of negative self-regard. Consideration of such matters might indeed indicate that a negative o to s relation would result in a net increase in the number of balanced semicycles. However, without detailed information regarding p's phenomenology, there is no way of knowing. This dilemma is one that we repeatedly encounter in subsequent discussion of various research problems. Balance theory is a theory about phenomenological processes. Application of the theory thus requires a knowledge of the elements that are phenomenologically represented.

Wiest (1965) has reported data bearing on the importance of self-regard. His subjects were 415 fifth-, sixth-, and seventh-grade students from 14 different classrooms in five public schools. The subjects were provided with a list of all the same-sex students in their classroom and were asked to indicate, first, the extent to which each of the other students was liked or disliked and, second, the extent to which each of the other students was perceived as liking or disliking them. After completing the two rating tasks, the subjects filled out a 50-item Self-Esteem Inventory (Coopersmith, 1959).

In order to check the balance theory prediction of reciprocated sentiment, Wiest calculated the correlation between each subject's liking–disliking of the other same-sex students and the extent of perceived reciprocation of this sentiment. The average correlation (with appropriate z transformation) was $+.74$. Given our previous reservation regarding at least some aspects of reciprocated sentiment, this correlation appears remarkably high. More relevant to the present concern, however, is the moderation of this tendency toward reciprocated sentiment by self-esteem. Wiest investigated this matter by correlating the measure of self-esteem with each subject's reciprocated-sentiment correlation. If the reciprocated-sentiment correlation is taken as a measure of the balance tendency, it is reasonable to expect that this correlation (for each subject) would in turn be correlated with self-esteem (across subjects). The correlation was low but significant: $+.240$ for males and $+.222$ for females. Wiest's results do provide some evidence for a relationship between self-esteem and the tendency to reciprocate sentiment. Evidence for such a relationship was also found by Fillenbaum (1968).

Although the foregoing results are consistent with the generalization that the level of self-esteem has an effect on the extent to which other balance processes occur (reciprocated sentiment, for example), it is important to point out that alternative causal sequences could give rise to the foregoing correlational results.

It could well be, for example, that a lack of reciprocated sentiment with one's friends causes a lowering of self-esteem. Actually, from a balance theory point of view, this causal sequence is just as reasonable as is one that goes in the opposite direction (from lowered self-esteem to a lesser degree of perceived reciprocated sentiment).

Balance and Motivation

A final issue relating to balance theory concerns the role of motivation in balance theory. Does balance theory assume the existence of a need or drive to reduce imbalance and achieve balance, or is balance theory simply a set of rules specifying the manner in which the organism functions? The answer to this question is not clear. Cottrell (1975) regards balance theory as a "conceptual rule" relating to the processing of information. This perspective appears to reflect balance theory's ancestral connection with the Gestalt laws of perceptual grouping. Consider, for example, the law that states that elements will be grouped according to their proximity and equality. The proximity part of the law dictates that the array of elements, XX XX XX XX, will be perceived as four groups rather than as eight single elements. On the other hand, this tendency will be weakened to the extent that the elements are not "equal" or similar, X! @# $% ¢&.

Heider (1960) has an extensive discussion of the question of whether or not balance theory is a motivational theory. Paraphrasing a somewhat complex discussion, his answer appears to be that it depends on what is meant by the term *motivational theory*. If by a motivational theory is meant a theory based on analogy with biological needs for food, sex, and pain avoidance, the answer is no. Imbalance is not conceived as a negative goal state, nor is balance conceived as a positive goal state. On the other hand, if by motivational theory is meant a theory about how tension in the organism can lead to change, balance theory is a motivational theory. Heider identifies (1960) balance theory with the Gestalt theory of motivation—a theory concerning "a system of interrelated factors or parts with whole properties defining states of equilibrium or disequilibrium [p. 171]."

If tension is used as the criterion for the existence of motivation, the next question concerns when balance theory assumes the existence of tension. Consider, for example, a situation in which p perceives that o and q live together (are connected by a positive unit relation) and also are continually fighting with each other (express mutual negative sentiment). From p's perspective, this is an imbalanced dyad, and p may attempt to "make sense" of the situation (create a balanced cycle) by believing that "they must enjoy fighting." On the other hand, to the extent that p has no strong sentiment or unit relation with either o or q, it seems likely that the initial amount of tension for p would be minimal and possibly nonexistent. The situation appears analogous to the already described example of the Gestalt law of proximity and equality. When p's level of involvement is low, perhaps it is better to regard balance theory as a set of principles regarding cognitive functioning. On the other hand, suppose that p is personally involved. Following the foregoing example, suppose that p has a strong positive sentiment relation with both o and q. In this altered situation, it is reasonable to suppose that p will experience considerable tension. It is thus proposed that polarity of the sentiment and unit relations relating p to the relevant elements is the determiner of tension in an imbalanced system. With high polarity imbalance will create a greater degree of tension.[1]

SELECTED TOPICS IN ATTITUDE CHANGE

Balance theory is first and foremost a theory about phenomenology. In view of this fact, it is quite possible to misrepresent the theory's predictions through a more or less routine application of balance rules and an unwillingness to consider the complexity of phenomenology. Thus a critic of balance theory may assert: "It is foolish to suppose that because I disagree with my friend about some issue, I am therefore going to change my attitude about my friend or about the issue." Indeed it may be. Recognize, however, that balance theory does not say that imbalance will be resolved but rather that there is a tendency to resolve imbalance. Recognize further that the tendency to resolve imbalance in this particular p-o-x triad does not exist in a phenomenological vacuum. If p changes his or her attitude toward x, there is some possibility that the newly acquired attitude will be inconsistent with other attitudes existing in a more or less consistent or balanced ideology. And if p changes his or her attitude toward o, there is potential imbalance with other perceived similarities with o or further interaction with o, and so forth. Balance theory must always be applied with a sensitive eye to p's phenomenology.

Balance theory has wide-ranging implications for various areas of social psychology—person perception, interpersonal attraction, attitude change, and the like. Present discussion, however, is limited to just a few topics in attitude change.

Attitude Structure

Rosenberg (1953, 1956) was one of the first persons to call major attention to what he refers to as an "attitude structure" (see Chapter 1). His concern was with the structural relationship between a person's attitude and values. Attitudes

---

[1]As is partially illustrated in a subsequent section, balance theory provides competing explanations for various phenomena traditionally explained by dissonance theory. These explanations always assume high self-involvement. It is thus of more than passing interest to note that Kiesler and Pallak (1976) have made a convincing case for the motivational consequences of various "dissonance" manipulations (see also Cooper, Zanna, & Taves, 1978).

stand in an "instrumental" relationship to values in that the attitude can be perceived as either facilitating or interfering with the attainment of those values. By a structure, Rosenberg does not mean a set of steel girders standing in space but rather a set of relations among component parts such that a change in one relation will set up pressure for a change in one or more additional components. These changes are in the direction of consistency or balance. Rosenberg provided a mathematical summary of this structural relationship, one that bears some similarity to the attitude "equations" of Fishbein (Chapter 15) and Anderson (Chapter 16).

Rosenberg's general position can be simply illustrated with the hypothetical attitude structure contained in Fig. 14.1. Suppose that some individual has a positive attitude toward the building of nuclear power-generating plants. In addition to feeling favorable toward this x, however, he also has certain beliefs about the building of nuclear power-generating plants. He believes, for example, that the building of such plants would facilitate ($+$) conservation of oil and gas and would interfere with ($-$) dependence on foreign oil. In Heiderian language, these beliefs are unit relations. "Facilitates" is a positive unit relation, and "interferes with" is a negative unit relation. These unit relations or beliefs (Rosenberg's term is "*instrumental cognitiions*") link the building of nuclear plants to different x's (or values) around the "circumference" of the structure. Thus "continued industrial growth" and "conservation of oil and gas" are positive values, and "high unemployment" and "dependence on foreign oil" are negative values. The sign of the value corresponds to the sign of the sentiment relationship between the person (or p) and the values. An attitude structure is composed of what Rosenberg refers to as "cognitive bands"—for example: "The building of nuclear power-generating plants facilities conservation of oil and gas." There are four such bands in Fig. 14.1, one for each value.

For each of the four bands in the structure, balance theory can predict the sign of the attitude given knowledge of the sign of the value and the instrumental or unit bond. As a corollary of the "multiplicative rule," this sign is simply the product of the two known signs. This coincides exactly with Rosenberg's mathematical index. He proposed that attitude is the sum of the products of the degree of satisfaction represented by a value (which subjects rate on a $+3$ to -3 scale) and the extent to which the attitude facilitates or interferes with attainment of the value (as rated on a $+3$ to -3 scale). Assume that the hypothetical person in Fig. 14.1 rated the two positive values as $+3$ and believed they were facilitated at $+3$, and that the two negative values were rated at -3 and believed they were interfered with at -3. In this case, each of the four triads in the structure would contribute a product of $+9$, and the sum would total $+36$. Assuming that all of the relevant aspects of any particular individual's phenomenology have been measured, it should be the case that the greater the sum of products, the more positive or the less negative the attitude toward the central attitude object will be.

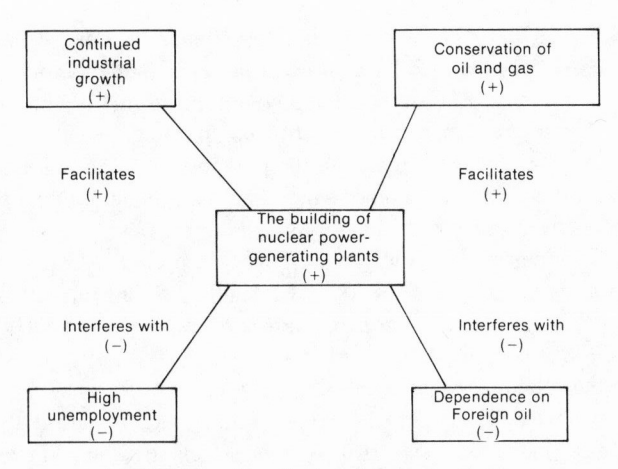

FIG. 14.1.   Hypothetical attitude structure.

In his research, Rosenberg (1953, 1956) dealt with two different attitude issues: free speech for Communists and segregated black housing. For both issues, Rosenberg found a significant relation between the sum of products and an assessment of the central attitude. Additional data consistent with this structural model has been reported by Woodruff and DiVesta (1948) with attitude toward the abolishment of fraternities and sororities, by Fishbein (1963) with attitude toward blacks, and by Insko, Blake, Cialdini, and Mulaik (1970) with attitude toward the use of birth control. This literature generally makes a convincing case for a relationship between attitude and the sum of products. The relationship provides evidence that people, in general, tend to have balanced attitude structures.

It is important to comment briefly regarding the difference between the sum of products and the mean, or average, of products. In the foregoing illustration, the sum of products is +36, and the simple average is +9. Anderson (Chapter 16) has systematically investigated this matter, where the concern is with the overall evaluation of an attitude object (e.g., a hypothetical person) as a function of assigned items of information that differ in evaluation. His results have convincingly supported the averaging as opposed to the summing, or adding, procedure. He, furthermore, makes the interesting observation that the averaging procedure is more consistent with Gestalt psychology, because influence of any one part is dependent on the whole when the more complex, differential weighting model is used. The issue has not been systematically investigated within the balance theory interpretation of attitude structure.

An alternative procedure for gaining information regarding attitude structure is to use a more open-ended assessment in which people are simply asked for their thoughts on some issue. Early examples of this are reported in Chapter 1. More recent examples of open-ended assessment (described in Chapter 2) are

Greenwald's (1967, 1968b) and Brock's (1967) use of a listed-thought technique. The essential idea is to have subjects list their thoughts, one thought per line, following exposure to a persuasive communication. In Greenwald's version, the subjects are subsequently instructed to categorize their thoughts as favorable, unfavorable, or unrelated to the position advocated in the persuasive communication. Brock, on the other hand, used independent judges to score the listed thoughts for number of counterarguments to the position advocated by the persuasive communication. Both the originally reported research and various follow-up investigations (e.g., Insko, Turnbull, & Yandell, 1974; Petty & Cacioppo, 1977) have found consistent and strong relationships between attitude and various thought indices.

What is the relationship between such evidence and Rosenberg's concept of an attitude structure? Following the example of attitude toward the building of nuclear power plants, suppose that someone lists the thought "problem of radioactive waste." According to Greenwald's scheme, this is an unfavorable thought; according to Brock's, a counterargument. From the perspective of an attitude structure, this is an implied cognitive band: "The building of nuclear power plants (?) would result in (+) radioactive waste (−)." The implication of the muliplicative rule for this one band or thought is that nuclear plants are negative.

The listed-thought technique has not typically assessed the polarity of the belief linkage or the polarity of the related x (or value). The technique, however, does have the virtue of tailoring the assessment to each individual's phenomenology.

One methodological-theoretical issue that has been raised concerning the listed-thought technique relates to causal sequence. Do the thoughts cause the attitude, or does the attitude cause the thoughts? The latter "rationalization" sequence has been advocated by Miller (1971; see Chapter 5). It may be that in some particular circumstance, the causal sequence proceeds in one direction, but balance theory in general clearly has the implication that the relationship between attitude and thoughts is reciprocal, or goes in both directions. Rosenberg (1960a), in fact, makes a major point of this when he states that sometimes affective change may lead to cognitive change and sometimes cognitive change may lead to affective change. Referring to Fig. 14.1, a change in the central attitude will have implications for the belief linkages, and a change in the belief linkages will have implications for the central attitude.

Attitudinal Verbal Reinforcement

The first experiment on attitudinal verbal reinforcement was reported by Hildum and Brown (1956). A sample of Harvard students were called on the telephone and asked to participate in a survey concerning the "Harvard philosophy of general education." The survey consisted of 15 statements, with each of which the students were asked to agree strongly, agree slightly, disagree slightly, or disagree strongly. Each statement was a cognitive triad with either favorable or unfavorable implications for Harvard's philosophy of general education. The experiment contained two conditions—pro and con. In the pro condition the experimenter played the role of someone who favored the philosophy of general education. Every time the subject agreed with a favorable statement or disagreed with an unfavorable statement, the experimenter said "good." In the con condition, the experimenter played the role of someone who was unfavorable to the philosophy of general education. Every time the subject agreed with an unfavorable statement or disagreed with a favorable statement, the experimenter said "good." The results were scored by assigning numerical values to the four possible responses to each statement such that the higher the score, the more unfavorable the attitude toward the Harvard philosophy of general education. The results, in fact, indicated that the mean score in the con condition was significantly higher than the mean score in the pro condition.

An obvious question concerning such results relates to whether the attitudinal verbal reinforcement effect is simply a temporary alteration in interview-specific responses or the occurrence of genuine attitude change. Recall from Chapter 1 the study by Insko (1965) in which a sample of students from two large, introductory psychology classes at the University of Hawaii were called on the telephone and asked to agree or disagree with a series of belief statements relating to the creation of a "Springtime Aloha Week." (Ordinarily, Aloha Week is a fall festival in Hawaii.) Half the subjects were reinforced (with the word "good") for a favorable attitude, and half were reinforced for an unfavorable attitude. Approximately 1 week later, a "Local Issues Questionnaire" was passed out in the two psychology classes, and all the students were asked to fill it out. One of the rating scales on this questionnaire related to the creation of a "Springtime Aloha Week." The results indicated that the pro–con direction of reinforcement significantly influenced the interview responses (in agreement with Hildum and Brown's results) and also that the effect was still present in the follow-up questionnaire. Apparently, then, something other than the temporary modification of interview-specific responses does occur as a result of attitudinal verbal reinforcement.

Why does attitudinal verbal reinforcement produce attitude change? There are at least four possible explanations. The first of these explanations is in terms of demand characteristics (Orne, 1962; see Chapter 3). Perhaps subjects are motivated to please the experimenter by giving the results for which he or she is looking. They thus go through a problem-solving sequence in which they initially ascertain the experimental hypothesis and then subsequently alter their behavior so as to support this hypothesis. A moment's reflection, however, indicates that this interpretation does not fit the already described results. In both the Hildum and Brown and Insko experiments, the subjects did not know that they were participating in an experiment. Of course, they may have been motivated to get along with the interviewer, but it is highly unlikely that the source of the motivation was a desire to support an experimental hypothesis. Insko and Melson (1969) directly confronted this issue by testing subjects either in a laboratory setting or in a telephone interview. Subjects from the introductory psychology course at the University of North Carolina were either called on the telephone or tested in a laboratory setting. In two separate experiments, Insko and Melson found a significant effect for direction of reinforcement but no significant difference in the magnitude of that effect between phone and lab settings. This type of bridging experiment is the crucial test of the demand characteristics perspective on laboratory results, and in this one instance, the demand characteristics interpretation was found lacking.

The second interpreation is in terms of hedonism. Perhaps subjects alter their interview responses so as to maximize the pleasant affect or feeling associated with "good" and possibly so as to minimize the unpleasant affect or feeling with lack of a "good." Insko and Cialdini (1969), in fact, found that verbally reinforced subjects retrospectively report that the "good" was pleasant. Such reported pleasantness, however, is not correlated with the extent of influence. Cialdini and Insko (1969) asked their subjects two postexperimental questions designed to provide relevant information for the hedonism interpretation: "How did you feel when I said 'good'?" and "How hard were you trying to make me say 'good' [p. 345]?" Responses to both questions were minimally correlated with the extent of influence.

A third possible interpretation of attitudinal verbal reinforcement is in terms of conveyed information. According to this interpretation, the experimenter's "good" informs the subject of the experimenter's position on the attitude issue, and a simple conformity effect follows. Cialdini and Insko (1969) tested this interpretation in an experiement in which the direction of reinforcement was either consistent or inconsistent with the experimenter's professional affiliation. The interview consisted of a series of 18 statements, each of which pitted experimental psychology against clinical psychology. The experimenter initially introduced himself either as a graduate student in experimental psychology or as a graduate student in clinical psychology. In a so-called informationally consistent condition, the direction of reinforcement was consistent with the experimenter's reported affiliation; that is, experimental reinforcement went with experimental affiliation, and clinical reinforcement went with clinical affiliation. In a so-called informationally inconsistent condition, the direction of reinforcement was inconsistent with the experimenter's reported affiliation; that is, experimental reinforcement went with clinical affiliation, and clinical reinforcement went with experimental affiliation. The results indicated that reinforcement had an effect only in the consistent condition. This experiment, then, appears to provide compelling evidence for the importance of information.

Is the simple conveying of information, however, a sufficient explanation for attitudinal verbal reinforcement? Insko and Cialdini argued that an additional factor beyond information is also important. They thus advanced an additional or fourth interpretation of attitudinal verbal reinforcement—a two-factor interpretation. According to this interpretation, the "good" does two things. First, it conveys information regarding the experimenter's attitude. Second, it creates positive rapport with the experimenter. It is the second factor, liking for the experimenter, that serves to motivate conformity to the experimenter's assumed attitude.

Two questions can be raised about the liking or rapport factor. First, does the experimenter's "good" in fact create liking? Caildini and Insko (1969) investigated this matter by comparing liking for the experimenter in the experimental conditions (in which reinforcements were delivered) with the control conditions (in which the experimenter identified himself either as a clinical or an experimental psychologist but did not deliver reinforcements). The results indicated that the experimenter was liked better in the experimental than in the control conditions. The experimenter's use of "good" does create positive rapport.

The second question concerns whether rapport has a causal effect upon attitudinal verbal reinforcement. This matter was investigaged in two experiments: Insko and Butzine (1967) and Insko and Cialdini (1969). Insko and Butzine manipulated rapport through an initial exchange between experimenter and subject prior to the beginning of the interview. In a positive rapport condition the experimenter was initially complimentary, and in a negative rapport condition the experimenter was initially insulting. Rapport was found to interact with the direction of reinforcement in the expected manner; that is, the direction of reinforcement had a greater effect in the positive rapport condition than in the negative rapport condition. Insko and Cialdini (1969) got at rapport through a direct manipulation of the potentially reinforcing responses of the experimenter to the subject's interview responses. In one condition, for example, the experimenter said "huh" after the to-be-discouraged interview responses. It was supposed that "huh" would convey as much information as "good" but that "huh" and "good" would differ in rapport. A postexperimental assessment, in fact, revealed that "huh" created as much awareness of the experimenter's behavior as did "good." In terms of influence, however, "huh" had no effect, whereas "good" produced the usual effect.

Overall, the evidence in support of the two-factor interpretation is fairly compelling. The two-factor interpretation derives from a more thorough understanding of the subject's phenomenology. We tend to agree with people we like—a commonsense observation that is, of course, a simple balance theory implication. By altering interview responses so as to agree with the liked experimenter, the subject achieves balance or harmony in this one, small part of his or her social world.

Insko and Cialdini (1971) acknowledge the possibility that the two-factor interpretation may not be a sufficient explanation for everything that occurs in the attitudinal verbal reinforcement situation. One matter to which they refer relates to the fact that the subject is active and not passive. The actual semipublic responding may have an effect over and above that produced by the two factors of information and rapport. It is possible that such responding produces a commitment that is responsible for the persistence effect found in the "Aloha Week" study described earlier. Or, put somewhat differently, perhaps the subject observes his or her own responses and attributes an attitude to the self that is consistent with the responses. Ross, Insko, and Ross (1971) and Ross (1971) have obtained results indicating that the manipulation of subjects' supposed, but not actual, questionnaire responses has an effect on subsequently reported attitudes—even when steps are taken to assure "destruction" of the manipulated questionnaire responses. From a balance theory point of view, it is reasonable that a subject should have a tendency to evaluate positively those responses with which a positively evaluated self is associated.

"Dissonance" as a Function of Insufficient Reward

Balance theory can be regarded as a theory of cognitive consistency in that cognitive relations are expected to be consistent with one another. One of the most renowned of the consistency theories, and one that provoked a great amount of research activity, is the theory of "cognitive dissonance" (Festinger, 1957). Of all the experiments in the dissonance theory tradition, perhaps the best known is an experiment by Festinger and Carlsmith (1959). The experiment was intended as an exploration of the effect of reward on attitude change produced by counterattitudinal advocacy, or argument contrary to one's own point of view (as, for example, in a debate). According to Festinger and Carlsmith, counterattitudinal advocacy produces "dissonance." The magnitude of such dissonance, however, is dependent on the amount of reward offered to induce the counterattitudinal advocacy. If, for example, someone who disliked comic books was offered a million dollars to state publicly that he or she liked comic books, very little dissonance would be created. On the other hand, if the reward was only ten cents, the amount of dissonance would be considerably greater. As the argument is developed, it is postulated that dissonance may be reduced through attitude change consistent with the direction of advocacy (for example, by deciding that comic books are, after all, "pretty good"). Thus we have one of dissonance theory's most famous "nonobvious" predictions: The less the reward used to induce counterattitudinal advocacy, the greater the amount of attitude change consistent with the direction of advocacy.

Festinger and Carlsmith (1959) tested the nonobvious prediction in an experiment in which subjects were offered either a low reward or a high reward for engaging in counterattitudinal advocacy. After spending an hour at tasks designed to be boring (spool packing and peg turning), individual male subjects were informed that the experiment was over but that their help was need in introducing the next subject to the experiment. It was explained that the individual who normally did this had failed to arrive. Usually this individual acted like a person who had just finished the experiment and told the waiting subject that the experimental task was interesting and fun. As payment for deceiving the waiting subject and for being on call in case of future emergencies, the subjects were offered either $1 or $20. After talking to the waiting subject (who was actually a female stooge), the subjects were taken to another office and were introduced to an interviewer who was supposedly collecting data on subjects' reactions to having participated in experiments. In the course of the interview, the subjects were asked to rate their enjoyment of the experimental tasks. The results indicated that the subjects who received $1 rated the tasks as more enjoyable than the subjects who received $20. Such results, of course, confirm the original nonobvious prediction.

The Festinger and Carlsmith experiment attracted a lot of attention and was succeeded by a large number of follow-up investigations. The results of these investigations, however, were not consistent. Some investigators obtained dissonance results (an inverse or negative relation between reward and attitude change); some investigators obtained reinforcement results (a direct or positive relation between reward and attitude change); and some investigators obtained neither dissonance nor reinforcement results. (See Collins & Hoyt, 1972, for a review.) Research in recent years (e.g., Calder, Ross, & Insko, 1973; Collins & Hoyt, 1972; Cooper & Worchel, 1970; Nel, Helmreich, & Aronson, 1969), however, has finally succeeded in specifying the requisite conditions for the replication of Festinger and Carlsmith's dissonance effect. It now appears that the inverse relation between reward and attitude change will appear only if there is both high choice and what is called high consequences. By high choice is meant that the subject is given an explicit choice as to whether or not to accept the money and engage in the counterattitudinal advocacy. The subject cannot simply be given the money and told what to do. By high consequences is meant either that the subject anticipates that the counterattitudinal advocacy will be convincing or directly perceives that the counterattitudinal advocacy does have a persuasive impact.

Intuitively, it appears that the dissonance effect is dependent on the subject having an "Oh my God what have I done" reaction—a reaction of assumed responsibility for having misinformed someone. Although choice and consequences were not emphasized by Festinger and Carlsmith, their experiment did involve both high choice and high consequences. Subjects were given an explicit choice and did perceive that their counterattitudinal advocacy had a persuasive impact.

A study by Calder, Ross, and Insko (1973) illustrates the importance of choice and consequences. It was modeled after the original Festinger and Carlsmith "dull task paradigm" and included three factors. These were reward (high vs. low), choice (high vs. low), and consequences (high vs. low). Reward was operationalized in terms of extra hours credit that subjects would earn toward a requisite 5-hour total. Low reward was 1/2 hour, and high reward was 2 hours. In the low-consequences condition, the stooge was unconvinced by the subject's counterattitudinal advocacy. In the high-consequences condition, the stooge was convinced and also stated that since the experiment was interesting and enjoyable, he would stay and be a subject rather than leave and study for a quiz as he had originally intended. The latter matter relating to not studying for the coming quiz was intended as an added measure to produce the "Oh my God what have I done" reaction.

The results of the experiment (shown in Table 14.3) illustrate the importance of choice and consequences. Note the results in the first column in which there is both high choice and high consequences. These were the only conditions under which the expected dissonance effect was obtained—that is, an inverse relation between reward and attitude change. The mean of 21.33 in the high-dissonance cell is the only mean in the entire table that differs from the control mean, 13.20. In the second column, in which there is low choice and high consequences, there is a reinforcement effect—that is, a direct relation between reward and attitude change. The key role of high choice and high consequences in obtaining the dissonance effect was also verified in a study by Insko, Worchel, Folger, and Kutkus (1975), using a conceptually similar, but operationally different, variation in amount of reward.

Insko et al. (1975) advanced a balance theory interpretation of the dissonance effect. The argument is partially an elaboration of the "Oh my God what have I done" reaction. They state that the relevant cognitive band is one that involves the self: The self (+) is responsible for (?) misleading the waiting subject (?). Consistent with past discussion, the self is given a positive sign. Insko et al. further argue that within the context of the high-consequences condition, the counterattitudinal advocacy is most obviously misleading and negative. For the high-consequences condition: The self (+) is responsible for (?) misleading the waiting subject (−). The remaining undetermined sign relates to responsibility. It is clear that the subject should be motivated to avoid accepting responsibility for the negative act. From the perspective of balance theory, the reason for such

TABLE 14.3
Mean Enjoyableness Ratings in the Calder, Ross,
and Insko (1973) Experiment[a]

| | High Consequences | | Low Consequences | |
	High Choice	Low Choice	High Choice	Low Choice
1/2 Hour	21.33	9.60	13.20	12.33
2 Hours	14.80	16.20	16.40	9.40

Note. Control = 13.20, ratings on a 36-point scale with higher numbers indicating more enjoyment.
[a] Adapted from Calder, Ross, and Insko (1973).

reluctance is that assigning a positive sign to "is responsible for" would result in an imbalanced cognitive band.

Assume for the moment that the evidence for responsibility is sufficiently strong to prevent its denial. How could the subject escape imbalance? One possibility is through devaluation of the self. This is not too likely, however, in view of the fact that it would create further imbalance in the subject's interpersonal relations. Another possibility is for the subject to decide that is is not too bad to mislead someone. This, however, would also create further imbalance in related attitude structures. To the extent that responsibility is accepted, the subject appears to be "boxed in." A way out, however, is for the subject to decide that "I did not mislead the waiting subject, because I really did enjoy the task." Thus a shift is produced in the dependent variable. To the extent that such a shift removes one of the elements from the band, imbalance is resolved.

The key to the entire matter thus revolves around the acceptance of responsibility. In everyday usage, the term *responsibility* is assumed to have only one meaning. Actually, as Heider (1958) pointed out, the term has multiple meanings—meanings that can be arranged into "levels." Fishbein and Ajzen (1973) labeled and described these levels as follows:

(1) *Association:* At the first and most primitive level, the actor is held responsible for all effects that are in any way associated with him. (2) *Commission:* At the next level he is held responsible if he was instrumental in producing the observed effects (even if he could not have foreseen them). (3) *Foreseeability:* At this level the actor is held responsible only if he could have foreseen the effects even though he might not have intended to produce them. (4) *Intentionality:* At the fourth level he is held responsible for effects he foresaw and intended. (5) *Justification:* Finally, at the fifth level he is held responsible only to the extent that his intended behavior was not justified, i.e., not caused by environmental factors beyond his control [pp. 149–150].

These levels differ in the extent to which responsibility is attributed to the environment rather than to the person. At the fifth level, justification, responsibility is most likely shifted to the environment. According to Heider (1958), it is at this level that "The criminal may blame the environment for his ill-fated career and thereby excuse himself [p. 114]." The lower levels are illustrated by parents' acceptance of responsibility for the welfare of their children.

As previously indicated, the acceptance of responsibility for negative acts is imbalanced. Thus individuals are motivated to assert: "It's not my fault" or "I am not responsible." Such denial of responsibility, however, is difficult or impossible if "responsibility" has a meaning associated with one or more of the lower levels. It is therefore plausible that the subjects in the Festinger and Carlsmith experiment implicitly shifted the meaning of responsibility to one or more of the higher levels—intentionality and justification.

Insko et al. argue that choice and reward have implications for the acceptance of responsibility. High choice provides evidence for intentionality and also indicates that everyone might not have acted in the same way. Also, low choice provides evidence against intentionality and, further, indicates that everyone might have conformed to the pressure and acted in the same way. Therefore, choice provides evidence for responsibility regardless of whether responsibility is interpreted as intentionality or as justification. What about reward? When the reward is large, the subject may assume that other subjects would have behaved exactly as he or she did and, consistent with the justification conception of responsibility, deny responsibility. The subject in essence assumes: "Since anybody in the same circumstances would have done exactly what I did, I am not responsible." Low reward, on the otherhand, does not have such an implication. Indeed the very insufficiency of the reward is an argument that other subjects would not have behaved as he or she did.

The evidence for responsibility is therefore most convincing when choice is high and reward is low. This occurs in the high-dissonance cell and theoretically produces the "what have I done" reaction. In the remaining high-consequences cells, either choice is low or reward is high or both. One final complication is Insko et al.'s agreement with Bem's (1967) attribution argument regarding reward. Bem argues that low reward is a cue that the task was in fact enjoyed. Otherwise, how is the complaint behavior to be explained? The cue implications of low reward in the high-dissonance cell are particularly welcome, because acceptance of the implication allows the subject to resolve imbalance in the cognitive band.

Additional Topics

There are actually a large number of topics within attitude change that are potentially understandable in terms of balance theory. These include, for example, classical conditioning of attitudes, persistence of attitude change, generalization of attitude change, overevaluation of in-group products, spreading of the alternatives in free-choice situations, and some "way-out" possibilities like conversion. Generally, however, the relevance of balance theory to such matters has not been recognized and/or appreciated. Partially as a result of this fact, the potential relevance of balance theory to these matters has not been thoroughly investigated. Thorough investigation always involves an initial consideration or examination of the subject's phenomenology. If the phenomenology has not been accurately specified, the test of the theory will be inadequate.

Consider, for example, the potential applicability of balance theory to the overevaluation of in-group products (cf. Ferguson & Kelley, 1964). Does balance theory imply that the greater the attraction of the individual for his or her group, the higher the evaluation of the group's achievements? Yes, most certainly. However, the situation is quite likely much more complicated. The individual also has a positive unit relation with the group—even when the group is disliked. And what about anticipated future contact with group members? Further, what is the assumed impact of publicly expressed high evaluation of the group—leading, for example, to possible overconfidence in competitive situations (Worchel, Lind, & Kaufman, 1975)?

Despite a very favorable win-lose record, Dean Smith, our basketball coach at the University of North Carolina, always manages to be modest about his team and complimentary of an opposing team—no matter how inept the opposing team may actually be. The existence of such a Dean Smith effect does not necessarily demonstrate that the balance theory account is incorrect. A fair test of balance theory must consider any particular individual's phenomenology. Avoiding overconfidence, appearing modest, and moderating the disappointment of a loss can all be viewed as balance tendencies.

BALANCE THEORY, HEDONISM, AND TESTABILITY

The foregoing discussion illustrates a major problem with balance theory at its present stage of development. *In its current somewhat loose formulation, the theory is not testable.* It is not testable because its loose formulation makes it difficult or impossible to generate a prediction that, if disconfirmed, would lead to the theory's rejection.

Balance theory's slippery quality arises from two sources. First, the theory has not been completely developed so as to specify the utilized mode or modes of imbalance resolution or balance attainment in any particular situation (and, also, the specific quantitative changes produced by each mode). Second, because the empirical testing of balance theory always presupposes accurate specification of the subject's phenomenology, disconfirmation of a prediction may lead the defender of balance theory to claim that the failure is due, not to the inadequacy of balance theory, but rather to inaccurate or incorrect specification of the subject's phenomenology. Although the general formulation or balance theory is currently untestable, it is possible to test specific balance hypothesis that include specified phenomenology and specified dependent variable effects. One illustration of this is Insko and Cialdini's (1971) already described hypothesis that attitudinal verbal reinforcement is a result of agreement with a liked experimenter.

The situation for balance theory is analogous to the one for hedonism. Consider the individual who chooses to be burned at the stake rather than renounce his beliefs. Does such behavior disprove hedonism? Not necessarily. The individual may be concerned with the rewards of afterlife, the pain of renouncing deeply held beliefs, and so on. Whenever results are obtained in apparent contradiction to a hedonistic prediction, the defender of hedonism may maintain that the test was unfair due to an inadequate conceptualization of the pleasures and pains (rewards and costs) in the situation. This does not mean, however, that a hedonistic orientation is of no value. Experience with the use of so-called behavior modification techniques demonstrates quite the opposite. Without a general hedonistic orientation, an investigator might never discover the specific rewards in a given situation that allow for the modification of some behavior. Also there is no reason to assume that future advancement will never discover exactly what it is that makes a reward a reward.

In addition to sharing this testability dilemma, balance theory and hedonism also have an interesting degree of theoretical overlap. Thus the self (+) positively associated wth (+) reward (+) is balanced, as is the self (+) negatively associated with (−) cost (−). Also the self (+) positively associated with (+) cost (−) is imbalanced, as is the self (+) negatively associated with (−) reward (+). The parallel between hedonism and balance follows from the positive evaluation of the self. Assuming a positively evaluated self, that which is pleasant will imply balance in the relevant self-affect band, and that which is unpleasant will imply imbalance in the relevant self-affect band. This means that whatever effects are predicted by a hedonistic (or exchange) orientation can also be predicted by balance theory—assuming a positive self.

In the foregoing self-affect band (or triad) p's self-concept is directly involved; that is, one of the crucial signs for determination of balance or imbalance is for the self. It is for such triads that the parallel between balance and hedonism is most obvious. For triads or dyads in which the self is not an element, the parallel between hedonism and balance is less apparent. This is particularly true if p has no personal involvement with the elements. Suppose that p observes that o has continuing interaction with q. If p also observes that o likes q, the o–q dyad will be balanced (for p). On the other hand, assuming no sentiment relation between p and either o or q, the situation does not appear to be obviously pleasant for p. (This assumes no empathic identification with o or q.) Balance and imbalance are not necessarily self-related, whereas pleasure and pain are self-related. Thus balance theory is more general than is psychological hedonism and can possibly subsume hedonism as a special case.

The realization of this fact places the previously described Insko and Cialdini (1971) results relating to attitudinal verbal reinforcement in a somewhat different light. Insko and Cialdini argued that their results implied that the hedonistic interpretation in terms of the pleasant affect associated with "good" was incorrect, and that the balance interpretation in terms of agreement with a liked experimenter was correct. From the current perspective what they should have stated is that a hedonism–balance interpretation in terms of the self achieving the pleasant affect of "good" is incorrect, whereas a balance interpretation in terms of agreement with a liked experimenter is correct.

BEYOND LOGIC

The preceding discussion of the relevance of balance theory to the consistency of non-self-related matters is suggestive of logic, where the concern has traditionally been with such matters. Runkel and Peizer (1968) have pointed out an intriguing parallel between balance and logic. Traditional logic is said to be two-valued. What this means is that the relationship between two associated propositions is either consistent or inconsistent. Suppose that balance theory is similarly restricted. This would mean that if two attitude objects (or values) are associated, the association is either balanced or imbalanced. Despite our complaints, this is, in fact, the way in which Heider originally formulated balance theory. Such a two-valued formulation of balance theory flows from a decision to regard sentiment and unit relations as either positive or negative. There is no consideration of the polarity or strength of a relation or association. Runkel and Peizer point out that such a restriction of balance theory "virtually erases" the distinction between logic and balance.

Much of Runkel and Peizer's discussion is quite technical, but the essential argument can be easily described. Consider the first rectangle in Fig. 14.2. Elements within the universe represented by this rectangle are either associated or not associated; and if they are associated, the association is either positive ($+$) or negative ($-$). The two subsets of positive and negative associations are repre-

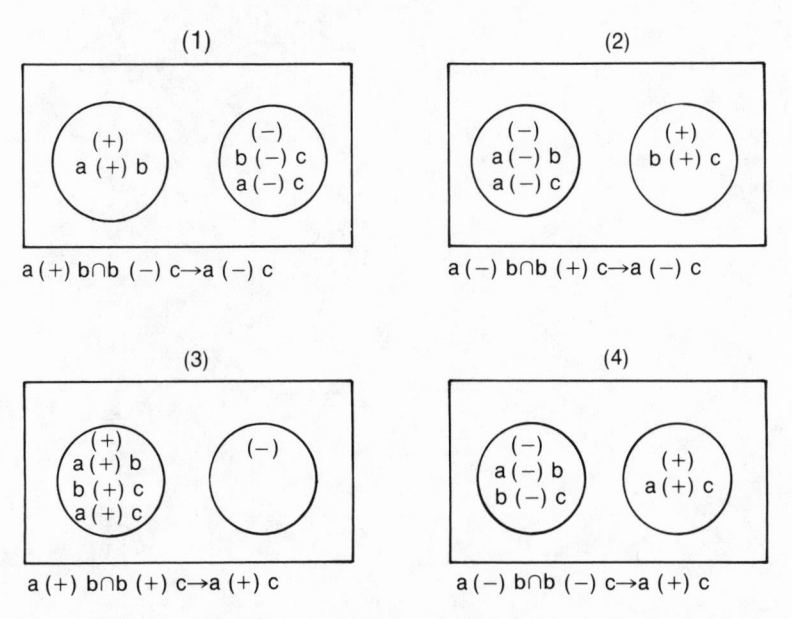

FIG. 14.2.   Logical and balanced implications for a two-valued World.

sented by circles. In this first example, elements a and b are associated in the positive subset and elements b and c are associated in the negative subset. Therefore, it logically follows that if a has a positive association with b and b has a negative association with c, then a has a negative association with c. Using the logical symbols: $a(+)b \cap b(-)c \rightarrow a(-)c$. This is, of course, the now familiar balance implication. The remaining three rectangles illustrate the three additional possibilities; for example, if a has a negative association with b and b has a negative association with c, then a has a positive association with c.

The realization of the conceptual bridge between balance theory and logic on one hand and balance theory and hedonism on the other suggests that balance theory specifies something of basic importance regarding human cognition. It appears, however, that just as two-valued logic is not accurately descriptive of all human thought, so two-valued balance theory is not a totally accurate description of p's phenomenology. Thus, what is needed is a theoretical formulation that goes beyond logic to what Runkel and Peizer refer to as a "many-valued" balance theory. Such a quantified statement of balance theory will need to include all the relevant semicycles in p's phenomenology and also take into account the numerous modes of imbalance resolution. The theoretical challenge is thus a formidable one.

15 Acceptance, Yielding and Impact: Cognitive Processes in Persuasion

Martin Fishbein
University of Illinois at Urbana-Champaign

Icek Ajzen
University of Massachusetts-Amherst

Information is the essence of the persuasion process. Receivers are exposed to a persuasive communication in the hope that they will be influenced by the information it contains. The effectiveness of the message depends in large measure on the nature of this information. It is therefore somewhat disconcerting to find that message content has rarely been the focus of much attention. Construction of an effective message has been left largely to the intuitive devices of the investigator, whereas most communication and persuasion research has been devoted to the discovery of factors that influence the effectiveness of the message as constructed. To be sure, order of presentation, type of appeal (e.g., high versus low fear appeal), and other global features of the message have not escaped scrutiny; but few attempts have been made to take account of the items of information actually contained in the message.

The purpose of the present chapter is to draw attention to the decisive role played by the content of a persuasive communication. In the first section we note that a message can be designed to influence different kinds of target variables, and we propose to distinguish between belief, attitude, intention, and behavior as potential targets of a communication. We discuss the differential determinants of these variables and demonstrate that the choice of a given target sets the stage for the selection of information that must be made part of the message in order to bring about the desired change. The chapter's second section turns to a consideration of the cognitive processes that mediate the effects of a message. The structure of a typical persuasive communication is described, and a distinction is made between acceptance of arguments contained in the message, yielding to those arguments, and possible impact effects on arguments not mentioned in the message. Acceptance, yielding, and impact are viewed as the critical cognitive processes in any persuasion situation. In the final section, the role of various source, message, and receiver factors is discussed. Our goal, then, is to present a general information-processing theory of persuasion and to try to show how this theory can provide a unifying framework for research on communication and persuasion.

TARGET VARIABLES AND
THEIR DETERMINANTS

Persuasive communication is usually viewed as a means of bringing about attitude change, where the term *attitude* is used in a generic sense to refer not only to a person's affective feelings toward some object but also to his or her cognitions (or beliefs) about the object and conations (or behavioral tendencies) with respect to the object. Given this all-inclusive definition of *attitude,* investigators have felt free to select their dependent measures in an arbitrary fashion, so long as the measure appeared to be related to the issue under consideration. The result has been an accumulation of largely contradictory and inconsistent research findings with few (if any) generalizable principles of effective communication.

In marked contrast, we have advocated a clear distinction between belief, attitude, intention, and behavior; and we have tried to show that, although interrelated, these variables have different determinants and are affected in very different ways by the same experimental manipulations (Fishbein & Ajzen, 1972, 1975). Because the effectiveness of a persuasive communication depends on the extent to which it influences the determinants of the target variable selected by the investigator, we must turn our attention to the determinants of the different kinds of target variables.

Influencing Intentions and Behaviors

Consider, first, a message designed to change the receiver's behavior. Over the past 10 years, we have developed and presented evidence in support of a theory for the prediction of behavioral intentions and overt behavior (Ajzen & Fishbein, 1970, 1972, 1973, 1980; Fishbein, 1967, 1972, 1973, 1980; Fishbein & Ajzen, 1972, 1975). A detailed description of this work is beyond the scope of the present chapter; the following is a brief outline of the theory of reasoned action.

According to the theory, an individual's behavior (B) is determined by his or her intention (I) to perform the behavior in question. Assuming that no unforeseen events have produced a change in plans, a measure of the individual's intention should be the best single predictor of behavior. The behavioral intention is viewed as a function of two factors: (1) the individual's attitude toward performing the behavior under consideration (A_B)—that is, his or her positive or negative feeling toward performing the behavior; and (2) the individual's subjective norm with respect to that behavior (SN)—that is, his or her belief that most important others think the individual should or should not perform the behavior. The relative importance or weights (w) of the attitudinal and normative factors may vary from intention to intention and from person to person. These relationships are shown in Equation 1.

$$B \sim I = f[w_1 A_B + w_2 SN] \tag{1}$$

It can be seen that a person's intention is a function of two factors—one personal in nature (A_B), and the other reflecting social influence (SN). Unlike the traditional tricomponent view of attitudes mentioned in the introduction, attitude toward a behavior is defined in our model strictly in terms of a bipolar evaluative or affective dimension. A person's attitude toward a behavior is simply that person's subjective judgment that performing the behavior is good or bad, desirable or undesirable.

Looking for the determinants of this attitude, we are led to a consideration of beliefs. According to the theory of reasoned action, an individual's attitude toward a behavior is a function of his or her *salient* beliefs about performing the behavior. A belief about any object may be defined as the person's subjective probability that the object has a given attribute. The terms *object* and *attribute* are used in the generic sense, and they can refer to physical objects, people, actions, events, or any other discriminable aspect of the individual's world. In dealing with attitudes toward a behavior, the object of interest is, of course, performance of the behavior. The attributes associated with this object are usually the consequences or outcomes of performing the behavior in question. To illustrate, a person might indicate a 60% chance that her smoking leads to lung cancer. The belief object "my smoking" is linked to the attribute "leads to lung cancer" with a belief strength or subjective probability of .60.

Generally speaking, a person who believes that performing a given behavior will lead to mostly positive outcomes will hold a favorable attitude toward the behavior, whereas a person who believes that performing the behavior will lead to mostly negative outcomes will hold an unfavorable attitude toward it. Specifically, the belief that performing a given behavior will produce a certain outcome is assumed to contribute to the attitude toward the behavior in direct proportion to the subjective probability or strength of the belief (b) and to the degree to which the outcome is positively or negatively evaluated (e). The relation between a set of n beliefs about performing a behavior and attitude toward that behavior is summarized in Equation 2.

$$A_B = f[\sum_n b_i e_i] \tag{2}$$

It can be seen that A_B is determined by the sum of the products of belief strength and attribute evaluation over the set of beliefs that are salient for the individual.

The second factor in our model for the prediction of intention and behavior is the subjective norm (see Equation 1). Subjective norms with respect to a given behavior are defined as people's beliefs (i.e., subjective probabilities) that most people who are important to them think they should or should not perform the behavior in question. According to the theory of reasoned action, these general subjective norms are determined by salient normative beliefs (*b*) concerning the perceived normative prescriptions of specific referent groups or individuals (e.g., spouse, co-workers) and motivations to comply with each of these referents (*m*). The relation between a set of *n* salient normative beliefs and the subjective norm is given in Equation 3. It can be seen that each

$$SN = f[\sum_{n} b_i m_i] \tag{3}$$

belief as to what a specific referent thinks the person should do is multiplied by the person's motivation to comply with the referent, and the resulting products are summed across the *n* salient normative beliefs.

Our discussion up to this point is summarized in Fig. 15.1. Consider now the implications for any attempt to influence behavioral intentions or overt behavior. It can be seen in Fig. 15.1 that in the final analysis, behavior change is brought about by producing changes in beliefs. By influencing beliefs about the consequences of performing the behavior, we can produce change in the attitude toward the behavior; and by influencing beliefs about the expectations of specific referents, we can affect the subjective norm.[1] A change in the attitudinal or normative component is likely to be reflected in the person's intention and behavior, provided that the component affected carries a significant weight in the prediction of the intention. Two possible strategies suggest themselves with regard to the beliefs that are singled out for change: We can try to influence some of the beliefs that are salient in a subject population or try to introduce novel, previously nonsalient, beliefs.

A concrete example may be instructive. Suppose that a communicator would like to induce receivers of his message to donate blood. He would first assess the salient beliefs held by members of his target populations,[2] obtaining a set of beliefs concerning the perceived consequences of donating blood (e.g., "Donating blood is painful"; "Donating blood helps save lives") and a set of normative beliefs with respect to this behavior (e.g., "My spouse thinks I should not donate

---

[1] Note that attitudes toward the behavior can also be influenced by changing outcome evaluations and that subjective norms can also be influenced by changing motivations to comply with specific referents. However, in both cases we must ultimately again change beliefs. Because the evaluation of an outcome is nothing but the person's attitude toward that outcome, influencing the evaluation requires changing beliefs about the outcome. Although the determinants of motivation to comply are less well understood, it seems clear that a person's motivation to comply with a given referent is some function of his or her beliefs about that referent and, in particular, beliefs about the referent's power, expertise, trustworthiness, and so forth.

[2] For a description of belief elicitation procedures, see Fishbein and Ajzen (1975).

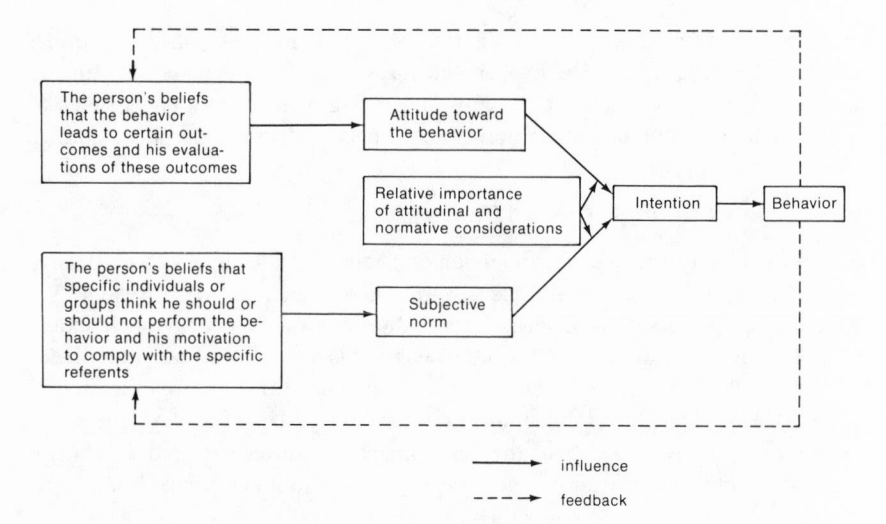

FIG. 15.1. Schematic presentation of conceptual framework for the prediction of intentions and behaviors.

blood''; ''My friends think I should donate blood''). In constructing his message, the communicator could attempt to change any one of these salient beliefs in the appropriate direction. Thus, in an attempt to produce more favorable attitudes toward this behavior, he could try to decrease the receivers' subjective probabilities that donating blood is painful. Alternatively, he could try to induce a more favorable subjective norm by increasing the receivers' subjective probabilities that their spouses think they should donate blood.

The second strategy open to the communicator involves the introduction of previously nonsalient beliefs, or of beliefs that were salient for only a minority of the target population. For example, the communicator might induce the receivers to believe that donating blood will assure them of access to the blood bank should they ever need it and that the President of the United States thinks they should donate blood. Assuming that receivers positively evaluate having access to the blood bank, this communication should produce more favorable attitudes toward donating blood. In the same manner, if the receivers are highly motivated to comply with the President, the communication should result in more favorable subjective norms.

It is important to note that the attitude toward a behavior is based on the *total set* of beliefs about performing the behavior and that the subjective norm is similarly determined by the *total set* or normative beliefs. Although a message that is successful in changing one or two beliefs concerning the behavior's consequences may at times influence the person's attitude toward the behavior, it will often have little or no effect, because the changes produced as intended may be offset by unexpected changes in other relevant beliefs. For the same reason, a message that influences one or two normative beliefs may also have little effect on the subjective norm. Only when the message brings about a shift in the summed products across the total set of underlying beliefs can it be expected to influence attitudes or subjective norms and, hence, intentions and behavior.

Influencing Attitudes Toward Targets

Rather than being directed at an intention or a behavior, the target of a persuasive communication is often an attitude toward some object, person, or event. We have already discussed the determinants of attitude toward a behavior. It should be clear, however, that attitude toward a behavior is but a special case of attitudes in general. We have singled it out for special consideration because of its importance as a determinant of intentions and, indirectly, behaviors. Nevertheless, everything we have said about the determinants of attitude toward a behavior can, with slight modifications, also be applied to attitudes toward any other target.

Consistent with the work of other theorists (Rosenberg, 1956; Zajonc, 1954), Fishbein (1963) has argued that an attitude toward any object is based on beliefs (b) that the object has certain attributes and evaluations (e) of those attributes. The terms *object* and *attribute* are again used in the generic sense to refer to any discriminable aspect of the individual's world. As noted earlier, we use the phrase "attitude toward a *behavior*" when the object refers to an action; attitudes involving other objects will be called "attitudes toward *targets*" (A_t). Our present discussion deals with the determinants of a person's attitude toward a target.

Consider, for example, an individual's attitude toward another person. According to Fishbein's theory, the individual's attitude toward the other person will be favorable if most of his or her salient beliefs link that person to such positively evaluated attributes as "intelligent," "friendly," "reliable," and so forth. Conversely, if the individual associates mostly negative attributes with the other person ("dishonest," "rude," "immature"), his or her attitude toward that person will be negative.

The relation between a set of n salient beliefs about a target and attitude toward that target is shown in Equation 4. This equation is identical to Equation 2 except that the beliefs involve the perceived attributes of

$$A_t = f[\sum_n b_i e_i] \tag{4}$$

some target rather than the perceived outcomes of a behavior. Considerable evidence in support of this theory has been presented elsewhere (e.g., Ajzen, 1974, 1977a; Fishbein, 1963; Fishbein & Ajzen, 1975; Jaccard & Fishbein, 1975).

The implications of this theory for persuasive communication are obvious. If a message is to influence a person's attitude toward a target, it must produce change in the beliefs on which this attitude is based—that is, in the person's beliefs concerning the target's attributes. Again, a change in one or two beliefs may be insufficient to influence the person's attitude, which is based on the entire set of salient beliefs about the target. As in the case of attitude toward a behavior, the communicator may attempt to influence some of the beliefs that are salient in the receiver population or to introduce new, previously nonsalient beliefs about the target under consideration. Whichever strategy is chosen, the communicator's message must contain information that links the target to various positive or negative attributes if it is to be successful in bringing about change in the receivers' attitudes toward that target.

Influencing Beliefs

In many cases, a persuasive communication is intended to influence a given belief held by the potential receivers of the message. For example, the communicator may attempt to persuade receivers that smoking is dangerous to their health or that TV violence produces antisocial behavior. To understand how changes in beliefs of this kind can be brought about, we have to examine the processes whereby beliefs are formed. Although certain attributes of an object or person (size, texture, color, and the like) can be directly observed, most of our beliefs are the result of some inference process (see Fishbein & Ajzen, 1975). Another person's intelligence or honesty, the likelihood that smoking causes emphysema, the probable stimulation of the economy following a tax rebate—all have to be inferred from other information we have about the person, behavior, or policy under consideration. In other words, inferential beliefs are the *conclusions* we reach on the basis of other relevant beliefs we happen to hold.

Various processes have been proposed whereby inferential beliefs may be formed. Perhaps the best known of these is the logical syllogism where the conclusion follows logically from a major and minor premise. For instance, the beliefs "Communists are atheists" (major premise) and "Albanians are Communists" (minor premise) imply the conclusion "Albanians are atheists." As described in Chapter 13, McGuire (1960c) and, more recently, Wyer and Goldberg (1970) have provided evidence for syllogistic reasoning among receivers of a persuasive communication.

Other formal probability models, including Bayes's theorem, have also been found to provide quite accurate predictions of inferential belief formation (see Fishbein & Ajzen, 1975; Peterson & Beach, 1967; Wyer, 1974). According to all these models, people base their inferences on a consideration of their prior beliefs and the relation of those beliefs to the conclusion. Although people appear capable of using such relatively sophisticated information-processing strategies, recent theory and research suggest that they often employ rather simple cognitive processes that rely more on intuition than on formal logic (Abelson, 1976; Ajzen, 1977b; Kahneman & Tversky, 1974). A review of this work is beyond the scope of the present chapter; suffice it to note that even though the proposed information-processing strategies differ markedly from those implied by the formal probability models, it is again assumed that inferences are based on the prior beliefs held by the individual and on his or her perception of the relations between these beliefs and the conclusion under consideration (for a review, see Slovic, Fischhoff, & Lichtenstein, 1977).

As far as construction of a persuasive communication is concerned, therefore, a message that is intended to change the subjective probability of a conclusion must influence beliefs that are known to be inferentially related to that conclusion. It must again be noted that any given conclusion may be based on a set of many different beliefs held by the individual; change in only one or two of those beliefs may fail to have the desired effect on the conclusion. As before, the communicator may concentrate his or her efforts on changing some of the underlying beliefs that are salient in the receiver population or on attempting to introduce new beliefs known to be inferentially related to the conclusion. For example, the message might be directed at major or minor premises of a syllogism already familiar to the audience, or it might attempt to present new major and minor premises from which the conclusion in question could be inferred.

We have argued that a persuasive communication may be designed to change either a belief (conclusion), an attitude, an intention, or a behavior. Whatever the target of the communication, we have seen that in the final analysis, we have to change the set of beliefs on which it is based. From our point of view, a message can be effective in changing its intended target only if it influences these *primary beliefs*—that is, the beliefs that are functionally related to (or primary determinants of) the target in question.

It is of utmost importance to realize that the primary beliefs determining intentions and behaviors differ greatly from the beliefs that are functionally related to attitude toward a target, and that both types of beliefs may bear little resemblance to the primary beliefs that are inferentially related to a conclusion. Although obviously not the only possible approach, the conceptual framework just discussed specifies appropriate primary beliefs for any given target variable. Thus, to change intentions or behaviors, the primary beliefs that need to be influenced are beliefs about the consequences of the behavior or normative beliefs with respect to the behavior. In the case of attitude toward a target, the appropriate primary beliefs are beliefs linking the target to various positive or negative attributes. Finally, if the target variable is a belief or conclusion, other beliefs that are inferentially related to the conclusion have to be changed.

STRUCTURE AND CONTENT OF
A PERSUASIVE COMMUNICATION

From our point of view, the purpose of a persuasive communication is to change the primary beliefs that underlie the target variable of interest—be it a conclusion, an attitude, an intention, or a behavior. The present section deals with the cognitive processes that mediate the message's effects on primary beliefs. Before turning to this analysis, however, we must take a brief look at the structure of a persuasive communication.

Structure of a Message

As a general rule, a message consists of two parts: a set of *arguments* and factual *evidence* designed to support the arguments. When the ultimate target variable is behavior (or intention), the message usually also includes one or more recommended actions; when the target is a conclusion, the message typically makes explicit reference to that conclusion.

As an illustration, consider the persuasive communications used by Eagly (1974) in a series of experiments dealing with, among other things, the discrepancy of the source's position from that of the receiver.[3] In one study, this message was used in an attempt to change receivers' acceptance of the conclusion that either 6, 4, or 2 hours of sleep were desirable for the average adult for maximum happiness, well-being, and success in life. In a second study, the same message was used to change the conclusion that the *receiver* (rather than the average adult) should get 6 hours or 1 hour of sleep. After stating the general conclusion, the message proceeded with a series of six arguments, each supported by several items of "factual" evidence. The six arguments can be paraphrased as follows:

1. The amount we sleep is culturally determined and arbitrary.
2. How rested a person feels upon waking up depends on how much "rapid eye movement" sleep he or she gets rather than on the total amount of sleep.
3. A person can sleep fewer hours per day if he or she learns to take naps rather than sleep one 8-hour period.
4. Sleeping for long periods is bad for a person physically.
5. People often sleep as a defensive escape from their problems.
6. Many successful people sleep considerably less than 8 hours.

To bolster these arguments, the message provided various factual items of evidence. For example, the argument that the amount we sleep is culturally determined and arbitrary was supported by the following set of statements:

People believe that 8 hours are necessary because they have been told this is so and have been taught to sleep a lot when they were children. A University of California anthropologist pointed out that in some cultures, the norm is markedly less sleep than 8 hours; while in other cultures, people are expected to sleep even more than in our society. Also anthropologists point out that the amount of sleep people get varies with the season, especially for primitive and peasant peoples who live close

---

[3]We are grateful to Alice Eagly for providing us with the text of her message.

to the land—they sleep when it is dark, so sleep more in the winter. Northern people—like Lapplanders and Eskimos—sleep, according to one study, 1.8 times more in the winter than in the summer. In industrialized civilizations, we are not so affected by these rhythms of nature—sleep patterns become more purely cultural.

In constructing a message of this kind, two basic assumptions are made: (1) that acceptance of the supportive evidence will result in acceptance of the arguments, and (2) that acceptance of the arguments will lead to a change in the target variable. Unfortunately, these assumptions are rarely, if ever, tested. Although investigators will usually try their best to construct an effective message, they have no clear guidelines to aid in the selection of arguments and appropriate evidence. As a result, they may select arguments and evidence that fail to meet the foregoing assumptions; thus, the message may be ineffective.

Some of the difficulties created by this state of affairs can be illustrated with respect to Eagly's sleep communication already described. The same set of six arguments was used in attempts to change quite different conclusions. However, an argument or set of arguments perceived to be supportive of one conclusion may not be perceived as supportive of some other conclusion. It follows that an argument that, if accepted, leads to a change in the conclusion that "6 hours of sleep are desirable for the average adult for maximum happiness, well-being, and success in life" may have much less effect on the conclusion advocating 2 hours of sleep for the same goals, or on the conclusion that the *receiver* should get 6 hours of sleep. The situation would have been even more problematic if the dependent variable had been attitude toward sleep, intention to sleep less, or actual sleeping behavior. The reason for this is that these variables are increasingly removed from the immediate target of the communication. The belief that a certain amount of sleep is necessary is only one of the beliefs that may determine attitude toward sleeping less, which in turn is only one of the two major determinants of sleeping intention and behavior. By traditional criteria, however, any one of these variables could legitimately be considered a target of the communication in question.

Processing of Message Content

According to our approach, the first step in the construction of a persuasive communication is the selection of an appropriate set of arguments. That is, the arguments selected should either constitute some of the primary beliefs underlying the target variable, or they should be known to determine or influence those primary beliefs.

Suppose, for example, that in an attempt to increase the favorability of attitudes toward a presidential candidate, one of the primary beliefs to be attacked is the belief that the candidate will protect the interests of the average citizen. To increase the receiver's subjective probability associated with this belief, the statement could simply be used as one of the arguments in the message. Alternatively, it could be viewed as, say, the conclusion of a logical syllogism. McGuire (1960c) and Wyer and Goldberg (1970) have shown that a syllogistic conclusion can be affected indirectly by exposing receivers to a message that produces a change in the minor premise. To return to our example, imagine we know that our receiver population believes, with a high probability, that if the presidential candidate is compassionate, he will protect the interests of the average citizen. By raising the strength of the belief that the presidential candidate is compassionate, we will indirectly bring about the desired change in the primary belief.

One of the problems in research on communication and persuasion is that arguments are usually selected, not on the basis of a systematic and empirically validated theory, but quite arbitrarily on the basis of intuition and often fallacious assumptions. This can be seen clearly in many messages designed to change one or more specific actions. Empirical research has demonstrated that the assumption of a strong relation between a person's attitude toward a target and any given behavior with respect to that target is clearly unwarranted. [See Ajzen & Fishbein (1977) for a review of research on the attitude–behavior relation.] Still, the arguments of a message intended to influence a specific behavior are often belief statements that link the target of the behavior to various positive or negative attributes. Such a message may be quite effective in changing the receiver's attitude toward the target because the arguments it contains constitute the primary beliefs for this variable, but it is unlikely to have the desired effect on behavior.[4]

As we saw in the first section, to produce a change in behavior or behavioral intention, the primary beliefs that have to be attacked are beliefs about the performance of the behavior. It follows that the arguments included in the message must be statements about the likely consequences of the behavior—and not about the attributes of the target of the behavior. The latter arguments are appropriate only when the attitude toward the target serves as the dependent variable. When the dependent variable is a conclusion, the arguments in the message should be statements of belief known to be inferentially related to the conclusion.[5]

Acceptance, Yielding, and Impact Effects

The mere presentation of an argument (without any supportive evidence) may lead to a change in the corresponding belief of the receiver, particularly if it is a novel, previously nonsalient argument. It is important, however, to distinguish

---

[4]One exception to this rule occurs when the arguments influence not only beliefs about the target but also beliefs about the behavior.

[5]It is not sufficient to simply to *assume* that change in a given belief will produce change in the conclusion. To construct an effective message, it will often be necessary to demonstrate empirically (e.g., in a pilot study) that the argument is in fact related to the conclusion.

between *acceptance* of an argument and *yielding*—that is, change in the corresponding belief.[6] Consider, for example, the argument that "smoking is hazardous to your health." A person may strongly believe (i.e., accept) that smoking is hazardous to one's health without ever having been exposed to the message containing the argument in question. Yielding, on the other hand, refers to the change in acceptance of the belief statement resulting from exposure to the message. Thus, a receiver who shifted his or her subjective probability that smoking is dangerous to one's health from .40 to .70 would exhibit yielding of 30 percentage points on the probability scale.

In addition to acceptance of, and yielding to, a persuasive argument, the presentation of an argument may have indirect effects; that is, it may have *impact effects* on one or more other beliefs that were not explicitly mentioned. For example, suppose that a television commercial contains the statement: "Detergent X is strong." Apart from any possible yielding to this argument, the receiver may also infer that "detergent X is harmful to clothes," and the persuasive effect of the message may be very different from that intended. Clearly, to understand fully the effects of a persuasive communication, it is important to assess not only the receiver's acceptance of, and yielding to, the arguments it contains but also its impact effects on other, unmentioned, primary beliefs.

In other chapters of this book, various cognitive mediating processes are proposed in an attempt to explain the effects of persuasive communication. In fact, the major common theme underlying this book is the premise that the effectiveness of a message is mediated by such cognitive processes. From our perspective, the most essential cognitive processes that mediate persuasion are acceptance, yielding, and impact.

As we have noted, a persuasive communication usually provides a set of arguments as well as factual evidence in support of those arguments. We can now see that the effectiveness of this strategy is contingent on three conditions. First, the receiver must accept and yield to the item of evidence. If the evidence is not accepted as valid, or if it is accepted but involves no change on the receiver's part, it is unlikely to influence acceptance of the arguments it was designed to support. Second, the receiver must view the evidence as related to, or relevant for, the arguments in question. If the evidence is irrelevant to the arguments, the receiver will show little change in beliefs corresponding to those arguments regardless of the extent to which he or she accepts the evidence. In fact, an item of evidence may even have a negative relation to the argument it is intended to support such that yielding to the evidence has a boomerang effect on acceptance of the argument; that is, yielding to the evidence may *reduce* the receiver's subjective probability associated with the argument.

---

[6]The term *yielding* is used here in a more restricted sense than is usually implied (e.g., McGuire, 1968b). We use it to refer solely to change in the subjective probability associated with a belief corresponding directly to a statement contained in the message.

It is worth noting that yielding to the evidence and a positive relation between evidence and argument do not ensure that exposure to the evidence will increase *yielding* to the argument. The reason for this is that the receiver may accept the argument in question even before being exposed to the supportive evidence, in which case no change in his or her belief corresponding to the argument can be expected.

Finally, presentation of supportive evidence may not only produce yielding to the arguments contained in the message but may also have an impact on other primary beliefs. Because change in the dependent variable is a function of change in the total set of underlying primary beliefs, the possibility of impact effects must also be taken into account.

A major problem in research on persuasive communication is that none of these issues have received much attention. To reiterate our position, we postulate a set of primary beliefs as the determinants of any given target variable—be it a belief, an attitude, an intention, or a behavior. To be effective, a message must influence these primary beliefs. The effects of the message can be direct in that it can produce acceptance of, and yielding to, the arguments it contains. Equally important, the message may have indirect effects by its impact on primary beliefs not explicitly mentioned in the communication. Some of these impact effects may, of course, be intended; but others may not have been foreseen, and they may produce unexpected results.

To illustrate the importance of impact effects, consider Janis and Feshbach's (1953) classic study on fear appeals. In this experiment, high school students were exposed to a lecture on dental hygiene. For the most part, the lecture presented information about the consequences of improper dental care, as well as five specific recommendations concerning appropriate oral hygiene practices. For example, in the high-fear condition the possible outcomes of improper dental care were described, among other things, as pain from toothaches; cancer, paralysis, and blindness; having teeth pulled and cavities drilled; sore, swollen, and inflamed gums; and "decayed" teeth.

Although not explicitly mentioned in the message, it was apparently assumed that the receivers of this communication would draw the inference that performing the five recommended actions (e.g., spending about 3 minutes on each brushing, brushing after breakfast rather than before) will help prevent the negative consequences of improper dental care. From the communicator's point of view, such an impact would have been highly desirable and was probably intended. Unfortunately, the investigators did not measure changes in beliefs concerning the consequences of the recommended toothbrushing practices. It is possible that receivers were unwilling to accept the implied claim that proper ways of brushing one's teeth are sufficient to prevent the frightening consequences mentioned in the high-fear message. If so, the message would not have had the desired impact effect—a possibility that might explain the relatively weak influence the high-fear message was found to have on behavior.

Another possible explanation for the ineffectiveness of the high-fear appeal is its potential for additional unintended and undesirable impact effects. Assuming that the message's main arguments were accepted, a receiver of the high-fear appeal would come to believe that improper dental care leads to having teeth pulled; to cancer, paralysis, and blindness; to sore, swollen, and inflamed gums; and so on.[7] Since it is unlikely that the receiver's own dental hygiene practices have actually resulted in any of these consequences, the individual would probably infer that he or she has been taking proper dental care and thus would see no need to change toothbrushing behavior. Again we can only speculate about these possible impact effects, because no measures of such cognitive responses to the message were obtained.

A study by McArdle (1972; see also Fishbein, 1976) provided more direct evidence for both anticipated and unanticipated impact effects. In this study, receivers were exposed to one of three messages designed to persuade alcoholics to sign up for the Alcoholic Treatment Unit (ATU) in a VA hospital. Each message consisted of 10 arguments. The *fear appeal* linked "continued drinking" with 10 undesirable consequences, such as ruined physical and mental health, a poorer relationship with family and employer, less personal attention from the hospital staff, and less freedom to leave the hospital. The *negative message* linked "not signing up for the ATU" to the same 10 undesirable consequences, where the *positive message* linked "signing up for the ATU" to 10 desirable consequences, which were constructed by reversing the undesirable consequences. For example, signing up for the ATU was said to lead to improved physical and mental health, a better relationship with family and employer, and so forth. The final paragraph in all three messages recommended that in order to avoid the negative consequences (or attain the positive consequences), receivers should sign up for the ATU.

It can be seen that taken together, the three messages contained a total of 30 arguments. Each receiver was exposed to 10 of these arguments but not to the remaining 20. Following exposure to one of the three messages, receivers' acceptance of each of the 30 arguments was assessed and compared to acceptance of the arguments by a control group of respondents who had not been exposed to any communication.

The results showed that the three messages had very different direct and indirect effects. Whereas receivers were found to yield to the arguments in the positive and negative messages, they showed little yielding when they were exposed to the arguments in the fear appeal. These latter receivers were no more

---

[7]Note that these beliefs about the consequences of improper dental care are primary beliefs determining attitudes toward improper dental care. It follows that if the arguments were indeed accepted, receivers would hold negative attitudes toward improper dental care. Nevertheless, we may find little effect on actual toothbrushing behavior since the primary beliefs of relevance for that behavior would be beliefs about the consequences of the specific recommended practices. As noted, such beliefs could have been affected only through impact effects.

likely to accept the arguments concerning the negative consequences of continued drinking than were the no-message control subjects. More important in the present context, the three messages also produced differential impact effects on the acceptance of arguments not contained in a given receiver's message. Exposure to the positive message not only produced yielding to the arguments contained in that message but also produced changes in beliefs corresponding to the arguments contained in the negative message, and vice versa. For example, receivers who increased their belief (in comparison to the control group) that signing up for the ATU would improve physical and mental health also tended to increase their belief that not signing up for the ATU would ruin physical and mental health. These impact effects thus tended to bolster the direct effects of the positive and negative messages.

In contrast, the fear appeal's impact effects were unexpected, producing changes contrary to those intended in receivers' beliefs about the consequences of signing up and not signing up for the ATU. Receivers exposed to the fear appeal were *less* likely to believe that signing up leads to positive consequences or that not signing up leads to negative consequences than were subjects in the control group. As might be expected, these detrimental impact effects were reflected in behavior. Whereas the positive and negative messages increased the percentage of receivers who signed up for the ATU, the fear appeal actually produced a reduction in that percentage.

It can be seen that it is of the utmost importance to assess both the direct and indirect effects of a message on primary beliefs. Without such data, we will often be at a loss to explain why a persuasive communication has had little effect on our dependent variable (as in the case of Janis & Feshbach's high-fear appeal) or even a boomerang effect (as in the case of McArdle's fear appeal).

We realize, of course, that a message is usually pilot tested before being used in experimental research, and that most messages do show some effect on the dependent target variable in comparison to a no-message control group. However, few attempts have been made to explain why some persuasive communications are found to be effective whereas others constructed for use in experiments are found to be ineffective and have to be discarded (see, for example, Millman, 1968). According to our analysis and, we might add, from a practical point of view, this question is probably more important than any other issue investigated in persuasive communication research.

It is an encouraging sign that the present book is devoted to "cognitive responses in persuasion." Recent years have witnessed an increased awareness of the need to study the receiver's reactions to the content of a persuasive communication, and we welcome this general trend. From our point of view, however, it appears that many of these efforts are somewhat misdirected. Consider, for example, the question of reception (Eagly, 1974; McGuire, 1968b; Millman, 1968). It is assumed that, to be effective, a message has to be attended to and comprehended; that is, accurate reception is considered a necessary, although not sufficient, condition for change in a dependent variable. In contrast, our analysis suggests that reception may not even be a necessary condition for change. What determines change in a target variable is the extent to which the message influences the primary beliefs relevant to that variable. Receivers may fail to pay much attention to a message; they may misperceive it or misunderstand it and still display change in primary beliefs. For example, all a message may do is stimulate receivers to think about the issue under consideration, and this may be sufficient to bring about change in some of the primary beliefs and, hence, in the dependent variable (see, for example, Tesser & Conlee, 1975). Alternatively, receivers may pay little attention to the factual evidence provided by a communicator (and thus fail a reception test), but they may still yield to that communicator's main arguments. Although a measure of reception can provide some useful information about the persuasion situation, it is clearly not a precondition for persuasion. The failure of empirical research to reveal a strong or consistent relation between reception of message content and amount of change produced by the message (see McGuire, 1968; Table 5.1, Chapter 5) supports this line of reasoning.

In a similar manner, such cognitive responses as counterarguing and derogation of the communicator are also not essential mediators of persuasion. Although it is possible to treat such responses as impact effects, the beliefs affected may not be primary determinants of the dependent variable in question. In fact, counterarguing and derogation may sometimes be correlates or consequences, rather than antecedents, of acceptance and yielding (see Chapter 5 for a discussion of this issue). Although measures of these responses can shed light on various peripheral aspects of the persuasion situation, they often do little to further our basic understanding of the factors determining persuasion. As in the case of reception, subjects can yield to arguments and change their primary beliefs whether or not they engage in counterarguing or derogation of the communicator. More important than these issues are the direct and indirect effects of the message on the primary beliefs that determine the target variable under consideration.

EFFECTS OF INDEPENDENT VARIABLES

Beginning with the work of Hovland and his associates (Hovland, Janis, & Kelley, 1953), most research on persuasive communication has investigated variations in source, message, and audience factors and how they influence the effectiveness of a given message. Much of the work stimulated by the Hovland school has been based on the assumption that experimental manipulations of source, message, or receiver factors can influence change in the dependent target variable to the extent that the manipulations affect either reception of the message or yielding to what is received (see McGuire, 1968b).[8] At first glance, this approach appears quite reasonable, and it seems to have come as a considerable surprise that the concerted efforts of many able and well-trained investigators have produced few, if any, consistent findings concerning the effects of various independent variable manipulations. (For reviews of this literature, see Eagly & Himmelfarb, 1974; Fishbein & Ajzen, 1972, 1975; McGuire, 1969a.) In the remainder of this chapter we examine the role of source, message, and receiver factors in light of the theory of persuasion we have outlined in the preceding sections.

We have argued that the effectiveness of a persuasive communication depends on its direct and indirect effect on the primary beliefs that serve as the basis for the target variable that is to be changed. It follows that a source, message, or receiver factor will influence the effectiveness of a given message only if it affects the extent to which the message exerts direct or indirect effects on primary beliefs. To be more specific, manipulation of an independent variable can influence the effectiveness of a message in several ways. It can affect acceptance of, and yielding to, the evidence provided in support of the communication's major arguments. Alternatively, it can affect acceptance of, and yielding to, the arguments themselves. Finally, the experimental manipulation can influence the extent to which the message has an impact on primary beliefs not mentioned by the communicator.

To take a concrete example, consider the effect of variation in communicator credibility on the effectiveness of a message designed to change attitudes toward nuclear power plants. Suppose that the main arguments contained in the message deal with various dangerous and otherwise undesirable attributes of nuclear power plants and that each argument is supported by some factual evidence. Because the arguments represent primary beliefs with respect to attitudes toward nuclear power plants, yielding to those arguments should produce more unfavorable attitudes. In addition, attitudes toward nuclear power plants could change if the message had impact effects on primary beliefs not explicitly mentioned.

Attributing this message to sources of varying credibility might very well influence the amount of attitude change produced. Factual evidence presented by an expert (e.g., a nuclear physicist) may be more accepted and yielded to than the same factual evidence provided by a nonexpert (e.g., a street vendor). Assuming that the factual evidence is related to the arguments, greater yielding to the arguments might result. A credible communicator may also be more likely to produce acceptance of, and yielding to, the arguments themselves. Moreover, it is conceivable that in comparison to a message attributed to a communicator of low credibility, a message attributed to a highly credible source will have more

---

[8]Note that in this context, *yielding* is used in its broadest sense to refer to all processes (other than reception) that mediate change in the dependent variable. For a discussion of the differences between this broad view of the term *yielding* and our more restricted use, see Fishbein and Ajzen (1975).

impact effects on unmentioned primary beliefs. For example, the message might argue that nuclear power plants produce radioactive waste. Whatever the acceptance of this argument, when it is attributed to a credible communicator, it may also lead receivers to infer that nuclear power plants are dangerous, whereas this inference might not be made in the case of a low-credibility source.

Of course, all these possibilities are pure speculation unless measures of changes in primary beliefs (both mentioned and unmentioned) are obtained. It may turn out that, in a particular study, variations in communicator credibility have no effect on the amount of change in primary beliefs that result from exposure to the message. In that case, we would also expect no effect of the credibility manipulation on the amount of change in attitudes toward nuclear power plants.

Efforts to discover variables that influence the effectiveness of a given communication have involved a multitude of source, message, and audience factors. Elsewhere (Fishbein & Ajzen, 1975) we have suggested that factors of this kind may serve to facilitate or inhibit acceptance or arguments contained in the message and that they may be viewed as having a cumulative effect on the overall facilitation present in the situation. We have further proposed that acceptance of a given argument increases with overall facilitation and decreases with the discrepancy between the belief of the source and that of the receiver. One implication of this approach is that such potentially facilitating factors as source credibility or the receiver's self-esteem will influence acceptance of an argument primarily at high levels of discrepancy. Another implication is that the addition of any given facilitating factor may do little to increase acceptance of an argument if the overall facilitation in the situation is very high to begin with.

These considerations may help explain some of the inconsistent and inconclusive research findings on communication and persuasion. However, a much more fundamental difficulty inherent in this research may be responsible for many of the conflicting findings reported in the literature. As we have emphasized repeatedly, investigations of the persuasion process have, with a few notable exceptions (e.g., McGuire, 1960c; Wyer & Goldberg, 1970), tended to neglect the content of the message: the items of factual evidence, their relevance for the major arguments, and the relation of those arguments to the dependent target variable. It is our contention that the effect of varying a source, message, or receiver factor cannot be understood in isolation from the content of the message. An independent variable found to be positively related to the effectiveness of one message may be found to have little influence on, or even be negatively related to, the effectiveness of another message.

Message Factors

The validity of this argument is most readily apparent with regard to manipulations of message factors. Over the years, investigators have examined the relative effectiveness of various types of persuasive appeals. Studies have compared "rational" to "emotional" messages; high-fear appeals to low-fear appeals; one-sided to two-sided communications; stating the conclusion of a message to leaving it unstated; and one order of presenting the arguments to another. None of these factors has been found to have consistent and replicable effects on the persuasiveness of the message.

It is important to note that, except for order of presentation, all message manipulations directly vary the kind or amount of information to which receivers are exposed. For example, we saw earlier that in their high-fear appeal, Janis and Feshbach (1953) linked improper dental care to pain from toothaches; cancer, paralysis, and blindness; sore, swollen, and inflamed gums; decayed teeth, and so on. In contrast, their low-fear message made reference primarily to decayed teeth and cavities as resulting from improper dental care. The same case can be made for rational versus emotional appeals or one-sided versus two-sided messages. Clearly, such variations in type of appeal are confounded with differences in the content of the communication. It follows that any effect of a message manipulation cannot be unambiguously attributed to the message factor in question; instead, it may be due to differences in the information provided. Thus, if a high-fear appeal is found to produce more change (or less change) than a low-fear appeal, this effect may be due, not to differential fear aroused, but rather to the difference in the content of the high- and low-fear messages. In fact, by carefully selecting the arguments and supportive evidence used in the different types of messages, it is possible to construct a high-fear appeal that will be either more effective or less effective than a low-fear appeal. Our foregoing discussion made it clear that a message will be relatively ineffective if it includes evidence unrelated to the arguments, or arguments unrelated to the primary beliefs underlying the dependent variable. Although an investigator will usually try to select equally effective evidence and arguments for the different messages, he or she may unwittingly include more effective evidence or arguments in either the low-fear appeal or the high-fear appeal. Clearly, then, comparing the relative effectiveness of different types of appeal is rather meaningless. Whether one type of appeal is more or less persuasive than another will depend primarily on the content of the messages employed.

Source Factors

Although perhaps less evident, the content of a communication is equally important in regard to the effects of source and receiver factors. Consider, again, the case of communicator credibility. The effects of attributing a message to sources varying in expertise or trustworthiness have been studied more intensely than any other issue in communication and persuasion, with rather mixed results. Although a source low in credibility has seldom been found to produce more change than a high-credibility source, some studies have reported a positive relation between credibility and amount of change, whereas others have reported no difference between high- and low-credibility sources. From our point of view, such inconsistent findings are to be expected, because the effects of source credibility on amount of change will depend on the content of the message employed. It stands to reason that a communication that provides cogent and believable evidence in support of rather novel arguments may influence the target variable irrespective of the source of the communication. In contrast, a relatively weak message may well benefit from the facilitating effect of a highly credible communicator.

Some support for this line of reasoning can be found in a study by McCroskey (1970), who attempted to change attitudes toward federal control of education. In one experimental condition, the message provided strong supportive evidence for its main arguments, and in another condition the arguments were stated with minimal supportive evidence. Variations in source credibility had a significant effect on attitude change only when minimal evidence was provided. When the message contained strong supportive evidence, equal amounts of attitude change were observed. It may be argued that in this condition, receivers changed their primary beliefs on the basis of the supportive evidence, irrespective of the source's credibility.

Research concerning the effects of such other source characteristics as attractiveness or power has, if anything, produced even less consistent findings than research on communicator credibility. We would again propose that factors of this kind may influence amount of change produced by some messages but not by others depending on the content of the message employed.

Receiver Factors

The same is true for factors related to the receiver of a persuasive communication. In fact, it is often not clear why a given individual-difference variable should be related in a consistent fashion to the amount of change produced by a message. Consider the case of self-esteem. It might be suggested that receivers high in self-esteem should have more confidence in the validity of their own beliefs than receivers low in self-esteem and hence be swayed less by the arguments contained in the message. On the other hand, it might also be suggested that high-self-esteem individuals would find it easier to admit that they were wrong and accept the communicator's position than would individuals low in self-esteem. The first hypothesis would predict a negative relation between self-esteem and amount of change, whereas the second hypothesis would predict a positive relation. Similarly conflicting hypotheses could be derived for such other audience factors as intelligence, locus of control, authoritarianism, religiosity, or sex of receiver.

To make matters worse, it again appears likely that factors of this kind will interact with message content in their effects on amount of change produced by the communication. From our point of view, there is no reason to expect systematic effects of receiver variables across all messages and content areas. Consider, again, the case of self-esteem. It is conceivable that a receiver with low self-esteem will, in comparison to a high-self-esteem individual, yield more to forcefully stated arguments, whereas the reverse might be true in the case of arguments stated in a qualified manner. For still other arguments we may find little or no difference between high- or low-self-esteem receivers.

SUMMARY AND CONCLUSION

We have seen that the effectiveness of a communication in bringing about change in some target variable depends first and foremost on the content of the persuasive message. The general neglect of the information contained in a message and its relation to the dependent variable is probably the most serious problem in communication and persuasion research. We have argued that to be effective, the statements contained in a message must either directly or indirectly influence the primary beliefs that determine the target variable that is to be changed. Different arguments have to be constructed for changing a belief or conclusion, an attitude, and an intention or behavior. To increase acceptance of, and yielding to, these arguments, we may add relevant supportive evidence.

In order to understand the effects of such a message, we have to assess acceptance of, and yielding to, the statements it contains, as well as its impact effects on primary beliefs not contained in the message. These cognitive processes—rather than reception of message content, counterarguing, or derogation of the communicator—represent the essence of persuasion.

Manipulations of source, message, or receiver factors may influence the effectiveness of a persuasive communication to the extent that they affect the message's direct or indirect effects on primary beliefs. Whether and how they influence amount of change in the target variable will depend on the content of the persuasive communication. It is unfortunate that so much research effort has gone into assessing the effects of source, message, and receiver factors without much attention to the information contained in the message. We are convinced that the persuasiveness of a communication can be increased much more easily and dramatically by paying careful attention to its content (and the relation of that content to the dependent target variable) than by manipulation of credibility, attractiveness, fear, self-esteem, distraction, or any of the other myriad factors that have caught the fancy of investigators in the area of communication and persuasion.

16 Integration Theory Applied to Cognitive Responses and Attitudes

Norman H. Anderson
University of California-San Diego

NATURE OF
INFORMATION INTEGRATION THEORY

Information integration theory is a unified, general theory of judgment and decision. It has had substantial success in diverse areas of psychology, including person perception, psycholinguistics, attribution theory, and group dynamics, as well as in attitude theory (Anderson, 1974a, 1974b, 1974c, 1978, in press). Attitude theory is viewed as part of a more encompassing theory of judgment and decision. This section outlines basic ideas in the integration-theoretical approach.

The Principle of Information Integration

Multiple causation is a basic theme of the theory of information integration. Virtually all thought and behavior is multiply caused, the resultant of numerous coacting factors. The theory conceptualizes these causal factors in informational terms and assumes that their combined action is governed by a general principle of information integration.

Multiple causation has long been a concern of attitude theory, but it presents difficult problems. When several causal factors are at work, each pushing in different directions, their combined effect is hard to predict or analyze. The usual experimental tactic of showing that factor A has greater effect than factor B is no longer adequate. Quantitative theory is vital to the study of multiple causation.

Multiple causation involves two complementary problems, synthesis and analysis. The problem of *synthesis* or *integration* has already been noted: Given a set of causal factors, how are they integrated to yield the attitudinal response?

361

Analysis considers the inverse causal question: Given an attitudinal response, what was the set of causal factors that produced it? This problem of *analysis,* which is central in attribution theory, is closely connected with the valuation operation discussed later.

The cutting edge of integration theory is *cognitive algebra.* The accumulated evidence has shown that much of human judgment and decision obeys simple algebraic models (Anderson, 1974c, 1978, in press). Establishing an algebraic model provides a formal solution to the problem of synthesis or integration. Moreover, by virtue of *functional measurement methodology,* the model provides a way to dissect the observed response into its effective components. Once established, therefore, the integration model can play a further role in analysis, for it can measure the meaning of the information to each individual.

Cognitive Responses

A basic tenet of information integration theory is that information must be considered in terms of its meaning and value to the individual. If two persons hear the same message, they may disagree about what was actually said. If they agree about what was actually said, they may still disagree about the implications. And even if they agree about the implications, they may nevertheless disagree about their desirability.

These three stages all involve cognitive responses. Even bare comprehension of a message requires a complex of perceptual and linguistic skills. Inferences from the comprehended content require further cognitive operations, as does the evaluation of these implications. This processing chain corresponds to the *valuation operation.* Valuation is harder to study than integration. Although different persons may be expected to obey the same integration rule, they will react differently to the same situation because their perceptions and values are different. A complete determination of what goes on inside the individual head is clearly impossible. Nevertheless, functional measurement makes a unique contribution because it can measure values at the individual level.

Illustrative Example

A concrete example illustrates the foregoing theoretical concepts. For this purpose, the following imaginary experiment is used.

Imaginary Experiment on Attitudes Toward Automobiles. Jim and Dora were in the same psychology class, and both had signed up for the same psychology experiment. When they arrived at the laboratory, they found that the experiment was on automobile preferences. Each car was described by the company that made it, by a line drawing that showed its body style, and by its engine size. Jim and Dora rated each car on a 0–100 scale according to how much they personally would like to own it.

The psychologist had a specific hypothesis in mind. He believed that Jim, Dora, and other people made their attitudinal judgments according to an unconscious averaging process. That is, their preference for any car was an *average* of the values of its various attributes. Some of his colleagues disagreed with him and adhered to a different theory in which the preference for any car was the *sum* of its attribute values. He hoped this experiment would prove his averaging hypothesis and eliminate the rival theory.

Table 16.1 gives a numerical illustration of what went on in the heads of Jim and Dora as they made their judgments. This table represents one car, a four-door Buick sedan with a six-cylinder, 231-cc engine, which both Jim and Dora rated at 50. The numbers in the table show how they arrived at this judgment.

Jim's preference values for the attributes of this particular car are in the top row. His value for make is 20, which is quite low, a consequence of the fact that Jim's present car is a Buick and has given continual trouble. However, Jim puts a high value on four-door sedans because he lives at home as part of a large family. His family is not well-off, so the six-cylinder engine also gets a high value because it gives relatively good fuel economy.

But more is involved than the preference values for the various attributes. Attribute importance must also be taken into account. If paint color had been considered in this experiment, Jim would have given a very high value to green, a very low value to red. However, color would not be nearly as important in his judgment as other attributes.

The integration process, therefore, must allow for attribute importance. The second row of numbers in Table 16.1 represents how important Jim considers these three attributes. Make is most important, followed by body style and engine size, in that order.

According to the psychologist's theory, Jim's attitudinal judgment for this particular car should equal the average of the three attribute values in Table 16.1, each weighted by its importance. Theoretically,

$$\text{Attitude} = [(3 \times 20) + (2 \times 80) + (1 \times 80)]/(3 + 2 + 1).$$

TABLE 16.1
Weights and Scale Values for Auto Preference Experiment

		Make	*Body Style*	*Engine Size*
		(Buick)	(Four-door sedan)	(6-cylinder, 231 cc)
Jim	Value	20	80	80
	Importance	3	2	1
Dora	Value	90	30	?*
	Importance	1	2	0

*The ? sign means that the value of this attribute is indeterminate.

The numerator in this equation is the weighted sum of the attributes. Division by the sum of the weights converts this sum into a weighted average.

Dora's values are different from Jim's. Her family has always owned Buicks, and she thinks very highly of them. She is away from home, however, and much prefers a small coupe to a four-door sedan. Since her family is well-to-do, she has never worried about fuel economy. Indeed, she is largely ignorant of mechanical matters and ignores engine size in her judgment, so that this attribute has indeterminate preference value. Dora's importance values are listed in the bottom row. The importance value of 2 shows that she considers body style to be most *important,* even though she has a low preference *value* for this particular body style. Engine size has zero importance for the reasons just noted.

Despite these differences in personal values, Dora integrates the attributes in the same way as Jim—namely, as a weighted average. For Dora, therefore,

$$\text{Attitude} = [(1 \times 90) + (2 \times 30) + (0 \times ?)]/(1 + 2 + 0).$$

Note that the zero weight on engine size effectively eliminates this attribute, so the indeterminacy of its value is not a problem.

It should be emphasized that the psychologist did not claim that Jim and Dora went through this arithmetic in any conscious way. On the contrary, the calculations just tabulated were considered to be intuitive, at an unconscious level. Thus, the problem the psychologist faced was to deduce from the pattern of their actual preference responses what was going on in some unconscious part of their minds. How the psychologist was able to do this is shown shortly.

Attitudes Toward Persons. As Jim and Dora left the laboratory, Dora mentioned that there was a movie in the student union that evening and wondered if Jim was interested in going. This was unexpected to Jim, for his acquaintance with Dora was limited to this experiment and two sessions of their discussion section in which she hadn't said much. He had to "make up his mind" on the spot with only a little information to go on.

The psychologist heard them talking as they went out the door. He said to himself: "If my theory is correct, then Jim is averaging up Dora's attributes in exactly the same way as he did in my experiment on car preferences." And, in fact, Jim was doing exactly that. His attitudinal judgment toward Dora was an average of three of Dora's attributes:

$$\text{Attitude} = (\text{Personality} + \text{Face Appearance} + \text{Body Style}) \div 3.$$

To prove this attribute equation would be easy if Dora's attributes could be experimentally manipulated as in the auto preference experiment. That is not possible, naturally, and some alternative approach must be sought. Some ways of handling this problem are discussed later in this chapter.

Constructive Process in Attitudinal Judgment

Attitudinal judgments generally involve constructive processes. This is well illustrated by Jim's cogitations when Dora asked him to go to the movie. Because this came unexpectedly, Jim literally had to construct his judgment on the spot, pulling together various bits of information that he recollected about Dora. His immediate judgment thus resulted from an integration of information stored in memory and recalled by the occasion.

Although Jim's immediate reaction was based primarily on information retrieved from semantic memory, the constructive process can be extended to search for additional external information. If Jim had not recalled very much about Dora, for example, he might have stalled, asking Dora questions about the movie, for example, thereby obtaining additional information about Dora as well as about the movie. In theory, all this information is integrated according to the attitude model presented below.

Constructive Process in Formation of Attitudes

The constructive process has a further role, for it is continually operative in the formation or learning of attitudes. If Jim does go to the movie with Dora, then her subsequent behavior provides additional information that is evaluated and integrated in the same way as the earlier information. In this view, the attitude is a dynamic entity, continuously modified by incoming information.

All of Jim's attitudes have this same dynamic, constructive nature. His attitudes toward his parents and siblings, toward his life goals, toward social issues or presidential candidates all develop and change over time. This development of attitudes reflects the continuing process of information integration over the course of his life.

Attitudes and Attitudinal Judgments

As Jim talks to Dora, he is forming an attitude toward her as a movie date. If their acquaintance ripens into friendship, he will be forming attitudes toward her on other judgment dimensions, including politics, conservation, sex, neatness, and thoughtfulness, to name but a few. None of these seems to be "the" attitude. Some of these dimensions are quite unrelated, and no one-dimensional attitude can mediate them all.

A distinction is needed, therefore, between attitudes and attitudinal judgments. The not uncommon practice of defining attitude as a generalized good-bad dimension is inadequate as a basis for general theory (Anderson & Lopes, 1974). An advantage of integration theory is that it makes the attitude–judgment distinction explicit and provides explicitly for multiple dimensions of judgment.

The immediate object of study is the attitudinal judgment. That allows the precision of a dimensional approach without forcing the concept of attitude into the same mold. The concept of attitudinal judgment has explicit definition, both conceptual and operational. Further, attitudinal judgments follow a cognitive algebra much like other judgments.

Attitudes and Behavior

Attitudes are typically poor predictors of behavior, a result that has been repeatedly obtained over 40 years of research. This finding has caused much concern, for it has been widely assumed that a person's behavior is largely controlled by his or her attitudes. In this view, the weak relations between attitude and behavior are not theoretically correct.

A different outlook emerges from information integration theory. From this standpoint, attitudes typically must be weakly related to actual behavior. The reason lies in the fact of multiple causation. For example, Jim's response to Dora's invitation is determined not simply by his attitude toward Dora but also by his attraction to the movie, the pressure of school work, and other forces. This example illustrates a general truth, that an attitude is only one of many determinants of action. Hence attitude and action must be weakly related.

This emphasis on multiple causation is similar to the "other forces" interpretation considered by various writers (see Wicker, 1971). Integration theory has the advantage that it makes a direct attack on multiple causation. Furthermore, it allows for nonattitudinal determinants of behavior, for it places attitudes within a general theory of judgment and decision. Only this more comprehensive approach can provide an adequate analysis of attitudes.

Cognitive Algebra and Construct Validity

Information integration theory has placed heavy emphasis on algebraic models of attitudinal judgment. This approach has been reasonably successful, and the accumulated evidence points to the operation of a general *cognitive algebra*. Beyond the intrinsic interest of discovering that much of human judgment follows simple algebraic rules, these models serve several useful functions in the study of multiple causation.

Perhaps the most important function of the models is that they provide a rigorous basis for construct validity. For example, the common distinction between importance weight and scale value turns out to be rather subtle behind its face validity. The averaging model provides a theoretical basis for disentangling and measuring weight and scale value, and the success of the model provides construct validity for this theoretical representation.

More important is that models provide construct validity for theoretical concepts. Stimulus constructs such as subjective probability and motivation and response constructs such as attitudinal judgment, blame, and intention begin to rise above the level of common sense to become true theoretical entities.

TESTING THE INTEGRATION MODEL: THE PARALLELISM THEOREM

It was the psychologist's hypothesis in the auto preference experiment that Jim and Dora made their attitudinal judgments by averaging the attributes. This averaging hypothesis was illustrated in the numerical examples of Table 16.1. However, the psychologist thought that this averaging process was done intuitively, not as conscious arithmetic, for he believed that people were largely unaware of how their minds operated. But the fact that these judgment processes were unconscious made it difficult to convince some of his colleagues who disagreed with his theory and adhered to a different one.

How could the psychologist find evidence so compelling that his colleagues could no longer doubt his theory? How could he prove to them that the averaging hypothesis must be true? He had two ways to go about this.

The first way would be to ask Jim and Dora to judge each separate attribute of each car. That is, they would rate the preference value and the importance separately for make, for body style, and for engine size. These ratings would be used instead of the numbers listed in Table 16.1. Then it would be straightforward to check whether the weighted average of these attribute ratings was indeed equal to the actual preference value for the auto.

This first way seems direct and simple, but it has numerous quicksands to trap the unwary. To avoid these difficulties, the psychologist developed a second way, which, though seemingly roundabout, is actually much more powerful.

This second way is the functional measurement way. It has a touch of magic about it. If the psychologist's theory is indeed true, then it is only necessary to measure the overall preference for the autos. The pattern of these overall preference judgments will provide a test of the model without one's having to know the values of the separate attributes. Moreover, if the model succeeds in this test, then it can be used to dissect the overall preference into its causal components. Knowing only the overall attitudinal judgment, 50 in the example of Table 16.1, it will be possible to determine what values Jim and Dora placed on each separate attribute. Thus, the psychologist has a way to look into Jim's and Dora's heads to read their unconscious thoughts.

The Averaging Model

At this point, it is necessary to give a formal statement of the averaging model. Attitudinal judgments will ordinarily be determined by several pieces of stimulus information. These may be physical stimuli manipulated by the experimenter as in the auto preference experiment, or they may be memory stimuli as in Jim's evaluation of Dora as a date. Within the theory, each such informational stimulus is represented by two parameters: a scale value s and a weight w. The scale value represents the location of the information on the dimension of judgment—that is, how favorable or unfavorable it is. The weight represents the importance of the information (see following).

One piece of information has unique importance—namely, the prior attitude. Attitudes are seldom constant but change continually as new information is received and integrated. At any point in time, therefore, the prior attitude is that attitude developed in the person's previous history. In the car preference experiment, for example, Jim's evaluation of make would represent a prior attitude formed from his previous experience with Buicks. For going to the movie with Dora, however, his prior attitude was almost nonexistent.

The prior attitude has a scale value and weight just like any other piece of information, and these are denoted by A_0 and w_0, respectively. If the person receives several pieces of stimulus information, his or her new attitude, denoted by A, is theoretically just the average of the prior attitude and the new information. This averaging model can be written:

$$A = [w_0 A_0 + \Sigma w_i s_i]/[w_0 + \Sigma w_i]. \tag{1}$$

Conceptually, this averaging model is quite simple. The numerator is just the sum of the values of all the stimuli, each weighted by its importance. The denominator is just the sum of the weights; its effect is to convert the weighted sum of the numerator into a weighted average. A simple, rigorous test of this averaging model can be obtained with the following parallelism theorem.

The Parallelism Theorem

The parallelism theorem can be illustrated with the experiment of Fig. 16.1. Subjects received pairs of trait adjectives that described a person. They judged how much they would like such a person.

A key feature of this experiment is that the trait adjectives were combined in a "factorial design." This is just a rectangular, row × column matrix, each cell of which represents one combination of adjectives. In Fig. 16.1, the row adjectives are *level-headed, unsophisticated,* and *ungrateful;* the column adjectives are *good-natured, bold,* and *humorless.* Altogether, there are nine pairs of adjectives, each of which describes a different person. Note that each adjective actually appears in three different person descriptions. This interlocking feature of the factorial design provides the key to the analysis.

Look at the nine data points for Subject FF. Each point represents FF's judgment for one of the nine person descriptions. The important feature of these data is that the three curves are parallel. This pattern of parallelism provides the required support for the theoretical model.

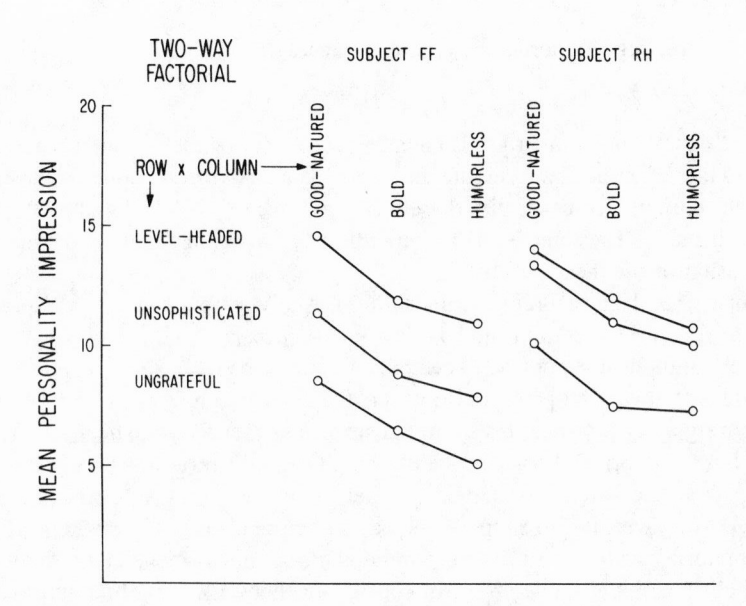

FIG. 16.1. Judgments of likableness of persons described by pairs of personality-trait adjectives. The observed parallelism supports the averaging model of person perception. Data after Anderson (1962). (From CONTEMPORARY DEVELOPMENTS IN MATHEMATICAL PSYCHOLOGY, Volume II, edited by David H. Krantz, Richard C. Atkinson, R. Duncan Luce, and Patrick Suppes. W. H. Freeman and Company. Copyright © 1974.)

The parallelism theorem will be proved for the case of a row × column factorial design like that in Fig. 16.1. Scale values of the row adjectives are denoted by s_i, and scale values of the column adjectives are denoted by t_j. Weights w_1 and w_2 apply to the row and column adjectives, respectively. From Equation 1, the response to the pair of adjectives in row i, column j is

$$R_{ij} = (w_0 A_0 + w_1 s_i + w_2 t_j)/(w_0 + w_1 + w_2). \tag{2}$$

Will the observed data obey this model? This can be readily tested by virtue of the following parallelism theorem.

If (1) the model of Equation 2 is true,

(2) each adjective has the same constant value in all sets, and

(3) the rating response is a linear or "equal-interval" scale,

then (1) the data will plot as a group of parallel curves and

(2) the row means of the design will estimate the row stimulus values on a validated linear (equal-interval) scale.

The proof is straightforward. Consider rows 1 and 2. In column j, the theoretical responses in rows 1 and 2, respectively, are

$$R_{1j} = (w_0 A_0 + w_1 s_1 + w_2 t_j)/(w_0 + w_1 + w_2), \tag{3a}$$

$$R_{2j} = (w_0 A_0 + w_1 s_2 + w_2 t_j)/(w_0 + w_1 + w_2). \tag{3b}$$

Upon subtracting, the terms in A_0 and t_j cancel. Thus,

$$R_{1j} - R_{2j} = [w_1/(w_0 + w_1 + w_2)] (s_1 - s_2). \qquad (4)$$

But the expression on the right is constant, the same for each column j. In other words, the difference between the theoretical values in rows 1 and 2 is the same in each column. Geometrically, therefore, these two rows of data will plot as two parallel curves. The same holds for any other two rows, and that proves the first conclusion of the theorem.

This parallelism theorem provides a remarkably simple and yet very precise way to test the integration model. *Just do the experiment, and plot the data.* Perfect parallelism cannot be expected, of course, because some response variability will always be present. However, the ordinary analysis of variance provides a rigorous statistical test. Parallelism means that the statistical interaction term is zero in principle and so should be nonsignificant in practice.

By this theorem, the observed parallelism in Fig. 16.1 supports the basic model. Moreover, it also supports the other two premises of the theorem. If any one premise is not correct, then parallelism will not in general be obtained. Parallelism is not absolute proof, of course, for there is a logical possibility that two incorrect premises could just counteract each other. As far as one experiment may go, however, these data provide joint support for three conclusions:

1. The averaging model is correct.
2. Each adjective has the same meaning and value regardless of what other adjective it is paired with.
3. The rating response is a linear (equal-interval) scale.

Later work has amply supported the outcome of this initial experiment.

Measurement Theory

The parallelism test is striking because it rests solely on the pattern in the responses. There is no need to get separate scale values for the single adjectives. The success of integration theory rests in part on its ability to bypass stimulus scaling until the basic integration model is established.

Once established, however, the model can be used to obtain the scale values. This is called *functional measurement* because the integration model (*function*) provides the base and frame for scaling. Further, these values are the ones that were functional in the judgments in question (Anderson, 1974c, 1977, 1979).

In fact, it is straightforward to show from Equation 2 that the stimulus values are proportional to the marginal means of the factorial data table. In Fig. 16.1, therefore, the vertical spacing of the three curves represents the relative values of the three row adjectives. For Subject FF, therefore, *unsophisticated* lies midway in value between *ungrateful* and *level-headed*. But for Subject RH, *unsophisticated* is almost equal to *level-headed*. It is no surprise that FF and RH have different values. The point is that functional measurement can measure each subject's personal values.

Actually, two distinct problems of measurement arise in testing the integration model. One is the problem of *stimulus scaling,* which has just been discussed; the other, more fundamental, is the problem of *response scaling.*

The parallelism theorem includes the assumption that the rating response is a linear scale—that is, a faithful reflection of the subject's preference. Rating scales, however, have often been criticized on the ground that the ratings are merely English words and that it is presumptuous to use them as true numbers. The psychological difference between 18 and 19, near the end of the scale, may be quite different from the psychological difference between 11 and 12, near the center of the scale.

Such criticism must be answered. A way must be found to show that the rating response is a true linear scale—or to show that it is not. The answer is simple. It is found in the parallelism theorem itself. Unless the rating scale is a linear response measure, the data will not exhibit parallelism even though the model is true. Observed parallelism therefore supports the validity of the rating response.

Not any rating scale will be a valid linear scale. Certain experimental precautions are employed to avoid known biases (Anderson, 1974c, pp. 245–246; in press). The development of these procedures constitutes an important contribution of the work on information integration theory.

The Meaning Constancy Hypothesis

Parallelism has one final implication: It supports the hypothesis of *meaning constancy,* that each personality adjective has a fixed meaning and value regardless of what other adjective it may be combined with. This is an interesting and important result, especially because it seems contrary to intuition.

Asch's (1946) oft-cited article on person perception was devoted almost exclusively to one thesis, that the adjectives do change one another's meanings. Asch relied essentially on the introspective reports of his subjects, who claimed that an adjective did indeed seem to have a different meaning in one combination than in another. But several lines of research have shown this to be a semantic illusion. It is a strong and compelling illusion, as is the Muller–Lyer arrow illusion, but it is an illusion (Anderson, 1971b, in press).

One line of evidence comes from the parallelism. In Equations 3a and 3b, suppose that the adjective in column j did have different meanings when it was paired with the adjectives in row 1 and row 2. Then the values of t_j in these two equations would not be equal and so would not cancel upon subtraction. Hence Equation 4 would not hold, and so parallelism would not be expected. Observed parallelism, therefore, supports the hypothesis of meaning constancy.

Parallelism in Attitudinal Judgments

Many experiments have found parallelism in support of the averaging model for attitudinal judgment. A few are noted here.

Attitudes Toward Presidents. Figure 16.2 shows judgments of statesmanship of presidents of the United States, each described by paragraphs about his life and deeds. Each point on the solid curves represents the attitude produced by two paragraphs—one of low or high value (as listed by each curve); the other of low, medium, or high value (as listed on the horizontal). The parallelism of the solid curves strongly supports the attitude integration model.

This experiment has added interest because the stimuli were complete paragraphs, not single words. Each paragraph conveyed information about a number of different attributes, with each attribute having its own $w-s$ representation. The parallelism thus supports not only the attitude model but also the molar unitization hypothesis, by virtue of which the complex paragraph can be treated as a unitary stimulus.

Attitudes Toward Outstanding Women. Figure 16.3 shows attitudinal judgments about United States women of outstanding achievement. This experiment (Simms, 1978) was patterned on the foregoing president experiment, and it

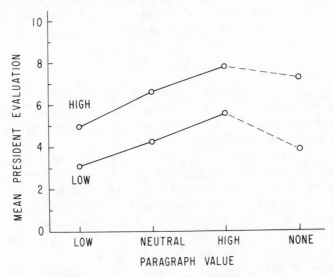

FIG. 16.2. Judgments of statesmanship of U.S. Presidents described by paragraphs of graded value about their lives and deeds. Data after Anderson (1973). (From CONTEMPORARY DEVELOPMENTS IN MATHEMATICAL PSYCHOLOGY, Volume II, edited by David H. Krantz, Richard C. Atkinson, R. Duncan Luce, and Patrick Suppes. W. H. Freeman and Company. Copyright © 1974.)

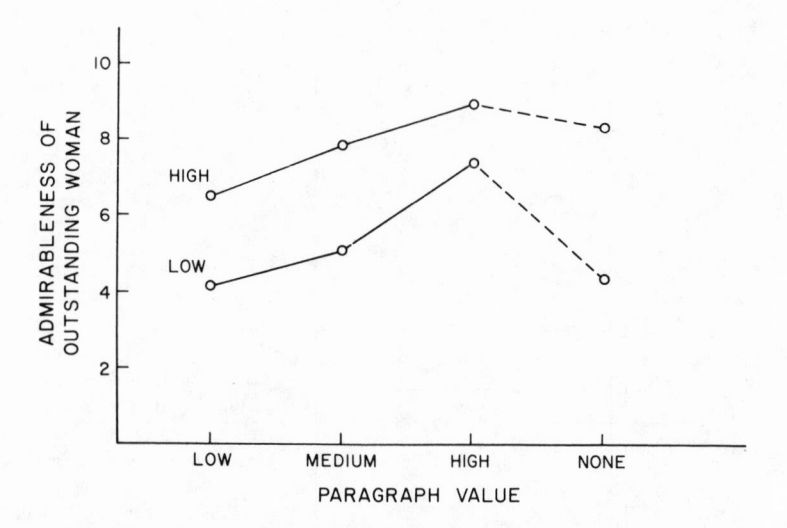

FIG. 16.3.   Judgments of admirableness of outstanding American women described by paragraphs of graded value about their lives and deeds. Data after Simms (1978).

yielded virtually identical results. Further, Simms obtained quite similar results in a laboratory experiment and in a more naturalistic classroom setting.

Person Perception.   Numerous tests of the parallelism prediction have been made in studies of person perception (Anderson, 1974c, in press). One with special interest (Kaplan & Kemmerick, 1974) showed that personal qualities of a defendant in a criminal trial affected judged guiltiness and recommended punishment. Other studies have also shown that legally irrelevant information affects legal decision making (Brooks & Doob, 1975), as expected from the theory.

Attitudes Toward Consumer Products.   Theoretically, the attributes of any consumer product should be integrated by an averaging rule to determine the attitudinal judgment. In the experiment of Fig. 16.4, expectant couples judged the value of diapers characterized by absorbency and durability (Troutman & Shanteau, 1976). Each attribute had four possible values, ranging from low to high. The near parallelism of the four solid curves in the upper panel implies that these two attributes are integrated by averaging.

Averaging versus Adding: Critical Tests

Many investigators have argued that people integrate information by adding rather than averaging. It is easy to show that adding-type models also predict parallelism. The foregoing results support adding and averaging models equally, therefore, and some other test is needed to discriminate between them.

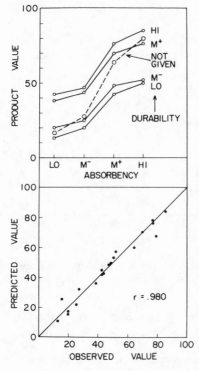

FIG. 16.4. Upper panel: Judged value of diapers by expectant couples as a function of their absorbency and durability; crossover supports averaging model, rules out linear or summation model. Lower panel: Predicted values from linear model plotted as function of observed values from upper panel; weak inference methods of regression analysis fail to reveal that the linear model is incorrect. Data after Troutman and Shanteau (1976). (Copyright 1977 by the American Psychological Association. Reprinted by Permission.)

One critical test between averaging and adding is illustrated by the dashed curve in Fig. 16.4. This curve gives the judgment for diapers specified by absorbency alone, no information being given about durability. Judgments for these same diapers, with the added information that durability was somewhat above average, are given by the second curve from the top labeled M^+. The critical test comes from comparing the dashed curve with the M^+ curve. An adding-type model requires that the M^+ curve lie above the dashed curve at every point. This follows because the added information that the diaper is somewhat above average in durability has a moderately positive value. Adding it should increase the diaper value over that given by the absorbency information alone. Hence, the M^+ curve would have to be above the dashed curve at every point. That is not true; the two curves cross over. No form of adding model can account for this crossover.

The averaging model explains the crossover. Since the M^+ durability information is moderately positive, it should average up the very negative LO value of absorbency, but average down the very positive HI value of absorbency. That is what the data show. The same conclusion follows from comparison of the dashed curve to the M^- curve.

Another critical test appears in the experiment on presidents of Fig. 16.2. The two points at the right connected by dashed lines represent the judgment based on high or low paragraphs alone, 7.2 and 3.8, respectively. When a neutral paragraph is added, it averages both these judgments in toward the neutral center of the scale. Indeed, these values, plotted above the neutral label on the horizontal, were 6.6 and 4.3, respectively. Any adding formulation must predict that both changes will go in the same direction, contrary to fact. In the same way, Fig. 16.3, for attitudes toward outstanding women, also shows that the adding or summation model is wrong.

Besides its theoretical importance, the averaging model has practical relevance for it shows that adding favorable information can actually boomerang to produce a less favorable response. This is something to keep in mind in applying for a job or otherwise trying to make a good impression.

The Set-Size Effect

Two pieces of information that have the same value will produce a more extreme attitude than either one alone (Anderson, 1959). This "set-size effect" seems to pose a critical problem for the averaging hypothesis. Because the average value of the two given pieces of information is the same as the value of either one alone, a simple averaging model would predict the same response. How can averaging theory account for the fact that adding information of equal value produces a more extreme attitude?

The answer to this question is found in the concept of prior attitude, A_0 in Equation 1. This prior attitude is averaged in along with the stimulus information presented by the experimenter. To illustrate, suppose that $A_0 = 50$, the neutral point on a 0–100 scale, and $w_0 = 1$. Suppose that every piece of stimulus information has value 100 and weight 1. From Equation 1, the response to a set of k pieces of information is

$$A_k = (50 + 100k)/(1 + k). \tag{5}$$

This expression takes on the values 50, 75, 83.3, 87.5, ... for 0, 1, 2, 3, ... pieces of information, approaching 100 as asymptote. Equation 5 is the set-size curve for averaging theory. The observed data agree with this theoretical prediction (Anderson, 1974c, p. 254).

Molar Unitization

A fundamental problem in attitude theory concerns the representation of complex stimuli. In a general way, any stimulus can be conceptualized as a set of features or attributes. These attributes may be properties of some object, as in the auto experiment of Table 16.1, or they may be meanings and implications of a person's actions, as in the president experiment of Fig. 16.2. These are the attributes that enter into the construction process.

But this view presents two formidable problems—determining the attributes and assessing their values. One major obstacle is that large parts of the constructive process may never become conscious. Thus, Dora's reactions to Jim's face and voice will depend on subtle, momentary stimuli such as the shape of a smile, the richness of a laugh, or the glint of a filled tooth that give her a warm feeling without her being aware of the causal stimuli. Moreover, such self-reports as she might give are susceptible to halo effects as discussed later. Finally, even if all the relevant attributes were known, it would still be necessary to allow for Dora's personal valuation of these attributes.

How can it be possible to study the effects of unobservable memory traces? How can it be possible to handle stimulus cues whose meanings are strictly personal and different for each subject? If the operative stimuli and processes are not conscious to the experiencing person, how can any external observer hope to unravel them?

Fortunately, there is an effective method of attack based on the principle of *molar unitization*. By virtue of this principle, a complex stimulus can be treated as a cognitive unit. Let w_i and s_i be the weights and scale values of the molecular attributes of some complex stimulus. Theoretically (Anderson, 1971a), the aggregated effect of these attributes can be treated as a unitary molar stimulus, with molar parameters w and s defined by

$$w = \Sigma w_i, \tag{6a}$$

$$s = \Sigma w_i s_i / \Sigma w_i, \tag{6b}$$

where the sum is taken over all the cognitive attributes. Thus, the weight of the molar stimulus is the sum of the weights of its attributes, and its scale value is the mean value of its attributes. In other words, the combined effect of these molecular attributes also has the simple two-parameter, w–s representation and hence can be treated as a molar unit.

Molar unitization has fundamental theoretical importance. Molar analysis does not neglect the molecular effects; they are all represented in the molar outcome. The complex of cognitive responses to the information stimulus—be it a word, an essay, or a video scene—reduces to the simple w–s representation of Equations 6a and 6b. Valid and exact model analyses can thus be made at the molar level without the immediate need to consider the molecular detail.

Molar unitization has special methodological importance because experimental control is feasible with molar level stimuli. Consequently, the integration model can be subjected to the exacting scrutiny of the parallelism theorem. No matter how complex the molecular structure of the stimulus, no matter how intricate the cognitive inferences of the valuation operation, the end result is the simple pattern of parallelism. By virtue of the principle of molar unitization, therefore, information integration theory can provide exact quantitative analyses at the level of the individual person in a direct and simple way.

Source–Message–Receiver Schema

It is useful to relate the information integration model to the source–message–receiver schema studied by the Yale group (see McGuire, 1969a). In this schema, stimuli are considered as messages that come from some source to some receiver. For advertising and for market displays, the application of this schema is straightforward. A favorite device is to attribute the message to some positive source, such as a famous athlete or movie star. Similarly, the visual appearance of the package on the supermarket shelf is a message to the shopper, and much effort may go into making the package attractive. In the same way, Jim's manner of dress is a message to Dora, for it conveys information about Jim's personality.

The source–message–receiver schema is helpful for it calls attention to the basic elements in attitudinal judgment. These elements must be related to the w–s representation and to the integration rules.

Message–Message Integration.   Typically, a person will receive many different messages. Thus, the package on the supermarket shelf contains at least two distinct messages—namely, visual appearance and cost. These different messages have to be integrated with each other and with the prior attitude in order to determine the new attitude. For message–message integration, the averaging model of Equation 1 has had substantial success.

Source–Message Integration.   Reliability or credibility of the source will affect the weight placed on the message. Source-plus-message is thus a unit whose w value is governed by the source and whose s value is governed by the content of the message. Equation 1 then implies that source and message should be integrated by a w-times-s rule as verified in Fig. 16.7.

Message–Receiver Integration.   Even a single message presents an integration problem—namely, that of integrating the message with the receiver's prior attitude A_0. For this case, the averaging model has the simple form,

$$A = (w_0 A_0 + ws)/(w_0 + w). \tag{7}$$

Accordingly, the change in attitude can be written as

$$\text{Attitude Change} = A - A_0 = [w/(w_0 + w)](s - A_0). \tag{8}$$

This is the distance-proportional model (Anderson & Hovland, 1957). The change in attitude ($A - A_0$) is proportional to the distance ($s - A_0$) between message position and prior attitude. The coefficient of proportionality $[w/(w_0 + w)]$ is an increasing function of the weight of the message, a decreasing function of the weight of the prior attitude. A sequence of messages of equal scale value s would produce a learning curve of attitude formation asymptoting at s.

The Concepts of Scale Value and Weight

The concepts of scale value and weight are fundamental to integration theory and deserve more explicit discussion. In attitude research, the scale value of a stimulus can be viewed as its location on the dimension of judgment. This intuitive idea can be made theoretically precise within the averaging model. In the distance-proportional form of Equation 8, no change occurs when $s = A_0$. Conceptually, therefore, the scale value of a stimulus is defined to be equal to the value of that attitude that is left unchanged by the stimulus.

The concept of weight may be intuitively clear in terms of source reliability. A given message generally has greater impact when attributed to a more reliable source. However, source reliability does not of itself argue for any particular position on the dimension of judgment. It cannot be a scale value, therefore, but can readily be treated as a weight.

There are four main determinants of the weight parameter. *Relevance* refers to the implicational relation between the stimulus information and the dimension of judgment. Dora's facial appearance would have high relevance for dating, low relevance for playing tennis. *Salience* refers primarily to attentional factors. Primacy and recency effects have been found to result mainly from salience weighting. *Reliability* is a probabilistic concept, referring to the subjective probability that the information is valid. Source factors typically operate on reliability, as in the experiment of Fig. 16.7. *Quantity* refers to the amount of information. Thus, two messages would generally carry more information than one, and so the pair would have greater weight than either one alone, without regard to scale value.

MEASUREMENT OF COGNITIVE RESPONSES

Measurement of cognitive responses may seem easy, but various quicksands await the unwary investigator. This section takes up results from information integration theory that bear on "thought listing" and other self-report procedures. Some related problems of measurement are also considered, together with some applications of functional measurement methodology.

The Problem of Self-Report

Do people know their own minds? Can they give valid reports about their thought processes? Are they aware of what causes them to think and act the way they do? A good part of the research on cognitive processes reported in other chapters of this book rests heavily on the assumption that people do know their own minds and can give valid lists of their thoughts. Yet this assumption is certainly not true in general, as suggested by the failure of the introspectionist school at the beginning of this century and by the Freudian emphasis on unconscious motivation.

Much of the mind is inaccessible to consciousness, and as the psychology of testimony shows, much of what people do report is not really true.

On the other hand, it does seem that people know something about what is going on in their minds. If a woman says she is happy, hungry, or resentful, there is likely to be some truth in what she says. It is important, therefore, to determine what biases can affect self-reports and what conditions may give rise to valid self-reports.

Halo Effect

Consider the following two person descriptions from Fig. 16.1:

Person A	Person B
good-natured	humorless
unsophisticated	unsophisticated

Subjects form an impression of each person, then rate *unsophisticated* according to "how much you like that particular trait of that particular person." The outcome is simple. *Unsophisticated* is rated as more likable in Person A than in Person B. This "positive context effect," which was discovered early in the work on integration theory (Anderson, 1966), has fundamental importance.

The obvious interpretation of the positive context effect takes the ratings at face value: Because it is rated differently, *unsophisticated* must mean different things in the two persons. This difference in meaning can be explained by assuming that *unsophisticated* has various shades of meaning represented by different implied attributes. In forming an impression of each person, the subject strives for cognitive consistency and accordingly selects those attributes that fit with the other adjective, discounting those that do not fit. Thus, the more favorable attributes of *unsophisticated* would be selected to fit with *good-natured* in Person A, whereas the less favorable attributes would be selected to fit with *humorless* in Person B. In this view, whose main sense originated with Asch (1946), the operative meaning of each adjective depends on the others. This may be called the *change-of-meaning hypothesis*.

But an alternative interpretation is also possible—one in which *unsophisticated* does not change its meaning. This is the *meaning constancy hypothesis* already discussed. The difference in rated likableness of *unsophisticated* is considered as a kind of halo effect, derivative from but not causal in the overall person impressions. The theoretical rationale is straightforward. The subject's first task is to form an impression of Persons A and B, and it is assumed that *unsophisticated* has exactly the same meaning in both cases. The subject's next task is to rate the likableness of the trait *unsophisticated* in each person. This trait rating is colored by the overall impression and so is higher in *good-natured* Person A than in *humorless* Person B.

In this view, the positive context effect is a generalized halo effect. It is analogous to the traditional halo effect, which says that the overall impression of a person acts as a causal mediator in judgments of specific traits. Curiously, the evidence on the traditional halo effect does not rule out an interpretation in terms of change of meaning. A novel contribution of integration theory is that it provides a solid empirical and theoretical base for the halo concept. This work rules out the change-of-meaning interpretation and shows that the general impression of the person acts as a causal mediator in judging specific traits of that person (Anderson, 1974c, in press).

The difference between these two interpretations might seem subtle, but straightforward experimental tests are available to discriminate between them. One such test is based on the parallelism theorem. As pointed out in the discussion of this theorem, the change-of-meaning hypothesis implies systematic deviations from parallelism, whereas the meaning constancy hypothesis implies parallelism. Therefore, the observed parallelism (e.g., Fig. 16.1) rules out change of meaning and supports the halo interpretation. A second kind of test is presented in the experiment on thought listing later.

Two Implications of the Halo Effect

The halo interpretation of the positive context effect has far-reaching implications for cognitive response theory. It represents a proven case in which subjects are unable to give veridical reports about their cognitive processes. On the contrary, they give invalid reports with great confidence in their validity. Cognitive responses cannot be taken at face value, therefore, but require validation. This halo view has recently been adopted by Nisbett and Wilson (1977a, 1977b).

A more particular implication is that halo confoundings may occur whenever judgments are made about attributes of some object. One illustration of this problem appears in the report of Wright (1973) in which women received a message advocating a line of consumer products made from soybeans, and then listed their thoughts about soybeans and the soybean message. Wright followed the usual assumption that these listed thoughts were causal mediators of the final attitude. However, the halo effect implies a causal chain in the opposite direction, in which the initial attitude toward soybeans is a causal mediator in the thought production. These thought lists are ambiguous about causal direction, therefore, and so do not constitute valid explanations of the attitude.

An Experiment With Thought Listing

This experiment (Anderson, 1971b) tested two theoretical issues about thought listing. Subjects received three trait adjectives that described a person and rated the likableness of the person under one of two conditions. In the no-paragraph condition, subjects read the three adjectives and immediately rated the person. In the paragraph or thought-listing condition, subjects first wrote a paragraph describing the person in their own words and only then rated the person. In the paragraph condition, therefore, subjects were generating additional thoughts and inferences about the person.

The first theoretical issue is whether the additional thoughts and inferences generated in writing the paragraph have a causal influence on the attitude toward the person. If so, then the attitude will be based on more information—not just the three given adjectives but also the additional thoughts and inferences. Hence, by virtue of the set-size effect already discussed, the paragraph writing will polarize the attitude, making it more extreme.

No such polarization was found. In fact, the person judgments were a little *less* polarized in the paragraph condition. This finding has been corroborated in a nice series of experiments by Simpson and Ostrom (1975) and in a study of group polarization by Burnstein and Vinokur (1975, Condition III).

This finding implies that the added thoughts and inferences generated in writing the paragraph have no essential causal role in the person judgments. Listed thoughts may sometimes have a causal role, as when a constructive process is involved, but they cannot be taken at face value as causal mediators.

The second theoretical issue concerns the change-of-meaning and halo hypotheses discussed earlier. After rating the person, subjects also rated the likableness of each separate trait of the person. If the adjectives really do affect one another's meanings, they should do so more in the paragraph condition, because these subjects worked over the given stimulus information in much greater detail. This would appear as a larger positive context effect. No such difference appeared in either of two large experiments. This finding provides further support for the halo interpretation of the positive context effect.

Attitude Memory

Verbal messages are common in attitude research. According to the *verbal learning hypothesis,* the attitude is based directly on the verbal material that is learned. This hypothesis, which was dominant in the work of the Yale group (see Chapter 1; McGuire, 1969a), promised a fruitful relation between attitude research and the large mass of research on verbal learning.

The first theoretical alternative to the verbal learning hypothesis seems to be that of Anderson and Hubert (1963), who obtained evidence for two distinct memory systems. In this view, the relevant meaning of an incoming message is extracted and integrated into the developing attitude. Once the meaning has been extracted, the verbal forms of the message are no longer needed and may be stored in a different memory system or even forgotten. The hypothesis of distinct memory systems has been supported by Greenwald (1968a), Rywick and Schaye (1974), and Brink (1974, p. 564), as well as by Dreben, Fiske, and Hastie (1979) and Riskey (1979). This *two-memory hypothesis* also accounts for the generally small correlations between attitude and amount learned, an awkward result for the verbal memory hypothesis.

The operation of distinct memory systems does not mean that attitudes are completely independent of verbal memory. Any attitudinal judgment could depend in part on constructive processes that require a search through semantic memory, especially on some new issue. Nevertheless, this conceptualization of attitude memory stands as another limitation on the usefulness of thought lists in cognitive response analysis.

Methodological Problems

It has been truly said that the correlation coefficient is an "instrument of the devil." Correlation does not imply causation, of course, and the covariance analyses that have been applied to thought-list data have not been appropriate to clarify the causal chain. Moreover, there are several other shortcomings of the correlation coefficient that, though well known, have not received adequate consideration. These problems can only be outlined here (see Anderson, in press; Anderson & Shanteau, 1977; Cooper & Crano, 1974; Eagly & Himmelfarb, 1978, p. 521).

Correlations Depend on Reliability and Range.   The size of a correlation depends not only on the true relation between the variables but also on their reliabilities and on their ranges. Comparisons of two correlations may be invalid, therefore, if the variables differ in reliability or range. Here is an example.

In Jaccard and Fishbein (1975), subjects were read a list of 12 trait adjectives that described a person. Then they wrote down all the adjectives they could remember (the recalled adjectives) and also any other adjectives they thought might characterize the person (the inferred adjectives). Finally, they judged the person on social desirability. A central hypothesis in this experiment was that the inferred adjectives played a causal role in the judgment of the person. Jaccard and Fishbein attempted to prove this by correlating the person judgment with a weighted sum of the values of the separate traits. The correlation was .47 when only recalled traits were used, .67 when both recalled and inferred traits were used. This increase in correlation from .47 to .67 was taken to mean that the inferred traits were causal determinants of the attitudinal judgment. However, the correlation could increase even though the inferred traits had no causal role, merely because their inclusion would increase both reliability and range of the predictor. It may well be true that the inferred traits do have a causal role; but the design and analysis used by Jaccard and Fishbein are incapable of demonstrating this.

Correlations Are Invalid as Model Tests.   A common practice in testing attitude models has been to correlate the predictions from the model with the observed data. When these correlations are high, it is tempting to claim support for the model. Unfortunately, such claims are not valid; extremely high correlations can be obtained from models that are seriously incorrect.

One illustrative example is shown in Fig. 16.4, which appears earlier. The dashed curve in the upper panel is markedly nonparallel to the four solid curves, clear evidence against an adding or summation model. But suppose that this fact is ignored and the adding model is fit to these data. The resulting predictions from the adding model are plotted against the observed values in the lower panel of Fig. 16.4. The points cluster closely around the diagonal line of perfect fit. The correlation between predicted and observed is remarkably high, .980. Thus, correlation and scatter plot seem to support the summation model, even though it is seriously in error. This methodological issue is important in attitude theory. For example, tests of Fishbein's summation model (Fishbein & Ajzen, 1975) rest almost entirely on such correlations (Anderson & Shanteau, 1977, p. 1164; Wyer, 1974, p. 146).

Comparing and Measuring Importance. A frequent question in many areas of psychology is whether one variable is more important than another. It is a surprising fact, not generally appreciated, that this question is very difficult and that the methods of answering it in common use are valid only under very special conditions. The correlation coefficient is subject to the problems noted in the previous section. Percentage of variance accounted for depends on arbitrary choice of stimulus ranges and so has little comparative meaning. Regression coefficients are confounded with scale unit, and standardization does not remove the confounding.

When the averaging model holds, valid comparisons can be obtained (Anderson, 1976a, in press). With suitable design, the weight parameters are on ratio scales with the same unit, and hence are directly comparable across variables. Further, the scale values are on linear scales with common zero and common unit, and hence are also directly comparable across variables. In this way, it becomes meaningful and possible to compare quite distinct concepts, such as money and love.

Measurement of Cognitive Inferences. If you know one characteristic of a person, you can make reasonable guesses about many other characteristics. If you are told that a man is kind, for example, you expect him to be helpful, not critical, probably soft-spoken, cheerful, somewhat older, neatly dressed, and so forth. As this example suggests, there is a ramified network of inferential relations among the vast array of traits and behaviors that might go with any person.

Various attempts to assess the inference network have been summarized by Hastorf, Schneider, and Polefka (1970), but these all use arbitrary ways of measuring inferences. For example, the commonly used trait–trait correlations taken over a group of subjects are almost self-contradictory, because such correlations are nonzero only to the extent that different subjects have different inference values for the traits. Further, the correlations are symmetrical between stimulus and response, whereas trait implications are asymmetrical (Warr & Knapper, 1968, p. 135). None of the other methods are really satisfactory, because, among other things, none of them provides a valid measure of importance or weight.

When the averaging model holds, however, functional measurement may be used to assess the inference network. In the person perception experiment of Fig. 16.1, for example, the inferences are from the listed stimulus adjectives (*unsophisticated, good-natured,* and so on) to the response dimension of likableness. Formally, each inference has the w–s representation in which s is the magnitude of the inference and w its importance for the given dimension of judgment.

This small experiment looks only at a small part of the inference network, but it is straightforward to enlarge the analysis. On the stimulus side, many more adjectives could be used, both singly and in pairs, and other stimuli such as actions, photographs, or videotaped interviews could be included. On the response side, the subject would judge not only likableness but thoughtfulness, cynicism, happiness in marriage, and so on. The end result is a stimulus-response matrix of w–s values. This matrix represents the inference network.

Self-Estimated Parameters

In the method of self-estimated parameters, the subject is asked to make direct ratings of weight and scale value of specified attributes or pieces of stimulus information. If these self-estimates are valid, they can be extremely useful. However, self-estimates are subject to biases, as was illustrated in the halo interpretation of the positive context effect. Clearly, some criterion is needed to determine whether the self-estimates are valid or not.

Integration theory can provide a validational base for self-estimated parameters. By the functional measurement logic, illustrated in the parallelism theorem, integration models can provide validated parameter values. Self-estimated parameters can then be validated by comparing them to these functional values. In the few studies that have used this approach (e.g., Shanteau, 1974, 1975; Shanteau & Anderson, 1969), the self-estimates did moderately well.

This approach has more general importance because it provides a direct measure of any bias in the self-estimates. That can suggest improvements in procedure that will reduce or eliminate the bias. In this way, it may be possible to develop a general methodology for self-estimation. That would be valuable if not vital for situations in which attributes and information are not under experimental control so that the parallelism theorem is not applicable.

An alternative way to validate self-estimates is to employ them in the integration model. By functional measurement logic, success of the model provides joint support for the model and for the self-estimated parameters. Applications of this method are rare. Although many investigations have used self-estimates, nearly all have relied on the invalid correlation methods already discussed and have failed to provide the necessary test of goodness of fit. However, two successful applications are given in the next section on integration-theoretical analyses of group discussion and of dating.

SIX APPLICATIONS OF INTEGRATION THEORY

Group Discussion

Group discussion is an important area for attitude research. Group discussion affects attitudes in dating couples, in the family, and at every social level. All group members are oriented toward their own goals and use various arguments to support those goals or to modify another's goals. The informational flow in the group discussion plays a basic role in the formation and change of members' attitudes.

It is not easy to study group discussion, however, for the informational flow is complex and largely uncontrolled. The impact of one group member on another is fragmented over time; controlled by interpersonal affect, by motivations to influence and to conform; dependent on prior knowledge; and conditioned by expressive factors such as clarity of thought and eye contact. Thus, the attitude of each group member reflects a time-dependent process whose detailed molecular structure seems close to unknowable.

Nevertheless, simple analysis is possible with the methods of information priming and self-estimated parameters, together with the concept of molar unitization. In the following experiment (Anderson & Graesser, 1976), each of three subjects in a group was initially given a different paragraph of information about some U.S. president. This information priming provides a needed measure of experimental control. The subjects then verbally exchanged and discussed their information and evaluated the president on statesmanship.

For theoretical analysis, each person–paragraph combination is treated as a molar unit. Consider Member 1 in the group. Although his paragraph may require a complex evaluation process, it can still be treated as a molar unit, exactly as in the president experiment of Fig. 16.2. This paragraph information can therefore be represented by a molar scale value and molar weight, denoted by s_1 and w_1. Person 1 also receives information from Member 2, this being an amalgam of Member 2's paragraph and personal opinion. Even though the transmission of this information is intricately embedded in the entire discussion, its resultant effect can be represented as a molar unit, with parameters s_2 and w_2. Similarly, the impact of Member 3 on the attitude of Member 1 can be represented with molar parameters s_3 and w_3. Theoretically, therefore, the final attitude of Member 1 should obey the averaging rule,

$$A = (w_1 s_1 + w_2 s_2 + w_3 s_3)/(w_1 + w_2 + w_3).$$

For simplicity, the prior attitude A_0 is omitted in this equation, but it was included in the actual analysis. Analogous equations hold for the attitudes of Members 2 and 3, although, of course, their parameter values will be different.

Each subject was also asked, in effect, to self-estimate his or her own parameters. Thus, Member 1 judged the scale value of his or her own paragraph and of

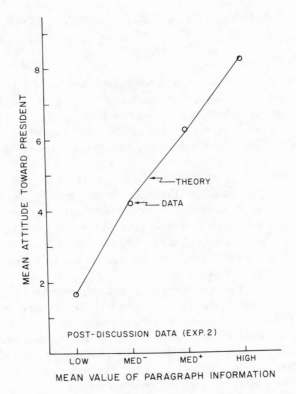

FIG. 16.5.   Observed (open circles) and predicted (solid line) attitudes developed in group discussion. Predictions based on integration theory model in conjunction with self-estimated parameters. Data after Anderson and Graesser (1976).

the positions presented by Members 2 and 3. Analogous judgments were made of importance. These self-estimates may then be substituted in the right side of the foregoing expression to obtain a predicted value of Member 1's final attitude. If subjects give valid self-estimates, and if the averaging model is correct, then this predicted value of A should equal the actual observed value of A.

This test of the theory is shown in Fig. 16.5. The data points lie very close to the theoretical curve. This experiment thus provides promising support for the integration-theoretical approach to group discussion. Rigorous, quantitative analyses can be obtained even for the intricate informational field of a group discussion. An extension to group bargaining is given by Graesser (1977).

Group Polarization (Risky Shift)

Group discussion tends to accentuate preexisting opinion. If the average attitude of the members is positive (negative) prior to discussion, then it will typically be more positive (negative) after discussion (see Chapter 9). To an informational view, group polarization presents two puzzles. The first puzzle is that it occurs even though no new information is injected into the group. Where does the information come from that is presumed to mediate the changes in members' attitudes?

A plausible answer to this first puzzle is that each individual member contributes information that is new to other members. Discussion does not change the information pool of the group, but it does increase the information pool for the individual members. This interpretation was developed by Vinokur and Burnstein (1974) and Bishop and Myers (1974), and their work illustrates a good application of thought-listing procedures (see Chapter 9).

But a second puzzle remains. Exactly how does this sharing of information make the group attitude more extreme? Intuitively, that might seem obvious: Direct analogy to the set-size effect says that more information of the same value will produce a more extreme attitude. But the set-size effect is only an empirical result, and a theoretical interpretation is still needed.

The simplest averaging rule is not adequate. Suppose that the scale value of the information transmitted by each member is equal to the value of his or her attitude. Pooling this information will increase attitudes for some group members and will decrease attitudes for others. Thus, the attitude of each member will move toward the average attitude. The average attitude, however, will remain constant, and so no polarization will be obtained. The model of Vinokur and Burnstein (1974) has a similar flaw and so does not really explain group polarization (Anderson & Graesser, 1976, p. 219).

However, averaging theory can account for group polarization if the information transmitted by each member is more extreme than his or her attitude. That might seem odd, but it actually follows from the theory. To illustrate the theoretical rationale, consider a simplified case in which each member initially has just one piece of information. Assume that all members have different pieces of information but that every piece has the same value s. From Equation 7, each member's prediscussion attitude A can be represented as a weighted average of prior attitude A_0 and information value s:

$$A = w_0 A_0 + ws. \qquad (w_0 + w = 1)$$

The essential assumption is that A_0 is less extreme than s. Although this need not always be true, it seems justified for the experiments in question on the basis of experimental studies of the set-size effect in similar situations (Anderson & Graesser, 1976; Kaplan, 1977; Kaplan & Miller, 1977).

Now when the members transmit their information, each receives from the others information of value s. This is integrated with their prediscussion attitude A to form the postdiscussion attitude. Because s is more extreme than A, the discussion will polarize each member's attitude.

Figure 16.6 provides a quantitative test. Subjects listened to acted but realistic group discussions deliberately constructed to contain specified proportions of positive to negative arguments (Ebbesen & Bowers, 1974). The shift in attitude

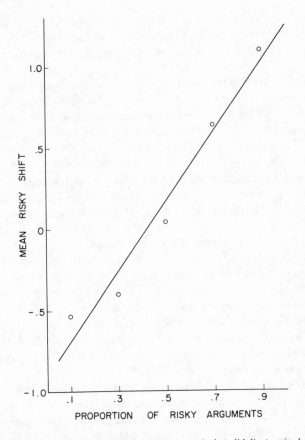

FIG. 16.6.   Observed (open circles) and theoretical (solid line) attitudes developed in a risky shift experiment. Predictions from integration theory model. Data after Ebbesen and Bowers (1974).

is approximately a linear function of argument proportion, in line with theoretical prediction (Anderson, 1971a, p. 191).

In this way, the averaging model can provide a consistent account of group polarization. Further predictions are that polarization should increase with group size, that discussion will make the group more homogeneous in attitude, and that amount of polarization will be an inverted-U function of initial attitude, in agreement with available data (see Anderson & Graesser, 1976, pp. 218–221, who also discuss active effects of group discussion).

Justice in the Courtroom

A seminal extension of the concepts of information integration theory has been made in a study of bail setting by Ebbesen and Konečni (1974, 1975). Their work has exceptional significance, for its theoretical and social relevance and also for its exploration of methodological problems in analyzing field data.

Bail Setting as Information Integration. An accused person posts bail to stay out of jail while awaiting trial. That is a hardship, for the accused must often borrow at high interest from a bail bondsman. Social justice requires that bail should not be excessive but graded to each individual. A more severe crime indicates higher bail, as does a more serious prior criminal record. An accused with stronger job-family ties is less likely to jump bail and so deserves lower bail. In addition, both the defense and district attorneys make specific bail recommendations. This and other case information must be integrated by the judge in arriving at a decision.

How well do the judges do their integrations? Apparently, not very well.

The Judge's Ideal of Justice. Bail setting involves many subjective factors. Different judges will evaluate the same information in different ways and reach different decisions. Each judge has his or her own ideal of justice. Integration theory provides a ready way to determine a judge's ideal of justice. Hypothetical but realistic cases may be constructed using factorial design as illustrated in the experiments of Figs. 16.1 and 16.2. These cases may be presented to each judge in chambers. Because the information is under experimental control, the analysis is straightforward. Theoretically, the judge's decision should obey the averaging rule for information integration. Ebbesen and Konečni followed this procedure in their initial study, and the results were consistent with averaging theory.

The Judge's Courtroom Decisions. In the courtroom setting, the information about the accused is not listed in neat order on a sheet of paper as it was in the experimental study just described. Under courtroom pressures, with many distractions, the judge cannot give the same careful attention to each case that would be possible in the privacy of chambers. Hence, the judge's decisions from the bench must be expected to fall short of his or her ideal of justice.

This expectation was more than fulfilled. The main trend of the bail decisions in the courtroom cases was simple: The judge's decision appeared to depend largely on the recommendation of the district attorney. In turn, the recommendation of the district attorney depended largely on the severity of the crime. Prior criminal record had essentially no effect. These results disagree sharply with the ideal of justice.

Potential of Bail-Setting Studies. Bail setting has exceptional potential as an area of study, not only for social relevance but also with respect to two major problems in analysis of naturalistic data. First is the relevant variable problem. When the variables are not controlled experimentally but are coded by the investigators, as with the courtroom observations, some relevant variable may be overlooked.

This problem arose in the interpretation of a paradoxical interaction in the courtroom decisions. For mild crimes, bail was set lower for cases with stronger job-family ties, as is just. But for more severe crimes, bail was set much higher for cases with stronger job-family ties, contrary to justice. Ebbesen and Konečni gave an ingenious interpretation of this paradoxical interaction in terms of the averaging model. It cannot be completely ruled out, however, that the paradoxical interaction resulted from a hidden variable, such as race, that was not included in the coding of the case information.

A great advantage of bail setting is that defining the relevant attributes is about as simple as one could hope for in a field setting. The three case variables of severity of crime, prior record, and job-family ties are the main determinants. They did very well in the predictive model for the judges' decisions, leaving little unexplained variance. Only a few other attributes, such as race, age, or appearance (Brooks & Doob, 1975), would seem likely to play any role. Thus, the problem of determining the relevant variables can probably be essentially solved for the bail-setting situation.

The second methodological problem is the correlation-versus-causation conundrum. The strong dependence of the judge's decision on the district attorney's recommendation may have been correlational, not causal. That is, the judge may have evaluated and integrated the case information independently of, but in the same manner as, the district attorney. This correlation–causation problem also seems tractable for bail setting, and Ebbesen and Konečni took some important steps to resolve it.

The bail-setting situation has additional advantages. The decision task is simple as social decisions go, and substantial data can be gathered at reasonable cost. The numerical dollar response facilitates analysis for individual judges. Overall, the bail-setting situation offers an exceptionally attractive base for development of theory and method. Such development could provide a valuable model for other less tractable field situations.

Research Strategy.   The bail-setting investigation nicely illustrates the usefulness and need for laboratory-type experiments jointly with naturalistic field studies. The averaging rule became important in the interpretation of the courtroom data. However, it could not have been established without experimental studies that allowed control of the stimulus information.

Ebbesen and Konečni, it should be noted, took a somewhat different view of research strategy. Indeed, they concluded that their initial experiment was misleading because different results were obtained from the courtroom data. Ebbesen and Konečni (1975) suggested that the judges in their chambers "may have attempted to present themselves as unbiased [p. 810]," as though they were somehow covering up a courtroom bias. The present view is that the judge was trying to do an honest job in both situations. In this view, the judge's decisions in chambers represent his or her ideal of justice. An explanation for the difference in courtroom decisions would be sought, not in the judge's character, but in the information field prevailing in the courtroom.

The judge's mind presumably operates in the same basic way in chambers and on the bench. The same integration model should apply in both situations. The difference in the judge's decisions in the two environments would reflect differences in the w–s parameters caused by differences in the information field. The information was laid out in compact form in the controlled experiment but not in the courtroom, where the flow of information is complex; and in fact, some major piece of information was missing in about 35% of the cases. Much might be accomplished for social justice, therefore, just by providing the judge on the bench with a summary sheet of relevant information, as in the controlled experiment.

Moreover, the integration model can be used in treatment. Judges may well be unaware that they virtually limit their attention to the recommendation of the district attorney. The model analysis can make this clear and confront judges with their actual decision models. The contrast between a judge's ideal and real models would provide a useful aid to improvement. This gives another reason for a research strategy of joint experimental–naturalistic studies.

Source Effects

Any message has some source, implicit or explicit, and source characteristics such as expertise or credibility will influence the integration process. A senior thesis conducted in the writer's laboratory by Becky Wong (1973), with able guidance from Michael Birnbaum, provides striking support for an averaging interpretation of source effects.

In this experiment, hypothetical persons were described by two acquaintances, each of whom contributed one trait adjective that was high, medium, or low in likableness value. Source credibility was manipulated by specifying how long the acquaintance had known the person: 1 meeting, 3 months, or 3 years. This source credibility variable is assumed to affect the weight parameter.

Theoretically, the response should obey the equation:

$$R = (w_0A_0 + w_1s_1 + w_2s_2)/(w_0 + w_1 + w_2), \tag{9}$$

where s_1 and s_2 are the scale values of the adjectives contributed by Source 1 and Source 2; w_1 and w_2 are their respective weights; and A_0 and w_0 represent the prior attitude or "initial impression." If Equation 9 is averaged over the three values of s_2, the term in s_2 drops out because the average of the low, medium, and high adjectives from Source 2 is approximately zero. Further, because the person is hypothetical, A_0 is also near the neutral zero value. Accordingly, Equation 9 reduces to the following approximate form:

$$R = [w_1/(w_0 + w_1 + w_2)]s_1. \tag{10}$$

Three predictions follow from this equation and are illustrated in Fig. 16.7.

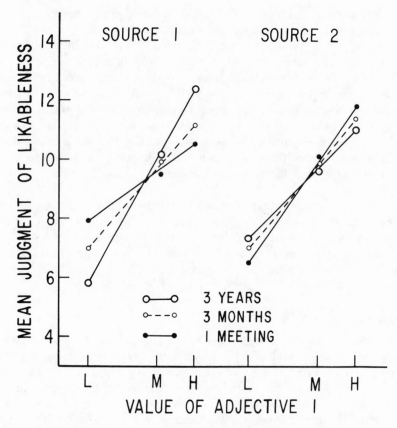

FIG. 16.7.   Judged likableness of persons described by two trait adjectives of
varied value, each contributed by one of two sources of varied reliability. Linear
fan patterns in each panel predicted by averaging model, which also accounts for
the inverse effect of reliability of Sources 1 and 2. Data after Wong (1973).

First, consider how the credibility information about Source 1 is integrated
with the trait adjective contributed by Source 1. Equation 10 can be considered as
a multiplying model, s_1 times the function of w_1 in the brackets. Hence, the data
should plot as a linear fan (Anderson, 1974c, 1976a). This linear fan pattern is
clear in the left panel of Fig. 16.7.

Second, consider how the credibility information about Source 2 is integrated
with the trait information given by Source 1. Again Equation 10 can be considered as a multiplying model, s_1 times the function of w_2 in the brackets. For this
case also, the data should plot as a linear fan, and this prediction is verified in the
right panel of Fig. 16.7.

Third, note that the effect of source credibility goes in opposite directions in
the two panels of Fig. 16.7. That agrees with Equation 10, as the term in brackets
is a direct function of w_1, an inverse function of w_2.

This experiment also provided support for the concept of prior attitude. Birnbaum, Wong, and Wong (1976) and Birnbaum and Stegner (1979) give further details and supplementary work, and Birnbaum (1976) reports a replication for intuitive prediction.

The Distraction Effect

It is an odd fact that distraction can actually increase the persuasive impact of a message that attacks one's attitudes (Chapter 3). Festinger and Maccoby (1964) had fraternity members listen to an antifraternity speech. Subjects were more persuaded by the speech when they simultaneously watched a humorous silent film than when they did not. This outcome is surprising; the film would be expected to distract the subjects from the arguments in the speech, thereby reducing its persuasive impact.

To explain this result, Festinger and Maccoby assumed that distraction did not interfere with the message but did inhibit subvocal "counterarguing" that helped defend beliefs against attack. Counterarguing is thus seen as a separate process, one that occurs after message evaluation and that subtracts from the effect of the message itself. In addition, belief threat is necessary to produce counterarguing.

An Integration-Theoretical Approach.   In the present theory, counterarguments may occur as part of the normal valuation operation *regardless of belief threat* (Farkas & Anderson, 1976). Counterarguing is thus not a distinct process from message reception, as Festinger and Maccoby assumed. Instead, distraction has a unitary effect of interfering with the one operation of evaluating the information in the message.

The present informational analysis has many similarities to the positions of Regan and Cheng (1973) and Petty, Wells, and Brock (1976) and is much indebted to their work. Regan and Cheng made the key observation that distraction could have opposite effects for different messages, depending on their informational structure. Analogous results were obtained by Petty et al., who concluded that distraction operated by interfering with the dominant cognitive response to the message. This conclusion, however, is almost tautological; the important questions concern the nature of this cognitive processing.

For this purpose, the message is viewed as an aggregate of molecular arguments (Anderson, 1971a, p. 198), each with its own w-s representation. From Equation 1, the attitude A produced by the message is then,

$$A = [w_0 A_0 + \Sigma w_i s_i]/[w_0 + \Sigma w_i],$$

where the sum is taken over all molecular arguments in the message.

Distraction is assumed to affect the valuation operation that determines the w-s parameters in this equation. These w-s parameters control the attitude. The key question, therefore, is how distraction affects the valuation operation. This can occur in various ways, both obvious and subtle, and can best be illustrated by a molecular look at some specific messages.

Petty et al. found opposite effects of distraction for different messages. Both messages advocated the same tuition increase, an unpopular issue with the Ohio State students who were subjects. When the message contained strong arguments ("hard to counterargue"), distraction decreased attitude change; when the message contained weak arguments ("easy to counterargue"), distraction increased attitude change. Only means–end arguments are considered here. A more detailed discussion, including source credibility arguments, is given in Anderson (1976b).

Means–End Arguments.   In a means–end argument, the tuition increase is justified as a means toward some end. In model terms, scale value represents the desirability of that end; weight represents the importance of that end to the subject.

Means–end arguments abound in both messages. The strong message refers to the "potential of becoming one of the great state universities," the need to recruit "quality" faculty, and so forth. The weak message refers to the "potential of becoming better" and the need to "beautify the campus"; it concludes with a superficial argument about the need to improve classroom lighting. The weights and scale values of these means–end arguments are obviously greater for the strong message. The critical question, however, concerns distraction.

The main assumption in the present interpretation is that there are two successive stages in the valuation operation. The first stage is an immediate affective reaction to the face value of the argument. The second stage involves a more leisurely, thoughtful consideration of the pragmatic merits of the argument. This two-stage assumption has special importance for the valuation of the weak message. Two separate cases must be considered.

First, the effective scale values of weak-message arguments may be positive, as would seem to apply in Experiment 1 of Petty et al. For example, consider an argument from the weak message such as: Classroom lighting must be improved because it is inadequate and because a number of students have reported headaches. From its affective, surface content, this argument has moderately large w–s parameters. With more time for thought, however, the listener may realize that the lighting actually seems to be quite adequate, and that "a number of students" may not be very many. This pragmatic stage would thus reduce the w–s parameters of this argument. Distraction, of course, would interfere especially with the more complex processing of the second, pragmatic stage. For the weak message, therefore, distraction would actually produce more attitude change.

This same two-stage valuation operation would, of course, also be at work in the strong message. But there, the second, pragmatic stage would reinforce the first, affective stage and so increase the w–s parameters. The strong message, therefore, would have greater impact with no distraction.

It is also necessary to consider the case in which the effective scale values of the weak arguments are negative—that is, opposite to the ostensible position of the message. This case may seem odd, but it appears in Experiment 2 of Petty et al., in which the weak message argued for a tuition decrease using means–end arguments that the subjects would see as undesirable (e.g., money can be saved by compelling students to take unpopular, low-enrollment courses). In this case, the first, affective stage is reinforced by the second, pragmatic stage. Distraction should therefore reduce the persuasive impact of the message and the amount of attitude change. But the direction of change is opposite to the ostensible position of the message. Relative to this ostensible position, therefore, the resultant attitude will be more favorable in the distraction condition. The two-stage interpretation thus provides a complete account of the two experiments of Petty et al.

Research Strategy.   This integration-theoretical analysis indicates the need to shift research emphasis from the molar to the molecular. Distraction can act in either direction, depending on the nature of the arguments. Any molar outcome is possible, depending on the construction of the message. The molecular thought-listing procedures have some uses, but they have great trouble with correlation-causation. Experimental control of the molecular structure of the message is essential for theoretical analysis.

Real progress will require development of molecular-level arguments of simple structure that can be used in constructing molar messages to specification. This is necessary because distraction, not to mention other factors, will have different effects on different molecular units. Without knowledge of the informational structure of the molar message, little prediction or understanding will be possible. This approach has relevance far beyond the distraction effect itself, for the valuation operation is present in any attitudinal judgment.

Cognitive Algebra in Dating

The studies of dating judgments by Shanteau and Nagy (1976) have two important implications. First, they reveal a cognitive algebra of dating judgments. Second, they illustrate how self-estimated parameters can be employed to analyze cognitive responses.

Utility Model for Dates.   In the first experiment, females were shown photographs of a male together with a verbal statement of the probability that he would go out with them. The theoretical hypothesis was that the information should be integrated by a multiplying rule from utility theory:

Date Preference = Probability × Physical Attractiveness.

The success of this model can be seen in Fig. 16.8, which plots the mean response to the 35 probability–photo combinations. This graph has a simple story and tells it clearly. If the multiplying model is correct, then the data curves should form a linear fan of diverging lines. That is exactly the form they take, thus supporting the model.

Testing the Model with Cognitive Response Data. In the second experiment, females received only a photograph of the male. It was assumed that the photograph would elicit two cognitive responses: one of physical attractiveness, the other of the probability that the male would go out with them. Hence, the same utility model should apply as in the first experiment. Unlike the first experiment, however, these two cognitive responses are not under experimental control, and so the simple linear fan analysis of Fig. 16.8 cannot be used. Accordingly, the method of self-estimated parameters was applied to get numerical values for each cognitive response.

The observed date preferences for three representative females are given by the solid curves in Fig. 16.9. The theoretical predictions, obtained by using the self-estimated parameters in the model analysis, are given by the dotted curves. Data and theory agree very closely.

As these results illustrate, the work of Shanteau and Nagy brings a new level of theoretical penetration to the study of face perception and dating. At the

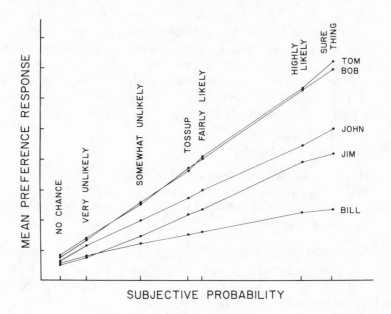

FIG. 16.8. Date preferences of women for men as a function of physical appearance and the probability that the men would ask them for a date. Linear fan shape supports the multiplying model—subjective probability × value. Data after Shanteau and Nagy (1976).

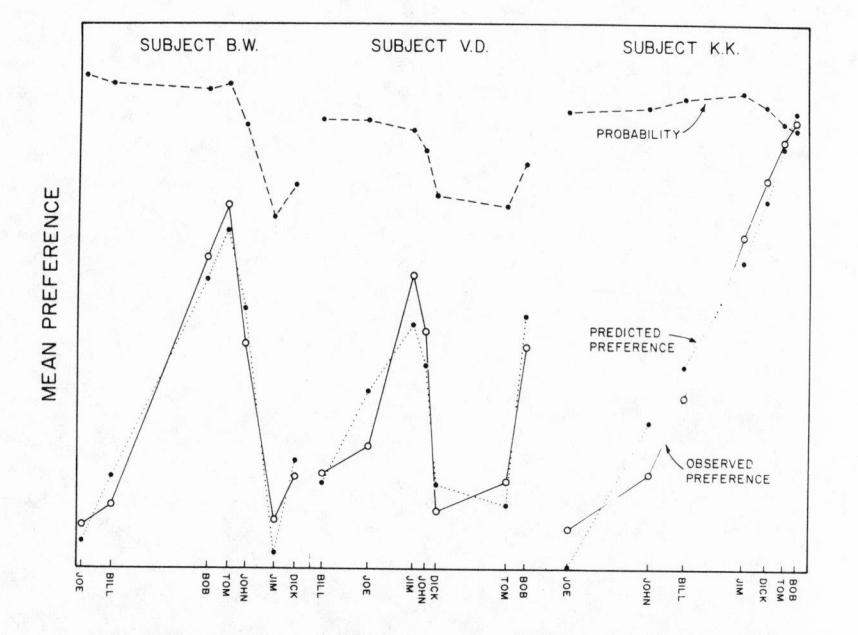

FIG. 16.9.   Date preferences of women for men as a function of physical appearance, each man listed on the horizontal axis having been described by a photograph. Solid and dotted curves compare observed and predicted date preferences.
Predictions from integration theory model. Data after Shanteau and Nagy (1976).

same time, their self-estimation procedures have general interest for cognitive
response analysis.

ACKNOWLEDGMENTS

This work has supported by National Science Foundation Grant BNS 75-21235 and by
grants from the National Institute of Mental Health to the Center for Human Information
Processing, University of California, San Diego. I wish to thank Tom Ostrom for helpful
advice and Rich Petty for providing copies of the messages discussed in the section on the
distraction effect. A longer version of this chapter that contains considerable supplementary detail is in technical report form (Anderson, 1976b).

17 Principles of Memory and Cognition in Attitude Formation

John H. Lingle
Livingston College
Rutgers—The State University

Thomas M. Ostrom
Ohio State University

One important contribution of the cognitive response approach to attitudes is that it raises anew the question of what an attitude is. Our concern in this chapter is with the question of whether an attitude is conceptually distinct from its constituent beliefs. Several existing theoretical approaches (see the chapters by Anderson and by Fishbein and Ajzen in this volume) posit that attitudes derive from the information and beliefs people hold about attitude objects. These views argue that every thought about the attitude object, when considered by itself, falls along an attitude continuum. The overall attitude is viewed as being a statistical composite (e.g., a weighted average) of these separate attitude-relevant thoughts. For example, if you were asked to form an attitude about Richard Nixon's ability as an international statesman, these theoretical approaches suggest that you might review relevant information such as: "He reestablished relations with mainland China"; "He opened disarmament talks with the Soviet Union"; or "He extended America's involvement in the Vietnam conflict into Cambodia." Accordingly, each such item of remembered information would be assigned a value depending on its position along the statesman continuum (running from "outstanding" to "inept"), and the several values would be weighted and algebraically combined (e.g., averaged or summed) to form an overall attitude concerning Nixon's effectiveness as a statesman.

What is not addressed by these theoretical approaches is whether or not such an attitude judgment (e.g., Nixon was a moderately effective statesman) has a cognitive representation that is in any way conceptually distinct from the beliefs upon which it is based. Several possibilities exist. It may be that people always review their beliefs about an attitude object prior to making an attitudinal judgment. A more likely possibility, however, is that when people have made one or more judgments in the past, they simply recall their past judgment(s) as a basis for their present one and do not systematically review all of their judgment-relevant beliefs. However, even if such a process represents how people make judgments, it does not necessarily imply that an attitude is conceptually distinct from its constituent beliefs. Consider, for example, the situation in which two different people ask for your attitude toward Nixon as a statesman. As long as your set of beliefs did not change between the time the first and second judgments were made, you would say the same thing to the second person as you did to the first, regardless of whether you based your response on your relevant beliefs or your earlier judgment. As a result, the attitude would have the same effect on subsequent responses as would the set of attitude-relevant beliefs, and there would be no conceptual advantage in distinguishing between the two.

For an attitude to be considered conceptually distinct from its constituent beliefs, it must influence subsequent attitude responses in ways that cannot be produced by the beliefs alone, either singly or in combination with one another. To determine whether or not this is indeed the case, in the present chapter we go beyond the traditional question of how attitudes are derived from a set of information items or beliefs and examine (1) how attitude judgments influence the organization of, and memory for, attitude-relevant beliefs and (2) whether people draw upon their memory for prior attitude judgments rather than their beliefs when responding to an attitude object. In answering these questions we argue that attitudes are indeed conceptually distinct from the beliefs upon which they are based.

We begin the chapter by reviewing a body of research from the area of cognitive psychology that examines the role that thematic frameworks play when people process information. This research suggests several specific ways in which attitudes are likely to differ from their constituent beliefs, as well as some general principles about how people are likely to process attitude-relevant information. Next, we describe some of our own research investigating how attitude judgments influence the manner in which subjects process and remember information about people.

SOME PRINCIPLES OF
THEMATIC STRUCTURE AND HUMAN THOUGHT

Cognitive psychologists generally agree that people are very active processors, rather than passive recorders, of even the simplest stimulus events. New information is constantly being compared with subsets of people's preexisting knowledge. Such prior knowledge provides frameworks within which new information can be organized, interpreted, and understood. As early as 1920, the neurologist Henry Head wrote:

> The sensory cortex is the store house of past impressions. They [these impressions] may rise into consciousness as images, but more often . . . remain outside central consciousness. Here they form organized models of ourselves which may be called schemata. Such schemata modify the impressions produced by incoming sensory impulses in such a way that final sensations of position or of locality rise into consciousness charged with a relation to something that has gone before [p. 607].

Head's early concept of schemata was subsequently noted and elaborated upon by Bartlett (1932), many of whose ideas about memory continue to be a focus of modern-day psychological research. Since 1920, a number of new terms have been suggested in place of the word *schemata,* including "cognitive structures" (Krech & Crutchfield, 1948), "frames" (Minsky, 1975), "focus elements" (Bobrow & Norman, 1975), "prototypical frames" (Thorndyke, 1976), and "scripts" (Abelson, 1975). Each of these expressions has been defined slightly differently and used within a distinct theoretical framework. Because the points we wish to make in the present chapter are not meant to be limited to any single theoretical structure, we have chosen to use the more general term *theme* or *thematic framework.* In general, each of these several expressions, as well as the term *theme,* is used to refer to *a subset of existing knowledge, based upon prior experience and relevant to a limited domain, that people use as a framework to guide their observation, organization, and retrieval from memory of perceived events.* Although the expression "subset of existing knowledge" is relatively broad and ill defined, in the following pages we specify some of the functional properties of themes. We do this by identifying several empirically based principles that describe how themes influence the manner in which information is interpreted, organized in memory, and remembered. Our purpose in discussing these principles is not only to define more clearly what a thematic framework is but also to pose the question of whether or not attitude judgments serve as thematic frameworks for organizing attitude-relevant thoughts and beliefs.

Principle I

The manner in which multiattribute stimuli are mentally encoded is dependent on the thematic framework(s) that is (are) salient at the time the stimuli are initially processed.

The essence of this first principle is easily demonstrated. Consider for the moment the impression you might form of a person upon hearing each of the following sentences:

> "He spent the afternoon lying in the grass."
> "He spent the afternoon smoking grass."

Most people would form very different impressions of the term *grass* based upon these two statements. The reason for this is that the verb in each case (*lie in* vs. *smoke*) elicits a distinct subset of existing knowledge (or theme) within which to interpret and encode the multiple attributes of the word *grass* (i.e., *lawn* vs. marijuana). Although the stimulus word is identical, its cognitive referents (or elicited meanings) are different when considered within the two different thematic contexts.

The ability of a salient theme to determine how stimuli are mentally encoded has been demonstrated by psychologists for a variety of stimulus materials. For example, it has been shown that a salient theme influences how subjects perceive ambiguous drawings. One such drawing (developed by Boring, 1930) consists of a picture that can be seen either as an old woman with her head bowed or a young girl looking over her shoulder. Leeper (1935) discovered that when this figure was shown after a drawing of a young girl, 25 out of 25 subjects reported that they saw a picture of a girl. However, when the figure was shown following a sketch of an old woman, 30 out of 31 subjects said the drawing was a picture of an old woman. Thus, by controlling which one of two themes was salient in subjects' minds, Leeper was able to control how the subjects interpreted and cognitively represented the figure.

In a more recent study, Johnston and Chesney (1974) have provided physiological data showing that a salient thematic framework can influence the neurological activity that accompanies the encoding of a visual stimulus. Johnston and Chesney used a figure that could be interpreted either as the capital letter *B* or the number 13 (see Fig. 17.1). They found that when they showed subjects this figure in a sequence of numbers, the pattern of neuronal firings in the subjects' brains was different from the pattern that resulted when they showed the figure in a sequence of letters.

In addition to such studies demonstrating the importance of salient themes in determining how simple stimuli are perceived, evidence exists that a similar process occurs with more complex stimulus information, such as a sequence of human behaviors. For instance, based on earlier work by Solomon Asch (1946), Kelley (1950) conducted an experiment in which an invited lecturer gave a brief presentation to several of his university classes. In each case the lecturer was introduced by a biographical sketch. This sketch was identical for all the students except that in half of the cases, the speaker was described as being a *warm* person, whereas for the other half he was said to be a *cold* person. Even though all the students heard the same presentation by the same lecturer, their subsequent impressions of the speaker were quite different depending on whether he had been introduced as being warm or cold. Although the results of the experiment can be interpreted in several ways, they are consistent with the idea that an imposed thematic structure (i.e., warm vs. cold) influenced how subjects cognitively represented the speaker's actions. If it is true that a salient theme influences how stimuli are cognitively represented, a second general principle naturally follows.

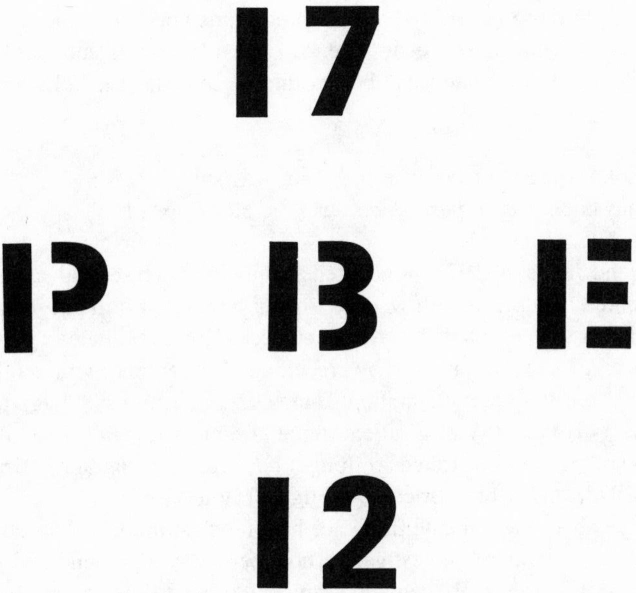

17

P B E

12

FIG. 17.1. Example of ambiguous stimuli used by Johnston and Chesney (1974).

Principle II

The manner in which stimulus information can later be remembered is dependent on the thematic framework(s) that is (are) salient at the time the stimulus information is initially processed.

As an illustration of Principle II, consider a situation in which you and a friend begin to discuss Richard Nixon's final year as President. Suppose for the moment that back in 1973 you had been most interested in determining whether Nixon was guilty of tax evasion, whereas your friend had been more concerned at that time with the consequences of Nixon's actions for the American economy. It is likely that your and your friend's memories for the facts would be quite different. Your different interests would have influenced how you interpreted and organized various events in your memory. Even if both of you were capable of recalling the same set of occurrences, the salience and ease with which you could remember the events would probably differ. Each of you would most likely remember the general theme that had been most salient to you [e.g., he was guilty (innocent) of tax evasion vs. his decisions harmed (helped) the economy] and would remember the particular events that had most directly led to your conclusion. Whereas you might first remember how much money Nixon had to repay the Internal Revenue Service, your friend would be more likely to recall first the amount of wheat Nixon agreed to sell to the Russians.

One procedure used to study how thematic frameworks influence memory has been to see how the presence or absence of a title affects subjects' ability to remember a series of sentences. For example, consider the following pair of sentences:

"The notes were sour because the seam was split."
"The haystack was important because the cloth ripped."

Bransford and Johnson (1973) conducted a study in which several such sentences were presented to subjects followed by a recall test. As you might imagine, their subjects had trouble remembering the sentences. However, memory for the sentences was significantly improved by preceding each sentence with a title capable of eliciting a relevant thematic framework, such as "bagpipes" and "parachute." This ability of a salient theme to improve recall for written materials has also been demonstrated for longer descriptive paragraphs (Bransford & Johnson, 1973) and short stories (Dooling & Mullet, 1973).

Not only can a salient theme influence how much stimulus information is later remembered, but research investigating how people comprehend and remember written texts indicates that thematic frameworks also determine what specific items of information will later be recalled. In this type of research, organizational schemes have been used to classify hierarchically the major ideas, or episodes, in written passages. One such classification procedure, developed by Schank (1975a, 1975b), hierarchically orders episodes and ideas according to their causal dependencies. For example, in the statement, "John hit Mary because he hated her for her indecision," the episode "John hit Mary" would represent a superordinate episode under which "because he hated her" and "for her indecision" would be subordinate, causative episodes. Although several different categorization schemes have been developed for classifying texts (cf. Frederiksen, 1975; Mandler & Johnson, 1977; Rumelhart, 1975; Thorndyke, 1977), all of them have found that there is a marked difference in how easily different levels of the hierarchy can later be recalled. Subjects are most easily able to remember the central theme of a passage and less able to remember lower-order, descriptive episodes. For instance, in the foregoing example, "John hit Mary" would be more likely to be remembered than "because he hated her," which in turn would be more easily remembered than "for her indecision." Thus, a central theme is one determinant of how easily specific information items, within a set of items, can later be remembered.

Finally, it has been shown by several investigators that a salient theme influences the conditions under which stimulus information can later be remembered. Tulving and Thomson (1973) have referred to this phenomenon as the "encoding specificity principle," according to which "the memory trace of an event and hence the properties of effective retrieval cues are determined by the specific encoding operations performed by the system on the input stimuli [p. 352]." An example of the principle is provided in a study conducted by Funkhouser (1968). Funkhouser had his subjects sort two-dimensional figures drawn on cards according to one of two different attributes (color or shape). Later, the subjects were able to remember the items more quickly, and with greater accuracy, when they were allowed to use the same attribute during recall that they had used in sorting the materials. You can experience this phenomenon for yourself by trying to say the months of the year in alphabetical order. The time it takes you to list all 12 months (if you can do it) is much longer than when you say them in temporal order. Your predicament is similar to that of the subjects in Funkhouser's experiment. The thematic structure you used in learning the months was their temporal, not alphabetical, order.

The first two principles we have discussed deal with how thematic structures influence the way in which items of stimulus information are cognitively represented and remembered. However, cognitive organization of specific stimulus events is only one facet of information processing. When comparing sensory information with preexisting knowledge, people often generate abstractions, inferences, or associated thoughts. Such "implicational associates," as we refer to them, are important in understanding attitude formation and change to the degree that they influence how people interpret information and make later judgments. Indeed, this concern is at the heart of the cognitive response approach to persuasion. Our last two general principles concern the way in which implicational associates are remembered and used, as well as how they relate to thematic frameworks.

Principle III

The implicational associates people generate when they consider stimulus information tend to be stored in memory and can be recalled to form the bases of subsequent judgments.

As an example of Principle III, if someone were to ask you today what you thought about Richard Nixon, you might respond with a statement such as "I think he was dishonest" or "I think he made substantial contributions to foreign policy." If you were asked why you felt the way you did, however, you might not be able to recall all of the specific incidents that led to your reaction. In short, the implicational associates you have formed about Richard Nixon are stored in memory separately from the factual information items upon which they are based. Furthermore, these implicational associates can be accessed in memory as the bases of subsequent judgments without recalling all of the factual information upon which they are based (e.g., I would not vote for him again, because I think he is dishonest).

Several studies (cf. Anderson & Hubert, 1963; Bahrick & Boucher, 1968) have shown that the meaning subjects abstract from stimulus materials is often stored separately in memory from the stimulus information itself. Bahrick and

Boucher (1968), for example, showed subjects pictures of different common items such as a teacup. In a recall test administered 2 weeks later, subjects were first asked to list as many of the items as possible and then to choose from a group of similar items (e.g., six different teacups) the particular item they had seen. It was found that the subjects' ability to recall having seen a member of a class of items (e.g., I saw a teacup) was not correlated with their ability to identify the specific item that had been shown to them (e.g., I saw that particular teacup). Such a correlation would be expected if subjects had been remembering each class of items by first recalling an image of the particular item they had seen. The fact that no such correlation existed suggests that subjects stored the class names of the items separately in memory from the identifying physical attributes of the objects, and that they could access one type of information in memory without accessing the other.

Cognitive psychologists, as well as attitude researchers, have provided evidence that people remember and use abstract characteristics of the stimulus information in judgment tasks. Posner and Snyder (1975), for example, found that subjects' performance on a simple memory task was influenced by information they spontaneously abstracted from sets of stimulus items. In this study subjects were first presented with descriptive traits in the format: "Jim is articulate, friendly, and outgoing." Each such set of traits always consisted of descriptive characteristics that were either all positive or all negative in evaluative tone. Shortly thereafter, subjects were shown a single probe word and were asked whether the word was one of the traits that had been used to describe the person. Two factors were varied in the experiment: (1) the number of traits presented in the initially displayed stimulus set, and (2) whether the incorrect probe word was similar or dissimilar in evaluative tone to the memory set. Posner and Snyder found that subjects took increasing amounts of time to determine if a probe trait (either correct or incorrect) was a member of a stimulus set as the number of traits in the set increased. This indicated that subjects needed increasing amounts of time to compare the probe trait with the several stimulus items as more stimulus traits were presented. However, Posner and Snyder also found that when an incorrect probe word was different in evaluative tone from the descriptive traits, subjects were able to identify that it was incorrect faster and with fewer errors than when the probe word was a new trait similar in evaluative tone to the displayed traits. Thus, even though subjects were not asked to consider the evaluative nature of the described stimulus person, they did so spontaneously and used this abstracted impression to help them determine if the probe trait was one that had previously been used to describe the person.

Several examples from the attitude change literature could be cited as supporting the notion that people remember and use implicational associates to make judgments. As but one example, Greenwald (1968b) found that the number of persuasive arguments subjects remembered from a particular message was a poor predictor of how much their attitude changed as a result of reading the message.

A better predictor of final attitude change was the set of inferences and abstractions subjects generated and reported when they considered the persuasive communication. This suggests that subjects recalled and relied upon their generated inferences, rather than the stimulus arguments, in making their evaluative responses.

Just as thematic frameworks determine how stimulus events are remembered (as described in Principle II), they also influence memory for implicational associates. This is expressed in Principle IV.

Principle IV

The set of implicational associates likely to be remembered as being true about a stimulus event is dependent on the thematic framework(s) that is (are) salient at the time the stimulus information is initially processed.

Principle IV is intended to refer to two classes of inferences: inferences that are remembered as inferences, and inferences that are remembered as facts. As we illustrate in a moment, it happens that people sometimes remember seeing or hearing things that have not actually occurred. It appears that this phenomenon can occur as a result of two different processes, both of which are susceptible to influence from a salient theme. One such process is for people to generate and store inferred information in memory at the time stimulus information is initially considered, as suggested in Principle III. In the case that such inferences are not clearly marked in memory as inferences, they may later be recalled as events that have actually occurred rather than as inferences.

A second way in which people may generate inferences and remember them as facts is to engage in a reconstructive process when they try to remember something that has previously transpired. That is, when people try to remember things, they often reconstruct, or fabricate, facts that "must" have happened from the facts they can remember. When this occurs, the fabricated or inferred facts are sometimes stored in memory and become indistinguishable from actual facts.

In point of fact, it is extremely difficult to determine whether a particular inference has been generated when a set of information items is initially considered or at the point in time when the information is recalled. Be that as it may, in either case, a salient thematic structure is likely to be an important determinant of what specific inferences will be generated and remembered, as has been illustrated in several studies (cf. Picek, Sherman, & Shiffrin, 1975; Potts, 1972; Sulin & Dooling, 1974). In one study, for example, Sulin and Dooling (1974) had subjects read a biographical passage. Half of the subjects were told that the passage was about a famous person (Adolf Hitler), whereas half were told that the passage described a fictitious character (Robert Martin). Thus, subjects in one group were able to use their preexisting knowledge about the central character as a thematic framework for comprehending and remembering the passage, whereas subjects in the other group were not. One week after the subjects had read the passage, they were shown eight test sentences and were asked which of the sentences were identical to sentences they had read in the passage. Seven of the test sentences were identical to ones in the passage; the eighth was a new sentence. This sentence was one of two types. For half of the subjects it was a sentence high in thematic relatedness (i.e., it stated a well-known fact about the famous person). For the remaining subjects, the eighth sentence was a low-thematic sentence that described a less well known characteristic of the famous person.

By varying the thematic relatedness of the false sentence, Sulin and Dooling hoped to determine whether the tendency to recognize a new sentence as an old one was influenced by the thematic framework within which the paragraph was processed. If this were the case, they reasoned that subjects who read about the famous main character should make more recognition errors on the high- than on the low-thematic key sentence; however, the thematic relatedness of the new sentence should not influence the number of recognition errors for the subjects who read the paragraph about Robert Martin. This was, in fact, what Sulin and Dooling found. Subjects who read about Adolf Hitler were much more likely to say that both new sentences were ones they had seen before than were the subjects who read about Robert Martin. Furthermore, the thematic relatedness of the test sentence influenced how likely subjects who read about Adolf Hitler were to say that they had seen it before. The thematic relatedness of the test sentence, however, did not affect the probability of recognition errors among the ''Robert Martin'' subjects.

ATTITUDES AS THEMATIC FRAMEWORKS

To this point in the chapter, we have documented the fact that people are very active processors of incoming information and that they constantly compare and contrast new information with existing knowledge. We have referred to subsets of existing knowledge that people use to interpret stimulus information as themes or thematic frameworks and have identified several of their functional properties. Included among these properties are the facts that salient themes can determine (1) how multiattributed stimuli are represented in memory, (2) how and under what circumstances stimulus information can later be remembered, and (3) what set of inferences people are likely to make and remember about stimuli such as attitude objects. In addition, we presented evidence that the inferences people generate when they process stimulus information can be stored separately in memory from the facts upon which they are based and can be used as the basis of future judgments.

The purpose of the research reported in the remainder of this chapter is to explore the possibility that an attitude judgment, once made, plays a role in the organization of cognitive responses that is independent of the information on which the attitude was initially based. That is, we are interested in determining whether an attitude acts as a theme, and whether the principles of thematic organization that we have described are applicable to attitudinal judgments. If so, this would not only establish that an attitude judgment possesses organizational properties that distinguish it conceptually from the constituent beliefs upon which it is based; it would also link attitudes to a rapidly expanding body of literature in cognitive psychology related to the role that themes play in cognitive organization, memory, and judgment.

The research we report deals with attitude judgments about only one category of attitude objects—persons—and one type of subjective continuum—occupational proficiency. Concern over whether a person with certain characteristics would be good or bad at a particular job underlies much of the work in voting behavior, counseling psychology, and personnel selection. Consequently, such attitudes represent an important area of study. In addition, we have no reason to believe that thematic processes that operate with this kind of attitude would not be equally applicable to other classes of social attitudes. The primary reason for selecting person attitudes was that it allowed us to study thematic processes at the stage of attitude formation. This was possible because we could have people form attitudes about hypothetical strangers on the basis of information we provided.

Two related series of experiments are reported. In the first experiments we discuss how the act of making an attitudinal judgment influences (1) what information subjects remember about a stimulus person and (2) what associated characteristics they think the person is likely to possess. In the second series of studies, we attempt to determine how an initial attitude judgment influences the manner in which subjects cognitively process information when they make subsequent decisions about a stimulus person.

Effects of an Initial Attitude Judgment on the Recall of Attitude-Relevant Information

If an attitudinal judgment, once made, acquires thematic properties, then according to Principle II the judgment (i.e., the central theme) itself should be relatively well remembered. How well specific information items are remembered should depend on their relevancy to the judgment. Judgment-relevant information should be remembered better than judgment-irrelevant information. This idea was tested in an experiment by Lingle, Geva, Ostrom, Leippe, and Baumgardner (1979) in which subjects were asked to make a judgment concerning a stimulus person's suitability for a particular occupation. The person was described by a photograph and 11 personality traits. For half of the subjects the descriptive traits had been selected to be relevant to the occupational judgment they had to make; for the other half, the descriptive traits were selected to be irrelevant to the occupational judgment (for example, the traits "good eyesight," "thorough," and "accurate" would be more relevant to whether a person would be a good pilot than to whether he or she would make a good comedian). After making the evaluative judgment, the subject was scheduled to return for a second session either 1 day or 1 week later. In this session, all of the subjects received a booklet in which they first were asked to recall the occupation for which they had evaluated the person. Next, they were presented with a 21-point evaluative scale, identical to the one they had used to make their initial judgment, and were asked to indicate their previous rating as accurately as possible. Finally, subjects were shown 33 traits and were asked to identify the 11 traits that had initially been used to describe the stimulus person.

The results of the several recall tests showed that the subjects' memory for the traits used to describe the stimulus person was significantly affected both by the passage of time and by whether the traits had been relevant or irrelevant to their occupational judgment. Subjects who took the test after a week's delay made significantly more errors in recognizing the traits than subjects taking the test the following day. Furthermore, subjects who had seen traits irrelevant (as opposed to relevant) to their judgment made significantly more errors in the trait-recognition test both after 1 day and after 1 week (this difference in error level was the same for both time periods).

If the occupational judgment acted as a theme, memory for that judgment should have been less affected by the passage of time and the relevancy of the trait information. Two different measures were used to test this. The first measure was subjects' ability to recall the occupation they had judged. Out of 123 subjects, only 5 were unable to remember their judged occupation. All 5 were in the week-delay condition, indicating that the passage of time did have some effect on subjects' ability to remember which occupation they had judged. However, the relevancy of the trait information had no effect on subjects' ability to remember the occupation. Neither the passage of time nor the relevancy of the occupation affected subjects' ability to recall the judgment they had made on the 21-point scale. Furthermore, their memory for their previous rating was extremely accurate. The average error in recalling the first ratings was less than 1 point on the 21-point scale in all four of the experimental conditions.

Thus, the experimental results provided qualified support for the thesis that an attitude judgment acts in a similar manner to a salient theme when person information is processed. The judgment itself was relatively well remembered and not affected by the nature of the descriptive traits. The traits, on the other hand, were better remembered when they were relevant, as opposed to irrelevant, to the judgment.

Effects of an Attitude Judgment on Implicational Associates

If a judgment serves as a thematic framework for processing attitude information, according to Principle IV it should also influence the inferences subjects make about a stimulus person. Two separate studies have been conducted that show this to be the case (Baumgardner, Leippe, & Ostrom, 1976; Lingle et al., 1979). In both studies subjects were first asked to make an occupational judgment about a stimulus person and then later were asked to list other traits they thought might be characteristic of the person. The person descriptions (a set of traits) seen by different groups of subjects were identical, the only treatment difference being the type of occupational judgment each group of subjects made. In both studies the traits that subjects generated were subsequently submitted to a separate group of judges to determine their occupational relevancy. In one study, Lingle et al. (1979) found that the characteristic traits that subjects generated were always more relevant to the judged occupation than to the nonjudged occupation. In the second study, Baumgardner et al. (1976) found that the resulting person descriptions were more characteristic of abilities that were stereotypical of the judged occupation than the nonjudged occupation. Thus, both studies found that an attitudinal judgment influenced the set of associated characteristics subjects generate about a described person.

Persistence of the Organizational Properties of an Attitude Judgment

Although the results of the studies we have discussed so far are consistent with the idea that a newly formed attitude thematically organizes attitude-relevant cognitions in memory, an alternative explanation exists. In the first study, subjects were reminded of their judgment immediately prior to the trait-recognition test; and in the last two studies, subjects wrote their descriptions of the stimulus persons immediately after making an occupational judgment. In each case the experimental procedure provided stimulus cues immediately prior to the memory and implicational-associate tasks, which could have predisposed subjects to give theme-related responses. That is, having just recently thought about the occupation may have increased the salience of occupation-relevant responses. To show that a judgment thematically structures attitude information in memory, it is necessary to demonstrate that an initial judgment influences how subjects remember stimulus information even when a second, unrelated judgment has just been made.

This, in fact, was demonstrated in a recent study by Geva (1977) in which there were three main conditions. In one condition all of the subjects saw the same set of 10 traits describing a stimulus person. Five of these traits were relevant to Occupation A, and 5 were relevant to Occupation B. Half of the subjects in this condition were asked to judge the stimulus person on Occupation A, and half were asked to judge the person on Occupation B. Following a short intervening task, all of the subjects were asked to recall as many of the traits describing the person as possible. Consistent with the previous experiment, it was expected that subjects would recall more relevant traits than irrelevant traits.

The second two conditions were identical to the first condition except that the subjects were required to make a second occupational judgment (without seeing the traits again) immediately prior to the recall test. In one of these conditions, the second occupation judged was the occupation relevant to the second half of the stimulus traits that had been shown. In the other condition, subjects judged the suitability of the stimulus person for a third occupation chosen to be unrelated to any of the stimulus traits.

The results of the study showed that subjects remembered significantly more of the traits that were relevant (as opposed to irrelevant) to their initial occupational judgment. This was true regardless of whether or not the subjects had made a second judgment immediately prior to the recall test. Neither type of second judgment significantly altered either the total number of stimulus traits recalled or subjects' tendency to recall traits relevant to their first judgment.

The data of this study rule out the possibility that the earlier findings resulted merely from the required occupational judgments cuing, or making salient, judgment-relevant cognitions. The thematic influences of an initial judgment on subjects' memory for descriptive information persisted even in the face of a new occupational judgment. Thus, there would appear to be a good deal of truth to the old saw that first impressions are the most enduring, at least when the impression is expressed in an overt judgment.

The results of the study are interesting in yet another way. One might expect that when someone makes a judgment about a person, he or she would think back to the information received that was most relevant to the decision that needed to be made. But if subjects had been doing this, one would expect that their memory for traits relevant to their second judgment would have improved, because they would have just recently recalled them. The fact that subjects' memory for these traits was not improved by their second judgment suggests that they either (1) remembered and relied upon the same set of descriptive traits regardless of the type of judgment they made, or (2) remembered and relied upon some other set of cognitions, such as their initial attitude judgment, so that their memory for the descriptive traits was not affected by making a new decision. In the next section we describe a series of studies that examined more closely how subjects process attitude-relevant information when they make a second decision about a person.

Contribution of an Initial Attitude Judgment to Subsequent Judgments

The task of determining what stimulus information is recalled and what implicational associates are generated when people form an attitude and make an attitudinal response is not straightforward. Recall tests and implicational-associate responses provide only a partial glimpse of people's actual thoughts. Just because the subjects in the reported experiments were able to remember several traits when specifically asked to do so does not mean that they recalled these same traits prior to making their judgments.

A method frequently used for inferring what people are thinking while making attitude judgments is to have them list their thoughts either while they are thinking them or retrospectively. Unfortunately, as discussed in Chapters 2 and 5, this procedure has a number of shortcomings, including the fact that it may interfere with the natural judgment process. The studies described in this and the next section employed a measure of cognitive response that is free from many of the shortcomings of the thought-listing method and that does not disrupt the normal judgmental processes—decision time. Since mental activity takes time, it is possible to make inferences about how people process information by determining how long it takes them to make a judgment. A study we conducted (Lingle & Ostrom, 1979) illustrates this fact and provides additional evidence that an initial attitude judgment acts as a thematic framework for processing attitude-relevant information.

In this study we reasoned that if an initial judgment acts as an organizing theme for descriptive information, subsequent judgments of the same stimulus person should be made more swiftly if they are similar, as opposed to dissimilar, to the first judgment. When the second judgment is similar to the first, people may not try to recall all the items of information they had when making the initial judgment. They may either recall their first judgment and generalize to the second (see Principle III) or they may use the theme of the first judgment as a cue to recall theme-relevant items of information (see Principle II). When a second judgment is thematically dissimilar to the first, however, people may require extra time to recall each of the original items of stimulus information and average (or sum) their weighted values anew to produce their second judgment.

To test this idea, we had subjects make pairs of occupational judgments about different stimulus persons. Subjects first saw an occupation projected on a screen. This initial occupation was followed by four traits describing a person, and subjects were asked to think about the suitability of the person for the occupation they had seen. After 20 seconds, the initial occupation was again shown, and subjects indicated whether or not they thought the person would be good or bad in the occupation by moving a two-poled toggle switch. Three seconds later a different occupation was shown, and subjects were required to make a second decision about the same person's suitability for this new occupation. This sequence was repeated for several different stimulus persons.

The pairs of judgments subjects made about the various stimulus persons were of two types. In some cases they were two occupations that required people with similar characteristics (e.g., store clerk and salesman); in other cases the occupations required people with different characteristics (e.g., dentist and salesman). Our concern in each case was with the amount of time it took subjects to make their second occupational judgments. The thematic view of attitudes predicts that subjects' average decision times for second similar occupational judgments should be shorter than their decision times for second dissimilar judgments. The results supported this prediction. Subjects took significantly longer on the average to make a second dissimilar occupational judgment than a similar judgment (6.3 vs. 5.2 seconds, respectively). Thus, consistent with the recall studies, the thematic structure imposed on a set of stimulus traits by an initial attitude judgment did influence how quickly subjects made different types of subsequent judgments. It should be emphasized that a subject's first judgment provided no new information about a stimulus person. Its effects on a second judgment could only have been due to its organizational influence on the thoughts a subject had about the stimulus person.

The results of this first decision-time experiment give no indication as to what subjects were thinking about during the extra time they spent making dissimilar occupational judgments. To investigate this question, we conducted a second set of experiments, again using decision time as the primary dependent measure.

Is Descriptive Information Used in Making Judgments?

Several investigators have found that the amount of time people need to review a set of items in memory increases as the number of items in the set increases (cf. Kintsch, 1974; Posner & Snyder, 1975; Sternberg, 1969). This finding suggested a procedure for using decision time to determine the types of information subjects call to mind prior to making a second occupational judgment about a stimulus person.

What we did (Lingle & Ostrom, 1979) was again to have subjects make pairs of occupational judgments about several stimulus persons. However, besides varying whether or not subjects' second occupational judgments were similar or dissimilar to their first judgments, we varied how many traits were used to describe the stimulus persons. In panels A, B, and C of Fig. 17.2, we have displayed three different patterns of decision times that might be expected, depending on the types of information subjects bring to mind when making their second judgments. Note that, consistent with the previous study, each of these patterns shows subjects taking longer to make dissimilar (as opposed to similar) second judgments when the stimulus person is described by four traits.

Panel A pictures the expected results if subjects try to recall and consider the original stimulus traits prior to making a second judgment. Since search time is known to increase as the number of items in a memory set (i.e., set size) increases, subjects in both the similar and dissimilar conditions should take longer to review the information and make their judgments as set size increases. At the same time, however, something else should happen as set size increases. It follows from Principle IV, and the research we have reported, that subjects in both the similar and dissimilar conditions will most readily remember traits relevant to their first judgment. If it is assumed that some percent of the traits used to describe each stimulus person are relevant to the first judgment (e.g., 50%), the absolute number of relevant traits—and the time required to recall these traits—will increase with set size. When subjects are making a similar second occupational judgment, these traits—being relevant to the second judgment as well—should be sufficient to make a decision. However, when making a dissimilar second judgment, subjects should not find these traits particularly helpful, because the dissimilar occupation was selected to require dissimilar abilities. In the dissimilar condition, subjects should therefore have to recall the remaining traits in the set. Because the number of these remaining traits will also increase as set size increases, subjects will have to spend additional time remembering and reviewing them. As a result, the average *difference* in decision time for similar and dissimilar second judgments should increase as set size increases. One additional implication of this decision model is that no difference in decision time should result between the similar and dissimilar conditions when people are given only one item of information about the person.

It is apparent from the earlier described study by Lingle et al. (1979) that subjects' initial occupational judgments remain salient in memory. As a result,

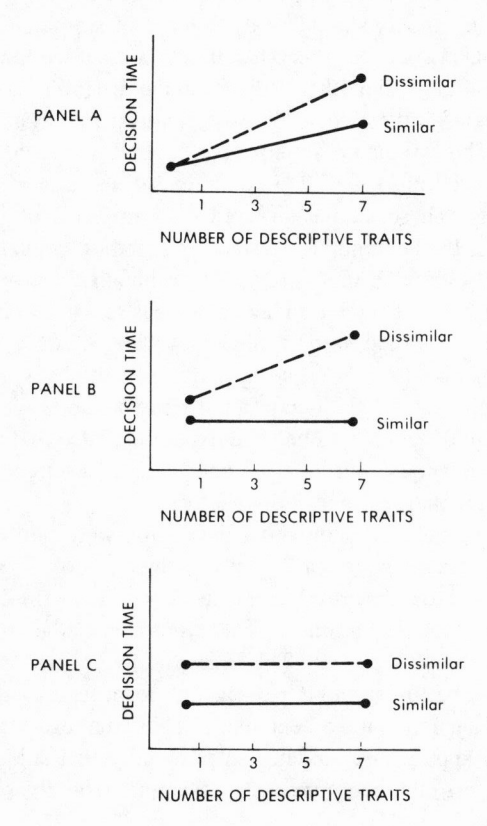

FIG. 17.2.   Predicted results of second occupational judgment times for three different ways of cognitively processing information, depending on the type of initial judgment and the amount of descriptive information received.

subjects may only spend time trying to recall the original stimulus traits when their second judgments are dissimilar to their first. When subjects make two very similar judgments, they may simply generalize from their first judgment to their second (e.g., "Since he would be a good lawyer, he is also bound to be a good judge"). In panel B of Fig. 17.2, we have drawn the expected pattern of results if this were the case. For similar second judgments, subjects' decision times are independent of the number of traits initially presented, because they are not considering them. However, for dissimilar decisions, decision time increases with the number of stimulus traits as subjects have to spend more time reviewing more information.

Finally, it is possible that subjects do not recall and review the stimulus traits for either type of second judgment. That is, they may simply remember the attitude theme (their first judgment), generate theme-related implicational associates, and base their second judgment on these thoughts in both the similar and dissimilar conditions. Set size would not influence second decision times, because subjects' ability to recall their first judgment and generate implicational associates should be independent of the amount of information on which the first judgment was based (in accordance with Principle III). For all set sizes, dissimilar judgments should take longer than similar judgments because the implicational associates generated in the similar condition are more relevant to the second judgment than they are in the dissimilar condition. In this case, subjects' response times would be expected to parallel panel C of Fig. 17.2.

Three separate set-size experiments were conducted to test the predictions depicted in Fig. 17.2. Experiments 1 and 2 used set sizes of two, four, and six traits. These studies differed only in terms of whether the trait sets used to describe the stimulus persons consisted of evaluatively homogeneous or evaluatively heterogeneous traits. Even though Experiment 1 used homogeneous sets and Experiment 2 used heterogeneous sets, they obtained similar results and have been combined for presentation in panel A of Fig. 17.3. Experiment 3 (see panel B of Fig. 17.3) used a wider range of set sizes (one, three, five, and seven) to insure that the findings of the first two studies were not the result of a restricted range of set sizes. The third experiment also included a manipulation of trait-set homogeneity, but it was found to have no effect, so the displayed results have been collapsed across this factor.

Figure 17.3 shows that the results were quite consistent. As in the initially reported response-time study, subjects took significantly more time to make second dissimilar judgments as compared to similar judgments. However, judgment time did not increase as a function of the number of traits used to describe the stimulus person. This was true regardless of the type of trait sets used to describe the stimulus person, and regardless of whether a similar or dissimilar prior judgment had been made. Thus, the results paralleled panel C of Fig. 17.2 and appear to eliminate the possibility that subjects were using any cognitive process that incorporates the assumption that their second judgments in each case were based on a review of a representative proportion of the original stimulus information.

This conclusion is further supported by a consideration of the one-trait set-size condition of Experiment 3. Even in this condition, subjects took longer to make a second dissimilar judgment than a similar one. Because of controls incorporated into the experimental design, there was no systematic difference in the relevance of the single trait description to the similar and dissimilar judgments. If subjects were simply recalling that one trait and using it alone as the basis of their second judgment, no differences should have emerged between the similar and dissimilar conditions. Thus, the differences in information processing that resulted from making an initial attitude judgment did not seem to be caused by subjects' processing a greater percentage of the original stimulus information. Rather, subjects must have been relying upon some other set of cognitions (such as the

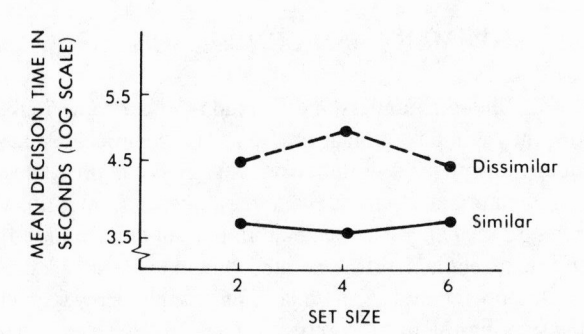

PANEL A: COMBINED DATA FROM EXPERIMENTS 1 & 2

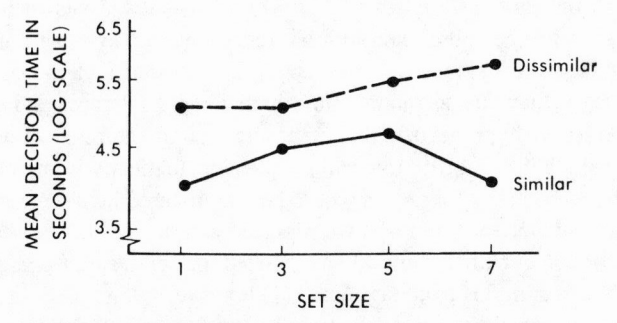

PANEL B: EXPERIMENT 3

FIG. 17.3.   Mean decision time for subjects' second occupational judgments as a function of type of initial judgment and trait-set size.

theme and its implicational associates) that differed in relevance to the two types of occupational judgments.

Finally, in Experiment 3, after subjects had made their last judgment, they were asked to list as many of the traits describing the final stimulus person as they could remember. Consistent with the study reported earlier by Geva (1977) the type of second judgment subjects made did not significantly affect how many traits they were able to remember. However, subjects were able to recall increasingly more traits as the number of traits used to describe the stimulus person increased. The mean number of recalled traits when subjects had seen descriptions containing 1, 3, 5, or 7 traits was 1.0, 2.6, 2.9, and 3.2, respectively. Thus, subjects were capable of recalling more traits prior to their second judgment as set size increased, even though there was no evidence that they were doing so.

SUMMARY AND CONCLUSIONS

If attitude researchers hope to understand the judgments people make (and the actions they take), they will have to learn more about the processes people use to encode and organize information in memory, as well as the processes by which they access from memory attitude-relevant thoughts. The cognitive response approach toward attitude change has made an important contribution in this area by demonstrating that people's self-generated thoughts about persuasive communications are remembered and mediate later judgments. However, this is only the first step in answering the more complex question of what factors determine the specific information items a person will think about in a particular decision situation.

In the present chapter we provide one part of the answer to this question. We began by posing the question of whether or not an attitude judgment is conceptually distinct from its constituent beliefs. We noted that for this to be true, an attitude must influence subsequent attitude responses in ways that could not be produced by the beliefs alone. After reviewing several studies demonstrating that salient themes influence the manner in which people interpret and remember stimulus events, we hypothesized that an attitude judgment might differ from its constituent beliefs in its ability to organize ideas thematically in memory and in this way influence what information would be remembered in making subsequent judgments. In support of this idea, we reported a series of studies that showed that, in accordance with several theme-related principles, an initial attitude judgment about a stimulus person affected (1) how well subjects could remember different traits that had been used to describe the person, (2) the set of inferred characteristics subjects thought would typify the person, and (3) the cognitive processing time subjects required to make different types of subsequent judgments about the person. In addition, it was found that the effects of an initial attitude judgment on memory for original stimulus information persisted even following different types of subsequent judgments.

A final study used decision time to identify the specific difference in information processing that resulted from subjects having made an earlier similar or dissimilar attiude judgment. The results of the study showed that decision time was not affected by the amount of information available to review. This finding indicated that subjects' second decisions tended to be based on their initial attitude rather than on a systematic review of the stimulus information items.

Although the research reported in this chapter shows that an initial attitude judgment can influence the information a person will think about when making later judgments, it should not be concluded that initial judgments always form the basis of an organizing theme. There are times (for example, when more information is forthcoming) when people may resist organizing their attitudes prematurely. No doubt there are also conditions under which an organizing theme can be changed by a subsequent judgment, despite the findings by Geva (1977) to the contrary. The principles presented in this chapter need to be elaborated to allow the identification of conditions under which an attitude judgment does and does not become an organizing theme for attitude-relevant beliefs and thoughts.

The role that attitudes play in organizing thought has been a source of speculation by some of the earliest attitude theorists (e.g., Krech & Crutchfield, 1948; Lippmann, 1922). Some clues regarding when a judgment may serve as the basis of an organizing theme are provided by Smith, Bruner, and White (1956) in their classic discussion of the "object appraisal" function that attitudes can serve:

> Presented with an object or event, a person may categorize it in some class of objects and events for which a predisposition to action and experience exists. Once thus categorized, it becomes the focus of an already-established repertory of reactions and feelings, and the person is saved the energy-consuming and sometimes painful process of figuring out *de novo* how he shall relate himself to it. If the environmental fact either defies categorization or is categorized in such a way as to bring harmful consequences to the person, new attitudes may be developed or shifts in categorization may occur. In sum, then, attitudes aid us in classifying for action the objects of the environment, and they make appropriate response tendencies available for coping with these objects [p. 41].

Thus, it may be that an attitude judgment only becomes an organizing theme under the conditions that a previous categorization (1) has not been made, (2) is inconsistent with new information, or (3) proves inadequate for a current decision need.

An additional question requiring further research is how the judgment task influences the items of information that are recalled and considered when a judgment is made. Although the results of our reseach (Lingle & Ostrom, 1979; Lingle et al., 1979) suggest that people have a tendency to rely on an initial attitude judgment rather than a systematic review of the stimulus information, this does not imply that people never review the factual information they are given when they make a decision. Quite possibly, if a high-involvement decision task had been used in our procedure, subjects would have spent more time trying to recall the specific information items upon which their earlier attitude judgments had been based, and decision time would have increased as the amount of stimulus information increased.

As a concluding note, as attitude researchers attempt to understand how people process attitude-relevant information, they will undoubtedly find it beneficial to become familiar with the conceptual and methodological advances that have recently taken place in the area of cognitive psychology. Cognitive psychologists have begun to use a broad range of new experimental paradigms and dependent measures based on the fact that information processing requires both cognitive capacity and execution time. These have included reaction-time measures (e.g., Pachella, 1974), recall errors (e.g., Loftus, 1975), stimulus interference or masking tasks (e.g., Sperling, 1967), and stimulus-probe recognition time (Warren, 1974). These various methods, in combination with the sequential judgment task used in the experiments discussed in this chapter, would seem to offer one profitable approach for understanding how people process information when they make attitude judgments.

ACKNOWLEDGMENTS

The research reported in this chapter was supported by National Science Foundation Grant GS-38604. Preparation of the manuscript was supported in part by a Rutgers University Research Council Grant. We are grateful to R. Hastie for comments on an earlier draft.

References

Abelson, R. P. Modes of resolution of belief dilemmas. *Journal of Conflict Resolution*, 1959, *3*, 343–352.

Abelson, R. P. Computer simulation of "hot" cognition. In S. S. Tomkins & S. Messick (Eds.), *Computer simulation of personality*. New York: Wiley, 1963.

Abelson, R. P. Are attitudes necessary? In B. T. King & E. McGinnies (Eds.), *Attitudes, conflict, and social change*. New York: Academic Press, 1972.

Abelson, R. P. Representing mundane reality in plans. In D. Bobrow & A. Collins (Eds.), *Representation and understanding: Studies in cognitive science*. New York: Academic Press, 1975.

Abelson, R. P. Script processing in attitude formation and decision-making. In J. S. Carroll and J. W. Payne (Eds.), *Cognition and social behavior*. Hillsdale, N.J.: Lawrence Erlbaum Associates, 1976.

Abelson, R. P., Aronson, E., McGuire, W. J., Newcomb, T. M., Rosenberg, M. J., & Tannenbaum, P. H. (Eds.) *Theories of Cognitive Consistency:* A Sourcebook. Chicago: Rand McNally, 1968.

Abelson, R. P., & Rosenberg, J. J. Symbolic psycho-logic: A model of attitude cognition. *Behavioral Science*, 1958, *3*, 1–13.

Acker, L. E., & Edwards, A. E. Transfer of vasoconstriction over a bipolar meaning dimension. *Journal of Experimental Psychology*, 1964, *67*, 1–6.

Adams, H. F. *Advertising and its mental laws*. New York: Macmillan, 1916.

Adorno, T. W., Frenkel-Brunswik, E., Levinson, D. J., & Sanford, R. N. *The authoritarian personality*. New York: Harper, 1950.

Ajzen, I. Effects of information on interpersonal attraction: Similarity versus affective value. *Journal of Personality and Social Psychology*, 1974, *29*, 374–380.

Ajzen, I. Information processing approaches to interpersonal attraction. In S. W. Duck (Eds.), *Theory and practice in interpersonal attraction*. London: Academic Press, 1977. (a)

Ajzen, I. Intuitive theories of events and the effects of base rate information on prediction. *Journal of Personality and Social Psychology*, 1977, *35*, 303–314. (b)

Ajzen, I., & Fishbein, M. The prediction of behavior from attitudinal and normative variables. *Journal of Experimental Social Psychology*, 1970, *6*, 466–487.

Ajzen, I., & Fishbein, M. Attitudes and normative beliefs as factors influencing behavioral intentions. *Journal of Personality and Social Psychology,* 1972, *21,* 1-9.

Ajzen, I., & Fishbein, M. Attitudinal and normative variables as predictors of specific behavior. *Journal of Personality and Social Psychology,* 1973, *27,* 41-57.

Ajzen, I., & Fishbein, M. Factors influencing intentions and the intention–behavior relation. *Human Relations,* 1974, *27,* 1-15.

Ajzen, I., & Fishbein, M. Attitude–behavior relations: A theoretical analysis and review of empirical research. *Psychological Bulletin,* 1977, *84,* 888-918.

Ajzen, I., & Fishbein, M. *Understanding attitudes and predicting social behavior.* Englewood Cliffs, N.J.: Prentice-Hall, 1980.

Allen, V. L. Situational factors in conformity. In L. Berkowitz (Ed.), *Advances in experimental social psychology* (Vol. 2). New York: Academic Press, 1965.

Allport, G. W. Attitudes. In C. Murchison (Ed.), *Handbook of social psychology* (Vol. 2). Worchester, Mass.: Clark University Press, 1935.

Allyn, J., & Festinger, L.:The effectiveness of unanticipated persuasive communications. *Journal of Abnormal and Social Psychology,* 1961, *62,* 35-40.

Alwin, D. F., & Tessler, R. C. Causal models, unobserved variables and experimental data. *American Journal of Sociology,* 1974, *80,* 58-86.

Amir, Y. Contact hypothesis in ethnic relations. *Psychological Bulletin,* 1969, *71,* 319-342.

Amster, H., & Glassman, L. D. Verbal repetition and connotative change. *Journal of Experimental Psychology,* 1966, *71,* 389-395.

Anderson, N. H. Test of a model for opinion change. *Journal of Abnormal and Social Psychology,* 1959, *59,* 371-381.

Anderson, N. H. Application of an additive model to impression formation. *Science,* 1962, *138,* 817-818.

Anderson, N. H. Component rating in impression formation. *Psychonomic Science,* 1966, *6,* 279-380.

Anderson, N. H. Integration theory and attitude change. *Psychological Review,* 1971, *78,* 171-206. (a)

Anderson, N. H. Two more tests against change of meaning in adjective combinations. *Journal of Verbal Learning and Verbal Behavior,* 1971, *10,* 75-85. (b)

Anderson, N. H. Information integration theory applied to attitudes about U.S. Presidents. *Journal of Educational Psychology,* 1973, *64,* 1-8.

Anderson, N. H. Algebraic models in perception. In E. C. Carterette & M. P. Friedman (Eds.), *Handbook of perception* (Vol. 2). New York: Academic Press, 1974. (a)

Anderson, N. H. Cognitive algebra. In L. Berkowitz (Ed.), *Advances in experimental social psychology* (Vol. 7). New York: Academic Press, 1974. (b)

Anderson, N. H. Information integration theory: A brief survey. In D. H. Krantz, R. C. Atkinson, R. D. Luce, & P. Suppes (Eds.), *Contemporary developments in mathematical psychology* (Vol. 2). San Francisco: Freeman, 1974. (c)

Anderson, N. H. How functional measurement can yield validated interval scales of mental quantities. *Journal of Applied Psychology,* 1976, *61,* 677-692. (a)

Anderson, N. H. *Integration theory applied to cognitive responses and attitudes* (Tech. Rep. CHIP 68). La Jolla, Calif.: University of California, San Diego, Center for Human Information Processing, December 1976. (b)

Anderson, N. H. Note on functional measurement and data analysis. *Perception & Psychophysics,* 1977, *21,* 201-215.

Anderson, N. H. Progress in cognitive algebra. In L. Berkowitz (Ed.), *Cognitive theories in social psychology.* New York: Academic Press, 1978.

Anderson, N. H. Algebraic rules in psychological measurement. *American Scientist,* 1979, *67,* 555-563.

Anderson, N. H. *Information integration theory: A case history in experimental science* (Vol. 1). New York: Academic Press, in press.

Anderson, N. H., & Graesser, C. C. An information integration analysis of attitude change in group discussion. *Journal of Personality and Social Psychology*, 1976, *34*, 210-222.

Anderson, N. H., & Hovland, C. I. The representation of order effects in communication research. In C. I. Hovland (Ed.), *The order of presentation in persuasion*. New Haven Conn.: Yale University Press, 1957.

Anderson, N. H., & Hubert, S. Effects of concomitant verbal recall on order effects in personality impression formation. *Journal of Verbal Learning and Verbal Behavior*, 1963, *2*, 379-391.

Anderson, N. H., & Lopes, L. L. Some psycholinguistic aspects of person perception. *Memory & Cognition*, 1974, *2*, 67-74.

Anderson, N. H., & Shanteau, J. Weak inference with linear models. *Psychological Bulletin*, 1977, *84*, 1155-1170.

Apsler, R., & Sears, D. O. Warning, personal involvement, and attitude change. *Journal of Personality and Social Psychology*, 1968, *9*, 162-168.

Arkin, R. M. *Self-presentation: The effects of anticipated approach and public commitment on attitudes*. Unpublished doctoral dissertation, University of Southern California, 1976.

Aronson, E. Dissonance theory: Progress and problems. In R. Abelson, E. Aronson, W. McGuire, T. Newcomb, M. Rosenberg, & P. Tannenbaum (Eds.), *Theories of cognitive consistency: A sourcebook*. Chicago: Rand McNally, 1968.

Aronson, E., & Carlsmith, J. M. Effect of the severity of threat on the devaluation of forbidden behavior. *Journal of Abnormal and Social Psychology*, 1963, *66*, 584-588.

Aronson, E., & Carlsmith, J. M. Experimentation in social psychology. In G. Lindzey & E. Aronson (Eds.), *The handbook of social psychology* (2nd ed., Vol. 2). Reading, Mass.: Addison-Wesley, 1968.

Aronson, E., Turner, J. A., & Carlsmith, J. M. Communicator credibility and cummunication discrepancy as determinants of opinion change. *Journal of Abnormal and Social Psychology*, 1963, *67*, 31-36.

Asch, S. E. Forming impressions of personality. *Journal of Abnormal and Social Psychology*, 1946, *41*, 258-290.

Asch, S. E. The doctrine of suggestion, prestige and imitation in social psychology. *Psychological Review*, 1948, *55*, 250-276.

Asch, S. E. Effects of group pressure on the modification and distortion of judgments. In H. Geutzkow (Ed.), *Groups, leadership, and men*. Pittsburg, Pa.: Carnegie, 1951.

Asch, S. E. Studies of independence and conformities. *Psychological Monographs*, 1956, *70*(9, Whole No. 416).

Atkins, A. L., Deaux, K. K., & Bieri, J. Latitude of acceptance and attitude change: Empirical evidence for a reformulation. *Journal of Personality and Social Psychology*, 1967, *6*, 47-54.

Averill, J. R. Autonomic response patterns during sadness and mirth. *Psychophysiology*, 1969, *5*, 399-414.

Ax, A. F. The physiological differentiation between fear and anger in humans. *Psychosomatic Medicine*, 1953, *15*, 433-442.

Bahrick, H. P., & Boucher, B. Retention of visual and verbal codes of the same stimuli. *Journal of Experimental Psychology*, 1968, *78*, 417-422.

Baker, W. M., Sandman, C. A., & Pepinsky, H. B. Affectivity of task, rehearsal time, and physiological response. *Journal of Abnormal Psychology*, 1975, *84*, 539-544.

Barber, T. X. *Pitfalls in human research: Ten pivotal points*. New York: Pergamon Press, 1976.

Barlow, J. D. Pupillary size as an index of preference in political candidates. *Perceptual and Motor Skills*, 1969, *28*, 587-590.

Baron, R. S., Baron, P. H., & Miller, N. The relation between distraction and persuasion. *Psychological Bulletin*, 1973, *80*, 310-323.

Baron, R. S., & Miller, N. Credibility, distraction, and counterargument in a forewarning situation. *Proceedings of the 77th Annual Convention of the American Psychological Association,* 1969, *4,* 411–412.

Bartlett, F. C. *Remembering: A study in experimental and social psychology.* Cambridge, England: Cambridge University Press, 1932.

Bauer, R. A. *A revised model of source effect.* Presidential address of the Division of Consumer Psychology, American Psychological Association Annual Convention, Chicago, Ill., September 1965.

Baumgardner, M. H., Leippe, M. R., & Ostrom, T. M. *The role of criterial attributes in the organization of cognitive representations.* Paper presented at the Mid-Western Psychological Association, Chicago, May 1976.

Beaber, R. J. *The general characteristics of covert resistance mechanisms, and their relationship to attitude change and speaker perception.* Unpublished doctoral dissertation, University of Southern California, 1975.

Beach, F. A. It's all in your mind. *Psychology Today,* 1969, *3,* 33–35.

Bechterew, V. M., & deLange, M. Die Ergebnisse des Experiments auf dem Gebiete der Kollectiven. Reflexologie, *Zietschrift für Angewandte Psychologie,* 1924, *24,* 305–344.

Becknell, J. C., Wilson, W. R., and Baird, J. C. The effect of frequency of presentation on the choice of nonsense syllables. *Journal of Psychology,* 1963, *56,* 165–170.

Bell, P. R., & Jamieson, B. D. Publicity of initial decisions and the risky shift phenomenon. *Journal of Personality and Social Psychology,* 1970, *6,* 329–345.

Bem, D. J. Self-perception: An alternative interpretation of cognitive dissonance phenomena. *Psychological Review,* 1967, *74,* 182–200.

Bem, D. J. Attitudes as self-descriptions: Another look at the attitude–behavior link. In A. Greenwald, T. Brock, & T. Ostrom (Eds.), *Psychological foundations of attitudes.* New York: Academic Press, 1968.

Bem, D. J. *Beliefs, attitudes and human affairs.* Belmont, Calif: Brooks/Cole, 1970.

Bergin, A. The effect of dissonant persuasive communications upon changes in a self-referring attitude. *Journal of Personality,* 1962, *30,* 423–438.

Bergman, G. The problem of relations in classical psychology. *Philosophical Quarterly,* 1952, *7,* 140–152.

Berkowitz, L., & Cottingham, D. R.The interest value and relevance of fear-arousing communications. *Journal of Abnormal and Social Psychology,* 1960, *60,* 37–43.

Berkowitz, L., & Lundy, R. M. Personality characteristics related to susceptibility to influence by peers or authority figures. *Journal of Personality,* 1957, *25,* 306–316.

Berlyne, D. E. *Conflict, arousal, and curiosity.* New York: McGraw-Hill, 1960.

Berlyne, D. E. Curiosity and exploration. *Science,* 1966, *153,* 25–33.

Berlyne, D. E. Novelty, complexity, and hedonic value. *Perception & Psychophysics,* 1970, *8,* 279–286.

Berlyne, D. E. *Aesthetics and psychobiology.* New York: Appleton-Century-Crofts, 1971.

Berscheid, E. Opinion change and communicator–communicatee similarity and dissimilarity. *Journal of Personality and Social Psychology,* 1966, *4,* 670–680.

Bieri, J. Cognitive complexity–simplicity and predictive behavior. *Journal of Abnormal and Social Psychology,* 1955, *51,* 263–268.

Biferno, M. A., & Dawson, M. E. The onset of contingency awareness and electrodermal classical conditioning: An analysis of temporal relationships during acquisition and extinction. *Psychophysiology,* 1977, *14,* 164–171.

Biondo, J., & MacDonald, A. P. Internal–external locus of control and response to influence attempts. *Journal of Personality,* 1971, *39,* 407–419.

Birnbaum, M. H. Intuitive numerical prediction. *American Journal of Psychology,* 1976, *89,* 417–429.

Birnbaum, M. H., & Mellers, B. A. One-mediator model of exposure effects is still viable. *Journal of Personality and Social Psychology*, 1979, *37*, 1090–1096 (a).

Birnbaum, M. H., & Mellers, B. A. Stimulus recognition may mediate exposure effects. *Journal of Personality and Social Psychology*, 1979, *37*, 391–394 (b).

Birnbaum, M. H., & Stegner, S. E. Source credibility in social judgment: Bias, expertise, and the judge's point of view. *Journal of Personality and Social Psychology*, 1979, *37*, 48–74.

Birnbaum, M. H., Wong, R., & Wong, L. Combining information from sources that vary in credibility. *Memory & Cognition*, 1976, *4*, 330–336.

Bishop, G. D., & Myers, D. G. Information influence in group discussion. *Organizational Behavior and Human Performance*, 1974, *12*, 92–104.

Bither, S. W., & Wright, P. L. The self-confidence-advertising response relationship: A function of situational distraction. *Journal of Marketing Research*, 1973, *10*, 146–152.

Blaylock, B. Some antecedents of directional fractionation: Effects of "intake-rejection," verbalization requirements, and threat of shock on heart rate and skin conductance. *Psychophysiology*, 1972, *9*, 40–52.

Bobrow, D. G., & Norman, D. A. Some principles of memory schemata. In D. Bobrow & A. Collins (Eds.), *Representation and understanding: Studies in cognitive science*. New York: Academic Press, 1975.

Bochner, S., & Insko, C. A. Communicator discrepancy, source credibility, and opinion change. *Journal of Personality and Social Psychology*, 1966, *4*, 614–621.

Bogart, L., Tolley, B. S., & Orenstein, F. What one little ad can do. *Journal of Advertising Research*, 1970, *10*, 3–13.

Bonvallet, M., & Allen, M. B. Prolonged spontaneous and evolved reticular activation following discrete bulbar lesions. *Electroencephalography and Clinical Neurophysiology*, 1963, *15*, 969–988.

Bonvallet, M., Dell, P., & Hiebel, G. Tanus sympathique et activite electrique corticale. *Electroencephalography and Clinical Neurophysiology*, 1954, *6*, 119–144.

Boring, E. G. *A history of experimental psychology*. New York: Century, 1929.

Boring, E. G. A new ambiguous figure. *American Journal of Psychology*, 1930, *42*, 444–445.

Boucher, J., & Osgood, C. E. The Pollyanna hypothesis. *Journal of Verbal Learning and Verbal Behavior*, 1969, *8*, 1–8.

Bransford, J. D., & Johnson, M. K. Considerations of some problems of comprehension. In W. Chase (Ed.), *Visual information processing*. New York: Academic Press, 1973.

Brehm, J. W. *A theory of psychological reactance*. New York: Academic Press, 1966.

Brehm, J. W., & Cohen, A. R. *Explorations in cognitive dissonance*. New York: Wiley, 1962.

Brickman, P., & D'Amato, B. Exposure effects in a free-choice situation. *Journal of Personality and Social Psychology*, 1975, *32*, 415–420.

Brickman, P., Redfield, J., Harrison, A. A., & Crandall, R. Drive and predisposition as factors in the attitudinal effects of mere exposure. *Journal of Experimental Social Psychology*, 1972, *8*, 31–44.

Brink, J. H. Impression order effects as a function of the personal relevance of the object of description. *Memory & Cognition*, 1974, *2*, 561–565.

Brock, T. C. Cognitive restructuring and attitude change. *Journal of Abnormal and Social Psychology*, 1962, *64*, 264–271.

Brock, T. C. Communicator-recipient similarity and decision change. *Journal of Personality and Social Psychology*, 1965, *1*, 650–654.

Brock, T. C. Communication discrepancy and intent to persuade as determinants of counterargument production. *Journal of Experimental Social Psychology*, 1967, *3*, 296–309.

Brock, T. C. Implications of commodity theory for value change. In A. Greenwald, T. Brock, & T. Ostrom (Eds.), *Psychological foundations of attitudes*. New York: Academic Press, 1968.

Brock, T. C., & Becker, L. A. Ineffectiveness of "overheard" counterpropaganda. *Journal of Personality and Social Psychology*, 1965, *2*, 654–660.

Brock, T. C., & Blackwood, J. Dissonance reduction, social comparison, and modification of other's opinion. *Journal of Abnormal and Social Psychology*, 1962, *65*, 197–201.

Brooks, W. N., & Doob, A. N. Justice and the jury. *Journal of Social Issues*, 1975, *31*, 171–182.

Brown, R. *Social psychology*. New York: Free Press, 1965.

Buckhout, R. Changes in heart rate accompanying attitude change. *Journal of Personality and Social Psychology*, 1966, *4*, 695–699.

Burdick, J. A. Cardiac activity and attitude. *Journal of Personality and Social Psychology*, 1972, *22*, 80–86.

Burgess, T. D. G., & Sales, S. M. Attitudinal effects of mere exposure: A re-evaluation. *Journal of Experimental Social Psychology*, 1971, *7*, 461–472.

Burnstein, E., Stotland, E., & Zander, A. Similarity to a model and self-evaluation. *Journal of Abnormal and Social Psychology*, 1961, *62*, 257–264.

Burnstein, E., & Vinokur, A. Testing two classes of theories about group-induced shifts in individual choice. *Journal of Experimental Social Psychology*, 1973, *9*, 123–137.

Burnstein, E., & Vinokur, A. What a person thinks upon learning he has chosen differently from others: Nice evidence for the persuasive-arguments explanation of choice shifts. *Journal of Experimental Social Psychology*, 1975, *11*, 412–426.

Burnstein, E., & Vinokur, A. Persuasive argumentation and social comparison as determinants of attitude polarization. *Journal of Experimental Social Psychology*, 1977, *13*, 315–332.

Burnstein, E., Vinokur, A., & Trope, Y. Interpersonal comparison versus persuasive argumentation: A more direct test of alternative explanations for group-induced shifts in individual choice. *Journal of Experimental Social Psychology*, 1973, *9*, 236–245.

Byrne, D. Interpersonal attraction and attitude similarity. *Journal of Abnormal and Social Psychology*, 1961, *62*, 713–715.

Byrne, D. Attitudes and attraction. In L. Berkowitz (Ed.), *Advances in experimental social psychology* (Vol. 4). New York: Academic Press, 1969.

Byrne, D. Sexual imagery. In J. Money & H. Musaph (Eds.), *Handbook of sexology*. Amsterdam: Excerpta Medica, 1976.

Cacioppo, J. T. *Heart rate, cognitive response, and persuasion*. Unpublished doctoral dissertation, Ohio State University, 1977.

Cacioppo, J. T. The effects of exogenous changes in heart rate on the facilitation of thought and resistance to persuasion. *Journal of Personality and Social Psychology*, 1979, *37*, 480–489.

Cacioppo, J. T., & Petty, R. E. Attitudes and cognitive responses: An electrophysiological approach. *Journal of Personality and Social Psychology*, 1979, 37, 2181–2199. (a)

Cacioppo, J. T., & Petty, R. E. The effects of message repetition and position on cognitive response, recall, and persuasion. *Journal of Personality and Social Psychology*, 1979, *37*, 97–109. (b)

Cacioppo, J. T., & Petty, R. E. Lip and nonpreferred forearm EMG activity as a function of orienting task. *Journal of Biological Psychology*, 1979, *9*, 103–113. (c)

Cacioppo, J. T., Petty, R. E., & Snyder, C. Cognitive and affective response as a function of relative hemispheric involvement. *International Journal of Neuroscience*, 1979, *9*, 81–89.

Cacioppo, J. T., & Sandman, C. A. Physiological differentiation of sensory and cognitive tasks as a function of warning, processing demands, and reported unpleasantness. *Journal of Biological Psychology*, 1978, *6*, 181–192.

Cacioppo, J. T., Sandman, C., & Walker, B. The effects of operant heart rate conditioning on cognitive elaboration and attitude change. *Psychophysiology*, 1978, *15*, 330–338.

Calder, B. J., Insko, C. A., & Yandell, B. The relation of cognitive and memorial processes to persuasion in a simulated jury trial. *Journal of Applied Social Psychology*, 1974, *4*, 62–93.

Calder, B. J., Ross, M. A., & Insko, C. A. Attitude change and attitude attribution: Effects of incentive, choice, and consequences. *Journal of Personality and Social Psychology*, 1973, *25*, 84–99.

Calder, B. J., & Sternthal, B. Television commercial wearout: An information processing view. *Journal of Marketing Research,* in press.

Campbell, D. T. Social attitudes and other acquired behavioral dispositions. In S. Kock (Ed.), *Psychology: A study of science* (Vol. 6). New York: McGraw-Hill, 1963.

Campbell, D. T. Prospective: Artifact and control. In R. Rosenthal & R. Rosnow (Eds.), *Artifact in behavioral research.* New York: Academic Press, 1969.

Campbell, D. T., & Fiske, D. W. Convergent and discriminant validation by the multitrait multimethod matrix. *Psychological Bulletin,* 1959, *56,* 91–105.

Campbell, D. T., & Stanley, J. C. *Experimental and quasi-experimental designs for research.* Chicago: Rand McNally, 1966.

Cannon, W. B. The James–Lange theory of emotions: A critical examination and alternate theory. *American Journal of Psychology,* 1927, *39,* 106–124.

Cantor, G. N. Children's "like–dislike" ratings of familiarized and nonfamiliarized visual stimuli. *Journal of Experimental Child Psychology,* 1968, *6,* 651–657.

Carlsmith, J. M., Ellsworth, P. C., & Aronson, E. *Methods of research in social psychology.* Reading, Mass.: Addison-Wesley, 1976.

Carlson, E. R. Attitude change through modification of attitude structure. *Journal of Abnormal and Social Psychology,* 1956, *52,* 256–261.

Carr, L., & Roberts, S. Correlates of civil rights participation. *Journal of Social Psychology,* 1965, *65,* 259–267.

Carter, R. F., Ruggels, W. L., Jackson, K. M., & Heffner, M. B. Application of signaled stopping technique to communication research. In P. Clarke (Ed.), *New models for mass communication research.* Beverly Hills, Calif: Sage Publications, 1973.

Carter, R. F., & Simpson, R. (1970) cited in P. Clark (Ed.), *New models for mass communication research.* Beverly Hills, Calif.: Sage Publications, 1973.

Cartwright, D. Some principles of mass persuasion. *Human Relations,* 1949, *2,* 253–267.

Cartwright, D., & Harary, F. Structural balance: A generalization of Heider's theory. *Psychological Review,* 1956, *63,* 277–293.

Carver, C. S. Physical aggression as a function of objective self-awareness and attitudes towards punishment. *Journal of Experimental Social Psychology,* 1975, *11,* 510–519.

Chaiken, S. *Locus of control beliefs and responsiveness to social influence: A critical review.* Unpublished manuscript, University of Massachusetts, 1975.

Chaiken, S. Communicator physical attractiveness and persuasion. *Journal of Personality and Social Psychology,* 1979, *37,* 1387–1397.

Chaiken, S., & Eagly, A. H. Communication modality as a determinant of message persuasiveness and message comprehensibility. *Journal of Personality and Social Psychology,* 1976, *34,* 605–614.

Chen, W. K. C. The influence of oral propaganda material upon students' attitudes. *Archives Psychology* (New York), 1935, No. 150.

Chu, G. Prior familiarity, perceived bias, and one-sided versus two-sided communications. *Journal of Experimental Social Psychology,* 1967, *3,* 243–254.

Cialdini, R. B. Attitudinal advocacy in the verbal conditioner. *Journal of Personality and Social Psychology,* 1971, *17,* 350–358.

Cialdini, R. B., & Insko, C. A. Attitudinal verbal reinforcement as a function if informational consistency: A further test of the two-factor theory. *Journal of Personality and Social Psychology,* 1969, *12,* 342–350.

Cialdini, R. B., Levy, A., Herman, C. P., & Evenbeck, S. Attitudinal politics: The strategy of moderation. *Journal of Personality and Social Psychology,* 1973, *25,* 100–108.

Cialdini, R. B., Levy, A., Herman, C. P., Kozlowski, L. T., & Petty, R. E. Elastic shifts of opinion: Determinants of direction and durability. *Journal of Personality and Social Psychology,* 1976, *34,* 663–672.

Clark, R. D., Crockett, W. H., & Archer, R. L. Risk as value hypothesis: The relationship between perception of self, others, and the risky shift. *Journal of Personality and Social Psychology,* 1971, *20,* 425-429.

Clark, R. D., & Willems, E. P. Where is the risky shift? *Journal of Personality and Social Psychology,* 1969, *13,* 215-221.

Cohen, A. R. Need for cognition and order of communication as determinants of opinion change. In C. Hovland, W. Mandell, E. Campbell, T. Brock, A. Luchins, A. Cohen, W. McGuire, I. Janis, R. Feierabend, & N. Anderson (Eds.), *The order of presentation in persuasion.* New Haven, Conn.: Yale University Press, 1957.

Cohen, A. R. Some implications of self-esteem for social influence. In C. I. Hovland & I. L. Janis (Eds.), *Personality and persuasibility.* New Haven, Conn.: Yale University Press, 1959.

Cohen, A. R. *Attitude change and social influence.* New York: Basic Books, 1964.

Cohen, J. *Statistical power analysis for the behavioral sciences.* New York: Academic Press, 1977.

Collins, B. E.;*Social psychology.* Reading, Mass: Addison-Wesley, 1970.

Collins, B. E. Four components of the Rotter internal-external scale: Belief in a difficult world, a just world, a predictable world, and a politically responsive world. *Journal of Personality and Social Psychology,* 1974, *29,* 381-391.

Collins, B. E., Ellsworth, P. C., & Helmreich, R. L. Correlations between pupil size and the semantic differential: An experimental paradigm and pilot study. *Psychonomic Science,* 1967, *9,* 627-628.

Collins, B. E., & Hoyt, M. F. Personal responsibility-for-consequences: An integration and extension of the "forced-compliance" literature. *Journal of Experimental Social Psychology,* 1972, *6,* 558-593.

Condry, J., & Dyer, S. Fear of success: Attribution of cause to the victim. *Journal of Social Issues,* 1976, *32,* 63-83.

Cook, S. W., & Selltiz, C. A multiple-indicator approach to attitude measurement. *Psychological Bulletin,* 1964, *62,* 36-55.

Cook, T. D. Competence, counterarguing, and attitude change. *Journal of Personality,* 1969, *37,* 342-358.

Cook, T. D., & Campbell, D. T. The design and conduct of quasi-experiments and true experiments in field settings. In M. Dunnette (Ed.), *Handbook of industrial and organizational psychology.* Chicago: Rand McNally, 1976.

Cook, T. D., & Flay, B. R. The temporal persistence of experimentally induced attitude change: An evaluative review. In L. Berkowitz (Ed.), *Advances in experimental social psychology.* New York: Academic Press, 1978.

Cook, T. D., & Insko, C. A. Persistence of induced attitude change as a function of conclusion re-exposure. *Journal of Personality and Social Psychology,* 1968, *9,* 322-328.

Cooley, C. H. *Human nature and the social order.* Boston: Scribner, 1902.

Coombs, C. H. *A theory of psychological scaling.* Ann Arbor, Mich.: Engineering Research Institute, University of Michigan, 1952.

Coombs, C. H., Dawes, R. M., & Tversky, A. *Mathematical psychology,* Englewood Cliffs, N.J.: Prentice-Hall, 1970.

Cooper, E., & Dinerman, H. Analysis of the film "Don't Be A Sucker": A study of communication. *Public Opinion Quarterly,* 1951, *15,* 243-264.

Cooper, J., & Jones, E. E. Opinion divergence as a strategy to avoid being miscast. *Journal of Personality and Social Psychology,* 1969, *13,* 23-30.

Cooper, J., & Jones, R. A. Self-esteem and consistency as determinants of anticipatory opinion change. *Journal of Personality and Social Psychology,* 1970, *14,* 312-320.

Cooper, J., & Worchel, S. Rule of undesired consequences in arousing cognitive dissonance. *Journal of Personality and Social Psychology,* 1970, *16,* 199-206.

Cooper, J., Zanna, M. P., & Taves, P. A. Arousal as a necessary condition for attitude change following forced compliance. *Journal of Personality and Social Psychology,* 1978, *36,* 1101-1106.

Cooper, J. B. Emotion in prejudice. *Science,* 1959, *130,* 314-318.

Cooper, J. B., & Pollock, D. The identification of prejudicial attitudes by the galvanic skin response. *Journal of Social Psychology,* 1959, *50,* 241-245.

Cooper, J. B., & Siegel, H. E. The galvanic skin response as a measure of emotion in prejudice. *Journal of Psychology,* 1956, *42,* 149-155.

Cooper, J. B., & Singer, D. N. The role of emotion in prejudice. *Journal of Social Psychology,* 1956, *44,* 241-247.

Cooper, R. E., & Crano, W. D. Sources of bias in the comparison of attitude change models. *Sociometry,* 1974, *37,* 66-78.

Coopersmith, S. A method for determining types of self-esteem. *Journal of Abnormal and Social Psychology,* 1959, *59,* 87-94.

Corey, S. M. Professed attitudes and actual behavior. *Journal of Educational Psychology,* 1937, *28,* 271-280.

Cottrell, N. B. Heider's structural balance principle as a conceptual rule. *Journal of Personality and Social Psychology,* 1975, *31,* 713-720.

Couch, A., & Keniston, K. Yeasayers and naysayers: Agreeing response set as a personality variable. *Journal of Abnormal and Social Psychology,* 1960, *60,* 151-174.

Cox, D. F., & Bauer, R. A. Self-confidence and persuasibility in women. *Public Opinion Quarterly,* 1964, *28,* 453-466.

Crandall, J. E. Predictive value and confirmability of traits as determinants of judged trait importance. *Journal of Personality,* 1970, *38,* 77-90.

Crandall, J. E., Montgomery, V. E., & Reese, W. W. Mere exposure versus familiarity, with implications for response competition and expectancy arousal hypothesis. *Journal of General Psychology,* 1973, *88,* 105-120.

Crandall, R. Field extension of the frequency-affect findings. *Psychological Reports,* 1972, *31,* 371-374.

Crandall, R. The measurement of self-esteem and related constructs. In J. P. Robinson & P. R. Shaver (Eds.), *Measures of social psychological attitudes* (Rev. ed.). Ann Arbor, Mich.: Institute for Social Research, 1973.

Crandall, R., Harrison, A. A., & Zajonc, R. B. *The permanence of the positive and negative effects of stimulus exposure: A "sleeper effect"?* Unpublished manuscript, University of Michigan, 1975.

Crano, W. D., & Brewer, M. D. *Principles of research in social psychology.* New York: McGraw-Hill, 1973.

Crowne, D. P., & Liverant, S. Conformity under varying conditions of personal commitment. *Journal of Abnormal and Social Psychology,* 1963, *66,* 547-555.

Crutchfield, R. S. Conformity and character. *American Psychologist,* 1955, *10,* 191-198.

Cullen, D. M. *Attitude measurement by cognitive sampling.* Unpublished doctoral dissertation, Ohio State University, 1968.

Dabbs, J. M., & Leventhal, H. Effects of varying the recommendations in a fear-arousing communication. *Journal of Personality and Social Psychology,* 1966, *4,* 525-531.

Darley, J. M., & Aronson, E. Self-evaluation versus direct anxiety reduction as determinants of the fear-affiliation relationship. *Journal of Experimental Social Psychology,* 1966, Supplement 1, pp. 66-79.

Darrow, C. W. Differences in the physiological reactions to sensory and ideational stimuli. *Psychological Bulletin,* 1929, *26,* 185-201.

Darrow, C. W. The galvanic skin reflex (sweating) and blood pressure as preparatory and facilitative functions. *Psychological Bulletin,* 1936, *33,* 73-94.

Darwin, C. *The expressions of the emotions in man and animals.* London: Murray, 1872.

Davis, J. H. Group decision and social interaction: A theory of social decision schemes. *Psychological Review,* 1973, *80,* 97-125.

Davis, R. C. Response patterns. *Transactions of the New York Academy of Science*, 1957, *19*, 731–739.

Dawson, M. E., & Reardon, P. Effects of facilitory and inhibitory sets on GSR conditioning and extinction. *Journal of Experimental Psychology*, 1969, *82*, 462–466.

Deaux, K. K. Variations in warning, information preference, and anticipatory attitude change. *Journal of Personality and Social Psychology*, 1968, *9*, 157–161.

Deaux, K. K. Anticipatory attitude change: A direct test of the self-esteem hypothesis. *Journal of Experimental Social Psychology*, 1972, *8*, 143–155.

Dembroski, T. M. Locus of control and the effectiveness of persuasive communications: Changing dental health practices as measured by a chemical agent. *Dissertation Abstracts International*. 1969, *30*, 2614.

Detweiler, R. A., & Zanna, M. P. On the physiological mediation of attitudinal responses. *Journal of Personality and Social Psychology*, 1976, *33*, 107–116.

Deutsch, M., & Gerard, H. B. A study of normative and informational social influence upon individual judgment. *Journal of Abnormal Social Psychology*, 1955, *51*, 629–630.

Dillehay, R. On the irrelevance of the classical negative evidence concerning the effect of attitudes on behavior. *American Psychologist*, 1973, *28*, 887–891.

Dillehay, R. C., Insko, C. A., & Smith, M. B. Logical consistency and attitude change. *Journal of Personality and Social Psychology*, 1966, *3*, 646–654.

Dinner, S. H., Lewkowicz, B. E., & Copper, J. Anticipatory attitude change as a function of self-esteem and issue familiarity. *Journal of Personality and Social Psychology*, 1972, *24*, 407–412.

Doob, L. The behavior of attitudes. *Psychological Review*, 1947, *54*, 135–156.

Dooling, D. J., & Mullet, R. L. Locus of thematic effects in retention of prose. *Journal of Experimental Psychology*, 1973, *97*, 404–406.

Dreben, E. K., Fiske, S. T., & Hastie, R. The independence of evaluative and item information: Impression and order effects in behavior-based impression formation. *Journal of Personality and Social Psychology*, 1979, *37*, 1758–1768.

Dysinger, D. W. A comparative study of affective responses by means of the impressive and expressive methods. *Psychological Monographs*, 1931, *41*, No. 187, 14–31.

Eagly, A. H. Involvement as a determinant of response to favorable and unfavorable information. *Journal of Personality and Social Psychology*, 1967, *7* (1–15, Whole No. 643).

Eagly, A. H. Responses to attitude-discrepant information as a function of intolerance of inconsistency and category width. *Journal of Personality*, 1969, *37*, 601–617. (a)

Eagly, A. H. Sex differences in the relationship between self-esteem and susceptibility to social influence. *Journal of Personality*, 1969, *37*, 581–591. (b)

Eagly, A. H. Comprehensibility of persuasive arguments as a determinant of opinion change. *Journal of Personality and Social Psychology*, 1974, *29*, 758–773.

Eagly, A. H. Sex differences in influenceability. *Psychological Bulletin*, 1978, *85*, 86–116.

Eagly, A. H., & Himmelfarb, S. Current trends in attitude theory and research. In S. Himmelfarb & A. H. Eagly (Eds.), *Readings in attitude change*. New York: Wiley, 1974.

Eagly, A. H., & Himmelfarb, S. Attitudes and opinions. *Annual Review of Psychology*, 1978, *29*, 517–554.

Eagly, A. H., & Telaak, K. Width of the latitude of acceptance as a determinant of attitude change. *Journal of Personality and Social Psychology*, 1972, *23*, 388–397.

Eagly, A. H., & Warren, R. Intelligence, comprehension, and opinion change. *Journal of Personality*, 1976, *44*, 226–242.

Eagly, A. H., & Whitehead, G. I., III. Effect of choice on receptivity to favorable and unfavorable evaluations of oneself. *Journal of Personality and Social Psychology*, 1972, *22*, 223–230.

Eagly, A. H., Wood, W., & Chaiken, S. Causal inferences about communicators and their effect on opinion change. *Journal of Personality and Social Psychology*, 1978, *36*, 424–435.

Ebbesen, E. B., & Bowers, R. J. Proportion of risky to conservative arguments in a group discussion and choice shift. *Journal of Personality and Social Psychology*, 1974, *29*, 316–327.

Ebbesen, E. B., & Konečni, V. J. *Cognitive algebra in legal decision making.* (Tech. Rep. CHIP 46). La Jolla, Calif.: University of California, San Diego, Center for Human Information Processing, September 1974.

Ebbesen, E. B., & Konečni, V. J. Decision making and information intergration in the courts: The setting of bail. *Journal of Personality and Social Psychology*, 1975, *32*, 805–821.

Ebel, R. L. *And still the dryands linger.* Presidential address, American Psychological Association, Division 5. Honolulu, Hawaii, September 1972.

Edelberg, R. Electrical activity of the skin: Its measurement and uses in psychophysiology. In N. S. Greenfield & R. A. Sternbach (Eds.), *Handbook of psychophysiology*. New York: Holt, Rinehart & Winston, 1972.

Edfeldt, A. W. *Silent speech and silent reading.* Chicago: University of Chicago Press, 1960.

Edwards, A. L. *The social desirability variable in personality assessment and research.* New York: Dryden, 1957. (a)

Edwards, A. L. *Techniques of attitude scale construction.* New York: Appleton-Century-Crofts, 1957. (b)

Edwards, D. C., & Alsip, J. E. Stimulus detection during periods of high and low heart rate. *Psychophsiology*, 1969, *5*, 431–434.

Endler, N. S., & Magnusson, D. Toward an interactional psychology of personality. *Psychological Bulletin*, 1976, *83*, 956–974.

Epstein, S. The self-concept revisited, or a theory of a theory. *American Psychologist*, 1973, *28*, 404–416.

Epstein, S. Traits are alive and well. In D. Magnusson & N. S. Endler (Eds.), *Personality at the crossroads: Current issues in interactional psychology*. Hillsdale, N.J.: Lawrence Erlbaum Associates, 1977.

Epstein, S. The stability of behavior: I. On predicting most of the people much of the time. *Journal of Personality and Social Psychology*, 1979, *37*, 1097–1126.

Ericson, K. A., & Simon, H. A. Retrospective verbal reports as data. C.I.P. Working Paper No. 388, Carnegie-Mellon University, August 4, 1978.

Faison, E. W. J. Effectiveness of one-sided and two-sided mass communications in advertising. *Public Opinion Quarterly*, 1961, *25*, 468–469.

Farkas, A. J., & Anderson, N. H. Inoculation theory and integration theory as explanations of the "paper tiger" effect. *Journal of Social Psychology*, 1976, *98*, 253–268.

Feather, N. T. Balance approach to communication effects. In L. Berkowitz (Ed.), *Advances in experimental social psychology* (Vol. 3). New York: Academic Press, 1967.

Feather, N. T. Organization and discrepancy in cognitive structures. *Psychological Review*, 1971, *78*, 355–379.

Fehr, F. S., & Stern, J. A. Peripheral physiological variables and emotion: The James–Lange theory revisited. *Psychological Bulletin*, 1970, *74*, 411–424.

Feldman, S. (Ed.) *Cognitive Consistency.* New York: Academic Press, 1966.

Ferguson, C., & Kelley, H. Significant factors in overevaluation of own-group's product. *Journal of Abnormal and Social Psychology*, 1964, *69*, 223–228.

Festinger, L. A theory of social comparison processes. *Human Relations*, 1954, *7*, 117–140.

Festinger, L. *A theory of cognitive dissonance.* Stanford, Calif.: Stanford University Press, 1957.

Festinger, L. *Conflict, decision and dissonance.* Stanford, Calif.: Stanford University Press, 1964.

Festinger, L., & Carlsmith, J. M. Cognitive consequences of forced compliance. *Journal of Abnormal and Social Psychology*, 1959, *58*, 203–210.

Festinger, L., & Freedman, J. L. Dissonance reduction and moral values. In P. Worchel & D. Byrne (Eds.), *Personality change*. New York: Wiley, 1964.

Festinger, L., & Maccoby, N. On resistance to persuasive communications. *Journal of Abnormal and Social Psychology,* 1964, *68,* 359–366.

Fillenbaum, G. G. Heider's theory of balance: Internal distinctions and population generality. *Human Relations,* 1968, *21,* 177–210.

Fishbein, M. An investigation of the relationships between beliefs about an object and the attitude toward that object. *Human Relations,* 1963, *16,* 233–240.

Fishbein, M. *Sexual behavior and propositional control.* Paper read at the Psychonomic Society meetings, 1966.

Fishbein, M. Attitudes and the prediction of behavior. In M. Fishbein (Ed.), *Readings in attitude theory and measurement.* New York: Wiley, 1967.

Fishbein, M. The search for attitudinal–behavioral consistency. In J. Cohen (Ed.), *Behavioral science foundations of consumer behavior.* Glencoe, Ill.: Free Press, 1972.

Fishbein, M. The prediction of behaviors from attitudinal variables. In C. Mortenson & K. Sereno (Eds.), *Advances in communication research.* New York: Harper & Row, 1973.

Fishbein, M. Persuasive communication: A social psychological perspective on factors influencing communication effectiveness. In A. E. Bennett (Ed.), *Communication between doctors and patients.* London: Oxford University Press, 1976.

Fishbein, M. A theory of reasoned action: Some aplications and implications. In H. Howe & M. Page (Eds.), *Nebraska Symposium on Motivation, 1979.* Lincoln: University of Nebraska Press, 1980.

Fishbein, M., & Ajzen, I. Attitudes and opinions. *Annual Review of Psychology,* 1972, *23,* 487–544.

Fishbein, M., & Ajzen, I. Attribution of responsibility: A theoretical note. *Journal of Experimental Social Psychology,* 1973, *9,* 148–153.

Fishbein, M., & Ajzen, I. Attitudes towards objects as predictors of single and multiple behavioral criteria. *Psychological Review,* 1974, *81,* 59–74.

Fishbein, M., & Ajzen, I. *Belief, attitude, intention, and behavior: An introduction to theory and research.* Reading, Mass.: Addison-Wesley, 1975.

Fisher, S., Rubinstein, I. I., & Freeman, R. W. Intertrial effects of immediate self-committal in a continuous social influence situation. *Journal of Abnormal and Social Psychology,* 1956, *52,* 200–207.

Flanagan, J. Galvanic skin response: Emotion or attention? *Proceedings of the 75th Annual Convention of the American Psychological Association,* 1967, *2,* 7–8.

Fleming, D. Attitude: The history of a concept. *Perspectives in American History,* 1967, *1,* 287–365.

Foley, L. A. Personality and situational influences on changes in prejudice: A replication of Cook's railroad game in a prison setting. *Journal of Personality and Social Psychology,* 1976, *34,* 846–856.

Frederiksen, C. H. Representing logical and sematic structure of knowledge acquired from discourse. *Cognitive Psychology,* 1975, *7,* 371–458.

Freedman, J. L., & Sears, D. O. Warning, distraction and resistance to influence. *Journal of Personality and Social Psychology,* 1965, *1,* 262–266.

Freedman, J. L., Sears, D. O., & O'Connor, E. F. The effects of anticipated debate and commitment on the polarization of audience opinion. *Public Opinion Quarterly,* 1964, *28,* 615–627.

French, V. L. The structure of sentiments. *Journal of Personality,* 1947, *15,* 247–286.

Freud, S. (1900) [The interpretation of dreams.] In A. A. Brill (Ed. and trans.), *The basic writings of Sigmund Freud.* New York: Random House, 1939.

Freud, S. *Collected papers.* London: The Hogarth Press, Ltd., 1924.

Freund, K., Sedlacek, F., & Knob, K. A simple transducer for mechanical plethysmograph of the male genital. *Journal of the Experimental Analysis of Behavior,* 1965, *8,* 169–170.

Fryrear, R. L., & Cottrell, N. B. *Effects of stimulus complexity and repeated exposures on affective ratings.* Unpublished mansucript, 1975.

Funkhouser, G. R. Effects of differential encoding on recall. *Journal of Verbal Learning and Verbal Behavior*, 1968, *7*, 1016-1023.

Gaes, G. G., & Tedeschi, J. T. An evaluation of self-esteem and impression management theories of anticipatory belief change. *Journal of Experimental Social Psychology*, 1978, *14*, 579-587.

Gardner, R. W., & Schoen, R. A. Differentiation and abstraction in concept formation. *Psychological Monographs*, 1962, *76* (41, Whole No. 560).

Garrity, L. Electromyography: A review of the current status of subvocal speech research. *Memory & Cognition*, 1977, *5*, 615-622.

Geer, J. H., & Fuhr, R. Cognitive factors in sexual arousal: The role of distraction. *Journal of Clinical and Consulting Psychology*, 1976, *44*, 238-243.

Gerard, H. B. Choice difficulty, dissonance, and the decision sequence. *Journal of Personality*, 1967, *35*, 91-108.

Gerard, H. B. Basic features of commitment. In R. P. Abelson, E. Aronson, W. J. McGuires, T. M. Newcomb, M. J. Rosenberg, & P. H. Tannenbaum (Eds.), *Theories of cognitive consistency: A sourcebook*. Chicago: Rand McNally, 1968.

Gergen, K. J., & Bauer, R. A. Interactive effects of self-esteem and task difficulty on social conformity. *Journal of Personality and Social Psychology*, 1967, *6*, 16-22.

Geva, N. *The role of memory in impression formation*. Unpublished doctoral dissertation, Ohio State University, 1977.

Gillig, P. M., & Greenwald, A. G. Is it time to lay the sleeper effect to rest? *Journal of Personality and Social Psychology*, 1974, *29*, 132-139.

Glass, D. C. Theories of consistency and the study of personality. In E. F. Borgatta & W. W. Lambert (Eds.), *Handbook of personality theory and research*. Chicago: Rand McNally, 1968.

Goethals, G. R. Consensus and modality in the attribution process: The role of similarity and information. *Journal of Personality and Social Psychology*, 1972, *21*, 84-92.

Goethals, G. R., & Nelson, R. E. Similarity in the influence process: The belief-value distinction. *Journal of Personality and Social Psychology*, 1973, *25*, 117-122.

Goldstein, M. J. The relationship between coping and avoiding behavior and response to fear-arousing propaganda. *Journal of Abnormal and Social Psychology*, 1959, *58*, 247-252.

Goldwater, B. C. Psychological significance of pupillary movements. *Psychological Bulletin*, 1972, *77*, 340-355.

Gollin, E. S. Forming impressions of personality. *Journal of Personality*, 1954, *23*, 65-76.

Gouge, C., & Fraser, C. A further demonstration of group polarization. *European Journal of Social Psychology*, 1972, *2*, 95-97.

Graesser, C. C. *A social averaging theorem for group decisions*. Unpublished doctoral dissertation, University of California, San Diego, 1977.

Graham, D. T. Some research on psychophysiologic specificity and its relation to psychosomatic disease. In R. Roessler & N. S. Greenfield (Eds.), *Physiological correlates of psychological disorder*. Madison: University of Wisconsin Press, 1962.

Graham, D. T., Kabler, J. D., & Graham, F. K Physiological response to the suggestion of attitudes specific for hives and hypertension. *Psychosomatic Medicine*, 1962, *24*, 159-169.

Grass, R. C., & Wallace, W. H. Satiation effects of T.V. commercials. *Journal of Advertising Research*, 1969, *9*, 3-8.

Greenberg, A., & Suttoni, C. Television commercial wearout. *Journal of Advertising Research*, 1973, *13*, 45-57.

Greenberg, B. S., & Miller, G. R. The effects of low-credible sources on message acceptance. *Speech Monographs*, 1966, *33*, 127-136.

Greenberg, B. S., & Tannenbaum, P. H. The effects of bylines on attitude change. *Journalism Quarterly*, 1961, *38*, 535-537.

Greenwald, A. G. *An amended learning model of persuasion*. Paper read at American Psychological Association meeting, Washington, D.C., 1967.

Greenwald, A. G. Cognitive learning, cognitive response to persuasion and attitude change. In A.

G. Greenwald, T. C. Brock, & T. M. Ostrom (Eds.), *Psychological foundations of attitudes.* New York: Academic Press, 1968. (a)

Greenwald, A. G. On defining attitude and attitude theory. In A. G. Greenwald, T. C. Brock, & T. M. Ostrom (Eds.), *Psychological foundations of attitudes.* New York: Academic Press, 1968. (b)

Greenwald, A. G. Consequences of prejudice against the null hypothesis, *Psychological Bulletin,* 1975, *82,* 1-20.

Greenwald, A. G. The totalitarian ego: Fabrication and revision of personal history. *American Psychologist,* 1980, *35,* 603-618.

Greenwald, A. G., & Albert, R. D. Acceptance and recall of improvised arguments. *Journal of Personality and Social Psychology,* 1968, *8,* 31-34.

Greenwald, A. G., Brock, T. C., & Ostrom, T. M. (Eds.). *Psychological foundations of attitudes.* New York: Academic Press, 1968.

Grings, W. W. The role of consciousness and cognition in autonomic behavior change. In F. J. McQuigan & R. A. Schoonover (Eds.), *The psychophysiology of thinking: Studies of covert processes.* New York: Academic Press, 1973.

Gruder, C. L., Cook, T. D., Hennigan, K. M., Flay, B. R., Alessis, C., & Halamaj, J. Empirical tests of the absolute sleeper effect predicted from the discounting cue hypothesis. *Journal of Personality and Social Psychology,* 1978, *36,* 1061-1074.

Grush, J. E. Attitude formation and mere exposure phenomena: A nonartificial explanation of empirical findings. *Journal of Personality and Social Psychology,* 1976, *33,* 281-290.

Guttman, L. An outline of the statistical theory of prediction. In P. Horst, P. Wallin, & L. Guttman, (Eds.), *The prediction of personal adjustment.* New York: Social Science Research Council, 1941.

Guttman, L. A basis for scaling qualitative data. *American Sociological Review,* 1944, *9,* 139-150.

Haaland, G. A., & Venkatesan, M. Resistance to persuasive communications: An examination of the distraction hypothesis. *Journal of Personality and Social Psychology,* 1968, *9,* 167-170.

Hallonquist, T., & Suchman, E. A. Listening to the listener. In P. Lazarsfeld & F. Stanton (Eds.), *Radio research 1943-1945.* New York: Duell, Sloan and Pearce, 1944.

Hamid, P. N. Exposure frequency and stimulus preference. *British Journal of Psychology,* 1973, *64,* 569-577.

Hamid, P. N., & Flay, B. R. Changes in locus of control as a function of value modification. *British Journal of Social and Clinical Psychology,* 1974, *13,* 143-150.

Hammond, K. R. Measuring attitudes by error-choice: An indirect method. *Journal of Abnormal and Social Psychology,* 1948, *43,* 38-48.

Hansen, F. C. C., & Lehmann, A. Ueber unwillkürliches Flüstern. *Philo. Studien,* 1895, *11,* 471-530. Cited in Edfeldt, 1960.

Harding, J., Kutner, B., Proshansky, H., & Chein, I. Prejudice and ethnic relations. In G. Lindzey (Ed.), *Handbook of social psychology.* Reading, Mass.: Addison-Wesley, 1954.

Hardyck, J. A. *Cognitive interrelationships and resistance to influence.* Unpublished doctoral dissertation, Stanford University, 1962.

Harrison, A. A. Response competition, frequency, exploratory behavior, and liking. *Journal of Personality and Social Psychology,* 1968, *9,* 363-368.

Harrison, A. A. Exposure and popularity. *Journal of Personality,* 1969, *37,* 359-377.

Harrison, A. A. Mere exposure. In L. Berkowitz (Ed.), *Advances in experimental social psychology* (Vol. 10). New York: Academic Press, 1977.

Harrison, A. A., & Crandall, R. Heterogeneity-homogeneity of exposure sequence and the attitudinal effects of exposure. *Journal of Personality and Social Psychology,* 1972, *21,* 234-238.

Harrison, A. A., & Fisicaro, S. A. Stimulus familiarity and alley illumination as determinants of approach response latencies of house crickets. *Perceptual and Motor Skills,* 1974, *39,* 147-152.

Harrison, A. A., & Hines, P. Effects of frequency of exposure at three short exposure times on affective ratings and exploratory behavior. *Proceedings of the 78th Annual Convention of the American Psychological Association,* 1970, *5,* 391-392.

Harrison, A. A., Tutone, R. M., & McFadgen, D. G. Effects of frequency of exposure of changing and unchanging stimulus pairs on affective ratings. *Journal of Personality and Social Psychology*, 1971, *29*, 102-111.

Harrison, A. A., & Zajonc, R. B. The effects of frequency and duration of exposure on response competition and affective ratings. *Journal of Psychology*, 1970, *75*, 163-169.

Harvey, O., & Beverly, G. Some personality correlates of concept change through role playing. *Journal of Abnormal and Social Psychology*, 1961, *63*, 125-130.

Haslett, D. M. Distracting stimuli: Do they elicit or inhibit counter-argumentation and attitude shift? *European Journal of Social Psychology*, 1976, *6*, 81-94.

Hass, R. G. Resisting persuasion and examining message content: The effects of source credibility and recipient commitment on counterargument production (Doctoral dissertation, Duke University, 1972). *Dissertation Abstracts International*, 1972, *33*, 1305-B.

Hass, R. G. Persuasion or moderation? Two experiments on anticipatory belief change. *Journal of Personality and Social Psychology*, 1975, *31*, 1155-1162.

Hass, R. G. To say or not to say? And if so, when? In N. C. Weissberg (Ed.), *Basic and current studies in social psychology*. New York: Holt, Rinehart & Winston, in press.

Hass, R. G., & Grady, K. Temporal delay, type of forewarning and resistance to influence. *Journal of Experimental Social Psychology*, 1975, *11*, 459-469.

Hass, R. G., & Linder, D. E. Counterargument availability and the effects of message structure on persuasion. *Journal of Personality and Social Psychology*, 1972, *23*, 219-233.

Hass, R. G., & Mann, R. W. Anticipatory belief change: Persuasion or impression management? *Journal of Personality and Social Psychology*, 1976, *34*, 105-111.

Hass, R. G., Mann, R., & Stevens, R. *Anticipatory changes within the latitude of acceptance.* Unpublished manuscript, Brooklyn College, 1977.

Hass, R. G., & Reichig, D. *The effects of source credibility and message structure on persuasion.* Unpublished manuscript, Brooklyn College CUNY, 1977.

Hastorff, A. H., Schneider, D. J., & Polefka, J. *Person perception.* Reading, Mass.: Addison-Wesley, 1970.

Head, H. *Studies in neurology.* London: Frowde, 1920.

Heberlein, T. A., & Black, J. S. Attitudinal specificity and the prediction of behavior in a field setting. *Journal of Personality and Social Psychology*, 1976, *33*, 474-479.

Heeler, R. M. *Laboratory investigation of inter-related effects of mixed insertions in advertising campaigns.* Unpublished doctoral dissertation, Stanford University, 1972.

Heider, F. Attitudes and cognitive organization. *Journal of Psychology*, 1946, *21*, 107-112.

Heider, F. *The psychology of interpersonal relations.* New York: Wiley, 1958.

Heider, F. The gestalt theory of motivation. In M. R. Jones (Ed.), *Nebraska Symposium on Motivation* (Vol. 8). Lincoln: University of Nebraska Press, 1960.

Heingartner, A., & Hall, J. V. Affective consequences in adults and children of repeated exposure to auditory stimuli. *Journal of Personality and Social Psychology*, 1974, *29*, 719-723.

Henninger, M., & Wyer, R. S. The recognition and elimination of inconsistencies among syllogistically related beliefs: Some new light on the "Socratic effect." *Journal of Personality and Social Psychology*, 1976, *34*, 680-693.

Hess, E. H. Attitude and pupil size. *Scientific American*, 1965, *212*, 46-54.

Hess, E. H. Pupillometrics: A method of studying mental, emotional, and sensory processes. In N. S. Greenfield & R. A. Sternbach (Eds.), *Handbook of psychophysiology*. New York: Holt, Rinehart & Winston, 1972.

Hess, E. H., & Polt, J. M. Pupil size as related to interest value of visual stimuli. *Science*, 1960, *132*, 349-350.

Hess, E. H., Seltzer, A. L., & Shlien, J. M. Pupil response of hetero- and homosexual males to pictures of men and women. *Journal of Abnormal Psychology*, 1965, *70*, 165-168.

Hicks, R. A., & LePage, S. *A pupillometric test of the bidirectional hypothesis.* Paper presented at the meeting of the Western Psychological Association, Los Angeles, April 1976.

Higbee, K. L. Fifteen years of fear arousal: Research on threat appeals: 1953-1968. *Psychological Bulletin*, 1969, *72*, 426-444.

Hildum, D. C., & Brown, R. W. Verbal reinforcement and interviewer bias. *Journal of Abnormal and Social Psychology*, 1956, *53*, 108-111.

Hill, F. A. Effects of instructions and subject's need for approval on the conditioned galvanic skin response. *Journal of Experimental Psychology*, 1967, *73*, 461-467.

Hilton, S. Hypothalamic regulation of the cardiovascular system. *British Medical Bulletin*, 1966, *22*, 243-248.

Himmelfarb, S., & Eagly, A. H. Orientations to the study of attitudes and their change. In S. Himmelfarb and A. H. Eagly (Eds.), *Readings in attitude change*. New York: Wiley, 1974.

Hjelle, L. A., & Clouser, R. Susceptibility to attitude change as a function of internal-external control. *Psychological Record*, 1970, *20*, 305-310.

Hoerl, A. E. Application of ridge analysis to regression problems. *Chemical Engineering Progress*, 1962, *58*, 54-59.

Hoerl, A. E., & Kennard, R. W. Ridge regression: Biased estimation for non-orthogonal problems. *Technometrics*, 1970, *72*, 55-67.

Holt, L. E. Resistance to persuasion on explicit beliefs as a function of commitment to and desirability of logically related beliefs. *Journal of Personality and Social Psychology*, 1970, *16*, 583-591.

Holt, L. E., & Watts, W. A. Salience of logical relationships among beliefs as a factor in persuasion. *Journal of Personality and Social Psychology*, 1969, *11*, 193-203.

Horowitz, M. W. Changes in cognitive structure as a function of attributed motive. *Journal of Social Psychology*, 1963, *59*, 53-64.

Horst, P. *Factor analysis of data matrices*. New York: Holt, Rinehart & Winston, 1965.

Horwitz, M. W., & Pastore, N. Relationship of motive to author and statement. *Science*, 1955, *121*, 110-111.

Hovland, C. I. Changes in attitude through communication. *Journal of Abnormal and Social Psychology*, 1951, *46*, 424-437.

Hovland, C. I. Reconciling conflicting results derived from experimental and survey studies of attitude change. *American Psychologist*, 1959, *14*, 8-17.

Hovland, C. I., Janis, I. L., & Kelley, H. H. *Communication and persuasion*. New Haven, Conn.: Yale University Press, 1953.

Hovland, C. I., & Janis, I.L. (Eds.) *Personality and persuasibility*. New Haven, Conn.: Yale University, Press, 1959.

Hovland, C. I., Luchins, A. S., Mandell, W., Campbell, E. H., Brock, T. C., McGuire, W. J., Feierabend, R. L., & Anderson, N. H. (Eds.). *The order of presentation in persuasion*. New Haven, Conn.: Yale University Press, 1957.

Hovland, C. I., Lumsdaine, A. A., & Sheffield, F. D. *Experiments on mass communication*. Princeton, N.J.: Princeton University Press, 1949.

Hovland, C. I., & Mandell, W. An experimental comparison of conclusion-drawing by the communicator and by the audience. *Journal of Abnormal and Social Psychology*, 1952, *47*, 581-588.

Hovland, C. I., & Pritzker, H. A. Extent of opinion change as a function of amount of change advocated. *Journal of Abnormal and Social Psychology*, 1957, *54*, 257-261.

Hovland, C. I., & Weiss, W. The influence of source credibility on communication effectiveness. *Public Opinion Quarterly*, 1951, *15*, 635-650.

Hoyt, M. F., & Janis, I. L. Increasing adherence to a stressful decision via a motivational balance-sheet procedure: A field experiment. *Journal of Personality and Social Psychology*, 1975, *31*, 833-840.

Hyman, H. *Political socialization*. Glencoe, Ill.: Free Press, 1959.

Ikemi, Y., & Nakagawa, S. A psychosomatic study of contagious dermatitis. *Kyushu Journal of Medical Science*, 1962, *13*, 335-350.

Insko, C. A. One-sided versus two-sided communications and counter-communications. *Journal of Abnormal and Social Psychology,* 1962, *65,* 203-206.

Insko, C. A. Primacy versus recency in persuasion as a function of the timing of arguments and measures. *Journal of Abnormal and Social Psychology,* 1964, *69,* 381-391.

Insko, C. A. Verbal reinforcement of attitude. *Journal of Personality and Social Psychology,* 1965, *2,* 621-623.

Insko, C. A. *Theories of attitude change.* New York: Appleton-Century-Crofts, 1967.

Insko, C. A., Blake, R. R., Cialdini, R. B., & Mulaik, S. A. Attitude toward birth control and cognitive consistency: Theoretical and practical implications of survey data. *Journal of Personality and Social Psychology,* 1970, *16,* 228-237.

Insko, C. A., & Butzine, K. W. Rapport, awareness, and verbal reinforcement of attitude. *Journal of Personality and Social Psychology,* 1967, *6,* 225-228.

Insko, C. A., & Cialdini, R. B. A test of three interpretations of attitudinal verbal reinforcement. *Journal of Personality and Social Psychology,* 1969, *12,* 333-341.

Insko, C. A., & Cialdini, R. B. *Interpersonal influence in a controlled setting: The verbal reinforcement of attitude.* New York: General Learning Press, 1971.

Insko, C. A., Lind, E. A., & LaTour, S. Persuasion, recall, and thoughts. *Representative Research in Social Psychology,* 1976, *7,* 66-78.

Insko, C. A., & Melson, W. H. Verbal reinforcement of attitude in laboratory and nonlaboratory contexts. *Journal of Personality,* 1969, *37,* 25-40.

Insko, C. A., & Schopler, J. Triadic consistency: A statement of affective–cognitive–conative consistency. *Psychological Review,* 1967, *74,* 361-376.

Insko, C. A., & Schopler, J. *Experimental social psychology.* New York: Academic Press, 1972.

Insko, C. A., Turnbull, W., & Yandell, B. Facilitating and inhibiting effects of distraction on attitude change. *Sociometry,* 1974, *37,* 508-528.

Insko, C. A., Worchel, S., Folger, R., & Kutkus, A. A balance theory interpretation of dissonance. *Psychological Review,* 1975, *82,* 169-183.

Jaccard, J. J., & Fishbein, M. Inferential beliefs and order effects in personality impression formation. *Journal of Personality and Social Psychology,* 1975, *31,* 1031-1040.

Jacobsen, E. Electrophysiology of mental activities and introduction to the psychological process of thinking. In F. J. McGuigan & R. A. Schoonover (Eds.), *The psychophysiology of thinking: Studies of covert processes.* New York: Academic Press, 1973.

James, W. *The principles of psychology.* New York: Holt, 1890.

James, W. H., Woodruff, A. B., & Werner, W. Effect of internal and external control upon changes in smoking behavior. *Journal of Consulting Psychology,* 1965, *29,* 184-186.

Janis, I. L. Personality correlates of susceptibility to persuasion. *Journal of Personality,* 1954, *22,* 504-518.

Janis, I. L. Anxiety indices related to susceptibility to persuasion. *Journal of Abnormal and Social Psychology,* 1955, *51,* 663-667.

Janis, I. L. Effects of fear arousal on attitude change: Recent developments in theory and experimental research. In L. Berkowitz (Ed.), *Advances in experimental social psychology* (Vol. 3). New York: Academic Press, 1967.

Janis, I. L. *Victims of groupthink: A psychological study of foreign-policy decisions and fiascoes.* Boston: Houghton Mifflin, 1972.

Janis, I. L., & Feshbach, S. Effects of fear-arousing communications. *Journal of Abnormal and Social Psychology,* 1953, *48,* 78-92.

Janis, I. L., & Field, P. B. Sex differences and personality factors related to persuasibility. In C. I. Hovland & I. L. Janis (Eds.), *Personality and persuasibility.* New Haven, Conn.: Yale University Press, 1959.

Janis, I. L., & Hovland, C. I. An overview of persuasibility research. In C. I. Hovland & I. L. Janis (Eds.), *Personality and persuasibility.* New Haven, Conn.: Yale University Press, 1959.

Janis, I. L., Kaye, D., & Kirschner, P. Facilitating effects of "eating-while-reading" on responsiveness to persuasive communications. *Journal of Personality and Social Psychology*, 1965, *1*, 181–186.

Janis, I. L., & King, B. The influence of role-playing on opinion change. *Journal of Abnormal and Social Psychology*, 1954, *49*, 211–218.

Janis, I. L., & Rife, D. Persuasibility and emotional disorder. In C. I. Hovland & I. L Janis (Eds.), *Personality and persuasibility*. New Haven, Conn.: Yale University Press, 1959.

Janis, I. L., & Terwilliger, R. An experimental study of psychological resistance to fear-arousing communication. *Journal of Abnormal and Social Psychology*, 1962, *65*, 403–410.

Janisse, M. P. Attitudinal effects of mere exposure: A replication and extension. *Psychonomic Science*, 1970, *22*, 101–103.

Janisse, M. P. (Ed.). *Pupillary dynamics and behavior*. New York: Plenum Press, 1974.

Jellison, J. M., & Arkin, R. M. Social comparison of abilities: A self-presentational interpretation of decision making in small groups. In J. M. Suls & R. L. Miller (Eds.), *Social comparison processes*. Washington, D.C.: Hemisphere Publishing, 1977.

Jellison, J. M., Jackson-White, R., Bruder, R. A., & Martyna, W. Achievement behavior: A situational interpretation. *Sex Roles*, 1975, *2*, 369–384.

Jellison, J. M., & Mills, J. Effects of public commitment upon opinions. *Journal of Experimental Social Psychology*, 1969, *5*, 340–346.

Jellison, J. M., & Riskind, J. A social comparison of abilities and interpretation of risk taking behavior. *Journal of Personality and Social Psychology*, 1970, *15*, 375–390.

Johnson, H. H., & Izzett, R. R. Relationship between authoritarianism and attitude change as a function of source credibility and type of communication. *Journal of Personality and Social Psychology*, 1969, *13*, 317–321.

Johnson, H. H., & Stanicek, F. F. Relationship between authoritarianism and attitude change as a function of implicit and explicit communications. *Proceedings of the 77th Annual Convention of the American Psychological Association*, 1969, *4*, 415–416.

Johnson, H. H., Torcivia, J. M., & Poprick, M. A. Effects of source credibility on the relationship between authoritarianism and attitude change. *Journal of Personality and Social Psychology*, 1968, *9*, 179–183.

Johnson, H. H., & Watkins, T. A. *The effects of message repetition on attitude change*. Paper presented at the meeting of the Midwestern Psychological Association, Cincinnati, Ohio, 1970.

Johnson, H. H., & Watkins, T. A. The effects of message repetitions on immediate and delayed attitude change. *Psychonomic Science*, 1971, *22*, 101–103.

Johnson, M. A. *The attitudinal effects of mere exposure and the experimental environment*. Paper presented at Western Psychological Association meeting, 1973.

Johnston, V. S., & Chesney, C. L. Electrophysiological correlates of meaning. *Science*, 1974, *186*, 944–946.

Jones, E. E. *Ingratiation: A social psychological analysis*. New York: Appleton-Century-Crofts, 1964.

Jones, E. E., & Aneshansel, J. The learning and utilization of contravaluant material. *Journal of Abnormal and Social Psychology*, 1956, *53*, 27–33.

Jones, E. E., & Gerard, H. B. *Foundations of social psychology*. New York: Wiley, 1967.

Jones, E. E., & Kohler, R. The effects of plausibility on the learning of controversial statements. *Journal of Abnormal and Social Psychology*, 1958, *57*, 315–320.

Jones, G. E., & Johnson, H. J. Physiological responding during self-generated imagery of contextually complete stimuli. *Psychophysiology*, 1978, *15*, 439–446.

Jones, R. A., & Brehm, J. W. Attitudinal effects of communicator attractiveness when one chooses to listen. *Journal of Personality and Social Psychology*, 1967, *6*, 64–70.

Jones, R. A., & Brehm, J. W. Persuasiveness of one and two-sided communications as a function of awareness that there are two sides. *Journal of Experimental Social Psychology*, 1970, *6*, 47–56.

Joreskog, K. G.   Analyzing psychological data by structural analysis of covariance matrices. In D. J. Krantz (Ed.), *Contemporary developments in mathematical psychology* (Vol. 2). San Francisco: Freeman, 1974.

Joreskog, K. G., & van Thillo, M.   *LISREL—A general computer program for estimating a linear structural equation system involving multiple indicators of unmeasured variables* (Research Report 73-5). Uppsala, Sweden: Uppsala University, Statistical Department, 1973.

Kahan, J. P.   A subjective probability interpretation of the risky shift. *Journal of Personality and Social Psychology*, 1975, *31*, 977–982.

Kahneman, D.   *Attention and effort.* Englewood Cliffs, N.J.: Prentice-Hall, 1973.

Kaiser, D. N., & Sandman, C. A.   Physiological patterns accompanying complex problem solving during warning and nonwarning conditions. *Journal of Comparative and Physiological Psychology*, 1975, *89*, 357–363.

Kapferer, J. N.   *Repetition, persistence of induced attitude change and retention of the inducing content.* Doctoral dissertation, Northwestern University, 1975.

Kaplan, M. F.   *Group discussion effects in a modified jury decision paradigm: Informational influences.* Paper presented at the meeting of the Psychonomic Society, Denver, November 1976.

Kaplan, M. F.   Judgment by juries. In M. F. Kaplan & S. Schwartz (Eds.), *Human judgment and decision making in applied settings.* New York: Academic Press, 1977. (a)

Kaplan, M. F.   Discussion polarization effects in a modified jury decision paradigm: Informational influences. *Sociometry,* 1977, 40, 262–271. (b)

Kaplan, M. F., & Kemmerick, G. D.   Juror judgment as information integration: Combining evidential and nonevidential information. *Journal of Personality and Social Psychology,* 1974, *30,* 493–499.

Kaplan, M. F., & Miller, C. E.   *Juror judgments and discussion: Effects of variety of shared information on amount of polarization.* Paper presented at the meeting of the Psychonomic Society, St. Louis, November 1976.

Kaplan, M. F., & Miller, C. E.   Judgments and group discussion: Effect of presentation and memory factors on polarization. *Sociometry,* 1977, 40, 337–343.

Katz, D.   The functional approach to the study of attitudes. *Public Opinion Quarterly,* 1960, *24,* 163–204.

Katz, D., McClintock, C., & Sarnoff, I.   The measurement of ego defense as related to attitude change. *Journal of Personality,* 1957, *25,* 465–474.

Katz, D., & Stotland, E.   A preliminary statement to a theory of attitude structure and change. In S. Koch (Ed.), *Psychology: A study of science* (Vol. 3). New York: McGraw-Hill, 1959.

Katz, H., Cadoret, R. J., Hughes, K. R., & Abbey, D. S.   Physiological correlates of acceptable and unacceptable attitude statements. *Psychological Reports,* 1965, *17,* 78.

Keating, J. P., & Brock, T. C.   Acceptance of persuasion and the inhibition of counterargumentation under various distraction tasks. *Journal of Experimental Social Psychology,* 1974, *10,* 301–309.

Keating, J. P., & Latané, B.   Distorted television reception, distraction and attitude change. *Proceedings, 80th Annual Convention, American Psychological Association,* 1972, *7,* 141–142.

Kelley, H. H.   The warm-cold variable in first impressions of persons. *Journal of Personality,* 1950, *18,* 431–439.

Kelley, H. H.   Two functions of reference groups. In G. E. Swanson, T. M. Newcomb, & E. L. Hartley (Eds.), *Readings in social psychology* (2nd ed.). New York: Holt, Rinehart & Winston, 1952.

Kelman, H.   Attitude change as a function of response restriction. *Human Relations,* 1953, *6,* 185–214.

Kelman, H.   Compliance, identification and internalization: Three processes of attitude change. *Journal of Conflict Resolution,* 1958, *2,* 51–60.

Kelman, H.   Processes of opinion change. *Public Opinion Quarterly,* 1961, *25,* 57–58.

Kelman, H. C. Attitudes are alive and well and gainfully employed in the sphere of action. *American Psychologist*, 1974, *29*, 310-324.

Kelman, H. C., & Cohler, J. *Reactions to persuasive communication as a function of cognitive needs and styles*. Paper presented at the meetings of the Eastern Psychological Association, Atlantic City, April 1959.

Kelman, H. C., & Hovland, C. I. "Reinstatement" of the communicator in delayed measurement of opinion change. *Journal of Abnormal and Social Psychology*, 1953, *48*, 327-335.

Kenny, D. A. An empirical application of confirmatory factor analysis to the multitrait-multimethod matrix. *Journal of Experimental Social Psychology*, 1976, *12*, 247-252.

Kiesler, C. A. *The psychology of commitment*. New York: Academic Press, 1971.

Kiesler, C. A., Collins, B. E., & Miller, N. *Attitude change: A critical analysis of theoretical approaches*. New York: Wiley, 1969.

Kiesler, C. A., & Kiesler, S. B. Role of forewarning in persuasive communications. *Journal of Abnormal and Social Psychology*, 1964, *68*, 547-549.

Kiesler, C. A., & Kiesler, S. B. *Conformity*. Reading, Mass: Addison-Wesley, 1969.

Kiesler, C. A., & Pallak, M. S. Arousal properties of dissonance manipulations. *Psychological Bulletin*, 1976, *83*, 1014-1025.

Kiesler, S. B. Post hoc justification of family size. *Sociometry*, 1977, *40*, 59-67.

Kiesler, S. B., & Mathog, R. The distraction hypothesis in attitude change: Effects of effectiveness. *Psychological Reports*, 1968, *23*, 1123-1133.

King, B. T., & Janis, I. L. Comparison of the effectiveness of improvised versus non-improvised role-playing in producing opinion changes. *Human Relations*, 1956, *9*, 177-186.

Kintsch, W. *The representation of meaning in memory*. Hillsdale, N.J.: Lawrence Erlbaum Associates, 1974.

Kirby, M. W. *The pupil reaction in response to an unpleasant odor as an index of affect*. Unpublished master's thesis, Wake Forest University, 1968.

Knower, F. H. Experimental studies of change in attitude: I. A study of the effect of oral arguments on changes of attitudes. *Journal of Social Psychology*, 1935, *6*, 315-347.

Knower, F. H. Experimental studies of change in attitudes: II. A study of the effect of printed arguments on changes in attitudes. *Journal of Abnormal and Social Psychology*, 1936, *30*, 522-532.

Kogan, N., & Wallach, M. A. *Risk taking: A study in cognition and personality*. New York: Holt, Rinehart, and Winston, 1964.

Kogan, N., & Wallach, M. A. The risky-shift phenomenon in small decision-making groups: A test of the information-exchange hypothesis. *Journal of Experimental Social Psychology*, 1967, *3*, 75-85.

Konečni, V. J. Annoyance, type and duration of past annoyance activity, and aggression: The "cathartic" effect. *Journal of Experimental Psychology: General*, 1975, *104*, 76-102.

Konečni, V. J. The role of aversive events in the development of intergroup conflict. In W. Austin & S. Worchel (Eds.), *The psychology of intergroup relations*. Monterey, Calif.: Brooks/Cole, 1978.

Koslin, B. L., & Paragament, R. Effects of attitude on the discrimination of opinion statements. *Journal of Experimental Social Psychology*, 1969, *5*, 245-264.

Krech, D., & Crutchfield, R. S. *Theory and problems of social psychology*. New York: McGraw-Hill, 1948.

Krugman, H.E. An application of learning theory to T.V. copy testing. *Public Opinion Quarterly*, 1962, *26*, 622-634.

Krugman, H. E. The impact of television learning: Learning without involvement. *Public Opinion Quarterly*, 1965, *29*, 349-356.

Krugman, H. E. Answering some unanswered questions in measuring advertising effectiveness. *Proceedings of the 12th Annual Conference, Advertising Research Foundation,* 1966, 18–23.

Krugman, H. E. The measurement of advertising involvement. *Public Opinion Quarterly,* 1967, *30,* 583–596.

Krugman, H. E. Processes underlying exposure to advertising. *American Psychologist,* 1968, *23,* 245–253.

Kutner, B., Wilkins, C., & Yarrow, P. Verbal attitudes and overt behavior involving racial prejudice. *Journal of Abnormal and Social Psychology,* 1952, *47,* 649–652.

LaBerge, D. Acquisition of automatic processing in perceptual and associative learning. In P. M. A. Rabbitt & S. Dornic (Eds.), *Attention and performance V.* London: Academic Press, 1975.

Lacey, B. C., & Lacey, J. I. Studies of heart rate and other bodily processes in sensorimotor behavior. In P. A. Obrist, A. H. Black, J. Brener, & L. V. DiCara (Eds.), *Cardiovascular psychophysiology.* Chicago: Aldine, 1974.

Lacey, J. I. Psychophysiological approaches to the evaluation of psychotherapeutic process and outcome. In E. A. Rubinstein & M. B. Parloff (Eds.), *Research in psychotherapy.* Washington, D.C.: American Psychological Association, 1959.

Lacey, J. I. Somatic response patterning and stress: Some revisions of activation theory. In M. H. Appley & R. Trumbull (Eds.), *Psychological stress: Issues in research.* New York: Appleton, 1967.

Lacey, J. I., Kagan, J., Lacey, B., & Moss, H. A. The visceral level: Situational determinants and behavioral correlates of autonomic response patterns. In P. H. Knapp (Ed.), *Expression of the emotions in man.* New York: International Universities Press, 1963.

Lacey, J. I., & Lacey, B. C. Some autonomic-central nervous system interrelationships. In P. Black (Ed.), *Physiological correlates of emotion.* New York: Academic Press, 1970.

Lamm, H. Will an observer advise higher risk-taking after hearing a discussion of the decision problem? *Journal of Personality and Social Psychology,* 1967, *6,* 467–471.

Lamm, H., Trommsdorff, G., & Rost-Schaude, E. Self-image, perception of peers' risk acceptance and risky shift. *European Journal of Social Psychology,* 1972, *2,* 255–272.

Lammers, H. B., & Becker, L. A. Distraction effects on the perceived extremity of a communication and on cognitive responses. *Personality and Social Psychology Bulletin,* 1980, *6,* 261–266.

Lang, P. J., Rice, D. G., & Sternbach, R. A. The psychophysiology of emotion. In N. S. Greenfield & R. A. Sternbach (Eds.), *Handbook of psychophysiology.* New York: Holt, Rinehart & Winston, 1972.

Lange, L. Neue experimente uber den vorgang der einfacher reaktion auf sinnesindrucke. *Phil Stud,* 1888, *4,* 472–510.

LaPiere, R. Attitudes versus actions. *Social Forces,* 1934, *13,* 230–237.

Lasswell, H. D. The structure and function of communication in society. In L. Bryson (Ed.), *Communication of ideas.* New York: Harper, 1948.

Laughlin, P. R., & Bitz, D. S. Individual versus dyadic performance on a disjunctive task as a function of initial ability level. *Journal of Personality and Social Psychology,* 1975, *31,* 487–496.

Laughlin, P. R., Kerr, N. L., Davis, J. H., Halff, H. M., & Marciniak, K. A. Group size, member ability, and social decision schemas on an intellective task. *Journal of Personality and Social Psychology,* 1975, *31,* 522–535.

Lawless, J. F., & Wang, P. A simulation study of ridge and other regression estimators. *Communications,* 1976, *5,* 307–323.

Lazarus, R. S. *Psychological stress and coping process.* New York: McGraw-Hill, 1966.

Lazarus, R. S. Cognitive and personality factors underlying threat and coping. In M. H. Appley & R. Trumbull (Eds.), *Psychological stress.* New York: Appleton-Century-Crofts, 1967.

Lazarus, R. S., Opton, E. M., Nomikos, M. S., & Rankin, N. O. The principle of short-circuiting of threat: Further evidence. *Journal of Personality,* 1965, *33,* 622–635.

Leavitt, C., Waddell, C., & Wells, W. Improving day-after recall techniques. *Journal of Advertising Research,* 1970, *10,* 13–17.

Leber, W., & Johnson, H. J. Rated activity of verbal stimuli as a determinant of physiological arousal to internally evoked images. *Psychophysiology,* 1976, *13,* 170. (Abstract)

Leeper, R. A. A study of a neglected portion of the field of learning—the development of sensory organization. *Journal of Genetic Psychology,* 1935, *46,* 41–75.

Lefcourt, H. M. Recent developments in the study of locus of control. In B. A. Maher (Ed.), *Progress in experimental personality research* (Vol. 6). New York: Academic Press, 1972.

Lehman, S. Personality and compliance: A study of anxiety and self-esteem in opinion and behavior change. *Journal of Personality and Social Psychology,* 1970, *15,* 76–86.

Lemon, N. *Attitudes and their measurement.* New York: Wiley, 1973.

Lesser, G. W., & Abelson, R. P. Personality correlates of persuasibility in children. In C. I. Hovland & I. L. Janis (Eds.), *Personality and persuasibility.* New Haven, Conn.: Yale University Press, 1959.

Leventhal, H. Findings and theory in the study of fear communications. In L. Berkowitz (Ed.), *Advances in experimental social psychology* (Vol. 5). New York: Academic Press, 1970.

Leventhal, H., & Perloe, S. I. A relationship between self-esteem and persuasibility. *Journal of Abnormal and Social Psychology,* 1962, *64,* 385–388.

Leventhal, H., & Trembly, G. Negative emotions and persuasion. *Journal of Personality,* 1968, *36,* 154–168.

Leventhal, H., & Watts, J. C. Sources of resistance to fear-arousing communications on smoking and lung cancer. *Journal of Personality,* 1966, *34,* 155–175.

Levinger, G. A three-level approach to attraction: Toward an understanding of pair relatedness. In T. L. Huston (Ed.), *Foundations of Interpersonal Attraction.* New York: Academic Press, 1974.

Levinger, G., & Schneider, D. J. A test of risk as a value hypothesis. *Journal of Personality and Social Psychology,* 1969, *11,* 165–169.

Lewin, K. Group decision and social change. In T. Newcomb & E. Hartley (Eds.), *Readings in social psychology.* New York: Holt, Rinehart & Winston, 1947.

Libby, W. L., Jr., Lacey, B. C., & Lacey, J. I. Pupillary and cardiac activity during visual attention. *Psychophysiology,* 1973, *10,* 270–294.

Likert, R. A technique for the measurement of attitudes. *Archives of Psychology,* 1932, *140,* 1–55 (whole).

Linder, D. E., Cooper, J., & Jones, E. E. Decision freedom as a determinant of the role of incentive magnitude in attitude change. *Journal of Personality and Social Psychology,* 1967, *6,* 245–254.

Lingle, J. H., Geva, N., Ostrom, T. M., Leippe, M. R., & Baumgardner, M. H. Thematic effects of person judgments on impression organization. *Journal of Personality and Social Psychology,* 1979, *37,* 675–687.

Lingle, J. H., & Ostrom, T. M. Retrieval selectivity in memory-based impression judgments. *Journal of Personality and Social Psychology,* 1979, *37,* 180–194.

Linton, H., & Graham, E. Personality correlates of persuasibility. In C. I. Hovland & I. L. Janis (Eds.), *Personality and persuasibility.* New Haven, Conn.: Yale University Press, 1959.

Lippmann, W. *Public opinion.* New York: Harcourt, Brace, 1922.

Liska, A. E. *The consistency controversy.* New York: Halsted, 1975.

Loewenfeld, I. E. Mechanisms of reflex dilation of the pupil: Historical review and experimental analysis. *Documenta Ophthalmologica,* 1958, *12,* 185–448.

Loewenfeld, I. E. Comment on Hess' findings. *Survey of Ophthalmology,* 1966, *11,* 293–294.

Loftus, E. F. Leading questions and eyewitness report. *Cognitive Psychology,* 1975, *7,* 560–572.

Lott, A. J., & Lott, B. E. A learning theory approach to interpersonal attitudes. In A. G. Greenwald,

T. C. Brock, & T. M. Ostrom (Eds.), *Psychological foundations of attitudes.* New York: Academic Press, 1968.

Love, R. E. *Unobtrusive measurement of cognitive reactions to persuasive communications.* Unpublished doctoral dissertation, Ohio State University, 1972.

Lowenstein, O. Experimentelle beitrage zur lehre von den katatonischen pupillenveranderungen. *Monatschrift fur Psychiatrie and Neurologie,* 1920, *47,* 194–215.

Lowenstein, O., & Loefield, I. E. The pupil. In H. Davson (Ed.), *The eye* (Vol. 3). New York: Academic Press, 1962.

Lumsdaine, A. A., & Janis, I. L. Resistance to "counterpropaganda" produced by one-sided and two-sided "propaganda" presentations. *Public Opinion Quarterly,* 1953, *17,* 311–318.

Lund, F. H. The psychology of belief: IV. The law of primacy in persuasion. *Journal of Abnormal and Social Psychology,* 1925, *20,* 183–191.

Lynd, R. S., & Lynd, H. M. *Middletown: A study in American culture.* New York: Harcourt, Brace, Jovanovich, 1929.

MacLeod, R. B. Phenomenology: A challenge to experimental psychology. In T. W. Wann (Ed.), *Behaviorism and phenomenology.* Chicago: University of Chicago Press, 1964.

Maddi, S. R. Meaning, novelty, and affect: Comment on Zajonc's paper. *Journal of Personality and Social Psychology, Monograph Supplement,* 1968, *9,* 28–29.

Malmo, R. B. Overview. In N. S. Greenfield & R. A. Sternbach (Eds.), *Handbook of psychophysiology.* New York: Holt, Rinehart & Winston, 1972.

Marquardt, D. W., & Snee, R. D. Ridge regression in practice. *American Statistician,* 1975, *29,* 3–19.

Markus, H. Self-schemata and processing information about the self. *Journal of Personality and Social Psychology,* 1977, *35,* 63–78.

Marquis, D. G. Individual responsibility and group decision involving risk. *Industrial Management Review,* 1962, *3,* 8–23.

Martin, I., & Venables, P. H. Mechanisms of palmar skin resistance and skin potential. *Psychological Bulletin,* 1966, *65,* 347–357.

Matlin, M. W. Response competition as a mediating factor in the frequency–affect relationship. *Journal of Personality and Social Psychology,* 1970, *16,* 536–552.

Matlin, M. W. Response competition, recognition, and affect. *Journal of Personality and Social Psychology,* 1971, *19,* 295–300.

Matlin, M. W. Frequency–affect relationship in a simultaneous spatial presentation. *Psychology Reports,* 1974, *35,* 379–383.

Matlin, M. W., & Stang, D. J. *The Pollyanna principle.* Unpublished manuscript, State University of New York at Geneseo, 1975.

Mazis, M. B. *A theoretical and empirical examination of comparative advertising.* Faculty Working Paper, College of Business Administration, University of Florida, 1976.

McArdle, J. B. *Positive and negative communications and subsequent attitude and behavior change in alcoholics.* Unpublished doctoral dissertation, University of Illinois, Urbana-Champaign, 1972.

McCanne, T. R., & Sandman, C. A. Instrumental heart-rate responses and visual perception: A preliminary study. *Psychophysiology,* 1974, *11,* 283–287.

McCollough, J. L., & Ostrom, T. M. Repetion of highly similar messages and attitude change. *Journal of Applied Psychology,* 1974, *59,* 395–397.

McCroskey, J. C. The effects of evidence as an inhibitor of counterpersuasion. *Speech Monographs,* 1970, *37,* 188–194.

McCurdy, H. G. Consciousness and the galvanometer. *Psychological Review,* 1950, *57,* 322–327.

McFall, R. M., & Schenkein, D. Experimenter expectancy effects, need for achievement, and field dependence. *Journal of Experimental Research in Personality,* 1970, *4,* 122–128.

McFarland, S. G., & Thistlethwaite, D. L. An analysis of a logical consistency model of belief change. *Journal of Personality and Social Psychology*, 1970, *15*, 133-143.

McGinnies, E., & Ward, C. D. Persuasibility as a function of source credibility and locus of control: Five cross-cultural experiments. *Journal of Personality*, 1974, *42*, 360-371.

McGuigan, F. J. *Subvocal speech during silent reading* (Contract OE J-10-073. Project No. 2643). Washington, D.C.: Office of Education, U.S. Department of Health, Education and Welfare, 1967.

McGuigan, F. J. Covert oral behavior during the silent performance of language task. *Psychological Bulletin*, 1970, *74*, 309-326.

McGuigan, F. J. *Cognitive psychophysiology: Principles of covert behavior.* New York: Appleton-Century-Crofts, 1978.

McGuigan, F. J., & Bailey, S. C. Covert response patterns during the processing of language stimuli. *Interamerican Journal of Psychology*, 1969, *3*, 289-299.

McGuigan, F. J., & Rodier, W. I., III. Effects of auditory stimulation on covert oral behavior during silent reading. *Journal of Experimental Psychology*, 1968, *76*, 649-655.

McGuire, W. J. Cognitive consistency and attitude change. *Journal of Abnormal and Social Psychology*, 1960, *60*, 345-353. (a)

McGuire, W. J. Direct and indirect persuasive effects of dissonance-producing messages. *Journal of Abnormal and Social Psychology*, 1960, *60*, 354-358. (b)

McGuire, W. J. A syllogistic analysis of cognitive relationships. In C. I. Hovland & M. J. Rosenberg (Eds.), *Attitude organization and change.* New Haven, Conn.: Yale University Press, 1960. (c)

McGuire, W. J. Effectiveness of forewarning in developing resistance to persuasion. *Public Opinion Quarterly*, 1962, *26*, 24-34.

McGuire, W. J. Inducing resistance to persuasion: Some contemporary approaches. In L. Berkowitz (Ed.), *Advances in experimental social psychology.* Vol. 1 New York: Academic Press, 1964.

McGuire, W. J. Attitudes and opinion. *Annual Review of Psychology*, 1966, *17*, 475-514. (a)

McGuire, W. J. Current status of cognitive consistency theories. In S. Feldman (Ed.), *Cognitive consistency.* New York: Academic Press, 1966. (b)

McGuire, W. J. Personality and susceptibility to social influence. In E. F. Borgatta & W. W. Lambert (Eds.), *Handbook of personality theory and research.* Chicago: Rand McNally, 1968. (a)

McGuire, W. J. Theory of the structure of human thought. In R. Abelson, E. Aronson, W. McGuire, T. Newcomb, M. Rosenberg, & P. Tannenbaum (Eds.), *Theories of cognitive consistency: A sourcebook.* Chicago: Rand McNally, 1968. (b)

McGuire, W. J. The nature of attitudes and attitude change. In G. Lindzey & E. Aronson (Eds.), *The handbook of social psychology* (2nd ed., Vol. 3), *The individual in a social context.* Reading, Mass.: Addison-Wesley, 1969. (a)

McGuire, W. J. Suspiciousness of experimenter's intent. In R. Rosenthal & R. Rosnow (Eds.), *Artifact in behavioral research.* New York: Academic Press, 1969. (b)

McGuire, W. Attitude change: The information-processing paradigm. In C. G. McClintock (Ed.), *Experimental social psychology.* New York: Holt, Rinehart & Winston, 1972.

McGuire, W. J. The yin and yang of progress in social psychology: Seven Koan. *Journal of Personality and Social Psychology*, 1973, *26*, 446-456.

McGuire, W.J. An information-processing model of advertising effectiveness. In H. L. Davis & A. J. Silk (Eds.) *Behavioral and Management Sciences in Marketing.* New York: Ronald (Wiley), 1978.

McGuire, W. J., & Millman, S. Anticipatory belief lowering following forewarning of a persuasive attack. *Journal of Personality and Social Psychology*, 1965, *2*, 471-479.

McGuire, W., & Papageorgis, D. The relative efficacy of various types of prior belief defense in producing immunity against persuasion. *Journal of Abnormal and Social Psychology*, 1961, *62*, 327–337.

McGuire, W. J., & Papageorgis, D. Effectiveness of forewarning in developing resistance to persuasion. *Public Opinion Quarterly*, 1962, *26*, 24–34.

Mead, G. H. *Mind, self, and society: From the standpoint of a social behaviorist*. Chicago: University of Chicago Press, 1934.

Mehrabian, A. Some referents and measures of nonverbal behavior. *Behavior Research Methods and Instrumentation*, 1969, *1*, 203–207.

Meichenbaum, D., & Cameron, R. *An examination of cognitive and contingency variables in anxiety relief procedures*. Unpublished manuscript, University of Waterloo, 1973.

Miller, N. *On measuring counterarguing*. Paper presented at American Psychological Association meeting, Washington, D.C., 1971.

Miller, N., & Baron, R. *Distraction, communicator credibility, and attitude change*. Unpublished manuscript, University of Minnesota, 1968.

Miller, N., & Baron, R. S. On measuring counterarguing. *Journal of the Theory of Social Behavior*, 1973, *1*, 101–118.

Miller, N., & Campbell, D. T. Recency and primacy in persuasion as a function of the timing of speeches and measurements. *Journal of Abnormal and Social Psychology*, 1959, *59*, 1–9.

Miller, N., & Levy, B. H. Defaming and agreeing with the communicator as a function of emotional arousal, communication extremity, and evaluative set. *Sociometry*, 1967, *30*, 158–175.

Miller, N., Maruyama, G., Beaber, R. J., & Valone, K. Speed of speech and persuasion. *Journal of Personality and Social Psychology*, 1976, *34*, 615–625.

Miller, R. L. Mere exposure, psychological reactance and attitude change. *Public Opinion Quarterly*, 1976, *40*, 229–233.

Miller, S. A., & Brownell, C. A. Peers, persuasion, and Piaget: Dyadic interaction between conservers and non-conservers. *Child Development*, 1975, *46*, 992–997.

Miller, S. J., Mazis, M. B., & Wright, P. L. The influence of brand ambiguity on brand attitude development. *Journal of Marketing Research*, 1971, *8*, 445–449.

Millman, S. Anxiety, comprehension, and suceptibility to social influences. *Journal of Personality and Social Psychology*, 1968, *9*, 251–256.

Mills, J. Opinion change as a function of the communicator's desire to influence and liking for the audience. *Journal of Experimental Social Psychology*, 1966, *2*, 152–159.

Mills, J., & Aronson, E. Opinion change as a function of the communicator's attractiveness and desire to influence. *Journal of Personality and Social Psychology*, 1965, *1*, 173–177.

Mills, J., & Harvey, J. Opinion change as a function of when information about the communicator is received and whether he is attractive or expert. *Journal of Personality and Social Psychology*, 1972, *21*, 52–55.

Mills, J., & Jellison, J. M. Effect on opinion change of how desirable the communication is to the audience the communicator addressed. *Journal of Personality and Social Psychology*, 1967, *6*, 98–101.

Mills, J., & Kimble, C. Opinion change as a function of perceived similarity of the communicator and subjectivity of the issue. *Bulletin of the Psychonomic Society*, 1973, *2*, 35–36.

Minsky, M. A framework for representing knowledge. In P. Winston (Ed.), *The psychology of computer vision*. New York: McGraw-Hill, 1975.

Mischel, W. *Personality and assessment*. New York: Wiley, 1968.

Mischel, W. Toward a cognitive social learning reconceptualization of personality. *Psychological Review*, 1973, *80*, 252–283.

Moreland, R. I., & Zajonc, R. B. A strong test of the exposure effect. *Journal of Experimental Social Psychology*, 1976, *12*, 170–178.

Moreno, J. L. *Who shall survive? A new approach to the problem of human relations*. Washington, D.C.: Nervous and Mental Disease Publishing House, 1934.

Morgan, C. P., & Aram, J. D. The preponderance of arguments in the risky shift phenomenon. *Journal of Experimental Social Psychology,* 1975, *11,* 25–34.

Mueller, D. J. Physiological techniques of attitude measurement. In G. F. Summers (Ed.), *Attitude measurement.* Chicago: Rand McNally, 1970.

Myers, D. G., & Lamm, H. The group polarization phenomenon. *Psychological Bulletin,* 1976, *83,* 602–627.

Natsoulas, T. Concerning introspective "knowledge." *Psychological Bulletin,* 1970, *73,* 89–111.

Neisser, U. *Cognitive psychology.* New York: Appleton, 1967.

Nel, E., Helmreich, R., & Aronson, E. Opinion change in the advocate as a function of the persuasibility of his audience: A clarification of the meaning of dissonance. *Journal of Personality and Social Psychology,* 1969, *12,* 117–124.

Nelson, C. E. Anchoring to accepted values as a technique for immunizing beliefs against persuasion. *Journal of Personality and Social Psychology,* 1968, *9,* 329–334.

Nelson, P. J. The economic value of advertising. In Y. Brozen (Ed.), *Advertising and society.* New York: New York University Press, 1974.

Newcomb, T. M. Individual systems of orientation. In S. Koch (Ed.), *Psychology: A study of a science* (Vol. 3). New York: McGraw-Hill, 1959.

Newcomb, T. M., Koenig, K. E., Flacks, R., & Warwick, D. P. *Persistence and change: Bennington College and its students after twenty-five years.* New York: Wiley, 1967.

Newell, A., & Simon, H. A. *Human problem solving.* Englewood Cliffs, N.J.: Prentice-Hall, 1972.

Newman, J. R. *Comparison of least squares versus Bayes: Estimates of regression weights.* Unpublished manuscript, Social Science Research Institute, University of Southern California, 1977.

Nisbett, R. E., & Bellows, N. Verbal reports about causal influences on social judgments: Private access versus public theories. *Journal of Personality and Social Psychology,* 1977, *35,* 613–624.

Nisbett, R. E., & Gordon, A. Self-esteem and susceptibility to social influence. *Journal of Personality and Social Psychology,* 1967, *5,* 268–276.

Nisbett, R. E., & Wilson, T. D. The halo effect: Evidence for unconscious alteration of judgment. *Journal of Personality and Social Psychology,* 1977, *35,* 250–256. (a)

Nisbett, R. E., & Wilson, T. D. Telling more than we can know: Verbal reports on mental processes. *Psychological Review,* 1977, *84,* 231–259. (b)

Norman, D. A. *Memory and attention.* New York: Wiley, 1976.

Norman, R. When what is said is important: A comparison of expert and attractive sources. *Journal of Experimental Social Psychology,* 1976, *12,* 294–300.

Nowicki, S., & Strickland, B. R. A locus of control scale for children. *Journal of Consulting and Clinical Psychology,* 1973, *40,* 148–154.

Orne, M. T. On the social psychology of the psychological experiment: With particular reference to demand characteristics and their implications. *American Psychologist,* 1962, *17,* 776–783.

Orne, M. T. Demand characteristics and the concept of quasi-controls. In R. Rosenthal & R. L. Rosnow (Eds.), *Artifact in behavioral research.* New York: Academic Press, 1969.

Orne, M. T., & Evans, F. J. Social control in the psychological experiment: Antisocial behavior and hypnosis. *Journal of Personality and Social Psychology,* 1965, *1,* 189–200.

Osgood, C. E. Cross-cultural comparability of attitude measurement via multi-lingual semantic differentials. In I. S. Steiner & M. Fishbein (Eds.), *Recent studies in social psychology.* New York: Holt, Rinehart & Winston, 1965.

Osgood, C. E., Suci, G. J., & Tannenbaum, P. H. *The measurement of meaning.* Urbana, Ill.: University of Illinois Press, 1957.

Osgood, C. E., & Tannenbaum, P. H. The principle of congruity in the prediction of attitude change. *Psychological Review,* 1955, *62,* 42–55.

Oskamp, S. *Attitudes and opinions.* Englewood Cliffs, N.J.: Prentice-Hall, 1977.

Osterhouse, R. A., & Brock, T. C. Distraction increases yielding to propaganda by inhibiting counterarguing. *Journal of Personality and Social Psychology,* 1970, *15,* 344–358.

Ostrom, T. M. The emergence of attitude theory: 1930-1950. In A. Greenwald, T. Brock, & T. Ostrom (Eds.) *Psychological foundations of attitudes*. New York: Academic Press, 1968.

Ostrom, T. M. The relationship between the affective, behavioral, and cognitive components of attitude. *Journal of Experimental Social Psychology*, 1969, *5*, 12-30.

Ostrom, T. M., & Brock, T. C. A cognitive model of attitudinal involvement. In R. P. Abelson, E. Aronson, W. J. McGuire, T. M. Newcomb, J. J. Rosenberg, & P. H. Tannenbaum (Eds.), *Theories of cognitive consistency: A sourcebook*. Chicago: Rand McNally, 1968.

Pachella, R. G. The interpretation of reaction time in information processing research. In B. H. Kantowitz (Ed.), *Human information processing: Tutorials in performance and cognition*. Hillsdale, N.J.: Lawrence Erlbaum Associates, 1974.

Page, M. M. Social psychology of a clasical conditioning of attitudes experiment. *Journal of Personality and Social Psychology*, 1969, *11*, 177-186.

Papageorgis, D. Anticipation of exposure to persuasive messages and belief change. *Journal of Personality and Social Psychology*, 1967, *5*, 490-496.

Papageorgis, D. Warning and persuasion. *Psychological Bulletin*, 1968, *70*, 271-282.

Papageorgis, D., & McGuire, W. The generality of immunity to persuasion by pre-exposure to weakened counterarguments. *Journal of Abnormal and Social Psychology*, 1961, *62*, 475-481.

Pavlov, I. P. *Conditioned reflexes*. New York: Oxford University Press, 1927.

Peak, H. Psychological structure and psychological activity. *Psychological Review*, 1958, *65*, 325-347.

Peak, H., & Morrison, H. W. The acceptance of information into attitude structure. *Journal of Abnormal and Social Psychology*, 1958, *57*, 127-135.

Perlman, D., & Oskamp, S. The effects of picture content and exposure frequency on evaluations of Negroes and whites. *Journal of Experimental Social Psychology*, 1971, *7*, 503-514.

Peavler, W. S., & McLaughlin, J. P. The question of stimulus content and pupil size. *Psychonomic Science*, 1967, *8*, 505-506.

Pepitone, A. *Attraction and hostility: An experimental analysis of interpersonal and self-evaluation*. New York: Atherton Press, 1964.

Peterson, C. R., & Beach, L. R. Man as an intuitive statistician. *Psychological Bulletin*, 1967, *68*, 29-46.

Peterson, P. D., & Koulack, D. Attitude change as a function of latitudes of acceptance and rejection. *Journal of Personality and Social Psychology*, 1969, *11*, 309-311.

Pettigrew, T. F. Regional differences in anti-Negro prejudice. *Journal of Abnormal and Social Psychology*, 1959, *59*, 28-36.

Petty, R. E. *Distraction can enhance or reduce yielding to propoganda by interfering with cognitive responses*. Master's thesis, Ohio State University, 1975.

Petty, R. E. *A cognitive response analysis of the temporal persistence of attitude changes induced by persuasive communications*. Doctoral dissertation, Ohio State University, 1977. (a)

Petty, R. E. The importance of cognitive responses in persuasion. In W. D. Perreault (Ed.), *Advances in consumer research* (Volume 4). Atlanta, Ga.: Association for Consumer Research, 1977. (b)

Petty, R. E., & Cacioppo, J. T. Forewarning, cognitive responding, and resistance to persuasion. *Journal of Personality and Social Psychology*, 1977, *35*, 645-655.

Petty, R. E., & Cacioppo, J. T. Effects of forewarning of persuasive intent and involvement on cognitive responses and persuasion. *Personality and Social Psychology Bulletin*, 1979, *5*, 173-176. (a)

Petty, R. E., & Cacioppo, J. T. Issue involvement can increase or decrease persuasion by enhancing message-relevant cognitive responses. *Journal of Personality and Social Psychology*, 1979, *37*, 1915-1926. (b)

Petty, R. E., & Cialdini, R. B. The role of argumentation in lasting attitude polarization. Unpublished manuscript, Ohio State University, 1976 (Cited in Petty, 1977b).

Petty, R. E., Harkins, S. G., & Williams, K. D. The effects of group diffusion of cognitive effort on attitudes: An information processing view. *Journal of Personality and Social Psychology,* 1980, *38,* 81–92.

Petty, R. E., Wells, G. L., & Brock, T. C. Distraction can enhance or reduce yielding to propaganda: Thought disruption versus effort justification. *Journal of Personality and Social Psychology,* 1976, *34,* 874–884.

Phares, E. J. *Locus of control: A personality determinant of behavior.* Morristown, N.J.: General Learning Press, 1973.

Picek, J. S., Sherman, S. J., & Shiffrin, R. M. Cognitive organization and coding of social structures. *Journal of Personality and Social Psychology,* 1975, *31,* 758–768.

Platt, J. R. Strong inference. *Science,* 1964, *146,* 347–353.

Poffenberger, A. T. *Psychology in advertising.* New York: Shaw, 1925.

Politz, A. The Rochester study. *Saturday Evening Post,* 1960.

Porier, G. W., & Lott, A. J. Galvanic skin responses and prejudice. *Journal of Personality and Social Psychology,* 1967, *5,* 253–259.

Posner, M. I. *Cognition: An introduction.* Glenview, Ill.: Scott, Foresman, 1973.

Posner, M. I., & Snyder, C. R. R. Attention and cognitive control. In R. Solso (Ed.), *Information processing and cognition: The Loyola Symposium.* Hillsdale, N.J.: Lawrence Erlbaum Associates, 1975.

Potts, G. R. Information processing strategies used in the encoding of linear orderings. *Journal of Verbal Learning and Verbal Behavior,* 1972, *11,* 727–740.

Prokasy, W. F., & Raskin, D. C. (Eds.). *Electrodermal activity in psychological research.* New York: Academic Press, 1973.

Proshansky, H. A preobjective method for the study of attitudes. *Journal of Abnormal and Social Psychology,* 1943, *38,* 393–395.

Pruitt, D. B. Choice shifts in group discussion: An introductory review. *Journal of Personality and Social Psychology,* 1971, *20,* 339–360.

Pylyshyn, Z. W. What the mind's eye tells the mind's brain: A critique of mental imagery. *Psychological Bulletin,* 1973, *80,* 1–24.

Rajecki, D. W. Imprinting in precocial birds: Interpretation, evidence, and evaluation. *Psychological Bulletin,* 1973, *79,* 48–58.

Rajecki, D. W., & Wolfson, C. The rating of materials found in the mailbox: Effects of frequency of receipt. *Public Opinion Quarterly,* 1973, *37,* 110–114.

Rankin, R. E., & Campbell, D. T. Galvanic skin response to Negro and white experimenters. *Journal of Abnormal and Social Psychology,* 1955, *51,* 30–33.

Ray, M. L. Can order effect in copy tests be used as an indicator of long-term advertising effect? *Journal of Advertising Research,* 1969, *9,* 45–52.

Ray, M. L. Marketing communication and the hierarchy of effects. In P. Clarke (Ed.), *New models for communication research.* Beverly Hills, Calif.: Sage Publishing, 1974.

Ray, M. L. When does consumer information processing research actually have anything to do with information processing? *Advances in Consumer Research,* 1977, *4,* 372–375.

Ray, M. L., & Sawyer, A. G. Behavioral measurement for marketing models: Estimating the effects of advertising repetion for media planning. *Management Science,* 1971, *18,* 73–89. (a)

Ray, M. L., & Sawyer, A. G. A laboratory technique for estimating the repetition function for advertising media models. *Journal of Marketing Research,* 1971, *8,* 20–29. (b)

Ray, M. L., Ward, S., & Lesser, G. *Experimentation to improve pretesting of drug abuse education and information campaigns.* Cambridge, Mass.: Marketing Science Institute, 1973.

Ray, M. L., & Webb, P. *Experimental research on the effects of TV clutter: Dealing with a difficult media environment.* City: Marketing Science Institute, Working Paper 102, 1976.

Razran, G. A quantitative study of meaning by conditioned salivary technique (semantic conditioning). *Science,* 1939, *90,* 89–91.

Razran, G. The observable unconscious and the inferable conscious in current Soviet psychophysiology. *Psychological Review,* 1961, *68,* 81-147.

Reeves, K. *Reality in advertising.* New York: Knopf, 1961.

Regan, D. T., & Cheng, J. B. Distraction and attitude change: A resolution. *Journal of Experimental Social Psychology,* 1973, *9,* 138-147.

Regan, D., & Fazio, R. On the consistency between attitudes and behavior: Look to the method of attitude formation. *Journal of Experimental Social Psychology,* 1977, *13,* 28-45.

Reich, J. W., & Moody, C. A. Stimulus properties, frequency of exposure, and affective responding. *Perceptual and Motor Skills,* 1970, *30,* 27-35.

Reich, J., & Sherif, M. *Ego involvement as a factor in attitude assessment by the own categories technique.* Norman: University of Oklahoma, 1963 (mimeographed).

Riley, R. T., & Pettigrew, T. F. Dramatic events and attitude change. *Journal of Personality and Social Psychology,* 1976, *34,* 1004-1015.

Riskey, D. R. Verbal memory processes in impression formation. *Journal of Experimental Psychology: Human Learning and Memory,* 1979, *5,* 271-281.

Ritchie, E., & Phares, E. J. Attitude change as a function of internal-external control and communicator status. *Journal of Personality,* 1969, *37,* 429-443.

Roberts, D. F., & Maccoby, N. Information processing and persuasion: Counterarguing behavior. In P. Clarke (Ed.), *New models for mass communication research.* Beverly Hills, Calif.: Sage, 1973.

Rogers, C. R. *Client-centered therapy: Its current practice, implications, and theory.* Boston: Houghton Mifflin, 1951.

Rogers, C. R. A theory of therapy, personality and interpersonal relationships, as developed in the client-centered framework. In S. Koch (Ed.), *Psychology: A study of science* (Volume 3). New York: McGraw-Hill, 1959.

Rogers, R. W., & Mewborn, C. R. Fear appeals and attitude change: Effects of a threat's noxiousness, probability of occurrence, and the efficacy of coping responses. *Journal of Personality and Social Psychology,* 1976, *34,* 54-61.

Rogers, T. B., Kuiper, N. A., & Kirker, W. Self-reference and the encoding of personal information. *Journal of Personality and Social Psychology,* 1977, *35,* 677-688.

Rokeach, M. *The open and closed mind.* New York: Basic Books, 1960.

Rokeach, M. The organization and modification of beliefs. *The Centennial Review,* Volume VII, No. 4, Fall 1963.

Romer, D. Distraction, counterarguing, and the internalization of attitude change. *European Journal of Social Psychology,* 1979, *9,* 1-18.

Rosen, N. A., & Wyer, R. S. Some further evidence for the "Socratic effect" using a subjective probability model of cognitive organization. *Journal of Personality and Social Psychology,* 1972, *24,* 420-425.

Rosenberg, M. J. *The experimental investigation of a value theory of attitude structure.* Unpublished doctoral dissertation, University of Michigan, 1953.

Rosenberg, M. J. Cognitive structure and attitudinal affect. *Journal of Abnormal and Social Psychology,* 1956, *53,* 367-372.

Rosenberg, M. J. An analysis of affective-cognitive consistency. In M. J. Rosenberg, C. I. Hovland, W. J. McGuire, R. P. Abelson, & J. W. Brehm (Eds.), *Attitude organization and change.* New Haven, Conn.: Yale University Press, 1960. (a)

Rosenberg, M. J. Cognitive reorganization in response to the hypnotic reversal of attitudinal affect. *Journal of Personality,* 1960, *28,* 39-63. (b)

Rosenberg, M. J. The conditions and consequences of evaluation apprehension. In R. Rosenthal & R. L. Rosnow (Eds.), *Artifact in behavioral research.* New York: Academic Press, 1969.

Rosenberg, M. J., & Abelson, R. P. An analysis of cognitive balancing. In M. J. Rosenberg, C. I.

Hovland, W. J. McGuire, R. P. Abelson, & J. W. Brehm (Eds.), *Attitude organization and change*. New Haven: Yale University Press, 1960.

Rosenberg, M. J., & Hovland, C. Cognitive, affective, and behavioral components of attitudes. In M. J. Rosenberg, C. I. Hovland, W. J. McGuire, R. P. Abelson, & J. W. Brehm (Eds.), *Attitude organization and change*. New Haven, Conn.: Yale University Press, 1960.

Rosenblatt, P. C. Persuasion as a function of varying amounts of distraction. *Psychonomic Science*, 1966, *5*, 85–86.

Rosenblood, L., & Ostrom, T. M. Is "mere exposure" merely adaption? Paper presented at the meeting of the Midwestern Psychological Association, Detroit, May 1971.

Rosenthal, R. *Experimenter effects in behavioral research*. New York: Appleton-Century-Crofts, 1966.

Rosenthal, R. Combining results of independent studies. *Psychological Bulletin*, 1978, *85*, 185–193.

Rosenthal, R., & Fode, K. L. The effect of experimenter bias on the performance of the albino rat. *Behavioral Science*, 1963, *8*, 183–189.

Rosenthal, R., Persinger, G. W., Mulry, R. C., Vikan-Kline, L., & Grothe, M. Changes in experimental hypotheses as determinants of experimental results. *Journal of Projective Techniques and Personality Assessment*, 1964, *28*, 465–469.

Rosenthal, R., & Rosnow, R. L. *Artifact in behavioral research*. New York: Academic Press, 1969.

Ross, M. A. *Attribution of attitude to self and to another*. Unpublished doctoral dissertation, University of North Carolina, 1971.

Ross, M. A., Insko, C. A., & Ross, H. Self-attribution of attitude. *Journal of Personality and Social Psychology*, 1971, *17*, 292–297.

Rothschild, M. L. *The effects of political advertising on the voting behavior of a low-involvement electorate*. Unpublished doctoral dissertation, Stanford University, 1975.

Rothschild, M. L., & Ray, M. L. Involvement and political advertising effect: An exploratory experiment. *Communications Research*, 1, 1974.

Rotter, J. B. *Social learning and clinical psychology*. Englewood Cliffs, N.J.: Prentice-Hall, 1954.

Rotter, J. B. Generalized expectancies for internal versus external control of reinforcement. *Psychological Monographs*, 1966, *80* (1, Whole No. 609).

Rule, B. G., & Rehill, D. Distraction and self-esteem effects on attitude change. *Journal of Personality and Social Psychology*, 1970, *15*, 359–365.

Rumelhart, D. E. Notes on schema for stories. In D. Bobrow & A. Collins (Eds.), *Representation and understanding: Studies in cognitive science*. New York: Academic Press, 1975.

Runkel, P. J., & Peizer, D. B. The two-valued orientation of current equilibrium theory. *Behavioral Science*, 1968, *13*, 56–65.

Ryckman, R. M., Rodda, W. C., & Sherman, M. F. Locus of control and expertise relevance as determinants of changes in opinion about student activism. *Journal of Social Psychology*, 1972, *88*, 107–114.

Rywick, T., & Schaye, P. Use of long-term memory in impression formation. *Psychological Reports*, 1974, *34*, 939–945.

Sadler, O., & Tesser, A. Some effects of salience and time upon interpersonal hostility and attraction during social isolation. *Sociometry*, 1973, *36*, 99–112.

Saegert, S. C., & Jellison, J. M. Effects of initial level of response competiton and frequency of exposure on liking and exploratory behavior. *Journal of Personality and Social Psychology*, 1970, *16*, 553–558.

Saegert, S., Swap, W. C., & Zajonc, R. B. Exposure, context, and interpersonal attraction. *Journal of Personality and Social Psychology*, 1973, *25*, 234–242.

St. Jean, R. Reformation of the value hypothesis in group risk taking. *Proceedings of the 78th Annual Convention of the American Psychological Association*, 1970, *5*, 339–340.

St. Jean, R., & Percival, E. The role of argumentation and comparison processes in choice shifts: Another assessment. *Canadian Journal of Behavioral Science,* 1974, *6,* 297–308.

Sanders, G. S., & Baron, R. S. Is social comparison irrelevant for producing choice shifts? *Journal of Experimental Social Psychology,* 1977, *13,* 303–314.

Sandman, C. *Psychophysiological parameters of emotional expression.* Unpublished doctoral dissertation, Louisiana State University, 1971.

Sandman, C. A. Physiological responses during escape and non-escape from stress in field-independent and field-dependent subjects. *Biological Psychology,* 1975, *2,* 205–216.

Sandman, C. A., McCanne, T. R., Kaiser, D. N., & Diamond, B. Heart rate and cardiac phase influences on visual perception. *Journal of Comparative and Physiological Psychology,* 1977, *91,* 189–202.

Sarnoff, I. Psychoanalytic theory and social attitudes. *Public Opinion Quarterly,* 1960, *24,* 251–279.

Sawyer, A. G. *A laboratory experimental investigation of the effects of advertising.* Unpublished doctoral dissertation, Stanford University, 1971.

Sawyer, A. G. The effects of repetition of refutational and supportive advertising appeals. *Journal of Marketing Research,* 1973, *10,* 23–33.

Sawyer, A. G. The effects of repetition: Conclusions and suggestions about experimental laboratory research. In G. D. Hughes, & M. L. Ray, (Eds.), *Buyer/consumer information processing.* Chapel Hill: University of North Carolina Press, 1974.

Sawyer, A. G. Demand artifacts in consumer research. *Journal of Consumer Research,* 1975, *1,* 20–30. (a)

Sawyer, A. G. Detecting demand characteristics in laboratory experiments in consumer research: The case of repetition-affect research. In M. J. Schlinger (Ed.), *Advances in Consumer Research,* 1975, *2,* 713–724. (b)

Sawyer, A. G. Repetition and affect: Recent empirical and theoretical development. In A. G. Woodside, P. Bennett, & J. Sheth (Eds.), *Foundations of consumer and industrial buying behavior.* New York: American Elsevier, 1977.

Schaie, W. K., & Parham, I. A. Stability of adult personality traits: Fact or fable. *Journal of Personality and Social Psychology,* 1976, *34,* 146–158.

Schank, R. C. *Conceptual information processing.* Amsterdam: North-Holland, 1975. (a)

Schank, R. C. The structure of episodes in memory. In D. Bobrow & A. Collins (Eds.), *Representation and understanding: Studies in cognitive science.* New York: Academic Press, 1975. (b)

Schick, C., McGlynn, R. P., & Woolam, D. Perception of cartoon humor as a function of familiarity and anxiety level. *Journal of Personality and Social Psychology,* 1972, *24,* 22–25.

Schlesinger, A. M. Jr. *A thousand days.* Boston: Houghton Mifflin, 1965.

Schneider, W., & Shiffrin, R. M. Controlled and automatic human information processing: I. Detection, search, and attention. *Psychological Review,* 1977, *84,* 1–66.

Schwartz, G. E. Biofeedback, self-regulation, and the patterning of physiological processes. *American Scientist,* 1975, *63,* 314–324.

Schwartz, G. E., Davidson, R. J., & Pugash, E. Voluntary control of patterns of EEG parietal asymmetry: Cognitive concomitants. *Psychophysiology,* 1976, *13,* 498–504.

Schwartz, G. E., Fair, P. L., Greenberg, P. S., Freedman, M., & Klerman, J. L. Facial electromyography in assessment of emotion. *Psychophysiology,* 1974, *11,* 237.

Schwartz, G. E., Fair, P. L., Greenberg, P. S., Mandel, M. R., & Klerman, J. L. Facial expression and depression: An electromyographic study. *Psychosomatic Medicine,* 1974, *36,* 458.

Schwartz, G., Fair, P., Mandel, M., & Klerman, G. Facial expression and imagery in depression: An electromyographic study. *Psychosomatic Medicine,* 1976, *38,* 337–347.

Schwartz, G. E., Fair, P. L., Salt, P., Mandel, M. R., & Klerman, G. L. Facial muscle patterning to affective imagery in depressed and nondepressed subjects. *Science,* 1976, *192,* 489–491.

Schwartz, S. Temporal instability as a moderator of the attitude–behavior relationship. *Journal of Personality and Social Psychology,* 1978, *36,* 715–724.

Scott, W. Attitude change through reward of verbal behavior. *Journal of Abnormal and Social Psychology,* 1957, *55,* 72–75.

Scott, W. A. Cognitive consistency, response reinforcement, and attitude change. *Sociometry,* 1959, *22,* 219–229.

Scott, W. A. Cognitive complexity and cognitive flexibility. *Sociometry,* 1962, *25,* 405–414.

Scott, W. A. Cognitive complexity and cognitive balance. *Sociometry,* 1963, *26,* 66–74.

Scott, W. A. Attitude measurement. In G. Lindzey & E. Aronson (Eds.), *The handbook of social psychology* (2nd ed., Vol. 2). Reading, Mass.: Addison-Wesley, 1968.

Scott, W. A. Varieties of cognitive integration. *Journal of Personality and Social Psychology,* 1974, *30,* 563–578.

Sears, D. O. Social anxiety, opinion structure, and opinion change. *Journal of Personality and Social Psychology,* 1967, *7,* 142–151.

Shamo, G. W., & Meador, L. M. The effect of visual distraction upon recall and attitude change. *Journal of Communication,* 1969, *19,* 157–162.

Shanteau, J. Component processes in risky decision making. *Journal of Experimental Psychology,* 1974, *103,* 680–691.

Shanteau, J. An information analysis of risky decision making. In M. F. Kaplan & S. Schwartz (Eds.), *Human judgment and decision processes.* New York: Academic Press, 1975.

Shanteau, J. C., & Anderson, N. H. Test of a conflict model for preference judgment. *Journal of Mathematical Psychology,* 1969, *6,* 312–325.

Shanteau, J., & Nagy, G. Decisions made about other people: A human judgment analysis of dating choice. In J. Carroll & J. Payne (Eds.), *Cognition and social behavior.* Hillsdale, N.J.: Lawrence Erlbaum Associates, 1976.

Shaw, M. E. A comparison of individuals and small groups in the rational solution of complex problems. *American Journal of Psychology,* 1932, *44,* 491–504.

Shaw, M. E., & Wright, J. M. *Scales for the measurement of attitudes.* New York: McGraw-Hill, 1967.

Sherif, M. A study of some social factors in perception. *Archives of Psychology,* 1935, No. 187.

Sherif, M., & Cantril, H. The psychology of attitudes: I *Psychological Review,* 1945, *52,* 295–319.

Sherif, M., & Cantril, H. The psychology of attitudes: II *Psychological Review,* 1946, *53,* 1–24.

Sherif, M., & Hovland, C. *Social Judgment: Assimilation and contrast effects in communication and attitude change.* New Haven, Conn.: Yale University Press, 1961.

Sherif, C. W., & Sherif, M. *Attitudes, ego-involvement, and change.* New York: Wiley, 1967.

Sherif, C. W., Kelly, M., Rodgers, H. L., Sarup, G., & Titler, B. I. Personal involvement, social judgment, and action. *Journal of Personality and Social Psychology,* 1973, *27,* 311–327.

Sherif, C. W., Sherif, M., & Nebergall, R. E. *Attitude and attitude change: The social judgment-involvement approach.* Philadelphia: Saunders, 1965.

Sherman, S. J. Internal–external control and its relationship to attitude change under different social influence techniques. *Journal of Personality and Social Psychology,* 1973, *26,* 23–29.

Sherrington, C. S. *The integrative action of the nervous system.* New York: C. Scribner's Sons, 1906.

Silk, A. J., & Vavra, T. G. The influence of advertising's affective qualities on consumer response. In G. D. Hughes, & M. L. Ray (Eds.), *Buyer/consumer information processing.* Chapel Hill: University of North Carlina Press, 1974.

Silverman, I. Differential effects of ego-threat upon persuasibility for high and low self-esteem subjects. *Journal of Abnormal and Social Psychology,* 1964, *69,* 567–572.

Silverman, I. *The human subject in the psychological laboratory.* New York: Pergamon Press, 1977.

Silverman, I., Ford, L. H., Jr., & Morganti, J. B. Inter-related effects of social desirability, sex, self-esteem, and complexity of argument on persuasibility. *Journal of Personality*, 1966, *34*, 555–568.

Silverman, I., & Regula, C. Evaluation apprehension, demand characteristics, and the effects of distraction on persuasibility. *Journal of Social Psychology*, 1968, *75*, 273–281.

Silverthorne, C. P. Information input and the group shift phenomenon in risk taking. *Journal of Personality and Social Psychology*, 1971, *20*, 456–461.

Simms, E. S. *Averaging model of information integration theory applied in the classroom. Journal of Educational Psychology*, 1978, *70*, 740–744.

Simon, H. A. Motivational and emotional controls of cognition. *Psychological Review*, 1967, *74*, 29–39.

Simpson, D. D., & Ostrom, T. M. Effect of snap and thoughtful judgments on person judgments. *European Journal of Social Psychology*, 1975, *5*, 197–208.

Sistrunk, F., & McDavid, J. W. Sex variable in conforming behavior. *Journal of Personality and Social Psychology*, 1971, *17*, 200–207.

Slovic, P., Fischhoff, B., & Lichtenstein, S. Behavioral decision theory. *Annual Review of Psychology*, 1977, *27*, 1–39.

Smith, G. F., & Dorfman, D. D. The effect of stimulus uncertainty on the relationship between frequency of exposure and liking. *Journal of Personality and Social Psychology*, 1975, *31*, 150–155.

Smith, M. B. Personal values as determinants of a political attitude. *Journal of Psychology*, 1949, *28*, 477–486.

Smith, M. B. The self and cognitive consistency. In R. P. Abelson, E. Aronson, W. J. McGuire, T. M. Newcomb, M. J. Rosenberg, & P. H. Tannenbaum (Eds.), *Theories of cognitive consistency: A sourcebook*. Chicago: Rand McNally, 1968.

Smith, M. B., Bruner, J. S., & White, R. W. *Opinions and personality*. New York: Wiley, 1956.

Smith, S. M., Brown H. O., Toman, J. E. P., & Goodman, L. S. The lack of cerebral effects of d-Tubocurarine. *Anesthesiology*, 1947, *8*, 1–14.

Smith, W. *The measurement of emotion*. London: Paul, 1922.

Snyder, C. R., & Larson, G. R. A further look at student acceptance of general personality interpretations. *Journal of Consulting and Clinical Psychology*, 1972, *38*, 384–388.

Snyder, M., & Monson, T. C. Persons, situations, and the control of social behavior. *Journal of Personality and Social Psychology*, 1975, *32*, 637–644.

Snyder, M., & Swann, W. B., Jr. When actions reflect attitudes: The politics of impression management. *Journal of Personality and Social Psychology*, 1976, *34*, 1034–1042.

Snyder, M., & Tanke, E. D. Behavior and attitude: Some people are more consistent than others. *Journal of Personality*, 1976, *44*, 501–517.

Sokolov, A. N. *Perception and the conditioned reflex*. Oxford: Pergamon Press, 1963.

Sokolov, A. N. Speech-motor afferentiation and the problem of brain mechanisms. *Soviet Psychology*, 1967, *6*, 3–15.

Sokolov, A. N. Studies of the speech mechanisms of thinking. In M. Cole & I. Maltzman (Eds.), *A handbook of contemporary Soviet psychology*. New York: Basic Books, 1969.

Spencer, H. *First principles*. New York: Appleton, 1895. (Preface dated 1862.)

Sperling, G. A. Successive approximations to a model for short-term memory. In A. F. Sanders (Ed.), *Attention and performance*. Amsterdam: North-Holland, 1967.

Staats, A. W. An outline of an integrated learning theory of attitude formation and function. In M. Fishbein (Ed.), *Readings in attitude theory and measurement*. New York: Wiley, 1967.

Stang, D. J. Six theories of repeated exposure and affect. *JSAS Catalogue of Selected Documents in Psychology*, 1973, *3*, 126.

Stang, D. J. Intuition as artifact in mere exposure studies. *Journal of Personality and Social Psychology*, 1974, *30*, 647–653. (a)

Stang, D. J. Methodological factors in mere exposure research. *Psychological Bulletin,* 1974, *81,* 1014–1025. (b)

Stang, D. J. *A critical examination of the response competition hypothesis. Bulletin of the Psychonomic Society,* 1976, *7,* 530–532.

Stang, D. J. Effects of mere exposure on learning and affect. *Journal of Personality and Social Psychology,* 1975, *31,* 7–12.

Steiner, I. D. Sex differences in the resolution of A-B-X conflicts. *Journal of Personality,* 1960, *28,* 118–128.

Steiner, I.D. Personality and the resolution of interpersonal disagreements. In B. A. Maher (Ed.), *Progress in experimental personality research* (Vol. 3). New York: Academic Press, 1966.

Sternberg, S. Memory-scanning: Mental processes revealed by reaction-time experiments. *American Scientist,* 1969, *57,* 421–457.

Sternthal, B., Dholakia, R., & Leavitt, C. The persuasive effect of source credibility: A test of cognitive response analysis. *Journal of Consumer Research,* 1978, *4,* 252–260.

Sternthal, B., Phillips, L., & Dholakia, R. The persuasive effect of source credibility: A situational analysis. *Public Opinion Quarterly,* 1978, *42,* 285–314.

Stinchcombe, A. L. *Constructing social theories.* New York: Harcourt, Brace & World, 1968.

Stokes, J. P. Effects of familiarization and knowledge of others' odd choices on shifts to risk and caution. *Journal of Personality and Social Psychology,* 1971, *20,* 407–412.

Stoner, J. A. F. *A comparison of individual and group decisions involving risk.* Unpublished master's thesis, School of Industrial Management, Massachusetts Institute of Technology, 1961.

Stoner, J. P. Risky and cautious shifts in group decisions: The influence of widely held values. *Journal of Experimental Social Psychology,* 1968, *4,* 442–459.

Stotland, E., Katz, D., & Patchen, M. The reduction of prejudice through the arousal of self-insight. *Journal of Personality,* 1959, *27,* 507–531.

Stroebe, W., Eagly, A. H. & Stroebe, M. S. Friendly or just polite? The effect of self-esteem on attribution. *European Journal of Social Psychology,* 1977, *7,* 265–274.

Stroebe, W., & Fraser, C. The relationship between riskiness and confidence in choice dilemma decision. *European Journal of Social Psychology,* 1971, *1,* 519–526.

Stroebe, W., Thompson, V. D., Insko, C. A., & Reisman, S. R. Balance and differentiation in the evaluation of linked attitude objects. *Journal of Personality and Social Psychology,* 1970, *16,* 48–54.

Strongman, K. T. *The psychology of emotion.* London: Wiley, 1973.

Suedfeld, P., Epstein, Y. M., Buchanan, E., & Landon, P. B. Effects of set on the "effects of mere exposure." *Journal of Personality and Social Psychology,* 1971, *17,* 121–123.

Suedfeld, P., Rank, D., & Borrie, R. A. Frequency of exposure and evaluation of candidates and campaign speeches. *Journal of Applied Social Psychology,* 1975, *5,* 118–126.

Sulin, R. A., & Dooling, D. J. Intrusion of thematic ideas in retention of prose. *Journal of Experimental Psychology,* 1974, *103,* 255–262.

Summers, G. F. *Attitude measurement.* Chicago: Rand McNally and Company, 1970.

Surwillo, W. W. Human reaction time and endogenous heart rate changes in normal subjects. *Psychophysiology,* 1971, *8,* 680–682.

Swap, W. Effects of repeated exposure of meaningful stimuli on attitude information and change. *Proceedings of 81st annual convention of the American Psychology Association,* 1973, 107–108.

Tannenbaum, P., II. The congruity principle revisited: Studies in the reduction, induction, and generalization of persuasion. In L. Berkowitz (Ed.), *Advances in experimental social psychology* (Vol. 3). New York: Academic Press, 1967.

Tedeschi, J. T., Schlenker, B. R., & Bonoma, T. V. Cognitive dissonance: Private ratiocination or public spectacle? *American Psychologist,* 1971, *26,* 685–695.

Teger, A. I., & Pruitt, D. G. Components of group risk taking. *Journal of Experimental Social Psychology,* 1967, *3,* 189–205.

Tesser, A. Self-generated attitude change. In L. Berkowitz (Ed.), *Advances in experimental social psychology* (Vol. 2). New York: Academic Press, 1978.

Tesser, A., & Conlee, M. C. Some effects of time and thought on attitude polarization. *Journal of Personality and Social Psychology,* 1975, *31,* 262–270.

Thomas, W. I., & Znaniecki, F. *The Polish peasant in Europe and America* (Vol. 1). New York: Alfred A. Knopf, 1927.

Thorndike, R. L. The effect of discussion upon the correctness of group decisions, when the factor of majority is allowed for. *Journal of Social Psychology,* 1938, *9,* 343–362. (a)

Thorndike, R. L. On what type of task will a group do well? *Journal of Abnormal and Social Psychology,* 1938, *33,* 409–413. (b)

Thorndyke, P. W. The role of inferences in discourse comprehension. *Journal of Verbal Learning and Verbal Behavior,* 1976, *15,* 437–446.

Thorndyke, P. W. Cognitive structures in comprehension and memory of narrative discourse. *Cognitive Psychology,* 1977, *9,* 77–110.

Thurstone, L. L. Attitudes can be measured. *American Journal of Sociology,* 1928, *33,* 529–544.

Thurstone, L. L. The measurement of social attitudes. *Journal of Abnormal and Social Psychology,* 1931, *26,* 249–269.

Timmons, W. M. *Decisions and attitudes as outcomes of the discussion of a social problem.* New York: Teachers College, Columbia University, Contributions to Education, No. 77, 1939.

Tognacci, L. N., & Cook, S. Conditioned autonomic responses as bi-directional indicators of racial attitude. *Journal of Personality and Social Psychology,* 1975, *31,* 137–144.

Treisman, A. M. Monitoring and storage of irrelevant messages in selective attention. *Journal of Verbal Learning and Verbal Behavior,* 1964, *3,* 449–459.

Tresselt, M. E., & Volkmann, J. The production of uniform opinion by non-social stimulation. *Journal of Abnormal and Social Psychology,* 1942, *37,* 234–243.

Troutman, C. M., & Shanteau, J. Do consumers evaluate products by adding or averaging attribute information? *Journal of Consumer Research,* 1976, *3,* 101–106.

Tulving, E., & Thomson, D. M. Encoding specificity and retrieval processes in episodic memory. *Psychological Review,* 1973, *5,* 352–373.

Turner, R. G. Self-consciousness and anticipatory belief change. *Personality and Social Psychology Bulletin,* 1977, *3,* 438–441.

Tursky, B., Schwartz, G., & Crider, A. Differential patterns of heart rate and skin resistance during a digit-transformation task. *Journal of Experimental Psychology,* 1970, *83,* 451–457.

Uttal, W. R. *Cellular neurophysiology and integration.* Hillsdale, N. J.: Lawrence Erlbaum Assoc., 1975.

Vidulich, R. N., & Krevanick, F. W. Racial attitudes and emotional response to visual representations of the Negro. *Journal of Social Psychology,* 1966, *68,* 85–93.

Vinokur, A., & Burnstein, E. The effects of partially shared persuasive arguments on group-induced shifts: A group problem-solving approach. *Journal of Personality and Social Psychology,* 1974, *29,* 305–315.

Vinokur, A., & Burnstein, E. The depolarization of attitudes in groups. *Journal of Personality and Social Psychology,* 1978, *36,* 872–885. (a)

Vinokur, A., & Burnstein, E. Novel argumentation and attitude change: The case of polarization following group discussion. *European Journal of Social Psychology,* 1978, *8,* 335–348. (b)

Vinokur, A., Trope, Y., & Burnstein, E. A decision making analysis of persuasive-argumentation and the choice-shift effect. *Journal of Experimental Social Psychology,* 1975, *11,* 127–148.

Vohs, J. L., & Garrett, R. L. Resistance to persuasion: An integrative framework. *Public Opinion Quarterly,* 1968, *32,* 445–452.

Volkova, B. C. Some characteristics of conditioned reflex formation to verbal stimuli in children. *Sechenov Journal of Physiology,* 1953, *39,* 540–548.

Wallach, M. A., & Kogan N. The role of information and consequences in group in risk taking. *Journal of Experimental Social Psychology,* 1965, *1,* 1–19.

Wallach, M. A., Kogan, N., & Bem, G. Group influence on individual risk taking. *Journal of Abnormal and Social Psychology*, 1962, *65*, 75-86.

Walster, E., Aronson, E., & Abrahams, D. On increasing the persuasiveness of a low prestige communicator. *Journal of Experimental Social Psychology*, 1966, *2*, 325-342.

Walster, E., & Festinger, L. The effectiveness of "overheard" persuasive communications. *Journal of Abnormal and Social Psychology*, 1962, *65*, 395-402.

Waly, P., & Cook, S. Effect of attitude on judgments of plausibility. *Journal of Personality and Social Psychology*, 1965, *2*, 745-749.

Wang, G. H., & Lu, T. W. On the intensity of the GSR induced by stimulation of postganglionic sympathetic nerve fibers with single induction shocks. *Chinese Journal of Physiology*, 1930, *4*, 393-400.

Warr, P. B., & Knapper, C. *The perception of people and events.* New York: Wiley, 1968.

Warren, R. E. Association, directionality, and stimulus encoding. *Journal of Experimental Psychology*, 1974, *102*, 151-158.

Washburn, M. F. *Movement and mental imagery. Outlines of a motor theory of the complexer mental processes.* Boston: Houghton Mufflin Co., 1916.

Watson, J. B. *Psychology from the standpoint of the behaviorist.* Philedelphia: Lippincott, 1919.

Watts, W. A., & Holt, L. E. Logical relationships among beliefs and timing as factors in persuasion. *Journal of Personality and Social Psychology*, 1970, *16*, 571-582.

Watts, W. A., & Holt, L. E. Persistence of opinion change induced under conditions of forewarning and distraction. *Journal of Personality and Social Psychology*, 1979, *37*, 778-789.

Watts, W., & McGuire, W. J. Persistence of induced opinion change and retention of the inducing message contents. *Journal of Abnormal and Social Psychology*, 1964, *68*, 233-241.

Webb, P. Consumer initial processing in a difficult media environment, *Journal of Consumer Research*, 1979, *6*, 225-236.

Weber, S. J., & Cook, T. D. Subject effects in laboratory research: An examination of subject roles, demand characteristics, and valid inference. *Psychological Bulletin*, 1972, *77*, 273-295.

Weigel, R. H., & Newman, L. S. Increasing attitude-behavior correspondence by broadening the scope of the behavioral measure. *Journal of Personality and Social Psychology*, 1976, *33*, 793-802.

Weigel, R. H., Vernon, D. T. A., & Tognacci, L. N. The specificity of the attitude as a determinant of attitude-behavior congruence. *Journal of Personality and Social Psychology*, 1974, *30*, 724-728.

Weiss, W. Modes of resolution and reasoning in attitude change experiments. In R. P. Abelson, E. Aronson, W. J. McGuire, T. M. Newcomb, M. J. Rosenberg, & P. H. Tannenbaum (Eds.), *Theories of cognitive consistency: A sourcebook.* Chicago: Rand McNally, 1968.

Wellens, A. R., & Thistlethwaite, D. L. An analysis of two quantitative theories of cognitive balance. *Psychological Review*, 1971, *78*, 141-150. (a)

Wellens, A. R., & Thistlethwaite, D. L. Comparison of three theories of cognitive balance. *Journal of Personality and Social Psychology*, 1971, *20*, 82-92. (b)

Wells, G. L., Petty, R. E., Harkins, S., Kagehiro, D., & Harvey, J. Anticipated discussion of interpretation eliminates actor-observer differences in the attribution of causality. *Sociometry*, 1977, *40*, 247-253.

Werts, C. E., Rock, A., Linn, R. L., & Joreskog, K. G. Comparison of correlations, variances, covariances and regression weights with or without measurement error. *Psychological Bulletin*, 1976, *83*, 1007-1013.

Weschler, I. R. An investigation of attitudes toward labor and management by means of the error-choice method. *Journal of Social Psychology*, 1950, *32*, 51-67.

Westie, F. R., & DeFleur, M. L. Autonomic responses and their relationship to race attitudes. *Journal of Abnormal and Social Psychology*, 1959, *58*, 340-347.

White, G. M. Contextual determinants of opinion judgments: Field experimental probes of judgmental relativity boundary conditions. *Journal of Personality and Social Psychology*, 1975, *32*, 1047–1054.

Wicker, A. W. Attitudes versus actions: The relationship of verbal and overt behavioral responses to attitude objects. *Journal of Social Issues*, 1969, *25*, 41–78.

Wicker, A. W. An examination of the "other-variables" explanation of attitude–behavior inconsistency. *Journal of Personality and Social Psychology*, 1971, *19*, 18–30.

Wicker, A., & Pomazal, R. The relationship between attitudes and behavior as a function of specificity of attitude object and presence of a significant person during assessment conditions. *Representative Research in Social Psychology*, 1971, *2*, 26–31.

Wicklund, R., & Brehm, J. *Perspectives on cognitive dissonance*. Hillsdale, N.J.: Lawrence Erlbaum Associates, 1976.

Wicklund, R. A., Cooper, J., & Linder, D. E. Effects of expected effort on attitude change prior to exposure. *Journal of Experimental Social Psychology*, 1967, *2*, 416–428.

Wiest, W. M. A quantitative extension of Heider's theory of cognitive balance applied to interpersonal perception and self-esteem. *Psychological Monographs*, 1965, *79* (14, Whole No. 607).

Wilson, W., & Miller, H. Repetition, order of presentation, and timing of arguments and measures as determinants of opinion change. *Journal of Personality and Social Psychology*, 1968, *9*, 184–188.

Winter, F. W. A laboratory experiment of individual attitude response to advertising exposure. *Journal of Marketing Research*, 1973, *10*, 130–140.

Wong, R. *A theory for integration of two source-adjective combinations in a personality impression formation task*. Senior honors thesis, University of California, San Diego, 1973.

Woodmanseee, J. J. *An evaluation of the pupil response as a measure of attitude toward Negroes*. Unpublished doctoral dissertation, University of Colorado, 1965.

Woodmansee, J. J. Methodological problems in pupillographic experiments. *Proceedings of the 74th Annual Convention of the American Psychological Association*, 1966, *1*, 133–134.

Woodmansee, J. J. The pupil response as a measure of social attitudes. In G. F. Summers (Ed.), *Attitude measurement*. Chicago: Rand McNally, 1970.

Woodruff, A. D. Personal values and the direction of behavior. *Scholastic Review*, 1942, *50*, 32–42.

Woodruff, H., & DiVesta, F. The relationship between values, concepts, and attitudes. *Educational and Psychological Measurement*, 1948, *8*, 645–660.

Worchel, S., Lind, A., & Kaufman, K. Evaluations of group products as a function of expectations of group longevity, outcome of competition, and publicity of evaluations. *Journal of Personality and Social Psychology*, 1975, *31*, 1089–1097.

Wright, P. L. *The role of cognitive response in the advertising influence process*. Unpublished doctoral dissertation, Pennsylvania State University, 1971.

Wright, P. L. The cognitive processes mediating acceptance of advertising. *Journal of Marketing Research*, 1973, *4*, 53–62.

Wright, P. L. Analyzing media effects on advertising responses. *Public Opinion Quarterly*, 1974, *38*, 192–205. (a)

Wright, P. The harassed decision maker: Time pressure, distraction, and the use of evidence. *Journal of Applied Psychology*, 1974, *59*, 555–561. (b)

Wright, P. L. On the direct monitoring of cognitive response to advertising. In G. D. Hughes & M. L. Ray (Eds.), *Buyer/consumer information processing*. Chapel Hill: University of North Carolina Press, 1974. (c)

Wright, P., Factors affecting cognitive resistance to advertising, *Journal of Consumer Research*, 1975, *2*, 1–9.

Wright, P. *Research on ad-stimulated thought processes: A review*. Faculty Working Paper, Graduate School of Business, Stanford University, 1977.

Wright, P., Concrete action plans in TV messages to increase reading of drug warnings, *Journal of Consumer Research*, 1979, *6*, 256–269.

Wright, P., & Barbour, F. The relevance of decision process models in structuring persuasive messages. *Communications Research*, 1975, *2*, 246–259.

Wright, P., & Rip, P. Advocacy message streams as guides to decision strategy: Effects of cross-advocate consensus and imagery instructions on the college choice process. Unpublished working paper, Stanford Graduate School of Business, 1979.

Wright, P., & Weitz, B. Time horizon effects on product evaluation strategies. *Journal of Marketing Research*, 1977, *14*, 429–443.

Wyer, R. S. *Cognitive organization and change: An information-processing approach*. Hillsdale, N.J.: Lawrence Erlbaum Associates, 1974. (a)

Wyer, R. S. Some implications of the "socratic effect" for alternative models of cognitive consistency. *Journal of Personality*, 1974, *42*, 399–419. (b)

Wyer, R. S. The role of probabilistic and syllogistic reasoning in cognitive organization and social inference. In M. Kaplan & S. Schwartz (Eds.), *Human judgment and decision processes*. New York: Academic Press, 1975.

Wyer, R. S., & Goldberg, L. A probabilistic analysis of the relationships between beliefs and attitudes. *Psychological Review*, 1970, *77*, 100–120.

Zajonc, R. B. *Structure of the cognitive field*. Unpublished doctoral dissertation, University of Michigan, 1954.

Zajonc, R. B. The process of cognitive tuning in communication. *Journal of Abnormal and Social Psychology*, 1960, *61*, 159–167.

Zajonc, R. B. Cognitive theories in social psychology. In G. Lindzey & E. Aronson (Eds.), *The handbook of social psychology* (Vol. 1). Reading, Mass.: Addison-Wesley, 1968.

Zajonc, R. B., & Rajecki, D. W. Exposure and affect: A field experiment. *Psychonomic Science*, 1969, *17*, 216–217.

Zajonc, R. B. Brainwash: Familiarity breeds comfort. *Psychology Today*, 1970, *3*, 32–35; 60–62.

Zajonc, R. B., Crandall, R., Kail, R. B., & Swap, W. Effect of extreme exposure frequencies on different affective ratings of stimuli. *Perceptual and Motor Skills*, 1974, *38*, 667–678.

Zajonc, R. B., Markus, H., & Wilson, W. R. Exposure effects and associative learning. *Journal of Experimental Social Psychology*, 1974, *10*, 248–263. (a)

Zajonc, R. B., Markus, H., & Wilson, W. R. Exposure, object preference, and distress in the domestic chick. *Journal of Comparative and Physiological Psychology*, 1974, *86*, 581–585. (b)

Zajonc, R. B., Reimer, D. J., & Hausser, D. Imprinting and the development of object preference in chicks by mere repeated exposure. *Journal of Comparative and Physiological Psychology*, 1973, *83*, 434–440.

Zajonc, R. B., Shaver, P., Tavris, C., & VanKreveld, D. Exposure, satiation, and stimulus discriminability. *Journal of Personality and Social Psychology*, 1972, *21*, 270–280.

Zajonc, R. B., Swap, W. C., Harrison, A. A., & Roberts, P. Limiting conditions of the exposure effect: Satiation and relativity. *Journal of Personality and Social Psychology*, 1971, *18*, 384–391.

Zanna, M. P., Kiesler, C., & Pilkonis, P. A. Positive and negative attitudinal affect established by classical conditioning. *Journal of Personality and Social Psychology*, 1970, *14*, 321–328.

Zellner, M. Self-esteem, reception, and influenceability. *Journal of Personality and Social Psychology*, 1970, *15*, 87–93.

Ziller, R. C. *The social self*. New York: Pergamon Press, 1973.

Zimbardo, P. G. Involvement and communication discrepancy as determinants of opinion conformity. *Journal of Abnormal and Social Psychology*, 1960, *60*, 86–94.

Zimbardo, P. G. The effect of effort and improvisation on self-persuasion produced by role-playing. *Journal of Experimental Social Psychology*, 1965, *1*, 103–120.

Zimbardo, P. G., & Ebbesen, E. B. The experimental modification of the relationship between effort, attitude and behavior. *Journal of Personality and Social Psychology,* 1970, *16,* 207-213.

Zimbardo, P., Ebbesen, E., & Maslach, C. *Influencing attitudes and changing behavior.* Reading, Mass.: Addison-Wesley, 1977.

Zimbardo, P. G., Snyder, M., Thomas, J., Gold, A., & Gurwitz, S. Modifying the impact of persuasive communications with external distraction. *Journal of Personality and Social Psychology,* 1970, *16,* 669-680.

Zimbardo, P. G., Weisenberg, M., Firestone, I., & Levy, B. Communicator effectiveness in producing public conformity and private attitude change. *Journal of Personality,* 1965, *33,* 233-255.

Zobel, E. J., & Lehman, R. S. Interaction of subject and experimenter expectancy effects in a tone-length discrimination task. *Behavioral Science,* 1969, *14,* 357-363.

Author Index

Subject Index